Communicating at Work

Principles and Practices for Business and the Professions

Tenth Edition

Ronald B. Adler
Santa Barbara City College, Emeritus

Jeanne Marquardt Elmhorst
Central New Mexico Community College

The McGraw-Hill Companies

Connect
Learn
Succeed™

Published by McGraw-Hill, an imprint of The McGraw-Hill Companies, Inc., 1221 Avenue of the
Americas, New York, NY 10020. Copyright © 2010, 2008, 2005, 2002, 1999, 1996, 1992, 1989, 1986,
1983. All rights reserved. No part of this publication may be reproduced or distributed in any form
or by any means, or stored in a database or retrieval system, without the prior written consent of The
McGraw-Hill Companies, Inc., including, but not limited to, in any network or other electronic storage
or transmission, or broadcast for distance learning.

This book is printed on acid-free paper.

2 3 4 5 6 7 8 9 0 DOW/DOW 0

ISBN: 978-0-07-338517-4
MHID: 0-07-338517-4

Editor in Chief: *Michael Ryan*
Executive Sponsoring Editor: *Katie Stevens*
Senior Development Editor: *Jennie Katsaros*
Director of Development: *Rhona Robbin*
Editorial Coordinator: *Erika Lake*
Executive Marketing Manager: *Leslie Oberhuber*
Senior Production Editor: *Carey Eisner*
Design Manager: *Laurie Entringer*
Cover and Interior Design: *Jesi Lazar*
Photo Research Coordinator: *Alexandra Ambrose*
Photo Researcher: *Sherri Alder*
Production Supervisor: *Tandra Jorgensen*
Composition: *10.5/12 Goudy by Laserwords Private Limited*
Printing: *45# New Era Matte Plus, R.R. Donnelley & Sons*

Cover: © Stockbyte/Getty Images.

Credits: The credits appear at the end of the book and are considered an extension of the copyright page.

Library of Congress Cataloging-in-Publication Data

Adler, Ronald B. (Ronald Brian), 1946-
    Communicating at work : principles and practices for business and the professions / Ronald
B. Adler.—10th ed.
        p. cm.
    Includes bibliographical references and index.
    ISBN-13: 978-0-07-338517-4 (pbk. : alk. paper)
    ISBN-10: 0-07-338517-4
        1. Business communication. 2. Interpersonal communication. I. Title.
HF5718.A33 2010
658.4'5—dc22

                                                                2009034536

The Internet addresses listed in the text were accurate at the time of publication. The inclusion of a
Web site does not indicate an endorsement by the authors or McGraw-Hill, and McGraw-Hill does not
guarantee the accuracy of the information presented at these sites.

www.mhhe.com

Ronald B. Adler is professor emeritus at Santa Barbara City College. Throughout his career, he has specialized in the study of organizational and interpersonal communication. He is the author of *Confidence in Communication: A Guide to Assertive and Social Skills* and coauthor of *Understanding Human Communication, Interplay: The Process of Interpersonal Communication* as well as the widely used text *Looking Out/Looking In*. Professor Adler is a consultant for a number of corporate, professional, and government clients and leads workshops in such areas as conflict resolution, presentational speaking, team building, and interviewing.

Jeanne Marquardt Elmhorst is an instructor in communication studies at Central New Mexico Community College in Albuquerque, New Mexico. Her courses reflect the variety in the communication discipline: business and professional, public speaking, listening, intercultural, and interpersonal. Jeanne lived and taught in Asia for three years and continues to find opportunities to travel, study, and volunteer in other countries. She enjoys designing and presenting communication training for business and not-for-profit clients.

preface

Some courses (and textbooks) are easily forgettable. Once the final exam is over, memories of the course fade quickly. But a few academic experiences are different: Lessons learned are transformative, making a difference for the rest of the student's life.

Our goal in writing *Communicating at Work* has been to help put the business and professional communication course in the second category. This book aims to give students insights and tools that will help them achieve their career goals more ethically and effectively, and contribute to the success of the enterprises they undertake. If we've done our jobs, the information in this book will benefit readers long after their class has finished.

While *Communicating at Work* is clearly a university-level textbook, it contains information that can help all career-minded readers. Novices to the business world will be introduced to skills they will need for on-the-job success. Readers who have ample job experience but recognize that there is always potential for communicating more effectively will also find useful tips and tools.

What's Familiar

The tenth edition of *Communicating at Work* retains the approach that has made it a perennial market leader. Most important is a practical, real-world focus: Every page contains useful information, advice, and examples on how to communicate successfully. Extensive coverage of communication technology offers insights on when and how to use a multitude of electronic channels, along with more traditional ones. Thorough attention to workplace diversity helps readers communicate with others from different backgrounds and choose approaches that work for everyone involved. Finally, an emphasis on ethical communication discusses how communicators can achieve their goals in a way that doesn't compromise moral integrity. All of this material is presented in a no-nonsense writing style and packaged in an inviting design that aims to capture the sophistication of today's workplace.

New to This Edition

Several new features enhance the timeliness and effectiveness of this edition:

- **More concise, efficient organizational plan.** A new, condensed chapter lineup makes it easier to cover material within an academic term, without sacrificing content. Chapter 13 now covers both informative and persuasive presentations, as well as guidelines for group and special occasion speaking. Annotated transcripts of sample informative and persuasive presentations are now accessible in Appendix II.
- **New *Technology Tip* sidebars.** These boxes show readers how to use a variety of communication tools to achieve their goals. Topics include guidelines for advancing career goals using blogs, text and instant messaging, and creating an electronic portfolio, tips for working in virtual teams, and managing conflicts in cyberspace.

- **New *Case Study* sidebars.** Appearing in every chapter, these boxes describe both the communication triumphs and blunders of real-life business and professional communicators. Critical Analysis questions following each case help students analyze communication principles and apply insights to their own lives.

- **Expanded coverage of important topics.** These include informal communication networks, how cultural differences affect communication, the appropriate uses of both mindful and "mindless" listening, strategies for addressing sexual harassment, and advice for communicating with diverse audiences.

- **New pedagogy and resources.** End-of-chapter Review Points summarize key elements clearly and efficiently. Thoroughly updated Instructor's Resource Manual provides tools to make teaching more efficient and learning more effective. Expanded Online Learning Center (OLC) provides a wealth of new web-based information, readings, and study aids that enhance student success.

- **Sample Speech Appendix (Appendix I).** Appendix I now contains annotated samples of both informative and persuasive presentations.

- **Updated Business Writing Appendix (Appendix II).** Appendix II has been updated to reflect changes in how business documents are created and shared in an era when electronic communication is becoming the norm.

Resources for Instructors and Students

An array of resources makes teaching and learning both more efficient and effective.

The Online Learning Center at **www.mhhe.com/adler10e** provides instructors with downloadable supplements and provides students with learning tools to help them master course concepts. It includes an updated Instructor's Manual, Resource Integrator, and Test Bank and PowerPoint slides for instructors. The student side includes self-quizzes, videos, business document templates, a PowerPoint tutorial, and glossary flash cards.

Communication Concepts video, available on the book's Web site, provides scenarios of common types of business and professional interaction for analysis.

Tegrity Campus

Tegrity Campus is a service that makes class time available all the time by automatically capturing every lecture in a searchable format for students to review when they study and complete assignments. With a simple one-click start and stop process, you can capture all computer screens and corresponding audio. Students replay any part of any class with easy-to-use browser-based viewing on a PC or Mac.

Educators know that the more students can see, hear, and experience class resources, the better they learn. With Tegrity Campus, students quickly recall key moments by using Tegrity Campus's unique search feature. This search helps students efficiently find what they need, when they need it across an entire semester of class recordings. Help turn all your students' study time into learning moments immediately supported by your lecture.

To learn more about Tegrity watch a two minute Flash demo at **http://tegritycampus .mhhe.com.**

CourseSmart

CourseSmart is a new way for faculty to find and review eTextbooks. It's also a great option for students who are interested in accessing their course materials digitally and saving money. CourseSmart offers thousands of the most commonly adopted textbooks across hundreds of courses from a wide variety of higher education publishers. It is the only place for faculty to review and compare the full text of a textbook online, providing immediate access without the environmental impact of requesting a print exam copy. At CourseSmart, students can save up to 50% off the cost of a print book, reduce their impact on the environment, and gain access to powerful Web tools for learning including full text search, notes and highlighting, and e-mail tools for sharing notes between classmates.

acknowledgments

We are indebted to the colleagues whose reviews helped improve this edition:

Carolyn Clark, Salt Lake Community College

Charlotte Cottrell, Paris Junior College—Greenville Center

Carrie Cropley, Santa Barbara City College

Tasha Davis, Austin Community College—NRG

Mark S. Gallup, Lansing Community College

Robert Harrison, Gallaudet University

Pamela D. Hopkins, East Carolina University

Brendan B. Kelly, University of West Florida

M. Sean Limon, University of Florida

Kelly Petkus, Austin Community College

Jennifer Reem, Nova Southeastern University

Molly Steen, University of California, Santa Barbara

Bryan P. Townsend, Louisiana Tech University

Wendy Yarberry, Florida Community College-Jacksonville

We are grateful to Carolyn Clark for updating the Instructor's Manual and new end-of-chapter activities, as well as for many other insightful suggestions. Special thanks to Bryan P. Townsend for writing the online quizzes and internet activities and to Kelly Petkus for creating the PowerPoint presentations for the Online Learning Center. Our thanks also to the people at McGraw-Hill whose efforts have helped bring *Communicating at Work* to market: Jennie Katsaros, Leslie Oberhuber, Katie Stevens, Erika Lake, Carey Eisner, Laurie Entringer, and Alexandra Ambrose.

A hardworking and talented group of freelance professionals also contributed to the book you are holding. As always, Sherri Adler's selection of photos contributed to the appealing design of this edition. Darlene Blesdoe's copyediting transformed a rather confusing manuscript into the clear copy you can behold between these covers. Carole Quandt proofread every word of the page proofs to make sure the book is error-free.

a visual walkthrough

A Practical, Real-World Focus

career tip

Finding Photographs and Videos

Anyone with an Internet connection and Web browser can search among millions of online photos and videos quickly and easily by using Google, YouTube, and other Web sites. Once on Google's home page, type in a description of the photo or drawing you are seeking and click on "Images" or "Video" right above the search box. To refine your search, click on "Advanced" and enter the criteria into the on-screen form. Once you activate your search, your screen will display a list of thumbnail photos of the images or video stills. Click on any images that you want to view more closely and a larger version will appear.

When you have found an image you want to use in your presentation, you can copy and paste it into PowerPoint or another presentation program, or you can save it for future use.

Be sure to give credit to the source for any photos or videos you use, and honor any restrictions that are posted on the Web site where you find an image or footage.

Career Tips

Career Tip boxes give practical advice on how to be more successful in work-related situations. New topics include getting recognized by your bosses, cubicle etiquette, difference as advantage, and using a telephone log.

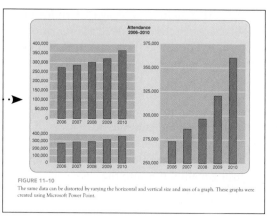

FIGURE 11–10
The same data can be distorted by varying the horizontal and vertical size and axes of a graph. These graphs were created using Microsoft Power Point.

Presentations

Coverage includes basic steps for organizing business presentations and preparing PowerPoint presentations.

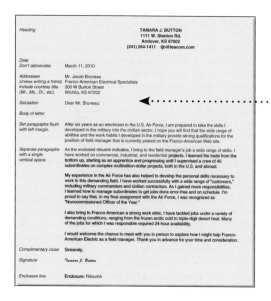

Business Writing—Appendix II

Updated coverage of business writing includes information on choosing the best format for résumés and job applications. Business document templates on the book's Web site provide additional templates so students can create cover letters, résumés, agendas, and memos.

viii

Pedagogy

on your feet

Storytelling to Make a Point

Well-chosen and well-told stories can help you make a point in an interesting and compelling way. In a brief presentation of 2 minutes or less, use a story to illustrate an important lesson regarding professional communication. The story you tell may be based on your personal experience, something you observed, or something you read or heard about from others.

Organize your presentation in one of two ways: Either state your thesis first and then show how the story supports it or tell the story first, and then show how it illustrates your thesis. In either case, conclude by showing audience members how your thesis and the story that illustrates it relate to their professional lives.

On Your Feet

This feature provides activities to get students speaking comfortably from the very beginning of the course. Examples include describing one's "dream team" of co-workers and recalling a unique organizational culture.

Technology

New Technology Tip sidebars

These boxes show readers how to use a variety of communication tools to achieve their goals. Topics include guidelines for advancing career goals using blogs, text and instant messaging, and creating an electronic portfolio, tips for working in virtual teams, and managing conflicts in cyberspace.

technology tip

Generational Preferences in Communication Technology

Age often matters when choosing the best technology for exchanging messages on the job. The channels that communicators prefer are often a function of the era in which they came of age.

When boomers entered the workforce, typewriters and telephones were the principal communication technologies. Over 80 percent now use the Internet in one way or another, and most have embraced e-mail. But they are less likely than younger communicators to use or appreciate the value of text messaging, blogging, social networking, or instant messaging. Differences even exist between Gen X-ers and their Gen Y counterparts. For example, about half of the Y's in one survey reported sending or receiving at least one text message within the past day—roughly double the proportion of those in Gen X.

Beyond technology, generational differences also arise in communication style. Gen Y workers are used to the speed and brevity of texting and IM-ing. As a consequence, they often aren't sticklers for correct spelling and syntax. By contrast, matures, boomers, and even Gen X-ers grew up learning that accuracy is essential. They are likely to regard careless writing as a sign of incompetence.

Keeping differences like these in mind can help you choose the communication channel and style that best suits the people you are trying to reach. As always, generalizations don't apply to every person: Some boomers are avid users of all technologies, and some members of Generation Y resemble their grandparents when it comes to using digital media. Despite exceptions to the rule, it often pays to be mindful of generational differences when communicating strategically.

Sources: T. Erickson, "Where Are My Corduroy Pants? Is Gen Y's Texting Obsession Headed for the Workplace?" *Harvard Business Online*, May 29, 2007. Retrieved http://discussionleader.hbsp.com/erickson/2007/05/where_are_my_corduroy_pants_is.html. S. Fox, and M. Madden, *Generations Online* (Washington, DC: Pew Internet and American Life Project, 2006).

case study

Mosquitoes Create a Buzz over Bill Gates' Speech

Microsoft founder Bill Gates is passionate about eliminating the scourge of malaria from the world. The disease kills millions of people each year, but Gates told an elite California audience that it's hard for Westerners to appreciate the impact of the disease because the majority of deaths occur in the developing world.

Then Gates used a unique strategy to show his listeners the risk faced by so many less fortunate people in tropical parts of the world. "There's no reason only poor people should have the experience," he calmly remarked as he opened a jar and released a swarm of mosquitoes. Nervous laughter erupted as the tiny insects flew into the audience.

The stir caused by the mosquito stunt was immediate and widespread. Audience members tweeted the news into cyberspace, where it spread around the world faster than any infectious disease.

Gates' simple strategy of using mosquitoes as props dramatized his point far more effectively than would otherwise have been possible.

CRITICAL ANALYSIS:

1. Gates' mosquito stunt obviously made his speech more interesting. Did it also make his material more clear? How well did it help prove his thesis? Did it further his goal of advancing the cause of malaria prevention?

2. Imagine that Gates had not reassured his audience immediately that the mosquitoes were malaria-free. What (if any) responsibility does a speaker have to protect an audience from becoming disturbed or upset?

Source: Bill Gates, "How I'm trying to change the world now." Speech delivered at the TED conference, Long Beach, California, February 4, 2009. Retrieved March 10, 2009 from www.ted.com/talks/bill_gates_unplugged.html.

Case Studies

New Case Study sidebars

Appearing in every chapter, these boxes describe both the communication triumphs and blunders of real-life business and professional communicators. Critical Analysis questions following each case help students analyze communication principles and apply insights to their own lives.

Self-Assessment

These statements reflect different facets of cultural intelligence. For each set, add up your scores and divide by four to produce an average. Our work with large groups of managers shows that for purposes of your own development, it is most useful to think about your three scores in comparison to one another. Generally, an average of less than 3 would indicate an area calling for improvement, while an average of greater than 4-5 reflects a true CQ strength.

Rate the extent to which you agree with each statement, using the scale:
1 = strongly disagree, 2 = disagree, 3 = neutral, 4 = agree, 5 = strongly agree.

_____ Before I interact with people from a new culture, I ask myself what I hope to achieve.

_____ If I encounter something unexpected while working in a new culture, I use this experience to figure out new ways to approach *other* cultures in the future.

_____ I plan how I'm going to relate to people from a different culture before I meet them.

+ _____ When I come into a new cultural situation, I can immediately sense whether something is going well or something is wrong.

Total _____ ÷ 4 = [ ] Cognitive CQ

Self-Assessments help students see how well they are applying concepts. For example, they can diagnose their cultural intelligence, assess their personal conflict style, and assess the way they present themselves nonverbally.

Ethics

Ethical Considerations

Throughout the text, and in Ethical Challenge boxes, students are invited to consider ways of incorporating ethical considerations into day-to-day work contexts.

ethical challenge

Cherrypicking Support?

Imagine you are planning a sales presentation to a prospective client. To back up your claims that the product or service you are offering is outstanding, you know you need to use examples of outstanding service and testimonials of satisfied customers. You do have a few good examples of each, but sadly they aren't a representative of the kind of feedback your organization usually receives. It would be easier to come up with examples and complaints that reflect unhappy clients.

How can you reconcile the need to be honest with the desire to sign up a new customer?

Diversity

Focus on Diversity

Working with people from different backgrounds is more important and more common than ever. *Communicating at Work* encourages cultural understanding by exploring issues of diversity throughout the text.

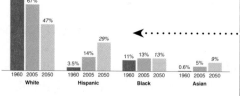

FIGURE 2–1
Population by Race and Ethnicity

Note: American Indian/Alaska Native not shown.

Source: J. S. Passel and D. Cohn, *U.S. Population Projections: 2005–2050* (Washington, DC: Pew Research Center, 2008).

perspective gives DuPont a competitive edge."[10] Stona Fitch, vice president of manufacturing for Procter & Gamble, says, "Diversity provides a much richer environment, a variety of viewpoints, greater productivity. And, not unimportantly, it makes work more fun and interesting."[11] A spokesperson for the American Society of Civil Engineers states, "Without embracing diversity, the engineering profession will be unable to compete effectively in the global marketplace."[12] Whether you are working abroad, for or with foreign nationals at home, or with native-born people from different backgrounds, understanding cultural differences is an essential part of being an effective communicator.

Quick Guide to
Communicating at Work

This handy reference tool offers a step-by-step guide for planning the most common types of business and professional presentations: meetings, interviews, and problem-solving negotiations.

Quick Guide to
Communicating at Work

Parenthetical references refer to pages in *Communicating at Work* where each tip is discussed in detail.

Effective Interviewing

Before the Interview

1. Define your goal as specifically as possible. (161)
2. Consider the setting: time, place, etc. (170–172)
3. Identify/analyze the other party. (161–163)
   - Knowledge, self-concept, view of you, attitude about the subject.
4. Consider the structure. (165–166)
   - Highly structured, moderately structured, or unstructured.
5. Prepare a list of topics to be discussed and likely questions. (164–170)
   If you are the interviewer, anticipate questions.
   - Consider question types: open/closed, fact/opinion, direct/indirect, hypothetical.
   - Avoid loaded and leading questions.

During the Interview

1. Begin with a sociable greeting to build rapport. (172)
2. Include orientation. (Clarify reason for the interview, information needed, how it will be used.) Describe approximate length of interview. (173–174)
3. During body
   - Interviewer should control focus of conversation and follow up with secondary questions as needed. (174–176)
   - Interviewee should give clear, detailed answers, correct misunderstandings, cover own agenda, and ask questions as necessary. (174–176)
4. Conclude the interview with review of results, establish future actions, and close with pleasantries. (177)

Successful Meetings

Planning a Meeting

1. Decide whether a meeting is appropriate. (274–277)
2. Choose the right attendees. (281)
   - Seek optimal size of group. Include only essential people and exclude unproductive members, if possible.
3. Schedule enough time for tasks at hand. (280)
4. Choose/propose meeting time and location convenient for most members. (280)
5. Arrange the necessary room and facilities. (283)
   - Convenient for attendees, necessary facilities (e.g., Internet connection, flip chart, etc.), free from distractions.
6. Circulate agenda. (280–283)
   - Distribute far enough in advance to give members sufficient notice.
   - Include particulars of meeting (date, time, length, location, attendees).
   - Provide sufficient background information.
   - List goals for each item.

» continued on the inside back cover

Media Resources for Students and Instructors

The Online Learning Center at www.mhhe.com/adler10e provides a variety of resources to help students review key course content. Icons in the text prompt students to use corresponding features on the Web site.

brief contents

part one — Basics of Business and Professional Communication
Strategic Case: Sundown Bakery 2

1 Communicating at Work 4
2 Communication, Culture, and Work 34

part two — Personal Skills
Strategic Case: Computer Solutions 66

3 Listening 68
4 Verbal and Nonverbal Messages 90
5 Interpersonal Skills 124

part three — Interviewing
Strategic Case: Platinum Sounds 156

6 Principles of Interviewing 161
7 Types of Interviews 186

part four — Working in Groups
Strategic Case: Museum of Springfield 232

8 Working in Teams 234
9 Effective Meetings 272

part five — Making Effective Presentations
Strategic Case: Fresh Air Sports 300

10 Developing and Organizing the Presentation 302
11 Verbal and Visual Support in Presentations 346
12 Delivering the Presentation 376
13 Types of Business Presentations 400

Appendix I: Sample Presentations 444
Appendix II: Business Writing 457
Glossary 478
Notes 485
Credits 505
Index 508

table of contents

part one

**Basics of Business
and Professional Communication
Strategic Case: Sundown Bakery   2**

1 Communicating
at Work   4

The Importance of Communication   5

The Nature of Communication   7

The Process of Communication   7

Communication Principles   9

Ethical Dimensions of Communication   10

Using Communication Networks   12

Formal Communication Networks   12

Informal Communication Networks   17

**Face-to-Face and Electronic Communication
Channels   23**

Face-to-Face Communication   23

Telephone and Voice Mail   24

Teleconferencing and
Videoconferencing   25

Instant Messaging   25

Twitter and Text Messaging   26

E-mail and Written Communication   27

Which Channel to Use   28

Review Points   30
Key Terms   31
Activities   31
Resources   33

2 Communication,
Culture, and Work   34

**Cultural Diversity
and Communication   35**

The Nature of Culture   36

Cultural Differences in Doing
Business   37

Fundamental Dimensions of Cultural
Diversity   40

Co-cultural Dimensions of a Diverse
Society   45

Diversity and Ethical Issues   52

Communicating across Diversity   53

**Organizational Culture
and Communication   56**

The Importance of Organizational
Culture   58

Dimensions of Organizational
Culture   58

Creating and Maintaining Organizational
Cultures   60

Organizational Culture and Career
Planning   61

Review Points   62
Key Terms   63
Activities   63
Resources   65

part two

**Personal Skills
Strategic Case: Computer
Solutions   66**

3 Listening   68

The Importance of Listening   69

Barriers to Effective Listening   72
Physiological Barriers   72
Environmental Barriers   73
Attitudinal Barriers and False
Assumptions   74
Sociocultural Differences   76
Lack of Training   78

Listening Styles   78
People-Oriented   78
Action-Oriented   79
Content-Oriented   79
Time-Oriented   79

Listening More Effectively   81
Listening to Understand   81
Listening to Evaluate   85
Review Points   86
Key Terms   87
Activities   87
Resources   89

4 Verbal and Nonverbal
Messages   90

Verbal Messages   92
Clarity and Ambiguity   93

Inflammatory Language   98
Masculine and Feminine Language
Use   99

Nonverbal Communication   103
Characteristics of Nonverbal
Communication   103
Types of Nonverbal Communication   105
Improving Nonverbal Effectiveness   116

Sexual Harassment   117
Avoiding Sexual Harassment
Problems   118
Responding to Sexual Harassment   118
Review Points   120
Key Terms   120
Activities   121
Resources   123

5 Interpersonal
Skills   124

Building Positive Relationships   125
Communication Climate   127
Giving Praise   131

Dealing with Criticism   133
Offering Constructive Feedback   133
Responding to Criticism   135

Managing Conflict   137
What Are Conflicts About?   138
Approaches to Conflict   139
Handling Conflicts Constructively   143

Win–Win Problem Solving in Action   149
Review Points   151
Key Terms   152
Activities   152
Resources   155

part three

Interviewing
Strategic Case: Platinum Sounds   156

6 Principles of Interviewing   158

Planning the Interview   161
Define the Goal   161
Identify and Analyze the Other Party   161
Prepare a List of Topics   164
Choose the Best Interview Structure   165
Consider Possible Questions   166
Arrange the Setting   170

Conducting the Interview   172
Opening   172
Body   174
Closing   177

The Ethics of Interviewing   178
Obligations of the Interviewer   179
Obligations of the Interviewee   180

Sample Interview Plan   180
Review Points   183
Key Terms   183
Activities   184
Resources   185

7 Types of Interviews   186

The Information-Gathering Interview   187
Collect Background Information   188
Define Interview Goals and Questions   188
Choose the Right Interviewee   189

The Career Research Interview   190
The Value of Personal Contacts   190
Choosing Interviewees   190
Contacting Prospective Interviewees   192
Following Up   193

The Employment Interview   194
Pre-Interview Steps   194
During the Interview   200
Post-Interview Follow-up   212
Interviewing and the Law   213
Sample Employment Interview   216

The Performance Appraisal Interview   223
Definition and Importance   223
Steps in the Appraisal Process   225
Review Points   228
Key Terms   229
Activities   229
Resources   231

part four

Working in Groups
Strategic Case:
Museum of Springfield   232

8 Working in Teams   234

The Nature of Teams   235
Teams Are Essential   236
Characteristics of Work Groups   237
What Makes a Group a Team?   239
Virtual Teams   240

Leadership and Influence in Groups and Teams   242
Centralized Leadership   242
Becoming a Leader   245
Power and Influence of Members   246

Problem-Solving Communication   248

Systematic Problem Solving   248

Stages in Group Problem Solving   250

Functional Role Analysis   252

Decision-Making Methods   254

Effective Communication in Groups and Teams   258

Recognize Both Group and Personal Goals   258

Promote Desirable Norms   261

Promote an Optimal Level of Cohesiveness   263

Avoid Excessive Conformity   265

Encourage Creativity   267

Review Points   268
Key Terms   268
Activities   269
Resources   271

9 Effective Meetings   272

Types of Meetings   274

Information-Sharing Meetings   274

Problem-Solving or Decision-Making Meetings   275

Ritual Activities   275

Virtual Meetings   275

Planning a Problem-Solving Meeting   277

When to Hold a Meeting   278

Setting an Agenda   280

Conducting the Meeting   283

Beginning the Meeting   284

Conducting Business   285

Concluding the Meeting   292

Following Up the Meeting   294

Review Points   296

Key Terms   296
Activities   297
Resources   299

part five

**Making Effective Presentations
Strategic Case: Fresh Air Sports   300**

10 Developing and Organizing the Presentation   302

Analyzing the Situation   305

Analyzing the Audience   306

Analyzing Yourself as the Speaker   310

Analyzing the Occasion   311

Setting Your Goal and Developing the Thesis   313

General and Specific Goals   313

Developing the Thesis   316

Organizing the Body   317

Brainstorming Ideas   318

Basic Organizational Plan   318

Identify Main Points and Subpoints   320

Choose the Best Organizational Pattern   321

Rules for Main Points   329

Planning the Introduction and Conclusion   332

Functions of the Introduction   332

Types of Opening Statements   333

Functions of the Conclusion   336

Types of Closing Statements   337

Adding Transitions   338

Functions of Transitions   338

Characteristics of Effective Transitions   341

Review Points 341
Key Terms 342
Activities 343
Resources 345

11   Verbal and Visual Support in Presentations 346

Functions of Supporting Material 348
Clarity 348

Interest 349

Proof 349

Verbal Support 349
Definitions 349

Examples 351

Stories 351

Statistics 354

Comparisons 355

Quotations 356

Citing Your Sources 356

Visual Aids 357
Types of Visual Aids 359

Media for Presenting Visual Aids 364

Presentation Software 366

Guidelines for Using Visual Aids 369

Review Points 372
Key Terms 373
Activities 373
Resources 375

12   Delivering the Presentation 376

Types of Delivery 377
Manuscript Presentations 378

Memorized Presentations 378

Extemporaneous Presentations 379

Impromptu Presentations 380

Guidelines for Delivery 381
Visual Elements 381

Verbal Elements 384

Vocal Elements 387

Question-and-Answer Sessions 389
When to Answer Questions 390

How to Manage Questions 391

Speaking with Confidence 393
Accept a Moderate Amount of Nervousness 394

Speak More Often 394

Rehearse Your Presentation 395

Focus on Your Topic and Audience, Not on Yourself 395

Think Rationally about Your Presentation 396

Review Points 397
Key Terms 397
Activities 397
Resources 399

13   Types of Business Presentations 400

Informative Presentations 401
Briefings 402

Reports 403

Training 406

Persuasive Presentations 413
Organizing Persuasive Messages 413

Types of Persuasive Messages 417

Strategies for Ethical Persuasion 422

Group Presentations 432
Approaches to Organizing a Group Presentation 432

Planning Introductions, Conclusions, and Transitions in Group Presentations   433

Delivering a Group Presentation   433

Special-Occasion Speaking   435

Welcoming a Guest or Group   435

Introducing Another Speaker   436

Honoring a Person or Institution   437

Giving a Toast   438

Presenting an Award   439

Accepting an Award   440

Review Points   441
Key Terms   442
Activities   442
Resources   443

Appendix I: Sample Presentations   444

Appendix II: Business Writing   457

Glossary   478

Notes   485

Credits   505

Index   508

Communicating at Work

Sundown Bakery

When Carol Teinchek and Bruce Marshall first started Sundown Bakery, the business was fairly simple. Carol ran the shop up front, while Bruce ran the bakery and ordered supplies. When the business began to grow, Carol hired two part-time clerks to help out in the shop. Marina had moved to the country 2 years ago from El Salvador, and Kim was a newly arrived Korean who was working his way through college. Bruce hired Maurice, a French Canadian, as an assistant.

The ovens were soon running 24 hours a day, supervised by Maurice, who was now master baker, and two assistants on each of three shifts. Marina and Kim supervised the shop, since Carol was usually too busy managing general sales distribution to spend much time with customers. Bruce still spent 3 or 4 hours a day in the bakery whenever he could get out of his office, but he spent most of that time coordinating production and solving problems with Maurice.

Within the next year, Sundown expanded from its original location, adding two new shops as well as two kiosks in local malls. Carol and Bruce hired a new operations manager, Hans Mikelson, who had formerly been regional manager of a national chain of coffee shops. Mikelson had plenty of new ideas about how to operate an expanding business: He had a Web site created, added an extensive range of drinks and meal items to the menu, and instituted two dress codes—one for all counter help and another for kitchen employees. He also put together an employee manual to save time orienting new employees. All of these changes were announced by memos from Mikelson, which were distributed to employees by the store managers.

The expanding size of Sundown led to a change in the company. The family feeling that was strong when Sundown was a small operation was less noticeable. The new employees barely knew Bruce and Carol, and, as a result, there was less give-and-take of ideas between the owners and workers.

Mikelson's memos on the dress code and the employee manual created a crisis. Old-time employees were furious about receiving orders from "the bureaucrats," as management came to be called.

Bruce and Carol recognized the problem and wanted to keep the lines of communication open, but they weren't sure how to do so. "I'm just a baker," Bruce confessed in exasperation. "I don't know how to run a big company."

Another set of challenges grew out of the changing character of the employees. In the original location alone, Sundown now employed workers from seven different countries. José, who was born in Brazil, confessed to Bruce that he felt uncomfortable being managed by Carol. "It's nothing personal," he said, "but where I come from, a man doesn't take orders from a woman." The Sundown employee profile was different in other ways. Two of the assistant bakers were openly gay; one of the sales clerks got around by wheelchair.

Carol, Bruce, and Hans know that good products alone aren't enough to guarantee the continuing success of Sundown Bakeries. They need to improve the quality of communication among the growing team who make and sell their products.

As you read the chapters in this unit, consider the following questions:

Chapter 1

1. Analyze the likely causes of the resentment over the employee manual and uniforms by considering the impact of the sender, message, decoding, feedback, context, and probable sources of noise. Describe how the problems you identified could have been minimized by different communication strategies.

2. Identify the changes in communication channels between employees and management as Sundown has grown. What channels can be used to make communication about changes in the business most productive?

3. Consider the relational messages employees seem to have received from management as Sundown's business grew.

4. How have Sundown's formal and informal communication networks changed as the company expanded? In what ways have both the formal

and informal networks contributed to Sundown's growing pains? In what ways can these networks be used to improve the relationships between management and employees?

Chapter 2

1. How do changes in the demographic makeup of Sundown Bakeries reflect transformation of the larger workforce?

2. Consider the following dimensions of culture as you describe the impact of culture on communication within the company: high- and low-context styles, individualism and collectivism, and power distance.

3. How would you describe the early organizational culture of Sundown? How has the culture changed as the company grew? Consider the issues listed on pages 58–60 as you answer this question.

4. What advice would you give to Sundown's management team about how to maintain the most effective culture in the face of the company's growth?

1

Communicating at Work

chapter outline

The Importance of Communication

The Nature of Communication
  The Process of Communication
  Communication Principles

Ethical Dimensions of Communication

Using Communication Networks
  Formal Communication Networks
  Informal Communication Networks

Face-to-Face and Electronic Communication Channels
  Face-to-Face Communication
  Telephone and Voice Mail
  Teleconferencing and Videoconferencing
  Instant Messaging
  Twitter and Text Messaging
  E-mail and Written Communication
  Which Channel to Use
  Review Points
  Key Terms
  Activities
  Resources

chapter objectives

After reading this chapter you should be able to

1. Explain the role of communication in career success, providing examples to support your claims.
2. Apply the basic elements, the process, and key principles of communication to a specific situation, showing how each one affects the outcome of the interaction.
3. Apply the concepts of ethical communication discussed here to one or more ethically challenging situations.
4. Describe how formal and informal communication networks operate in a given situation, and how you can use various networks to accomplish your goals within an organization.
5. Analyze the advantages and disadvantages of various face-to-face and electronic communication channels and choose the most appropriate and effective one for a given situation.

The Importance of Communication

Virtually everyone communicates at work. No matter what the field, specialized knowledge alone isn't enough to guarantee success; communication skills are also vital. Table 1-1 summarizes the results of one annual survey in which employers list the skills and qualities for their ideal candidate. Communication skills always top the list.[1] Subscribers to the *Harvard Business Review* rated "the ability to communicate" the most

Table 1–1	Top Ten Qualities/Skills Employers Want

1. Communication skills
2. Strong work ethic
3. Teamwork skills (works well with others)
4. Initiative
5. Analytical skills
6. Computer skills
7. Flexibility/adaptability
8. Interpersonal skills (relates well to others)
9. Problem-solving skills
10. Technical skills

Source: Reprinted from *Job Outlook 2009—Student Version*, from JobWeb (**www.jobweb.com**), with permission of the National Association of Colleges and Employers, copyright holder.

career tip

Careers in Communication

While communication plays an important role in every job, it is the focus of many careers. The National Communication Association (**www.natcom.org**) publishes a list of communication-related fields and some typical specialties within them. While a degree in communication may not be mandatory for jobs like these, academic study of the field is excellent preparation.

- **Advertising/marketing:** market researcher, copy writer, account executive, sales manager, media planner, media buyer, creative director, media sales representative.

- **Electronic media/radio-television/broadcasting:** archivist/librarian, community relations director, unit manager, video editor, news director, writer, technical director, advertising sales coordinator, traffic/continuity specialist, media buyer, announcer, disc jockey, newscaster, public relations manager, casting director, producer, business manager, account executive, floor manager, talk show host, director of broadcasting.

- **Journalism/publishing:** reporter, editor, author, writer, project manager, publisher, news service researcher, technical writer.

- **Public information/development:** public information officer, press agent, development officer, fund raiser, membership recruiter, media analyst/planner, creative director, public opinion researcher.

- **Organizational affairs:** human resources specialist or manager, director of organizational communication, industrial and labor relations representative, negotiator, ombudsman, customer service representative, newsletter editor, trainer, human resources manager.

- **Government/political affairs:** public information officer, speech writer, legislative assistant, campaign staffer/director, research specialist, lobbyist, press secretary.

---

important factor in making an executive "promotable," more important than ambition, education, and capacity for hard work.[2]

The need for communication skills is important in virtually every career,[3] not just those that are traditionally regarded as people-oriented. Practitioners in Big Six accounting firms spend 80 percent of their work time communicating with others, individually and in groups.[4] Likewise, engineers spend most of their professional lives speaking and listening, mostly in one-to-one and small group settings.[5] Communication skills are essential for doctors, nurses, and other medical professionals.[6] Technical people with good communication skills earn more, and those who are weak communicators suffer.[7] William Schaffer, international business development manager for computer giant Sun Microsystems, made the point emphatically: "If there's one skill that's required for success in this industry, it's communication skills."[8] Writing in *The Scientist*, author Jim Richman echoes this sentiment: "If I give any advice, it is that you can never do enough training around your overall communication skills."[9] Other high-tech experts back up this claim.

On-the-job communication skills can even make the difference between life and death. The Los Angeles Police Department cited "bad communication" among the most common reasons for errors in shooting by its officers.[10] Researchers discovered that "poor communication" was the root of over 60 percent of reported medical errors—including death, serious physical injury, and psychological trauma.[11] Research published in the *Journal of the American Medical Association* and elsewhere revealed a significant difference between the communication skills of physicians who had no malpractice claims against them and doctors with previous claims.[12]

The importance of communication is not surprising when you consider the staggering amount of time people spend communicating on the job. One study based on responses from over 1,000 employees at Fortune 1000 companies found that workers send and receive an average of 178 messages each day via telephone, e-mail, faxes, text messages, blogs, instant messages, and face-to-face communication.[13] Some experts have estimated that the average business executive spends 75 to 80 percent of the time communicating—about 45 minutes of every hour.[14] According to one authority, the primary source of clogged in-boxes isn't commercial spam, but messages from co-workers.[15]

The Nature of Communication

Understanding the importance of communication isn't the same thing as understanding how the process works. A close look at what happens when people try to communicate can offer clues about why some attempts succeed and others fail.

The Process of Communication

No matter what the setting or the number of people involved, all communication consists of the same elements. Although the process of communication is more than the total of these parts, understanding them can help explain what happens when one person tries to express an idea to others.

A Model of Communication   The communication process begins with a **sender,** the person who transmits a **message.** Some messages are deliberate, while others (such as sighs and yawns) may be unintentional. The sender must choose certain words or nonverbal methods to send an intentional message. This activity is called **encoding.** The **channel** (sometimes called the *medium*) is the method used to deliver a message. As a business communicator, you can often choose to write a letter or memo, send a fax or an e-mail, or deliver the message over the phone or in person.

Even if a message does get to its intended receiver intact, there's no guarantee that it will be understood as the sender intended it to be.[16] The **receiver** must still **decode** it, attaching meaning to the words or symbols. Receivers don't just absorb messages like sponges; they interpret and respond to them. The discernible response of a receiver to a sender's message is called **feedback.** Some feedback is nonverbal—smiles, sighs, and so on. Sometimes it is oral, as when you react to a colleague's ideas with questions or comments. Feedback can also be written, as when you respond by writing your co-worker a memo. In many cases, no message can be a type of feedback. Failure to answer a letter or to return a phone call can suggest how the noncommunicative person feels about the sender. When we add the element of feedback to our communication model, we begin to recognize that in face-to-face settings people are simultaneously senders and receivers of information. This explains why these two roles are superimposed in the communication model pictured in Figure 1–1 on page 8.

One of the greatest sources of communication problems is **noise**—the term communication scholars use for factors that interfere with the exchange of messages. The most obvious type of noise is *external* (also called *physical*) *noise.* This includes sounds that distract communicators—such as the babble of voices in the next room or the annoying ring of someone's cell phone in a meeting—an overcrowded room, or a smelly cigar. A second kind of noise is *physiological:* hearing disorders, illnesses, disabilities, and other factors make it difficult to send or receive messages. To appreciate the importance of physiological noise, recall how hard it is to pay attention when you are recovering from

case study

a late-night study session or have the flu. The third type of noise is *psychological*—forces within the sender or receiver that interfere with understanding, such as egotism, defensiveness, assumptions, stereotypes, biases, prejudices, hostility, preoccupation, and fear.

Communication Contexts Communication always takes place in some setting, and the **context** in which it occurs can have a powerful effect on what happens. For example, the *physical context* can influence the content and quality of interaction. Imagine how discussing a problem with your boss or asking for a raise might be received differently depending on whether the conversation took place in your boss's office or over lunch at a local restaurant.

FIGURE 1–1

Communication Model

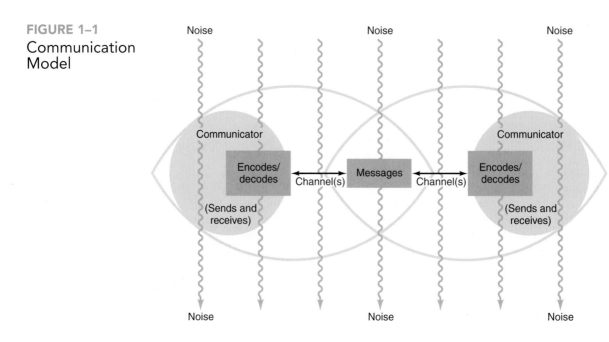

8

The *social context* refers to the nature of the relationship between the communicators, as well as others whose presence may affect the nature of communication. Imagine, for instance, the difference in asking a manager for a raise if you had a long history of friendship versus one of animosity, or if your ages were close or radically different. An interesting application of how changing the social context can shape interaction occurred during a round of secret negotiations in the 1990s between Israel and the Palestine Liberation Organization. The hosts, the Norwegian foreign minister and his wife, invited the negotiators to their home, where they played on the floor with the hosts' 4-year-old child. After changing the context, impasses were broken and a groundbreaking Mideast peace accord was hammered out.[17]

The *chronological context* refers to the ways in which time influences interaction. A sample of time-related considerations shows the importance of adapting to the chronological context: time of day (e.g., first appointment in the morning or last in the afternoon) or the time of year (e.g., holiday season, tax time). You can boost your chances for success by paying attention to chronological factors. When calling someone or requesting a person's help, consider asking, "Is this a good time?" or "Do you have time now, or would another time be more convenient?"

The *cultural context* of communication includes both the organizational and the ethnic and/or national backgrounds of the persons communicating. Chapter 2 discusses the role of culture in detail. For now, you can get a sense of the importance of culture by imagining how just a few differences in backgrounds might influence communication: baby boomers and generation X-ers or Y-ers, Euro-Americans and Hispanics, New Yorkers and Californians, or Americans and Chinese.

Communication Principles

The communication model pictured in Figure 1–1 is not yet complete. It is like a still picture of a live event: All the elements are present except action. Several characteristics describe the dynamic nature of the communication process.

Communication Is Unavoidable
A fundamental axiom of communication is "One cannot not communicate." As you will learn in Chapter 4, facial expression, posture, gesture, clothing, and a host of other behaviors offer cues about our attitudes. The impossibility of not communicating means that we send messages even by our absence. Failing to show up at an event or leaving the room suggests meanings to others. Because communication is unavoidable, it is essential to consider the unintentional messages you send.

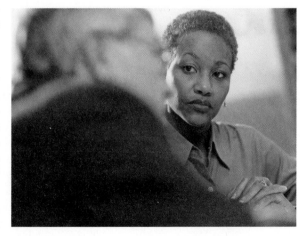

Communication Operates on Two Levels
Every time two or more people communicate, they exchange two kinds of messages. The most obvious ones are **content messages**—information about the topic under discussion. But at a less apparent level, the communicators also exchange **relational messages**—signals indicating how they feel about one another.[18] Relational messages indicate a variety of attitudes. An important one is *affinity*—the degree to which a communicator likes the other person in general or a

particular message that is being sent. Another kind of relational message deals with *control*—the amount of influence in that situation. Communication theorists sometimes talk about three self-explanatory distributions of control that can exist between communicators: "one up," "one down," and "straight across." A third type of relational message can reflect a communicator's degree of *respect* for the other person or people. Note that respect and affinity aren't always identical: It is possible to like others without respecting them and to respect them without liking them.

Communication Is Irreversible

At one time or another, we have all wished we could take back words we regretted uttering. Unfortunately, this isn't possible. Our words and deeds are recorded in others' memories, and we can't erase them. As the old saying goes, people may forgive, but they don't forget. In fact, often the more vigorously you try to erase an act, the more vividly it stands out.

Communication Is a Process

It isn't really accurate to talk about an "act" of communication as if sending or receiving a message were an isolated event. Rather, every communication event needs to be examined as part of its communication context. Suppose, for example, your boss responds to your request for a raise by saying, "I was going to ask you to take a *cut* in pay!" How would you react? The answer probably depends on several factors: Is your boss a joker or a serious person? How does the comment fit into the history of your relationship—have your boss's remarks been critical or supportive in the past? How does the message fit with ones you have received from other people? What mood are you in today? All these questions show that the meaning of a message depends in part on what has happened before. Each message is part of a process: It doesn't occur in isolation.

Communication Is Not a Panacea

Although communication can smooth out the bumps and straighten the road to success, it won't always get you what you want. Misunderstandings and ill feelings can arise even when people communicate carefully,[19] and they can increase when people communicate badly. This helps explain why some problems grow worse the longer they are discussed. Even effective communication won't solve all problems: There are some situations in which the parties understand one another perfectly and still disagree. These limitations are important to understand as you begin to study communication on the job. Boosting your communication skills can increase your effectiveness, but it isn't a cure-all.

Ethical Dimensions of Communication

One writer observed that the trouble with business ethics is that many people think the phrase is an oxymoron. Despite this cynical attitude, there is a growing recognition that behaving ethically is an essential part of being an effective, promotable employee. Scandalous business practices led to the downfall of major corporations like Enron and WorldCom and have cost others millions of dollars. As a result of these ethical lapses, sensitivity to communicating in a principled way has grown, and several hundred corporations and organizations now include an ethics officer in their organizational chart who reports directly to the chairman.[20] Employees share this concern for ethics. One survey of 800 recent MBA graduates revealed that virtually all were willing to forgo

ethical challenge

Ethical Communication Choices

See page 12 for descriptions of seven guidelines for judging ethical communication:

- Utilitarian Approach
- Rights Approach
- Fairness or Justice Approach
- Common-Good Approach
- Virtue Approach
- Professional Ethic
- Publicity Test

Outline the range of ways you could handle each situation below. Use one or more of the ethical guidelines to decide on a course of action that is both principled and realistic. Justify your decision.

1. A co-worker tells you he's about to buy an expensive car that will strain his budget to the maximum. You recently learned that he is slated to be laid off at the end of the month but were told to keep this information in strictest confidence. What do you do?

2. Your friend is applying for a job and has given you as a reference. A questionnaire sent by the employer asks if there is any reason you cannot recommend the applicant. You know that your friend is struggling with an alcohol problem, which led to dismissal from a previous job. Do you mention this problem on the reference form? If so, how?

3. Your boss calls you into her office and praises you for doing excellent work on a recent project. She suggests that this level of performance is likely to earn you a promotion and raise. In truth, a colleague made a far greater contribution to the project. How do you respond to your boss's praise?

4. As part of your job, you learn that some damaged equipment can be repaired for $15,000. Your supervisor tells you to claim the damage is much greater so the insurance company will pay closer to $100,000. What do you do?

5. While you are entertaining a customer, he makes a blatantly offensive joke. How do you respond?

Sources: Some of the scenarios above are adapted from the quiz "How Ethical Are You?" in John E. Richardson, ed., *Business Ethics 03/04*, 15th ed. (Guilford, CT: McGraw-Hill/Dushkin, 2003), p. 200, and "On Witnessing a Fraud" by Don Soeken in John E. Richardson, ed., *Business Ethics 07/08*, 19th ed. (Dubuque, IA: McGraw-Hill/Dushkin, 2008), p. 72.

---

some money to work for an organization with a better reputation for corporate social responsibility (CSR) and ethics.[21]

Doing the ethical thing isn't always easy. On a personal level, you are likely to face conflicts between what you believe is right and what is practical. For instance, you might have to deal with a customer or colleague whose business or approval you want, but who is behaving badly—perhaps making sexist or racist remarks. After a trip together, co-workers turn in inflated expenses and expect you to do the same. Your team is under pressure to finish a project, but you recognize potential safety issues being shortcut. Besides personal challenges, sooner or later you are likely to experience situations like these where others in your organization behave in ethically questionable ways. Do you speak up when a colleague makes promises to clients that you know the company can't keep? Should you challenge your boss when he or she treats other employees unfairly or illegally?

It has been said that ethics centers on a sense of responsibility for someone other than yourself.[22] A blanket obligation to communicate ethically can be too vague to be helpful in specific situations. Five philosophical principles offer standards that can help you decide how to behave in a principled manner:[23]

Utilitarian Approach (Jeremy Bentham and John Stuart Mill): Does this action provide the greatest good for the greatest number?

Rights Approach (Immanual Kant): Does this action respect the moral rights (truth, privacy, non-injury, promises) of everyone?

Fairness or Justice Approach (Aristotle, John Rawls): Is this action fair and free of discrimination or favoritism?

Common-Good Approach (Plato, Aristotle, Cicero, John Rawls): Does the action further the common or community good?

Virtue Approach: Does this action promote the development of moral virtue (character) in me and my community?

Two additional guidelines can help you evaluate whether you are behaving ethically:

Professional Ethic: How would this action be judged by an impartial jury of your professional peers?

Publicity Test: Would you be comfortable having the public learn about your behavior in the broadcast or print media?[24]

Using Communication Networks

The story of Sundown Bakery (page 2) shows that, as organizations grow, a system for managing the flow of communication has to develop. The regular patterns of communication between people are called **communication networks.**[25] Two kinds of networks exist: formal and informal.

Formal Communication Networks

Formal communication networks are systems designed by management to dictate who should talk to whom to get a job done.[26] In a small organization, networks are so simple that they may hardly be noticeable; in a larger organization, they become more intricate. The most common way of describing formal communication networks is with **organizational charts** like the one in Figure 1–2 on page 13. Organizational charts are more than a bureaucrat's toy; they provide a clear guideline of who is responsible for a given task and which employees are responsible for others' performance.

Downward Communication   **Downward communication** occurs whenever superiors initiate messages to their subordinates. There are several types of downward communication:

- *Job instructions:* "Bring in receipts for items under $20 that you pay for with cash. Anything over $20, charge to the company credit card."
- *Job rationale:* "We rotate the stock like that so the customers won't wind up with outdated merchandise."
- *Procedures and practices:* "Don't try to argue with unhappy customers. If you can't handle them yourself, call the manager."
- *Feedback:* "Backing up the files on your flash drive was a great idea. That saved us a lot of grief when the laptop didn't work."
- *Indoctrination:* "People can buy the stuff we sell at other places, but we can bring them in here by giving them what they want quickly and pleasantly. If we do that, we'll all come out ahead."

FIGURE 1–2

A Formal
Communication
Network

Organizational Chart

Chris
Manager

Jane
Administrative Assistant

Belle
Office Manager

Ted
Assistant Manager

Claire
Assistant Manager

Maria
Assistant Manager

Tara—CS Rep*

Bob—CS Rep

Malik—CS Rep

Todd—CS Rep

Dawn—CS Rep

Phil—CS Rep

Sue—CS Rep

Nancy—CS Rep

Jose—CS Rep

Steve—CS Rep

Pam—CS Rep

Kate—CS Rep

*CS Rep = Customer-Service Representative

Most managers would agree—at least in principle—that downward communication is important. It's hard to argue with the need for giving instructions, explaining rationale, describing procedures, and so on. Like their bosses, employees recognize the importance of downward communication. A study at General Electric (GE) revealed that "clear communication between boss and worker" was the most important factor in job satisfaction for most people. GE was so impressed with the findings of this study that it launched a program to encourage managers to communicate more, and more directly, with their employees, including holding informal meetings to encourage interaction.[27]

The desire for feedback is probably so strong among most employees because supervisors rarely provide enough of it. As two researchers in the field, Daniel Katz and Robert Kahn, put it: "The frequent complaint . . . by the individual is that he does not know where he stands with his superiors."[28] Many companies do take a more enlightened approach to feedback. Ed Carlson, former president of United Airlines, is generally credited with turning the company from a loser into a winner during his tenure. Part of his success was due to keeping United's employees—all of them—aware of how the company was doing. "Nothing is worse for morale than a lack of information down in the ranks," he said. "I call it NETMA—Nobody Ever Tells Me Anything—and I have tried hard to minimize that problem."[29] True to his word, Carlson passed along to the field staff information on United's operations that was previously considered too important to circulate.

career tip

Getting Recognized by Your Bosses

According to Muriel Solomon, "The big secret to getting recognized is to give creative thinking a priority." She and other career advisers recommend that you can showcase your talent, create interest in your work, and display your potential in several ways:

- **Present proposals to your boss.** Learn the history of a challenge, develop a specific plan that shows creativity and understanding of the company's needs. Don't wait for someone to recognize you or choose you for a prime assignment.

- **Volunteer for committees, to chair a committee, or to sponsor a workshop, hearing, or sports event.** Create opportunities to enlarge your working relationships with people at many levels of your organization. Prepare concise summaries and submit reports to your boss.

- **Get your thoughts printed.** Contribute quality writing in the company magazines, department newsletters, or association or professional journals. Distribute copies to your boss, bulletin boards, and company blogs.

- **Use thoughtful gestures to build bridges.** Devote 5 minutes a day to raising your visibility by thanking people who worked on your project, calling or sending notes of thanks to the supervisors of those who helped you (with a blind copy to the one whose help you received), and feeding your gratitude into the grapevine.

- **Be ready to share a story about your accomplishments.** Without bragging, be prepared to weave your accomplishments (be sure to include recent ones) into an interesting story you can tell whenever the opportunity arises: "Something like that happened to us last week . . ."

Sources: Peggy Klaus, *The Hard Truth About Soft Skills* (New York: Collins Business, 2007), and Muriel Solomon, *Getting Praised, Raised and Recognized* (Englewood Cliffs, NJ: Prentice-Hall, 1993).

Upward Communication   Messages flowing from subordinates to superiors are labeled **upward communication.** Virtually every organization *claims* to seek out upward messages, but many aren't as open to employee opinions as they claim. In some organizations, questioning the boss can be a recipe for professional suicide. "The disconnect between rhetoric and reality is why Scott Adams [creator of the 'Dilbert' comic strip] is a millionaire," says management expert Warren Bennis.[30]

Businesses that really are open to upward communication can profit from the opinions of employees.[31] Sam Walton, founder of Wal-Mart, the largest retailer in the United States, claimed that "our best ideas come from clerks and stockboys."[32] Industry observers credit the dramatic turnaround of Mattel Corporation to the openness to employee suggestions of its CEO, John Aberman.[33] Upward communication can convey four types of messages:[34]

- *What subordinates are doing:* "We'll have that job done by closing time today."

- *Unsolved work problems:* "We're still having trouble with the air conditioner in the accounting office."

- *Suggestions for improvement:* "I think I've figured a way to give people the vacation schedules they want and still keep our staffing up." As the Career Tip above suggests, getting recognized by your boss can pave the way to career advancement.

- *How subordinates feel about each other and the job:* "I'm having a hard time working with Louie. He seems to think I'm mad at him." Or, "I'm getting frustrated. I've been in the same job for over a year now, and I'd like more responsibility."

These messages can benefit both subordinates and superiors, and this explains why the most satisfied employees feel free to express dissent to their bosses.[35] Bennis emphasizes the critical role upward communication plays in the success of an organization:

> [T]he longer I study effective leaders, the more I am convinced of the underappreciated importance of effective followers. What makes a good follower? The single most important characteristic may well be a willingness to tell the truth. In a world of growing complexity, leaders are increasingly dependent on their subordinates for good information, whether the leaders want to or not. Followers who tell the truth, and leaders who listen, are an unbeatable combination.[36]

Upward communication is especially important for women. Females who engage in more interactions with their supervisors advance in the organizational hierarchy faster than those who do not spend as much time communicating upward.[37] A probable explanation for this fact is that women have fewer informal connections with powerful decision-makers in some organizations. Given this absence of connections, it makes sense that women would rely on official contacts to work efficiently and effectively.

Despite the importance of upward communication, employees find participation in upward communication extremely difficult. Being frank with superiors can be risky, especially when the news isn't what the boss wants to hear.[38] Busy superiors can also be too isolated, busy, or certain of their expertise to pay attention to employees. Some organizations have developed systems to promote upward communication in the face of challenges like these. Pillsbury Corporation employees can voice their messages on an anonymous voice mail system. An independent company creates transcripts of all calls and forwards them to Pillsbury's CEO.[39]

Most of the responsibility for improving upward communication rests with managers. They can begin the process by announcing their willingness to hear from subordinates. A number of vehicles facilitate upward messages: an open-door policy, grievance procedures, periodic interviews, group meetings, and the suggestion box, to name a few. Formal channels aren't the only way to promote upward messages. Informal contacts can often be most effective; chats during breaks, in the elevator, or at social gatherings can sometimes tell more than planned sessions. But no method will be effective unless a

Dilbert: © Scott Adams/Dist. by United Feature Syndicate, Inc. Reprinted by permission.

manager is sincerely interested in hearing from subordinates and genuinely values their ideas. Just talking about this isn't enough. Employees have to see evidence of a willingness to hear upward messages—both good and bad—before they will really open up.

Horizontal Communication

A third type of organizational interaction is **horizontal communication** (sometimes called **lateral communication**). It consists of messages between members of an organization with equal power.[40] The most obvious type of horizontal communication goes on between members of the same division of an organization: office workers in the same department, co-workers on a construction project, and so on. In other cases, lateral communication occurs between people from different areas: accounting calls maintenance to get a machine repaired, hospital admissions calls intensive care to reserve a bed, and so on. Horizontal communication serves five purposes:[41]

- *Task coordination:* "Let's get together this afternoon and set up a production schedule."

- *Problem solving:* "It takes 3 days for my department to get reports from yours. How can we speed things up?"

- *Sharing information:* "I just found out that a big convention is coming to town next week, so we ought to get ready for lots of business."

- *Conflict resolution:* "I've heard that you were complaining about my work to the boss. If you're not happy, I wish you'd tell me first."

- *Building rapport:* "I appreciate the way you got that rush job done on time. I'd like to say thanks by buying you lunch when it's convenient."

Research suggests that people in most organizations communicate horizontally, but the reasons for doing so in high-performing groups are different from those in less effective ones.[42] Low-performing groups are likely to reach out to different parts of the organization to get information on how to follow existing procedures. For example, an engineer might contact the purchasing department to check on the status of an equipment order. By contrast, lateral contacts in high-performing organizations are used to get the information needed to solve complex and difficult work problems. For instance, before starting design work on a new product, the same engineer might contact the sales manager to find out what features customers want most. Top-performing organizations encourage people from different areas to get together and share ideas. At Hewlett-Packard,

Worldwide Personnel Manager Barbara Waugh and her colleagues spent 5 years improving horizontal communication. "My role is to create mirrors that show the whole what the parts are doing—through coffee talks and small meetings, through building a network, through bringing people together who have similar or complementary ideas."[43]

Despite the importance of good horizontal communication, several forces work to discourage communication between peers.[44] *Rivalry* is one. People who feel threatened by one another aren't likely to be cooperative. The threat can come from competition for a promotion, raise, or other scarce resource. Sometimes rivalry occurs over an informal role. For example, two office comedians might feel threatened each time the other gets a laugh; that could inhibit their cooperation. Another challenge is the *specialization* that makes it hard for people with different technical specialties to understand one another. *Information overload* can also discourage employees from reaching out to others in different areas, and a simple *lack of motivation* is another problem. Finally, *physical barriers* can interfere with horizontal connections.

Informal Communication Networks

So far, we have focused on networks within organizations that are created by management. Alongside the formal networks, every organization also has **informal communication networks**—patterns of interaction based on friendships, shared personal or career interests, and proximity. One business writer described the value of informal networks:

> *A firm's organizational chart will tell you about authority. It doesn't always show how things get done or created. You know the rules, but you don't know the ropes. For that, you need a map to the network, the corresponding informal structure that is usually invisible.*[45]

Informal relationships within organizations operate in ways that have little to do with the formal relationships laid out in organizational charts.[46] Figure 1–3 shows how the actual flow of information in one firm is quite different from its formal structure. And beyond any sort of organizational connection, people are connected with one another through informal personal networks—with friends, neighbors, family members, and all sorts of other relationships.

Some informal networks arise because of personal interests. Two colleagues who are avid basketball fans or share a fascination with rare books are more likely to swap information on work than co-workers who have no such bonds. Personal friendships also create connections that can lead to increased communication. Finally, physical proximity increases the chances for interaction. Shared office space or frequent meetings around the copying machine make it likely that people will exchange information. Even sharing restrooms can lead to networking, as public relations executive James E. Lukaszewski observes in describing one anatomical difference that has benefited men.

> *This may sound facetious, even silly, but when these meetings break, where are the women and where are the men? The guys go to the porcelain in that little room with M-E-N on the door. . . . The guys are standing there, facing the wall, talking and deciding things. It's a critical opportunity for important verbal communication to take place during times of decision making.*[47]

Functions of Informal Networks within Organizations
As the following examples show, not all informal messages are idle rumors. Informal communication can serve several useful functions.

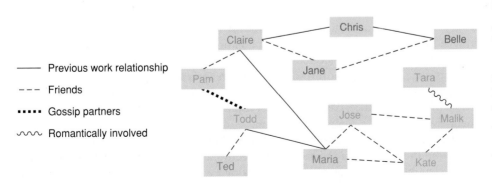

FIGURE 1–3

An Informal Communication Network

Source: Adapted from Mark P. Orbe and Carol J. Bruess, *Contemporary Issues Interpersonal Communication* (Los Angeles: Roxbury, 2005), p. 309.

- *Confirming formal messages:* "The boss is really serious this time about cutting down on overnight travel. I heard him yelling about it when I walked past his office."
- *Expanding on formal messages:* "The invitation to the office party says 'casual dress,' but don't make it too informal."
- *Expediting official messages:* You might learn about openings within an organization from people in your network long before the vacancies are published.
- *Contradicting official messages:* You might learn from a friend in accounting that the deadline for purchases on this year's budget isn't as firm as it sounded in the comptroller's recent memo.
- *Circumventing formal channels:* Your tennis partner who works in duplicating might sneak in an occasional rush job for you instead of putting it at the end of the line.

Many companies elevate informal communication to an official policy by encouraging open, unstructured contacts between people from various parts of the organization. For example, Hewlett-Packard's approach to problem solving has been termed MBWA, "management by wandering around."

Some observers consider informal contacts to be the primary means of communication within an organization. In one survey, 57 percent of the respondents said that the grapevine is "the only way to find out what's really happening" in their organizations.[48] A decade of research shows that engineers and scientists were five times more likely to turn to a person for information than to impersonal sources like the databases or files.[49] Two well-known analysts flatly assert that as much as 90 percent of what goes on in a company has nothing to do with formal events.[50] Writing in the *Harvard Business Review*, David Krackhardt and Jeffrey Hanson capture the difference between formal and informal networks: "If the formal organization is the skeleton of a company, the informal is the central nervous system."[51]

Like the human nervous system, informal networks are faster, and often more dependable, than formal channels.[52] They also provide a shortcut (and sometimes a way around) for the slower and more cumbersome formal channels, making innovation easier.[53] This fact helps explain why organizational decision-makers tend to rely on verbal information from trusted associates.[54] Smart communicators don't just rely on informal contacts with peers for information; they take advantage of sources throughout the organization. One study revealed that general managers spent a great deal of time with people who were not direct subordinates, superiors, or peers—people with whom, according to the official chain of command, they had no need to deal. Although many of these people—secretaries, lower-level subordinates, and supervisors with little power— seemed relatively unimportant to outsiders, successful managers all seemed to cultivate such contacts.[55]

Enlightened organizations do everything possible to encourage constructive, informal interaction. Siemens Corp. leaves overhead projectors and empty pads of paper in its factory lunchrooms to facilitate informal meetings.[56] Corning Glass deliberately installed escalators in its new engineering building to boost the kind of face-to-face contacts that are less likely in elevators. 3M sponsors clubs for any group of employees that requests them, realizing that this sort of employee interaction is likely to encourage new ideas that will help the company. Other firms mingle workers from different departments in the same office, convinced that people who rub elbows will swap ideas and see themselves as part of a companywide team.

Informal networks don't just operate within organizations. Friends, neighbors, and community members increase their effectiveness by sharing information. In some cities, chambers of commerce host networking events to encourage these ties among

Your Elevator Speech

Often the chance to present yourself and your ideas lasts less than a minute. You meet a prospective customer at a party. You run into your boss on the street. You are introduced to a potential employer in a hallway. Whether networking opportunities like these turn out well or badly may depend on your foresight and preparation.

When the opportunity arises, you can make a good impression by delivering what has been called an "elevator speech." (This type of communication gets its name because it should be brief enough to deliver in the length of an elevator ride.) Elevator speeches can accomplish a variety of goals. Besides serving as introductions, they can be a tool for seeking help, establishing a relationship, gaining visibility, marketing yourself or your organization, getting feedback, expanding your personal network, and doing an end-run around someone who is blocking your progress.

Practice your skill at presenting yourself briefly and effectively by planning and delivering an elevator speech to your classmates. Your speech should contain four parts and take less than a minute to deliver.

1. State your name and your current job title or position.

   "Hi. I'm Claire Yoder. I'm a senior, graduating in December."
2. Describe some personal strengths or distinguishing information.

   "I'm completing my accounting major this semester with a 3.8 GPA and I've developed additional skills in tax preparation through volunteer work with Tax-Help USA."
3. Depending on your audience, state what you can do for others *or* ask for their help:

   "If you or someone you know needs help with tax preparation, I can help," *or* "If you know of any openings in accounting, I'd like to hear about them."
4. Indicate how the person can get in touch with you or how you plan to contact this person:

   "Here's my card with my e-mail address. I'd like to hear from you."

While modesty is a virtue, don't be bashful about presenting yourself as an interesting and competent person. Whether or not you want to, you are always presenting yourself to others. Brevity and sincerity are the keys to an elevator speech. Don't overwhelm your audience with information; present enough to make sure you create a positive impression and, ideally, to be asked for more information.

For more help planning your elevator speech, see **www.saleslinks.com/sideline/99c/11v1.htm** and **www.work.com/creating-an-elevator-pitch-for-your-startup-319/**.

Source: After Marie Wallace, "The Elevator Speech—It's There for You," retrieved June 21, 2006, from Law Library Resource Exchange at **www.llrx.com/columns/guide18.htm**.

community businesses. Even without these organized contacts, most people are surprised to realize just how many people they know who can offer useful information. Consider all the networks to which you already belong: family members, friends, neighbors, social acquaintances, fellow workers, members of your religious community, professionals (doctors, dentists, accountants, attorneys, etc.), school contacts (faculty, fellow students, counselors, etc.).

Cultivating Personal Networks   Everyone is part of informal networks. As one writer put it, "Shared information is the foundation upon which civilization has been built. . . . We always networked. We just called it being 'neighborly.'"[57] While all of us have personal contacts, **networking,** as the term is usually used, has a strategic dimension that goes beyond being sociable. It is the process of deliberately meeting people and maintaining contacts to get career information, advice, and leads—and in turn to help others. Some professionals use social networks such as Facebook for business contacts, while others are networking at sites like LinkedIn that were designed expressly for business purposes. As you explore and expand your network, keep the following tips in mind.[58]

View everyone as a networking prospect   The Self-Assessment tool on page 22 will help you identify many people in your personal networks who can help you achieve your goals. Beyond the people you already know, almost everyone you meet has the potential to be a source of useful information. The passenger seated next to you on a plane or train might be acquainted with people who can help you. The neighbor who chats with you at a block party might have the knowledge or skill to help you solve a problem. Within an organization, the best informants are often people you might overlook. Administrative assistants are exposed to most of the information addressed to their bosses, and they usually serve as gatekeepers who can give or deny access to them. Custodial and maintenance people travel around the building and, in their rounds, see and hear many interesting things. Of course, treating everyone you deal with respectfully is ethical as well as smart.

Be sensitive to personal and cultural factors   While everyone you meet is a potential networking prospect, it's important to think of each person as an individual. Some welcome the chance to share information, whereas others may object to more than occasional contacts.

It's also important to recognize that culture plays a role in networking practices. As Table 1–2 shows, the relationships you have with others can vary depending on their nationality and background.

Treat your contacts with gratitude and respect   Don't make the mistake of equating networking with being dishonest or exploitive. As long as you express a genuine desire for information openly, there's nothing to be ashamed of. Furthermore, seeking information doesn't mean you have to stop enjoying others' company for social reasons.

Table 1–2	Chinese–Western Networking Differences

Chinese	Western
Personal and trust-based	Contract-oriented
Personal relationships have organizational implications and vice versa	Clear distinction between individual and organizational relationships
Symbiotic relationship between networked organizations	High independence of networked organizations
Motivated by economic and social concerns	Motivated primarily by economic concerns
Flexibility and informality	Formality and clearly defined roles

Source: M. J. Chen, *Inside Chinese Business: A Guide for Managers Worldwide.* Boston, MA: Harvard Business School Press, 2001, p. 64.

When others do give you information, be sure to express your appreciation. At the very least, a "thank you" is in order. Even better, let your networking contacts know exactly *how* the information they gave you was helpful.

Help others   Don't just be an information-seeker. Whenever possible, make an effort to put people who will benefit from contact in touch with one another: "You're looking for a new bookkeeper? I know someone who might be right for you!" Besides being the right thing to do, helping others will earn you a reputation for generosity that can serve you well.[59] The Self-Assessment on page 22 offers a tool for noting ways that you can use your personal networks to help meet others' needs.

Get referrals to secondary sources   The benefits of personal networks don't stop with your personal acquaintances. Each person you know has his or her own connections, some of whom could be useful to you. Social scientists have demonstrated the "small world" phenomenon: Research on the "six degrees of separation" hypothesis involving over 45,000 messages and over 150 countries has demonstrated that the average number of links separating any two people in the world is indeed a half-dozen.[60] You can apply this principle to your own information by only seeking people removed from your personal network by one degree: If you ask 10 people for referrals and each of them knows 10 others who might be able to help, you have the potential of support from 100 information-givers.

Secondary sources are so valuable that some online networking groups sites exist to help users find the contacts they need. For tips about how to find these groups, see the Online Learning Center Web site at **www.mhhe.com/adler10e**. Having a network of people who can refer you to others can be especially helpful in today's workforce, where people often stay in a job for only a year or two.

Seek a mentor   A mentor is a person who acts as a guide, trainer, coach, and counselor; who teaches you the informal rules of an organization or a field; and who imparts the kinds of wisdom that come from firsthand experience. Many organizations have formal programs that match new employees with experienced ones. Other mentor–protégé relationships develop informally and unofficially. However you find one, a mentor can be invaluable. This is especially true for women, minorities, and people trying to break into nontraditional fields where "good old boy" networks can be hard to penetrate.[61]

A successful mentoring relationship isn't a one-time affair. Instead, it passes through several stages.[62] In the initial phase, the parties get to know one another and gain confidence in each other's commitment to the relationship. After the initial stage, a period of cultivation occurs in which the mentor guides his or her protégé through a series of conversations and tasks with the goal of buiding knowledge, confidence, and skill. By the third phase of the relationship, the protégé can function mostly on his or her own, with occasional guidance from the mentor. Finally, the fourth stage involves either separation or a redefinition of the relationship as one of peers. Not all mentoring relationships are this involved or long-lasting; but whether they are relatively brief or ongoing, they can provide great value and satisfaction for both mentor and protégé.

Whatever the relationship, some rules guide mentoring relationships.[63] Look for someone with a position in a field that interests you. Don't be bashful about aiming high: You may be surprised by the willingness of successful people to give back by helping aspiring newcomers. Approach your mentor professionally, showing that you are serious about growing in your career. See "The Career Research Interview" in Chapter 7 for guidelines on how to handle this process.

Complete the table below to get a sense of some key people who are already members of your personal networks, and who can help you be more successful in your career. After completing the inventory, develop an action plan by choosing which contacts you can pursue. Keep yourself on target by setting deadlines for contacting the people you have identified.

	Name	Type of information this person could provide	Questions I could ask this person	Best channel to contact this person	How I can reciprocate/ acknowledge help
Family members					
Friends*					
Neighbors*					
Social acquaintances*					
Fellow workers and bosses*					
Members of religious and charitable community*					
Professionals (doctors, dentists, accountants, etc.)*					
School contacts (faculty, students, etc.)*					
Online acquaintances or friends (e.g., Facebook, MySpace)					

Past and present.

Once you have found a mentor, show respect for his or her time by keeping most of your contacts to regularly scheduled times. Be sure to follow up on your mentor's suggestions about reading, checking Web sites, and attending activities.

Realize that a mentoring relationship should be primarily professional. If you have serious personal problems, turn to a counselor. A mentor may be able to help you with some personal problems as they affect your work life, but a mentor should not become an emotional crutch. Remember that any personal insights shared by mentors and protégés should be kept confidential. Finally, don't expect a mentor to grant you special favors, intervene on your behalf with your boss, or boost your chances for promotion. The advice you receive should be reward enough.

Face-to-Face and Electronic Communication Channels

As a business communicator, you often can choose how to deliver a message. Deciding which communication channel to use isn't a trivial matter; communication researchers have studied extensively the factors that lead to good channel choice.[64] Sometimes a written message succeeds where an oral one fails; at other times, talking to the recipient will produce results that the printed word can't match. An understanding of these two channels will help you make the best choice about how to deliver your important messages.

Face-to-Face Communication

Talking to others in person has several apparent advantages:

- *Richness.*[65] Richness refers to the number of channels available: facial expression, tone of voice, eye and body movement. In person, a wide array of nonverbal cues help you better understand another person. Is the customer in a hurry? Is your boss angry? Is a colleague joking or serious? Seeing and hearing others can help you answer questions like these.

- *Speed.* Once you make contact with your audience, there's no time lag between the transmission of a message and its reception. If you need a price or have to have the funds in an account released *now*, putting your request in a letter or memo won't be much help.

- *Control.* You might spend hours drafting a memo, letter, or report only to have the recipient scan it superficially or not read it at all. In a personal contact, however, you have much more command over the receiver's attention. Another enormous advantage of face-to-face communication is that it permits *instantaneous feedback.* You can respond to questions as soon as they arise and rephrase or elaborate as necessary.

- *Personal quality.* Face-to-face contact has the potential to create personal bonds that are more difficult in other types of communication. One corporate manager, whose company spends over $4 million annually on employee travel, makes the case for face-to-face contact: "Nothing takes the place of a handshake, going to lunch, seeing their eyes."[66]

Although face-to-face communication has many advantages, it isn't always the best approach. The biggest drawback of personal contacts is the difficulty in arranging them. Even when communicators are in the same building, scheduling a meeting can be

career tip

Cell Phone and Voice Mail Do's and Dont's

Cell Phone

- Know your company's policy regarding personal cell phone calls in the office. Also, be sensitive to the informal norms about cell phone use in your work group.

- Avoid using your cell phone where others will be forced to overhear you. If you must receive calls, use the phone's vibrate function and move to a more private place to talk.

- Don't interrupt an ongoing face-to-face conversation to speak on the phone. It gives the impression that those you are talking with are not as important as the caller. If you know you will be receiving a business-related call that you must take, forewarn the others and take only that call, not other calls. If you must respond to a caller, excuse yourself and make it short—less than 30 seconds.

- Avoid using potentially annoying ringtones. If possible, use the vibrate function or a plain ring.

Voice Mail

- Know the schedule of the person you're trying to reach. Doing so can boost the odds of reaching (or not reaching) the person you're seeking (or avoiding).

- Leave the name of the person for whom the message is directed if the mailbox is shared by more than one person. Don't make the recipient guess who you're trying to reach.

- State your name and phone number and your company at the beginning of the message, and again at the end if the recipient doesn't know you well. Doing so will save the recipient from having to replay the whole message to figure out who you are. If there's any possibility of misunderstanding, spell your last name.

- Organize your message in advance. Don't confuse the recipient by leaving a rambling message that makes you sound muddle-headed and is likely to annoy the recipient.

- Keep the message as short as possible. If you have a great deal to say, consider alerting your receiver to the main points, and then send the details via fax, memo, or e-mail.

- Speak slowly and clearly. The vocal fidelity of some voice mail systems is poor, and you don't want your message to be misunderstood.

---

difficult and frustrating. A crosstown trip for a half-hour meeting can take most of the morning or afternoon. Personal factors can also be problematic in some relationships. Distance notwithstanding, a personal encounter might also be unproductive if it involves incompatible personalities or a sore subject. In cases like these, less confrontational forms of communication might be better.

Telephone and Voice Mail

While a phone conversation lacks the rich visual feedback that often reveals how your message is getting across, vocal cues—tone of voice, pauses, interruptions, pitch, and rate—can give you a good idea of the other person's reaction to your message.

As with face-to-face conversations, timing is important in phone communication. Your chances of having a successful conversation will drop if the other person is hurried, angry, or distracted. For this reason, it's smart to ask, "Is this a good time?" before launching into your conversation.

Voice mail might seem like a poor alternative to a real phone conversation, and it does have its potential drawbacks. (See the Career Tip box on this page.) But sometimes leaving a message can be preferable to a real conversation. If you're rushing to meet a deadline and don't have time to talk, voice mails can allow you to touch base without getting involved in long, unproductive conversations. And a voice mail message can give the recipient a chance to digest bad news before you discuss it in person or over the phone. Services like Slydial (**www.slydial.com**) allow callers to avoid unwanted conversations by sending messages directly to the receiver's voice mail box without ever ringing his or her phone.

Despite its advantages, oral communication isn't a perfect medium. Possibly the greatest disadvantage of speech is its *transience*. Listeners quickly forget much of what they hear—half of a message almost immediately and half of the remainder 2 days later. Thus, a customer might forget three of the five product features you mentioned, or your boss might forget exactly *why* you need more staff support and recall only the dollar amount you requested.

Even if they remember an oral message, listeners are likely to distort it. Some details drop out with each telling of a story. Facts and figures change. The farther the message travels in space and time from its original sender, the greater the chance of distortion.

Teleconferencing and Videoconferencing

Teleconferencing allows more than two participants to talk with each other via telephones, while **videoconferencing** lets people both speak with and see each other. With a fast Internet connection and a simple microphone and webcam, many conferencing services allow users all over the world to communicate with one another at no cost. Chapter 9 offers tips on how to set up and communicate effectively in teleconferences and videoconferences.

Instant Messaging

Instant messaging (IM) lets you exchange messages in real time via your computer. IM isn't just a tool for recreation: The technology has real utility on the job. For example, people who IM at work report being interrupted less often than non-users, and they engage in *more* frequent computer-mediated communication than non-users—work-related as well as personal.[67] Instant messaging allows users to send urgent information or queries to others currently logged on to the network or online. For example, customer support agents at many companies can instantly get help from their colleagues when stumped by a customer's problem. When speed is important, instant messaging can beat both e-mail and telephones in efficiency. Connecting is almost instantaneous, and there is less need to socialize when time is of the essence. "One thing about the telephone is the first thing you're supposed to say is 'how's the wife and kids?' With instant messaging you can just say, 'I want this.'"[68]

In one poll of 50 Fortune 1000 companies, 36 percent had employees who used instant messaging to keep in touch.[69] Another survey revealed that almost a quarter of American workers use instant messaging on the job, often informally.[70]

Along with its advantages, instant messaging does have drawbacks. Typing is certainly more cumbersome than talking on the phone, and text-only messages lack the richness of spoken conversations. For better or worse, instant messaging can make you available to others almost constantly. Failure to respond quickly to others' messages can be perceived by senders as lack of interest, especially if they know you are logged on at your computer.

technology tip

Instant Messaging at Work

Instant messaging (IM) is less intrusive than a phone call and more immediate than e-mail. It can be a business blessing or curse, depending on its use. Follow these guidelines for respectful and effective IM communication:[71]

- Check your organization's policy on IM software. Make sure it allows IM-ing on the job and that it authorizes you to download the software you want to use.

- Ask whether the other person is available to IM rather than assuming he or she is. Respect others' responses that they are busy.

- Save yourself from interruptions by using the "busy" or "away" feature to tell others you aren't available.

- Don't make IM your main form of communication. It can be the right channel for a quick answer or to open a door. For long conversations, delicate issues, or complex transactions, use the phone, e-mail, or have a face-to-face conversation.

- Keep messages brief and to the point.

- Use IMs for short, nonconfrontational messages, not for arguments or heated discussions.

- Don't write anything you wouldn't put on company letterhead because IMs can be permanent and they are easy to forward.

- Avoid acronyms that may not be widely understood by your correspondent. TTFN ("Ta ta for now") might be fine for casual personal exchanges; at work, this approach may not create the impression you want.

- Avoid poor grammar or general sloppiness that could create a bad impression of you and your company.

- Focus on what you're doing. Too much multitasking can lead to major slip-ups and embarrassments.

Twitter and Text Messaging

Twitter and similar services let users send short messages ("tweets") to interested parties who can read and reply to them via mobile phone, instant message, or the Web. At first, Twitter was criticized as a narcissistic form of microblogging ("Who cares what you are doing?"). Over time, though, business and professional applications have emerged. A small sample suggests the value of this medium:

- Communicate with customers: "See our Web site for new products!"
- Send messages to work teams: "Deadline for equipment requests is Friday at 5:00 p.m."
- Swap ideas with others in your field: "Great article on cost cutting in today's *Wall St. Journal.*"
- Extend invitations: "Please come to our grand opening party tonight."
- Express appreciation: "Thanks to all our volunteers. Great job!"
- Coordinate with those in your network: "Anybody going to the conference in Austin?"
- Monitor what people are saying about your organization, its product, and you via Twitter's search feature.

Text messaging (or *texting*) is the common term for sending brief text messages via mobile phones and personal digital assistants. Whereas Twitter is typically used to send messages to many recipients, most texting is aimed at just one receiver.

Texting is a useful tool when you don't want to interrupt the other person with a phone call, and the textual nature of your message provides a record that can be easier to manage than a voice mail message.

E-mail and Written Communication

Written communication comes in a variety of forms. Letters, memos, bulletins, and reports are familiar fixtures in almost everybody's career.

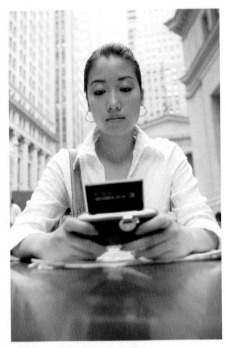

Written messages have a set of advantages and drawbacks different from their spoken counterparts. Unlike speech, written communication is *permanent.* Once your words are down on paper, they are saved for future reference—either to your delight or to your undying embarrassment and chagrin. While people may have trouble accurately recalling what you said a few hours ago, they can refer to your written remarks years later. Even if the receiver has lost or forgotten your message, you can always supply a copy from your files.

Along with its permanence, written communication can be *easier to understand* than speech. Readers can study complex passages as many times as necessary, a luxury they do not have when the same message is delivered orally. They can take a break if their interest wanes and, after a cup of coffee or a quick stretch, come back to what they were reading refreshed and ready to go on.

Perhaps the greatest advantage of written communication is that you can *compose it in advance.* You can take as much time as necessary to shape a message just as you want it, pondering every word if necessary. You can try out several versions on test readers to anticipate the reactions of your real audience, and you can make changes until you get the desired response.

Finally, written messages are *less prone to errors.* Even the best-rehearsed oral presentations can go awry. You can misplace an important set of papers or forget to mention a key idea. Furthermore, the spontaneity that makes spoken communication so effective can backfire. Your attempt to improvise might sound confusing or lame, and the joke you thought would make the perfect ice-breaker might fall flat. Every speaker has thought, hours after a conversation, "If only I'd said . . ." When you communicate in writing, you have time to choose exactly the right words.

E-mail has become the most-used communication tool on the job. According to one survey, 71 percent of managers use e-mail as their primary form of communication. By comparison, only 13 percent of managers polled use the telephone most often and just 14 percent rely on face-to-face meetings.[72] Just because e-mail is used commonly, it isn't always used well. For example, the length of time it takes a recipient to respond to a message can have serious consequences,[73] and a cordial tone can contribute to a positive communication climate, while an impersonal one can lower morale.[74]

Like voice mail, e-mail is asynchronous, so you can leave messages for others to pick up at their convenience. Because your ideas appear in writing, e-mail (like letters and faxes) makes it easier to comprehend lengthy, detailed messages. Along with speed and convenience, e-mail provides an astonishing degree of access to people you otherwise might not be able to reach.

The speed and easy-to-use nature of e-mail also make it a tool for improving personal relationships on the job.[75] Speeding up routine communication leaves more time for personal contacts, which the medium also makes more likely. Technology consultant Beau Carr explains: "It may sound backwards, but people who refuse to learn about technology are the ones losing the human touch. . . . Users can focus more energy and attention on relating to other people and at the same time deliver products and services faster, better, and probably less expensively."[76]

technology tip

Think Before Blogging

Free speech is a cornerstone of democratic society. But when it comes to your career, speaking freely can have serious costs. The information you publish on a personal blog or social networking site may come to the attention of employers—sometimes with shocking results. According to media sources, employees have been fired after opinionated blogging at a number of companies, including Starbucks, Wells Fargo, Kmart, and Silicon Valley firms Google and Friendster. Firms are most likely to discipline employees when posts bring discredit on the company. Delta Airlines terminated a flight attendant who posted suggestive photos of herself in uniform, and Microsoft dismissed a contractor who embarrassed the company by posting photos of Apple computers being delivered at a Microsoft loading dock.

Before posting information on a blog, consider the following guidelines:

1. **Understand company policy.** Ask about your employer's policy regarding blogging. Many firms support, and even host, employee blogs. Be sure you understand any boundaries about content that involve the organization, and whether any topics are off-limits.

2. **Don't blog on company time.** You are safer if you create and post content with your own equipment on your own time. Using company resources can increase your exposure to discipline.

3. **Think about what you say.** A blog is an extension of your own voice to a potentially enormous audience, so be sure you won't regret anything you post. If you wouldn't make a comment in person to a large audience, don't do so in a blog.

4. **Be prepared for controversy.** Sooner or later it's likely that something you say will displease readers. Your choice, then, is whether to play it safe and keep your thoughts to yourself, or accept the risks that come from having a public voice.

Sources: CNN, "Avoid Getting Fired for Blogging," **www.cnn .com/2005/US/Careers/04/05/blogging/**, and CBS News, "Fired for Blogging," **www.cbsnews.com/stories/2005/03/07/tech/ main678554.shtml.**

Along with its advantages, e-mail can easily become a drain on your productivity. The technology is so quick and easy that it is prone to overuse: Your in-box can fill up with unimportant messages, and you can go overboard in sending mail to others. At computer chip maker Intel Corp., employees spend an average of 2.5 hours per day sending and receiving e-mails.[77] See the appendix for more guidelines on composing and managing e-mail messages.

Which Channel to Use

New technologies have given businesspeople a wider range of choices for communication than ever before, and choosing the most efficient and effective way to communicate a message can mean the difference between success and failure.

The question is not which communication channel to use, but when to use each one most effectively.[78] As Table 1-3 shows, each communication channel has both advantages and drawbacks. Despite these pros and cons, there are guidelines that will help you decide how to deliver your message most effectively. Following these guidelines can produce dramatic results. In one survey, managers who were identified as "media sensitive"—those who matched the channel to the message—were almost twice as likely to receive top ratings in their performance reviews when compared with less media-sensitive peers.[79]

Table 1–3	Considerations in Choosing a Communication Channel				
	Time required for feedback	**Richness of information conveyed**	**Sender's control over how message is composed**	**Control over receiver's attention**	**Effectiveness for detailed messages**
Face-to-Face	Immediate	High	Moderate	Highest	Weak
Telephone Teleconferencing, and Videoconferencing	Immediate	Moderate	Moderate	Moderate	Weak
Voice Mail	Delayed	Moderate	High	Low	Weak
E-Mail	Varies	Low	High	Low	High
Instant Messaging	Varies	Low	High	Varies	Weak
Text Messaging and Twitter	Can be immediate	Low	High (given briefness of message)	Low	Good for brief messages
Hard Copy (e.g., handwritten or typed message)	Delayed	Low	High	Low	High

Consider the Desired Tone   In general, oral communication is best for messages that require a personal dimension. For example, relationships improve and problems decline when physicians and the administrators of hospitals and health care systems meet in person instead of exchanging messages through less personal channels.[80] Oral channels are also best for ideas that have a strong need for visual support—demonstration, photos or slides, and so on. Spoken communication is also especially useful when there is a need for immediate feedback, such as question-and-answer sessions or a quick reply to your ideas.

Written communication (with the exception of e-mail) works best when you want to create a relatively formal tone. Writing is almost always the best medium when you must choose your words carefully. Writing is also better than speaking when you want to convey complicated ideas that are likely to require much study and thought by the receiver. It is also smart to put your message in writing when you want it to be the final word, with no feedback or discussion. Finally, writing is best for *any* message if you want a record to exist. In business and the professions, sending confirming letters and memoranda is common practice, as is keeping minutes of meetings. These steps guarantee that what is said will be a matter of record, useful in case of later misunderstandings or disputes and in case anyone wants to review the history of an issue. Handwritten notes of thanks or sympathy express thoughtfulness and add a personal touch that typed messages lose.

Consider the Organization's Culture

Besides message-related considerations, the culture of the organization in which you work may favor some communication channels over others.[81] For example, Microsoft Corporation is so e-mail intensive that some voice mail greetings include the directive "If you're from Microsoft, please try to send electronic mail." In other organizations, voice mail is the preferred channel. Kirk Froggatt, a vice president at Silicon Graphics, offers one explanation: "There's something fundamentally more personal about voice mail. You can get the tone of voice, the passion. People like that."[82] A recent study even indicated that employees who followed corporate norms for e-mail and IM use received higher performance evaluations.[83] Along with an organization's overall preference for some channels, it's important to consider the preferences of departments, or even individuals. For example, the computer support staff in some organizations respond to e-mails, while in other companies a phone call to the help desk is the best way to get a quick response. And, if you know a co-worker or your boss responds only to face-to-face reminders, your best bet is to use that approach.

Consider Using Multiple Channels

In many cases, it is wise to send a message using both oral and written channels. This kind of redundancy captures the best of both media, and it works in a variety of settings:

- Distribute a written text or outline that parallels your presentation.
- Follow a letter, fax, or e-mail message with a phone call, or call first and then write.
- Send a report or proposal and then make appointments with your readers to discuss it.

You won't always have the luxury of choosing the communication channel. But when you do, the right decision can make your message clearer and more effective. The Career Tip on page 24 and the Technology Tips on pages 26 and 28 can help you use electronic channels with civility and effectiveness.

review points

- Communication occupies more time and is more crucial to success than other work activities.
- The process of communication involves people in different environments, specific contexts (physical, social, psychological, cultural), various channels, and verbal and nonverbal feedback.
- Noise can be physical, physiological, or psychological and can be present in the sender, receiver, message, or channel.
- To improve communication choose the most credible sender, pick the optimal receivers and address their needs, develop messages strategically, structure them clearly, minimize noise, and utilize feedback.
- Understand various ethical frameworks to make principled decisions around ethical challenges.
- Formal communication networks (flowcharts and organizational charts) represent management's view of organizational relationships: upward, downward, horizontal.

- Informal networks, based on proximity, shared interests, or friendships, serve to confirm, expand, expedite, contradict, circumvent, or supplement formal communication so effective communicators cultivate and use informal networks.

- Messages are exchanged face-to-face or electronically via oral and/or written channels. Each channel's advantages and drawbacks can have a strong influence on the effectiveness of a message.

- Communicators can choose the best channel by considering the situation, the nature of the message, the organizational culture, and the desired tone.

key terms

 Test your understanding of these key terms by visiting the Online Learning Center Web site at www.mhhe.com/adler10e.

channel   7
communication networks   12
content messages   9
context   8
decoding   7
downward communication   12
e-mail   27
encoding   7
feedback   7
formal communication networks   12
horizontal communication   16
informal communication networks   17
instant messaging (IM)   25

lateral communication   16
message   7
networking   19
noise   7
organizational charts   12
receiver   7
relational messages   9
sender   7
teleconferencing   25
text messaging   26
Twitter   26
upward communication   14
videoconferencing   25

activities

 Go to the self-quizzes at the Online Learning Center at www.mhhe.com/adler10e to test your knowledge of chapter concepts.

1. Invitation to Insight

Keep a log of your work- (or school-) related communication over a 3-day period. Include who you have communicated with (superior, subordinate, peer, external) and your level of satisfaction. Based on your findings, analyze

   a. How much time you spend communicating.
   b. With whom you communicate.
   c. Your level of satisfaction.
   d. Areas where improving your communication skills would be desirable.

2. Invitation to Insight

Think about a situation you have experienced in which communication went wrong. Diagnose the problem by finding the parts of the communication process that contributed to the trouble. Suggest a remedy for each problem you identify:

   a. Sender: Did the wrong person send the message?
   b. Encoding: Did the sender use words or nonverbal cues that were confusing, inappropriate, or irrelevant?

c. Message: Was the message too short or too long? Were there too many messages? Was the timing wrong?

d. Channel: Was the most appropriate channel chosen?

e. Receiver: Was there no receiver at all? Was the message poorly formulated for the person(s) at whom it was aimed? Was it received by the wrong person?

f. Decoding: Did the receiver read in meanings that were not intended?

g. Feedback: Was feedback adequate to ensure understanding? What impact did the feedback have on the sender?

h. Noise: Did external, physiological, or psychological noise distort the message? Provide specific examples.

i. Context: In what ways did physical, social, chronological, and cultural contexts impede the interaction?

3. Skill Builder

Identify at least two possible relational meanings for the following statements. For each relational meaning, envision the context in which it might have been stated. Based on your chosen context, decide which relational dimensions the message involves: affinity, control, and/or respect.

a. What's the matter with you?

b. It's about time!

c. I spent two days on this job.

d. I'd rather do it this way . . .

e. Let me pick up the lunch check.

f. You were a half-hour late. Is something wrong?

g. Give me a call sometime.

4. Invitation to Insight

Learn about upward communication in the workplace by asking several employees what types of information they share with their supervisors. What types of information do they avoid sharing with their supervisors? How does the organization encourage or discourage accurate upward communication?

5. Skill Builder

Develop your skill at cultivating informal communication networks by following these instructions:

a. Choose one of the following information goals, or identify a school- or work-related goal of your own.
    1. Decide which instructors and/or courses in an academic department of your institution are worth seeking out and which you might want to avoid.
    2. Identify the qualities that would help you get the job of your dreams.
    3. Determine which software program best suits your needs for a given application (e.g., word processing, database) and context (e.g., customer tracking, report writing).
b. Identify the people who can help you acquire the information you are seeking. Locate people from a variety of positions within the organization so you will gain a complete perspective. For each person, decide which channel you could use to begin to develop your network.

6. Skill Builder

With your group members, formulate a hypothetical context for each message below. Then use the information on pages 28–30 to decide which communication channel would be best for each message. Use the criteria from Table 1–3 to explain your choice:

a. Informing your supervisor about difficulties with a co-worker.
b. Asking for a few days of leave from work to attend a special reunion.
c. Training a new employee to operate a complicated computer program.
d. Notifying the manager of a local business that you still haven't received the refund you were promised.
e. Reminding your busy boss about a long overdue reimbursement for out-of-pocket expenses.
f. Apologizing to a customer for a mistake your company made.
g. Getting your boss's reaction to the idea of giving you more responsibility.

resources

→ For extensive readings and Web sites on business communication, networks, channels, and ethics, see the Online Learning Center Web site at www.mhhe.com/adler10e.

2

Communication, Culture, and Work

chapter outline

Cultural Diversity and Communication
The Nature of Culture
Cultural Differences in Doing Business
Fundamental Dimensions of Cultural Diversity
Co-cultural Dimensions of a Diverse Society
Diversity and Ethical Issues
Communicating across Diversity

Organizational Culture and Communication
The Importance of Organizational Culture
Dimensions of Organizational Culture
Creating and Maintaining Organizational Cultures
Organizational Culture and Career Planning
Review Points
Key Terms
Activities
Resources

chapter objectives

After reading this chapter you should be able to

1. Identify the cultures and co-cultures in a specific organization, field, or community and describe how their norms and values shape communication in the workplace.
2. Use the guidelines on pages 53–56 to describe the ways you and others can communicate most effectively in a diverse work environment.
3. Describe the culture in a specific organization or field and identify specific approaches to communicate most effectively within this culture.

Cultural Diversity and Communication

Diversity is a fact of life in today's working world. The population of Miami is two-thirds Hispanic;[1] over half of Washington, DC, residents are black; and one-third of San Franciscans are Asian Americans.[2] As Figure 2–1 on page 36 shows, the trend toward diversity will continue for the foreseeable future. According to U.S. Census Bureau, the nation's Hispanic and Asian populations will triple over the next half century, and non-Hispanic whites will represent about one-half of the total population by 2050.[3]

With the increase in international trade and immigration, the likelihood of working with people from different parts of the world is greater than ever. Over 10,000 foreign companies and their subsidiaries operate in the United States.[4] Some 300 Japanese companies operate in Michigan alone; German, British, and Dutch companies also have many U.S. sites. Immigrants accounted for over half of the growth in the U.S. labor force at the turn of the 21st century.[5] By 2016, experts predict that 2 million foreign-born workers will be moving to the United States every year.[6]

As more corporations become multi-national, Americans are moving abroad in growing numbers. Over 8 million were working overseas in 2003,[7] many for the 3,000 U.S. firms with global operations and others for over 36,000 foreign companies in more than 180 countries.[8]

Given figures like these, it's no surprise that over 80 percent of the human resources executives surveyed say that global talent will be a priority in the coming years.[9] For companies and individuals who can take advantage of the trend toward increasing cultural diversity, the opportunities are great. DuPont has a policy of hiring men and women of a variety of ages and cultures because "diversity of experience and

FIGURE 2–1

Population
by Race and
Ethnicity

*Note: American
Indian/Alaska Native
not shown.*

Source: J. S. Passel
and D. Cohn,
*U.S. Population
Projections: 2005–2050*
(Washington,
DC: Pew Research
Center, 2008).

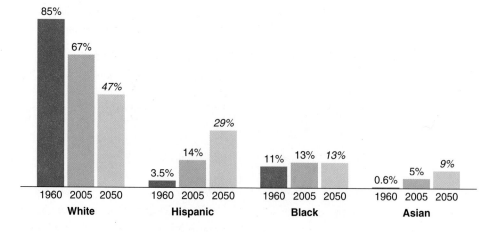

perspective gives DuPont a competitive edge."[10] Stona Fitch, vice president of manufacturing for Procter & Gamble, says, "Diversity provides a much richer environment, a variety of viewpoints, greater productivity. And, not unimportantly, it makes work more fun and interesting."[11] A spokesperson for the American Society of Civil Engineers states, "Without embracing diversity, the engineering profession will be unable to compete effectively in the global marketplace."[12] Whether you are working abroad, for or with foreign nationals at home, or with native-born people from different backgrounds, understanding cultural differences is an essential part of being an effective communicator.

The Nature of Culture

When most people use the word *culture*, they think of people from different national backgrounds. National cultures certainly do exist, and they play an important role in shaping the way people communicate. Other factors that define a culture and shape the way people communicate include race, ethnicity, age, socioeconomic status, gender identity, and language. Taking all these factors into account, we can define **culture** as a learned set of shared interpretations about beliefs, values, and norms, which affect the behaviors of a relatively large group of people.[13]

It's important to realize that culture is learned, not innate. A Korean-born infant adopted soon after birth by non-Korean parents and raised in the United States will think and act differently from his or her cousins who grew up in Seoul. An African American may view the world differently depending on whether he or she was raised in a small town, an inner city, or a middle-class suburb—or in a country like France or Zaire, where African heritage has a different significance from that in the United States. The overwhelming influence of culture on communication led famous anthropologist Edward Hall to assert that "culture is communication and communication is culture."[14]

Cultures are invisible to the people who are used to inhabiting them. But to people from different backgrounds, the power of dominant norms is obvious. One account of a corporate training session illustrates this point:

> [The trainer] would run a little experiment when she was talking to corporate audiences that were mixed—including white men, women, and minorities. She would ask the audience to do a simple task: "Please list," she would request, "the rules needed to be successful in a white male society." Immediately the women and the minorities would begin to write down all the things

they had to do to "fit in." Meanwhile, the white males in the audience just sat there, doing nothing, looking around at the women and the minorities writing for all they were worth.[15]

The author describing this experiment explains the important truth it reveals:

[Cultural] paradigms are like water to fish. They are invisible in many situations because it is "just the way we do things." Often they operate at an unconscious level. Yet they determine, to a large extent, our behavior. As a white male, I cannot write down all those rules. My wife can. My minority friends can.[16]

Cultural Differences in Doing Business

Some cultural differences in customs and behavior are obvious. For example, your work life will be simpler once you understand that punctuality is important in Switzerland and Germany but less important in most parts of Africa. Other differences, though, are much more subtle. We begin this section by looking at the more obvious differences in customs and behavior that distinguish cultures. Next we explore some fundamental dimensions of diversity that are less obvious but at least as important.

Differences in Customs and Behavior
Browse the travel and business sections of any decent bookstore and you're likely to find many volumes detailing the cultures and business practices around the world. The following categories are not an exhaustive list of differences between countries, but they suggest the importance of learning rules of the cultures in which you will operate.

Before going on, though, it is important to keep a sense of perspective about cultural influences on communication. Along with important differences, people from varied backgrounds also share many similarities. For example, computer engineers from Singapore, Lima, Tel Aviv, and Vancouver would find plenty of mutual interests and perspectives due to their shared occupational and socioeconomic backgrounds. Even when we acknowledge cultural variation, the fact remains that not everyone in a culture behaves identically. Figure 2–2 shows both the overlap in communication practices and the range of behavior within each one. Furthermore, within every culture, members display a wide range of communication styles. Ignoring cross-cultural similarities and intracultural variation can lead to stereotyping people from different backgrounds.

Formality
U.S. Americans take pleasure in their informality and their quickness in getting on a first-name basis with others. With the exception of a few countries, including Thailand and Australia, business exchanges with persons from other countries

FIGURE 2–2

Differences and Similarities within and between Cultures

Sources: Adapted from M. H. Bond, *Beyond the Chinese Face* (New York: Oxford University Press, 1991), p. 3, and F. Trompenaars, *Riding the Waves of Culture* (New York: McGraw-Hill/Irwin, 1994), p. 28.

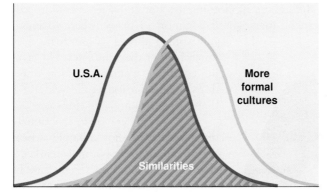

tend to be much more formal, especially toward the beginning of a relationship.[17] In the United States and Canada, first names are seen as friendly and indicative of fondness and attachment. In many other countries—Mexico, Germany, and Egypt, for example—titles are an important way of showing respect, and it's best to use them until you are invited to move to a first-name basis.[18]

Names and titles aren't the only way to express degrees of formality. The way people do—or don't—converse with strangers varies from one culture to another. In North America, it's not uncommon to strike up a conversation with a stranger; but this custom isn't universal. The U.S. retailing giant Wal-Mart made the strategic decision not to hire greeters at its German stores for reasons expressed by a public relations expert from that country: "As a German, I find the idea of being greeted at the door uncomfortable. I would feel astonished if someone I didn't know started talking to me."[19]

Social customs   Cultural differences begin as soon as communicators encounter one another. Greetings range from the bow (lower is more respectful) in Japan, to the *wai* (pressed palms with a head bow) in Thailand, to the handshake in Europe and South America.

In many countries, exchanging business cards is an important ritual. In Japan, especially, cards are given and received with care: The recipient should use two hands and study the card carefully, treating it with the same respect he or she would give its owner.[20] One U.S. businessperson lost a deal in Japan because his inattention to the Japanese businessmen's cards was taken as a measure of the lack of attention he would give to their business.[21]

In many cultures, gift giving is a part of business protocol. Knowing the details of a specific culture can be important. For example, in India, where cows are sacred, gifts of leather are to be avoided. In China, avoid giving white flowers (associated with death) or gifts in sets of four since the sound of that number is the same as the word for "death." Lavish gifts may put your host in an awkward position, so learn cultural specifics and choose carefully.

Another variable is the degree of overlap between doing business and socializing. While entertaining is part of business in virtually all cultures, in many parts of the world socializing after business hours is a central part of building a working relationship. In much of eastern Asia, drinking is regarded as a way of building bonds that carry over into working relationships. One consultant alerts travelers to be prepared for a turn singing in the karaoke bars that are part of the scene in China, Japan, and other countries in the region.[22]

Styles of dress   As travel and communication make the world feel like a smaller place, regional differences in clothing are becoming less pronounced. For men, the standard Western business suit is common in many urban settings. For both men

and women abroad, conservative dress will take you much further than the latest fad or fashion. In Muslim countries, women can show respect with modest dress, including longer sleeves and lower hemlines than may be fashionable elsewhere.

Even in an era of international business, local differences exist. For example, when United Parcel Service entered the German market, it belatedly discovered that the firm's signature brown uniforms evoked unpleasant memories of brown-shirted Nazi storm troopers. In Indonesia, the company had to modify its usual business suit dress rule, and allow executives to wear more casual attire that is common in that hot and humid climate.[23]

Time   In international business, the first shock for travelers from the United States may be the way members of other cultures understand and use time. North Americans, like most northern Europeans, have what anthropologists term a **monochronic** view of time, seeing it as an almost tangible substance. American speech reflects this attitude when people talk about saving time, making time, having time, wasting time, using time, and taking time. In U.S. culture, time is money, so it is rationed carefully. Appointments are scheduled and rigidly adhered to. Tasks are performed in a scheduled order, one at a time.

This monochronic orientation is not universal. Cultures with a **polychronic** orientation see time as taking a backseat to personal relationships. Meetings go on for as long as they take; they don't abruptly end because "it's time." Most Latin American cultures, as well as southern European and Middle Eastern cultures, have a polychronic orientation. In Mexico, for example, "you make friends first and do business later," according to R. C. Schrader, who heads California's trade office in Mexico City.[24]

Members of polychronic cultures are less concerned with punctuality than those raised with monochronic standards. It is not that being punctual is unimportant; it is just that other relational factors may take priority. This fact helps explain why the notion of being "on time" varies. Extremely monochronic cultures view even small delays as an offense. In polychronic cultures, varying degrees of lateness are acceptable—from roughly 15 minutes in southern Europe to part, or sometimes even all, of the day in the Middle East and Africa.[25]

Tolerance for conflict   In some cultures, each person is responsible for helping to maintain harmony of a group and of society. The maintenance and pursuit of harmony is expressed in the Japanese term *wa*. In Chinese, a similar term is *zhong he*.[26] In other places—the Middle East and southern Europe, for example—harmony takes a backseat to emotional expression. Figure 2–3 illustrates how the rules for expressing emotions vary around the world.

The cultural avoidance of conflict means most Asian businesspersons will probably not say "no" directly to you, fearing that you will lose face and suffer embarrassment. To help you maintain harmony and save face, they might spare you unpleasant news or

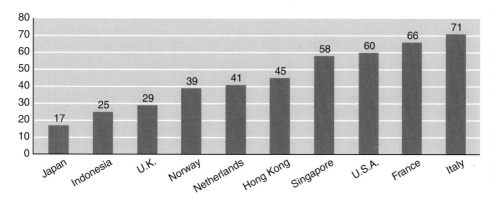

FIGURE 2–3

Percentage of Employees Who Would Openly Express Feeling Upset at Work

Source: F. Trompenaars, *Riding the Waves of Culture* (New York: McGraw-Hill/Irwin, 1994), p. 70.

information; it will be softened so that you don't suffer disgrace or shame, especially in front of others. You may be told that they will consider the matter or that it would be very difficult. Mexican business culture also values harmony and discourages confrontation. This attitude creates problems when it clashes with more aggressive standards that U.S. businesspeople usually bring to transactions. As president of Black & Decker Latin America, José Maria Gonzales is used to working with colleagues and suppliers from north of the border. Despite that fact, he says that coping with the difference between U.S. and Mexican approaches to conflict doesn't come easily:

> In a meeting Americans can argue, hit the table and leave as if nothing happened, while a Mexican might not forgive you for three months. I have to make sure not to personalize things sometimes.[27]

This sort of accommodation works both ways. People from cultures that seek harmony can learn to adapt to and accept conflict, and communicators from more aggressive societies like the United States can learn to appreciate the importance of harmony when communicating cross-culturally. Once communicators learn to appreciate different sets of rules about how to express and handle disagreements, conducting business becomes much easier.

Gender roles   Women from North America, western Europe, and Australia/New Zealand who travel internationally are likely to be astonished and chagrined by the way they are regarded in some overseas cultures, where ideas of appropriate feminine behavior can be quite different. In some countries, a woman who outranks a man may not be treated that way by hosts; they may still speak to and prefer to negotiate with the male, assuming he is her superior. In Asian countries and Muslim countries women may find they are omitted from substantive conversation or overlooked in negotiations because of designated gender roles. Sometimes, a woman can establish greater credibility by clarifying her title, role, and responsibilities in writing before a personal visit, but even this step won't guarantee the desired effect.

The kinds of differences described here can present challenges when workers from different cultures work together. Table 2–1 illustrates some of these challenges by listing differences between Chinese and Western businesspeople in both concerns and communication styles.

Fundamental Dimensions of Cultural Diversity

So far we have discussed obvious differences between cultures. As important as customs and norms are, they are only the tip of the cultural iceberg. Underlying what might appear to be idiosyncrasies in behavior are a number of fundamental values that shape the way members of a culture think, feel, and act. In the following pages, we look at some of these fundamental differences. Once you appreciate them, you will understand how and why people from different backgrounds behave as they do, and you will have ideas of how you can adapt to improve the quality of your communication with others.

High versus Low-Context   Anthropologist Edward Hall identified two distinct ways in which members of various cultures deliver messages.[28] A **low-context culture** uses language primarily to express thoughts, feelings, and ideas as clearly and logically as possible. To low-context communicators, the meaning of a statement is in the words spoken. By contrast, a **high-context culture** relies heavily on subtle, often

Table 2–1	Contrasting Chinese–Western Concerns and Communication Practices	
	Chinese	**Western**
Concerns	Saving face	Frankness, "honesty"
	Respect, politeness	Assertiveness
	Compromise, flexibility	Self-assurance
	General feeling, "spirit"	Specific terms
	Social status	Task at hand
	Patience	Time efficiency
Communication practices	Reserved	Extroverted
	Tentative	Firm
	Personal	Less personal
	No body contact	Hugging, backslapping acceptable
	No pointing	Index finger used to point

Source: Ming-Jer Chen, *Inside Chinese Business: A Guide for Managers Worldwide* (Boston: Harvard Business School Press, 2001), p. 136.

nonverbal cues to convey meaning, save face, and maintain social harmony. Communicators in these societies learn to discover meaning from the context in which a message is delivered: the nonverbal behaviors of the speaker, the history of the relationship, and the general social rules that govern interaction between people. When delivering difficult or awkward messages, high-context speakers often convey meaning through context rather than plainly stated words to avoid upsetting their listeners. Consider a few differences between how a low-context Westerner and a high-context Chinese might express the same idea:[29]

Western	Chinese
Do you understand? *(Responsibility placed on other.)*	Am I being clear? *(Speaker takes responsibility for understanding.)*
Is the project acceptable? *(Requires direct "yes" or "no" answer.)*	What do you think of the project? *(Gives respondent latitude to reply diplomatically.)*
We can't do that. *(Clear refusal could be perceived as harsh.)*	This may be a little difficult for us to do. *(Context makes it clear that the answer is still "no.")*

Mainstream culture in the United States and Canada falls toward the low-context end of the scale. Longtime residents generally value straight talk and grow impatient with "beating around the bush." By contrast, most Middle Eastern and Asian cultures fit the high-context pattern. In many Asian societies, for example, maintaining harmony is important, so communicators avoid speaking directly if that would threaten another person's dignity. One U.S. project manager describes how her insensitivity to high-context communication almost derailed an international team in developing a Japanese-language version of an Internet search service:

> As an American project manager, I was expecting that if I was proposing something stupid, I would hear it from the people on the team. In reality, I had a plan with a fatal flaw, and the Japanese team members knew it, but it was not their style of communication to embarrass me by telling me.[30]

Even within a single country, co-cultures can have different notions about the value of direct speech. For example, Puerto Rican language style resembles high-context Japanese or Korean more than low-context English. As a group, Puerto Ricans value social harmony and avoid confrontation, which leads them to systematically speak in indirect ways to avoid giving offense.[31] The same holds true for Mexican Americans, as communication researcher Don Locke explains:

> Whereas members of the dominant culture of the United States are taught to value openness, frankness, and directness, the traditional Mexican-American approach requires the use of much diplomacy and tact when communicating with another individual. Concern and respect for the feelings of others dictate that a screen be provided behind which an individual may preserve dignity. . . . The manner of expression is likely to be elaborate and indirect, since the aim is to make the personal relationship at least appear harmonious, to show respect for the other's individuality. To the Mexican-American, direct argument or contradiction appears rude and disrespectful.[32]

A preference for high- or low-context communication isn't the only factor that distinguishes one culture from another. One survey of 160,000 employees in 60 countries revealed several other ways in which the worldviews of one national culture can differ from those of another.[33] Table 2–2 lists those dimensions and the styles that are most common in some countries. We will look at those differences now.

Individualism and Collectivism   Members of **individualistic cultures** are inclined to put their own interests and those of their immediate family ahead of social concerns. Individualistic cultures offer their members a great deal of freedom, the belief being that this freedom makes it possible for each person to achieve personal success. **Collectivist cultures,** however, have tight social frameworks in which members of a group (such as an organization) feel primary loyalty toward one another and the group to which they belong. China, like most East Asian cultures, is highly collective.

In collectivist societies, members are expected to believe that the welfare of the organization is as important as their own.[34] Workers are less likely to strive to become organizational "stars," since that approach would dishonor other members of the team. "You seldom see an individual

Long-Term Orientation	Short-Term Orientation
China	Pakistan
Hong Kong	Philippines
Taiwan	Norway
Japan	Canada
South Korea	East Africa*
Individualistic	**Collectivistic**
U.S.	Guatamala
Australia	Ecuador
United Kingdom (England)	Panama
Canada	Venezuela
New Zealand	Pakistan, Indonesia
Avoid Uncertainty	**Tolerate Uncertainty**
Greece	Singapore
Portugal	Jamaica
Uraguay	Denmark
Guatemala	Sweden
Belgium and El Salvador	Hong Kong
High Power Distance	**Low Power Distance**
Malaysia	Austria
Philippines	Israel
Mexico	Denmark
Arab world**	New Zealand
China	Ireland
Task Oriented	**Socially Oriented**
Japan	Sweden
Hungary	Norway
Austria	Netherlands
Italy	Denmark
Switzerland	Costa Rica

Table 2–2 Cultural Values in Selected Countries

*Ethiopia, Kenya, Tanzania, Zambia.
**Egypt, Iraq, Kuwait, Lebanon, Libya, Saudi Arabia, United Arab Emirates.
Source: Adapted from *Cultures and Organizations: Software of the Mind* by G. Hofstede (New York: McGraw-Hill, 1997). Accessed from **http://www.geert-hofstede.com/hofstede-dimensions.php?culture1=95&culture2=14.**

Japanese executive who stands above the rest until he is the most senior individual in the company," says international corporate recruiter Richard M. Ferry.[35] The power of collectivist beliefs was illustrated when PepsiCo rewarded one of its managers in China with a sizable cash bonus that he divided equally among his subordinates.[36]

Power Distance

The term **power distance** refers to attitudes toward differences in authority. Cultures with high power distance, such as Mexico and the Philippines, accept the fact that power is distributed unequally—that some members have greater resources and influence than others. In these cultures, differences in organizational status and rank are expected, routine, and clear-cut. Employees respect those in high positions. Other cultures, such as the U.S., downplay differences in power. Employees are more comfortable approaching—and even challenging—their superiors and may expect to gain greater power.

Colleagues with different notions of power distance might find it difficult to work together. Imagine, for example, how a young business school graduate from a U.S. firm might grow frustrated after being transferred to the Guadalajara branch office, where the same relentless questioning that marked her as a free thinker in school is regarded as overly aggressive troublemaking.

Uncertainty Avoidance

The world is an uncertain place. International politics, economic trends, and the forces of nature make it impossible to predict the future with accuracy. **Uncertainty avoidance** is a measure of how accepting a culture is of a lack of predictability. Some cultures (e.g., Singapore and Hong Kong) are comfortable with this fact. Their acceptance of uncertainty allows them to take risks, and they are relatively tolerant of behavior that differs from the norm. Other cultures (e.g., Japan, Greece, and Portugal) are less comfortable with change. They value tradition and formal rules, and show less tolerance for different ideas.

Task versus Social Orientation[*]

Groups in societies with a strong **task orientation** (e.g., Japan, Austria, and Switzerland) focus heavily on getting the job done. By contrast, groups in cultures with a high degree of **social orientation** (Scandinavian countries, Chile, Portugal, and Thailand, and much of Latin America) are more likely to be concerned about the feelings of members and their smooth functioning as a team. When compared to other countries, the U.S. falls slightly toward the task-oriented end of the spectrum and Canada is almost exactly in the middle, balanced between task and social concerns.[37] For many Latinos in the U.S., *personalismo*, the interpersonal relationship between managers and employees, is of utmost importance.[38]

Task-oriented societies focus on making the team more competent through training and use of up-to-date methods and are highly concerned with individual success: advancing to more responsible jobs, better training, and so on. By contrast, groups in socially oriented societies focus more on collective concerns: cooperative problem solving, maintaining a friendly atmosphere, and good physical working conditions.

---

*These categories were originally labeled "masculine" and "feminine," based on traditional views that men are assertive and results-oriented, while women are nurturing. In an era of increasingly flexible sex roles these terms are considered sexist and misleading, so we have substituted different labels.

Difference as Advantage

Historically, being different from the norm was a disadvantage for many career-minded people. For that reason, job-seekers often tried to downplay differences such as being born abroad, speaking differently, or appearing visibly different from the mainstream. But as society becomes more diverse, tolerance grows, and world trade expands, diversity can be a career-enhancer.

Here are some tips that can help you use your unique background in your career:

1. If you are skilled at speaking other languages, feature that information in your resume. Being bi- or multilingual can make you a very attractive candidate. If you are already employed, show your bosses how fluency can help the organization.

2. If English isn't your first language, make sure your literacy skills and accent reduction are up to par. Most communities offer classes in English, public speaking, and writing where you can sharpen these skills.

3. Identify ways your cultural background will help you be an asset in marketing, sales, client support, management, and other areas. Make sure your bosses understand these advantages.

4. Don't overplay your unique identity and risk being pigeonholed as a "token minority employee." Career success depends on a variety of factors, including your personal background, but performance is the best measure of your value.

Source: C. Prasad, "Difference as Advantage: Maximize the Benefits of Your Cultural Identity on the Job," retrieved May 3, 2009, from **www.imdiversity.com/Villages/Careers/articles/careerjournal_languages_105.asp**.

Short-versus Long-Term Orientation   Cultures with a **short-term orientation** look for quick payoffs, while people with **long-term orientations** defer gratification in pursuit of long-range goals. The willingness to work hard today for a future payoff is especially common in East Asian cultures, while Western industrialized cultures are much more focused on short-term results.

As long as employees and employers share the same orientation toward payoffs, the chances for harmony are good. When some people push for a quick fix while others urge patience, conflicts are likely to arise.

It's easy to see how a society's task or social orientation, attitudes toward uncertainty, individuality, power distance, and short- or long-term results can make a tremendous difference in how work situations evolve. Cultural values shape what persons communicate about and how they interact. Cultural differences don't account for every aspect of workplace functioning, of course, but they do provide a set of assumptions that exert a subtle yet powerful effect on each person's workplace communication.

Co-cultural Dimensions of a Diverse Society

It isn't necessary to travel abroad to find cultural differences. Diversity at home exerts a powerful effect on communication at work. Society is made up of a variety of **co-cultures**—groups that have a clear identity within the majority culture.

Language   As society becomes more diverse, the mix of languages spoken and heard in the workplace increases. As the Case Study on page 46 shows, this trend presents real challenges: To what degree are non-native speakers obliged to learn the dominant language? How many accommodations are organizations and workers obliged to make

case study

A $48 Million Misunderstanding?

Jockey Jose Santos filed a libel claim against the Miami *Herald*, seeking $48 million in damages over a reporter's misunderstanding of his accented English. The *Herald* published a photograph showing Santos apparently holding an object in his hand as he rode thoroughbred Funny Cide across the finish line in the 2003 Kentucky Derby. In the accompanying story, reporter Frank Carlson misquoted the jockey as stating the object was an illegal "cue ring." The item turned out to be a Q-Ray, an ionized bracelet the jockey wore to help with his arthritis. As a result of the story, the Kentucky Racing Commission launched an investigation into what one official called "very suspicious" behavior.

The newspaper later printed a correction, but jockey Santos maintained that the story caused him emotional distress. The horse's owners were co-parties in the lawsuit, alleging that the article's allegation of underhanded racing tactics cost them potential business.

Santos' attorney said that the misunderstanding would never have happened if the *Herald* had chosen a Spanish-speaking reporter. In the same vein, the editor of Miami's alternative paper *New Times* commented: "Let me get this straight: In Miami, the most Hispanic city in the country, the newspaper of record screwed up because someone misunderstood a Spanish speaker?"

CRITICAL ANALYSIS: Answer the following questions as you consider this case.

1. What parties might have been harmed as a result of this misunderstanding?

2. How might the misunderstanding have been significantly reduced if the reporter and interviewee had been more familiar with each other's first language?

3. Describe at least one situation from your experience where misunderstandings could occur due to language differences. How could the chances of the misunderstanding(s) be reduced?

Sources: Based on "Santos, Sackatoga Sue Miami Herald for Libel," *Thoroughbred Times*, May 9, 2004; Richard Prince, "Latino Jockey's Case against Herald to Proceed," February 11, 2005, **www.maynardije.org/columns/dickprince/050211_prince/**, retrieved May 3, 2009; and "Photo of Kentucky Derby Winner Leads to Investigation," *Sports Illustrated.com* **http://sportsillustrated.cnn.com/horse_racing/news/2003/05/10/derby_photo_ap/**, retrieved May 3, 2009.

to help non-native speakers? Regardless of how you answer these difficult questions, it's indisputable that the ability to speak more than one language is an asset in virtually every career.

Even when communicators all speak the same language, accent can have a strong effect on how they are perceived. In the U.S., for example, a variety of accents can be heard in the workplace. Besides the standard dialect (think of speech by newscasters), regional and ethnic accents are common. Research suggests that speech differences are powerful. Speakers of standard dialect are rated higher than nonstandard speakers in a variety of ways: They are perceived as more competent and more self-confident, and the content of their messages is rated more favorably.[39] In one experiment, human resource directors listened to identical recorded passages of text spoken in different U.S. regional accents—and then recommended the best type of job for the speaker. Job-seekers with identifiable accents, such as a heavy southern drawl, were more often recommended for lower-level jobs that offer little client or customer contact, while those with a less identifiable accent were more likely to be recommended for higher-contact, higher-profile—and often higher-paying—jobs with more public contact.[40]

Regional Differences   Beyond accent, regional differences in communication can be significant. In the United States, for example, the unwritten rules about smiling differ from one part of the country to another. Communication researcher Ray Bird-whistell found that midwesterners from Ohio, Indiana, and Illinois smiled more than New Englanders from Massachusetts, New Hampshire, and Maine. None of those people smiled as much as people from southern and border states like Georgia, Kentucky, and Tennessee.[41] Given these differences, it is easy to imagine how a manufacturer from Memphis might regard a banker from Boston as unfriendly, and how the New Englander might view the southerner as overly demonstrative.

Ethnicity It is an oversimplification to describe a single "Hispanic," "Asian," "white," or "black" style of communication, just as it is dangerous to claim that all Arabs, baby boomers, Israelis, or women are alike. Each person's communication style is a combination of individual and cultural traits. Keeping in mind the risks of over-generalizing, scholars have found some patterns of communication that are common for many members of various groups. Understanding how communication is affected by cultural conditioning can help prevent jumping to mistaken conclusions about what a certain kind of behavior means.

The amount of talk and silence that is appropriate can differ from one co-culture to another. For example, most Native American and many Asian American cultures value silence more than mainstream U.S. culture does. By contrast, African American and Euro-American cultures place a high value on verbal skills, and their members tend to speak more. It is easy to imagine how the silence of, say, a Japanese American or Native American employee could be viewed by an African American or Euro-American colleague as a sign of dislike.

Attitudes toward conflict also differ from one ethnic co-culture to another. Because Asian cultures place a high value on saving face, some Asian Americans can display a preference for not disagreeing assertively and directly. Native Americans may prefer to deal with conflict through silence rather than direct confrontation. By contrast, many (though certainly not all) people with a Greek, Israeli, Italian, French, or South American background may prefer a direct, open conflict style.[42]

Even when communicators from different backgrounds speak roughly the same amount, the degree of personal information they reveal can differ dramatically. For example, Euro-Americans disclose more than African Americans or Puerto Ricans, who in turn reveal more than Mexican Americans.[43] (Of course, varying social and cultural contexts may create different disclosure patterns.)

Nonverbal standards also vary by co-culture. Most communicators unconsciously assume that their rules for behaviors such as eye contact are universal. Researchers, however, have found that eye behavior can vary significantly. One study found that widely opened eyes are often interpreted in mainstream U.S. culture as a sign of surprise or wonder and in Hispanic culture as a call for help, signifying "I don't understand." To some African Americans, the same kind of gaze is often regarded as a measure of innocence.[44] Chapter 4 has more to say about cultural differences in nonverbal behavior.

Since Euro-Americans often associate eye contact with honesty and respect, it is easy to misjudge others for whom steady eye contact would be a sign of disrespect. There are many cases where attempts by Puerto Ricans and Native Americans to show respect to persons in authority by not looking at them have been interpreted as dishonesty or disrespect by those accustomed to greater eye contact. Traditionally, Hopi and Navajo people generally avoid steady eye contact, as it is considered offensive, disrespectful, and rude. Blacks tend to make more eye contact when speaking but will not have such a steady gaze at someone they are listening to. Whites tend to make more continuous eye contact while listening to someone.[45]

technology tip

Generational Preferences in Communication Technology

Age often matters when choosing the best technology for exchanging messages on the job. The channels that communicators prefer are often a function of the era in which they came of age.

When boomers entered the workforce, typewriters and telephones were the principal communication technologies. Over 80 percent now use the Internet in one way or another, and most have embraced e-mail. But they are less likely than younger communicators to use or appreciate the value of text messaging, blogging, social networking, or instant messaging. Differences even exist between Gen X-ers and their Gen Y counterparts. For example, about half of the Y's in one survey reported sending or receiving at least one text message within the past day—roughly double the proportion of those in Gen X.

Beyond technology, generational differences also arise in communication style. Gen Y workers are used to the speed and brevity of texting and IM-ing. As a consequence, they often aren't sticklers for correct spelling and syntax. By contrast, matures, boomers, and even Gen X-ers grew up learning that accuracy is essential. They are likely to regard careless writing as a sign of incompetence.

Keeping differences like these in mind can help you choose the communication channel and style that best suits the people you are trying to reach. As always, generalizations don't apply to every person: Some boomers are avid users of all technologies, and some members of Generation Y resemble their grandparents when it comes to using digital media. Despite exceptions to the rule, it often pays to be mindful of generational differences when communicating strategically.

Sources: T. Erickson, "'Where Are My Corduroy Pants?' Is Gen Y's Texting Obsession Headed for the Workplace?" *Harvard Business Online*, May 29, 2007. Retrieved **http://discussionleader.hbsp.com/ erickson/2007/05/where_are_my_corduroy_pants_is.html**. S. Fox and M. Madden, *Generations Online* (Washington, DC: Pew Internet and American Life Project, 2006).

Generational Differences   Along with factors like ethnicity and regional differences, the era in which people have been raised can shape the way they communicate. Demographers, marketers, and social scientists often categorize people born in the Western world in the 20th century into four groups: "matures," "boomers," "Generation X," and "Generation Y." While generalizing can be risky, awareness of fundamental differences can make intergenerational communication more effective.[46]

Matures (born 1900–1945) have been called "The Greatest Generation." Their formative experiences included the Depression, World Wars I and II, and the dawn of the atomic era. These events led to a strong sense of self-control and self-sacrifice. Matures commonly have a strong respect for authority. In the workplace, they have traditionally been loyal to the organizations for which they work. They follow the rules, which they assume exist for good reason. Their work ethic includes timeliness and productivity.

Boomers (born 1946–1964) benefited from growing up in the post–World War II era of prosperity. They witnessed and participated in an era of social reform and upheaval that included the Civil Rights revolution. Social upheaval surrounding the Vietnam War and the degradation of the environment led many boomers to question the claims of authority figures—an ironic position now that they have become the authorities. Boomers have an optimistic, can-do belief in themselves and in the potential for society and organizations to change for the better. As a group, boomers have grown used to getting their way.

Generation X (born 1965–1982) has accepted technological advances as a fact of life. During their youth, gender roles for women became more flexible, contributing to the notion that anything is possible. Because of their many options, Generation X-ers characteristically explore what is desirable for themselves as individuals. They are adept with technology, skeptical, and independent, seeking a good balance between work and the rest of life. They don't accept orders uncritically, and they expect work and life to be meaningful. They respect performance over tenure and are loyal to people, not organizations.

Generation Y (born 1982–1991) also goes by a number of descriptive labels: the Why Generation, Net Generation, The First Globals, and Digital Natives. When compared to the preceding generation, they are hopeful and determined. They have an international worldview; over half have passports and one quarter expect to work outside the U.S.[47] They are technologically adept, and they like to learn by doing. They have high—sometimes unrealistic—expectations for salary, job, and duties. They are remarkably able to shift attention rapidly from one task to another. As a result, they are excellent at multitasking. On the other hand, they may ignore what doesn't interest them—at their own expense and that of their work.

Disabilities

Belonging to a co-culture based on ethnicity or nationality requires years of immersion. By contrast, says columnist Karen Stone, "Disability is a club anyone can join, anytime. It's very easy. Have a stroke and be paralyzed. . . . Be in a car wreck and never walk again."[48] The Americans with Disabilities Act of 1990 (ADA) seeks to guarantee that people with disabilities receive reasonable accommodations and equal access to employment, buildings, transportation, and services. These legal guarantees are important, but they don't change the fact that, in many ways, having a disability may change how one is regarded. Typical language habits reflect this fact. The tendency is to use labels like "blind," "wheelchair-bound," or "deaf" to describe a person, putting him or her in a category that emphasizes physical condition over all other attributes.

Advocates urge terms that treat a disability as one feature, not as a defining characteristic. Describing Mike as "a person who is blind" is both more accurate and less constricting than calling him a "blind person." The difference between "deaf person" and "person who is deaf" might seem subtle—until you imagine which label you would prefer if you lost your hearing.

There are no hard-and-fast rules about communicating with people who have disabilities. After 11 years of research, communication researcher Dawn Braithwaite found that strategies preferred by some were rejected by others.[49] This variability showed up in situations in which an able-bodied person might appropriately offer help. About half of the survey respondents were open to offers of assistance, while others preferred that able-bodied persons wait until they receive a request for help. In either case, though, one message came through clearly: It is important for the self-esteem and safety of a person with a disability to maintain control over if, when, and how help is given. If your offer of help is turned down, accept that fact. If it is accepted, either ask "How can I help?" or ask whether your intentions are acceptable: "Would you like me to open the door?"

Despite the lack of specific overall rules, there are some guidelines for interacting with people who have disabilities:

1. Speak directly to people with disabilities, rather than looking at and talking to their companion or sign language interpreter.

2. When introduced to a person with a disability, offer to shake hands. People with limited hand use or who wear an artificial limb can usually shake hands. (Shaking hands with the left hand is an acceptable greeting.)

3. When meeting a person who is visually impaired, identify yourself and others who may be with you. When conversing in a group, remember to identify the person to whom you are speaking. If you are leaving a group, tell the other person.

4. If you offer assistance, wait until your offer is accepted. Then listen to or ask for instructions.

5. Treat adults as adults. Address people who have disabilities by their first names only when extending the same familiarity to all others. Never patronize people who use wheelchairs by patting them on the head or shoulder.

6. Leaning on or hanging on to a person's wheelchair is similar to leaning or hanging on to a person and is generally considered annoying. The chair is part of the personal body space of the person who uses it.

7. Listen attentively when you're talking with a person who has difficulty speaking. Be patient and wait for the person to finish, rather than correcting or speaking for the person. If necessary, ask short questions that require short answers, a nod, or shake of the head. Never pretend to understand if you are having difficulty doing so. Instead, repeat what you have understood and allow the person to respond. The response will clue you in and guide your understanding.

8. When speaking with a person who uses a wheelchair or a person who uses crutches, place yourself at eye level in front of the person to facilitate the conversation.

9. To get the attention of a person who is deaf, tap the person on the shoulder or wave your hand. Look directly at the person and speak clearly, slowly, and expressively to determine whether the person can read your lips. Not all people who are deaf can read lips. For those who do lip read, be sensitive to their needs by placing yourself so that you face the light source and keep hands, cigarettes, and food away from your mouth when speaking.

10. Relax. Don't be embarrassed if you happen to use accepted, common expressions such as "See you later" or "Did you hear about that?" that seem to relate to a person's disability. Don't be afraid to ask questions when you're unsure of what to do.[50]

So far we have focused on guidelines for able-bodied communicators. People with disabilities also can take steps to improve communication. Braithwaite identified several strategies, including the following, that can minimize the impact of the disability and help put able-bodied people at ease:

- *Initiating a transaction:* "Excuse me. Would you mind looking up a phone number?"

- *Modeling behavior:* "If you move your lips more like this, I can understand you better."

- *Establishing normalcy:* "Don't you hate waiting in lines like this?"

These statements reflect different facets of cultural intelligence. For each set, add up your scores and divide by four to produce an average. Our work with large groups of managers shows that for purposes of your own development, it is most useful to think about your three scores in comparison to one another. Generally, an average of less than 3 would indicate an area calling for improvement, while an average of greater than 4–5 reflects a true CQ strength.

Rate the extent to which you agree with each statement, using the scale:
1 = strongly disagree, 2 = disagree, 3 = neutral, 4 = agree, 5 = strongly agree.

_____ Before I interact with people from a new culture, I ask myself what I hope to achieve.

_____ If I encounter something unexpected while working in a new culture, I use this experience to figure out new ways to approach *other* cultures in the future.

_____ I plan how I'm going to relate to people from a different culture before I meet them.

+ _____ When I come into a new cultural situation, I can immediately sense whether something is going well or something is wrong.

Total _____ **÷ 4 =** [   ] **Cognitive CQ**

_____ It's easy for me to change my body language (for example, eye contact or posture) to suit people from a different culture.

_____ I can alter my expression when a cultural encounter requires it.

_____ I modify my speech style (for example, accent or tone) to suit people from a different culture.

+ _____ I easily change the way I act when a cross-cultural encounter seems to require it.

Total _____ **÷ 4 =** [   ] **Physical CQ**

_____ I have confidence that I can deal well with people from a different culture.

_____ I am certain that I can befriend people whose cultural backgrounds are different from mine.

_____ I can adapt to the lifestyle of a different culture with relative ease.

+ _____ I am confident that I can deal with a cultural situation that's unfamiliar.

Total _____ **÷ 4 =** [   ] **Emotional/ motivational CQ**

Source: P.C. Earley and E. Mosakowski, "Cultural Intelligence," *Harvard Business Review*, October 2004, pp. 139–146.

- *Confronting the issue:* "I may have trouble speaking, but I can understand just fine!"
- *Using humor:* "Tony, they tell me your singing is so awful that even a guy like me who can't hear would hate it!"

Diversity and Ethical Issues

Some cultural differences may challenge your sense of what is normal or proper behavior without raising ethical questions. For example, you probably could readjust your sense of promptness or what to wear to a business meeting without facing any sort of moral dilemma. In other cases, though, doing business in an unfamiliar culture might challenge your fundamental sense of right and wrong. You might be offended by differing notions of gender equality. You could be shocked to learn that bribes or payoffs are considered a normal part of doing business. You could encounter favoritism toward friends and family members that offends your sense of fair play. You might see a profound disregard for the environment.

There is growing recognition that businesses that operate in a worldwide economy need a universal code of business ethics. Toward that end, a collaboration of business leaders in Japan, Europe, and the United States have developed a code of ethics based on ideals from both East Asia and the West. Called the Caux Round Table Principles for Business, this code includes many communication-related principles, such as treating all employees with honesty and dignity, listening to employee suggestions, avoiding discriminatory practices, dealing with all customers fairly, and avoiding industrial espionage and other dishonest means of acquiring commercial information.[51]

Despite this admirable effort, you may encounter ethical challenges arising out of cultural differences. In cases like these, you can respond in a variety of ways:

Avoiding: You might refuse to do business in cultures which operate according to ethical principles that are different from yours.

Accommodating: You could accept the different ethical system and conform to practices that are fundamentally different from yours.

Forcing: You could insist on doing business in a way that you believe is ethically proper.

Educating–Persuading: You could try to convince the people with whom you want to do business why your set of ethical principles is more appropriate.

Negotiating–Compromising: Both parties could give up something to negotiate a settlement.

Collaboration–Problem Solving: The parties could confront the conflict directly and work together to develop a mutually satisfying solution.[52]

All of these approaches have obvious drawbacks. It's easy to imagine a situation in which you may have to choose between compromising your principles to please your bosses and customers or being true to yourself and risking your career.

Facing ethical dilemmas you never anticipated can be especially hard. You can begin to prepare yourself by grounding yourself in ethical principles and learning about the ethical practices of a new culture. When you do encounter new situations, ask yourself the following questions to help you make the best possible decision:

- *How morally significant is this situation?* Not all ethical conflicts have the same moral significance. For example, while giving contracts to friends or family members may offend the sensibilities of a businessperson used to awarding jobs on the basis of merit, the practice may not be as morally offensive as one exploiting child labor or irreparably damaging the environment.[53]

- *Is there home culture consensus regarding the issue?* If there is not widespread agreement in your home culture about the ethical principle, you justifiably may have more latitude about how to act. For example, since corporations in the United States have a wide range of policies about supporting the families of employees, there might be less obligation for a company to provide family benefits in a host country.[54]

Communicating across Diversity

By now it should be clear that communicating with others from different backgrounds isn't always easy. Matters including culture, ethnicity, and gender may have made others' experiences quite different from yours.[55] Some of the responsibility for building bridges rests with management, and a growing number of businesses are taking this job seriously. But you don't need to join a corporate training program to benefit from cultural diversity. Figure 2–4 shows the range of attitudes about cultural differences, and Table 2–3 lists attitudes and behaviors that can promote more satisfying, productive relationships among members of different cultures. These principles can be summarized in the five categories on pages 53–56. Adopting a more perceptive attitude can go a long way toward opening the door to more rewarding and productive communication.

Become Culturally Literate   Many cultural problems are caused not by malice but by a lack of knowledge. Trainers in cultural sensitivity cite examples of how mistaken assumptions can lead to trouble.[56] In one West Coast bank, officials were dismayed when Filipino female employees didn't cooperate with the new "friendly teller" program. Management failed to realize that in Filipino culture overtly friendly women can be taken for prostitutes. A Taiwanese executive who was transferred to the midwestern offices of a large company was viewed as aloof and autocratic by his peers, who did not understand that Asian culture encourages a more distant managerial style.

Misunderstandings like these are less likely to cause problems when mainstream workers understand each other's cultural backgrounds. As Paulette Williams, former senior manager at Weyerhauser's nurseries in Southern California, put it, "If you don't learn how other people feel, you can hurt them unintentionally."[57]

Timothy Weiss, a U.S. professor who spent a year teaching at the Chinese University of Hong Kong, illustrates the kind of open-minded, inquiring attitude that can make communicators more effective when they encounter different cultural practices.

> *Why, in a culture that so dearly values every second and minute saved, will meetings and conversations last for what Americans would consider such inordinately long periods? . . . In these departmental meetings—which I find excruciating—I suspect that something else is going*

Denial	Defense	Minimization	Acceptance	Adaptation	Integration
No perception of differences	Hostility toward other cultures	Belief that cultural differences are superficial	Recognition and exploration of differences	Ability to empathize, shift frame of reference	Recognizing and embracing differences

Self-centered ◄──────────────────────────────────────► Other-centered

FIGURE 2–4
Stages of Intercultural Sensitivity

Table 2–3   Attitudes and Behaviors That Block or Promote Intercultural Relations

Assumptions That Block Authentic Relations

Assumptions Majority Makes	Assumptions Minorities Make
• Differences should not affect performance.	• All members of the majority have the same attitudes about minorities.
• Minorities will always welcome inclusion in the majority culture.	• There are no majority members who understand minorities.
• Open recognition of differences may embarrass minorities.	• Majority members are not really trying to understand minorities.
• Minorities are using their situation to take advantage of the majority.	• The only way to change the situation is by confrontation and force.
• "Liberal" members of the majority are free of discriminatory attitudes.	• All majority members will let you down in a "crunch."
• Minorities are oversensitive.	

Behaviors That Block Authentic Relations

Behaviors of Majority Cultures	Behaviors of Minority Cultures
• Interruptions.	• Confronting too early and too harshly.
• Condescending behavior.	• Rejecting offers of help and friendship.
• Expressions of too-easy acceptance and friendship.	• Giving answers majority members want to hear.
• Talking about, rather than to, minorities who are present.	• Isolationism.

Assumptions and Behaviors That Promote Authentic Relations

• Treating people as individuals as well as members of a culture.	• Staying with and working through difficult confrontations.
• Demonstrating interest in learning about other cultures.	• Acknowledging sincere attempts (even clumsy ones).
• Listening without interrupting.	• Dealing with others as they are, instead of expecting them to be perfect.
• Taking risks (e.g., being first to confront needed differences).	• Recognizing that interdependence is needed between members of majority and minority cultures.
• Expressing concerns directly and constructively.	

Source: From Philip R. Harris and Robert T. Moran, *Managing Cultural Differences: Global Leadership Strategies for the 21st Century.* (Boston: Elsevier/Butterworth-Heinemann, 2004), pp. 245–247.

on that a Westerner such as myself will understand sooner or later. Although I certainly am not ready to abandon my American sense of how departmental meetings should be conducted, in allowing myself to remain open-minded about other ways of conducting these meetings, I begin to learn something about other ways of approaching departmental issues and of communicating messages within a group.[58]

View Diversity as an Opportunity
It is easy to think of cultural differences as an annoyance that makes it harder to take care of business. Dealing with others who have different attitudes or customs takes patience and time—both scarce commodities in a busy work schedule. But with the right attitude, cultural diversity can stop being just a necessary cost of doing business and can become an opportunity.[59]

People with differing backgrounds can bring new strengths to a business. Women, for instance, are generally more skilled than men at reading nonverbal cues.[60] This makes them ideal members of a negotiating team, where they may be especially skilled at interpreting how the other people are feeling. Workers from diverse ethnic groups can offer new insights into how customers or other workers with similar backgrounds can be reached. A Hispanic supervisor, for example, may be especially effective at motivating and training other Hispanics, and a Korean team member can give new insights into how a Korean-managed competitor operates.

Avoid Ethnocentrism
Ethnocentrism is the inclination to see all events from the perspective of your own culture and to evaluate your own culture as superior. Ethnocentrism is evident when you judge someone to be less intelligent or less important because he or she doesn't keep up with your national teams, critique others as less sophisticated because their dress doesn't match your culture's notion of fashion, or assume others have less business acumen because they use different software programs. Taking advantage of intercultural communication training and opportunities for multicultural interactions may help reduce your ethnocentrism.[61]

Don't Condescend
It's easy to view people who are different as unequal. Your first reaction to a physically challenged colleague might be sympathy or pity. Immigrants who are learning English as a second language might sound less intelligent than native speakers. Even white males, members of the traditional majority, might seem like members of the "good old boy" club, undeserving of respect since their success seemingly owes more to personal connections than to merit.

Even excessive efforts to demonstrate an attitude of equality can come across as condescending. One African American woman listed three statements that white women who want to treat black women with respect and friendship should never utter: (1) "I never even notice that you're black"; (2) "You're different from most black people"; (3) "I understand what you're going through as a black woman, because I'm (Jewish, Italian, etc.)."[62]

Create Dialogue
Intercultural communication experts Judith Martin and Thomas Nakayama advise that an important first step toward intercultural competence is to enter into dialogue.[63] Dialogue occurs when persons acknowledge each other's common humanity and engage with each other authentically and spontaneously. Dialogue requires an attitude of mutual respect in which each person is listening to the other without preplanned agendas or past prejudices and distortions.

When people from differing backgrounds don't listen to and talk with one another constructively, misperceptions can take root. In a study of American corporations,

"After the merger, you may notice a few changes in our corporate culture."

© 2003 Ted Goff. Reprinted by permission.

Charles Kelly found that blacks perceived whites as being reserved and ambitious and having an attitude of superiority. He found that whites perceived blacks as being easygoing and ambitious and feeling as if they are owed something.[64] Without understanding each other's concerns, attitudes like these are less likely to disappear.

Not all talk about diversity is constructive: The way people talk about differences can determine whether relationships improve or suffer. Journalist Ellis Cose describes two nonproductive styles:

> Discussions tend to be conducted at one of two levels—either in shouts or whispers. The shouters are generally so twisted by pain or ignorance that spectators tune them out. The whisperers are so afraid of the sting of truth that they avoid saying much of anything at all.[65]

Experts agree with Cose that ignoring differences can be just as dangerous as emphasizing them. The challenge, then, is to discuss differences openly without using the kinds of inflammatory language described in Chapter 4. If you approach others with a constructive attitude, the odds of positive outcomes increase.

Organizational Culture and Communication

So far we have explored culture as a matter of geography, ethnicity, and physical condition. But even people with identical personal backgrounds can find themselves in very different cultures, depending on the organizations to which they belong. Just like individuals, organizations have personalities. Some are casual, energetic, even zany; others are formal, slow-moving, and serious. Social scientists call this personality an **organizational culture**—a relatively stable, shared set of rules about how to behave and set of values about what is important. In everyday language, culture is the insiders' view of "the way things are around here." Founder and former CEO of Southwest Airlines, Herb Kelleher, defined culture as "what people do when no one is looking."[66]

Like human personalities, organizational cultures that appeal to one kind of person repel others. Many people abhor bureaucracies, with their clearly defined job hierarchies and voluminous rules; others feel most comfortable in that sort of setting. Some people welcome the chaotic disorganization and constant change that often characterize new companies in emerging fields; others feel more at home in organizations with clearly defined jobs and products. Some people like a working environment in which employees are one big family; others prefer to keep their working and personal lives separate.

Belonging to an organizational culture means choosing a way of life. Consider one example of how cultures—and their effects—can differ.

> Tattoos, piercings, long hair and good books. It's an odd combination that helps bookselling superstore Borders distinguish itself from the competition. Borders goes for funky, edgy employees who use their personality and passion to sell the products. Barnes & Noble, its closest competitor, prefers clean-cut employees in pressed shirts who smile brightly while helping customers find whatever they're looking for.[67]

A Great Place to Work: Griffin Hospital

For eight consecutive years, *Fortune* magazine has honored Connecticut-based Griffin Hospital as one of the best companies to work for in the United States. The most important factor in choosing award winners is what employees themselves say about their organization.

Employees report that salary and benefits are important; but they are looking for something more basic. They want to have a voice in how the organization operates. They want to be told the truth, especially if the news is bad.

Griffin's culture of openness was tested in the dark days of 2001, when a rash of anthrax poisonings had the entire country on edge. A patient had become the nation's fifth victim of the deadly bacterium. The hospital's lab confirmed the diagnosis, and word was sure to leak out via the organizational grapevine. Despite pressure from the state's governor and the FBI to withhold the information, Griffin's administration felt obligated to honor its policy of openness and keep its workforce informed. The hospital held a briefing for 400 of its day-shift employees.

In light of Griffin's commitment to openness, a representative of the American Hospital Association endorsed the decision, saying, "If you do not follow the open and honest culture you have created at Griffin, you will destroy in one day what has taken you 10 years to build." Local opinion also supported the hospital. Griffin received an award from the New London newspaper for its commitment to keeping employees informed, calling the hospital's decision "nothing short of heroic."

Most organizations claim a commitment to a culture of open communication, but the real test is in what they do when faced with challenges. When choosing where to work, prospective employees would be wise to explore whether a company's deeds match its words.

CRITICAL ANALYSIS: Explore the importance of organizational culture by answering these questions:

1. How might the culture at Griffin have changed if administrators had been less open with employees in the anthrax case?

2. Why would a commitment to truth-telling and openness be at least as important as salary and benefits to employees at Griffin and elsewhere?

3. What elements of an organizational culture are most important to you? To what degree have these been present in organizations where you have worked and studied?

4. How can you use the guidelines on pages 61–62 ("Organizational Culture and Career Planning") to identify organizations with cultures that match your values and goals?

Sources: Carmine Gallo, "Creating a Great Place to Work," *Business Week*, February 4, 2008, p. 28, and "Changing the Face of Healthcare" **www.griffinhealth.org/Performance/FortuneSurvey .aspx**.

Cultures aren't limited to large corporations. Every organization has its own way of doing business and treating people. Anyone who has worked for more than one restaurant or retail store, attended more than one college or university, belonged to more than one team, or volunteered for more than one worthy cause knows that even when the same job is being performed, the way of doing business can be radically different. Furthermore, a person's "fit" with the culture of an organization can make all the difference between a satisfying and a disappointing job. Research shows that employees are more satisfied and committed to their jobs when their values match those of their supervisors and the organization.[68] They are also more successful. Harvard Business School professors John Kotter and James Heskett flatly claim that people who conform to the norms of their organization's culture will be rewarded, while those who do not will be penalized.[69]

Some of the rules for communicating in organizational settings are spelled out: "Customers come first" is one example. But in other cases, rules aren't made explicit. For instance, "don't complain" or "document *everything*" can be powerful rules, even though they aren't ever discussed.[70] One study revealed that the costs of employees not understanding the unspoken rules of an organization can be high—running into millions of dollars in lost time, reduced productivity, quality problems, and ill will.[71] Another study suggests that it is mid-level managers who best know, understand, and transmit company culture, perhaps making them the best source of information for new hires.[72]

The Importance of Organizational Culture

It's hard to overstate the importance of organizational culture. The cost of having a workforce that doesn't understand and play by the rules can be staggering. In one survey, respondents reported that the annual cost of workers not "knowing the ropes" ranged from less than $100 to as much as $10 million.[73] When employees didn't understand or accept their organization's culture, the results included lost time, lowered productivity, bad publicity for the firm, lowered morale and trust, lost customers, and lost opportunity. Poor fit between cultures may even cause organizational mergers to fail.[74]

Organizational culture can affect you in a variety of ways, both large and small. Among other things, the culture of your organization can determine where and how long you work, including options such as flextime and telecommuting. It can shape the emotional environment, including the degree of cooperation or competition, and notions of how much and what kinds of fun are appropriate. Culture will surely influence the way you and others dress and the space in which you work: its size, degree of privacy (or lack thereof), and decoration. Organizational culture will govern the amount and type of interaction you have (both on and off the job) with other employees, both co-workers and management.[75]

Dimensions of Organizational Culture

What elements distinguish one culture from another? In his well-known management book *The Human Side of Enterprise*, Douglas McGregor proposed two theories that shape organizational cultures. He referred to these opposing motivational theories as **Theory X** and **Theory Y**.[76] As Table 2–4 shows, the assumptions behind each theory are different. It's easy to imagine how the top-down, authoritarian structure in a Theory X organization would differ from the more optimistic, supportive culture in a Theory Y operation.

Several dimensions distinguish organizations, even those doing the same kind of work.

1. *Sociability.* Are employees involved with one another on a personal level, or do they limit interaction to job-related tasks? A "one big family" culture isn't necessarily superior to a less personal one, but shared notions about how much sociability is appropriate is an important ingredient of job satisfaction.

2. *Power distribution and job autonomy.* What is the degree of power distance between people at different levels within the organization? What are the demands to report and justify actions to higher management? How much freedom do employees have

Describing Organizational Cultures

The culture of an organization can be a powerful influence on the experience members have in it and the public has with it.

In 2 minutes or less, brief your class on the culture of an organization (e.g., a place where you have worked or an organization you have belonged to) or a field (e.g., construction, software design) that you are familiar with.

Begin with a brief description of the organization or field and your experience with it. Then use the qualities listed on pages 58–60 that best describe the kinds of communication that shape this culture and how the culture shapes the way communication operates in the organization or field. Include at least one example of an incident or practice that illustrates the culture you are describing.

Table 2–4	Theory X and Theory Y Organizational Cultures

Theory X Organizations	Theory Y Organizations
• Work is inherently distasteful to most people, and they will attempt to avoid work whenever possible.	• Work can be as natural as play, if the conditions are favorable.
• Most people are not ambitious, have little desire for responsibility, and prefer to be directed.	• People will be self-directed and creative to meet their work and organizational objectives if they are committed to them.
• Most people have little aptitude for creativity in solving organizational problems.	• The capacity for creativity spreads throughout organizations.
• Most people are self-centered. As a result, they must be closely controlled and often coerced to achieve organizational objectives.	• Most people can handle responsibility because creativity and ingenuity are common in the population.
• Most people resist change.	• Under these conditions, people will seek responsibility.
• Most people are gullible and unintelligent.	

to make decisions themselves? Some workers are most comfortable when they have both limited authority and responsibility; others prefer more freedom.

3. *Degree of structure.* Are job roles highly defined, with people operating within their own area of responsibility, or is it considered acceptable to get involved in other areas of the organization's work? Does the organization have a large number of policies and procedures, or are issues handled less formally?

4. *Achievement rewards.* How (if at all) are the accomplishments of employees acknowledged and rewarded? Are praise and other types of reinforcement commonplace or infrequent? Is recognition based on true ability or other, less fair reasons? Is the level of reinforcement suitable to meet your personal needs?

5. *Opportunities for growth.* Does the company encourage workers to develop their skills and take on new responsibilities, or does it focus exclusively on employees' handling their present jobs competently? Does it encourage education and training? Are you satisfied with the opportunities for growth provided by the organization?

ethical challenge

6. *Tolerance for risk and change.* Does management encourage employees to take well-reasoned chances, or is avoiding risk a high priority? Is change expected and welcomed, or are tradition, predictability, and stability highly valued?

7. *Conflict tolerance.* Does the company believe that disagreement is not necessarily a sign of disloyalty, or is harmony stressed? Are the organizational norms for managing conflict compatible with your personal style?

8. *Emotional support.* Does management show a genuine interest in the well-being of employees by seeking out and responding to their concerns? Do you feel like you are receiving the emotional support you want and deserve?[77]

Creating and Maintaining Organizational Cultures

Whether the culture is created deliberately or evolves without a grand design, the earliest phase of an organization's life is the best time to set the tone for its lifelong culture. Early events are enshrined in stories that can take on the quality of legends.[78] One of the most famous of these tales is told at IBM about former chairman of the board Thomas Watson Jr. Watson was barred from entering a high-security area of one of the company's plants because he was not wearing the proper identification badge. Rather than firing the assertive guard who blocked his entry, Watson acknowledged the policy and waited at the gate until the proper identification was found. The story confirms a policy central to IBM's culture: Everybody at the company obeys the rules.

An organization's culture takes on a life of its own. Customs and rituals develop that perpetuate a company's values.[79]

- The "work hard, play hard" culture of the Los Angeles Dodgers baseball club is apparent by a long history of practical jokes which included locking former manager Tommy Lasorda in his office, stealing the clothes of rookies while they are showering, and smearing shoe polish inside an unwitting player's cap in order to give him a black "halo." Players who have misconstrued these pranks as personal insults have overreacted until they understood the team's culture.[80]

- At Tupperware, the president and senior managers spend fully 1 month per year at celebrations honoring top salespersons and managers.[81]

- Some cultural practices involve changing labels. Employees are called crew members at McDonald's, hosts at Disney Productions, and associates at JCPenney, reflecting those companies' shared belief that every worker plays an important role in the corporation's success.

Practices like these both reflect a company's culture and continue to shape it, but they are nothing more than gimmicks unless they are backed up by day-to-day activities.

Not all cultural traditions are so positive. Supervisors often try to prod unproductive workers by issuing more and more rules, feeding the flames of unhappiness that they are trying to extinguish. In some organizations, negative customs perpetuate an unhappy state of affairs. Complaining can become a part of a company's culture: Bitter employees may spend time over coffee ridiculing management and criticizing the company. Unavailability is sometimes an organizational trait as well: Managers who dislike and fear subordinates often barricade themselves in offices, cutting off communication with the rank-and-file employees, who, in turn, feel increasingly alienated. One observer pointed out how corporate downsizing can be the ultimate measure of management's attitude toward employees.

> *Perhaps the most dramatic and egregious gestures companies make are layoffs. On one level, it looks as though the corporation has just gone feral and is chewing off its right leg because its left leg is in a trap. But when layoffs are particularly callous, an additional message is sent, one that speaks of arrogance, omnipotence and impunity. It's as if a gang of executives, clad in navy suits, were walking down a city sidewalk four abreast, bumping hapless strangers into gutters or shop windows. Downsizing's subtext is this: "We have the power and the money. We can do what we like, and there's not much you can do about it except whine."*[82]

Organizational Culture and Career Planning

As a prospective employee, you might be tempted to select a company on the basis of its most obvious characteristics. What is the starting salary? How are the working conditions? What are the chances for promotion? If you consider only these factors, you could wind up with an impressive title and income—but miserable.

When you are thinking about going to work for an organization, make an effort to pin down its personality, just as you would if you were choosing a mate. After all, you are likely to spend more hours per year at work than you will with a spouse. You can get a sense of a company's culture in five ways.[83]

Study the Physical Setting
An organization's physical plant and architecture says something about its personality. Even though most organizations don't make statements by building their environment, they do say something about themselves by choosing the space in which they operate. For example, choosing to locate in a high-rent or low-rent district might say something about the prosperity of the organization, its concern with controlling costs, the public it wants to serve, or even its competence. Likewise, the physical condition of the facilities makes a statement. Is the workplace clean or dirty? Are workers' areas personalized or standardized?

Read What the Company Says about Itself
Press releases, annual reports, and advertisements can all be revealing. Companies with strong values are proud to publicize them. An emphasis on only profit and loss raises doubts about the company's concern for its personnel. Pride about innovation, service to customers,

and commitment to the community—all are clues about an organization's culture. Of course, noble statements may be only lip service to praiseworthy values. Use the other suggestions in this section to see whether a company practices what it preaches.

Observe Communication Practices

How are you treated when you visit a company or deal with its employees? Do e-mails and other written correspondence suggest a welcoming culture?[84] A walking tour of the working areas can help give a feel for the organization's personality. "Vibrations" may not be a scientific term, but companies do have them.

Interview Company People

Communication scholar J. Kevin Barge talks about the importance of learning about an organization's culture from the people who know it best: "Corporate cultures come from the way people talk about their organization, the way they construct what values are important, what rituals are important, what standards for performance are important, and what it means to be a member of this organization."[85]

An employment interview probably isn't the best place to explore how a company treats its employees. Talking with employees off the record can provide valuable insights about the way the company operates. See what they say about the company. Even rehearsed answers can be revealing: The apparent enthusiasm and sincerity with which they are delivered offer a clue about whether employees believe in the company line. Even if you don't learn much about the organization as a whole, you'll get a good picture of the kind of people you will be working with.

Learn How People Spend Their Time

During your interview and observations, find out how employees spend their time at work. A surprising amount of effort might go into activities that are only remotely related to getting the job done: dealing with paperwork, playing office politics, struggling with balky equipment, or attending one unproductive meeting after another.

Check out the parking lot or garage on evenings and weekends: Lots of vehicles can be a tip-off that you will be expected to work long hours. Decide whether you are willing to accept this lifestyle. The way a company goes about its business reveals more about its culture than the kind of work it does.

review points

- U.S. society is increasingly diverse and communicating with many cultures (race, nationality, physical ability, gender identity, socioeconomics) and co-cultures (language, region, ethnicity, age) is a business necessity.
- Culture consists of learned beliefs, values, and norms of a group.
- Astute business communicators are aware of differences in formality, social customs, dress, time, tolerance for conflict, and gender roles as well as more "hidden" cultural dimensions of high/low context, individualism/collectivism, power distance, uncertainty avoidance, task/social orientation, and long-/short-term focus.
- Business communicators must consider the greater complexity of multicultural ethical issues.

- Employees must continuously update their cultural knowledge, view diversity as an opportunity, avoid ethnocentrism, treat everyone with equal respect, and develop dialogue.
- Prospective employees can understand organizational cultures (Theory X or Y, rules, customs, rituals, leaders, and history) by observation and interview and then evaluate the cultural "fit."

key terms

 Test your understanding of these key terms by visiting the Online Learning Center Web site at www.mhhe.com/adler10e.

boomers   48
co-cultures   45
collectivist cultures   42
culture   36
ethnocentrism   55
Generation X   48
Generation Y   49
high-context culture   40
individualistic cultures   42
long-term orientation   45
low-context culture   40

matures   48
monochronic time orientation   39
organizational culture   56
polychronic time orientation   39
power distance   44
short-term orientation   45
social orientation   44
task orientation   44
Theory X   58
Theory Y   58
uncertainty avoidance   44

activities

 Go to the self-quizzes at the Online Learning Center at www.mhhe.com/adler10e to test your knowledge of chapter concepts.

1. Invitation to Insight

a. Either through personal interviews or research, identify several differences in communication practices between your own culture and another culture that interests you.

b. If you were interacting with a person from that culture, how would you bridge the differences?

2. Invitation to Insight

Choose one set of cultural values summarized on pages 40–45 and identify the characteristic that is not representative of your own culture. For example, if you are used to a low-context culture, you might focus on high-context communication. Now consider both the advantages and the disadvantages of working in an environment in which this unfamiliar norm is the dominant one. For instance, how might interaction be more effective or otherwise desirable if most people communicated in a high-context manner?

3. Skill Builder

Select one form of disability. Collaborate with several of your classmates to create two role plays, illustrating effective and ineffective communication with a person who is challenged by the disability. Act out your role plays in front of the class.

4. Skill Builder

Develop your ability to identify and communicate effectively within an organization's culture. Choose an organization in a field that interests you, or focus on an organization to which you already belong. By analyzing the organization's physical setting and literature, interviewing others, and making your own observations, construct a description of the organizational culture that addresses the dimensions listed on pages 53–60. On the basis of your findings, describe an optimal way to communicate in the following areas:

a. Introducing new ideas.
b. Interacting with superiors.
c. Dealing with conflict.
d. Managing time.
e. Socializing with fellow workers.
f. Using preferred methods of exchanging information (e.g., telephone, e-mail, face-to-face interaction).

5. Skill Builder

Choose three cultures around the world with which you are likely to interact in the course of your career. To discover the keys to effective intercultural communication in your three chosen cultures, use the Internet sites listed in On the Web, World Cultures, on the Online Learning Center Web site at **www.mhhe.com/adler10e**. For each of the three cultures describe

a. The culture in general.
b. Business protocol for that culture.
c. The language(s).
d. Sources you could go to for additional training and/or e-mail contacts.

6. Skill Builder

Representatives from Japan, the United States, and European nations collaborated in an attempt to create an international code of business ethics. Read about the Caux Round Table by using a search engine to find articles on this process begun in 1994. Read the document at **http://www .cauxroundtable.org** and then

a. List the seven principles found in the document.
b. Describe how these seven principles relate to the ethical standards on page 12 of Chapter 1.
c. Write a short essay describing how your own personal sense of ethics corresponds to each of the seven principles.

7. Invitation to Insight

Choose one of the following options to better understand the importance of organizational culture. In each case, use the most relevant dimensions of communication described on pages 58–60 to structure your analysis and description.

a. Interview someone familiar with an organization or field that interests you to learn about its culture. Identify the kinds of communication that shape this culture and how the culture shapes the way communication operates in the organization or field.

b. Assume the administration of your college or university has asked you to brief newly hired faculty members about the academic culture of your school from an undergraduate student's perspective. Describe how communication practices at your school both shape and reflect its culture. You can make your remarks more clear and interesting by including one or more brief examples to illustrate how the culture operates.

resources

For extensive readings and Web sites on cultural diversity and organizational communication, see the Online Learning Center Web site at **www.mhhe.com/adler10e.**

Computer Solutions

From the outside, Marissa and Tran's partnership looks like a classic entrepreneurial success story. Their business, Computer Solutions, has doubled its volume annually in each of the 4 years since it began in an extra room of Tran's apartment. Tran has always been the technical expert, and Marissa has dealt with landing customers and making sure they are satisfied. Besides Tran and Marissa, Computer Solutions now has 16 talented employees and needs at least 4 more to cope with the backlog of business.

Despite their success, both Tran and Marissa feel like they are facing a crisis in their partnership—although each one views the problem differently. Tran sees Marissa as failing to carry her share of the load: "I work 12-hour days to give our customers the solutions they need. While I'm trapped here in the office, Marissa is off having 2-hour lunches or traveling to all sorts of great places. When we started this business, we agreed we would split the responsibilities 50-50, and now I'm doing much more than my share of work. And Marissa keeps saying we need to talk about this. But I'm too busy to talk. If I don't keep working, we're going to lose some of our customers."

Marissa sees the problem quite differently: "Tran doesn't seem to appreciate that I'm the one who brings in the business. We have plenty of good, strong competitors out there, and I have the job of making sure customers choose and stay with us. Believe me—all the business meals, travel, and trade shows aren't fun. I'd much rather stay near home and live a normal life." Marissa also has another concern: "Tran doesn't recognize how our chief engineer, Carlo, is making our female employees very uncomfortable. Three of the women who work for us have complained privately to me about how Carlo's stares and jokes with sexual content are affecting their ability to work. Tran is Carlo's manager, and he needs to deal with this problem soon. I'm afraid we're at risk of losing some of these women. I can even imagine a sexual harassment lawsuit in our future. I've tried to explain to Tran how important it is to have a positive climate in the office, but he doesn't seem to think feelings are worth considering. A typical engineer!"

Until recently, Tran and Marissa hadn't spoken openly about their feelings toward each other. Despite this fact, they knew each other well enough to realize that the tension was growing thicker by the week. Finally, at the end of an especially grueling month, the storm burst and they had the first shouting match of their partnership. Tran called Marissa a "glory hog," and she accused him of being a "sexist nerd." Since then, they have both suffered through a period of frigid politeness.

The strains of the unresolved conflict are beginning to affect the operation of Computer Solutions. Both partners realize that the success of the business depends on working through their differences. Marissa doubts they will be able to accomplish this without some outside help, and she is thinking about proposing to Tran that they hire a consultant to help them develop more productive ways of behaving. She also wants to propose that the company start a formal performance review process so problems like Carlo's can be managed and good employee performance is recognized. Tran is skeptical about "touchy-feely human relations types" becoming involved. He thinks they can use logic to solve their problems without bringing in outsiders.

As you read the chapters in this unit, consider the following questions:

Chapter 3

1. Which barriers to listening described in Chapter 3 might have contributed to Marissa and Tran's problems?
2. Describe how Marissa and Tran might have used the guidelines in Chapter 3 to deal more effectively with their disagreements.

Chapter 4

1. Describe a series of messages, ranging from highly ambiguous to highly specific, that Tran and Marissa could use to express their concerns to one another. Which approach(es) might have the best chance of success?

2. Give an example of how Marissa or Tran could use each type of inflammatory language described in this chapter to confront each other. For each statement, provide a noninflammatory alternative.

3. What kinds of behavior—verbal and nonverbal—might Carlo's subordinates have perceived as harassing? What options did they have for reducing these problem behaviors?

Chapter 5

1. What types of disconfirming messages do you suspect Marissa and Tran have been exchanging as their dispute escalated? How would you describe the communication climate of their relationship at this point?

2. Which types of confirming messages outlined on pages 128–131 could the partners use to improve the climate of their relationship?

3. How could Marissa, Tran, and Carlo use praise to improve the situation they are facing?

4. How might Marissa, Tran, and Carlo use the skills introduced on pages 135–137 to respond to criticism from one another and the other employees at Computer Solutions?

5. Describe likely scenarios if Tran and Marissa used each of the following approaches to dealing with their conflict: win–lose, compromise, win–win.

3

Listening

chapter outline

The Impoprtance of Listening
Environmental Barriers
Attitudinal Barriers and False Assumptions
Sociocultural Differences
Lack of Training

Listening Styles
People-Oriented
Action-Oriented
Content-Oriented
Time-Oriented

Listening More Effectively
Listening to Understand
Listening to Evaluate
Review Points
Key Terms
Activities
Resources

chapter objectives

After reading this chapter you should be able to

1. Identify how effective listening can contribute to your career success.
2. Describe barriers to your listening effectively and outline strategies for overcoming each barrier.
3. Identify your listening style(s), and describe how you might use them to better understand others and be understood.
4. Describe the best listening approaches you can use in a given situation to promote understanding, accomplish your goals, and enhance your relationship with others.

"I told her we were meeting *this* Tuesday, not next Tuesday. Now we have to reschedule the meeting, and we may not make the deadline."

"He said he was listening, but he didn't give me a minute to talk before he started interrupting. That's the last time I'll try to present a better way to do anything around here!"

"Something went wrong down the line. I warned those people to watch the temperature carefully, but they don't listen. Now a whole batch is spoiled. What does it take to get them to understand?"

Situations like these are disturbingly common in business. They show how frequent listening failures are and how costly they can be. You may not be able to make others listen better, but you can boost your own ability to listen carefully to the scores of important messages you are likely to hear every business day.

As you will learn in the following pages, listening effectively is hard work. It involves far more than sitting passively and absorbing others' words. It occurs far more frequently than speaking, reading, or writing and is just as demanding and important.

The Importance of Listening

Business experts agree that listening is a vitally important skill. In today's highly competitive global marketplace, most theorists agree that management has to listen to everyone—customers, employees, scholars, government, and the public at large—in order to survive and prosper.

Stephen Covey, in his best-selling book, identifies listening—understanding others' messages before making one's own understood—as one of the "seven habits of highly

SALES PER 100,000 WORDS SPOKEN

SALES PER 100,000 WORDS LISTENED TO

GOFF

effective people."[1] Tom Peters, business consultant and co-author of *In Search of Excellence* and *A Passion for Excellence*, emphasizes that one key to effective leadership is listening:

> Leaders listen to what the market is saying, to what the customer is saying, and to what the team is saying. No, you don't have to do everything that your constituents demand that you do. But just by showing that you're listening, really listening, you demonstrate the respect that you accord to them.[2]

Dennis Hastert, former Speaker of the U.S. House of Representatives, echoed Peters's sentiment about the value of paying attention when describing how he spent most of his time: "They call me the Speaker, but they ought to call me the Listener."[3]

Research backs up the claims of business leaders. When 1,000 executives were asked to list the ideal manager's skills, listening ranked number one.[4] Another study asked business executives what skills were most important on the job. Listening was mentioned more than any other skill or talent, including technical competence, computer knowledge, administrative talent, and creativity.[5]

Why is listening so important? One major reason is time: Listening is the most frequent—and, arguably, the most important—type of on-the-job communication. Studies conducted more than 60 years ago indicated that adults spent an average of 29.5 percent of their waking hours listening. This is almost a third more time than they spent talking and virtually twice as much time as they spent reading.[6] A more recent study focused on listening in business settings. Personnel at all levels—including top-, middle-, and lower-level managers as well as workers with no managerial responsibilities—were asked to note the time they spent engaged in various types of communication during a typical week.[7] The results were impressive:

Listening 32.7%	Writing 22.6%
Speaking 25.8%	Reading 18.8%

Top executives spend even more time listening than other employees. Researchers have found that executives spend between 65 and 90 percent of the working day listening to someone.[8] Another piece of research revealed that effective managers almost constantly ask questions of their subordinates; in a half-hour conversation, some ask literally hundreds.[9]

Listening on the job is not only frequent but important. When 282 members of the Academy of Certified Administrative Managers were asked to list the skills most crucial for managerial ability, "active listening" was rated number one and was placed in the "supercritical" category.[10] In another survey, 170 businesspeople were asked to describe the communication skills that they considered most important and that they wished had been taught in college; in each category, listening was the number-one response.[11]

Effective listening is vital to organizations. It can improve quality, boost productivity, and save money. Poor listening can have the opposite effect. As one consultant says:

With more than 100 million workers in this country, a simple $10 listening mistake by each of them, as a result of poor listening, would add up to a cost of a billion dollars. And most people make numerous listening mistakes every week.

Because of listening mistakes, letters have to be retyped, appointments rescheduled, shipments rerouted. Productivity is affected and profits suffer.[12]

Beyond avoiding costly and embarrassing errors, good listening skills can play a major role in career success. Job hunters can respond best in employment interviews by keeping their ears open.[13] Listening is just as important once you have found a new job. Career consultant Andrea Sutcliffe argues that listening should be the predominant communication style for new employees: "If you had to choose one interpersonal skill to work on in your first year on the job, pick listening. It will be the single most important tool you will have for getting along and getting ahead."[14]

A study of employees in the insurance industry revealed that better listeners occupied higher levels in their company and were more upwardly mobile.[15] In problem-solving groups, people who listen well are rated as having the best leadership skills.[16] In a study of managerial effectiveness, listening skill was the best factor in distinguishing good bank managers from poor ones.[17] Along with advancing in their careers, good listeners report being happier on the job, and others are more satisfied working with them.[18]

Listening skills are important in a variety of careers, and selling is a prime example. Writer and management professor David J. Schwartz makes the point more succinctly:

In an office recently I noticed a sign which said, "To sell John Brown what John Brown buys, you've got to see things through John Brown's eyes." And the way to get John Brown's vision is to listen to what John Brown has to say.[19]

Listening to what people want and focusing on their needs helps you to avoid sounding "canned" and helps you focus on what you have to sell. "The great salespeople ask questions and have great listening skills. Poor salespeople get locked into script mode," according to Kevin Hogan, sales trainer and author. "Our job as salespeople is to listen and acquire an understanding of the needs of the prospect."[20]

Listening well is just as important for health care providers. It enables them to build rapport, show empathy, gather information, and identify patients' concerns.[21] A Harris poll found that 97 percent of adult patients said a physician's ability to listen to concerns and discuss them in an understandable way was an "extremely important" or "very important" ingredient in satisfying care.[22] Listening to the patient is considered so important that medical students in the United States now must demonstrate their ability to listen to patients in clinical exams before receiving their licenses to practice medicine.[23]

From hotels to high-tech computer services, from auto repair to financial institutions, service industries are a vital segment of the U.S. economy. "Good service, in many respects, is good listening," according to Judi Brownell of Cornell University. "In order to thrive in highly competitive, rapidly changing environments, service employees must learn to listen well."[24] Feargal Quinn, entrepreneur and founder of the successful Superquinn grocery chain, believes that listening to the customers creates success. He expects all managers to "jump the counter" once a month. They shop, ask questions, wait in line, and "become" the customer so they learn to listen from a customer's point of view. According to Quinn, "Listening is not an activity you can delegate—no matter who you are."[25]

Golden and Platinum Rules

The Golden Rule tells us to treat others the way we would like to be treated, and the "Platinum Rule" is to treat others the way *they* would like to be treated. The best way to honor the Platinum Rule is to listen to others, discovering what they want. On the other hand, realists acknowledge that it is impossible to give equal attention to every message and still accomplish the multitude of tasks that occupy every workday.

How can you, as a busy worker, respond to non-essential messages without alienating the people who deliver them?

Barriers to Effective Listening

Despite the importance of understanding others, research suggests that misunderstandings are the rule, rather than the exception. Conversational partners typically achieve no more than 25 to 50 percent accuracy in interpreting each other's remarks.[26] Listening expert Ralph Nichols echoes this grim assessment. This dismal figure is supported by research showing that immediately after a 10-minute presentation, a normal listener can recall only 50 percent of the information presented. After 48 hours, the recall level drops to 25 percent.[27]

Despite the widespread problem of poor listening, most business communicators don't see themselves as lacking in this skill. In one study, subordinates were asked to rate the listening ability of their bosses. More than half put their managers in the "poor" category. When the same managers were asked to rate themselves, 94 percent described themselves as "good" or "very good" listeners! A number of studies have revealed reasons why people listen poorly, despite the advantages of doing just the opposite.[28]

Physiological Barriers

Chapter 1 described the various types of noise that can interfere with the decoding of a message. Sometimes physiological problems make it difficult to listen effectively. Fortunately, most of these limitations can be managed with medical attention and technology.

Hearing Problems   For some people, poor listening results from actual hearing deficiencies. Once recognized, they can usually be treated. An undetected hearing loss may cause employees to get annoyed about the boss ignoring them or cause a supervisor to get angry when her instructions are bungled. Other people may have auditory processing difficulties, such as auditory discrimination, sequencing, or memory, which create the appearance of not listening or paying attention to what is said but are actually the result of physiological involvement, not intentional disregard.

Rapid Thought   Listeners can process information at a rate of about 500 words per minute, while most speakers talk at around 125 words per minute. This difference leaves us with a great deal of mental spare time. While it is possible to use this time to explore the speaker's ideas, we most often let our minds wander to other matters—from the unfinished business just mentioned to romantic fantasies. Management expert Peter Senge puts it this way: "Ears operate at the speed of sound, which is far slower than the speed of light the eyes take in. Generative listening is the art of developing deeper

Listening to Voice Mail

Hearing problems aren't just an issue for physically impaired communicators. The racket of background noise often makes it difficult to hear and understand messages—especially those played back on tinny speakers in most telephones. A variety of products overcome the limitations of trying to discern voice mail messages by transcribing the caller's spoken words into text that can be viewed on the display of a cell phone, PDA, or computer. Besides saving you the time it takes to replay voice mail, these services allow you to check for calls in a noisy environment, do it unobtrusively, and have a text record of what callers said.

You can read about these services by typing the words "convert voice mail to text" into your favorite Internet search engine. Many of the companies providing voiced-to-text service offer free trials.

silences in yourself, so you can slow your mind's hearing to your ears' natural speed, and hear beneath the words to their meaning."[29]

Environmental Barriers

Some listening challenges reside outside the listener, in the environment. While none of these challenges can be eliminated, you can learn to deal with them.

Physical Distractions   A stuffy room, uncomfortable chairs, or a conversation going on nearby are only a few of the distractions that can make listening difficult. In a world of cell phones, PDAs, laptops, and other devices, "multicommunicating" is a challenge that previous generations never faced.[30]

Problems in the Communication Channel   Listening can be difficult when the communicators lack face-to-face contact. It's harder to receive ideas accurately over the telephone, for example, than it is to understand the same information in a face-to-face conversation. Some McDonald's restaurants are designed with this fact in mind: Instead of drive-through passengers delivering their orders over an intercom, they speak in person to the order-taker at the same window where food is dispensed. Company management reports that the face-to-face approach takes a little more time, but the results are much more accurate.[31]

Dilbert: © Scott Adams/Dist. by United Feature Syndicate, Inc. Reprinted by permission.

Message Overload   It is hard to listen carefully when the phone rings every few minutes, people keep dropping in to give you quick messages, a co-worker has just handed you cost estimates on a new product line, and your PDA continuously beeps to let you know you have incoming mail or scheduled appointments. Coping with a deluge of information is like juggling—you can keep only a few things going at one time.[32]

Attitudinal Barriers and False Assumptions

Some of the most daunting barriers to understanding come from attitudes and assumptions that discourage careful listening.

Preoccupation   Business and personal concerns can make it difficult to keep your mind on the subject at hand. Even when your current conversation is important, other unfinished business can divert your attention: the call to an angry customer, the questions your boss asked about your schedule delays, the new supplier you heard about and want to interview, and the problems you have with the baby-sitter or the auto mechanic. Figure 3–1 illustrates several ways in which preoccupation can cause listeners to lose focus on understanding a speaker. Some preoccupation is inescapable, but keeping your focus on the speaker as much as possible will have benefits for you, the other person, and your relationship.

Egocentrism   One common reason for listening poorly is the belief—usually mistaken—that your own ideas are more important or valuable than those of others. Besides preventing you from learning useful new information, this egocentric attitude is likely to alienate the very people with whom you need to work. Self-centered listeners are rated lower on social attractiveness than communicators who are open to others' ideas.[33] As an old saying puts it, Nobody ever listened themselves out of a job.

Fear of Appearing Ignorant   Some businesspeople think asking for clarification is a sign of ignorance. Rather than seek clarification, they pretend to understand

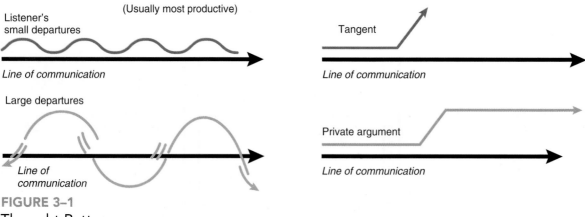

FIGURE 3–1
Thought Patterns
These four thought patterns represent different ways in which preoccupied listeners can ignore a speaker's message.

Source: A. D. Wolvin and C. G. Coakley, *Perspectives on Listening* (Norwood, NJ: Ablex, 1993), p. 115.

others—often with unfortunate consequences. In truth, a sincere desire to seek clarification can pay dividends, as management guru Tom Peters explains:

> *My first boss . . . is one of the smartest people I know. He was smart enough and comfortable enough with himself to ask really elementary (some would say dumb) questions. The rest of us were scared stiff; we assumed that since we were being paid an exorbitant fee, we shouldn't ask dumb questions. But the result was we'd lose 90 percent of the strategic value of the interview because we were afraid to display our ignorance.*
>
> *Mostly, it's the "dumb," elementary questions, followed up by a dozen more elementary questions, that yield the pay dirt.*[34]

Assuming That Effective Communication Is the Sender's Responsibility   Management expert Peter Drucker recognized that communication depends on the receiver as well as the sender when he wrote, "It is the recipient who communicates. The so-called communicator, the person who emits the communication, does not communicate. He utters. Unless there is someone who hears . . . there is only noise."[35]

As Drucker suggests, even the most thoughtful, well-expressed idea is wasted if the intended receiver fails to listen. Both the speaker *and* the listener share the burden of reaching an understanding.

Assuming That Listening Is Passive   Some communicators mistakenly assume that listening is basically a passive activity in which the receiver is a sponge, quietly absorbing the speaker's thoughts. In fact, good listening can be hard work. Sometimes you have to speak while listening—to ask questions or paraphrase the sender's ideas, making sure you have understood them. Even when you remain silent, silence should not be mistaken for passivity. Famous attorney Louis Nizer described how he would often emerge dripping with sweat from a day in court spent mostly listening. Sperry executive Del Kennedy, commenting on his company's well-known listening training program, says, "Most people don't know how exhausting listening can be."[36]

Assuming That Talking Has More Advantages Than Listening   At first glance, it seems that speakers control things while listeners are the followers. Western society seems to correlate listening with weakness, passivity, and lack of authority or power.[37] The people who do the talking are the ones who capture everyone's attention, so it is easy to understand how talking can be viewed as the pathway to success.

Talking instead of listening can lead professinals to miss important information. One analysis of physician–patient interviews revealed that the more doctors talked, the more they got off track and failed to address concerns raised by the patients.[38]

Despite the value of talking, savvy businesspeople understand that listening is equally important. Consider the advice of communication consultant Bill Acheson: "For every minute a salesperson spends listening, he or she will save four minutes overcoming objections."[39]

case study

Keynote Listening

Many business gatherings begin with a "keynote speech" in which a respected authority sets the tone for the entire program. Leaders of Washington State University and nearby Columbia Basin College turned this concept on its head by proclaiming themselves "keynote listeners" at a conference of Hispanic community members.

College and university leaders attended sessions without trying to promote their own ideas. Instead, they listened carefully to the concerns and ideas of the community members. Consultants had prepared the leaders to listen for differences in opinions, concerns, values, and interests, as well as for areas of common ground. Out of this approach came a vision of where the community was, where it wanted to go, and how it could get there.

Most of the time, powerful people try to speak. In this case, they showed respect and concern by listening.

CRITICAL ANALYSIS: Use the information from this case to answer the following questions:

1. How do you imagine the process and outcomes of the Washington conference differed from the usual "keynote speech" model as a result of the "keynote listening" approach?

2. How would the "keynote listening" approach change the nature of your workplace?

Source: K. Domenici, and S. W. Littlejohn, *Facework: Bridging Theory and Practice* (Thousand Oaks, CA: Sage, 2006), pp. 130–31.

Communication expert Susan Peterson reinforces the value of superior listening skills:

Too many times, whether it's with e-mail, voice mail or Internet, we are concentrating on the art of telling, not listening. Yet good listening, in my opinion, is 80 to 90 percent of being a good manager and an effective leader. . . . Listening is one of the best ways to keep high touch in your organization. In your day-to-day meetings with customers, clients, or employees, if you listen—really listen with full eye contact and attention—you can own the keys to the communication kingdom.[40]

Sociocultural Differences

Some listening problems come from the differing styles of each communicator. Some arise from cultural communication styles, while others come from differences between typically masculine and feminine communication styles.

Cultural Differences   Accent is often the most obvious difference when people from different cultures communicate. A different accent can be a source of psychological noise when it interferes with your ability to understand and appreciate the words of someone whose pronunciation differs from yours. Some communicators mistakenly assume that accented speakers are less intelligent and less able to understand spoken words.[41] Differing accents aren't just a problem in international communication. They can also interfere with communication between speakers from different co-cultures. For example, researchers have found that African American and Euro-American women hear very different things when speaking to each other.[42] White women tend to hear their own speech as being "normal or universal" and focus on African American women's pronunciation and grammar (instead of focusing on the message itself), whereas African American women (who are more used to hearing different styles of speech) find it easier to accept each accent as legitimate.

Some cultural differences are much more subtle than accent. The amount of time that should be spent listening is an example of one such difference. Monochronic Euro-Americans tend to put great value on time. Communicators raised with this orientation may view listening as wasting time, because it is not immediately clear what has been produced by taking the time to hear out another person. When interacting with Asians, U.S. businesspeople may find it very difficult to listen, as much time is spent engaging in small talk or having tea, rather than getting down to business.[43] The same issues may arise in U.S. business relationships with Latin Americans and Middle Easterners, who also value time spent on speaking and listening to information about families before business; however, time spent on listening in this way is of great importance to the overall relationship.

Culture also influences a communicator's attitude about silence—a big part of listening. African Americans and Euro-Americans tend to value speaking over listening and talk over silence.[44] Westerners often feel uncomfortable with long silences and want to fill them in with speech. By contrast, Native Americans and Japanese and other Asians regard silence as an important part of communication.[45] It is easy to imagine how a Westerner, uncomfortable with an Asian's silence, would fill in conversational gaps that seemed perfectly normal to a Korean or Navajo. In the same way, an Asian who wants to communicate successfully with a Euro-American would need to spend more time vocalizing.

Gender Differences
Popular magazines are fond of asking, Who listens better, men or women? This question is not as helpful as asking, Do men and women listen differently? Research shows that, to some degree, the answer is yes.[46] By understanding the differences, men and women can do a better job of listening to and understanding one another.

Women often pay more attention to the kinds of relational messages described in Chapter 1, while men often pay more attention to information on the content level. Both men and women may fail to recognize important messages because they listen for different purposes. Consider a simple example: A computer programmer, when asked by two users if a particular software package will work, may reply, "Sure." The male user may focus on the content of the answer and take the statement at face value. The female user may tune in to the speaker's vocal tone and hear some hesitation or annoyance. Later on, the two users might disagree about what the programmer meant because they listened to different aspects of the response.

Another gender-related difference involves "listening noises"—vocalizations such as "uh-huh" and "ummm" that signal attention. Researchers have discovered that men and women often use and interpret listening noises differently.[47] Women may use them to signal attention; men, to signal agreement. Thus, a woman who says "uh-huh" may mean "I'm listening," while a man hearing this utterance would think that his female partner agrees. Once communicators are aware of differences like these, they can clarify the meaning of ambiguous vocal cues: "You seem interested in the idea I'm presenting. Do you agree that we should get started on it?"[48]

Men and women may hear different parts of a message because they listen for different purposes. Women are more likely to catch the feelings behind a speaker's words, while men tend to listen for the facts.[49] For example, at a committee meeting, a colleague is asked to redo a report. He says, "Sure." After the meeting, a female colleague may comment on how upset the person was and his reluctance to redo the report. She "heard" the feelings. A male colleague may respond, "What's the problem? He said he'd do it." Communicators who recognize this difference may choose to make any important feelings explicit when they are speaking to one or more men.

Gender differences don't just affect *how* we listen to one another; they also influence *whether* we listen at all. Well-known sociolinguist Deborah Tannen says, "All else being equal, women are not as likely to be listened to as men, regardless of how they speak or what they say."[50] In business meetings, it is not uncommon for an idea presented by a woman to be ignored or downplayed, while the same idea presented by a man receives more attention. Listeners who are aware of this tendency can train themselves to give equal attention to the messages of every communicator regardless of sex. One way to be more attentive to the ideas of everyone in a meeting is to systematically give equal time and attention to each person or to post the ideas in writing.

Lack of Training

Listening may seem like a natural ability—like breathing. "After all," you might say, "I've been listening since I was a child." We could all say the same thing about talking; but even though almost everyone does it, this doesn't mean most people do it well. Former Chrysler chairman Lee Iacocca recognized the need for organized programs to train personnel to become better listeners:

> I only wish I could find an institute that teaches people how to listen. After all, a good manager needs to listen at least as much as he needs to talk. Too many people fail to realize that real communication goes in both directions. . . .
>
> You have to be able to listen well if you're going to motivate the people who work for you. Right there, that's the difference between a mediocre company and a great company. The most fulfilling thing for me as a manager is to watch someone the system has labeled as just average or mediocre really come into his own, all because someone has listened to his problems and helped him solve them.[51]

Some businesses spend thousands of dollars on training, yet they fail to include training on listening in their workshops.[52] Most organizations, including major corporations such as 3M, American Telephone and Telegraph, General Electric, and Dun and Bradstreet, know better. They have included listening skills in their training programs.[53] Xerox Corporation's program for improving listening has been used by over 1.5 million employees in 71,000 companies, and Sperry Corporation invested more than $4 million to advertise its message: "We know how important it is to listen." In addition, Sperry set up listening seminars for its 87,000 employees in an effort to make its advertising campaign more than a string of empty slogans.

Listening Styles

Not everyone listens the same way. Two decades of research have identified four common ways people listen to others' messages.[54] You can identify your own preferences by completing the Self-Assessment: Listener Preference Profile on page 80.

People-Oriented

People-oriented listeners are most concerned with creating and maintaining positive relationships. They are sensitive to others' moods, and they respond to speakers' feelings as well as their ideas. People-oriented listeners are usually nonjudgmental about what others have to say: They are more interested in understanding and supporting people than in evaluating them.

Along with the obvious strengths of a people-oriented style, a strong concern for relationships has some drawbacks. It is easy to become overinvolved with others' feelings, and even to internalize and adopt them. People-oriented listeners may lose their ability to assess the quality of information others are giving in an effort to be congenial and supportive. They also risk being perceived as overly expressive and even intrusive by speakers who don't want to connect on a personal level.

Action-Oriented

Unlike people-oriented listeners who focus on relationships, **action-oriented** listeners are most concerned with the task at hand. Their main goal is to understand the facts and ideas that are being communicated. They want to get to the heart of the matter quickly, and so they appreciate clear, concise messages and often translate others' remarks into well-organized mental outlines.

Action-oriented listeners are most welcome when taking care of business is the primary concern: They help others focus on the task at hand and encourage them to be organized and concise. Their no-nonsense approach may not be welcomed by speakers who don't have the skill or inclination to be clear and direct. They appear to minimize emotional issues and concerns, which may be an important part of business and personal transactions.

Content-Oriented

Content-oriented listeners are evaluators. They want to hear details and analyze an issue from a variety of perspectives. They prefer to listen to experts and other credible sources of information. Content-oriented listeners often enjoy ideas for their own sake and are willing to spend time exploring them in thorough exchanges of ideas.

Content-oriented listeners can be a big help when the goal is to assess the quality of ideas, and when there is value in looking at issues from a wide range of perspectives. They are especially valuable when the issues at hand are complicated. On the other hand, their detail-oriented approach may annoy others who don't share their analytical orientation. Their thorough approach can take more time than others may be willing to give and their frequent challenging can be perceived as overly critical, or even hostile.

Time-Oriented

As the label suggests, **time-oriented** listeners are most concerned with efficiency. They view time as a scarce and valuable commodity and get impatient with people whom they view as wasting it. In a fast-paced business environment, time-oriented listeners can help keep things functioning efficiently. On the other hand, their displays of impatience can sometimes put a strain on relationships. Also, an excessive focus on time can hamper the kind of thoughtful deliberation that some jobs require.

If you completed the Self-Assessment on page 80, you may have found that you have more than one of the four listening preferences. If so, you aren't alone: 40 percent of the people who have used this instrument indicate at least two strong listening preferences.[55] The key to success as a listener is to recognize that you can control the way you listen and to use the approaches that best suit the situation at hand. When your relationship with the speaker needs attention, adopt a people-oriented approach. When clarity is the issue, be an action-oriented listener. If analysis is called for, put on your content-oriented persona. And when the clock is what matters most, become a model of time-orientation.

Just as important, try to assess the listening preferences of your conversational partners and adapt your approach accordingly.

Instructions: Think of a specific listening role or situation that you are often in. For example, you may focus on your listening at work, as a friend, as a spouse, or as a parent. (Note: You can complete the instrument more than one time, with different roles and situations in mind.) As you read the series of statements below, keep the particular listening role or situation you have chosen in mind. Circle the appropriate number for each item, using the key below:

Always = 5   Frequently = 4   Sometimes = 3   Infrequently = 2   Never = 1

1. I focus my attention on other people's feelings when listening to them.	5 4 3 2 1
2. When listening to others, I quickly notice if they are pleased or disappointed.	5 4 3 2 1
3. I become involved when listening to the problems of others.	5 4 3 2 1
4. I try to find common areas of interest when listening to new acquaintances.	5 4 3 2 1
5. I nod my head and/or use eye contact to show interest in what others are saying.	5 4 3 2 1
6. I am frustrated when others don't present their ideas in an orderly, efficient way.	5 4 3 2 1
7. When listening to others, I focus on any inconsistencies and/or errors in what's being said.	5 4 3 2 1
8. I jump ahead and/or finish thoughts of speakers.	5 4 3 2 1
9. I am impatient with people who ramble on during conversations.	5 4 3 2 1
10. I ask questions to help speakers get to the point more quickly.	5 4 3 2 1
11. I wait until all the facts are presented before forming judgments and opinions.	5 4 3 2 1
12. I prefer to listen to technical information.	5 4 3 2 1
13. I prefer to hear facts and evidence so I can personally evaluate them.	5 4 3 2 1
14. I like the challenge of listening to complex information.	5 4 3 2 1
15. I ask questions to probe for additional information.	5 4 3 2 1
16. When hurried, I let others know that I have a limited amount of time to listen.	5 4 3 2 1
17. I begin a discussion by telling others how long I have to meet.	5 4 3 2 1
18. I interrupt others when I feel time pressure.	5 4 3 2 1
19. I look at my watch or clocks in the room when I have limited time to listen to others.	5 4 3 2 1
20. When I feel time pressure, my ability to concentrate on what others are saying suffers.	5 4 3 2 1

Scoring:

Tally the number of times you circled 4 or 5 for statements 1–5:

People-oriented = _____

Tally the number of times you circled 4 or 5 for statements 6–10:

Action-oriented = _____

Tally the number of times you circled 4 or 5 for statements 11–15:

Content-oriented = _____

Tally the number of times you circled 4 or 5 for statements 16–20:

Time-oriented = _____

Source: Adapted from L. Barker and K. Watson, *Listen Up* (New York: St. Martin's Press, 2000). Reprinted with permission.

Listening More Effectively

Social scientists have identified two levels of listening—mindless and mindful.[56] **Mindless listening** occurs when we react to others' messages automatically and routinely, without much mental investment. The term *mindless* sounds negative, but sometimes this sort of low-level processing can be useful, since it frees us to focus our minds on messages that require our careful attention.[57] The challenge, of course, is to pay enough attention to decide which messages need more careful attention. By contrast, **mindful listening** involves giving careful and thoughtful attention and responses to the messages we receive.

You might imagine that the value of mindful listening is so obvious that it hardly needs mentioning. But business and professional communicators recognize that thoughtful listening is difficult, and that it needs cultivating. At General Mills, for example, employees at all levels—including more than 80 vice presidents and directors—have voluntarily signed up for mindfulness programs ranging from a half day to 7 weeks.[58]

One important step toward mindful listening is to be clear about your goal in a given situation. Are you listening to *understand* the other person, or listening critically to *evaluate* the message? Once you've answered this fundamental question, the following tips can help you do a good job.

Listening to Understand

Most of us would claim that we always aim to understand what others are saying, but a little introspection will show that we're often focused on other tasks: mentally (or overtly) arguing with the speaker, daydreaming, thinking about other tasks, and so on. Following the advice here can boost your accuracy in listening mindfully to the message.

Withhold Judgment
In his study of highly effective people, Stephen Covey said it best: "Seek first to understand, then to be understood."[59] It is often difficult to try to understand another person's ideas before judging him or her, especially when you hold strong opinions on the matter under discussion. For example, you might ask for a customer's reaction to your company's product or service and then spend your mental energy judging the answer instead of trying to understand it. ("Doesn't this guy have anything better to do than make petty complaints?" "Yeah, sure, he'd like us to deliver on a tighter schedule, but he'd scream his head off if we billed him for the overtime.") Or you might find yourself judging the ideas of a boss, co-worker, or subordinate before he or she has finished explaining them. ("Uh-oh. I hope this doesn't mean I have to spend a week in the field, trying to get market information." "These college kids come in and want to take over right away.") Listen first. Make sure you understand. Then evaluate.

Talk and Interrupt Less
Sometimes the best approach to listening is to stay out of the way and encourage the other person to talk. One marketing expert explained how, even in selling, silence can be more effective than talking:

> The 20/80 rule is a standard in small-business principles. Twenty percent of your customers account for 80 percent of your business. Here's a variation of the theme. . . . When meeting with prospective customers for the first time, listen 80 percent of the time and talk the other 20 percent. Your job is to listen attentively and determine what your prospects require. Before they are prepared to listen to your pitch, they want to tell you what they're looking for.[60]

on your feet

If you are normally a talkative person, consider rationing your comments when trying to listen. Imagine that you have only a finite number of words available, so that you speak only when it is absolutely necessary. You may be surprised at how the quality of your conversations and your level of understanding improve.

Ask Questions **Sincere questions** are genuine requests for information. They can be a terrific way to gather facts and details, clarify meanings, and encourage a speaker to elaborate. Former University of Kentucky basketball coach Rick Pitino learned the importance of asking questions after he lost a key recruit by trying to sell the virtues of his program instead of listening to what concerned his prospect. Later, when he courted another potential star (Tony Delk), he used a more effective approach:

> This time, instead of trumpeting Kentucky's virtues, he asked questions: what Delk wanted from a coach, what the family wanted for their son in college. For an hour, he just asked questions and nodded a lot, listening to their answers. . . .
>
> Not only did Pitino get Delk, but four years later, Delk helped lead Kentucky to its sixth national championship and Pitino's first. "That's one of my favorites," Pitino says. "That's one I like to tell business groups because it illustrates how important it is to listen to people."[61]

While sincere, focused questions can be a powerful tool, **counterfeit questions** are really disguised forms of advice or subtle traps: "Have you ever considered offering more money to get experienced people?" or "Why haven't you told me about this?" Counterfeit questions like these can pollute a communication climate just as quickly as any direct attack.[62]

Paraphrase **Paraphrasing** involves restating a speaker's ideas in your own words to make sure that you have understood them correctly and to show the other person that fact. Paraphrasing is often preceded by phrases such as "Let me make sure I understand what you're saying . . ." or "In other words, you're saying . . ." When you are paraphrasing, it is important *not* to become a parrot, repeating the speaker's statements word for word. Understanding comes from translating the speaker's thoughts into your own language and then playing them back to ensure their accuracy. After paraphrasing, it is important that you invite the speaker to *verify* your paraphrase so you know if you accurately understood him or her or to *clarify* your paraphrase and clear up what you have misunderstood.

The following conversations illustrate the difference between effective and ineffective paraphrasing:

Ineffective

Print Supervisor: I'm having trouble getting the paper to run that job. That's why I'm behind schedule.

Plant Manager: I see. You can't get the paper to run the job, so you're running behind schedule.

Print Supervisor: Yeah. That's what I said.

"You haven't been listening. I keep telling you that I don't want a product fit for a king."

© 1996 Ted Goff. Reprinted by permission.

After this exchange, the plant manager still doesn't have a clear idea of the problem—why the print supervisor can't get the paper, or what he means when he says he can't get it. Effective paraphrasing, however, could help to get to the root of the problem:

Effective

Print Supervisor: I'm having trouble getting the paper to run that job. That's why I'm running behind schedule.

Plant Manager: In other words, your paper supplier hasn't shipped the paper you need for this job.

Print Supervisor: No, they shipped it, but it's full of flaws.

Plant Manager: So the whole shipment is bad?

Print Supervisor: No, only about a third of it. But I've got to get the whole batch replaced, or the dye lots won't match—the paper won't be exactly the same color.

Plant Manager: No problem—the colors can be a little off. But I have to have at least half of that order by Tuesday; the rest can wait a couple of weeks. Can you print on the good paper you have now, then do the rest when the new paper comes in?

Print Supervisor: Sure.

At first glance, questioning and paraphrasing may seem identical, but a closer look reveals that they are different tools. Questions seek new, additional information ("How far behind are we?" "When did it begin?"), while paraphrasing clarifies what a speaker has said. This is an important difference.

There are three types of paraphrasing. Although each of them reflects the speaker's message, each focuses on a different part of that statement.

Paraphrasing content   The example above illustrates this most basic kind of paraphrasing, which plays back the receiver's understanding of the explicit message. It is easy to think you understand another person, only to find later that you were wrong. At its most basic level, paraphrasing is a kind of safety check that can highlight and clarify misunderstandings. People who practice paraphrasing are astonished to find out how many times a speaker will correct or add information to a message that had seemed perfectly clear.

Paraphrasing intent   Besides helping you understand *what* others are saying, paraphrasing can help you learn *why* they have spoken up. Imagine that, at a staff meeting, the boss announces, "Next week, we'll start using this display board to show when we're out of the office and where we've gone." It's easy to imagine two quite different reasons for setting up this procedure: (1) to help keep customers and colleagues informed about where each person is and when he or she will return, or (2) to keep track of employees because the boss suspects that some are slacking off on company time. Paraphrasing intent can help you understand what people mean when they make statements that can be interpreted in more than one way.

Paraphrasing feeling   Often, the speaker's feelings are the most important part of a message.[63] Despite this fact, most people don't express—or even recognize—their emotions. Ask yourself which emotions might be contained in these statements:

> "That's the third time he canceled an appointment on me—who does he think he is?"

> "Whenever a deadline comes, I get excuses instead of results—this can't go on much longer."

> "One minute she says we have to spend money to make money, and the next minute she talks about cutting costs—I can't figure out what she really wants."

In each example there are at least two or three possible emotions:

> Anger, hurt, and self-doubt.

> Anger, frustration, and worry.

> Anger and confusion.

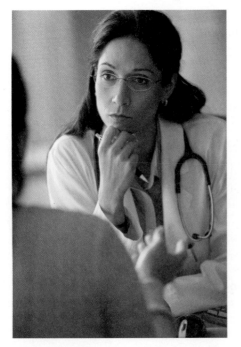

Paraphrasing the apparent emotion can give the speaker a chance to agree with or contradict your interpretation: "Yeah, I guess it did hurt my feelings," or "I'm more worried than mad." In either case, this sort of response can help the other person to clarify how he or she is feeling and to deal with the emotions.

Attend to Nonverbal Cues   Focusing on a speaker's nonverbal cues may tell you more than his or her words. Watch for the "iceberg tips" that let you know if the speaker might say more, especially if encouraged to do so.[64] Chapter 4 explains in detail the wealth of nonverbal cues that are always available to you: gestures, postures, vocal tones, facial expression, and more.

Nonverbal cues can be especially useful in figuring out another person's feelings and attitudes. You can get a sense of how emotions are communicated nonverbally by imagining all the different messages that might be conveyed by the following statements. How many different ways can you imagine each could be expressed? What different meaning might each set of nonverbal cues convey?

> "No, nothing's the matter."

> "We should get together one of these days."

Use a Telephone Log

E-mail provides a virtually automatic record of your correspondence, but telephone conversations are ephemeral. Recording phone calls is inconvenient and sometimes illegal, but a simple written log can help you maintain your records, prevent false claims, and reestablish contacts. For example, a log can remind you of the name of the agent you spoke to, the date and time of an appointment you've set up, or the model number of a product you're researching. Weeks later it may be important to tell a client, co-worker, or supervisor of all the attempts (successful and unsuccessful) you made to contact them.

You can also rely on your notes to remind others about information and commitments they have made, such as a reservation, promised delivery date, or a price quote: "The job won't be ready until November 15? But last Friday, Rose in your office promised me it would be done by the first of the month." A log can even remind people about what they *didn't* say or do. For example, you might respond to a complaint that you haven't kept a customer informed by explaining, "Actually I've phoned three times before today: On April 4, 11, and 18. Each time your voice mail picked up and I left a message telling you the job was ready."

For most purposes, a phone log doesn't have to be elaborate, but should usually include the following:

- Date and time the call was placed.
- Subject of the call.
- Phone number called.
- Whether this call is a part of a series (i.e., a follow-up or response to an earlier call).
- Unsuccessful attempts to contact (busy signal, no answer, malfunctioning voice mail).
- Messages left on voice mail or with another person.
- Name of person you spoke with.
- Key points you and the other person made.

"I'd like to talk with you in my office."

"Nobody's ever had that idea before."

Listening to Evaluate

Once you are sure you understand a message, you are ready to evaluate its quality. Most evaluations are based on two levels of analysis: logic and emotion.

Analyze the Speaker's Evidence   As a good critical listener, you need to ask yourself several questions about the evidence a speaker gives to support her or his statements. What evidence does the order fulfillment manager give that the current computer system is causing problems or that a new one will be better? Does a sales representative back up the claim that a product will pay for itself in less than a year?

Once you've identified the evidence, you need to make sure it is valid. The success of the flexible-hours program instituted in the New York office doesn't mean that the same program will work as well in the factory in West Virginia, where a certain number of people have to be operating the machinery at any given time. The two or three employees unhappy with the new office furniture might be the exceptions rather than representative of the majority, while the one or two satisfied customers you hear about could be the only happy ones. Carefully researched statistics that look at more than a few isolated cases are a much stronger form of proof than are a few random examples.

"I'm not convinced that's the best strategy.
Then again, I wasn't listening."

The following questions can help you to examine the overall validity of supporting material:

Is the evidence given true?

Are enough cases cited?

Are the cited cases representative of the whole being considered?

Are there any exceptions to the points the speaker is making?

Do these exceptions need to be considered?

Examine Emotional Appeals   Sometimes emotional reactions are a valid basis for action. The sympathy we feel for underprivileged children is a good reason for donating money to their welfare. The desire to cut down on your own fatigue may be a good reason to hire an assistant.

In some cases, though, emotional appeals can obscure important logical considerations that might dissuade you from accepting a proposal. We can see this by thinking about fund-raisers who seek money for underprivileged children. Your sympathy might not justify allowing a fund-raiser to wander around your building soliciting funds from employees: Your employees could resent being asked to give money to *your* favorite cause rather than one of theirs, especially if they have just been asked to donate to another cause. The particular agency asking for your donation might not be the best vehicle for helping underprivileged children: It may have excessive overhead so that much of your contribution never reaches any children, or other organizations might serve needier people.

review points

- Listening, the most frequent communication activity at work, contributes to career success by meeting organizational objectives, promoting career advancement, understanding organizational events, performing jobs well, and building networks and relationships.

- Physiological, environmental, attitudinal, sociocultural, and educational barriers interfere with effective listening.

- Analyze and improve your listening and tailor messages for others by understanding which of four major listening styles (people, content, action, or time) you and others prefer.

- Mindful listening to understand requires that you withhold judgment, talk and interrupt less, seek feedback by asking sincere (not counterfeit) questions and by paraphrasing content, feelings, and intentions.

- Insights come from paying attention to others' vocal and nonverbal cues as well as their words.

- Improve your evaluative listening effectiveness by analyzing a speaker's evidence and emotional appeals.

key terms

Test your understanding of these key terms by visiting the Online Learning Center Web site at www .mhhe.com/adler10e.

action-oriented listening style   79
content-oriented listening style   79
counterfeit questions   82
mindful listening   81
mindless listening   81

paraphrasing   82
people-oriented listening style   78
sincere questions   82
time-oriented listening style   80

activities

Go to the self-quizzes at the Online Learning Center at www.mhhe.com/adler10e to test your knowledge of chapter concepts.

1. Invitation to Insight

a. Recall three on-the-job incidents in which you had difficulty listening effectively. For each incident, describe which of the following factors interfered with your listening effectiveness:
  1. Physiological barriers
      Hearing problems
      Rapid thought
  2. Environmental barriers
      Physical distractions
      Problems in the communication channel
      Message overload
  3. Attitudinal barriers and faulty assumptions
      Preoccupation
      Egocentrism
      Fear of appearing ignorant
      Assuming that effective communication is the sender's responsibility
      Assuming that listening is passive
      Assuming that talking has more advantages than listening
  4. Sociocultural differences
      Culture
      Gender
  5. Lack of training

b. Develop a list of ways you could overcome the greatest barriers that prevent you from listening more effectively.

2. Invitation to Insight

For each of the listening styles listed below (see pp. 78–79), describe a specific work situation in which this style would be effective and one situation in which the style would probably not be appropriate. Defend your answers.

  People-oriented

  Action-oriented

  Content-oriented

  Time-oriented

3. Skill Builder

a. How can we differentiate between sincere questions and counterfeit questions?
b. What impact do counterfeit questions have on the receiver? On the interaction?
c. Write three examples of counterfeit questions. Supply a context that explains why the questions are counterfeit.
d. Convert the counterfeit questions to sincere questions.

4. Skill Builder

Practice your skill at questioning and paraphrasing in groups of four. Each group member should assume one of the following roles: speaker, listener1, listener2, and observer.

a. The **speaker** will talk about a problem he or she has recently experienced. If you can't think of a problem, talk about *one* of the following topics: how to perform a task you are familiar with, how to improve your chances for landing the job you want, or how to talk politely to a co-worker about a behavior you disapprove of.

b. The **listeners** should use vocalizations, sincere questions, and paraphrasing to *understand* the speaker's content, intent, and feeling.

c. After the conversation ends, the speaker will describe the degree to which s/he feels satisfied that the paraphrasing reflected his or her meaning accurately. This is the measure of success of the interaction.

d. The **observer** should point out specific examples of effective and ineffective techniques used by the listeners.

e. Listeners should answer the following questions:

 1. Was paraphrasing difficult or awkward? Why?
 2. How does this type of listening compare to your typical manner of responding?

3. What types of useful information did you gain from the conversations? Would you be likely to gain the same quality of information by responding in your more usual manner?

4. How could you use paraphrasing and sincere questioning to help in your everyday work?

5. Skill Builder

Practice your evaluative listening skills by following these steps:

a. Listen to a short persuasive presentation. Identify what the speaker is asking the listeners to believe or do.

b. Evaluate the speaker's evidence by answering the following questions.
 1. Does the speaker support the claim with evidence?
 2. Does the speaker cite references for the evidence?
 3. How accurate is the evidence? Explain.
 4. Does the speaker represent opposing evidence fairly?

c. Identify at least two emotional appeals used by the speaker.
 1. Do any of the emotional appeals obscure important logical considerations?
 2. Do the emotional appeals stretch the truth? Why or why not?

d. Based on this analysis, do you believe the speaker's argument is trustworthy?

resources

 For extensive readings and Web sites on listening, see the Online Learning Center Web site at **www.mhhe.com/adler10e.**

4

Verbal and Nonverbal Messages

chapter outline

Verbal Messages
   Clarity and Ambiguity
   Inflammatory Language
   Masculine and Feminine Language Use

Nonverbal Communication
   Characteristics of Nonverbal Communication
   Types of Nonverbal Communication
   Improving Nonverbal Effectiveness

Sexual Harassment
   Avoiding Sexual Harassment Problems
   Responding to Sexual Harassment

Review Points
Key Terms
Activities
Resources

chapter objectives

After reading this chapter you should be able to

1. Describe business situations in which ambiguous or specific language is preferable and create each type of statement.
2. Define, identify, and remedy examples of inflammatory language described in these pages.
3. Compare and contrast characteristically male and female speech and describe the potential benefits and problems arising from differences.
4. Describe how you can apply the information on nonverbal behavior in these pages in your own career.
5. Define and give examples of eight types of nonverbal behavior and summarize the importance of each in a specific organization or career field.
6. Predict the outcomes of various verbal and nonverbal behaviors with regard to sexual harassment and explain communication options for targets of harassment.

A lthough they are neighbors and see each other almost every day, Bob and Carolyn rarely speak to each other. Ever since their partnership broke up, the hard feelings have made even casual conversation painful.

"We both should have known better," Bob lamented. "It was such a simple misunderstanding. We went into the partnership agreeing that we would be 'equal partners,' but now I can see that we had different ideas about what being 'equals' meant. I saw each of us taking charge of the areas that we did best: I'm good at marketing and sales, and Carolyn knows product design and production backward and forward. So it made sense to me that, while we were each equally responsible for the business and deserving an equal share of the profits, we would each make the final decisions in the areas where we were experts."

"That's not what I meant by 'equal partners,'" stated Carolyn flatly. "Bob wasn't willing to take responsibility for the hard work of production. He kept saying, 'That's where you're the expert.' And he didn't have any faith in my ideas about sales and marketing. He wanted to make those decisions himself, whether or not I agreed. To me, being equal means you have just as much say as the other person in every part of the business."

In hindsight, both Bob and Carolyn realize that there had been signs of trouble from the beginning of their partnership. "Even before we opened for business, I could tell that Carolyn was unhappy," sighs Bob. "I always saw the venture as a chance to make a fortune. But whenever I'd get excited and talk about how much money we could make, Carolyn would clam up and get this grim look on her face."

Carolyn also remembers early, unspoken signs of trouble. "I've always wanted to have a business that my kids could be proud of," she said. "But when I'd talk about that, Bob wouldn't have much to say. Even though he never said so, at times I got the feeling that he was laughing at my high ideals."

This story illustrates the importance of paying close attention to verbal and non-verbal messages. The ill-fated partnership between Bob and Carolyn could have been

Online Translation Services

In the age of global business, sooner or later you will need to communicate with someone who speaks an unfamiliar language. If you type "online translation" into your Internet search engine, you will find a variety of services available to help you bridge the language gap. One excellent—and free—option is Google Translate (**www.translate.google.com**).

A good test of a computerized translation is to convert a message from one language to another, and then back to the original one. Because idioms don't rely on word-for-word meanings, they provide an especially tough challenge. Google Translate did

a surprisingly effective job at this task. It flawlessly retained the meanings of expressions such as "cross your fingers," "start from scratch," and "blessing in disguise" when those phrases were translated from English to Arabic and back again.

Even Google Translate wasn't perfect, though: It translated the phrase "from rags to riches" into "of the flags of wealth," and it mistakenly converted the idiom "go for broke" to "broken leg."

While computerized services can't match the talents of a skilled human translator, the better ones are surprisingly accurate for basic messages and are useful tools in the global village.

---

avoided if they had paid more attention to the unspoken but powerful nonverbal clues that warned of trouble. Examining more carefully just what an equal partnership meant also could have helped them avoid the clash that finally led to their breakup.

This chapter looks at the two channels by which you communicate: your words and your nonverbal behavior. By the time you have finished it, you will recognize that significant problems can lurk in even the simplest statements, and you will have discovered some ways to avoid or overcome such problems. You will also become more aware of the wordless messages that each of us constantly sends and receives.

Verbal Messages

As the case study on page 66 and the story that opened this chapter suggest, misunderstandings are a fact of life. In fact, most people vastly overestimate how well their explanations get through, and how well they understand others.[1] Linguistic theorists C. K. Ogden and I. A. Richards constructed a simple but profound model that explains the nature of many misunderstandings.[2] The broken line in their famous **triangle of meaning** model (Figure 4–1) shows that there is no direct relationship between an object, idea, process, or other referent and the word (or other symbol) used to represent it. Rather, the pathway to understanding—or misunderstanding—passes through

FIGURE 4–1

Ogden and Richards's Triangle of Meaning

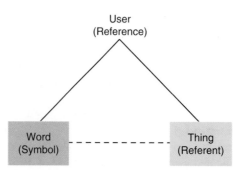

Table 4–1	Even Simple Messages Can Be Misunderstood	

What the Manager Said	What the Manager Meant	What the Subordinate Heard
I'll look into hiring another person for your department as soon as I complete my budget review.	We'll start interviewing for that job in about 3 weeks.	I'm tied up with more important things. Let's forget about hiring for the indefinite future.
Your performance was below par last quarter. I really expected more out of you.	You're going to have to try harder, but I know you can do it.	If you screw up one more time, you're out.
I'd like that report as soon as you can get to it.	I need that report within the week.	Drop that rush order you're working on and fill out that report today.
I talked to the boss, but at the present time, due to budget problems, we'll be unable to fully match your competitive salary offer.	We can give you 95 percent of that offer, and I know we'll be able to do even more for you next year.	If I were you, I'd take that competitive offer. We're certainly not going to pay that kind of salary to a person with your credentials.
We have a job opening in Los Angeles that we think would be just your cup of tea. We'd like you to go out there and look it over.	If you'd like the job, it's yours. If not, of course you can stay here in Denver. You be the judge.	You don't have to go out to L.A. if you don't want to. However, if you don't you can kiss good-bye to your career with this firm.
Your people seem to be having some problems getting their work out on time. I want you to look into this situation and straighten it out.	Talk to your people and find out what the problem is. Then get together with them and jointly solve it.	I don't care how many heads you bust, just get me that output. I've got enough problems around here without you screwing things up too.

Source: From Steven Altman, Enzo Valenzi, and Richard M. Hodgetts, *Organizational Behavior: Theory and Practice* (Academic Press, Inc., 1985).

the mind of the sender or receiver. As Table 4–1 shows, the listener can understand the meaning of every word perfectly and still interpret a message in a way that is completely different from its intended meaning.

Clarity and Ambiguity

Since the most basic language problems involve misunderstandings, we begin our study of language by examining how to prevent this sort of miscommunication. We also look at times when a lack of clarity can actually be desirable.

Use Unequivocal Terms to Avoid Misunderstandings   **Equivocal terms** are those with two different, but equally acceptable or common, meanings:

A shipment ordered for Portland goes to Oregon instead of Maine.

A client asks a contractor for a mid-project change: "Can you move that door from here to there?" The contractor replies, "No problem." Later, the client is astonished to find that she has been charged for the change order.

You agree to call on a client at home at "dinner time" in a part of the country where "dinner" is midday and "supper" is in the evening. When you appear at 6:00 P.M., the client asks why you didn't arrive at the promised time.

Most equivocal misunderstandings arise in casual conversation, where statements seem perfectly clear until you discover that others can interpret them differently.[3] Sometimes equivocal problems arise because communicators from different fields use the same term in specialized ways. Hollywood agent Jerry Katzman describes just such a situation. In a meeting with representatives of a Silicon Valley software publisher, he used the phrase "in development" to mean a project that was at the rough-idea stage. By contrast, the software people were used to using that phrase to describe a project that had been funded and was being created. Katzman reported, "It was like when the Japanese first came to Hollywood. They had to use interpreters, and we did too."[4]

Equivocation sometimes comes from different cultural values. Compared with U.S. businesspeople, Mexicans are less inclined to express conflict and are more polychronic and relaxed about managing time. The Spanish word *ahorita* means "right now" or "immediately" in English. Despite its dictionary meaning, North Americans have found that their Mexican counterparts use the term quite differently:

When are those photocopies going to be ready?

"*Ahorita*," answers the secretary who knows the copy machine is broken.

When will that delivery be made?

"*Ahorita*," answers the salesman who has no truck.

One U.S. financial officer sheepishly admits he finally prohibited his Mexican staff from giving him *ahorita* as an answer.[5]

At least some equivocation problems can be avoided if you double-check your understanding of terms that might be interpreted in more than one way. When you agree to meet "Wednesday" with someone, mention the date to be sure that you're both thinking of the same week. When your supervisor says that your ideas are "OK," make sure that the term means "well done" and not just "adequate."

Use Lower-Level Abstractions When Clarity Is Essential   Any object or idea can be described at various levels, some very general and others quite specific. **Low-level abstractions** are specific, concrete statements that refer directly to objects or events that can be observed. By contrast, **high-level abstractions** cover a broader range of possible objects or events without describing them in much detail. High-level abstractions can create problems because they are often subject to a wide variety of interpretations, such as the following examples:

Statement	Clarification
The job will take a little longer.	How much longer: Hours? Days? Weeks?
Straighten up the area.	A quick cleanup or a spit-and-polish job?
We need some market research.	A short questionnaire for a few customers or lengthy personal interviews and detailed surveys?
Give me your honest opinion.	Be diplomatic or blunt?

Since both abstract language and specific language have their advantages, it is often best to use both. One way to achieve maximum clarity is to begin explaining your proposal, problem, request, or appreciation with an abstract statement, which you then qualify with specifics:

"I'm worried about the amount of time we seem to be spending on relatively unimportant matters [abstract]. In our last meeting, for instance, we talked for 20 minutes about when to schedule the company picnic and then had only 15 minutes to discuss our hiring needs [specific]."

"I'd like to take on more responsibility [abstract]. Until now, the only decisions I've been involved in are about small matters [still abstract], such as daily schedules and customer refunds [more specific]. I'd like a chance to help decide issues such as buying and advertising [specific requests]."

Another type of ambiguous language that causes problems is the use of **relative words** such as *soon, often, large,* and *short* that have meaning only in relationship to other (unspecified) terms. Telling your supervisor that you'll have the memo done *soon* or agreeing to do a *short* report can cause problems. If *soon* means "in a few weeks" to you, but it means "in a few days" to your boss, a conflict is brewing. Replacing relative words with numeric words can eliminate most of these problems. Use "in 2 days" rather than *soon* and "two paragraphs" rather than *short,* for example.

Use Slang with Caution

Casual, slang-laden speech may be fine off the job, but it can create the wrong impression with bosses, clients, and even colleagues. Some slang simply won't be understandable to others. For example, the British term "gobsmacked" is likely to draw a blank stare when used in conversation with someone outside the U.K. ("I was gobsmacked when they gave me that assignment"). Other terms are also likely to cast you in an unprofessional light. You may call your friends "dude" and label anything that's positive as "the bomb," but it's smart to talk more professionally in professional settings.

Use Jargon Judiciously

Every profession has its own specialized vocabulary, often termed **jargon.** People who order office supplies talk about "NCR paper" and "three-up labels." Computer users talk about "64-bit architecture" and "image-compression boards."

In many cases, jargon serves a useful purpose. For one thing, it can save time. It's quicker for an accountant to use the term *liquidity* than to say "the degree to which an asset can be converted into cash." A specialized vocabulary is particularly vital when the subject matter is technical and complex. The phrase "sleeping pill" is unacceptable to health professionals because it says nothing about the dosage or the particular drug. Similarly, geologists can't discuss their findings by talking about "rocks."

A certain amount of jargon has its value for outsiders as well. Speakers who sprinkle their comments with jargon will

"O.K. What part of 'malignant regression and pathogenic reintrojection as a defense against psychic decompensation' don't you understand?"

ethical challenge

appear more credible to some listeners.[6] While incomprehensible language may *impress* listeners, it doesn't help them to *understand* an idea. Thus, if your goal is to explain yourself (and not merely to build your image), the ideal mixture may be a combination of clear language sprinkled with a bit of professional jargon.

Problems arise when insiders use their specialized vocabulary without explaining it to the uninitiated. According to one survey, people in computer support industries are the worst offenders when it comes to jargon.[7] A customer shopping for a computer might be mystified by a dealer's talk about bus speed, onboard circuitry, and data transfer rates. When the same information is translated into language the buyer can understand—the length of time it takes to download a file, for example—a sale is more likely.[8]

Certain words are used so often that they become clichés.[9] As one communication expert says, they "are brief and snappy, roll off the tongue easily, and can fool us into thinking that we know what we're talking about."[10] If you overuse buzzwords like "mission focused," "paradigm shift," and "at the end of the day," you run the risk of not clarifying your ideas in your own mind and not being clear to others.[11]

Use Ambiguous Language When It Is Strategically Desirable

In low-context cultures like the U.S. and Canada, speaking directly is valued. "Don't beat around the bush" is a common phrase. Vague language can be seen as a sign of deliberate deception, as an old joke shows: A reporter warned a state senator, "Sir, your constituents were confused by today's speech." "Good," the senator replied. "It took me two days to write it that way."

Despite its bad reputation, ambiguous language does have its place. High-context cultures have made an art of strategic ambiguity, finding ways to express difficult messages indirectly. One U.S. author describes how indirectness works:

> Instead of criticizing a report, the manager asks for more information. . . . When they say "I'd like to reflect on your proposal a while," when the decision must be [made] soon, it means "You are dead wrong, and you'd better come up with a better idea very soon. But I don't tell you so, because you should know that yourself!"
>
> It seems to me that such indirectness in interpersonal communication is a virtue; it is just as efficient, and it is certainly more mature and polite than the affront, "You are dead wrong." We need not talk to one another as if we were children (or characters out of the pages of pulp fiction)—yes, children need clarity—but adults can deal with indirectness and multiple meanings.[12]

Even in the normally low-context cultures like the U.S., Canada, Israel, and Germany, there are many times when indirect speech helps communicators achieve two useful goals.[13] The first is *to promote harmony*. A group of workers who have been feuding over everything from next year's budget to funding the office coffee supply can at least reach consensus on an abstraction like "the need to reduce waste," a small but important start toward more cooperation.

A second function of ambiguous speech is *to soften the blow of difficult messages.* Business communicators face the constant challenge of delivering difficult messages: "This work isn't good enough." "We don't want to do business with you anymore." While statements like these may be honest, they can also be brutal. Ambiguous language provides a way to deliver difficult messages that softens their blow and makes it possible to work smoothly with the recipients in the future. For example:

Brute Honesty	Strategic Ambiguity
This work isn't good enough.	I think the boss will want us to back up these predictions with some figures.
I don't want to work with you.	Right now I don't see any projects on the horizon.

A final function of strategic ambiguity is to make a *point indirectly that can't be expressed overtly.* In the current litigation-prone environment, business communicators often use strategic ambiguity to communicate critical messages without exposing themselves to lawsuits.[14] For example, consider this humorous letter of reference "endorsing" a former employee who was fired for being a slow, lazy, unmotivated worker with an inflated ego and who lacked qualifications, causing the company to lose money:

> *I am pleased to say John Doe is a former colleague of mine. John left this job the same way he came, fired with enthusiasm. We are deeply indebted for the services he has given our firm over the years.*
>
> *John will do nothing which will lower your high regard for him. His job requires few skills which he lacks. I honestly don't think he could have done a better job for us if he had tried. I most enthusiastically recommend John Doe with no qualifications whatsoever. It will not take John long to get up to speed. No salary would be too much for him. You won't find many people like John.*[15]

One problem with strategic ambiguity, of course, is that it can easily be misunderstood. This problem can be especially acute in medical settings, when health care providers try to deliver bad news to patients in a way that softens its impact. For example,

> *[A surgeon] took one look at a patient's badly infected foot and recognized that it would have to be amputated. "I don't think we're going to be able to deal with this with local treatments," he told the patient.*
>
> *When the surgeon left the examining room, the woman turned to the doctor and asked: "Does that mean I'm going to have to go to Los Angeles for treatment?"*[16]

Even when misunderstandings aren't a problem, strategic ambiguity works only when both sender and receiver are willing to tolerate a deliberate lack of clarity. Without that understanding, the result can be confusion, and often feelings of being betrayed or manipulated.[17]

Choose the Optimal Degree of Powerful Language   Some types of language make a speaker sound less powerful, while other types create an air of power and confidence.

Less Powerful Speech	More Powerful Speech
Tag questions "This report is good, *isn't it?*"	"This report is good."
Hesitations "I, *uh*, think we should, *um*, use the newer format."	"I think we should use the newer format."
Qualifiers "*I don't know if you'll like this idea, but* we could hire an outside consultant."	"We could hire an outside consultant."
Intensifiers "That was *such* a good job!"	"That was a good job!"
Questions "*Do you think we* should shorten the report?"	"I think we should shorten the report."

Speakers who use more powerful speech are rated as more competent, dynamic, and attractive than speakers who sound powerless.[18] One study revealed that even a single type of powerless speech mannerism can make a person appear less authoritative.[19] So, when your goal is to create an impression of power and conviction, it's best to avoid less powerful speech.

On the other hand, there are times when powerful individuals might intentionally use less powerful language to avoid throwing their weight around. In some situations less powerful forms of speech can even enhance a speaker's effectiveness.[20] For example, a boss might say to her assistant, "Would you mind making copies of these files before you go home?" Both the boss and the assistant know this is an order and not a request, but the questioning form is more considerate and leaves the assistant feeling better about the boss.[21] The importance of achieving both content and relational goals helps explain why a mixture of powerful and polite speech is usually most effective.[22]

Inflammatory Language

Language has the power to stir intense emotions. It can motivate, inspire, and amuse audiences. Unfortunately, it can also generate negative feelings: antagonism, defensiveness, and prejudice. You can prevent these negative outcomes by following two guidelines.

Avoid Biased Language

Emotional problems arise when speakers intentionally or unintentionally use **biased language**—terms that seem to be objective but actually conceal an emotional bias. Consider, for example, the range of words you could use to refer to a 25-year-old man who disagrees with your proposal: *gentleman, fellow, guy, young man,* or *dude.* Each one paints a different picture in the listener's mind. None of them is neutral.

When faced with biased language, it's wise to recognize that the speaker is editorializing. Tactfully restate the term in language that doesn't contain an evaluation, paraphrase with neutral language, or use terms that quantify:

Speaker Biased Language	Listener's Restatement
It's a *gamble.*	So you don't think the idea is a reasonable risk. Is that it? (paraphrase)
He's *long-winded.*	Bill *has* been talking for a half hour. (quantify)
She's so *wishy-washy.*	You think Susan isn't willing to make a decision? (rephrase in nonbiased language)

Beware of Trigger Words   Some terms have such strong emotional associations that they act almost like a trigger, setting off an intense emotional reaction in certain listeners. These **trigger words** can refer to specific people (your boss, the president), groups or categories of individuals (union stewards, the Human Resources department, customers with complaints), issues (affirmative action, flexible scheduling), or other topics (imports, downsizing).

What is the best way to deal with trigger words? The first thing to realize is that, like others, you almost certainly have your own trigger words. You, therefore, ought to begin by recognizing them, so that when one comes up you'll at least be aware of your sensitivity and, thus, avoid overreacting. If, for example, your parents are farmers and you are sensitive about people speaking condescendingly about farmers, you might catch yourself before you overreact when a co-worker refers to someone on Casual Friday as "dressed like a farmer." It could be an innocent or uninformed remark.

Sometimes, however, you will discover too late that a term that seems innocuous to you is a trigger word for others. After the other person vents his or her strong feelings, you can acknowledge the misunderstanding, apologize, choose a more agreeable term and proceed with the discussion.

Masculine and Feminine Language Use

Chapter 2 described how culture affects communication. Some social scientists have suggested that conversation between men and women is a kind of cross-cultural communication in which members of each sex are not speaking different dialects but **"genderlects."**[23]

"Sorry, Chief, but of course I didn't mean 'bimbo' in the pejorative sense."

They have argued that these different approaches affect the way men and women interact with one another in ways that are powerful but usually unnoticed.

As you read about differences in male and female speech, understand that the descriptions don't characterize all men and women. The relationship between gender and language is like the one between gender and height: Men are generally taller than women, but some women are taller than some men. In fact, the difference between the tallest man and the shortest man (or the tallest woman and the shortest woman) is greater than the difference between the average man and the average woman. For this reason, the words "masculine" and "feminine" are actually better adjectives to describe language differences, since they refer to traits characteristically linked to each gender and not to biological sex. Remember also that gender isn't the only factor that influences conversational style. Cultural, geographical, and occupational influences also play a role. Finally, understand that the differences outlined in this section reflect past communication patterns. As the roles of men and women in society evolve, speech styles may change as well.

Feminine Speech   From childhood, females learn to use speech for what some researchers refer to as **rapport talk:** to create connections, establish goodwill, show support, and build community.

For many women an important part of building rapport is using language as an *expressive tool*: to articulate emotions ("I'm worried about finishing those reports today"; "I'm glad everybody had a chance to speak") and clarify relationships ("We don't seem to be working well together").

Characteristically feminine speech often goes beyond just expressing emotions; it also is *supportive*. Women are most likely to listen and respond to spoken and unspoken conversational clues about the other person's feelings. A characteristically feminine reply to a description of difficulties at work is "I know what that's like. Last year I had so much trouble with a client on the Bustos case. . . ." This response lets the speaker know that she is not alone, that she is understood.

Another characteristic of feminine conversational style is its *tentative* nature. This is reflected in questioning forms ("Could we go now?" "Would you type that for me?"), hedges and disclaimers ("I'm not sure about these figures . . ."; "This might not be a good time to bring this up, but . . ."), and tag questions ("The report is due today, isn't it?"). While these forms exhibit the less powerful characteristics described earlier in this chapter on pages 97–98, linguist Deborah Tannen describes them more as a bid for solidarity than a sign of weakness:

> *Many women are frequently told, "Don't apologize" or "You're always apologizing." The reason "apologizing" is seen as something they should stop doing is that it seems synonymous with putting oneself down. But for many women, and a fair number of men, saying "I'm sorry" isn't literally an apology; it is a ritual way of restoring balance to a conversation. "I'm sorry," spoken in this spirit, if it has any literal meaning at all, does not mean "I apologize," which would be tantamount to accepting blame, but rather "I'm sorry that happened.".*[24]

Speech forms like apologizing, especially when used by women, can create the impression of less authority, status, certainty, accuracy, or credibility. However, tentative speech doesn't have to be regarded as weak.[25] Another interpretation is that it builds rapport by avoiding dogmatism and suggesting equality.

Conversational initiation and maintenance are also characteristic of feminine speech. Women have long been taught to ask questions to get a conversation going, to find out what others are interested in, and to show interest in a conversational part-ner. So, many women ask questions to start and maintain conversations: "Did you hear about . . . ?" "Are you going to . . . ?" "Did you know that . . . ?" In addition, women use "listening noises" ("Uh, huh." "Oh really?" "Is that right?") to show interest. If women do interrupt, it is often to support or affirm the speaker, not to challenge or threaten.

Masculine Speech Whereas women use talk to build rapport, men are more comfortable with what linguists have labeled **report talk**—speech that focuses less on feelings and relationships and more on information, facts, knowledge, and competence. Men are more inclined to use language to claim attention, assert a position, establish status, and show independence. Research shows that men need to be just as sensitive as women, but they may use that awareness differently: In one study, male managers who were more accurate at emotion perception received higher satisfaction ratings if they used the information to be more persuasive, whereas more emotionally perceptive female managers received higher satisfaction ratings when they demonstrated more supportiveness.[26]

Characteristically masculine speech uses language *instrumentally* (as opposed to expressively) to get things done: report information, solve visible problems, achieve, accomplish, attain, execute, perform. The results are often tangible and the reward is visible: "Fax these reports to accounting"; "I'll make reservations at Sara's"; "Finish that proposal by Monday." Language is often used by men to define status.

When dealing with personal problems, a characteristically masculine approach is to offer *advice* that will lead to a solution. Empathizing to show sympathy and establish solidarity just doesn't seem helpful or appropriate to many men.

Characteristically masculine speech is more *assertive, certain, direct,* and *authoritative.* Men often use statements of fact rather than opinion: "That deduction belongs on Schedule C" rather than "I think that's a Schedule C deduction." Declarative sentences and dropped pitch at the end create a sense of sureness and authority. Men are more likely to speak directly, giving clear and unambiguous commands or directions rather than couching requests in the form of questions.

Men's speech style typically includes several characteristics of conversational *dominance* or *control*: verbosity, topic control, and interruptions. Most research supports the statement that in public conversations between men and women, men talk at greater length.[27] Often in response to questions from women, men decide which topic of con-versation to pursue and talk longer than the women in the same conversation. Research on interruptions is mixed as to who interrupts more, but it appears that the purpose of men's interruptions is often to gain control of the conversational topic or the conversa-tion itself. Table 4-2 on page 102 summarizes research findings on characteristics of feminine and masculine speech styles.

Meeting Gender-Related Language Challenges Problems can arise when stereotypically masculine and feminine language styles clash on the job—often without anyone knowing exactly why. For instance, a woman who says, "I'm having difficulty with the Garcia account," may want to hear her concerns acknowledged and know that others have experienced similar problems. Her goal may be to gain support, establish connection, and seek rapport. Or she may just want to talk about the situa-tion. A man, conditioned to use speech to solve problems, might respond with advice: "Here's one way you could handle it . . ." If the woman wanted support and connection, being given advice might produce an effect that is just the opposite of the rapport she

Table 4–2	Characteristics of Feminine and Masculine Speech Styles

Characteristically Feminine Speech	Characteristically Masculine Speech
Builds rapport	Reports facts
Is expressive	Is instrumental
Offers support	Offers advice
Sounds tentative	Sounds certain
Initiates and maintains conversation	Controls conversation

was looking for: The woman might feel that her male colleague was trying to appear "one-up," coming across as a superior. From his frame of reference, the man *was* being helpful: He offered useful information at the request of someone in need.

Another gender-related problem can arise when a man pays attention to the content of a message while a woman focuses on the relational dimension of the words. If a male supervisor says, "I can't do anything about your hours; the boss says they're set and can't be changed," a woman may hear a relational message of "I don't care" or "I don't want to be bothered." The man, used to dealing with communication at the content level, isn't being unsympathetic; he is just responding to a request.

Both masculine and feminine language styles work well—as long as listeners use the the same rules. Frustrations result when people expect others to use the same style as theirs.[28] The following suggestions can help communicators understand and adapt to one another's differing uses of language:

- *Be aware of different styles.* Once you are aware that men and women have been taught to use language differently, there's less likelihood of being dismayed at a style that doesn't match yours. The cultural analogy is apt here: If you were traveling in another country, you wouldn't be offended by the customs of its inhabitants, even if they were different from yours. In the same way, accepting gender differences can lead to smoother relationships—even if members of the other sex behave differently from you.

- *Switch styles, when appropriate.* Being bilingual is an obvious advantage in a multicultural world. In the same way, using a communication style that isn't characteristic of you can be useful. If you routinely focus on the content of others' remarks, consider paying more attention to the unstated relational messages behind their words. If you generally focus on the unexpressed-feelings part of a message, consider being more task-oriented. If your first instinct is to be supportive, consider the value of offering advice; and if advice is your reflexive way of responding, think about whether offering support and understanding might sometimes be more helpful.

- *Combine styles.* Effective communication may not be an either–or matter of choosing one style. In many situations, you may get the best results by combining typically masculine and feminine approaches. Research confirms what common sense suggests: A "mixed-gender strategy" that balances the traditionally masculine, task-oriented approach with the characteristically feminine, relationship-oriented approach is rated most highly by both male and female respondents.[29] Choosing the approach that is right for the other communicator and the situation can create satisfaction far greater than that which comes from using a single stereotypical style.

Nonverbal Communication

Words are not the only way we communicate. You can appreciate this fact by imagining the following scenes:

> Your boss has told the staff that she welcomes any suggestions about how to improve the organization. You take her at her word and schedule an appointment to discuss some ideas you have had. As you begin to outline your proposed changes, she focuses her gaze directly on you, folds her arms across her chest, clenches her jaw muscles, and begins to frown. At the end of your remarks, she rises abruptly from her chair, says "Thank you for your ideas" in a monotone, and gives you a curt handshake.

> Despite the expense, you have decided to have a highly regarded CPA handle your tax matters. While waiting for the accountant to appear, you scan the impressive display of diplomas from prestigious universities and professional associations. The accountant enters, and as the conversation proceeds, he yawns repeatedly.

Most people would find these situations odd and disturbing. This reaction would have nothing to do with the verbal behavior of the people involved. In each case, nonverbal behavior sends messages above and beyond the words being spoken: The boss doesn't really seem to want to hear your suggestions, and you wonder whether the accountant is capable or caring with regard to your taxes.

In the following pages we examine the role of nonverbal communication in the working world. For our purposes, **nonverbal communication** involves messages expressed by other than linguistic means.

Characteristics of Nonverbal Communication

Now that we have defined nonverbal communication and discussed its importance, we need to take a look at some of its characteristics. Nonverbal communication resembles verbal communication in some ways and is quite different in others.

Nonverbal Behavior Always Has Communicative Value   You may not always *intend* to send nonverbal messages, but everything about your appearance, every movement, every facial expression, every nuance of your voice has the potential to convey meaning.[30] You can demonstrate this fact by imagining that your boss has "called you on the carpet," claiming that you haven't been working hard enough. How could you not send a nonverbal message? Nodding gravely would be a response; so would blushing, avoiding or making direct eye contact, or shaking your head affirmatively or negatively. While you can shut off your linguistic channels of communication by refusing to speak or write, it is impossible to avoid behaving nonverbally.

One writer learned this fact from movie producer Sam Goldwyn while presenting his proposal for a new film. "Mr. Goldwyn," the writer implored, "I'm telling you a sensational story. I'm only asking for your opinion, and you fall asleep." Goldwyn's reply: "Isn't sleeping an opinion?"

Nonverbal communication operates even in mediated communication. Some nonverbal elements are obvious: The use of emoticons, an abundance of exclamation points, and the impression of shouting when a message is typed in ALL CAPITAL LETTERS, are clear examples. But even *not* responding to an e-mail, IM, or text message can suggest a put-down.[31]

Nonverbal Communication Is Powerful

Despite folk sayings like "you can't judge a book from its cover," we form impressions of others mostly from nonverbal observations—about physical appearance and behavior. Once we form these impressions, they influence our subsequent impressions and judgments. Canadian communication consultant Lee McCoy gives an example:

> If I meet Susan and initially perceive her to be professional, attractive and intelligent, I'm also likely to begin to attribute other positive characteristics to her. I might see her as organized, successful and warm. This is not to suggest that I'll ignore negative characteristics, but it will take me longer to become aware of something negative if my initial perceptions of her are very positive. If, on the other hand, Susan presents herself to me as sloppily dressed, with bitten fingernails and a lack of eye contact, I may begin to attribute equally negative characteristics to her—insecurity, lack of knowledge, coldness.[32]

Even after first impressions have been made, the impact of nonverbal behavior is powerful. In fact, when nonverbal behavior seems to contradict a verbal message, the spoken words carry less weight than the nonverbal cues.[33]

Nonverbal Behavior Is Ambiguous

While nonverbal communication can create powerful impressions, the messages it conveys are ambiguous.[34] You don't have to be as clueless as the boss in the cartoon below to misinterpret nonverbal cues. Does a customer's yawn signal boredom or fatigue? Are your co-workers laughing with or at you? Does your boss's frown reflect disapproval or preoccupation? Most nonverbal behaviors have a multitude of possible meanings, and it is a serious mistake to assume that you can decide which is true in any given case.

Nonverbal Communication Primarily Expresses Attitudes

While it is relatively easy to infer general interest, liking, disagreement, amusement, and so on, from another's actions, messages about ideas or concepts don't lend themselves to nonverbal channels. How, for instance, would you express the following messages nonverbally?

Dilbert: © Scott Adams/Dist. by United Feature Syndicate, Inc. Reprinted by permission.

Sales are running 16 percent above last year's.

Management decided to cancel the sales meeting after all.

Let's meet at two to plan the agenda for tomorrow's meeting.

It's apparent that such thoughts are best expressed in speech and writing. It's also apparent, though, that nonverbal behavior will imply how the speaker *feels* about these statements: whether the speaker is pleased that sales are up or worried that they're not as high as expected, how urgently the cashier at checkstand 2 needs change, and so on.

Nonverbal Communication Affects Career Success

Not surprisingly, the ability to effectively manage your nonverbal behavior plays a strong role in communicative success. For example, salespeople who were better at reading nonverbal cues of potential clients make more sales and earn higher income than less astute colleagues.[35] Likewise, successful entrepreneurs owe a great measure of their success to social skills including the ability to manage their own nonverbal behavior and read those of others.[36] Managers who were good at reading and responding to nonverbal cues received higher performance ratings from both their bosses and their subordinates.[37]

Much Nonverbal Behavior Is Culture-Bound

Certain types of nonverbal behavior seem to be universal. For example, there is strong agreement among members of most literate cultures about which facial expressions represent happiness, fear, surprise, sadness, anger, and disgust or contempt.[38] On the other hand, many nonverbal expressions do vary from culture to culture, however. (See Table 4-3 on page 106 for a few examples.)

In this age of international communication in business, it is especially important to understand that there are cultural differences in the meaning assigned to nonverbal behaviors. Consider the different rules about what distance is appropriate between speakers. One study revealed that the "proper" space between two speakers varied considerably from one culture to another: To Japanese, a comfortable space was 40.2 inches; for a U.S. resident, 35.4 inches; and to Venezuelans, 32.2 inches.[39] It's easy to see how this could lead to problems for a U.S. native doing business overseas.

Types of Nonverbal Communication

We have already mentioned several types of nonverbal messages. We now discuss each in more detail.

Voice

Your own experience shows that the voice communicates in ways that have nothing to do with the words a speaker utters. You may recall, for instance, overhearing two people arguing in an adjoining room or apartment; even though you couldn't make out their words, their emotions and the fact that they were arguing were apparent from the sound of their voices. Similarly, you have probably overheard people talking in a language you didn't understand; yet the speakers' feelings—excitement, delight, exhaustion, boredom, grief—were conveyed by their voices.

Social scientists use the term **paralanguage** to describe a wide range of vocal characteristics, each of which helps express an attitude: pitch (high–low), resonance (resonant–thin), range (spread–narrow), tempo (rapid–slow), articulation (precise–imprecise), dysfluencies (*um, er,* etc.), rhythm (smooth–jerky), pauses (frequency and duration), and volume (loud–soft).

Not surprisingly, voice contributes dramatically to the success or failure of business and professional communicators. For example, surgeons with harsh, impatient voices

Table 4–3   Co-cultural Differences Can Lead to Misunderstandings

Behaviors that have one meaning for members of the same culture or co-culture can be interpreted differently by members of other groups.

Behavior (in Traditional Co-culture)	Probable In-Group Perception	Possible Out-Group Perception
Avoidance of direct eye contact (Latino/a)	Used to communicate attentiveness or respect.	A sign of inattentiveness; direct eye contact is preferred.
Aggressively challenging a point with which one disagrees (African American)	Acceptable means of dialogue; not regarded as verbal abuse, or a precursor to violence.	Arguments are viewed as inappropriate and a sign of potential imminent violence.
Use of finger gestures to beckon others (Asian American)	Appropriate if used by adults for children, but highly offensive if directed at adults.	Appropriate gesture to use with both children and adults.
Silence (Native American)	A sign of respect, thoughtfulness, and/or uncertainty/ambiguity.	Interpreted as boredom, disagreement, or refusal to participate/respond.
Touch (Latino/a)	Normal and appropriate for interpersonal interactions.	Deemed appropriate for some intimate or friendly interactions; otherwise perceived as a violation of personal space.
Public display of intense emotions (African American)	Accepted and valued as measure of expressiveness. Appropriate in most settings.	Violates expectations for self-controlled public behaviors; inappropriate in most public settings.
Touching or holding hands of same-sex friends (Asian American)	Acceptable behavior that signifies closeness in platonic relationships.	Perceived as inappropriate, especially for male friends.

Source: Adapted from M. P. Orbe and T. M. Harris, *Interracial Communication: Theory into Practice* (Belmont, CA: Wadsworth, 2001), p. 65.

were more likely to be sued by patients for malpractice than were those with more friendly speech mannerisms.[40] One distinctive vocal trait is "uptalk"—the tendency to end sentences on a rising pitch. This vocal pattern makes assertions sound like questions: "Mr. Chen? It's Eliza Palmer? From Accounts Receivable?" Since uptalk is more common among women, it's easy to imagine how this trait can contribute to perceptions of female unassertiveness. "If women always sound like they're asking for approval or agreement, they seem less sure of themselves," says communication consultant Mary-Ellen Drummond.[41]

Appearance   Appearance plays a tremendous role in determining how a communicator's messages will be received in business and elsewhere.[42] As a rule, people who *look* attractive are considered to be likable and persuasive, and they generally have successful careers.[43] For example, research suggests that beginning salaries increase about $2,000 for every 1-point increase on a 5-point attractiveness scale and that more attractive men

Models of Nonverbal Effectiveness

Think of an especially effective communicator you have encountered in business or professional settings. This may be someone you know (e.g., a boss, colleague, instructor) or a person you don't know personally but have dealt with (e.g., a medical professional, salesperson, public safety official). The person you choose may even be a character in a film.

Describe to your audience

1. Who this person is and the context in which you encountered him or her.

2. The nonverbal behaviors and attitudes that contribute to his or her effectiveness. Be as specific as possible: Give examples of how the person you are describing has used the types of behaviors described in this chapter: facial expression, voice, attire, etc.

3. What lessons you have learned from the person you've chosen, and how you can apply them in your life.

If time and the facilities permit, you may even share a photo of the person you are describing with your audience.

(but not more attractive women) are given higher starting salaries than their less handsome counterparts.

A number of factors contribute to how attractive a person seems. For instance, potential employers, customers, and co-workers are usually impressed by people who are trim, muscular, and in good shape. One study, in fact, shows that people who are overweight have more trouble getting job offers.[44] Some aspects of physical appearance cannot be changed very easily. One very significant factor in appearance, though—and one over which you may have the most control—is clothing.

The kind of clothing one wears can influence how people react. Boeing Aircraft CEO Philip Condit is aware of this fact. Having discovered that discussions were hard to get going when he appeared in a business suit and tie, Condit routinely dressed down when making trips to the shop floor to talk with the men and women who build Boeing aircraft.[45]

Attitudes about what clothing is acceptable keep changing. By the mid-1990s, even conservative IBM abandoned its decades-long policy of requiring employees to wear a dark business suit, even allowing male workers in some jobs to show up for work without a suit and tie. A spokesperson for IBM explained, "You try to dress like your customers do."[46] But the casual dress trends brought on by the 1990 dot-coms seem to be in decline.[47]

Whether to dress up or dress down depends on several factors, including the industry or field of work. California's outdoor gear clothing manufacturer Patagonia, Inc., may have one of the most liberal dress codes: Even shoes aren't required.[48] By contrast, financial services and public administration businesses have some of the most conservative dress standards, while high-tech, utilities, and natural resources tend to be the most informal.[49]

Geography also makes a difference in determining an appropriate working wardrobe. In one survey, Washington, DC, proved to have the most conservative attire, with New York and Philadelphia close behind. California and New England—the location of many high-tech companies—had more liberal standards.[50] Knowing an office has a "business casual" dress code isn't enough. As business etiquette expert Dana Casperson notes, business casual "means one thing on the West Coast, another thing on the East Coast, and no one knows in the middle."[51] The culture of an individual organization also makes a difference in how to dress. Two companies in the same field might have quite different appearance codes.

When choosing your wardrobe, consider the following tips:

- *Look around.* The best guide to an appropriate wardrobe is right in front of you. Look at key people in the industry and country where you work. Wearing a conservative, dark business suit in a freewheeling start-up company where everyone else comes to work in jeans would look just as odd as wearing wrinkled Levis in a Wall Street stock brokerage.

- *Be flexible.* Within your company's dress code, choose an outfit that fits your daily activities. If you are seeing an important client, a business suit may be the best look. If you will be working all day at your desk, more casual dress may be fine.

- *Don't confuse "casual" with "sloppy."* A T-shirt and grubby denims send a different message than well-fitting khakis and a sharp shirt or sweater. Looking good in casual dress can be at least as challenging (and expensive) as a more formal look.

- *Never risk offending.* Your definition of appropriate attire may not match those of people whose approval you need. For example, only a slight majority of respondents in one survey thought exposed underwear is inappropriate, although this is a look that would jeopardize success in most fields.[52]

- *Dress for the job you want.* If you are seeking advancement, consider dressing in a way that makes it easy for the people who have the power to promote you to visualize you in a position of more responsibility.

The Face and Eyes

On an obvious level, a person's face communicates emotions clearly: a subordinate's confused expression indicates the need to continue with an explanation; a customer's smile and nodding signal the time to close a sale; and a colleague's frown indicates that your request for help has come at a bad time. Facial expressions, like other nonverbal signals, are ambiguous (a co-worker's frown could come from a headache rather than the timing of your request). Nonetheless, researchers have found that accurate judgments of facial expressions can be made.[53]

The eyes themselves communicate a great deal. A skilled nonverbal communicator, for example, can control an interaction by knowing when and where to look to produce the desired results. Since visual contact is an invitation to speak, a speaker who does not want to be interrupted can avoid looking directly at people until it is time to field questions or get reactions.

Eye contact can be a good indicator of how involved a person is in a situation, although the advice to always look people straight in the eye has been partially contradicted by research. In most two-person conversations, people seem to look at their partners somewhere between 50 and 60 percent of the time, often alternating short gazes with glances away. Still, a person who makes little or no eye contact may seem to have little involvement in the situation.

The rules for eye contact and facial expressions vary from one culture to another. In some cultures—Diné (Navajo), for example—lack of eye contact may indicate respect for elders, not a lack of interest. In Japan, smiling is less common than in North America, which can confuse visitors who mistakenly perceive formality for unfriendliness. Clerks greet customers with a simple "Irasshaimase"—"Welcome"—but typically don't accompany the greeting with a smile.[54] Some foreign companies, including McDonald's Corp., have created "smile schools" to teach employees how to greet customers in a manner that seems more friendly.

Even among communicators who follow the rules of Euro-American culture, eye contact can be deceptive; some people *can* lie while looking you right in the eye. And even barely perceptible changes in eye contact can send messages that may or may not be accurate. The following story illustrates how eye contact can be misleading—with serious repercussions:

"You have until he rolls his eyes and looks at his watch."

> *Discussing his corporation's financial future in front of television cameras, the chief executive officer of a Fortune 500 company lowered his eyes just as he began to mention projected earnings. His downcast eyes gave the impression—on television—that the executive wasn't on the level. Wall Street observers discounted the CEO's optimistic forecast, and the company's stock price dropped four points over the next few trading days. It took two years to build it up again—even though the projection had proved to be accurate.*[55]

Posture and Movement   A person's body communicates messages in several ways. The first is through posture. The way you sit at your desk when you're working can reflect your attitude toward your job or how hard you're working to anyone who cares to look. A less obvious set of bodily clues comes from the small gestures and mannerisms that every communicator exhibits at one time or another. While most people pay reasonably close attention to their facial expression, they are less aware of hand, leg, and foot motions. Thus, fidgeting hands might betray nervousness; a tapping foot, impatience; and clenched fists or white knuckles, restrained anger. Table 4-4 describes the way others may be likely to interpret some of your gestures.

A study on privacy in the workplace by GF Business Equipment Company describes ways in which such gestures can be used to discourage visits from co-workers. In addition to avoiding eye contact with your visitor, the company suggests that you shuffle papers or make notes to indicate a desire to return to work . . . keep pen or pencil poised—that communicates an aversion to engage in conversation . . . and if interrupted when dialing a call, don't hang up the receiver.[56]

Good communicators are sensitive to small cues like this and tailor their behavior accordingly. They will notice a forward-leaning position as an indication that their remarks are being well received and will capitalize upon the point that led to this reaction. When a remark results in a pulling back, a smart communicator will uncover the damage and try to remedy it. Awareness of such subtle messages can make the difference between success and failure in a variety of business settings: interviews, presentations, group meetings, and one-to-one interactions.

Table 4–4	Common Gestures and Their Possible Perceived Meanings	
Gesture	**In Moderate Form**	**When Exaggerated**
Forward lean	Friendly feelings	Hostile feelings
Direct eye contact	Friendly feelings	Hostile feelings
Unique dress and hairstyle	Creativity	Rebelliousness
Upright posture	Expertise; self-confidence	Uprightness; hostility
Variability in voice pitch, rate, and loudness	Lively mind	Nervousness; anxiety; insecurity
Smiling	Friendliness; relaxed and secure composure	Masking hostility; submissiveness
Averting gaze	Shyness; modesty	Guilt; unreliability
Knitted brow	Involvement	Hostility
Nodding and reaching out the hands while talking	Self-confidence	Uncertainty

Source: Adapted from University of Northern Iowa College of Business Administration. Accessed from **http://www.cba.unl.edu/buscomm/nonverbal/body%20Language.htm.**

Body relaxation or tension is a strong indicator of who has the power in one-to-one relationships. As a rule, the more relaxed person in a given situation has the greater status.[57] This is most obvious in job interviews and high-stake situations in which subordinates meet with their superiors—requesting a raise or describing a problem, for example. The person in control can afford to relax, while the supplicant must be watchful and on guard. While excessive tension does little good for either the sender or receiver, total relaxation can be inappropriate for a subordinate. A job candidate who matched the interviewer's casual sprawl would probably create a poor impression. In superior–subordinate interactions, the best posture for the one-down person is probably one that is slightly more rigid than the powerholder's.

Height also affects perceptions of power: Tallness usually equates with dominance. Standing up tall can help you appear more authoritative, whereas slumped posture or slouched shoulders create an appearance of submissive or passive demeanor. Getting your body at the same level as others is a way of nonverbally diminishing status whether speaking with a colleague in a wheelchair or with others shorter than you. To literally have to look up to someone may make the shorter person feel like a subordinate. Sitting down with someone could signal your desire for collegiality rather than status, while standing over or behind someone signals power or status. Since women and persons from some minority co-cultures may not be as tall as the average American male, and since persons in wheelchairs interact at a shorter height, your relative height is a factor worth considering in professional interactions. If you are taller than others or are standing when others are sitting, they may be seeing you as an authority figure or higher-status individual, even if you don't wish to appear as one.[58]

Personal Space and Distance   The distance we put between ourselves and others also reflects feelings and attitudes, and thus it affects communication. Anthropologist

Edward Hall has identified four distance zones used by middle-class Americans: intimate (ranging from physical contact to about 18 inches), casual–personal (18 inches to 4 feet), social–consultative (4 to 12 feet), and public (12 feet and beyond).[59]

In some cases the distance zones don't apply at all—or at least the distances aren't flexible enough to reflect the attitudes of the parties. Dentists and barbers, for instance, work within intimate distance—actual physical contact; yet the relationship between dentist and patient or barber and client may be rather impersonal.

In other cases, though, the distance that people put between themselves and others is significant. For example, distance can reflect the attitude of the person who does the positioning. Research shows that a person who expects an unpleasant message or views the speaker as unfriendly takes a more distant position than does someone expecting good news or viewing the speaker as friendly.[60] An observant communicator can thus use the distance others choose with respect to him or her as a basis for hunches about their feelings. ("I get the feeling you're worried about something, Harry. Is there anything wrong?")

Besides reflecting attitudes, distance also creates feelings. In one study, subjects rated people who communicated at a greater distance as less friendly and understanding than those who positioned themselves closer.[61] (Closeness has its limits, of course. Intimate distance is rarely appropriate for business dealings.) Thus, an effective communicator will usually choose to operate at a casual–personal distance when a friendly atmosphere is the goal.

Interpersonal distance is another nonverbal indicator of power. One unspoken cultural rule is that the person with higher status generally controls the degree of approach. As Mehrabian puts it, "It is easy enough to picture an older person in this culture encouraging a younger business partner by patting him or her on the back; but it is very difficult to visualize this situation reversed; that is, with the younger person patting the older and more senior partner."[62] This principle of distance explains why subordinates rarely question the boss's right to drop in to their work area without invitation but are reluctant to approach their superior's office even when told the door is always open.

When a subordinate does wind up in the office of a superior, both tension and distance show who is in charge. The less powerful person usually stands until invited to take a seat and, when given the choice, will be reluctant to sit close to the boss. Wise managers often try to minimize the inhibiting factor of this status gap by including a table or comfortable easy chairs in their offices so that they can meet with subordinates on a more equal level.

Some managers try to promote informal communication by visiting employees in the employees' own offices. David Ogilvy, head of one of the largest advertising agencies in the country, says, "Do not summon people to your office—it frightens them. Instead, go to see them in *their* offices."[63]

Physical Environment   So far we have discussed how personal behavior sends nonverbal messages. The physical environment in which we operate also suggests how we feel and shapes how we communicate.

Consider the way space is allocated in an organization. Power locations become apparent when we look at the amount and location of existing space given to various employees and groups. In many organizations, for instance, an employee's status may be measured by whether his or her office is next to the boss's or is in a dark alcove. An office with a window or an office on the corner often indicates higher status than an inside office with no window, and any office usually signals higher status than a cubicle.

Another way in which environments shape communication is proximity. The distance that separates people is perhaps the most important factor in shaping who talks with whom. Other things being equal, officemates will talk with one another more than with the people next door, and workers in the same area deal with one another more than with similarly employed people in another area. Researcher Thomas J. Allen studied workers in research facilities, medical laboratories, and business schools. He found that the frequency with which a person spoke to colleagues was a direct function of the distance between their desks.[64]

Furniture arrangement also plays a big role in the way people communicate. For example, in one study of a medical office, only 10 percent of the patients were "at ease" when conversing with a doctor seated behind a desk, while the figure rose to 55 percent when the desk was removed.[65] Even when the location of furniture is fixed, choices about seating can influence interaction. Dominant, high-status persons often select the position at a table where they can see and be seen. This allows more interaction and more influence over the interactions at the table. Not surprisingly, the person who is seated at the head of a table is more often perceived as a leader. Persons who want to diminish their potential for interaction and leadership often seat themselves in less visible spots along the sides of a table.[66]

This sort of information can be useful on the job. You may be able to relocate your work to an area that will give you the interaction you want. Beyond this, realize that several places in your working environment will probably allow you to interact informally with desirable communication partners. Employee lounges, elevators, and dining areas are a few examples. If you are interested in making your bosses more aware of your work, it's important to be visible to them. On the other hand, if you would just as soon be left alone, the old axiom "Out of sight, out of mind" applies here.

If you are a manager, think about arranging your subordinates' working areas to increase communication between people who should interact and to separate those who don't need to talk to one another. You can encourage communication between groups of workers by arranging gathering spots where congregation is easy. A good setting for informal contact needs to meet three criteria.[67] First, it ought to be centrally located so that people have to pass through it on their way to other places. Second, it should contain places to sit or rest, to be comfortable. Finally, it must be large enough so that the people gathered there won't interfere with others passing through or working nearby. Of course, if you want to discourage contact at a central spot (the copying machine, for example), simply change one or more of these conditions.

When it comes to managing interaction between members of an organization and its public, you can create the most desirable degree of accessibility by use of space and barriers. Proximity and visibility encourage contact, while distance and closure discourage it.

Time   The way we use time provides a number of silent messages.[68] Leonard Berlin, senior financial analyst at ExxonMobil, attributes his reputation as a hard worker to the fact that he routinely arrives at work half an hour early. "That's a big thing to my boss," he says.

Many business advisers recommend that you be particularly scrupulous about your use of time during the first few months you are on the job:

> *If . . . in that first ninety days, you're late or absent frequently, or seen as a clock watcher, you may earn yourself . . . negative scrutiny for a long time thereafter by your superiors. Rather than excusing any "infractions" of the rules, they'll be looking for slip-ups and a reason potentially to discharge you.*[69]

Cubicle Etiquette

As the comic character Dilbert has shown the world, daily life in a cubicle (or cube) has its challenges. These tips can help you manage the communication dynamics of cubicle life.

Privacy

Treat others' cubicles as if they were private offices. Knock gently to avoid startling occupants. Don't enter without verbal invitation or eye-contact permission—act as if there were a door. Never read the occupant's computer screens or borrow items from their desks just because you have access. Let others know when you aren't available by a "Do Not Disturb" sign or by your lack of eye contact. Resist the urge to shout out an answer to another cube dweller's question just because you overheard it. Avoid popping up over the top of cubicles to talk to others; instead, walk over or send an e-mail or instant message. Remember that whatever you say can be heard by others, so conduct meetings and personal conversations elsewhere. Keep conversations with your banker, family, doctor, and/or sweetheart out of the cubicle. Be polite enough to not listen to others' conversations, and certainly don't repeat anything overheard. Don't use a speaker phone in a cubicle; it is rude to the person on the other end and to your colleagues.

Noise

Don't add to the noise of a cube farm. Keep your voice on the low side. Set your phone ringer on low and turn it off when you are away from your desk. Don't let your cell phone ring when you are on another call. Use headphones for radios or CDs, and use a screen saver without sounds.

Odors

Your favorite scent (whether perfume, lotion, after-shave, or hair product) may be someone else's allergen, so think about its effect on others. Think about eating in lunch areas, not at your desk as your colleagues may not appreciate the odor of your food.

Children

In most organizations, children (especially if they are too young for school) are best kept away from work except on special occasions. No matter how well behaved, children may not be welcome or allowed by company policy to a shared cubicle.

Illness

Your determination to work when sick may be commendable, but you aren't doing any favors if you infect everybody in the office. If you wouldn't want someone in your state of health coming to work, try to stay away yourself.

Note: For more information see G. M. Smith, "Cubicle Etiquette" *Intercom*, November 2000, pp. 12–13, retrieved June 23, 2006, from **http://www.stc.org/intercom/PDFs/2000/200011_12-13.pdf**; J. Bremmer, "Cubicle Etiquette," at **www.bremercommunications.com/Cubicle_Etiquette.htm**; and "Cube and Cubicle Etiquette," at **http://papa.essortment.com/cubicleetiquett_ppb.htm**.

Rules and customs about time vary widely from one culture to another. Whereas most North Americans and northern Europeans value punctuality, other cultures value taking time for important relationships more highly than routine appointments and deadlines. Chris Pagliaro, an American football coach, learned this lesson the hard way when he spent a season leading Milan's team in the Italian league. His realization that time is treated differently began to dawn on him when he arrived for the first practice sessions, scheduled for 8:30 P.M.:

> We got out there at 8:30 P.M. I'm dressed, I've got my whistle, my (American) assistant coach is there, the two American players are there. And there's no Italians. It's ten 'til nine and I don't see anybody: [not] the owner, nobody. Around 9 o'clock, a couple of them start trickling in.

Indicate in the space at the left of each item the degree to which you believe the statement applies to you, using the following five-point scale:

1 = Never

2 = Rarely

3 = Occasionally

4 = Often

5 = Very often

_____ 1. I use my hands and arms to gesture while talking to people.

_____ 2. I touch others on the shoulder or arm while talking to them.

_____ 3. I use a monotone or dull voice while talking to people.

_____ 4. I look over or away from others while talking to them.

_____ 5. I move away from others when they touch me while we are talking.

_____ 6. I have a relaxed body position when I talk to people.

_____ 7. I frown while talking to people.

_____ 8. I avoid eye contact while talking to people.

_____ 9. I have a tense body position while talking to people.

_____ 10. I sit close or stand close to people while talking with them.

_____ 11. My voice is monotonous or dull when I talk to people.

_____ 12. I use a variety of vocal expressions when I talk to people.

_____ 13. I gesture when I talk to people.

_____ 14. I am animated when I talk to people.

_____ 15. I have a bland facial expression when I talk to people.

_____ 16. I move closer to people when I talk to them.

_____ 17. I look directly at people while talking to them.

_____ 18. I am stiff when I talk to people.

_____ 19. I have a lot of vocal variety when I talk to people.

> _I had made a practice schedule—typical American coach: at 8:30 we do this, at 8:35 this, at 8:50 this. You might as well throw that one out the window. We got started around 9:20 or 9:30._[70]

The coach was smart and flexible enough to realize that he couldn't fight against a lifetime of cultural conditioning. He developed a compromise between the American need for punctuality and the casual Italian attitude about time:

> _By Friday, I knew it was useless. So what I did, I made a schedule and waited around. While the team ran laps, we set our watches back to 8:30. That's the only way I could do it. So we were always starting at 8:30, regardless of what time it was._

_____ 20. I avoid gesturing while I am talking to people.

_____ 21. I lean toward people when I talk to them.

_____ 22. I maintain eye contact with people when I talk to them.

_____ 23. I try not to sit or stand close to people when I talk with them.

_____ 24. I lean away from people when I talk to them.

_____ 25. I smile when I talk to people.

_____ 26. I avoid touching people when I talk to them.

Scoring Procedure:

1. Start with a score of 78. Add to that the scores from the following items: 1, 2, 6, 10, 12, 13, 14, 16, 17, 19, 21, 22, and 25.

2. Add only the scores from the following items: 3, 4, 5, 7, 8, 9, 11, 15, 18, 20, 23, 24, and 26.

3. Subtract your total score in step 2 from your total score in step 1. This is your final score.

When using this instrument it is important to recognize that the difference in these self-reports between females and males is statistically significant and socially significant (that is, substantial variance in the scores on this instrument can be attributed to biological sex). Whether these differences are "real" (that is, females may actually be more nonverbally immediate than males) or a function of social desirability (that is, females think they should be more immediate than males think they should be) or a function of actual behavior has not yet been determined.

Scoring Norms:

Females	Mean = 96.7	S.D. = 16.1	High = >112	Low = <81
Males	Mean = 91.6	S.D. = 15.0	High = >106	Low = <77
Combined	Mean = 94.2	S.D. = 15.6	High = >109	Low = <79

Sources: Adapted from V. P. Richmond, J. C. McCroskey, and A. D. Johnson, "Development of the Nonverbal Immediacy Scale (NIS): Measures of Self- and Other-Reported Nonverbal Immediacy," _Communication Quarterly_ 51 (2003), pp. 505–517; and J. C. McCroskey, Nonverbal Immediacy Scale-Observer Report. Retrieved May 12, 2009, from **www.jamescmccroskey.com/measures.**

In monochronic cultures, speaking within the allotted time generally shows good planning and concern for the audience. Speaking longer inconveniences the listeners and communicates lack of regard for their schedules. But in some polychronic cultures, speaking only for the allotted time would indicate lack of excitement or actual indifference toward the audience or the issue. Getting down to business quickly can be seen as a rude and insulting move on the part of a potential business associate. In many polychronic cultures, the relationship is an important part of the business at hand. If the personal relationship is not established by taking time for dialogue and discussion, the business relationship will be at risk.

ethical challenge

Improving Nonverbal Effectiveness

Now that you understand the elements of nonverbal communication, you can use the following guidelines to help achieve your professional goals.

Monitor Your Nonverbal Behavior

If you have ever asked yourself "how am I doing?" you know something about **self-monitoring**—the process of paying close attention to your behavior and using these observations to shape the way you behave.

High self-monitors are good at knowing when to adapt their nonverbal behavior to suit the situation.[71] By contrast, low self-monitors don't even recognize the negative impact of some of their behaviors. One study found low self-monitors were blissfully ignorant of their shortcomings and more likely to overestimate their skill than were better communicators.[72] For example, experimental subjects who scored in the lowest quartile on joke-telling skills were more likely than their funnier counterparts to grossly overestimate their sense of humor.

It's easy to see how self-monitoring can help you manage your nonverbal behavior. In a meeting or delivering a presentation, you might catch yourself droning on and losing your audience. When dealing with a difficult situation, your mental alarm will go off if you are losing your patience and showing irritation. Dealing with an unhappy client or customer, you can monitor and control your defensiveness.

While too much self-monitoring can make you overly self-conscious, keeping an eye on how you may look and sound to others is likely to enhance your image as a professional.

Demonstrate Interest in Others

Social scientists use the term **immediacy** to describe verbal and nonverbal behaviors that indicate closeness and liking. Among the nonverbal cues are closer proximity (within social conventions, of course), more direct eye gaze, more forward lean, more relaxed posture, positive facial expression, and warmer vocal qualities.[73]

There's a strong link between high immediacy and career success.[74] For example, supervisors perceived as having high immediacy are regarded by their subordinates as more competent, credible, and attractive than less immediate bosses, and the subordinates are more cooperative. By contrast, low immediacy cues can be a put-off. Recall from your own experience how you reacted when you encountered someone with an unfriendly expression, a flat or hostile voice, and lack of animation.

Immediacy cues are especially important in the beginning states of a relationship. First impressions are powerful, particularly when strangers don't have much other information available to form opinions of you. Even after you know someone well, there are times when immediacy is especially important.[75]

With practice and self-monitoring, you can manage your nonverbal immediacy most effectively. You can begin by evaluating your current level of immediacy using the Self-Assessment inventory on pages 114–115.

Be Positive   Emotions can be contagious. As one writer put it, "We catch feelings from one another as though they were some kind of social virus."[76] Psychologists use the term *emotional contagion* to describe this phenomenon. They have discovered that we can "infect" one another with our moods in as little as 2 minutes.[77] Given this fact, a professional identity that reflects calmness, confidence, and goodwill will serve you well.

Just as others might "catch" an emotional state from you, you can be infected by the tone of others' nonverbal behavior. That's not a problem when you are around positive communicators, but sometimes you will need to struggle not to be overcome by the attitude of negative people.

Observe Conventions   As you read in Chapter 2, some conventions are cultural. For example, in northern Europe you can expect to greet associates with a handshake, while in Mediterranean countries and Latin America, a hug and even a ritual kiss might be more appropriate. Likewise, an American woman traveling in an Islamic country probably would dress more conservatively and be more likely to wear a head covering than she would at home.

Some nonverbal conventions are just as strong within certain fields or organizations. The style of dress worn by personal trainers or Web page designers would look out of place at a meeting of investment bankers, and the way you would dress or act at a company picnic or weekend retreat would probably differ from the clothes you would wear or the way you would act back in the office on Monday morning.

Actually, violating others' expectations can be effective, as long as your unexpected behavior is judged positively.[78] Dressing better, and being more enthusiastic can all generate positive reactions—as long as you don't overdo it so that your violation is regarded as negative or phony.

Sexual Harassment

Verbal and nonverbal sexual harassment on the job has always existed, but in recent decades it has been identified as a problem requiring governmental response. The Civil Rights Act of 1964 and subsequent legislation and court decisions have identified two types of sexual harassment:

- **Quid pro quo** (a Latin term meaning "this for that"). Examples of this form of harassment include directly or indirectly threatening not to promote someone who won't date you or implying that employment depends on the giving of sexual favors.

- **Hostile work environment**. This category includes any verbal or nonverbal behavior that has the intention or effect of interfering with someone's work or creating an environment that is intimidating, offensive, or hostile. Unwelcome remarks ("babe," "hunk"), humor, stares ("elevator eyes"), hand or body signs, and invasions of physical space all can create a hostile work environment.

Of the two types of harassment, there is less confusion about blatant quid pro quo propositions, and most people agree on what constitutes blatant harassment.[79] There is less agreement, though, on what kinds of behavior create a hostile working environment. One person's harmless joke can be deeply offensive to someone else, and what seems like a sincere compliment to the person who offers it can sound like a come-on to the receiver.

Sexual harassment can occur in a variety of circumstances. It may arise between members of the same sex or between men and women. The harasser can be the target's supervisor, an agent of the employer, a supervisor in another area, or a co-worker. Even behavior by non-employees (e.g., customers or people from other organizations) can be grounds for a harassment claim. The target does not have to be the person harassed but could be anyone affected by the offensive conduct. (Situations like this are termed "third-party harassment.") Unlawful sexual harassment may occur without economic injury to or discharge of the target.[80]

Reports of harassment are widespread. In fiscal year 2000, a total of 15,836 complaints were filed in the United States.[81] For example, in addition to a $7.75 million cash settlement in a suit against Ford Motor Company by 900 female employees, sensitivity training must now be given at Ford plants across the nation, at an estimated cost of $10 million.[82] Furthermore, sensitivity training is now provided at every organizational level of every federal government agency.[83] In Los Angeles, harassment was so widespread that the mayor ordered training programs for every city worker.

Avoiding Sexual Harassment Problems

Beyond the normal precautions and courtesy, it is smart to be especially sensitive in situations where others might take offense at your words or behaviors. Look at the situation from the other person's point of view. Could your language be considered offensive? Could your actions lead to discomfort? Read your company's sexual harassment policies carefully, know what the EEOC guidelines are, and be very familiar with any training and other information provided by your Human Resources professionals. If you wonder whether a behavior might be construed as harassment, not engaging in it is probably the safest course of action.

Responding to Sexual Harassment

Most organizations have written policies prohibiting sexual harassment and procedures for people who believe they are being harassed. Options may include hotlines and Human Resources representatives. If you believe you have been the target of harassment, be sure you understand the policies and resources that are available to you.

In addition to company policy, targets of sexual harassment are entitled to legal protection. The EEOC, state and local agencies, and the court system all enforce civil rights acts relating to harassment.

Despite the determination of government to protect employees, fighting sexual harassment through legal channels can take stamina. The process can be time-consuming, and targets sometimes experience depression, ridicule, isolation, and reprisal.[84] For these reasons, taking care of harassment at the lowest, most informal level possible may solve the problem in a way that doesn't punish the target. Listed below are several options, in escalating order. They aren't meant as a step-by-step guide for how to respond, but they will help you decide which options may best suit a given situation.

1. *Consider dismissing the incident.* This approach is appropriate only if you truly believe that the remark or behavior isn't worth worrying about. Pretending to dismiss

case study

Sexual Harassment: Speak Up or Keep Quiet?

Susan Carter was one of the few female partners in a New York consulting firm. During an out-of-town planning meeting in her hotel room, the client made a clumsy pass, knocking her over. He later apologized, but Susan was unable to forget the incident. The next day, Susan's boss, Justin Peale, called to ask how her meeting went. She knew from the office grapevine that Justin only put her on this key account with reluctance, thinking that the clients would feel more comfortable working with a male account representative. Susan feared that telling her boss about the incident could prejudice him against giving her future assignments. On the other hand, she knew that keeping quiet compromises her dignity and that not reporting the incident could result in the client's firm being exposed to future lawsuits.

CRITICAL ANALYSIS: As you consider this situation, answer the following questions:

1. How can Susan balance her career advancement with her knowledge of what happened? Feelings of being treated badly?

2. Imagine that the incident described above happened to you, or to a female colleague who seeks your advice. Decide which of the seven alternatives listed on pages 118–119 is the most effective and appropriate response.

For a more detailed account of this incident and commentary by several executives, see J. Margetta, "Will She Fit In?" *Harvard Business Review*, March/April 1997, pp. 18–32.

---

incidents that you believe are important can lead to repetition of the offensive behavior, self-blame, and diminished self-esteem.

2. *Tell the harasser to stop.* Inform the harasser early that the behavior is unwelcome, and tell him or her to cease immediately. Your statement should be firm, but it doesn't have to be angry. Remember that many words or deeds that make you uncomfortable may not be deliberately hostile remarks. (See Chapter 5 for details on how to be assertive without being aggressive.)

3. *Keep notes.* Keep a record of every incident. Detail the date, time, place, witnesses, and exactly what happened in specific, concrete language. Describe how you responded and how you felt.

4. *Write a personal letter to the harasser.* A written statement may help the harasser to understand what behavior you find offensive. Just as important, it can show that you take the problem seriously. Put the letter in a sealed envelope (keeping a copy for yourself). Use information from your diary to detail specifics about what happened, what behavior you want stopped, and how you felt. You may want to include a copy of your organization's sexual harassment policy. Keep a record of when you delivered the letter. If you want to be certain that the delivery of the letter will be acknowledged, take a friend along when you present it or send it via certified mail. [See sample letters at **www.colorado.edu/Ombuds/InformalStrategies.pdf**.

5. *Ask a trusted third party to intervene.* Perhaps a mutual acquaintance can persuade the harasser to stop. The person you choose should be someone who you are convinced understands your discomfort and supports your opinion. Be sure this intermediary is also someone the harasser respects and trusts.

6. *Use company channels.* Report the situation to your supervisor, Human Resources office, or a committee that has been set up to consider harassment complaints.

7. *File a legal complaint.* You may file a complaint with the federal EEOC or with your state agency. You have the right to obtain the services of an attorney regarding your legal options. (See **www.eeoc.gov** for detailed explanations of this procedure.)

review points

- Verbal messages are clearest when they use unequivocal and nonabstract language, an appropriate level of power, with few relative words, slang and jargon. Strategically ambiguous messages are occasionally useful to promote harmony, facilitate change, and soften difficult messages.

- Stay effective by avoiding inflammatory language (biased terms and trigger words that convey speaker attitudes and generate strong listener emotions) and monitoring your own responses to others' inflammatory words.

- Masculine and feminine language differ in some significant ways. Feminine language emphasizes rapport and relationships, while masculine speech focuses on reporting, accomplishing tasks, and controling situations. Meet gender challenges by being aware of style differences and switching or combining styles to suit the situation.

- Nonverbal behavior is a part of every communication exchange. It expresses attitudes and emotions more than ideas, and needs to be interpreted with caution, because it tends to be ambiguous and culture-bound.

- Nonverbal messages can be expressed vocally, through appearance (physical stature and clothing), and through the face, eyes, posture, gesture, distance, physical environment, and time.

- Achieve your workplace goals by monitoring your nonverbal behavior, demonstrating interest in others through immediacy, remaining positive, being aware of emotional contagion, and observing nonverbal cultural and organizational conventions.

- Minimize problems of sexual harassment by understanding verbal and nonverbal behaviors that are inappropriate and illegal in the workplace and staying aware of others' perceptions of and reactions to your behaviors.

- People who perceive themselves as targets of harassment in the workplace have a number of options available, ranging from informal to formal.

key terms

→ Test your understanding of these key terms by visiting the Online Learning Center Web site at www.mhhe.com/adler10e.

biased language   98
equivocal terms   93
feminine style of speech   100
genderlects   99
high-level abstractions   94
hostile work environment   117
immediacy   116
jargon   95
low-level abstractions   94
masculine style of speech   101

nonverbal communication   103
paralanguage   105
quid pro quo sexual harassment   117
rapport talk   100
relative words   95
report talk   100
self-monitoring   116
triangle of meaning   92
trigger words   99

activities

→ Go to the self-quizzes at the Online Learning Center at www.mhhe.com/adler10e to test your knowledge of chapter concepts.

1. Skill Builder

Practice your skill at using unequivocal language by describing how each of the following sentences is likely to be misunderstood (or not understood at all). Then improve the clarity of each message by introducing your message with a high-level abstraction and qualifying it with low-level abstractions. To invent meaningful low-level abstractions, you will have to imagine a specific scenario.

 a. You did a heck of a job on that proposal.
 b. There are just a few small problems to clear up.
 c. I just need a little more time to finish the job.
 d. Your job performance hasn't been good this year.

2. Skill Builder

Practice clarifying your understanding of another person's ambiguous messages. For each sentence below, construct a polite question you could ask the speaker to help clarify the meaning.

 a. I need this report right away.
 b. This presentation needs to be perfect.
 c. Whenever I leave to go to a meeting, nothing gets done in this office.
 d. I'm on my own around here!

3. Invitation to Insight

Identify jargon in your own line of work, or interview a worker in a field that interests you and identify jargon that he or she uses. Then answer the following questions:

 a. How does each term make communication more efficient?
 b. What confusion might arise from the use of each term with certain listeners?
 c. In cases where confusion or misunderstandings might arise, suggest alternative words or phrases that could convey the meaning more clearly.

4. Skill Builder

Describe a former co-worker three times. In your first account, use positively biased terms. In the second description, discuss the same person, using words with negative connotations. Finally, describe the co-worker in low-level abstractions without using biased language of any sort.

5. Invitation to Insight

Become more aware of your own emotional triggers by following these instructions:

 a. In each category shown, identify two words that trigger positive reactions for you and two other words you react to negatively:
  1. A person's name.
  2. The label for a category of people (e.g., "fanatic").
  3. A rule, policy, or issue (e.g., gay marriage).
 b. How do you react, both internally and observably, when you hear these terms? Ponder the source of your reactions (the way you were raised? past experiences?). How might your reactions impact your communication?
 c. Use the same categories to identify words that trigger positive and negative reactions in a person you work with. What are the consequences of using these emotion-laden words with that person? Suggest neutral words you could use to replace the trigger words.

6. Invitation to Insight

Explore the characteristics of nonverbal communication as communicative yet ambiguous.

 a. Observe the nonverbal behaviors of a person you work with. What interpretations do you attach to your observations? Describe an alternative interpretation for each nonverbal behavior you have noticed. Speculate on which of your interpretations might be more accurate. Verify your perceptions by asking your co-worker what the behavior means.

b. Ask a co-worker to observe you during a meeting. After the meeting, have your co-worker describe some of your nonverbal behaviors and speculate what meanings you intended. Did your co-worker's perceptions match your intentions?

7. Skill Builder

Demonstrate the impact of nonverbal communication by describing effective and ineffective examples of behaviors in each of the following categories.

a. Voice.
b. Dress.
c. Face and eyes.
d. Posture and movement.
e. Personal space and use of distance.

8. Skill Builder

Using the Web sites in Nonverbal Communication around the World (go to the Online Learning Center at www.mhhe.com/adler10e), choose two countries that are likely to be a part of a specific career field or organization you may work for. Find two or more gestures that have different meanings in those countries. Categorize the gestures into those that appear similar to a gesture in your culture but have a different meaning, those that appear unlike any gesture that would be recognized in your culture, and those that are very different from the gestures with the same meaning in your culture.

9. Invitation to Insight

Visit the Indiana University Human Resource Web site at http://www.indiana.edu/~uhrs/policies/uwide/sexual_harass.html. Scroll down to Appendix A. Choose one of the examples of behavior that

could lead to allegations of sexual harassment and answer the following questions.

a. Do you agree that this situation could lead to allegations of sexual harassment? If so, identify whether this behavior would be classified as quid pro quo or hostile work environment.
b. Use the guidelines in the text on pages 118–119 to decide how you would respond if you were the recipient of the harassment.

10. Invitation to Insight

Explore your present level of nonverbal effectiveness and how you might improve it.

a. Using the format on the next page, identify an important business or professional context from your life (e.g., in meetings, with customers, on the phone). If you are not currently working, choose a context from school (e.g., in class discussions, meeting with professors).
b. Using the information in this chapter, describe in the format on the next page both the aspects of your nonverbal behavior that are effective and also those you could improve.
c. Interview someone who has seen you operate in the context you are analyzing (e.g., a colleague, supervisor, professor, fellow student). Explain the types of nonverbal behavior described on pages 105–115. Then learn your interviewee's opinion of your effective nonverbal communication in this context, and how you could communicate more effectively.
d. Based on the information you have compiled, develop an action plan that describes how you can improve your nonverbal effectiveness in the context you are analyzing.

Context _____

	Effective	Could Do Better (Describe How)
Self-appraisal		
Other's appraisal		
Action plan	1.	
	2.	
	etc.	

resources

For extensive readings and Web sites on verbal and nonverbal communication, see the Online Learning Center Web site at **www.mhhe.com/adler10e.**

Interpersonal Skills

chapter outline

Building Positive Relationships
  Communication Climate
  Giving Praise

Dealing with Criticism
  Offering Constructive Feedback
  Responding to Criticism

Managing Conflict
  What Are Conflicts About?
  Approaches to Conflict
  Handling Conflicts Constructively
  Win–Win Problem Solving in Action

Review Points
Key Terms
Activities
Resources

chapter objectives

After reading this chapter you should be able to

1. Describe the communication climate in a working environment, identify the messages that have helped create it, and suggest ways of communicating that can improve that climate.
2. Use the guidelines in this chapter to give effective praise and constructive feedback.
3. Use the guidelines in this chapter to respond to criticism in a nondefensive manner.
4. Identify various approaches to conflict and steps to conflict management.
5. Describe four styles of negotiating solutions in work-related conflicts and predict likely consequences of using each style.
6. Demonstrate how to seek a win–win solution in a work-related negotiation.

What does it take to succeed in your career? Talent, good ideas, a good education, technical expertise, skills, hard work, motivation, initiative—all of these are important. In addition, because all jobs require you to get things done with other people—co-workers, customers, managers, people in other companies—career success also depends on your ability to communicate effectively. That ability, often called people skills, is the ability to work with other people, contribute to a positive climate, give and receive feedback, and handle conflicts so that you can do your job effectively.

Building Positive Relationships

Numerous studies have revealed just how important communication skills are in a career. In one survey, 1,000 personnel directors in the United States were asked to describe the "ideal management profile." The number-one characteristic was "ability to work well with others one-on-one."[1] Even CEOs who manage technical workers need people skills to succeed, and poor interpersonal skills are often blamed for "derailed" CEOs.[2]

The ability to work well with others is just as important for newcomers as it is for managers. A survey of chief executive officers and human resource managers from leading organizations rated the ability to work cooperatively with others as a most desirable quality in college graduates.[3] Good interpersonal communication skills are important in careers as diverse as medicine, engineering, real estate, and franchise management.[4]

Everyone can tell stories about co-workers, bosses, and customers whose communication style made life unpleasant. Table 5–1 on page 126 details some types of communication that surveys have found are especially unpleasant. You can probably recognize at least some of these behaviors in people you have worked with, and possibly even in yourself.

Former Chrysler chairman Lee Iacocca summed up the importance of maintaining good interpersonal working relationships when he said,

Table 5–1	Some Communication Traits of Unpleasant Co-workers

Busybody

- Butts in to conversations
- Butts in to others' business
- Expresses opinion on matters that don't concern him/her

Controlling/Bossy

- Tries to control, boss others around
- Gives orders without having the proper authority
- Is condescending/talks down to others
- Wants his/her own way

Self-promotion

- Competitive, wants to be number one
- Tries to promote him/herself
- Is self-centered
- Tries to make him/herself look good

Unprofessional Behavior

- Is rude
- Gossips and bad-mouths others to a third party
- Criticizes others
- Yells or screams

Unprofessional Focus of Attention

- Talks about personal problems at work
- Brings personal problems to work
- Talks about non-work-related issues

Distracting

- Distracts others from work
- Behaves in irritating ways

Defensive and Judgmental

- Sees others as a threat to his/her job
- Attacks others' behavior and judgments
- Critical, rather than constructive

Source: After J. M. H. Fritz, "How Do I Dislike Thee? Let Me Count the Ways: Constructing Impressions of Troublesome Others at Work," *Management Communication Quarterly* 15 (2003), pp. 410–38.

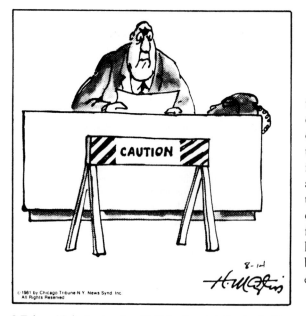

There's one phrase I hate to see on any executive's evaluation, no matter how talented he may be, and that's the line: "He has trouble getting along with other people." To me that's the kiss of death.[5]

Some social scientists have coined the terms **emotional intelligence (EQ)** and **social intelligence** to describe the ability and skills of interacting well with others.[6] According to emerging research, cognitive IQ takes a backseat to emotional intelligence in determining outstanding job performance.[7] Across the world and across the job spectrum, from copier repair technicians to scientists, IQ accounts for no more than 25 percent of entrepreneurial failure and success. The more difficult the job and the higher it is in an organization's hierarchy, the more important emotional intelligence becomes. Consultant Robert Dilenschneider contrasts emotional intelligence with intellectual aptitude:

Your cognitive IQ could be 145, and you could get a doctorate in business, but you'll never break away from the pack unless your interpersonal skills are top-drawer.[8]

Boss's Angry E-mail Sends Shares Plunging

A chief executive who sent his staff an email accusing them of being lazy and threatening them with the sack has seen the share price of his company plummet after his message was posted on the Internet.

In the three days after publication of his outburst—which gave managers a two-week ultimatum to shape up—stock in the American health care company dropped by 22 per cent over concerns about staff morale. It is now trading at more than a third less than it was before the email was sent. Neal Patterson, head of the Cerner Corporation, based in Kansas City, has spent the past three weeks trying to assuage investors.

His email to managers read: "We are getting less than 40 hours of work from a large number of our EMPLOYEES. The parking lot is sparsely used at 8am; likewise at 5pm. As managers, you either do not know what your EMPLOYEES are doing or you do not CARE. In either case, you have a problem and you will fix it or I will replace you."

His email read: "NEVER in my career have I allowed a team which worked for me to think they had a 40-hour job. I have allowed YOU to create a culture which is permitting this. NO LONGER." He added that "hell will freeze over" before he increased employee benefits. He wanted to see the car park nearly full by 7.30am and half full at weekends. He wrote: "You have two weeks. Tick, tock."

A week later, the email appeared on a Yahoo financial message board and Wall Street analysts began receiving calls from worried shareholders. Stephen Davas of Goldman Sachs said: "It raised two real questions for investors. Has anything changed at Cerner to cause such a seemingly violent reaction? And is this a chief executive that investors are comfortable with?"

CRITICAL ANALYSIS: As you think about this case, consider the following questions:

1. Which of the types of disconfirming communication described on page 128 does this memo exhibit? How would you expect employees who read this memo to react?

2. Construct an alternate memo expressing the same concerns, but using more confirming language.

3. Describe how a situation in your experience could have been handled using either confirming or disconfirming communication.

Source: Daily Telegraph of London, April 6, 2001.

Communication Climate

Social scientists use the term **communication climate** to describe the quality of personal relationships in an organization. Do people feel respected? Do they trust one another? Do they believe that they are appreciated? Organizations create an overall climate, which can be healthy or polluted, but within that environment individual relationships have their own microclimates. For example, your interactions with one colleague might be described as icy, while you and another person enjoy a warm relationship. There's no question that communication climate is a key factor in job satisfaction and commitment to the organization.[9] For this reason, communicators need to understand how to create positive climates.

The climate of an organization comes not so much from the specific tasks that members perform as from the feelings they have about those tasks and one another. In fact, a positive climate can exist under the worst working conditions: in a cramped, poorly furnished, understaffed office; during the graveyard shift of an urban newspaper; or even in a road gang cleaning up trash by the highway. Conversely, the most comfortable, prestigious settings can be polluted by a hostile climate. (See the Case Study above for an example of a hostile organizational climate.)

While communication climates are created by a variety of messages, they do share a common denominator. Positive climates result when people believe they are valued, and negative climates occur when people don't believe they are appreciated. Scholars have labeled messages that express feelings of value as **confirming** and those that fail to express value—or that explicitly show a lack of value—as **disconfirming**.[10] Psychologist Jack Gibb described six kinds of messages that are likely to promote a supportive, confirming climate and six types of disconfirming messages that are likely to generate a defensive climate (see Table 5–2). Gibb's supportive categories provide a list of ways to promote positive, confirming relationships.

Use Descriptive "I" Language

Many communicators unnecessarily attack the other person when delivering a message:

"Your report is too sloppy. You'll have to clean it up."

"You're always late."

"That was a dumb promise you made. We can never have the job done by the end of the month."

Statements like these are often called **"you" language** because they point a verbal finger of accusation at the receiver: "You're lazy." "You're wrong." By contrast, **descriptive statements** are often termed **"I" language** since they focus on the speaker instead of judging the other person. Notice how each of the evaluative statements above can be rephrased in descriptive "I" language:

"I'll take the blame if we turn in a report with this many errors. We'll get a better reaction if it's retyped."

"Since you've been coming in late, I've made a lot of excuses when people call asking for you. That's why I need you to start showing up on time."

"I'm worried about the promise you made. I don't see how we can get the job done by the end of the month."

Statements like these show that it's possible to be nonjudgmental and still say what you want without landing any verbal punches. In fact, descriptive statements like the

Table 5–2	Confirming and Disconfirming Message Identifiers
Supportive, Confirming Messages Are	**Defense-Arousing, Disconfirming Messages Are**
Descriptive (Use "I" language)	Evaluative
Focused on solving the problem	Controlling
Honest	Manipulative
Concerned with another's position	Indifferent
Equal	Superior
Open-minded, provisional	Dogmatic, certain

Is Total Honesty Always the Best Policy?

In principle, few people would dispute the ethical principle that honesty is the best policy. At the same time, it is hard to imagine a world in which everyone told the whole truth all the time.

Explore how you can reconcile the need to be honest with other goals by re-creating a list of all the opportunities you had to tell the truth during a typical day. Identify each occasion when you chose to either:

1. Tell even a partial lie (e.g., saying "Nothing's wrong" when you are bothered).
2. Hedge the truth by equivocating (e.g., saying "That's an unusual idea" instead of saying "I don't think that idea will work").
3. Keep quiet instead of volunteering the truth.

Based on your self-analysis, construct a principled yet pragmatic code of ethics involving honesty.

---

ones you just read are *more* complete than are typical everyday complaints since they express both the speaker's feelings and the reason for bringing up the matter—things most evaluative remarks don't do.

Focus on Solving Problems, Not Controlling Others   Even if you're in charge, others can get defensive if you force them to accept an idea they don't agree with or understand. If you're up against a tight deadline it's easy to say, "Just do it my way." Because control shows a lack of regard for the other person's needs, interests, or opinions, it can cause problems in the relationship even if it gets you what you want now.

In contrast, **problem-oriented messages** aim at solving both persons' needs. The goal isn't to solve a problem my way or your way but rather to develop a solution that meets everyone's needs. You will learn more about how to achieve problem-oriented solutions when we discuss win–win negotiating strategies later in this chapter.

Be Honest: Don't Manipulate   Once people discover that they have been manipulated, a defensive reaction is almost guaranteed. As Roger Fisher and Scott Brown explain, "If one statement of mine in a hundred is false, you may choose not to rely on me at all. Unless you can develop a theory of when I am honest and when I am not, your discovery of a small dishonesty will cast doubt over everything I say and do."[11]

By contrast, simple honesty is less likely to generate defensiveness, even when the news isn't welcome. Even though others might sometimes dislike what you have to say, your reputation for candor can earn you the respect of subordinates, co-workers, and management. (See the Case Study on page 57 in Chapter 2 for an example of how honesty in a difficult situation can produce good results.)

Show Concern for Others   Indifference—lack of acknowledgment or concern for others—is a strong disconfirming message. By contrast, a genuine message

"I'll take care of it impersonally."

on your feet

of interest can make a tremendous difference. A simple apology for making you wait can do wonders. The customer support agent who takes the time to find the right person to answer your questions can leave you feeling grateful and worthwhile, encouraging you to do business with that company again. The manager who seems genuinely concerned with your opinions—even if she doesn't agree with them—is easier to work with than one who brushes your concerns aside.

Demonstrate an Attitude of Equality

Neither talents nor job titles justify arrogance. Al Neuharth, founder of *USA Today*, earned a reputation as a tough, abrasive boss. His superior, evaluative comments like the following one suggest why: "When I criticize a female or when I criticize a grossly overweight person or anybody else, it's because, damn it, I think they ought to do better, just as I do."[12]

The essence of a more positive attitude is *respect*. Communication expert Kerry Patterson explains that respect is essential, just like the air we breathe: "If you take it away, it's all people can think about. At that point, the conversation is all about defending dignity."[13] Respect often comes from how we construct messages. Consider, for example, the difference between saying "Could you get me the files?" and demanding, "Get me the files." As this example illustrates, *how* we speak and act can be more important than the words themselves. Pay close attention not only to what you say but also to your nonverbal behavior, including your vocal tone and facial expression, when expressing yourself.

Keep an Open Mind

Listening with an open mind makes good sense. Whether the people you're dealing with are in your department or another, subordinates or customers, they probably have knowledge that you don't. Hearing them out may teach you something useful. Besides providing useful information, listening open-mindedly can promote good relationships. Take a moment and reflect on how much more you value people who consider your ideas carefully than those who dismiss them.

A tentative approach also works well when you are bringing up ideas. Paradoxically, you may get a better hearing if you present them as ideas, not facts. As one business

Respecting Spirituality in the Workplace

Research shows that spiritual practices can increase integrity and purposefulness, while decreasing stress and burnout. The challenge, of course, is to respect the rights and sensibilities of all employees and customers.

Here are some guidelines:

1. **Treat all faiths equally.** If an organization creates opportunity for any spiritual practices by its employees, it must welcome all equally. Some organizations create "quiet rooms" that can be used for prayers or meditation by people of all persuasions.

2. **Draw clear boundaries.** Personal practices and conversations are private matters. It isn't appropriate to make your beliefs an overt part of work. Open proselytizing is never acceptable. Neither is pressuring fellow workers to use any practice (such as prayer or meditation), even if it has been shown to be useful. Religious symbols, art, or sayings in public areas can create discomfort. In personal work spaces, discretion is the best principle.

3. **Don't be judgmental.** Sooner or later you will encounter beliefs that are contrary to yours. If you can't listen respectfully to beliefs that are different than yours, the best approach is to remove yourself from the situation as soon as possible.

4. **Defuse hot-button issues promptly.** Controversies are bound to arise. One person's idea of what is or isn't appropriate can offend someone else. If possible, the best way to resolve matters is via direct problem-solving among the people involved. (See the tips on pages 146–149 of this chapter for ideas.) If necessary, bringing in management or some other third party to help work out a constructive solution is far better than letting hostility escalate.

Source: P. M. Sullivan, "Spiritual Etiquette at Work," *Workforce Management*. Online at **http://www.workforce.com/section/09/feature/25/96/27/index.html.**

newsletter put it, "There's a certain irony here—the more forceful we are, the less influential we're likely to be."[14]

Giving Praise

There's truth to the old saying, You can catch more flies with honey than with vinegar. Sincere praise, delivered skillfully, can work wonders. The following tips can help make sure praise gets the desired results.

Praise Promptly The more quickly you can provide positive feedback, the more meaningful it will be. It doesn't take much time to praise positive behavior, and the results will most likely be well worth the investment.

Make Praise Specific Almost any sincere praise will be appreciated, but describing exactly *what* you appreciate makes it easier for the other person to continue that behavior. Notice how the following specific compliments add clarity:

Broad	Specific
Good job on handling that complaint.	You really kept your voice soft and spoke slowly when the customer complained.
I appreciate the support you've given me lately.	Thanks for being so flexible with my schedule while I was sick.
You've really been on top of your work lately.	You've finished every job this month within 2 days.

Being specific doesn't mean you have to avoid giving broad comments like the ones above. But along with giving general praise, consider the value of adding enough particulars to help the other person understand exactly what you appreciate.

Praise Progress, Not Just Perfection   You might wonder whether some people do much of anything that deserves sincere praise. If you look for outstanding performance, the answer may be no; but you can still deliver genuine compliments by looking for progress. Consider a few examples:

> "This draft of the report is a lot clearer. Adding a detailed budget really helps explain where the money will go. I think the same kind of detail would help make the schedule clearer."

> "I know we still see things differently, but I'm glad we were able to work so well together on the Baretti job."

Praise Intermittently   Too much praise can become as uncomfortable as too much rich food or too many jokes. Constant praise is also likely to sound insincere. In addition, social scientists have discovered that it isn't even as effective as occasional compliments. Praise others from time to time, when your remarks will have the best effect, but don't go overboard.

Relay Praise   If you already believe that complimenting someone sincerely can improve the communication climate in your relationship, wait until you see the benefits of singing their praises to others who deserve to know. You will win the gratitude of the person you are complimenting; you will show your own sense of security and team spirit; and you will be informing others about information they will probably find valuable. Praising others takes little time, and it benefits everyone.

You can also become a "praise messenger" by letting people know that you've heard others saying complimentary things about them. They will be more likely to continue the behavior, and they will feel better both about the person who praised them and about you for delivering the good news.

Praise Sincerely   Insincere praise is worse than no praise at all. It casts doubt on all your other compliments. It suggests that you can't think of anything the other person has done that deserves genuine acknowledgment, and it suggests that you think the recipient is naive enough to believe in your phony compliments.

When You Can't Think of Praise

think of anything about another person's performance to praise?

The value of praise is clear, and the guidelines in this section offer advice for when and how to compliment others. But what can you do when you cannot

As you consider when and how to praise, it is important to be aware of the cultural rules that may influence both the person receiving compliments and the audience to whom you are delivering them. In some collectivist cultures, it can be embarrassing to be singled out for praise, especially in front of others. In such cases, giving private reinforcement is probably wiser than lavishing compliments publicly.

Dealing with Criticism

Praise is a pleasure to give and receive, but it isn't always possible. In the real world of work, criticism is a fact of life. Sometimes you have to deliver a complaint, and other times you are on the receiving end of others' gripes. Either way, criticism can start a cycle of defensiveness that pollutes the communication climate between people or working groups. Despite their risks, critical messages don't have to create problems. With enough skill, you can learn to both deliver and respond to them in ways that can maintain—or even improve—working relationships.

Offering Constructive Feedback

Despite its faultfinding nature, criticism doesn't have to trigger a defensive reaction. As Table 5-3 on page 134 illustrates, the way you present your comments can make the difference between their being accepted and considered or being disputed and rejected.[15] You can maximize the chances of your comments being understood and accepted by carefully considering how they can be expressed.

Consider the Content The first concern is to edit your remarks so that they follow some important guidelines:

- *Limit the criticism to one topic.* You may have several complaints, but it is smart to focus on only one at a time. Your respondent may be able to handle a single problem, but he or she could grow understandably defensive if you pile on one gripe after another.

- *Make sure the criticism is accurate.* Be absolutely sure you get the facts straight before speaking out. If even a small detail is out of line, the other person can argue about that, sidetracking the discussion from the real problem at hand.

- *Define the problem clearly.* List the facts in enough detail that the recipient knows exactly what you are talking about. Be prepared to give some examples to back up your point, but don't overwhelm the other person with an avalanche of examples.

- *Show how your criticism can benefit the recipient.* Whenever possible, describe the payoffs for responding to your remarks. At the very least, the other person will get you off his or her back by heeding your complaints!

Table 5–3   Characteristics of Constructive Feedback

1. It is descriptive . . .

Tim, I like your report. The style was clear and concise and your ideas were organized logically. The documentation you used made the problem credible and vivid.

. . . not evaluative.

Tim, that was a terrific report.

2. It focuses on behavior . . .

Tim, slow down a little bit, and I think you can reduce the number of errors.

. . . not on personal characteristics.

Tim, you could be a lot faster on that machine if you were better coordinated.

3. It is specific . . .

Tim, I couldn't hear you from where I was sitting.

. . . not general.

Tim, your voice isn't effective.

4. It is timed appropriately . . .

Tim, let's get together around 2:00 p.m. and talk about your progress on the AMF.

. . . not delayed or left to chance.

Let's get together sometime.

5. It is offered . . .

Tim, perhaps my reactions to your report would help you in preparing for next week's meeting. Would you like to get together sometime this afternoon?

. . . not imposed.

Tim, I've got talk with you about that report before you give it at our meeting next week.

Source: J. Brownell, *Listening: Attitudes, Principles, and Skills,* 3rd ed. (Boston: Pearson Education, Inc., 2006), p. 23.

Consider the Sender   Who delivers the criticism can be as important as the content of the remarks. Two guidelines will help you in this area:

- *Choose the most credible critic.* Sometimes the recipient will be more receptive to one person than to another. If a choice is available, make sure that the message comes from whoever can deliver it most effectively.

- *Make sure the criticism is appropriate to the critic's role.* Even accurate criticism is likely to be rejected if you have no business delivering it. For example, most comments about someone's personal life are out of place unless they affect a working relationship. Job-related comments should be appropriate for your relationship to the other person.

Consider the Relational Climate   The framework in which your remarks are delivered can have an important impact on how they are received. Paying attention to three context-related factors can boost the odds of getting the desired reaction:

- *Deliver remarks as part of a positive relationship.* Let the other person know that your specific criticism doesn't diminish your respect or appreciation for the person in other areas. Sincerely acknowledging the positives can make the negatives easier to accept.

- *Accept partial responsibility for the problem.* If possible, show that you may have contributed in some degree to the issue. If nothing else, you might be able to say, "I probably should have brought this up sooner."

- *Accompany your criticism with an offer to help.* You can earn the goodwill of the other person by offering to play a role in solving the problem at hand.

Consider the Delivery   How you express a criticism can make a big difference in the way it is received. Two delivery-related guidelines can help:

- *Deliver criticism in a face-saving manner.* Probably the most important consideration is to make sure your remarks are delivered privately. Criticizing someone in front of others is likely to trigger resentment and embarrassment.

- *Avoid sounding and looking judgmental.* Avoid using the kind of emotive language described in Chapter 4. Don't call names or use inflammatory labels, and don't attribute motives to the other person. Try to use the kind of descriptive "I" language described earlier in this chapter instead of defense-arousing "you" statements. Avoid condescending nonverbal behaviors such as shaking your finger, raising your voice, or rolling your eyes.

Responding to Criticism

When people are faced with criticism, the two most common responses are "fight" and "flight." Fighters react by counterattacking and blaming others: "I'm not the only one who's at fault here." Your own experience probably shows that fighting with your critics seldom persuades them to back down.

Most businesspeople are too mature to actually run away from a critic, but there are other ways of evading negative remarks. Sometimes you *can* physically avoid critics—steering clear of their offices or not returning their phone calls, for example. Even when you can't escape unpleasant remarks, you can mentally disengage by refusing to listen thoughtfully to the criticism. While keeping quiet can seem to work in the short run, it is seldom a satisfying way to deal with an ongoing relationship in which you are constantly under attack.

Since neither fighting nor fleeing is likely to satisfy your critics or help you understand legitimate criticism, you need alternatives that allow you to listen nondefensively without losing face. Fortunately, two such alternatives exist.

Seek More Information   Asking your critic to explain the problem gives you a constructive option to fighting or fleeing. By asking your critic for more information, you are showing that you take the criticism seriously, but at the same time, you aren't accepting blame for the problem. There are several ways to seek more information:

- *Ask for examples or clarification.* "You've said I'm not presenting a good attitude to customers. Can you describe exactly what I'm doing?"

- *Guess about details of the criticism.* Even if the critic isn't willing or able to offer specifics, you can guess: "Was it the way I handled Mr. Tyson when the bank sent back his check for insufficient funds?"

- *Paraphrase the critic.* "When you say I have a bad attitude toward customers, it sounds like you think I'm not giving them the service they deserve."

- *Ask what the critic wants.* "How do you think I should behave differently around customers?"

It can be hard to listen sincerely when you are being criticized. But it's easier to keep your cool if you realize that trying to understand the objections doesn't mean you have to agree with them—at least not at this point. You may find that keeping notes of your critic's comments can give you something to do besides defend yourself. In addtion, this approach will show your critic that you take his or her comments seriously.

career tip

The Art of the Apology

When you have made a mistake, nothing is as honest and potentially effective as a genuine apology. Besides being the right thing to do, apologizing can be a smart business strategy. Research suggests that sincerely acknowledging mistakes can drastically reduce both resentment and legal actions by offended parties.[16]

A complete apology contains several elements:

- *Sincere regret.* The fundamental part of an apology is a genuine expression of regret. "I feel bad about not showing up for yesterday's shift. I'm really sorry I let you down."

- *Understanding that the person suffered harm.* Show that you recognize how the other person was affected and that you're sorry. "I know it was busy, and it must have been a nightmare."

- *An explanation of what happened.* Without offering excuses, consider explaining how the offending behavior came to happen. "I got a panicky call from my grandmother, and felt like I had to get over there and see what the matter was. It turned out to be nothing, but by the time I got her calmed down it was too late to call you."

- *Corrective action.* Show that you intend to prevent future problems. "I've asked her to call my sister if anything like this happens again, so unless there's a real emergency there shouldn't be any more problems like this."

- *Restoration.* Do what you can to compensate the other person for the misdeed. "If it would help, I'm happy to cover tomorrow's shift, even though I'm not scheduled."

Source: After Patrick J. Kiger, "The Art of the Apology," *Workforce Management,* October 2004, pp. 57–62.

Agree with the Criticism   An obvious but often overlooked way of responding is to agree with the criticism. Although this approach might seem like a form of self-punishment, it can be extremely effective. There are three ways to agree with a critic:

- *Agree with the facts.* Sometimes you are confronted with facts that can't be disputed. In these cases, your best approach is probably to face up to the truth: "You're right. I *have* been late three times this week." Notice that agreeing with the facts doesn't mean that you are accepting responsibility for every imaginable fault. In the case of being late to work, you might go on to point out that your lateness is a fluke in an otherwise spotless work record; but arguing with indisputable information isn't likely to satisfy your critic, and it will probably make you look bad.

- *Agree with the critic's right to his or her own perception.* Sometimes you can't honestly agree with the criticism. For example, a customer might unjustly accuse you of not caring about good service. After asking for more information to find out the basis of the criticism (a shipment didn't arrive on time, for example), you can acknowledge how the other person might view you as being at fault: "I can understand why it might seem that I don't care about your needs. After all, you did tell me that you absolutely had to have that shipment by last

© 1996 Ted Goff www.tedgoff.com

136

Friday, and I told you that it would be there. I'd be mad too if I were you." Notice that agreeing with the perception doesn't require you to *accept* your critic's evaluation as accurate, although you might indeed find that it does have some merit. What you are doing is acknowledging the other person's right to view the issue in a way that may differ from yours; you are agreeing that you can see how their perception makes sense to them, whether or not you see it the same way.

- *Emphasize areas of common ground.* As much as possible, point out areas where you and the other person share the same point of view. For example:

  Critic: The customers will never go for this idea!

  Response: We *do* have to keep the customers satisfied. What if we test market the idea? If they hate it, of course I'll drop the suggestion.

  Even when the criticism is extreme, you can probably find something in the other person's position to agree with:

  Hysterical Critic: You're going to ruin the whole job!

  Response: I know how important it is to you. (Then let the critic talk about the job's importance, reinforcing your agreement.)

Work for a Cooperative Solution Once your critic believes that you've understood his or her position and acknowledged at least some parts of it, he or she will be as ready as possible to hear your point of view. A few strategies can maximize the chances for a constructive solution.[17]

- *Ask for the chance to state your point of view.* If you push ahead and state your position before the critic is ready to listen, your words probably won't get through. It's far more productive to give your critic a thorough hearing, agree with whatever points you can, and then ask, "May I tell you my perspective?" Doing so won't guarantee that you'll get a respectful hearing, but it gives you the best chance of one.

- *Focus on a solution, not on finding fault.* Your own experience will show that playing the blame game rarely works. A far more productive approach is to focus on finding a solution that will work for both you and the critic by asking, "What would make this situation better?" or "How can we handle this situation in a way that both of us can accept?"

Managing Conflict

Like it or not, conflict is part of every job. In one study, human resource managers reported spending up to 60 percent of their time dealing with employee disputes, and over half of the workers said they lost time at work worrying about past confrontations or fretting about future conflicts.[18]

To most people, the fewer conflicts, the better. But since conflict is unavoidable, an inability or refusal to face problems can lead to job-hopping. Brenda Richard, director of human resources for the Radisson Hotel New Orleans, describes people who fit this pattern: "They don't want to solve problems, they don't want conflict."[19] The problem isn't conflict itself, but rather *the way in which it is handled*. With the right approach, conflict can produce good results. Management consultant and Harvard Medical School psychologist Steven Berglos argues flatly that constructive conflict is an essential ingredient in organizational success:

> If you're not looking for ways to promote healthful conflict between people of different backgrounds who cannot possibly see the world the same way, don't be surprised if anarchy ensues or if the best and the brightest abandon you.[20]

In Chinese, the ideogram for the word *crisis* is made up of two characters: danger and opportunity. A poorly handled organizational conflict can certainly be dangerous; relationships suffer and productivity declines. On the other hand, a skillfully handled conflict can result in several benefits.[21] It can function as a safety valve, letting people ventilate frustrations that are blocking their effective functioning, and it can lead to solving troublesome problems.

What Are Conflicts About?

Conflicts fall into several categories.[22] To understand them all, take another look at the dispute between business partners Marissa and Tran described in the "Computer Solutions" case study on page 66.

The Topic at Hand   The most obvious source of conflicts is the subject at hand. Topic-related disagreements are a fact of life in the workplace. They involve issues including

pay and other compensation	level of autonomy
resources	the quality of products and services
scheduling and job assignments	budgeting

The Process   Some disputes are more about *how* to do something than what to do. For example,

> A project team might all agree that the work at hand needs to be divided up, but they could disagree on how to decide who does what.

> Members of a community nonprofit group might decide to hold a fundraiser, but disagree on how to choose the type of event.

In the Computer Solutions case study, Tran and Marissa know they need to resolve their feelings about each other's contributions to the partnership, but each has trouble deciding how to proceed. Marissa wants to bring in an outside expert to mediate the problem, whereas Tran thinks they could work out the problems without any outsiders getting involved. So, the process has become a second area of conflict.

Relational Issues   As you read in Chapter 1, along with substantive content issues are *relational* disputes that center on how parties want to be treated by one another. Relational issues can involve control, affinity, and respect.

> Are we a big family, or are we a group of professionals who keep our personal lives separate from work? (affinity)

Should the company allow employees to book their own hotels and flights on business trips as long as costs are within the organization's cost guidelines? (respect, control)

Does management really welcome ideas from rank-and-file employees, or is the suggestion box just a prop? (respect, control)

In the Computer Solutions case, Marissa and Tran aren't just disagreeing about who is working harder. As the conflict escalates, each is probably feeling disrespected and resentful. Unless they can address and resolve these feelings, equalizing the workload won't resolve their conflict.

Ego/Identity Issues   Social scientists use the term "face" to describe the identity each of us strives to present. In a work context, most people try to present a face of

competence	honesty
commitment	reasonableness
fairness	professionalism

Relationships do well when others acknowledge our presenting face, and conflicts intensify when others communicate in face-threatening ways.[23] Marissa's calling Tran a "sexist nerd" is an obvious face-threatening attack. Such accusations open a whole new front in the dispute, in addition to the original disagreement about equalizing the workload.

Even though the four types of conflicts are listed separately here, most disputes involve a combination of issues. As the preceding paragraphs show, Tran and Marissa have conflicts in each area. When you deal with a conflict, it's important to explore all of the dimensions on which it operates.

Approaches to Conflict

When faced with a conflict, you have several choices about how to respond. Each of these approaches has different results.[24]

Avoiding   One way to deal with conflict is to avoid it whenever possible and withdraw when confronted. In some cases, avoidance is physical: refusing to take phone calls, staying barricaded in the office, and so on. In other cases, however, avoidance can be psychological: denying that a problem exists or that it is serious, repressing emotional reactions, and so on. In the workplace, a communicator who avoids conflicts might accept constant schedule delays or poor-quality work from a supplier to avoid a confrontation or might pretend not to see a co-worker's dishonest behavior. As these examples suggest, avoidance may have the short-term benefit of preventing a confrontation, but there are usually long-term costs, especially in ongoing relationships. "I think it's better to face whatever the conflict is head on and deal with the situation as it comes up and not side-step it or go to someone else about the problem," advises Jean Stefani, a senior operations analyst at Comcast Communication.[25]

Despite its drawbacks, avoidance may sometimes be a wise choice. Table 5–4 on page 141 lists some circumstances in which keeping quiet may be the most appropriate course of action. For example, when standing up for your rights would be hopeless, silence might be the best policy. You might simply tolerate a superior's unreasonable demands while you look for a new job, or you might steer clear of an angry co-worker who is out to get you. In many cases, however, avoidance has unacceptable costs: You lose self-respect, you become frustrated, and the problem may only get worse.

Accommodating

Whereas avoiders stay away from conflicts, accommodators give ground as a way of maintaining harmony. It can be equivalent to appeasement, sacrificing one's principles, and putting harmony above dealing with important issues. In her fascinating book *Talking from 9 to 5*, sociolinguist Deborah Tannen describes an extreme case in which accommodating led to disaster.[26] On January 13, 1982, Air Florida flight 90 crashed shortly after takeoff from Ronald Reagan National Airport in Washington, DC; 69 passengers were killed. The cause of the disaster was excessive ice on the airplane's wings. An analysis of cockpit recordings made on the heavily armored black box recovered after the accident revealed that the co-pilot had hinted about excessive ice several times to the pilot before takeoff but that his suggestions went unheeded. The command structure of aircraft operations dictates that the pilot has the final word on whether a plane is fit to fly. It is easy to imagine that a less accommodating approach might have caused the pilot to recheck the situation before making what turned out to be a catastrophic decision.

"It's not enough that we succeed, Cats must also fail."

Though it has obvious drawbacks, accommodating does have merit in some circumstances (see Table 5-4). If you are clearly wrong, then giving up your original position can be a sign of strength, not weakness. If harmony is more important than the issue at hand—especially if the issue is a minor one—then accommodating is probably justified. For example, if you don't care strongly whether the new stationery is printed on cream or gray paper and fighting for one color might be a big concern for others, then giving in is probably smart. Finally, you might accommodate if satisfying the other person is important enough to your welfare. You might, for example, put up with an overly demanding customer to make an important sale.

Competing

A competitive approach to conflicts is based on the assumption that the only way for one party to reach its goals is to overcome the other. This zero-sum approach is common in many negotiations, as you will see later in this chapter. Sometimes a power-based approach to conflict is based on simply disregarding the other person's concerns. Unsympathetic management might turn a deaf ear to the request of employees to make provisions for on-site exercise facilities, implying—or even stating outright—that the physical condition of employees is not the concern of the employer and that providing easy access to exercise would require a cash outlay and reduce time spent on the job.

In many cases, a competitive attitude is unnecessary. As the section of this chapter on win–win negotiating shows, it often *is* possible for both sides in a conflict to reach their goals (see pages 149–151). For instance, an employer might find that the cost of providing on-site exercise equipment is more than offset by reduced absenteeism and greater appeal when recruiting new employees. Furthermore, a competitive orientation

Table 5–4	Factors Governing Choice of a Conflict Style

Consider Avoiding
1. When an issue is genuinely trivial, or when more important issues are pressing.
2. When you have no chance of winning.
3. When the potential for disruption outweighs the benefits of resolution.
4. To let others cool down and regain perspective.
5. When the long-term costs of winning may outweigh short-term gains.
6. When others can resolve the conflict more effectively.

Consider Accommodating
1. When you find you are wrong.
2. When the issue is important to the other party and not important to you.
3. To build social credits for later issues.
4. To minimize loss when you are outmatched and losing.
5. When harmony and stability are more important than the subject at hand.
6. To allow others to learn by making their own mistakes.

Consider Competing
1. When quick, decisive action is vital (e.g., emergencies).
2. On important issues where unpopular actions need implementing (e.g., cost cutting, enforcing unpopular rules).
3. When others will take advantage of your noncompetitive behavior.

Consider Collaborating
1. To find solutions when both parties' concerns are too important to be compromised.
2. When a long-term relationship between the parties is important.
3. To gain commitment of all parties by building consensus.
4. When the other party is willing to take a collaborative approach.

Consider Compromising
1. When goals are important but not worth the effort or potential disruption of more assertive modes.
2. When opponents with equal power are committed to mutually exclusive goals.
3. To achieve temporary settlements of complex issues.
4. To arrive at expedient solutions under time pressure.
5. As a backup, when collaboration is unsuccessful.

Source: Kenneth W. Thomas, "Toward Multi-Dimensional Values in Teaching: The Example of Conflict Behavior," *Academy of Management Review* 2, no. 3 (1987), p. 487.

can generate ill will that is both costly and unpleasant. In our physical-fitness example, workers whose needs are ignored are likely to resent their employer and act in ways that ultimately wind up costing the company a great deal.

Despite its drawbacks, competition isn't always a bad approach. In some cases, an issue isn't important enough to spend time working it out. In other instances, there isn't time to collaborate on solutions. Finally, if others are determined to gain advantage at your expense, you might compete out of self-defense.

Instructions: Below are 15 statements that describe possible strategies for dealing with a conflict. Use the following scale to describe how you typically behave in conflicts.

1 = Always   2 = Usually   3 = Sometimes   4 = Not very often   5 = Rarely, if ever

____ a. I argue the merits of my position forcefully.

____ b. I try to work out compromises between my position and others.

____ c. I try to meet others' expectations as much as possible.

____ d. I try to explore differences with others in order to find solutions that are mutually acceptable.

____ e. I am firm in resolve when it comes to defending my side of the issue.

____ f. I prefer to avoid conflict, keeping disagreements to myself as much as possible.

____ g. I defend my solutions to problems.

____ h. I'm willing to compromise in order to reach solutions.

____ i. I like to exchange important information with others so our problems can be solved together.

____ j. I avoid discussing my differences with others.

____ k. I try to accommodate the wishes of my peers and colleagues.

____ l. I prefer to bring everyone's concerns out into the open in order to resolve disputes in the best possible way.

____ m. I advocate middle positions in efforts to break deadlocks.

____ n. I accept the recommendations of others about how to resolve conflicts.

____ o. I avoid hard feelings by keeping my feelings and ideas to myself.

Scoring

The 15 statements you just read are listed below under five categories. Each category contains the letters of 3 statements. Record the number you placed next to each statement. Calculate the total under each category.

Style				Total
Competing	a. ____	e. ____	g. ____	____
Collaborating	d. ____	i. ____	l. ____	____
Avoiding	f. ____	j. ____	o. ____	____
Accommodating	c. ____	k. ____	n. ____	____
Compromising	b. ____	h. ____	m. ____	____

Results

My dominant style is _____ (your **LOWEST** score)

and my back-up style is _____ (your second-lowest score).

Sources: Adapted from A. Falikowski, *Mastering Human Relations*, 4th ed. (Don Mills, Ontario, Canada: Pearson Education, 2007), and K. Hamilton, "What's Your Conflict Style?" http://webhome.idirect.com/~kehamilt/ipsyconstyle.html.

Collaborating   Rather than taking a competitive approach, collaborative communicators are committed to working together to resolve conflicts. Collaboration is based on the assumption that it is possible to meet one's own needs and those of the other person. This approach is reflected in Rabbi Hillel's statement, "If I am not for myself, who will be? If I am only for myself, what am I? If not now, when?"

Whereas avoiding and accommodating are based on the assumption that conflict should be avoided, and competing is based on the belief that conflict is a struggle, collaboration assumes that conflict is a natural part of life and that working with the other person will produce the best possible solution. The benefits of collaboration are clear: Not only can the issue at hand be resolved, but the relationship between the parties can also be improved.

Despite its advantages, collaborative communication isn't a panacea. It takes time to work with others, and a mutually satisfactory outcome isn't always possible. Furthermore, collaboration requires the cooperation of everyone involved. If the other party isn't disposed to work with you, then you may be setting yourself up for exploitation by communicating openly and offering to work cooperatively.

Compromising   In a **compromise,** each party sacrifices something he or she is seeking to gain an agreement. On one hand, this approach is cooperative, recognizing that both parties must agree to resolve a conflict. On the other, compromise is self-centered, since the parties act in their self-interest to get the best possible deal.

Compromise is a middle-range approach. It is more assertive than avoiding and accommodating yet less aggressive than competing. It is cooperative yet less so than collaboration. While it does not give any one of the parties in a dispute everything he or she seeks, it provides an outcome that, by definition, everyone involved can live with. As Table 5-4 shows, compromise may not be the perfect approach, but under many circumstances it produces the best possible outcome.

Handling Conflicts Constructively

When you avoid a conflict or accommodate another's demand, few communication skills are necessary. But if you decide to address an issue directly—either to collaborate, to compete, or to seek a compromise—you will need to negotiate.

Negotiation occurs when two or more parties—either individuals or groups—discuss specific proposals to find a mutually acceptable agreement. Although we don't always

technology tip

Managing Conflicts in Cyberspace

In a world where communicators are dispersed around the globe, conflicts often unfold online. The following tips can help you avoid unnecessary disagreements in cyberspace, and deal with them constructively when they arise.

1. **Reread the troublesome message, and share it with someone you trust.** Your first reaction to a message may be colored by how you're feeling at the time. Rereading it later may give you a different perspective. Sharing a troublesome message with someone whose judgment you trust can bring a new perspective. If you do share the message, use a printed version rather than forwarding any e-mails. This will reduce the chances of the message being forwarded electronically.

2. **Decide whether or not to respond.** The best response to some messages is no response at all. If the message directed at you is accusatory or inflammatory and the sender's style tends to be aggressive or bullying, the best strategy may be to ignore it.

3. **Don't respond right away.** When you are hurt or angry, it's tempting to respond immediately. Since you can't un-send a regrettable message, it's wise to hold on to a draft of your reply for at least 24 hours. The next day, see whether your message needs rewriting before sending.

4. **Compose your reply offline.** If you use the "Reply" function of your e-mail program to compose your response, you risk hitting the "Send" button before your message is complete. You can avoid this problem by composing your reply offline in a word processing program. When you are sure it's ready to send, copy and paste it into an e-mail.

Sources: Adapted from K. Monroe, "Conflict in Cyberspace," **www.kalimunro.com/article_conflict_online.html,** and J. Suler, "The Online Disinhibition Effect," *CyberPsychology and Behavior 7* (2004), pp. 321–26.

---

use the term, we negotiate every day. As one consultant explains, "Negotiations are seldom formal, sit-around-the-table affairs. In fact, almost any form of business problem or disagreement—from scheduling work shifts to 'Who's going to pay this $500 expense?'—is resolved by some form of negotiation."[27]

There's nothing magical about negotiation. When poorly handled, it can leave a problem still unsolved and perhaps worse than before. ("I tried to work things out, but he just tried to railroad me. I'm going to file a lawsuit this time.") When negotiation is handled skillfully, though, it can improve the position of one or even both parties. The remainder of this chapter will introduce communication strategies that can produce the best possible outcomes to your negotiations.

Negotiation Strategies and Outcomes   A common negotiating strategy is the competitive **win–lose** approach. It is based on the assumption that only one side can reach its goals and that any victory by that party will be matched by the other's loss. As Table 5-4 shows, you probably will need to take a competitive win–lose approach to protect your interests if others insist on gaining at your expense or when resources are truly scarce. For example, your company and another might compete for the same customers, and you might compete with another candidate for the same once-in-a-lifetime job.

Nobody seeks out **lose–lose** outcomes, but they can arise when competitors try to gain an advantage at one another's expense. Like armies that take mortal losses while trying to defeat their enemies, disputants who go for a competitive victory often find that they have hurt themselves as much as their opponents. For example, if you push for an unrealistically low price, you might antagonize the seller so much that you don't get the product you're seeking and the seller doesn't make the sale. On the job, feuding parties may ruin their own careers by gaining reputations as difficult employees or as poor team players.

Sometimes it seems better to *compromise* than to fight battles in a competitive manner and risk a lose-lose outcome. There certainly are cases in which compromise is the best obtainable outcome—usually when disputed resources are limited or scarce. If two managers each need a full-time assistant but budget restrictions make this impossible, they may have to compromise by sharing the services of one employee. While compromises may be necessary, they are less than ideal because both parties lose at least some of what they were seeking. Buyers, for instance, may pay more than they can afford, while sellers receive less than they need.

When negotiators collaborate, they can often—though not always—achieve a **win-win** outcome, in which everybody involved is satisfied. Win-win solutions are easiest when the needs of each party aren't incompatible, as in the following examples:

- *Shorter working hours.* Even though they were paid overtime, teachers at a preschool resented working weekends to keep school equipment clean and organized. A brainstorming session between the teachers and director produced a solution that satisfied everyone's needs: Substitutes covered for the teachers during some school hours while the teachers sorted and cleaned equipment. This approach had several benefits: Teachers' weekends were free, and teachers got a weekly change-of-pace from child care. Furthermore, the director welcomed the chance to observe the substitutes who were seeking full-time teaching jobs. She was also happy because the substitutes' pay was lower than the teachers' overtime.

- *Increasing employee compensation.* A contractor's employees wanted a raise. The contractor recognized that the employees deserved more, but couldn't afford to increase his payroll. After considering alternatives together, the boss and employees came up with a plan that pleased everyone. Workers were allowed to use company vehicles during nonworking hours, saving them the expense of an extra car or truck. The owner rented his vacation home to employees at a bargain rate. Finally, the boss negotiated lower prices for his employees on home furnishings and appliances at local merchants. These changes increased the employees' buying power—at little cost to the boss.

- *Blending business goals and community beauty.* A cellular phone company wanted to install a tower in the middle of a town, but residents didn't want an eyesore. The company agreed to build a long-needed new steeple for a local church, with the transmitter concealed inside. Furthermore, it paid the church $2,000 monthly rent. The result was a triple win: Expanded phone service, maintenance of the community's beauty, and both a new steeple and income for the church.[28]

As these few examples illustrate, the specific solutions that will work for a problem differ in each case. The important point is that parties working together *can* often find no-lose solutions to their problems. And, not surprisingly, research shows that a win-win approach is preferred to other problem-solving styles.[29] In one study, researchers compared the problem-solving styles used in six organizations. They found that the two highest-performing organizations used a win-win approach to a greater degree than did the less effective companies, while the lowest-performing organizations used that style less than the others.[30]

Win–win outcomes are ideal, but they aren't always realistic. Table 5–5 offers guidelines about when the chances are best for using this approach, as well as others.

Preparing to Negotiate

Successful negotiations begin before you say a word to the other person. You can take several steps to think out your position and approach your negotiating partners in a way that boosts the odds of getting your message across and getting a constructive response.

Clarify your interests and needs   Communicators can doom negotiations by prematurely focusing on means instead of ends. *Ends* are the goals you want, and *means* are ways of achieving those goals. In their best-selling book *Getting to Yes*, Roger Fisher and William Ury show that win–win results come from focusing on means instead of ends.[31] To illustrate the difference, we can adapt a story they tell.

Imagine a dispute between two office workers. John wants to open a window and Mary wants it closed. (This issue may seem trivial, but long-standing feuds have developed over smaller issues.) At this point the issue seems irreconcilable; but imagine that a colleague asks each worker what he wants. John replies, "To get some fresh air." To the same question, Mary replies, "To avoid a draft." "I have an idea," the mediating colleague suggests: "What if we open a window in the next room? That would give John the fresh air he needs and prevent the draft that Mary wants to avoid."

This simple example illustrates the difference between means and ends:

Issue	Ends	Means
John	Fresh air	Open window
		or
		Open window in adjoining room
Mary	No draft	Keep window closed
		or
		Open window in adjoining room

If Mary and John stayed focused on the first means that occurred to them, the issue would never be resolved to their satisfaction. But once they identified the ends each was seeking, the pathway to a mutually acceptable means was perfectly clear.

It's far better to identify the real end you are seeking and leave a discussion of means for later.

Consider the best time to raise the issue   Raising a difficult issue when the other person is tired, grumpy, or distracted by other business is likely to threaten the odds of getting the results you are seeking. Review the variables about chronological communication contexts in Chapter 1 (page 9) when you consider when to raise an issue.

Table 5–5	When to Use Competitive and Win-Win Negotiating Styles

Consider a Competitive Approach	Consider a Win–Win Approach
When your interests and the other party's clearly conflict.	When you and the other party have common interests.
When the other party insists on taking a win-lose approach.	When the other party is willing to consider a win–win approach.
When you do not need a long-term harmonious relationship.	When a continuing, harmonious relationship is important.
When you are powerful enough to prevail.	When you are weaker or power is approximately equal.
When short-term goals are more important.	When long-term goals are more important.

Table 5–6	Chinese and Western Negotiating Styles

Chinese	Western
Less direct communication (high context)	More direct communication (low context)
Incremental gains	Winner-takes-all
Finesse	Overt power
Avoidance of confrontation	Head-to-head disagreement expressed
Niche and local context focused	Broad-based and overall market dominance
Risk-averse	Prone to take bigger risks
Privacy valued	Transparent flow of information valued

Source: Adapted from M-J Chen, *Inside Chinese Business: A Guide for Managers Worldwide* (Boston: Harvard Business School Press, 2001), p. 119.

Consider cultural differences   As you plan your approach, consider the cultural sensibilities of your negotiating partners. As Chapter 2 explained in detail, the approach that seems comfortable to you may be quite alien to someone from a different background. Table 5–6 illustrates some of the differences that could distinguish the approaches of Western and Chinese negotiators.

Prepare your statement   Think over how you can best express yourself, following the advice for offering constructive feedback on pages 133–135 in this chapter. Practicing your message can help make your point quickly and clearly, and it will prevent you from blurting out an angry statement you'll regret later. When planning your remarks, be sure to think about how you can use "I" language instead of delivering defense-arousing "you" messages.

Rehearsing your statement doesn't mean you should memorize your remarks word for word; this approach would sound canned and insincere. Think about your general ideas and perhaps a few key phrases you'll use to make your ideas clear.

Conducting the Negotiation   The win–win approach is most successful when it follows the steps described below.

Identify the ends both parties are seeking   As you read earlier, seemingly irreconcilable conflicts can be resolved if negotiators focus on their needs, and not on positions. Consider the example of a parent who has found that the traditional work schedule isn't compatible with his child care responsibilities. Here are the ends that the employee and the boss identified:

Employee:	Make sure the children are cared for after school.
Boss:	Make sure employee's productivity doesn't drop.
Both:	Keep the employee on the job. Keep a positive relationship.

Brainstorm a list of possible solutions   Once both parties have identified the ends they are seeking, the next step is to develop a list of solutions that might satisfy each party's needs. Recall the problem-oriented approach introduced earlier in this chapter: Instead of working against one another (How can I defeat you?), the parties work together against the problem (How can we beat the problem?).

Consider again the case of the employee trying to have his child cared for after school. In this case, a number of potential win–win solutions are worth exploring:

- The employee could do some work at home during nonbusiness hours.
- The company could offer flexible work hours, so employees can get their jobs done when children are at school or being cared for by others.
- The employee could share his full-time position with another worker, giving the boss the coverage the boss needs and the employee the free time. If the employee needs additional income, he could take part-time work that could be done at home at his convenience.
- The boss could subsidize after-school child care, on the assumption that productivity would rise and absenteeism decline as children of employees are being cared for.

While not all of the above options are likely to be workable, the key to successful brainstorming is to avoid judging any possible solutions for the time being. Nothing deflates creativity and increases defensiveness as much as saying, "That won't work." You can judge the quality of each idea later; but for now, the key is quantity. Perhaps one person's unworkable idea will spark a productive suggestion.

Evaluate the alternative solutions   After brainstorming as many ideas as possible, decide which ones are most promising. During this stage, it is still critical to work for an answer that meets the important needs of all the parties. Cooperation will come only if everyone feels satisfied with the solution.

Implement and follow up on the solution   Once the best plan is chosen, make sure everyone understands it; then give it a try. Even the most appealing plans may need revision when put into action. After a reasonable amount of time, plan to meet

Ethical Communication Gets Positive Results

Stephen Covey, author of *The Seven Habits of Highly Effective People, Principle-Centered Leadership,* and *First Things First,* offers these guidelines for principled communication. Covey argues that, besides being ethical, this approach can increase your influence with others.

- *Refrain from saying the unkind or negative things.* When you are provoked or fatigued, the temptation to lash out at others is strong. Being kind under pressure will earn you the respect of others.

- *Distinguish between the person and the behavior or performance.* You may disapprove of bad behavior and poor performance, but separate your judgment of the work from the person who has done it.

- *Keep your promises.* Never make agreements unless you are prepared to keep them. Being known as a dependable person will generate trust that makes your word a powerful thing.

- *Reward open, honest expressions or questions.* Too often we punish honest, open expressions or questions. As a result others learn to hide their ideas, opinions, and feelings. You may not agree with someone, but you can always say, "Thank you for being honest with me."

- *Admit your mistakes.* Everyone makes mistakes. When you do, apologize. When personal problems occur, consider whether you are at least partly to blame. Resist the urge to offer excuses, explanations, or defenses: They rarely convince or impress anyone.

- *Accept the other person.* Nothing reinforces defensive behavior more than judgment, comparison, or rejection. Accepting others as they are frees them from the need to defend themselves. Acceptance doesn't necessarily require you to agree with the other person's opinion. Rather, it means accepting his or her right to hold a position, even when it is different from yours.

Source: Stephen Covey, "Seven Methods of Influence," *Incentive* 17 (October 1996), p. 22.

---

with the other parties to discuss how the solution is working out. If necessary, identify the needs that are still unmet, and then repeat the problem-solving procedure.

Win–Win Problem Solving in Action

The case of Marta, a senior manager, and Kurt, her assistant, shows how win–win problem solving can work. Kurt has learned that his department is about to launch a particularly ambitious project. He feels ready to take on more responsibility and thinks this could be a good chance to show what he can do. Kurt is disappointed that Marta hasn't offered him the chance to lead the effort, but he wisely has thought about how to approach her instead of unassertively nursing his grudge or aggressively attacking her. Knowing from experience that Marta is most receptive when not distracted by other matters, he makes an appointment to talk with her. They agree to meet at the end of the workday, after most employees have gone home and the office is quiet.

Identify the needs of both parties

Marta: What's up?

Kurt: I'm really excited about the KDM project, and I'd like a shot at taking the lead on managing it.

Marta:	Kurt, that's a major project. I need someone with more experience, especially in public relations, to handle that job. I've asked Greta to handle it. (*Marta explains her need–to have the job managed by someone with more experience.*)
Kurt:	Well, I guess I understand. But I'd really like to take on more responsibility. This is the second time a big job went to somebody else. I'd like to find some way of proving myself and showing what I can do for this company. (*Kurt wisely avoids arguing about the specific project and instead focuses on his real goal–to get a chance to show he can handle more responsibility.*)
Marta:	Fair enough. Let's try to figure out a way that you can have the responsibility and recognition you want and I can feel confident that the job is the right size. (*Like Kurt, Marta focuses on ends–Kurt growing in his job–instead of means.*)

Brainstorm a list of possible solutions

Kurt:	Great. What if you put me in charge of a major project—one not quite as big as this one, and I could just check everything with you along the way?
Marta:	Or I might be able to team you up with someone who has experience in areas where you're weak, and you could run the project together. Or I could get you to assist Greta on this project, so you could get some experience under her supervision and see how the aspects all fit together.
Kurt:	I'd really like to show I can take the lead. What if I took on a less important project—one that called for me to figure out problems in these areas? Or maybe I could manage just the public relations part of a bigger project, to show you that I can handle that. (*Notice that Kurt and Marta have brainstormed five options to consider, without judging any at this point.*)

Evaluate the alternative solutions

Marta:	All of these are possibilities. Let's see which of them will best suit us both. I could put you in charge of a major project, I guess, but you would need a lot of support, and I'm afraid I don't have enough time to give it to you.
Kurt:	Plus it would drive us both crazy if I had to check every detail with you. And I don't really want to team up with someone, either. The whole idea is for me to get some experience where I need it, and a person who has that experience will just handle those concerns—which gets me nowhere.
Marta:	On the other hand, I don't want to just put you on your own. How would you feel about handling the public relations on Greta's project? She could use some extra help, and having that help would give her time to train you. It would also help you get a sense of the whole project—not just part of it.

Implement the solution   Kurt agreed to the idea of handling Greta's public relations:

Kurt:	Just one thing. I want Greta to know that my job is to be responsible for that part of the project—not just be her assistant.

Marta: Sounds fair to me. I'll talk to Greta and make sure she's agreeable. I do think she has a lot of good advice to offer, though. You'd be foolish not to consider her opinions. And, of course, both she and I will have to support your decisions. But I'll be sure both of us give you the freedom to come up with your own plan—and the responsibility that goes with the freedom.

Follow up on the solution   Marta, Kurt, and Greta met several weeks after developing their plan to check its progress:

Kurt: I'm feeling pretty good about the arrangement. I appreciate the chance to be responsible for one part of such a big project. Just one thing, Greta. When we agree on the way I'll do a job, I feel uncomfortable when you keep checking on how I'm doing. It makes me wonder whether you think I'll mess it up.

Greta: Not at all, Kurt. I thought you'd want to know that I'm available for support. Of course, I do want to keep posted, but I don't have any intention of being a snoop. What do you suggest?

Kurt: How about letting me come to you. I promise to keep you on top of things, and I do appreciate your advice. I'd just like to have a little more operating room.

Marta: Sounds like a good arrangement. Let's give it a try and get together next week at this time to see how it works.

review points

- A positive communication climate is an important element in successful working relationships. Such a climate comes from messages that convey respect for others, even during conflicts.

- Confirming messages use descriptive "I" language rather than "you" language. They focus on solving problems, not imposing solutions. They are honest, not manipulative. They show concern for the other party and reflect attitudes of equality and open-mindedness.

- Effective praise creates and maintains positive communication climates when it follows these guidelines: Praise progress; praise specifically, promptly, and sincerely; and relay praise from others.

- Even criticism can enhance a relationship if offered constructively: (1) Frame the content so it is limited, accurate, clearly defined, and benefits the recipient. (2) Choose a sender who is credible, is in a legitimate position to deliver criticism, and can maximize criticism's beneficial effects. (3) Deliver remarks as part of a positive relationship, accept partial responsibility for the problem, and add an offer of help. (4) Deliver criticism in a face-saving, nonjudgmental manner.

- When receiving criticism, prevent defensiveness by (1) seeking more information: ask for examples or clarification, guess about details if necessary, paraphrase the critic, or ask what the critic wants; and (2) agreeing with facts or with a critic's right to his/her perception. (3) Work for cooperative solutions by asking to state your view and focusing on solutions, not fault.

- Handle the inevitable on-the-job conflicts constructively: (1) Explore whether the conflict is about a topic, a process, the relationship, or one's ego. (2) Choose the best conflict strategy (avoiding, accommodating, competing, collaborating, or compromising) for this situation. (3) Consider the best format (competitive, lose–lose, compromise, and win–win) to negotiate a mutually acceptable agreement.

- Successful negotiating includes these steps: Clarify your interests and needs by distinguishing between ends and means; pay attention to timing, culture, and non-defensiveness; and use a win–win approach (identify each party's needs, brainstorm then evaluate possible solutions, implement and follow up on a solution).

key terms

Test your understanding of these key terms by visiting the Online Learning Center Web site at www.mhhe.com/adler10e.

communication climate   127
compromise   143
confirming messages   128
descriptive statements   128
disconfirming messages   128
emotional intelligence (EQ)   126
"I" language   128

lose–lose orientation   144
negotiation   143
problem-oriented messages   129
social intelligence   126
win–lose orientation   144
win–win orientation   145
"you" language   128

activities

Go to the self-quizzes at the Online Learning Center at www.mhhe.com/adler10e to test your knowledge of chapter concepts.

1. Invitation to Insight

Recall two or three instances in which you have enacted troublesome communicative behaviors (see Table 5–1).

a. Identify which types of behaviors you enacted. What circumstances led you to enact these behaviors?

b. What were the results of these behaviors for you and the other people involved?

c. Describe specifically how you could have behaved in a more confirming manner.

2. Skill Builder

Convert each of the following disconfirming messages into a confirming message. In your messages, use descriptive "I" language (pp. 128–129) and unequivocal terms (pp. 93–94). Invent details about the situation as necessary.

a. "I sure wish I had someone to help me with this project."

b. "Look . . . stop asking questions and just get it done."

c. "You may think you know how to handle the situation, but you really don't have enough experience. I'm the boss and I know when an assignment is over your head."

d. "What a tacky idea. A formal reception with paper plates! I can't believe you'd even suggest that."

e. "If you want to keep your job, you had better round up 10 new accounts by Monday."

3. Invitation to Insight

Familiarize yourself with effective praise by completing the following exercise:

a. Recall three situations in which someone has praised you. Using the guidelines on pages 131–133, evaluate the praise you received. Was it specific? Sincere? How did the praise impact you?

b. Think of three co-workers or acquaintances you could praise sincerely. How could you deliver the praise effectively? For each, write a short statement or paragraph expressing your praise.

4. Skill Builder

Practice your ability to manage criticism constructively by creating a brief role play with a partner based on one of the scenarios below (or use any critical message you are likely to receive on the job).

A co-worker accuses you of trying to ingratiate yourself with (kiss up to) the boss.

A hard-to-please client snaps at you about not returning his phone calls in a timely manner.

You forgot to proofread the budget committee's minutes before you distributed them; you accidentally mistyped several of the budget figures and the boss is upset.

You walk through a co-worker's work area on the way to the drinking fountain. She barks, "Can't you give me some space to do my job?"

At a meeting, you present a proposal that angers one of your co-workers. He attacks you verbally, claiming that you don't have your facts right.

Your supervisor criticizes you for taking too long to finish a job.

Enact the role play three times as follows:

a. The sender of the message uses judgmental language and the receiver responds defensively.

b. The sender uses judgmental language. The receiver responds nondefensively, using the skills described on pages 136–137.

c. The sender delivers the criticism as constructive feedback, using the guidelines on pages 135–137. The receiver responds nondefensively.

Discuss the impact that each approach is likely to have (1) on the relational climate and (2) on future interactions between these employees. Explain your answer by using the communication model in Chapter 1, pp. 7–9.

5. Invitation to Insight

Recall two conflicts you've been involved in recently.

a. For each, identify the primary source of conflict described on pages 138–139 (topic, process, relational, ego/identity). Do you think the other party(ies) would agree about the primary source of the conflict? Why or why not?

b. Next, identify any secondary sources of each conflict.

c. How did each dimension affect the way the participants approached the conflict?

6. Skill Builder

Describe an avoiding, accommodating, competing, collaborating, and compromising response to each of the following situations. Then decide which approach you would recommend. Because the meaning of a message varies with the context, you will need to decide on the specifics of the situation in order to make an informed choice. Explain your choice, using the information on pages 139–143.

a. At 4:30 P.M. a boss asks her assistant to work late to retype a 25-page report due the next morning. The assistant has already purchased nonrefundable tickets to attend a concert that evening.

b. The co-worker with whom you share a small cubicle habitually leaves papers, files, and books strewn all over her desk. The litter bugs you. Besides, you are concerned that it gives your clients a bad impression.

c. The assistant manager of a bookstore is faced with a customer demanding a refund for a book he claims was a gift. The book has several crumpled pages and a torn cover.

d. You are facilitator of a student group that is writing a research report worth half of your grade for the term. One group member misses two meetings without contacting you. When he returns, he explains that he had a family emergency and asks what he can do to make up the work.

7. Skill Builder

Sharpen your skill at knowing when and how to communicate assertively by following these steps:

a. Develop an assertive message for each of the following situations in your professional life:
1. Making a request.
2. Describing a problem involving the recipient of your message.
3. Offering a suggestion.

b. Practice each message with a partner until you are confident that it is organized and delivered as effectively as possible. Recording your rehearsal can provide valuable feedback.

c. Now discuss with your partner the potential benefits and drawbacks of delivering each assertive message.

8. Skill Builder

In the following conflicts, identify the type(s) of conflict (topic, process, relational, ego/identity) and

the ends desired by each party. For each situation, identify solutions (means to the end) that can satisfy the needs of everyone involved.

a. A landlord and tenant disagree about who should pay for an obviously necessary paint job for the office space.

b. Two co-workers contributed equally to developing a proposal for an important client. They both want to be the one who delivers the final proposal.

c. A sales manager and sales representatives disagree over the quota necessary to earn bonuses.

d. In a company with limited resources to spend on a new project, the marketing manager wants more money to be spent on advertising, while the product development manager wants a greater budget for researching new product lines.

9. Skill Builder

With a partner, select one of the following situations. Plan how you would prepare for and conduct the negotiation, working through each step on pages 146–149. Provide details as necessary to explain the situation.

a. You want to ask for a raise.

b. You and your co-workers would like your boss to hire an additional worker so you can accomplish all the necessary work in a timely fashion, without burnout.

c. You want to rent office space for your small business at a rate that is 5 to 10 percent less than the advertised price.

d. You need an extra week to complete a long, complex assignment.

resources

→ For extensive readings and Web sites on the interpersonal skills discussed in this chapter (climate, criticism, conflict), see the Online Learning Center Web site at **www.mhhe.com/adler10e.**

Platinum Sounds

"Not bad for a 20-year-old," thinks Gina deSilva. "I'm the youngest store manager in the history of Platinum Sounds. With this job it will take me a little longer to get my degree, but I won't have to take out student loans and I'll leave school with some real management experience. That should make me lots more employable after I graduate."

Gina knows this job won't be an easy one. As a start she begins a mental "to do" list of the people with whom she needs to interview.

- *Clarify Marty's expectations of me.* Now that I'm store manager, Marty (the regional manager) will be my boss. I don't know him very well, and I need to understand what he wants me to do. What are his priorities? What problems does he see with the store? What does he think of me? Better find out.

- *Hire assistant manager to replace me.* Interview Rashid and Samantha, the top candidates. Rashid is more experienced and sociable, but can I count on him to put the store first when it conflicts with his band? Samantha is very serious, but her in-your-face style rubs some clerks the wrong way. Can she learn to be a little less aggressive? Also, I need to be sure that whoever I hire is committed to staying with the job for at least a year.

- *Hire two new clerks.* We need to hire two new salesclerks really soon. What skills and attitudes are we looking for? How can I handle the interviews to be sure we get the best people?

- *Schedule performance reviews.* At Platinum Sounds, semiannual performance reviews are a requirement. They also help determine who gets salary increases. Most people view these reviews as a stressful chore. How can I take the stress out of these interviews and make them really work for the company and the clerks?

- *Figure how to cut employee turnover.* We've had to replace 7 of our 10 salespeople in the last year. I'm not sure why so many people have left. Training new staff takes a lot of time, and new people don't serve the customers too well until they have figured out our routine. I need to talk with the three old-time clerks who are still here and the new ones. Maybe I should also track down people who left the store and find out why they quit.

- *Do market research with customers.* I know sales have been off since Mega-Hits opened in the mall. I need to talk with our customers to find out how to keep them here. I also need to track down customers we've lost and find out how to get them back.

- *Become the best manager I can be.* I know I take things too seriously, and I'm weak on the financial side of the business. I need to find people who are good managers in retail stores like this one and see what they can tell me about how to do a good job here at Platinum Sounds.

As you read the chapters in this unit, consider the following questions:

1. Who are the people Gina needs to interview? For each person, identify the type of interview described in Chapter 7 that would be most appropriate.

2. What will be her goal for each type of interview?

3. What topics does she need to cover for each interview?

4. Within each topic area, what primary questions does she need to ask? What types of questions described in Chapter 6 will be most effective in meeting her goals?

5. How can she plan the opening and closing of each interview to help achieve her goals?

Principles of Interviewing

chapter outline

Planning the Interview
Define the Goal
Identify and Analyze the Other Party
Prepare a List of Topics
Choose the Best Interview Structure
Consider Possible Questions
Arrange the Setting

Conducting the Interview
Opening
Body
Closing

The Ethics of Interviewing
Obligations of the Interviewer
Obligations of the Interviewee

Sample Interview Plan
Review Points
Key Terms
Activities
Resources

chapter objectives

After reading this chapter you should be able to

1. Prepare for each stage of an interview: opening, body, and closing.
2. Demonstrate knowledge of the uses and limitations of each type of interview question: open, closed, fact, opinion, primary, secondary, direct, indirect, hypothetical, and leading.
3. Describe and observe the ethical obligations of interviewers and interviewees.

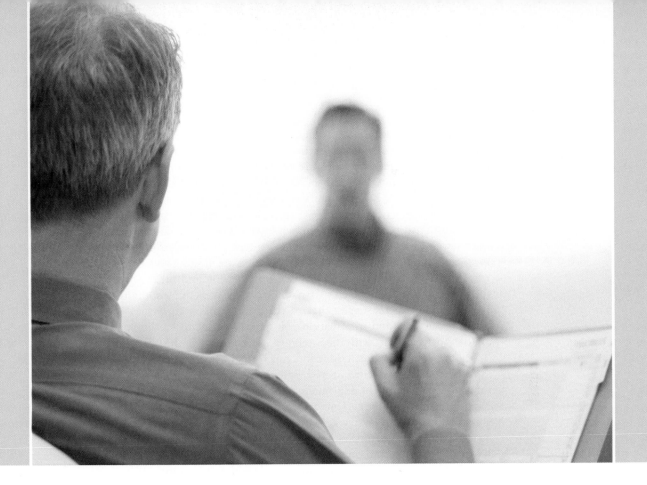

Daniel and Cecilia are co-owners of a small bookstore. A large national chain has opened in a nearby mall and is drawing away business. The partners think adding a small café to their store could recapture customers. They decide to travel around the state, asking other independent booksellers with cafés how well their plans have worked.

Sharon, a marketing manager for a building-supplies manufacturer, is preparing for a trade convention. Although her firm produces more than a thousand products, she can show only a few at the convention. She calls the convention coordinator and asks questions that will help her plan the exhibit: Are the builders who attend the convention concerned mostly with large public buildings, mostly with private homes, or a combination of both? How large will her exhibit space be? Will electrical outlets be available, and can they handle large power demands?

Ravi has just been appointed as new manager of a restaurant that has dropped from the leading producer in the chain to the bottom of the list in just over a year. His job is to figure out where the problem lies and turn the situation around. He begins by talking with virtually every employee, from shift managers to dishwashers.

Susan had worked in the accounting department for 3 months when Lloyd, her supervisor, calls her into his office. "Is there a problem?" she asks nervously. "No, no," Lloyd replies. "I wanted to let you know we've been pleased with your performance and to find out how you feel about your work in the last 3 months. I'd also like to know more about how you see yourself in the company in the future."

Each of these conversations is an **interview,** a two-party conversation in which at least one person has a specific, serious purpose. This definition makes it clear that interviewing is a special kind of conversation, differing from other types in several ways. Most important, interviewing is always *purposeful.* Unlike more spontaneous conversations, an interview includes at least one participant who has a serious, predetermined reason for being there. Interviews are also more *structured* than most conversations. As you will soon learn, every good interview has several distinct phases and always involves some sort of question-and-answer format. Interviews also have an element of *control* not present in more casual interaction. The interviewer's job is to keep the conversation moving toward a predetermined goal. Interviews always involve *two parties.* While there may be several interviewers (as sometimes occurs in employment situations) or multiple respondents (as in a "meet the press" journalistic format), there are always two parties: interviewer and respondent. A final difference between interviewing and other conversation involves the *amount of speaking* by each party. While the speakers in most informal conversations speak equally, experts suggest that participation in most interviews (with the possible exception of sales and information-giving types) ought to be distributed in roughly a 70 to 30 percent ratio, with the interviewee doing most of the talking.[1]

Some people in business spend much of their time in interviews. For example, salespeople interview current and potential customers to assess their needs. Health care professionals, including nurses, doctors, dental hygienists, and emergency-room receptionists, interview patients to learn about their problems. Most managerial jobs also require some interviews. Many consultants recommend that managers practice "management by walking around" and regularly interview their subordinates about progress, problems, and concerns. In fact, communication authorities claim that interviews are the most common form of planned communication.[2]

There are many kinds of interviews. *Selection interviews* help organizations and prospective employees explore the fit between applicant and employer. *Performance appraisal interviews* review the performance of employees and help set targets for the future. *Disciplinary interviews* deal with misconduct or poor performance. *Survey interviews* gather information from a number of people. They are used to provide information from which to draw conclusions, make interpretations, and determine future action. Manufacturers and advertisers use them to assess market needs and learn consumer reactions to new products. Employers use them to gather employees' ideas about how space should be allotted in a new location or how much a new benefits program might be needed. *Diagnostic interviews* allow health care professionals, attorneys, counselors, and other business and professional workers to gather information that helps them to respond to the needs of their clientele. *Research interviews* provide information upon which to base future decisions. An entrepreneur who is thinking about opening a chain of restaurants might interview others with related experience when developing the concept and question people familiar with the target area to collect ideas about locations and clientele. On a more personal level, an employee thinking about a career change might interview several people who work in the field she is considering to seek advice about how to proceed. *Investigative interviews* gather information to determine the causes of an event, usually a problem. Finally, *exit interviews* help to determine why a person is leaving an organization.

Each type of interview calls for a special approach, and Chapter 7 will discuss several of them in detail. Despite the differences, all interviews share some common characteristics and communication strategies. This chapter will introduce the skills that you can use in virtually every interview you face in your career, either as interviewer or interviewee.

Planning the Interview

A successful interview begins before the parties face each other. Whether you are the interviewer or the respondent, background work can mean the difference between success and disappointment.

Define the Goal

Sometimes the purpose of an interview isn't as obvious as it seems at first. For instance, if you are a hotel manager and have received several complaints about the surly manner of a desk clerk, you would certainly speak to the employee. What would your purpose be?

An obvious answer would be to change the clerk's behavior, but this goal isn't precise enough. Will you reprimand the clerk, insisting on a change in behavior? Will you act as a counselor, trying to correct the problem by understanding the causes of the employee's rudeness? Or will you take the role of an explainer, teaching the clerk some new customer-relations skills? While the general goal of each approach is identical (changing the clerk's behavior), the precise goal influences your approach.

The same principle operates in other types of interviews. In a selling situation, is the goal to get a single order or to build a long-term relationship? Is your goal in a grievance interview to ask for specific changes or simply to have your past concerns acknowledged?

In any interview, you should make your goal as clear as possible, as in the following examples:

Vague:	Improve clerk's behavior.
Better:	Teach clerk how to handle registration problems.
Best:	Teach clerk what to tell guests when rooms are not ready.
Vague:	Turn prospect into a customer.
Better:	Show customer features and benefits of my product.
Best:	Identify prospect's needs and show how my product can satisfy them, resulting in trial order.

The interviewee should also have a clear purpose. Notice, for example, the interviewee's purposes in regard to grievance and employment interviews:

Vague:	Complain about unfair supervisor.
Better:	Protest unfair scheduling of assignments.
Best:	Have supervisor develop fair method of scheduling future assignments.
Vague:	Get job offer.
Better:	Get job offer by demonstrating competence.
Best:	Get job offer by describing work experience, referring to favorable references, and describing ideas for the position.

Identify and Analyze the Other Party

Whether you are the interviewer or the interviewee, your interviews will be more useful and successful if you select the right person to talk to whenever you have a choice. If you are looking for information, the person you select to interview may greatly influence

case study

Interview Planning: Lessons from the Presidential Debates

The televised "debates" that have preceded every U.S. presidential election since 1960 are really interviews. Each candidate answers a series of questions—some by journalists and others by ordinary citizens. In most business and professional interviews the stakes are more modest and the conditions less public. Nonetheless, presidential debates provide lessons for more common interviews.

- *Prepare for the actual interview setting.* Since 1976, candidates have practiced by acting out their entire debates in conditions that precisely match the actual debate setting, with surrogates representing their opponents and the interviewers.

- *Identify your overall goals.* Beyond answering specific questions, candidates strive to leave voters with an overall impression about themselves. Both Barrack Obama (in 2008) and John F. Kennedy (in 1960) worked hard to overcome doubts about inexperience. By contrast, 73-year-old candidate Ronald Reagan defused concerns about his advanced age when he joked about his 56-year-old opponent's "youth and inexperience."

- *Anticipate likely questions.* Interviewers closely guard the questions they plan to ask, so surprises are possible. But the issues in every campaign are so widely known that candidates can anticipate most of them.

- *Give succinct answers.* The debate ground rules spell out the maximum amount of time a candidate has to answer each question—typically between 30 seconds and 2 minutes. Since the topics are complicated, candidates must struggle to craft answers that are succinct. Doing so is a special challenge for normally longwinded speakers, like vice president Joe Biden, who worked hard on brevity in his 2008 debate.

- *Avoid nonverbal blunders.* In his 1992 meeting with Bill Clinton, President George H. W. Bush created the impression he was eager for the debate to be over when he repeatedly glanced at his watch. In 2000, Al Gore damaged his image by sighing and looking exasperated when George W. Bush made statements with which he disagreed.

CRITICAL ANALYSIS: You can apply lessons from presidential debates to your own interviews by considering the following points:

1. Identify an interview you have experienced in the past, or one you will face in the future.

2. Describe how you can enhance your performance by applying each of the principles above to that situation.

Sources: A. Bosworth, "Presidential Debates: History News Network Scrapbook," September 27, 2004. Retrieved December 30, 2008, from http://hnn.us/articles/7569.html; M. Langley, "Stand-Ins, Naps Help Debate Preparation," *Wall Street Journal,* September 22, 2008. Retrieved December 30, 2008, from http://online.wsj.com/article/SB122204781847961747.html?mod=googlenews_wsj; "How to Prepare for the Big Debate," *Foreign Policy,* October 2008. Retrieved January 2, 2009, from www.foreignpolicy.com/story/cms.php?story_id=4484; "Memorable TV Debate Moments." Retrieved January 2, 2009, from www.foxnews.com/story/0,2933,133978,00.html.

the quality of the information you get. In sales, for example, identifying the appropriate interviewee—the person who makes purchasing decisions—is vital. Mark H. McCormack, owner of a sports promotion agency, describes the situation:

> One of the biggest problems we have had as a sales organization is figuring out who within another company will be making a decision on what. Very often in our business we don't know if it's the advertising department, the marketing department, or someone in PR or corporate communications. It may very well turn out to be the chairman and CEO of a multibillion-dollar corporation if the subject is of personal interest to him.[3]

Finding the right interviewee isn't only important in sales. For example, if you want to know more about the safety procedures in a manufacturing area, the plant manager or foreman can tell you more about them than, say, publicity staff—who probably get their information from the plant manager anyway. If you're preparing for a job interview, you'll want to know as much as possible about the person to whom you'll be talking.

As you decide who is ready, willing, and able to provide the information you need, consider several factors.

Knowledge Level
As an interviewer, your questions should be tailored to the information the other person has. A sales representative who bombarded a prospective client with overly technical information would probably be making a mistake, as would a supervisor who sought managerial advice from an employee who has no experience in leading others. As an interviewee, the same principle applies: You need to figure out the knowledge level of the person asking you questions so your answers won't be too simplistic or complex.

The Other's Concept of Self
The self-image of the other party can have a strong effect on what goes on in an interview. For example, if your boss is interviewing you about a project that isn't going well, consider whether she sees herself as a colleague who might be able to help you, an authority whose advice you should take, or an employee who will be in trouble if she has to defend a failure to her own superiors. Each attitude will call for a different approach on your part. If you're seeking career advice from a potential mentor, that person's willingness (or unwillingness) to listen to your thoughts should dictate how much you take charge of the conversation, or how much you follow the veteran's lead.

Your Image
Who you are isn't as important as who the other party *thinks* you are. In an employment interview, a knowledgeable applicant who *appears* uninformed is in trouble. In the same way, an employee may want to discuss constructively a problem with the boss, but if the boss thinks the subordinate only wants to complain, the employee's chances for success are limited.

Attitude
You may find three sources of information useful for identifying the interviewee's attitudes. First, you can listen to *what other people say.* Co-workers, friends, and even the media can be sources for learning about the other person. "I'm going to ask for a raise," you might tell a friend with whom you work. "How do you think I should bring it up?" If you interview an executive about career opportunities, knowing your subject's career history or education might help you build rapport and ask useful questions.

If you have known the other person before the interview, *what that person has said* can be a good source of information. For instance, you may have once heard your boss comment favorably about an employee who really had facts and figures to back up what he said. If you are asking for a raise, this information could give you an important clue about how to present your arguments.

Finally, you can discover a great deal about the person you will interview by *observation.* If you have seen the other party dress casually, use informal language, or joke around, you might behave differently than if you had observed more straight-laced behavior. Does he or she seem to encourage drop-in visits or prefer prearranged appointments?

Even if you are meeting the person for the first time, you can still learn something from observation. One sales authority recommends:

> *Be observant. Many times there are clues all around the office that will give you ideas that may assist you in talking the prospect's language and, thus, making the sale. Look for trophies, pictures, books, decor, awards, and plaques. It's a safe bet that the prospect is very proud of anything that is on display in the office.*[4]

career tip

Successfully Navigating Job Fairs

Job fairs offer the chance to network with employers and to secure job interviews, sometimes on the spot. In this respect, job fairs serve as initial interviews.

Some job fairs are set on college and university campuses, where employers look for graduating students. Community fairs are open to the public at large. Some target a specific field such as health care or engineering, while others offer a diverse array of organizations and fields.

Before you go

- Ask yourself what will make you stand out from the hundred people a recruiter might see in a day.
- Gain a competitive edge by learning about the employers that interest you. Learn what positions are they hiring for, and what qualifications are required. If possible, discover whether companies will be conducting job interviews at the fair or soon thereafter. You may be able to discover this sort of information from the career fair. Contact the company and you may be able to find out whether the person at the table will be the person who does the hiring, or if it is a Human Resources person who screens for quality candidates to recommend.
- Rehearse your "elevator" speech so you can present yourself clearly and professionally. (See Chapter 1, page 19.) Bring copies of both your generic résumé and customized versions for positions you will be seeking. Dress conservatively and professionally.
- Carry a briefcase (a shoulder strap leaves your hands free for handshakes and writing notes) with a professional portfolio that can easily be pulled out to retrieve résumés and letters of recommendation. Pack tissues and breath mints.

At the fair

- Arrive early. Spend a few minutes getting a feel for the way the fair operates. Is the atmosphere formal or informal?
- Don't ever ASK what an employer does. KNOW before you go.
- Manage your time efficiently: Approach your second-tier choices first to "warm up" so you are confident when approaching your first choices. Some employers pack up an hour or so before the designated closing time, so don't wait until the last minute.
- If you must stand in line, use that time to talk with other candidates: Find out what they've found about employers and positions.
- Approach the company's representative with confidence: "Hello. I'm Janya Greer. I'm a journalism and English major and I'm interested in the writing positions." Remember, you are being evaluated from the moment you make contact.
- Always think about how your career objectives and qualifications meet the employer's needs. Have specific questions that show you've done your homework.
- Ask for the business card of anyone you speak with.

After the fair

- For employers who look like a good match, follow up with a phone call or e-mail to express thanks and confirm your interest.
- Remind the person where you met, what you talked about, and about your skills and qualifications. Add any information you neglected to mention at the job fair. Express your interest in learning more about the fit between you and the organization.

Sources: **www.collegegrad.com** and **www.career.unm.edu**, University of New Mexico Career Center.

Prepare a List of Topics

Sometimes the topics an interview should cover will become clear as soon as you've listed your objectives. An insurance-claims investigator, for example, usually covers a standard agenda when collecting data on an accident: road conditions, positions of the vehicles, nature and extent of injuries, and so on. In other cases, however, some background research is necessary before you can be sure an agenda is complete. An office manager who is considering the purchase of new laptops might need to do some reading and talk with her staff before she can know which questions to ask the sales representatives who will be calling on her. She will probably want to learn about the topics listed below:

Objective: To purchase affordable wireless laptops that will be secure, reliable, and compatible with current equipment.

List of Topics:

Attitudes of the staff toward specific brands.

Funds available.

The general price range of the products.

Whether vendors have fixed or negotiable prices and quantity discounts.

Interviewees, too, should have goals and agendas. A job seeker approaching an employment interview might have a program like this:

Objective: To have the interviewer see me as a bright, ambitious, articulate person who knows about and can serve the company's needs.

List of Topics:

Discuss my short-term and long-term career goals.

Answer all questions completely and in an organized way.

Share my knowledge of the company's products and financial condition.

Choose the Best Interview Structure

There are several types of interview structures. As Table 6-1 illustrates, each calls for different levels of planning and produces different results.

A **highly structured interview** consists of a standardized list of questions. In its most extreme form, it even specifies their precise wording and the order in which they are asked. Highly structured interviews are most common in market research, opinion polls, and attitude surveys. Most of the questions allow only a limited range

Table 6–1	Differences between Highly Structured and Nonstructured Interviews

Highly Structured Interview	Nonstructured Interview
Usually takes less time	Usually takes more time
Easier for interviewer to control	More difficult for interviewer to control
Provides quantifiable results	Results more difficult to quantify
Requires less skill by interviewer	Requires high degree of interviewer skill
Low flexibility in exploring responses	High flexibility in exploring responses

of answers: "How many televisions do you own?" "Which of the following words best describes your evaluation of the company?" The answers to closed questions such as these are easy to tabulate, which makes this approach convenient for surveying large numbers of respondents. Because of their detailed structure, highly structured interviews call for less skill by the questioner.

Highly structured interviews have drawbacks, however, that make them unsuitable for many situations. The range of topics is limited by a predetermined list of questions, and there is no chance for the interviewer to follow up intriguing or unclear answers that might arise during the conversation.

The **nonstructured interview** stands in contrast to its highly structured counterpart. It might consist of a topical agenda without specific questions, or it might consist of just a few key questions and the interviewer builds on the answers given. Many managers make a point of regularly dropping in on their employees. The conversation may be generally directed at finding out how the employees are doing with their work, whether they are satisfied with their jobs, whether they have any problems—personal or work-related—that the manager should know about, but there are no specific, planned questions. Nonstructured interviews allow considerable flexibility about the amount of time and nature of the questioning in the various content areas. They permit the conversation to flow in whatever direction seems most productive.

Nonstructured interviewing looks easy when it's done with skill, but it's actually very difficult. It's easy to lose track of time or to focus too much on one topic and neglect others. When you're worried about what to ask next, you may forget to listen closely to the interviewee's answer and may miss clues to ask for more information.

The **moderately structured interview** combines features of the other types. The interviewer prepares a list of topics to be covered, anticipates their probable order, and lists several major questions and possible follow-up probes. These make up a flexible plan, which the interviewer can use or adapt as circumstances warrant. The planned questions ensure coverage of important areas, while allowing for examination of important but unforeseen topics.

Consider Possible Questions

After clarifying your purpose, setting an agenda, and deciding on a format, you are ready to think about specific questions. As you might expect, the type and quality of questions are the biggest factors in determining the success or failure of an interview.

The proper questions to ask might seem to be obvious once an agenda is finished, but this is not always the case. When planning questions, an interviewer may choose from many types:

Primary or secondary

Open or closed

Factual or opinion-seeking

Direct or indirect

Hypothetical or actual

General or focused on critical incidents

As you will see in the following pages, questions can fit into several of these categories. For example, an interviewer might ask a primary question that is open, opinion-seeking, and focused. Another question might be closed, direct, and factual. A good interviewer considers these question types as tools, and chooses the right combination to get the information he or she wants to uncover.

Primary and Secondary Questions

Primary questions introduce new topics or areas within topics: "How did you hear about our company?" "Do you have any questions for me?" "How often do you use the transit system?" **Secondary questions** aim at gathering additional information about a topic that has already been introduced: "Tell me more about it." "What do you mean by 'commitment'?" "Does that price include shipping costs?"

Secondary questions are useful in several circumstances:

- When a previous answer is *incomplete*: "What did Marilyn say then?"

- When a previous answer is *superficial* or *vague*: "What do you mean, you *think* the figures are right?"

- When a previous answer is *irrelevant*: "I understand that the job interests you. Can you tell me about your training in the field?"

- When a previous answer seems *inaccurate*: "You said everyone supports the idea. What about Herb?"

"Next question: I believe that life is a constant striving for balance, requiring frequent tradeoffs between morality and necessity, within a cyclic pattern of joy and sadness, forging a trail of bittersweet memories until one slips, inevitably, into the jaws of death. Agree or disagree?"

Open and Closed Questions

Closed questions restrict the interviewee's response. Closed questions form the backbone of most highly structured interviews, but they also have their place in moderately structured and nonstructured ones, too. Some ask the respondent to choose from a range of answers: "Which of the three shifts would you prefer to work on?" "Do you think Mary, Dave, or Leonard would be best for the job?" "Would you rather stay in this department or have a transfer?" Other closed questions ask for specific data: "How long have you worked here?" "When do you think the order will be ready?"

Open questions invite a broader, more detailed range of responses. Some questions are more open than others. Consider the difference between a wide-open one such as "What do you think is going on here?" and a more focused but still open query like "What would you do if you were in my position?" or "What makes you interested in working for this company?" As Table 6–2 on page 168 shows, both open and closed questions have their advantages.

As an interviewee, you may sometimes want to turn a closed question into an open one so that you can share more information:

Question: Do you have any experience as a manager?

Answer: Not on the job, but I've studied management in several college courses, and I'm looking forward to developing the skills I learned there. I'm especially excited about using the situational leadership approach I learned in my business communication course. I understand you've sent several of your people to workshops on the subject.

Table 6–2	Advantages of Open and Closed Questions

When to Use Open Questions	When to Use Closed Questions
1. To relax the interviewee (if the question is easy to answer and nonthreatening)	1. To maintain control over the conversation
2. To discover the interviewee's opinions	2. When specific information is needed and you are not interested in the interviewee's feelings or opinions
3. To evaluate the interviewee's communication skills	3. When time is short
4. To explore the interviewee's possession of information	4. When the interviewer is not highly skilled
5. To discover the interviewee's feelings or values	5. When a high degree of standardization between interviews is important

Source: Gerald L. Wilson and H. Lloyd Goodall Jr., *Interviewing in Context* (New York: McGraw-Hill, 1991), pp. 75–80.

Factual and Opinion Questions

Factual questions investigate matters of fact: "Have you taken any courses in accounting?" "Are you willing to relocate if we have an opening in another city?" "Can we apply lease payments to the purchase price, if we decide to buy?" **Opinion questions,** as their name implies, ask for the respondent's judgments: "Which vendor do you think gives the best service?" "Do you think Al is being sincere?" "Is the investment worth it?"

Whether you seek facts or opinions when approaching a topic can greatly influence the results. A manager trying to resolve a dispute between two employees could approach each one subjectively, asking, "What's the source of this problem?" This is a broad opinion-seeking question that invites disagreement between the disputants. A more factual question is "Tell me when you first noticed the problem, and describe what happened."

This doesn't mean that it is always better to ask factual questions. Opinions are often precisely what you are seeking. A client seeking financial advice from an investment counselor would be making a mistake by asking "How have energy stocks done in the past?" when the real question is "How do you expect they'll do in the future?" Your decision about whether to seek facts or opinions has to be based on your reason for asking the question.

Direct and Indirect Questions

The best way to get information is usually to ask **direct questions:** "What area of our business interests you most?" "I hear you've been unhappy with our service. What's the problem?"

Sometimes, however, a straightforward approach won't work. One such case occurs when the respondent isn't *able* to answer a direct question accurately. This inability may come from a lack of information, as when a supervisor's "Do you understand?" gets a "yes" from employees who mistakenly believe that they do. In another case, a respondent may not be *willing* to give a direct answer that would be risky or embarrassing. A boss who asks a subordinate, "Are you satisfied with my leadership?" isn't likely to get a straight answer if the employee thinks the boss is incompetent or unfair. In these

Planning Your Dream Interview

Imagine that you could interview anyone you want regarding a business or professional topic. Describe to your group how you would approach this topic, addressing the following points:

1. Who would you interview? Why did you choose this person?

2. What would be your goal for the interview? (Be as specific as possible.)

3. What topics would you cover, and what questions would you ask in each topic area?

4. How would your self-analysis and analysis of the interviewee affect your approach?

---

instances, an indirect approach would be better. **Indirect questions** elicit information without directly asking for it, as the following comparisons show:

Direct Question	Indirect Question
Do you understand?	Suppose you had to explain this policy to other people in the department. What would you say?
Are you satisfied with my leadership?	If you were manager of this department, what changes would you make?

Sometimes even the most skillful indirect questions won't generate a good response. But there is another indirect way of judging a response—the interviewee's nonverbal behavior. Facial expressions, posture, gestures, eye contact, and other nonverbal behaviors offer clues about another person's emotional state. Here is a description of how one attorney uses people's nonverbal behaviors as a guide when selecting members of a jury:

> To gauge nonverbal clues, Fahringer may ask the potential juror, "Mr. Jones, I'm going to ask you to do me a favor. Will you look at my client, Billy Williams, right now, and tell me whether you can think of him as being innocent." At that instant, Fahringer concentrates on the juror's face. "If he has difficulty looking at my client, or, when he glances at him, drops his eyes, rejecting him, he has told me all that I need to know."[5]

The same technique can work in the business world. For example, a manager who thinks an employee may be afraid to admit problems with a project can watch for clues by observing how the employee reacts nonverbally to a question such as "Is everything still on schedule for the September 15 opening?"

Hypothetical and Critical Incident Questions

Hypothetical questions seek the respondent's answer to a what-if question. They can be a useful way of indirectly getting a respondent to describe beliefs or attitudes: "If we were to take a poll about the morale level around here, what do you think the results would be?"

Hypothetical questions are also a useful way of learning how people would respond in certain situations. A bank manager might test candidates for promotion by asking "Suppose you became assistant operations manager and you had to talk to one of the tellers about her manner toward customers. What would you do if she accused you of acting bossy and forgetting your friends since your promotion?" Again, there is no guarantee that hypothetical answers will reflect a person's real behavior, but their specificity and realism can give strong clues.

Finally, hypothetical questions can be a useful way to get advice that will help you make a personal decision. For example, if your physician presents you with two options for treatment, you might ask, "Which one would you choose if you were me?" If you're talking to a trusted friend about whether to take a new job, you could ask, "What would you do?"

Critical incident questions ask the interviewee about a specific account of a real situation rather than a hypothetical one and are generally more reliable than hypothetical questions.[6] For example, a CEO may ask a "future" executive hopeful: "Think of a time when you felt you needed to break an implicit company policy in order to achieve the larger company vision. Describe the situation and how you handled it."

Leading Questions   **Leading questions** force or tempt the respondent to answer in one way. They frequently suggest the answer the interviewer expects: "How committed are you to our company's philosophy of customer service?" "You aren't really serious about asking for a raise now, are you?"

Some questions are highly leading. Using emotionally charged words and name-calling, they indicate the only acceptable answer: "You haven't fallen for those worn-out arguments, have you?" Other highly loaded questions rely on a bandwagon effect for pressure: "Do you agree with everyone else that it's best to put this incident behind us and forget the whole thing?"

Other leading questions signal the interviewer's position without being so intimidating: "Don't you think that idea is a little expensive?" In cases like this, you can consider the question as a chance to make the best argument to support your position: "Sure, it looks expensive at first, but in the long run this approach will save us money."[7]

A single question often falls into several categories. For instance, the question "Describe some experiences that demonstrate your leadership abilities" is open, direct, factual, and primary. A question could also be closed, hypothetical, and secondary: "You said you welcome challenges. If the chance arose, would you be interested in handling the next round of layoffs?"

Arrange the Setting

A manager at a major publishing company regularly interviews subordinates over lunch at a restaurant where company employees frequently eat together. The manager explains:

> The advantage of meeting here is we're both relaxed. They can talk about their work without feeling as though they've been called on the carpet to defend themselves. They're also more inclined to ask for help with a problem than if we were in the office, and I can ask for improvements and make suggestions without making it seem like a formal reprimand. We also have time to talk without people dropping in or the phone ringing. Of course, if I'm not happy with the person, or if I'm about to fire them, I certainly wouldn't do it over lunch. If that happened, or if they had a serious, confidential problem to discuss, I'd take them in my office, close the door, and have my secretary hold all calls.

The physical setting in which an interview occurs can have a great deal of influence on the results. With some planning of time and place, you can avoid the frustrations of trying to discuss a confidential matter with a co-worker within earshot of people who

Conducting Video Interviews

It isn't always easy to conduct an interview in person, especially when distance separates the parties. In these circumstances interviews can be a quick, affordable way to conduct a conversation. Besides being inexpensive, video technology boosts the odds that an interview can be arranged. Furthermore, it's easy to record a video interview for future analysis and sharing with others.

For all these reasons, video interviews are increasingly used by journalists. They are also becoming more common when employers want to screen candidates before investing resources in arranging a face-to-face meeting. For example, interviewers at software giant Oracle use the Internet to interview candidates thousands of miles away from its Silicon Valley headquarters. Market researchers can use video to conduct interviews and focus groups, gaining more information than could be gleaned via telephone. Finally, you can use video to conduct informational interviews, both as part of exploring career options and once on the job.

While elaborate options exist for video interviews, affordable technology is easy to use. All you (and the other party) need are an Internet connection, free communication software like Skype or Google Chat, and an inexpensive webcam with a built-in microphone.

The following tips will help make your video interviews a success:

Planning

- Make sure the date and time of your interview are confirmed in advance.

- Send the other party any background materials before the interview. For example, when interviewees must respond to visual information such as text or graphs, make sure they have received them in advance of the discussion.

- Test your equipment in advance and again shortly before the interview.

- Arrange an alternate way of contacting the other party (IM, phone) in case you need to communicate while establishing a connection.

During the Interview

- Make sure the field of vision your webcam picks up is clean and neat. (Use the picture-in-picture feature of your webcam to view exactly what the other party can see.)

- Be aware that the microphone picks up background noise as well as your voice. Try to choose a quiet setting, and don't tap your pen or shuffle papers.

- Plan on a shorter interview than you might have if you were in a face-to-face setting. A 15- or 20-minute phone conversation feels much longer than the same encounter would in person.

Sources: S. Davidson, "CNN Using Skype for Video Interviews," online at **http://share.skype.com/sites/business/2008/03/cnn _using_skype_for_video_inte.html**; and A. Doyle, "Tips for Successful Video Interviewing," online at **http://jobsearch.about.com/ od/interviewsnetworking/a/videointerview.htm**.

---

would love to overhear your conversation or of trying to stop your boss in the hall to ask for a raise when she's on her way to a meeting and the easiest way to get free of you is to say no.

Time   When you plan an interview, give careful thought to how much time you will need to accomplish your purpose and let the other person know how much time you expect to take. If you ask a co-worker in another department to spend half an hour with you to answer some questions about a mutual project, he can schedule his time so that you won't have to cut the session short or try to cram an important discussion into 15 minutes.

Other things to consider are the time of day and what the people involved have to do before and after the interview. For example, if you know your boss has an important meeting this afternoon, you can reasonably assume she will be too preoccupied or too busy to talk to you right before it and perhaps immediately afterward. You may also want to avoid scheduling an important interview right before lunch so that neither person will be more anxious to eat than to accomplish the goal of the interview.

Place   The right place is just as important as the right time. The first consideration here is to arrange a setting that is free of distractions. The request "Hold all my calls" is a good sign that you will have the attention of your interviewing partner. Sometimes it's best to choose a spot away from the normal habitat of either person. Not only does this lessen the chance of interruptions, but people often also speak more freely and think more creatively when they are in a neutral space, away from familiar settings that trigger habitual ways of responding.

The physical arrangement of the setting can also influence the interview. Generally, the person sitting behind a desk—whether interviewee or respondent—gains power and formality. On the other hand, a seating arrangement in which the parties face each other across a table or sit with no barrier between them promotes equality and informality. Distance, too, affects the relationship between interviewer and respondent. Other things being equal, two people seated 40 inches apart will have more immediacy in their conversation than will the same people discussing the same subject at a distance of 6 or 7 feet.

Isn't it usually desirable to create a casual atmosphere in an interview? As with other variables, the choice of closeness or distance depends on your goal. A supervisor who wants to assert his authority during a reprimand session might choose to increase distance and sit behind a desk. On the other hand, a sales representative who wants to gain the trust of a customer would probably avoid the barrier of a desk.

Conducting the Interview

After careful planning, the interview itself takes place. An interview consists of three stages: an opening (or introduction), a body, and a closing. Let's examine each one in detail.

Opening

A good introduction can shape the entire interview. Research suggests that people form lasting impressions of each other in the first few minutes of a conversation. Dave Deaver, a national management recruiter, describes the importance of first impressions in a job interview this way: "The first minute is all-important in an interview. Fifty percent of the decision is made within the first 30 to 60 seconds. About 25 percent of the evaluation is made during the first 15 minutes. It's very difficult to recover the last 25 percent if you've blown the first couple of minutes."[8] These initial impressions shape how a listener regards everything that follows.

A good introduction ought to contain two parts: a greeting and an orientation. The opening is also a time for motivating the interviewee to cooperate and giving a sense of what will follow.

Greeting and Building Rapport   The interviewer should begin with a greeting and a self-introduction, if necessary. In formal situations—taking a legal deposition or conducting a highly structured survey, for example—it is appropriate to get right down to

business. But in many situations, building rapport is both appropriate and useful. If the interviewer and interviewee are comfortable with each other, the results are likely to be better for both. This explains why a few minutes of informal conversation are often part of the opening of an interview. This small talk tends to set the emotional tone of the interview—whether it is formal or informal, nervous or relaxed, candid or guarded.

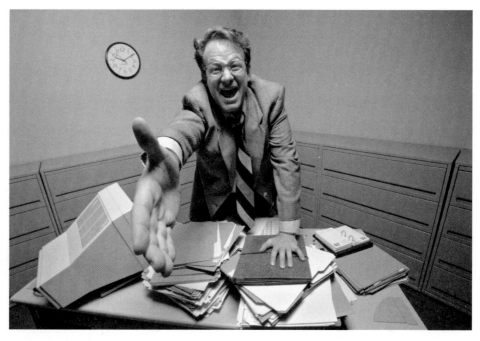

The most logical openers involve common ground: shared interests or experiences. "How are you coping with our record snowfall?" "Did you find your way around the airport construction?" Another type of common ground involves job-related topics, though usually unrelated to the subject of the interview itself. A manager interviewing employees to help design a new benefits package might start the conversation by asking, "How's the new parking plan we proposed last month working out?" Conversation in this rapport-building stage should be sincere. A phony-sounding compliment ("Are those pictures of your family? They certainly are attractive!") is likely to create the opposite reaction from what you want. On the other hand, you should be able to come up with genuine remarks: "What a great view!" "I'm really excited to be here!"

Orientation   In this stage of the opening, the interviewer gives the respondent a brief overview of what is to follow. This orientation helps put the interviewee at ease by removing a natural apprehension of the unknown. At the same time, it helps establish and strengthen the interviewer's control, since it is the interviewer who is clearly setting the agenda. In the orientation, be sure to do the following things.

Explain the reason for the interview   A description of the interview's purpose can both put the interviewee at ease and motivate him or her to respond. If your boss called you in for a "chat" about "how things are going," curiosity would probably be your mildest response. Are you headed for a promotion? Are you being softened up for a layoff? Did somebody complain about you? Sharing the reason for an interview can relieve these concerns: "As you know, we're thinking about opening a branch office soon, and we're trying to plan our staffing. I'd like to find out how you feel about your working situation now and what you want so we can consider your needs when we make the changes."

Explain what information is needed and how it will be used   A respondent who knows what the interviewer wants will have a greater likelihood of supplying it. In our example, the boss might be seeking two kinds of information. In one case, a statement of needed information might be "I'm not interested in having you name names of people you like or dislike. I want to know what parts of the business interest you and what you'd consider to be an ideal job." A quite different request for information might be "I'd like to hear your feelings about the people you work with. Who would you like to work with in the future, and who do you have trouble with?"

A description of how the information will be used is also important. In our current example, the boss might explain, "I won't be able to tell you today exactly what changes we'll be making, but I promise you we'll do the best we can to give you what you want." In many situations, it's important to define the confidentiality of the information you are seeking: "I promise you that this talk will be off the record. Nobody else will hear what you tell me."

Clarify any ground rules   Make sure that you and the other party understand any operating procedures. For example, you might say, "I'd like to tape our conversation instead of taking notes." An interviewer might say, "I'd like to spend the first part of our conversation going through the list of questions I've prepared. Then we can spend the rest of our time covering any questions or thoughts you might have."

Mention the approximate length of the interview   An interviewee who knows how long the session will last will feel more comfortable and give better answers.

Motivation

In some situations, such as a job interview, both people feel the interview is important to them personally. Sometimes, however, you need to give interviewees a reason that will make them feel the interview is worthwhile for them. In some cases, you can simply point out the payoffs: "If we can figure out a better way to handle these orders, it will save us both time." "We'd like to know what you'd like in the new office building so we can try to make everyone as comfortable as possible." If the interview won't directly benefit the other person, you might appeal to his or her ego or desire to help other people: "I'd like to try out a new promotional item, and you know more about them than anyone." "Although you're leaving the company, perhaps you can tell us something that will make it a better place for other people to work."

Body

It is here that the questions and answers are exchanged. While a smooth interview might look spontaneous to an outsider, you have already learned the importance of preparation.

It's unlikely that an interview will ever follow your exact expectations, and it would be a mistake to force it to do so. As an interviewer, you will think of important questions—both primary and secondary—during the session. As a respondent, you will probably be surprised by some of the things the interviewer asks. The best way to proceed is to prepare for the general areas you expect will be covered and do your best when unexpected issues come up.

Responsibilities of the Interviewer

The interviewer performs several tasks during the question-and-answer phase of the discussion.

Control and focus the conversation   If an interview is a conversation with a purpose, it is the interviewer's job to make sure that the discussion focuses on achieving the purpose and doesn't drift away from the agenda. A response can be so interesting that it pulls the discussion off track: "I see you traveled in Europe after college. Did you make it to Barcelona?" Such discussion about backgrounds might be appropriate for the rapport-building part of the opening, but it can get out of control and use up time that would better be spent achieving the interview's purpose.

A second loss of control occurs when the interviewer spends too much time in one legitimate area of discussion, thereby slighting another. Difficult as it may be, an interviewer needs to allot rough blocks of time to each agenda item and then to follow these guidelines during the interview.

Listen actively   Some interviewers—especially novices—become so caught up in budgeting time and planning upcoming questions that they fail to hear what the respondent is saying. Multitasking can present problems. It can be hard to juggle the tasks of asking and answering questions, taking notes, keeping eye contact, and budgeting time. With all these challenges, you can forget the most important task: To listen carefully and thoughtfully to what the other person is saying.

Use secondary questions to probe for important information   Sometimes an answer may be incomplete. At other times, it may be evasive or vague. Since it is impossible to know in advance when probes will be needed, the interviewer should be ready to use them as the occasion dictates.

An interviewer sometimes needs to *repeat* a question before getting a satisfactory answer:

Interviewer:	Your résumé shows you attended Arizona State for 4 years. I'm not clear about whether you earned a degree.
Respondent:	I completed all the required courses in my major field of study, as well as several electives.
Interviewer:	I see. Did you earn a degree?

When a primary question doesn't deliver enough information, the interviewer needs to seek *elaboration*:

Interviewer:	When we made this appointment, you said Bob has been insulting you. I'd like to hear about that.
Respondent:	He treats me like a child. I've been here almost as long as he has and I know what I'm doing!
Interviewer:	Exactly what does he do? Can you give me a few examples?

Sometimes an answer will be complete but unclear. This requires a request for *clarification*:

Respondent:	The certificate pays 6.3 percent interest.
Interviewer:	Is that rate simple or compounded?

A *paraphrasing* probe restates the answer in different words. It invites the respondent to clarify and elaborate on a previous answer:

Interviewer:	You've been with us for a year now and already have been promoted once. How do you feel about the direction your career is taking?
Respondent:	I'm satisfied for now.
Interviewer:	So far, so good. Is that how you feel?

Respondent:	Not exactly. I was happy to get the promotion, of course. But I don't see many chances for advancement from here.

Often *silence* is the best probe. A pause of up to 10 seconds (which feels like an eternity) lets the respondent know more information is expected. Depending on the interviewer's accompanying nonverbal messages, silence can indicate interest or dissatisfaction with the previous answer. *Prods* ("Uh-huh," "Hmmmm," "Go on," "Tell me more," and so on) accomplish the same purpose. For example:

Respondent:	I can't figure out where we can cut costs.
Interviewer:	Uh-huh.
Respondent:	We've already cut our travel and entertainment budget 5 percent.
Interviewer:	I know.
Respondent:	Some of our people probably still abuse it, but they'd be offended if we cut back more. They think of expense accounts as a fringe benefit.
Interviewer:	(silence)
Respondent:	Of course, if we could give them something in return for a cut, we might still be able to cut total costs. Maybe have the sales meeting at a resort—make it something of a vacation.

The Interviewee's Role   The interviewee can do several things to help make the interview a success.

Listen actively   Careful listening can assure that you understand the questions asked, so you do not go off on tangents or give answers unrelated to what is asked. Connecting your answers to what the interviewer has previously said shows both listening and critical thinking skills.

Give clear, detailed answers   A piece of obvious advice interviewees often ignore is to answer the question the interviewer has asked. An off-the-track answer suggests that the respondent hasn't understood the question, is a poor listener, or might even be evading the question. Put yourself in the interviewer's position, and think about what kind of information you would like to have. Then supply it.

Correct any misunderstandings   Being human, interviewers sometimes misinterpret comments. Most interviews are important enough for the respondent to want to be sure that the message given has been received accurately. Obviously, you can't ask the interviewer, "Were you listening carefully?" but two strategies can help get your message across. First, you can orally restate your message. This can be done in either the body or conclusion phase of the interview. For instance, in the body phase, while reporting on a list of exhibit preparations, the interviewee might mention that the brochures will have to be hand-carried; the following exchange could come later in the body phase or at the conclusion:

Interviewer:	So, everything will be at the exhibit booth when we get to the convention, and all we have to do is set up the exhibit.
Interviewee:	Not quite. The brochures won't be ready in time to ship to the convention, so you'll have to carry them with you on the plane.

Second, you can *put your ideas in writing.* It is sometimes wise to summarize important ideas in a memo that can be delivered before, during, or after the session. This enables the recipient to have a permanent record of your message.

Cover your own agenda   Interviewees often have their own goals. In a selection interview, the employer's goal is to pick the best candidate, while the applicant's aim is to prove that his or her qualifications make him or her the best. This may involve redefining the concept of best. For instance, a relatively inexperienced candidate might have the goal of showing the employer that experience isn't as important as education, enthusiasm, or social skills.

Closing

An interview shouldn't end with the last answer to the last question. As with most other types of communication, certain functions need to be performed to bring the interview to a satisfactory conclusion.

Review and Clarify the Results of the Interview
Either party can take responsibility for this step, though in different ways. The person with the greater power (usually the interviewer) is most likely to do so in the most forthright manner. For example, in an interview exploring a grievance between employees, a manager might say, "It sounds like you're saying that both of you could have handled it better." When the party with less power (usually the interviewee) does the reviewing and clarifying, the summary often takes the form of a question. A sales representative might close by saying, "So the product sounds good to you, but before you make your final decision you'd like to talk to a few of our clients to see how it has worked out for them. Is that right?"

Establish Future Actions
When the relationship between interviewer and respondent is a continuing one, it is important to clarify how the matter under discussion will be handled. A sales representative might close by saying, "I'll put a list of our customers in the mail to you tomorrow. Then why don't I give you a call next week to see what you're thinking?" A manager might clarify the future by saying, "I'd like you to try out the arrangement we discussed today. Then let's all get together in a few weeks to see how things are going. How does the first of next month sound?"

Conclude with Pleasantries
A sociable conclusion needn't be phony. You can express appreciation or concern, or you can mention future interaction:

"Your ideas were terrific. I know I can use them."

"I appreciate the time you've given me today."

"Good luck with the project."

Rate your skills in interview basics using the following scale:

1 = Not at all competent
2 = Somewhat comfortable
3 = Moderately competent
4 = Usually comfortable and competent
5 = Very comfortable and capable

1 2 3 4 5   1. I am able to greet the other person and introduce myself with sincere enthusiasm.

1 2 3 4 5   2. I am able to build rapport by establishing common ground and other ice-breaking conversation.

1 2 3 4 5   3. I am able to clarify the reason for the interview, the information that will be covered, and the estimated length of the interview.

4. *As an interviewer I understand how to (or I can)*

1 2 3 4 5   a. Control and focus the conversation.

1 2 3 4 5   b. Listen actively.

1 2 3 4 5   c. Use secondary questions, paraphrases, prods, and silence to gain elaboration and/or clarification.

5. *As an interviewee I understand how to*

1 2 3 4 5   a. Listen attentively to questions.

1 2 3 4 5   b. Give clear, detailed answers to the questions asked without getting sidetracked.

1 2 3 4 5   c. Correct any misunderstandings about me or my answers that the interviewer appears to have.

1 2 3 4 5   d. Cover my own agenda in addition to the interviewer's agenda.

1 2 3 4 5   6. Review and clarify the results of the interview and establish future actions.

1 2 3 4 5   7. Conclude with pleasantries.

The closer to 60 your score is, the more competent and comfortable you see yourself with interviewing basics.

The Ethics of Interviewing

The exchange of information that goes on between interviewer and interviewee should be guided by some basic ethical guidelines and responsibilities.[9] In addition to the moral reasons for following these guidelines, there is often a pragmatic basis for behaving ethically. Since the interview is likely to be part of an ongoing relationship, behaving

Handling Difficult Questions

1. You know that an employee has been leaving work early for the past several months. You hope he will volunteer this information, without your having to confront him. During a performance appraisal, how can you raise the issue with this employee?

2. You are conducting a series of half-hour interviews with consumers, exploring their attitudes toward a variety of social issues, as part of a market research project for your employer. In the first few minutes of one session, the interviewee makes several racist comments. How do you respond?

3. You are interviewing for a job you really want. The employer asks about your experience with a particular type of database software. You don't know much about this type of program, but you are confident that you can teach yourself before the job begins. How do you reply to the interviewer?

---

responsibly and honorably will serve you well in future interactions. Conversely, the costs of developing a poor reputation are usually greater than the benefits of gaining a temporary advantage by behaving unethically or irresponsibly.

Obligations of the Interviewer

A conscientious business communicator will follow several guidelines when conducting an interview.

Make Only Promises You Are Willing and Able to Keep   Don't make offers or claims that may later prove impossible to honor. For example, an employer should not encourage a job applicant about the chances of receiving an offer until he is sure an offer will be forthcoming. To make this sort of promise and then be overruled later by the boss or find out that the budget doesn't permit hiring at this time would be both dishonest and unfair. Likewise, a candidate should not indicate a willingness to start work immediately if she cannot begin work until she has sold her home and moved to the town where her new job is located. Despite the temptations, avoid making any commitments that sound good but are not firm.

Keep Confidences   Interviewers should not reveal confidential information to interviewees, nor should they disclose any private information gained during a session to people who have no legitimate reason to have it. For example, a supervisor who learns about an employee's personal problems should reveal them only with the employee's permission. Likewise, employees who learn confidential information in the course of their jobs—income levels, company plans, and so on—are obliged to make sure that such information stays private. Be certain to let the interviewee know it if you plan to record the session, and make it clear who else may be reviewing the recording.

Allow the Interviewee to Make Free Responses   An interview that coerces the subject into giving unwilling answers is a charade of an honest conversation. For example, a supervisor conducting a performance appraisal who asks a subordinate, "Who do you think is responsible for the problems in your area?" should be willing to accept whatever answer is given and not automatically expect the employee to accept the blame. Trying to *persuade* an interviewee is a normal part of doing business, but coercing one is not ethical.

Treat Every Interviewee with Respect

With rare exceptions, the interviewer's job is to help the interviewee do well. This means making sure that the interviewee feels comfortable and understands the nature of the session. It also means the interviewer must design questions that are clear and must help the interviewee answer them as well as possible.

Obligations of the Interviewee

The interviewee is also obliged to behave in an ethical and responsible way during a session. Several guidelines apply here.

Don't Misrepresent the Facts or Your Position

Whether the setting is an employment interview, a performance review session, or an information-gathering survey, it can be tempting to tell interviewers what they want to hear. The temptation is especially great if your welfare is at stake. But besides being unethical, misrepresenting the facts is likely to catch up with you sooner or later and harm you more than telling the truth in the first place would have.

Don't Waste the Interviewer's Time

If the choice exists, be sure you are qualified for the interview. For example, it would be a mistake to interview for a job you have little chance of landing or would not accept. Likewise, it would be unethical to volunteer for a customer survey if you aren't a member of the population being studied. If preparation for the interview is necessary, be sure to do your homework. Once the interview has begun, be sure to stick to the subject to use the time most wisely.

Sample Interview Plan

The following plan shows the kind of work that should go on before an interviewer and interviewee sit down to or even schedule a meeting. Every important interview requires the kind of planning exhibited here to achieve its goals. As you read this account, notice that it follows the advice outlined in this chapter.

Analysis and research	*I know that I'll never build the kind of financial security I am seeking by relying only on the income I earn from my job. Investing successfully will be the path to financial success. I also know that I'm very unsophisticated when it comes to investing, so I want to get a financial advisor who can teach me about the world of finance and who can help me set up and follow a plan.*
	Picking a financial advisor is like choosing a doctor. Skill is important, but it's not the only thing that matters. I need to find someone who has a personal style that I'm comfortable with and whose philosophy matches mine. I also need to find someone who is willing to devote time to me even though I don't have a great deal of money to invest . . . yet!
	I've compiled a list of possible advisors from friends, newspaper articles, and listings in the phone directory. I will call several of the people on this list to set up appointments for interviews.
Goal	*Based on my needs, the goal for my interviews will be to identify a financial planner with expertise in the field, whose investment philosophy matches mine, and who has a personal style that I am comfortable with.*

Interview strategy   *I definitely want to conduct these interviews in the offices of each financial planner. Seeing where and how they do business will probably give me a good idea of my comfort level before asking any questions. For instance, seeing a shabby or dis-organized office would cause me to doubt the competence of an advisor. On the other hand, a very plush office might make me wonder if I was being charged too much just to support a lavish lifestyle.*

I'll also be interested in seeing how much time each person gives me for the interview. If the person is rushed when trying to get a new client, this could mean I won't get the time or atten-tion I need once my money is in the planner's hands.

It will be interesting to see how much each person lets me explain my concerns and how much each controls the conversa-tion. I'm no financial expert, but I don't like the attitude "I'm the expert, so don't waste time asking too many questions." Since I would like someone who is willing to explain investing to me in a way that I can understand, I'll be looking for a good teacher.

Topics and questions   *As my goal suggests, I want to explore three topics. The following list shows the questions I'm planning to ask in each topic area as well as follow-up questions I can anticipate asking. I'm sure there will be a need for other secondary questions, but I can't predict all of them. I'll have to think of them on the spot*

TOPIC A: Expertise in Investments and Financial Planning

[This series of open questions explores the interviewee's qualifications and also provides an opportunity for her to talk about herself.]

1. What credentials do you have that qualify you as a financial planner? How important are credentials? If they aren't important, what is the best measure of a financial planner's qualifications?

[These questions move from a narrow to a broader focus.]

2. Do you have any areas of specialization? How and why did you specialize in this area?

[These indirect questions are a way of finding out whether the advisor's per-formance has been satisfactory.]

3. How many clients have you served in the last 5 years? What is the length of the relationship with your clients? How many have you retained, and how many are no longer with you?

[The average portfolio size is one measure of the advisor's expertise.]

4. What's the average amount of money you have managed for your clients?

[A closed question, designed to give interviewer references.]

5. May I see a list of your past and cur-rent clients and call some of them for references?

[The first question is a broad, open one. The second, closed question will produce a specific answer that can be compared with those of other potential advisors.]

6. How would you describe your track record in terms of investment advice? Specifically, what has been the ratio of successful to unsuccessful advice?

TOPIC B: Investment Philosophy

[This broad, open question gives the advisor a chance to describe his or her approach.]

1. How would you describe your investment philosophy?

[This hypothetical question will provide specific information about how a client–advisor relationship might operate.]

2. If I became your client, what steps would you recommend to start and maintain a financial program?

[This sequence of questions moves from specific to broad topics in a logical order.]

3. What kind of products do you like to deal in? Which specific ones might you recommend for me? Why?

[This two-question sequence again moves from a narrow to a broader focus. The most important information for the client is contained in the second question.]

4. I've read that some financial advisors make their income from commissions earned when their clients buy and sell investments. Other advisors charge a fee for their time. What approach do you take? Can you explain how this approach is in my interest as well as yours?

[Although this sounds like a closed question, it is likely to generate a long answer.]

5. How much should I expect to pay for your advice?

TOPIC C: Personal Style

[This indirect question really asks, "Would we work well together?"]

1. What kind of clients do you like to work with? What kinds don't you work well with?

[The first question here is really an indirect way of discovering how much attention the advisor has paid to the potential client.]

2. Have you looked over the papers I sent you about my financial condition? What did you think of them?

[This clever hypothetical question has a better chance of generating a useful answer than the more direct "What can you tell me about the kind of service I can expect?"]

3. If I were to call one of your clients at random, what would he or she tell me about the type of service and frequency of communication I can expect with you?

[This is a straightforward, open question.]

4. If we were to develop a relationship, what would you expect of me?

[This hypothetical question anticipates an important issue.]

5. Suppose I were to disagree with your advice. What would you say and do?

review points

- Interviewing is a conversation in which at least one party has a specific purpose. Unlike simple social conversations, interviews are purposeful, structured, and unbalanced in terms of control and speaking.

- Successful interview participants plan well by defining their objectives and identifying and analyzing the other party (self-concept, knowledge, image, and attitude toward the topic), and assuring an appropriate setting.

- Both interviewer and interviewee prepare agendas, while the interviewer determines the amount of structure desired.

- Interviewers plan important primary and secondary questions in advance of the interview and carefully consider the advantages of various types of questions: open or closed, direct or indirect, fact or opinion, hypothetical or critical incident. Leading questions ought to be avoided.

- Interviews consist of three parts: The opening establishes rapport, orients the respondent, and offers motivation for contributing.

- During the body, the interviewer keeps the conversation focused, listens actively, and probes for additional information as necessary. The respondent gives clear and detailed answers, corrects any misunderstandings, and covers his or her own agenda.

- The closing reviews and clarifies what has occurred, confirms future actions, and concludes with pleasantries.

- Ethical interviewers treat interviewees respectfully, keep confidences, make only promises they will honor, and avoid any coercion. Ethical interviewees do not waste an interviewer's time with insincerity, "practice," or poor preparation and present their facts and positions honestly.

key terms

Test your understanding of these key terms by visiting the Online Learning Center Web site at www.mhhe.com/adler10e.

closed questions   167
critical incident questions   170
direct questions   168
factual questions   168
highly structured interview   165
hypothetical questions   169
indirect questions   169
interview   160

leading questions   170
moderately structured interview   166
nonstructured interview   166
open questions   167
opinion questions   168
primary questions   167
secondary questions   167

activities

Go to the self-quizzes at the Online Learning Center at www.mhhe.com/adler10e to test your knowledge of chapter concepts.

1. Invitation to Insight

Learn more about the frequency and importance of interviewing. Choose a person whose work interests you and who spends much of his or her time interviewing in the course of a typical week. Ask your interviewee what kinds of interviews are common and what role they play in making his or her work successful.

2. Skill Builder

Imagine that you are conducting a research interview with an employee of a company where you might like to work.

a. Develop a list of topics that you will need to cover to get a complete picture of the organization.
b. Decide what structure (highly structured, moderately structured, nonstructured) would be best for this interview. Defend your choice.
c. For each topic, write several appropriate questions.

3. Skill Builder

Become more familiar with types of questions with the following activity.

a. Identify the problem with the following leading questions, and rephrase each question so that it is more effective:
   1. In a problem-solving interview: "If everyone works one Saturday morning per month, we can catch up on our backlog by the end of the quarter. How does that sound to you?"
   2. In a selection interview: "You don't mind traveling once or twice a month, do you?"
   3. In a survey interview: "We think the best features of our product are its price and durability. What do you think?"
   4. In a performance appraisal review: "Are you still bothered by not getting that promotion?"
   5. In a problem-solving interview: "We're really optimistic about the new job-sharing plan. What do you think?"
b. For each of the following situations, describe whether an open or closed question would be more appropriate, explaining your choice. If you think more than one question is necessary to discover the essential information, list each one.
   1. You want to find out whether your boss would support your request to attend a convention in a distant city.
   2. A manager wants to know whether a project will exceed its projected budget.
   3. An insurance sales representative wants to determine whether a customer has adequate coverage.
   4. An employer wants to find out why an applicant has held four jobs in 5 years.
c. For each of the following situations, write one factual and one opinion question. Decide which of these questions is most appropriate for the situation, and write two secondary questions as follows-ups for the primary question you have chosen:
   1. You want to know whether you are justified in asking your boss for a raise, and you decide to question a co-worker.
   2. A supervisor wants to discover whether an employee's request for a 1-month personal leave of absence to visit a sick parent is essential.

3. You are planning to buy a laptop or a desktop PC. You want to decide whether the laptop computer is worth the extra $250 it will cost.

d. For each of the following direct questions, create an indirect question that could elicit the same information:

1. "How hard a worker are you?" (selection)
2. "Do you agree with my evaluation?" (appraisal)
3. "Does the product have any drawbacks?" (sales)
4. "Are you telling me the real reason you're leaving?" (exit)
5. "Do you really believe my idea is a good one, or are you just going along?" (problem solving)

4. Skill Builder

With a partner, role-play how you, as an interviewer, could follow the guidelines in this section as you conduct the opening stages of each of the following interviews:

a. You are a real-estate broker meeting a potential home-buying client for the first time.
b. You are considering opening a new restaurant in town (you choose the kind), and you are interviewing the owner of a similar type of establishment in another city about how you can be successful.
c. You are thinking about taking a specific college course (you choose which one) that will help you in your career, and you are meeting with the professor to get a better idea of what is involved.
d. You are interviewing the manager of an assisted care facility to see if it would be a suitable place for your grandmother.

5. Invitation to Insight

Increase your awareness of ethical issues of interviewing by analyzing a televised interview (such as *Larry King Live*, the *Oprah Winfrey Show*, or a judicial or legislative hearing).

a. Evaluate the ethics of the interview by considering how well the interviewer and interviewee comply with the ethical obligations covered on pp. 178–180. Support your comments with specific examples.
b. What role did nonverbal communication play in your assessment?
c. Are there situations in which it would be advisable to breach any of the ethical obligations?

resources

For extensive readings and Web sites on principles of interviewing, see the Online Learning Center Web Site at **www.mhhe.com/adler10e.**

7

Types of Interviews

chapter outline

The Information-Gathering Interview
  Collect Background Information
  Define Interview Goals and Questions
  Choose the Right Interviewee

The Career Research Interview
  The Value of Personal Contacts
  Choosing Interviewees
  Contacting Prospective Interviewees
  Following Up

The Employment Interview
  Pre-Interview Steps
  During the Interview
  Post-Interview Follow-up
  Interviewing and the Law
  Sample Employment Interview

The Performance Appraisal Interview
  Definition and Importance
  Steps in the Appraisal Process
  Review Points
  Key Terms
  Activities
  Resources

chapter objectives

After reading this chapter you should be able to

1. Plan and conduct an information-gathering or career research interview that will help you clarify and/or achieve your career-related goals.
2. Identify and demonstrate the steps to prepare for, participate in, and follow up after an employment interview.
3. List various types of employment interviews and describe how you can prepare for each one.
4. Distinguish between legal and illegal employment interview questions and identify several methods of responding to illegal ones.
5. Describe how you can prepare for and effectively participate in a performance appraisal.

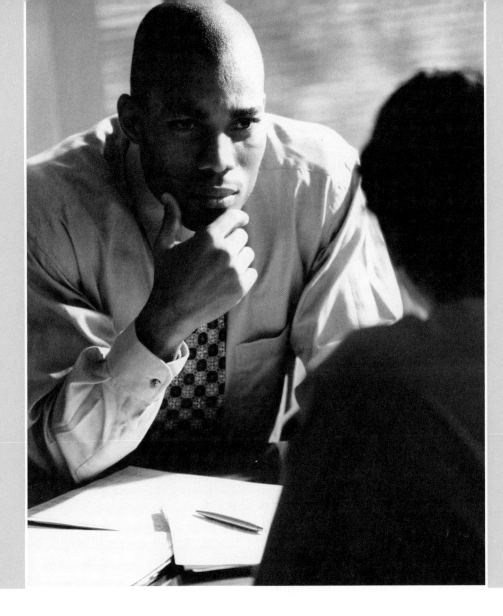

Of all the interview types described in Chapter 6, four are essential in almost every occupation: information-gathering, career research, employment, and performance appraisal. This chapter outlines the skills required for each of these important types of interview.

The Information-Gathering Interview

Information-gathering interviews come in many forms. For example, **investigative interviews** help answer the question, "What happened?" **Survey interviews** are used for various types of research to sample large groups of people. **Diagnostic interviews** are used by professionals in health care, law, counseling, and other areas to assess and treat clients. **Research interviews** turn up information that can help individuals and organizations perform more effectively. Finally, **exit interviews** help an organization learn why employees are leaving.

Many businesspeople owe their success in great part to the lessons they learned in information-gathering interviews. Sam Walton, founder of the Wal-Mart empire, explains how he used this approach early in his career to interview executives who had information that would help him:

> I would just show up and say, "Hi, I'm Sam Walton from Bentonville, Arkansas. We've got a few stores out there, and I'd like to speak with Mr. So-and-So"—whoever the head of the company was—"about his business." And as often as not, they'd let me in, maybe out of curiosity, and I'd ask lots of questions about pricing and distribution, whatever. I learned a lot that way.[1]

Another start-up tale reinforces the value of informational interviews. Three years out of college and jobless, entrepreneur Michael Mellinger created a thriving computer programming business in Barbados, where a staff of talented workers from second- and third-world Asian countries develop software for clients from wealthy, industrialized economies. He developed this idea by interviewing executives of Fortune 500 companies, whom he asked what services they needed. Despite his inexperience, Mellinger's approach captured the interest of top-level people. Before long, his mentors included the chief information officers of Pepsi, Merrill Lynch, and Chase Bank.[2]

Whatever their form, all types of information-gathering interviews follow the same general approach described in the following pages.

Collect Background Information

In many cases, pre-interview research is well worth the effort. Suppose, for instance, that you are interested in proposing a job-sharing plan—a system in which two people would share the responsibilities and salary of one full-time job. You decide you need to interview several people in your company before presenting your idea formally. Before conducting these interviews, however, you need to research the answers to some basic questions: How common is job sharing? In what industries does it occur? What forms does it take? Has it been tried by any firms in your field? What have the results of such arrangements been? Until you know at least the rough answers to these questions, you won't be ready to bring up the idea in your company.

Besides conducting traditional library research, you can get answers to questions like these by interviewing knowledgeable people. In this sense, talking about a single information-gathering interview is really an oversimplification, for you will usually conduct several during various stages of a task. You might, indeed, collect some fundamental background information during your first round of interviews. Perhaps you know someone who worked for a company that already has a job-sharing policy. An acquaintance might have mentioned a recent newspaper article on the subject, and you can get the reference that will help you locate it. During this phase, your questions will necessarily be vague, similar to the request you might make of a reference librarian: "I'm looking for information about job sharing. How do you think I ought to go about it?"

Once you have collected the necessary background information, you can use this knowledge to plan an intelligent approach to your second round of interviews—perhaps with people suggested by your earlier research or with the key decision makers who are your ultimate target.

Define Interview Goals and Questions

Defining the specific goal of your interview is always a key step. Your goal ought to be as specific as possible and be worded in a way that will tell you whether you have the answers you were seeking. Here are examples of how you might define a goal for an information-gathering interview:

Vague	Specific
I want to learn about tax-free municipal bonds.	Will tax-free municipal bonds give me liquidity, appreciation, safety, and tax shelter better than my present investments?
What happened at the accident yesterday?	What caused the accident, and could it have been prevented?
Should I buy a database management system?	Will a database management system improve my efficiency enough to justify the purchase?

Once you have identified your purpose, you must develop questions that will help you achieve it. For example:

Purpose: To learn what steps I need to take to have a job-sharing arrangement approved by management.

Questions:

Whom should I approach first?

Who will be the key decision maker on this issue?

Should I present my formal proposal first, or should I start by mentioning the subject informally?

What objections might management have to the proposal?

Is anyone else in the company (nonmanagement personnel) likely to oppose or support the idea?

What arguments (such as precedent, cost savings, employee morale) will most impress management?

What influential people might support this idea?

As you develop your questions, use the guidelines in Chapter 6. Make sure you gather both facts and opinions—and recognize which is which. Be prepared to follow up your primary questions with secondary queries as necessary.

Choose the Right Interviewee

The ideal respondent within an organization will be part of an informal communication network and may have no official relationship with you on the organizational chart. It might be naive to talk with your boss about the job-sharing proposal until you have consulted other sources who could suggest how to broach the subject: Perhaps a politically astute co-worker, someone who has experience making proposals to management, or even the boss's administrative assistant, if you are friends, will be helpful.

After you have established the purpose and the appropriate person to interview, follow the guidelines in Chapter 6 to plan and conduct the interview.

The Career Research Interview

The **career research interview** is a special type of informational interview in which you meet with someone who can provide information that will help you define and achieve your career goals. It is based on the principle that speaking with the right people can give you valuable ideas and contacts that you simply can't find from books, magazines, the Internet, or any other source.

The Value of Personal Contacts

The old phrase "It isn't what you know, it's who you know" is certainly true when it comes to getting a job. Over 30 years of research confirm that the vast majority of people don't find jobs from advertisements, headhunters, or other "formal" means.[3] Like these traditional sources, Web-based services like Monster.com aren't as useful as they might seem: Job-finding expert Richard Bolles cites research suggesting that less than 10 percent at best of job seekers find employment by using the Internet.[4] Other research backs up the value of personal contacts. A study of over 150,000 jobs found that more people were hired by referrals than by any other source.[5] Other research confirms this fact. A survey conducted by global resources company DBM revealed that 75 percent of job-seekers obtained their current positions through personal networking.[6]

Instead of using impersonal means, the majority of new hires get offers for employment through personal contacts. The reverse is also true: Most employers find good employees through their personal networks.[7] One corporate recruiter explained why networking is superior to Web-based employment sites:

> . . . in the rare instances where I actually post a position online, I get résumés from all over the world. Many of them bear no relationship to the job I am trying to fill. It's as though people just "point and shoot."
>
> The last professional position I posted—with extremely explicit qualifications laid out in the posting—received almost 1,000 responses, of whom only 25 or so even met the technical and educational qualifications for the position. My time is much better spent networking personally with people to find good candidates than reviewing and responding to these résumés.[8]

Finding a job is only one goal of career research interviews. These conversations can serve three purposes:

To conduct research that helps you learn more about the field and specific organizations that interest you.

To be remembered by making contacts who will recall you at an appropriate time and either offer you a position, inform you of employment opportunities, or suggest you to a potential employer.

To gain referrals to other people whom you might contact for help in your job search. These referrals can easily lead to meetings with more useful contacts, all of whom might mention you to *their* friends and associates.

Choosing Interviewees

The key to finding the wealth of unadvertised positions is to cultivate a network of contacts who can let you know about job opportunities and pass along your name to potential employers. Chapter 1 (pages 19–23) offered tips on how to build and nurture a personal network.

Getting Through Gatekeepers

Many potential career research interviewees are guarded by **gatekeepers**—personal assistants, receptionists, secretaries, etc. Even your most carefully crafted request for help may not gain you an interview if the gatekeeper is zealously guarding his or her boss's precious time. Here are some strategies for getting in touch with the person you want to interview.

Make your first request in writing

Your letter or e-mail has a much better chance of getting through to your target than an introductory phone call. Be sure your message follows the approach outlined in these pages, and that it is impeccably correct. Be sure to include your e-mail address and phone number so your target can reply.

Phone early or late

If you need to follow your introductory letter or e-mail with a phone call, the best time to reach your potential interviewee may be before or after regular business hours—when the gatekeeper isn't around to screen the boss's phone calls. If you are greeted by voice mail, be prepared to leave a fluent and concise reply: "Hi Ms. Allen. This is Daniel Mosher [phone number], following up on my letter to you from last week. I'm hoping to arrange a time when we can meet so I can get your advice about the best ways to prepare myself for breaking into the field of _____. My professor, Dr. Joy Chen, says you've been very helpful to other graduating seniors, and I would be very grateful for any ideas you're willing to share. I can be very flexible about when and where to meet. Again, my phone number is _____. I'll look forward to hearing from you at your earliest convenience."

Enlist gatekeepers as allies

If you find yourself speaking to the gatekeeper, begin by confidently asking to be put through to your prospective interviewee: "This is Daniel Mosher calling for Ms. Allen." If the reply is something like "She's in a meeting now. May I help?" your best approach may be to enlist the gatekeeper's assistance: "Certainly. I'd appreciate your advice. I'm following up on a letter I sent to Ms. Allen last week, and would like to set up a meeting with her. Could you suggest a time for an appointment, or maybe a time when I could call back and talk to her?" Be sure you get the gatekeeper's name, and address him/her personally from this point on.

Be flexible

Since you are asking for a favor, make yourself available for a meeting whenever it's convenient for your interviewee. Consider offering to conduct your interview over a meal or cup of coffee. One ambitious student even offered to chauffer his interviewee to the airport—a 90-minute drive. He argued that the chance to have an uninterrupted conversation made the effort well worthwhile.

There's no doubt that the people in your immediate networks can be helpful; but surprisingly, you can benefit even more from more-distant connections. In his classic study "The Strength of Weak Ties," Mark Granovetter surveyed over 280 residents of a Boston suburb who had taken a new job within the past year. While only 17 percent of the people surveyed found their jobs through close friends or relatives, the majority learned about their new positions from people who were only distant associates—old college friends, former colleagues, parents of a child's playmate, and so on.[9] Weak ties are often more useful than close acquaintances in finding jobs because your close associates rarely know more than you do about career opportunities. Distant acquaintances, however, are connected to other, less familiar communication networks, networks that often contain valuable information about new jobs.[10]

You might wonder why the kind of important person you would like to interview would be willing to meet with you. There are actually several reasons. First, if you have made contact through a referral, your subject will probably see you in deference to your mutual acquaintance. If you can gain a referral, you are most likely to get a friendly reception. Second, interviewees might be willing to see you for ego gratification. It is flattering to have someone say "I respect your accomplishments and ideas" and difficult for even a busy person to say no to a request that accompanies such a comment. A third reason is simple altruism. Most successful people realize they received help somewhere along the line, and many are willing to do for you what others did for them. Finally, you may get an interview because the person recognizes you as ambitious, someone who might have something to offer his or her organization.

Contacting Prospective Interviewees

When you approach a career research interviewee—especially one you don't know well—it can be smart to make your first contact in writing. A telephone call runs the risk of not getting through; and even if you do reach the interviewee, your call may come at a bad time. While e-mail can be quick and efficient, a traditional letter can make a strong, positive first impression. Your first message, like the one in Figure 7–1, should introduce yourself, explain your reason for the interview (stressing that you are *not* seeking employment), state your availability for a meeting, and promise a follow-up telephone call.

Unless you'll be conducting the interview within a day or two of the time your interviewee agrees to meet with you, a second letter, e-mail, or phone call should precede the interview and confirm its date, place, and time. This sort of follow-up can save you the

FIGURE 7–1

Request for an Informational Interview

From: Emily Park <eprk112@sunnet.net>
Sent: Tuesday, May 25, 2010 12:51 PM
To: Vanessa J. Yoder <v.yoder@DGHattysatlaw.com>
Subject: Seeking your advice

Dear Ms. Yoder:

I am currently a junior at the University of New Mexico, majoring in political science and communication. After graduating from UNM, I plan to attend law school and focus my studies on immigration law.

From several news accounts and also from several of my professors, I've learned that you are an expert in immigration law and have a stellar reputation for representing women when the cases involve both domestic violence and immigration issues. I also heard of your work during my internship at the Women's Workforce Training Center.

I would appreciate the opportunity to meet with you to discuss how I might best prepare myself for an eventual career in immigration law. I would also like to know which law schools you would recommend and hear about the challenges and rewards of this type of practice.

Let me stress that I am not seeking employment at this time. Your advice would be invaluable as I prepare myself for a career in law. I will call your office next week hoping to schedule an appointment. I know you are a busy person and I would be grateful for 30-45 minutes of your time.

I look forward to benefiting from your insights and recommendations.

Sincerely,
Emily Park
9971 Washoe St., NE
Albuquerque, NM 87112
(505) 793-3510

frustration of being stood up by a forgetful interviewee. Just as important, it shows that you know how to handle business engagements in a professional manner.

Giving your interviewee an advance list of topic areas and questions you hope to cover will distinguish you as a serious person, worth the interviewee's time and effort. Also, supplying this list will give your interviewee a chance to think about the areas you want to discuss and ideally come to your meeting best prepared to help you. Figure 7–2 illustrates a confirming e-mail with list of questions.

Following Up

In a post-interview letter or e-mail, express thanks for the interviewee's time and mention how helpful the information was. Besides demonstrating common courtesy, these messages become a tangible reminder of you and provide a record of your name and address that will be useful if the interviewee wants to contact you in the future.

FIGURE 7–2

Confirming E-mail with List of Questions

Subject: Interview confirmation and questions
Date: Fri, 11 June 2010, 8:26 a.m. (MDT)
From: Emily Park <eprk112@sunnet.net>
To: Vanessa J. Yoder <v.yoder@DGHattysatlaw.com>

Dear Ms. Yoder:

Thank you again for agreeing to speak with me about how I can best prepare myself for a career in immigration law. I am looking forward to our meeting at your office this coming Thursday, June 17, at 2:00 p.m. I know how busy you must be, and I'm grateful for your giving me 45 minutes of your time.

In order to use our time together most efficiently, here is a list of some questions I hope we can discuss at our meeting:

TRENDS IN IMMIGRATION AND LAW
- What trends do you anticipate in immigration patterns?
- How do you view the field of immigration law changing to reflect these conditions?

EDUCATION
- What law schools do you recommend for someone interested in practicing immigration law?
- Do you recommend any courses I should take in my senior year at the university?

EXPERIENCE
- What types of work experience (paid or volunteer) could help prepare me for law school and eventual employment?
- Can you recommend ways I might pursue positions in these areas?

EMPLOYMENT
- What types of jobs are there for attorneys who specialize in immigration law?
- How easy/difficult do you anticipate it will be to secure employment in these sorts of jobs?
- What, if any, are the pros and cons I might expect as a woman practicing law in this area?

LIFESTYLE
- How would you describe the benefits and challenges of working in the field of immigration law?
- How compatible is a career in this area with being a parent?

OTHER CONTACTS
- Can you recommend other people who might be willing to talk with me about preparing for a career in immigration law?

Of course, all correspondence should be typed neatly with impeccable format, spelling, and grammar: Your letters are a reflection of you.

The Employment Interview

An **employment interview** is designed to explore how well a candidate might fit a job. The exploration of fit works both ways: Employers certainly measure prospective candidates during this conversation, and prospective employees can decide whether the job in question is right for them. The Bureau of Labor Statistics reports that the typical American worker holds nearly nine different jobs before age 32, so the probability of facing at least one employment interview in the near future is high.[11]

The short time spent in an employment interview can have major consequences. Consider the stakes: Most workers spend the greatest part of their adult lives on the job—roughly 2,000 hours per year or upward of 80,000 hours during a career. The financial difference between a well-paid position and an unrewarding one can also be staggering. Even without considering the effects of inflation, a gap of only $200 per month can amount to almost $100,000 over the course of a career. Finally, the emotional results of having the right job are considerable. A frustrating job not only makes for unhappiness at work but these dissatisfactions also have a way of leaking into nonworking hours as well.

How important is an interview in getting the right job? The Bureau of National Affairs, a private research firm that serves both government and industry, conducted a survey to answer this question. It polled 196 personnel executives, seeking the factors that were most important in hiring applicants. The results showed that the employment interview is the single most important factor in landing a job.[12] Further research revealed that the most important factor during these critically decisive interviews was communication skills. Employers identified the ability to communicate effectively as more important in shaping a hiring decision than grade-point average, work experience, extracurricular activities, appearance, and preference for job location.[13]

Even though interviews can play an important role in hiring, research shows that potential employers—at least those who aren't trained in employment interviewing—are not very good at using interviews to choose the best applicant for a job.[14] They fail to recognize the potential in some candidates who would make fine employees, and they are impressed by others who prove to be less than satisfactory as workers. In other words, the best candidate does not necessarily get the job offer.

In many situations, the person who knows the most about getting hired gets the desired position. "Chemistry is the paramount factor in hiring," states Wilhelmus B. Bryan III, executive vice president of William H. Clark Associates, a New York recruiting firm.[15] While job-getting skills are no guarantee of qualifications once the actual work begins, they are necessary to get hired in the first place.

Pre-Interview Steps

Scanning the newspaper for openings and then filing an application with the company's personnel or human resources department is one way of looking for a job

"You don't look like a Dave."

but often not the most effective. Many employers never advertise jobs, and depending on the salary sought, only 5 to 24 percent of job seekers find a job solely through local newspaper ads.[16] Employment expert Richard Bolles explains:

> *I know too many stories about people who have been turned down by a particular company's personnel department, who then went back to square one, found out who, in that very same company, had the power to hire for the position they wanted, went to that woman or man, and got hired—ten floors up from the personnel department that had just rejected them.*[17]

Even when a company does advertise, the odds don't favor an applicant who replies with an application and résumé. Since most job announcements attract many more applicants than an employer needs, the job of the personnel department becomes *elimination*, not selection. The goal is to reduce the pool of job seekers to a manageable number by rejecting as many applicants as possible. Given this process of elimination, any shortcoming becomes welcome grounds for rejecting the application and the applicant. Many consultants, therefore, suggest identifying and contacting the person who has the power to hire you *before* an opening exists. The process has several steps.

Conduct Background Research

The first step is to explore the types of work and specific organizations that sound appealing to you. This involves doing Internet research, reading magazines and newspaper articles, taking classes, and simply fantasizing about jobs you might find interesting. The result of your research should be a list of organizations and names of people who can tell you more about your chosen field.

Besides helping you find organizations where you want to work, your knowledge of a company will distinguish you as a candidate worth considering for a job. Desiree Crips of Salus Media in Carpinteria, California, reflects the view of most potential employers: "If someone walks in here and doesn't know anything about our company, that's a real negative. There's just no excuse for not being up to speed on any company you're applying to these days."[18] Doing your homework is just as important in the workforce as in school.

Contact Potential Employers

At some point, your research and networking will uncover one or more job leads. You might read a newspaper story about the need of a local employer for people with interests or training like yours. Perhaps a career research interview subject will say, "I know someone over at _____ who is looking for a person like you." You might learn through a friendly contact that a desirable firm is about to expand its operations. In such a case, it is time to approach the person who has the power to hire you and explore how you can help meet the company's needs.

Whether the job lead comes from a formal announcement or a contact from your personal network, your first step is to let the organization know about your interest in a job. In most cases, the best way to do this is with written correspondence, usually a cover letter and a copy of your résumé. The Appendix of this book has advice on constructing and formatting résumés. A cover letter like the one in Figure 7–3 on page 196 that takes the following approach will serve you well.

In the first paragraph, introduce yourself to the reader. Clearly state your purpose for writing (e.g., in response to an advertisement, at the suggestion of a mutual acquaintance, as a result of your research) and describe your ability to meet the company's needs. When appropriate, mention any mutual acquaintances that the addressee will recognize. If you are writing to the human resources department of a medium- or large-sized

FIGURE 7–3

Sample
Message
Requesting an
Employment
Interview

*The writer identifies
her reason for writing,
and makes reference to
a mutual acquaintance,
who presumably can
vouch for her.*

*This paragraph links the
writer's experience to the
job being sought.*

*This paragraph details
professional accomplish-
ments that are relevant to
the job being advertised.*

*The applicant closes by
clearly expressing her
desire to meet and discuss
the job, indicating when
she will be available.*

*The applicant includes
her mailing address and
phone number, in case
the employer wishes to
contact her in one of
these ways.*

From: Krista Dudley [krista.dudley@rockycast.net]
Sent: Friday, April 16, 2010 5:41 PM
To: John Waldmann [john.waldmann@boulderarts.org]
Subject: Events Coordinator application

Attached: K Dudley Resume.doc

Dear Mr. Waldmann:

Our mutual friend Marcia Sherwood recently alerted me to the open position of Events Coordinator for the Boulder Arts Council, and I am writing to express my interest in that position.

I would welcome the chance to use skills acquired over the past 12 years planning events for a variety of community organizations in the Denver area to help the Council extend its reach in the community. The attached resume will help you gain a sense of my experience.

As a person who has coordinated a wide range of community events for nonprofit organizations, I can bring the Arts Council demonstrated ability to motivate and coordinate the work of volunteers and to generate widespread publicity for events on a limited budget. Most recently, I was chairperson for Aurora's Earth Day festival, and I was the public information coordinator for last year's Halloween auction and dance to benefit Denver's Shelter Services for Women. The enclosed résumé details a variety of other activities that have helped prepare me for the position of Events coordinator.

I would welcome the chance to discuss how I might help the Boulder Arts Council. I will be available any time in the next month, except for the weekend of April 23–24.

I look forward to hearing from you soon.

Sincerely,
Kristina Dudley
387 Blythe St.
Aurora, CO 80017
(303) 654-7909

organization, be sure to give the job number if there is one; a company that has many job openings won't know which one you're applying for unless you identify it.

In the next paragraph or two, highlight one or two of your most impressive accomplishments that are *relevant to the job at hand.* Don't just say you can help the organization: Offer some objective evidence that backs up your claim.

In the closing paragraph, describe the next step you hope to take—usually requesting an interview. Detail any information about limits on your availability (though you should keep these to an absolute minimum). Supply any other information that the prospective employer may have requested. Finally, close with a cordial expression of gratitude.

Most career counselors recommend directing your request for an interview to the person who has the ability to hire you, rather than to the company's human resources department. We have already discussed why personnel departments aren't the best avenue for getting hired: Employees there are usually screening large numbers of applicants, so they are looking for reasons to reject as many as possible to arrive at a manageable number of finalists to interview. Also, personnel screeners are usually not familiar with the position, so they may reject candidates for superficial or mistaken reasons.

The mechanical nature of this screening process is best illustrated by the growing use of **scannable résumés.** These documents are "read" by document scanning devices, not humans. The software searches for keywords and phrases that describe the skills and education required for the position. Applications that contain these words are passed on to a human who evaluates them further. The Appendix of this book offers tips on creating effective scannable résumés; but even the best document may not capture the unique traits you can offer an employer. For this reason, you will maximize your chances at being recognized by developing a relationship with people who know both your talents and the characteristics of the job.

Another screening technique are job interviews by computer. Retailers such as Target, Macy's, and Hollywood Video are replacing paper applications and in-person interviews with computer kiosks in the initial screening of applicants.[19]

Prepare for Possible Interview Formats   The standard one-on-one, question-and-answer interview format isn't the only one you may encounter. Employers use a variety of interview formats. If you are prepared for all of them, you aren't likely to be surprised.

In a **panel interview** (sometimes called a *team* or *group interview*), the candidate is questioned by several people. Panel interviews save the company time and provide the people with whom you may work an opportunity to compare their perceptions of you. When setting up an interview, it is appropriate to ask whether you will be facing a team of questioners. If you are, do your best to learn and use the names of each person. When you answer questions, make sure you look at everyone in the group. Some employers use a **stress interview** to evaluate your behavior under pressure; you can find tips to prepare for this at the Online Learning Center at **www.mhhe.com/ adler10e.**

In an **audition interview** you will be asked to demonstrate whatever skills the employer is looking for. You might be asked to create a project, solve a problem, or respond to a typical scenario in the job, such as dealing with a difficult client. The audition shows the potential employer how you are likely to do on the job. The prospect of an audition can be especially helpful if you will be competing against candidates with more experience or stronger credentials. For that reason, you might even volunteer for an audition if you are confident you can handle the job well.[20]

A **behavioral interview** is based on the assumption that past experience is the best predictor of future performance. In this approach interviewers explore specifics about the candidate's past accomplishments. John Madigan, a vice president at The Hartford Financial Services Group, explains the way behavioral interviews work: "We actually ask what you did in specific situations. Concrete examples will demonstrate a person's preferred way of dealing with those situations and give you a better idea of that person and how they're likely to act on the job."[21]

Here are some questions you might hear in a behavioral interview:

- Give me a specific example of when you sold your supervisor or professor on an idea or concept. What was the result?

- Tell me about a time when you came up with an innovative solution to a challenge you or your company was facing. What was the challenge? What role did others play?

- Describe a situation where you faced multiple projects. How did you handle it?[22]

on your feet

Preparing for Behavioral Interviews

Interviewers often ask questions about your past behavior in order to judge the way you are likely to handle a job if hired.

Each answer to a behavioral question should include (1) one or more specific examples of what you did and (2) what the example(s) you've chosen say about you as a prospective employee. Choose examples that showcase some of your best qualities. If it is a question about something you did wrong or a mistake you made, show how you learned something or how something positive resulted from the experience. For example, if asked to describe a time when you were faced with a stressful situation that demonstrated your coping skills, you might answer: "In the middle of my last semester as a senior, my father had emergency surgery. That put a big load on my family, and I moved back home for about 2 months to lend a hand. During that time I managed to finish all my classes with As and Bs, and I also covered every shift on my job after the first week. It wasn't fun, but that experience taught me that I can handle a lot of demands."

Practice your skill at behavioral interviews by answering the questions below in a group:

- Describe a time that you needed to work as part of a team.
- Tell about a time that you had to use creativity and problem-solving skills to solve an important problem.
- Explain how you handled a situation when you had to make an important ethical decision.
- Describe a time when you didn't succeed at something you were trying to accomplish.
- Give an example of a time when you took on a greater share of responsibility or decision making than was required by your job.

For more examples of behavioral interview questions, see **www.quintcareers.com/sample_behavioral.html**.

If you have a proven record of accomplishments that will clearly work well in the job you are seeking, a behavioral interview should sound ideal. If you don't have work experience that is clearly relevant to the new position, find ways to demonstrate how things you have done in other contexts apply to the job you are seeking. For example, you might be able to show how experience in retail sales taught you how to deal with difficult customers you'll encounter in a customer service job, or how being a volunteer for a nonprofit charity gave you an appreciation for working with limited resources—an attitude most employers will welcome.

Think Constructively   The way you think about an upcoming interview can affect how you feel and act during the session. A research team at Washington State University interviewed both highly anxious and more confident students to discover what causes some people to become especially apprehensive during the process of meeting prospective employers.[23] The differences between the groups were startling. Anxious students avoided thinking about an interview in advance, so they did little in the way of research or preparation. When they did think about an upcoming interview, they dwelled on negative self-talk: "I won't do well" or "I don't know why I'm doing this." It's no surprise that thoughts like these created negative self-fulfilling prophecies that led to poor interview performances. Students who handled interviews better weren't anxiety-free, but they thought about the upcoming challenge in more productive ways. We can imagine them thinking, "The interviewer isn't trying to trick me or trip me up" and "I'll do a lot better if I prepare."

Recovering from Interview Blunders

Most job seekers plan carefully for employment interviews. But occasionally an applicant blunders so spectacularly that his or her performance earns a place in the Communication Hall of Fame. The following true stories were reported by employment interviewers.

> "A man who forgot dark socks to wear with his suit colored in his ankles with a black felt-tip marker."

> "The candidate said that by crossing the Maryland state line he was in violation of his probation but felt the interview was worth risking possible jail time."

> "A candidate was asked what person they would most like to meet, living or dead, and their response was the living one."

> "I was interviewing someone who took a cell-phone call and asked me to leave my office while they talked."

> "When a candidate was asked about his greatest accomplishment, he replied that it was writing a short novel. When the interviewer said, 'No, I mean something you did while at work,' the candidate replied, 'But I did write it while at work!'"

No employer would hire an applicant who behaved so poorly in an interview. But job candidates do make less serious, though egregious, mistakes. According to experts in the field, some of the most common blunders are

arriving late

being rude to other employees

calling someone by the wrong name

an error in résumé or cover letter

referencing a potential employer's competitor

CRITICAL ANALYSIS: One way to avoid bungling an interview is to anticipate—and thereby avoid mindless errors. You can prepare yourself for an error-free interview by considering the following points.

1. What other kinds of careless mistakes might an otherwise prepared job candidate make in an interview situation?

2. How could you guard against making each of the mistakes you listed in the question above?

3. Devise a strategy for recovering from each of the five mistakes above and those that you have identified. Compare your strategies with those suggested by experts at **http://m.cnn.com/cnn/ne/living/detail/217858/full;jsessionid=F6AA 61F989728D95410C0E6E9C5BD7E1.live4ib.**

Sources: "Great Places to Work: Interview Horror Stories," *Washingtonian*, November 1, 2005, retrieved January 3, 2009, from **www.washingtonian.com/articles/businesscareers/2159.html;** and "Job Search Mistakes," CNN.com, December 24, 2008, retrieved December 30, 2008, from **http://m.cnn.com/cnn/ne/living/detail/217858/full;jsessionid=F6AA61F989728D95410C0E6E9C 5BD7E1.live4ib.**

Dress Appropriately and Act Professionally Looking good when you meet a potential employer is vitally important. In one survey, recruiters ranked clothing as the leading factor in shaping their initial impressions of applicants (ahead of physical attractiveness and résumé). Furthermore, 79 percent of the recruiters stated that their initial impressions influenced the rest of the interview.[24] The best attire to wear will depend on the job you are seeking: The professional business suit that would be appropriate for a banking job would almost certainly look out of place if you were interviewing for a job in the construction industry, and it might look overly formal at many software companies. When in doubt, it is always safest to dress on the conservative side. Of course, cleanliness and personal hygiene are essential.

Be sure to arrive at the interview 5 to 10 minutes early. Be polite to everyone in the office. While you wait, choose reading material about the business or company, not about current TV personalities. When introduced, shake hands firmly, no more than three shakes, avoiding a limp or hand-crushing grip. Smile, make eye contact, and take your lead from the interviewer about how to proceed.

During the Interview

If your fate in the selection process were determined by a skilled, objective interviewer, the need for strategic communication might not be essential. Research shows, however, that the rating you are likely to receive from an interviewer can be influenced by a variety of factors as varied as the time of day, the sex of the interviewer and interviewee, whether the candidates before you did well or poorly, and the employer's mood.[25] Since the interview is not a scientific measure of your skills, it is especially important to do everything possible to make the best impression. Interviewing expert Anthony Medley describes one memorable job candidate who illustrates the importance of first impressions:

> She was attractive, presentable, and had good references. But after showing up ten minutes late, she called me "Mr. Melody" throughout the interview.
>
> The two things I remembered about her were that she had kept me waiting and constantly mispronounced my name. I finally offered the position to someone whose . . . skills were not nearly so good.[26]

Your background research will pay dividends during the employment interview. One criterion most interviewers use in rating applicants is "knowledge of the position," and a lack of information in this area can be damaging. One example illustrates the advantages that come from knowing even a small amount about a position:

> When I first took a job as a young attorney for Litton Industries, I was interviewing for the position as an assistant division counsel for their Guidance Control Systems Division. That name alone was enough to boggle my mind. A scientist I was not. After a little research, I found that they made something called an inertial navigation system. That was worse than the name of the division. What was an inertial navigation system?
>
> Finally I went to a fraternity brother who had majored in engineering and asked him if he knew what it was all about. He explained to me that inertial navigation was a method of navigating whereby the system allows you, if you know your starting point, to measure speed and distance and therefore know where you are at all times. He also explained the components of the system.
>
> When I went into my interview with the division counsel, I astounded him by my ability to talk the jargon of inertial navigation . . .
>
> He later told me that I was the first person he had interviewed for the job to whom he did not have to explain inertial navigation. Since he didn't understand it any better than I did, his being relieved of this obligation was a big plus in my favor. Also he said that he knew that it was not an easy task for me to find someone who could explain the subject and understand it well enough to have the confidence to discuss it. My initiative and interest in going to this extent to prepare for the interview had impressed him.[27]

Table 7–1 lists common interviewer complaints about interviewees.

Anticipate Key Questions

Most employment interviewers ask questions in five areas:

Educational background. Does the candidate possess adequate training for a successful career? Do the candidate's grades and other activities predict success in this organization?

Work experience. Do any previous jobs prepare the candidate for this position? What does the candidate's employment history suggest about his or her work habits and ability to work well with others?

Table 7–1	Most Frequent Interviewer Complaints about Interviewees

1. Poor personality, manners; lack of poise, confidence; arrogant; egotistical; conceited
2. Poor appearance, lack of neatness, careless dress
3. Lack of enthusiasm, shows little interest, no evidence of initiative, lack of drive
4. Lack of goals and objectives, lack of ambition, poorly motivated, does not know interests, uncertain, indecisive, poor planning
5. Inability to express self well, poor oral expression, poor habits of speech
6. Unrealistic salary demands, overemphasis on money, more interested in salary than opportunity, unrealistic concerning promotion to top jobs
7. Lack of maturity, no leadership potential
8. Lack of extracurricular activities, inadequate reasons for not participating in activities
9. Failure to get information about our company, lack of preparation for the interview, inability to ask intelligent questions
10. Excessive interest in security and benefits, "what can you do for me" attitude
11. Objects to travel, unwilling to relocate

Source: Victor R. Lindquest, *The Northwestern Endicott Report 1988* (Evanston, IL.: The placement Center, Northwestern University, 1988).

Career goals. Does the candidate have clear goals? Are they compatible with a career in this organization?

Personal traits. Do the actions and attitudes of the candidate predict good work habits and good interpersonal skills?

Knowledge of organization and job. Does the candidate know the job and organization well enough to be certain that he or she will feel happy in them?

While the specifics of each job are different, many questions are the same for any position. Table 7–2 on page 202 lists the most common questions asked by interviewers. In addition, knowledge of the company and job should suggest other specific questions to you.

There's a good chance you will be asked at least some of the common questions listed below. Here are some tips about how to approach them, keeping the focus on what you can do for the organization.

Question	What to Emphasize
Why should we hire you?	Don't give a generic answer: Nearly everyone says they are hardworking and motivated. Briefly list your unique strengths and qualifications, showing how they **will help you perform the job in question.**
Why do you want to work here?	If you have researched the organization, this question gives you an opportunity to explain how your experience and qualifications match the **company's needs.**

Table 7–2	Commonly Asked Questions in Employment Interviews

Educational Background

How has your education prepared you for a career?

Why did you choose your college or university?

Describe your greatest success (biggest problem) in college.

What subjects in school did you like best? Why?

What subjects did you like least? Why?

What was your most rewarding college experience?

Work Experience

Tell me about your past jobs. (What did you do in each?)

Which of your past jobs did you enjoy most? Why?

Why did you leave your past jobs?

Describe your greatest accomplishments in your past jobs.

What were your biggest failures? What did you learn from them?

How have your past jobs prepared you for this position?

What were the good and bad features of your last job?

This job requires initiative and hard work. What in your experience demonstrates these qualities?

Have you supervised people in the past? In what capacities? How did you do?

How do you think your present boss (subordinates, co-workers) would describe you?

How do you feel about the way your present company (past companies) is (were) managed?

Career Goals

Why are you interested in this position?

Where do you see yourself in 5 years? 10 years?

What is your eventual career goal?

Why did you choose the career you are now pursuing?

Tell me about yourself.

Keep your answer focused on parts of your life that relate to the job. Pick a couple of points that show how you possess skills and/or experiences that show **what you can contribute to this organization.**

You can't anticipate every question a prospective employer will ask. Still, if you go into the interview with a clear sense of yourself—both strengths and limitations—and the nature of the job you are seeking, you can probably handle almost any question. Consider a few examples of unusual questions, and what the interviewers who asked them were seeking.

What are your financial goals?

How would you describe the ideal job?

How would you define success?

What things are most important to you in a career?

Self-Assessment

In your own words, how would you describe yourself?

How have you grown in the last years?

What are your greatest strengths? Your greatest weaknesses?

What things give you the greatest satisfaction?

How do you feel about your career up to this point?

What is the biggest mistake you have made in your career?

Do you prefer working alone or with others?

How do you work under pressure?

What are the most important features of your personality?

Are you a leader? (a creative person? a problem solver?) Give examples.

Knowledge of the Job

Why are you interested in this particular job? Our company?

What can you contribute to this job? Our company?

Why should we hire you? What qualifies you for this position?

What do you think about _____ (job-related topic)?

What part of this job do you think would be most difficult?

Other Topics

Do you have any geographical preferences? Why?

Would you be willing to travel? To relocate?

Do you have any questions for me?

Question	What the Interviewer Was Seeking
What's the biggest career mistake you've made so far?	Have you learned from your errors? What mistakes are you not likely to make if you work for us?
If I asked your previous co-workers what I'd better watch out for from you, what would they say?	How aware are you of your own strengths and weaknesses?
Who else are you interviewing with, and how close are you to accepting an offer?	How committed are you to our organization? How do others view your potential as an employee?[28]

"Will my office be near an ice machine?"

Since most employers are untrained in interviewing, you can't expect them to ask every important question.[29] If your interviewer doesn't touch on an important area, look for ways of volunteering information that he or she probably would want to have. For instance, you could show your knowledge of the industry and the company when you respond to a question about your past work experience: "As my résumé shows, I've been working in this field for 5 years, first at Marston-Keenan and then with Evergreen. In both jobs we were constantly trying to keep up with the pace you set here. For example, the VT-17 was our biggest competitor at Evergreen. . . ."

Respond to the Employer's Needs and Concerns   While you may need a job to repay a college loan or finance your new Porsche, these concerns won't impress a potential employer. Companies hire employees to satisfy *their* needs, not yours. Although employers will rarely say so outright, the fundamental question that is *always* being asked in an employment interview is, *"Are you a person who can help this organization?"* That is, *"What can you do for us?"* One career guidance book makes the point clearly:

> It is easy to get the impression during an interview that the subject of the interview, the star (so to speak) of the interview is, well, you. After all, you're the one in the hot seat. You're the one whose life is being dissected. Don't be too flattered. The real subject of the interview is the company. The company is what the interviewer ultimately thinks is important.
>
> Of course, you will be very concerned about what opportunities and skills the company has to offer you, but if you're smart, you'll keep that to yourself. It's not that it isn't proper to be interested in advancement and money—in fact, that's a given. What is not a given is your ability to put the interests of your company ahead of your own from time to time; to make personal sacrifices for the good of an important project. The interviewer will be extremely interested in these things if you can find a way to communicate them.[30]

Your approach in an interview, then, should be to show your potential employer how your skills match the company's concerns. Background research will pay off here, too: If you have spent time learning about what the employer needs, you will be in a good position to show how you can satisfy company needs and concerns. Consider an example:

Interviewer:	What was your major in college?
Poor Answer:	I was a communication major.
Better Answer:	I was a communication major. I'm really glad I studied that subject, because the skills I learned in school could help me in this job in so many ways: dealing with customers, working with you and the other people in the department, and also with all the external contractors who are part of the job. . . .

Interviewer:	Tell me about your last job as a sales rep.
Poor Answer:	I handled outside sales. I called on about 35 customers. My job was to keep them supplied and show them new products.
Better Answer:	(elaborating on previous answer) I learned how important it is to provide outstanding customer service. Even though the products I sold in my last job are different from the ones I'd be selling here, I know that the competitive edge comes from making sure the customers get what they want, when they need it. I know that this company has a reputation for good service, so I'm really excited about working here.

Just because you respond to the employer's needs doesn't mean you should ignore your own goals; but as you are in an interview, keep in mind that you need to demonstrate how you can help the organization or you won't have a job offer to consider.

Because most employers have had bad experiences with some of the people they have hired, they are likely to be concerned about what might go wrong if they hire you. In Richard Bolles's words, employers worry that

> *you won't be able to do the job, you lack the skills, you won't work full days, regularly, you'll quit unexpectedly, it will take you a long time to master the job, you won't get along with others, you'll do the minimum, you'll need constant supervision, you'll be dishonest, irresponsible, negative, substance abuser, incompetent, you'll discredit the organization or cost them a lot of money.*[31]

You can allay these fears without ever addressing them directly by answering questions in a way that showcases your good work habits:

Interviewer:	What were the biggest challenges in your last job?
Answer:	The work always seemed to come in spurts. When it was busy, we had to work especially hard to stay caught up. I can remember some weeks when we never seemed to leave the office. It was hard, but we did whatever it took to get the job done.
Interviewer:	How did you get along with your last boss?
Answer:	My last manager had a very hands-off approach. That was a little scary at times, but it taught me that I can solve problems without a lot of supervision. I was always glad to get guidance, but when it didn't come, I learned that I can figure out things for myself.

Be Honest   Whatever else an employer may be seeking, honesty is a mandatory job requirement. If an interviewer finds out that you have misrepresented yourself by lying or exaggerating about even one answer, then everything else you say will be suspect.[32]

Being honest doesn't mean you have to confess to every self-doubt and shortcoming. As in almost every type of situation, both parties in an employment interview try to create desirable impressions. In fact, some ethicists have noted that the ability to "sell" yourself honestly but persuasively is a desirable attribute, since it shows that you can represent an employer well after being hired.[33] So, highlight your strengths and downplay your weaknesses, but always be honest.

career tip

Negotiating a Salary

It is usually best to save a discussion of salary until you have been offered a job. Compensation is almost always negotiable to some degree. It becomes increasingly so for positions that require more expertise and experience. The way you handle this issue can make a significant difference in the pay and benefits you receive. The following tips can help you negotiate the best possible compensation package.

Find Out the Prevailing Compensation for Your Type of Job

Discover what others are paid for the kind of work you do. Begin by exploring compensation levels in your field or industry. Several strategies will help you come up with realistic figures:

- *Online information:* Glassdoor.com, Payscale.com, Jobstar.org, and Careerbuilder.com provide useful ways to compare salaries. You can also use a search engine like MetaCrawler (**www.metacrawler.com**) to seek out compensation. Combine terms like "wages" or "salary" with the name of your field (e.g., "sales" or "programming") to find the numbers you are seeking. The Salary Calculator (**www.homefair.com/calc/salcalc.html**) and Salary.com (**www.salary.com**) provide additional salary comparisons and information.

- *Personal contacts:* Your personal network can provide very useful information on prevailing salaries and benefits. Career counselors, recruiters, and outplacement counselors can be useful sources of information. An informational interview with people like this can be extremely useful. Contacts within a specific geographical area or company where you hope to work can be especially helpful. Rather than embarrassing people by asking for personal information ("How much do you earn?") or proprietary data ("What's the top salary the company would pay for a job like this?"), it's better to ask questions like, "What is the salary range in this company for a job like mine?" A good follow-up is, "What might lead an employer to offer a salary at the top end of this scale?"

Learn How Much the Company Wants You

Your leverage will be greatest under two conditions: first if the company needs to hire someone quickly, and if it is specifically interested in you. Your personal network is, again, the ideal way to determine whether these conditions exist. You can also determine how motivated the company is to hire you from your knowledge of the job market—both nationally and locally—for positions like the one you are seeking.

Consider Negotiating for Nonsalary Compensation

Even if the salary offer isn't everything you hope for, you may be able to get benefits such as the following that improve the overall compensation package:

- Nonsalary financial gains: commissions, bonuses (for signing or future performance), money in lieu of unneeded benefits (e.g., health insurance when you already have coverage), profit sharing, stock options.

- Time: personal leave days, extra vacation, flexible scheduling of work hours, telecommuting, job sharing.

- Educational benefits: tuition reimbursement, training programs.

- Perquisites: better office, expense account, company car, reserved or paid parking.

- Relocation expenses: house-hunting trips, moving costs, realty fees for home purchase/sale.

- Support: free on-site child care, company time for volunteering in your child's school.

- Lifestyle: use of company apartment, upgraded business travel (hotel, air), company tickets to sporting events and theaters, health club membership.

Promoting Yourself with Honesty

Think of a job that you are probably capable of handling well but for which you would most likely not be the candidate hired. Develop a list of questions you would probably be asked in an interview for this position. Then develop a list of answers that show you in the best possible light while being honest.

Emphasize the Positive   Although you should always be honest, it is also wise to phrase your answers in a way that casts you in the most positive light. Consider the difference between positive and negative responses to this question:

Interviewer:	I notice you've held several jobs, but you haven't had any experience in the field you've applied for.
Negative Answer:	Uh, that's right. I only decided that I wanted to go into this field last year. I wish I had known that earlier.
Positive Answer:	That's right. I've worked in a number of fields, and I've been successful in learning each one quickly. I'd like to think that this kind of adaptability will help me learn this job and grow with it as technology changes the way the company does business.

Notice how the second answer converted a potential negative into a positive answer. If you anticipate questions that have the ability to harm you, you can compose honest answers that present you in a favorable manner.

Even if you are confronted with comments that cast you in a negative light, you can recast yourself more positively. Notice how each negative trait below could be reframed as a positive attribute:[34]

Negative Trait	Positive Attribute
Overly detailed	Thorough, reliable
Cautious	Careful, accurate
Intense	Focused
Slow	Methodical, careful
Naive	Open, honest
Aggressive	Assertive

Don't misunderstand: Arguing with the interviewer or claiming that you have no faults isn't likely to win you a job offer. Still, reframing shortcomings as strengths can shift the employer's view of you:

Employer:	If I were to ask your colleagues to describe your biggest weaknesses, what do you think they'd say?

| Candidate: | Well, some might say that I could work faster, especially when things get frantic. On the other hand, I think they would agree that I'm very careful about my work and that I don't make careless errors. In the long run, I think that saves the company and our customers a lot of grief. I want to work faster, but never at the cost of making mistakes. |

Another important rule is to avoid criticizing others in an employment interview. Consider the difference between the answers below:

Interviewer:	From your transcript, I notice that you graduated with a 2.3 grade-point average. Isn't that a little low?
Negative Answer:	Sure, but it wasn't my fault. I had some terrible teachers during my first 2 years of college. We had to memorize a lot of useless information that didn't have anything to do with the real world. Besides, professors give you high grades if they like you. If you don't play their game, they grade you down.
Positive Answer:	My low grade-point average came mostly from very bad freshman and sophomore years. I wasn't serious about school then, but you can see that my later grades are much higher. I've grown a lot in the past few years, and I'd like to think that I can use what I've learned in this job.

Most job candidates have been raised to regard modesty as a virtue, which makes it hard to toot their own horns. Excessive boasting certainly is likely to put off an interviewer, but experts flatly state that showcasing your strengths is essential. Florida State University management professor Michele Kacmar found that job seekers who talked about their good qualities were rated higher than those who focused on the interviewer.[35] Pre-interview rehearsals will help you find ways of saying positive things about yourself in a confident, nonboastful manner.

Back Up Your Answers with Evidence   As you read a few pages ago, behavioral interviewers figure that the best predictor of a potential employee's performance is what he or she has done in the past. Even if you aren't in a behavioral interview, it is usually effective to back up any claims you make with evidence of your performance.

One good framework for answering questions is the "PAR" approach. These initials stand for the three parts of a good answer: Identifying the *problem*, describing the *action* you took, and stating the *results* that your actions produced. You can see the value of this approach by comparing the two answers below:

Interviewer:	What strengths would you bring to this job?
Weak Answer:	I'm a self-starter who can work without close supervision [unsupported claim].
Stronger Answer:	I'm a self-starter who can work without close supervision [claim]. For example, in my last job, my immediate supervisor was away from the office off and on for 3 months because of some health issues [problem]. We were switching over to a new accounting system during that time, and I worked with the software company to make the change [action]. We made the changeover without losing a single day's work, and without any loss of data [results].

Creating a Digital Portfolio

Showing a prospective employer what you can do is much more effective than simply talking about your qualifications. This is especially true for jobs that involve tangible products like graphic design, commercial art, journalism, and technical writing.

Portfolios can also work in less obvious fields. You might, for example, demonstrate your ability to do solid work by sharing a report you helped create, a training you devised, or a collection of letters from satisfied customers praising your work.

The nature of your work may lend itself to a digital portfolio that can be posted online. You can include links to this site in your print material, as well as in any electronic correspondence with potential employers and references. To keep a professional appearance, make sure your digital portfolio has its own Web address: Don't embed it in any social networking sites that include personal information. If you are applying for different types of positions, such as training and marketing, consider creating two different electronic portfolios that showcase your work for each type of position.

You can find extensive guides to constructing portfolios at the career centers of many colleges and universities, including

- Ball State University
  **http://www.bsu.edu/art/article/0,25305~,00
  .html** and **http://www.bsu.edu/commstudies/
  article/0,,16720~,00.html**
- University of Wisconsin–River Falls
  www.uwrf.edu/ccs/portfolio-steps.htm

For specific tips on creating a digital portfolio, see

- EFolio Minnesota: **www.efoliomn.com**
- Eduscapes: **http://eduscapes.com/tap/topic82.htm**
- E-portfolios at Penn State: **www.portfolio.psu.edu/**
- EIFEL: **www.eifel.org/publications/eportfolio/
  proceedings2/ep2008/presentations**
- Quintcareers: **www.quintcareers.com/QuintZine/
  archives/20021014.html**

Keep Your Answers Brief   It is easy to rattle on in an interview out of enthusiasm, a desire to show off your knowledge, or nervousness, but in most cases highly detailed answers are not a good idea. The interviewer probably has a lot of ground to cover, and long-winded answers won't help. A general rule is to keep your responses under 2 minutes. An interviewer who wants additional information can always ask for it.

Be Enthusiastic   If you are applying for jobs that genuinely excite you, the challenge isn't to manufacture enthusiasm, but to show it. This can be difficult when you are nervous during what feels like a make-or-break session. Just remember that the interviewer wants to know how you really feel about the job and organization, so all you have to do is share your enthusiasm. Sharing your interest and excitement in the job and company can give you a competitive edge. Career Center director Gregory D. Hayes says, "If I talk to five deadbeat people and have one who is upbeat, that's the one I'm going to hire."[36]

Have Your Own Questions Answered   Any good employer will recognize that you have your own concerns about the job. After you have answered the interviewer's questions, you should be prepared to ask a few of your own. Realize that your questions make indirect statements about you just as your answers to the interviewer's inquiries did. Be sure your questions aren't all greedy ones that focus on salary, vacation time, benefits, and so on. Table 7–3 on page 210 lists some questions to consider asking when you are invited to do so.

Table 7–3	Questions to Consider Asking the Interviewer during an Employment Interview

Why is this position open?

How often has it been filled during the past 5 years?

What have been the reasons for people leaving in the past?

Why did the person who most recently held this position leave?

What would you like the next person who holds this job to do differently?

What are the most pressing issues and problems in this position?

What support does this position have (people, budget, equipment, etc.)?

What are the criteria for success in this position?

What might be the next career steps for a person who does well in this position?

What do you see as the future of this position? This organization?

What are the most important qualities you will look for in the person who will occupy this position?

Rehearsing an Interview   No athlete would expect to win without practicing, and no performer would face an audience without practicing long and hard. The same principle holds when you are facing an important employment interview: You should practice enough to be your very best when facing a prospective employer.

Effective practicing involves several steps:

1. Use your pre-interview research to identify the nature of the job you are seeking. What skills are required? What personal qualities are most desirable for this position? What kind of person will fit best with the culture of the organization?

2. Draft a series of questions that explore the job description you have created; use the lists in Table 7–2 as a guide. Be sure to include questions in each key area: educational background, work experience, career goals, personal traits, and knowledge of the organization and job.

3. Think about how you can answer each question. Each answer should contain a *claim* ("I have experience making presentations using Microsoft PowerPoint") and *evidence* to back it up ("I learned PowerPoint in a college business communications course and used it to train customer service reps in my last job"). In every case, make sure your answer shows how you can satisfy the employer's needs.

4. Role-play the interview several times with the help of a friend. Be sure you include the orientation and conclusion phases of the interview, as well as practice the questions you plan to ask the interviewer. If possible, videotape and review your performance twice: once to evaluate the content of your answers and again to check your appearance and the image you are projecting.

Many colleges have student job placement centers that have tremendous print resources on interviewing as well as a way of scheduling and recording a mock interview with a professional job counselor who will go over your video with you and give you constructive advice. Alternatively, use interview simulators listed at the end of the chapter to practice your answers to interview questions and to get feedback about a variety of responses.

Assess how ready you are to handle employment interviews skillfully by answering the questions below, using the following scale:

> 5 = strongly agree; 4 = agree; 3 = maybe, not certain; 2 = disagree; 1 = definitely not.

Pre-Interview Planning

1. I have conducted background research and understand the organization and the field. 5 4 3 2 1
2. I know the nature of the job (responsibilities, skills, how it fits in the company). 5 4 3 2 1
3. When possible and appropriate, I have asked members of my personal network to give the prospective employer favorable information about me. 5 4 3 2 1
4. I am prepared for any interview format. 5 4 3 2 1
5. I think constructively about the upcoming interview, rather than dwell on negative thoughts. 5 4 3 2 1
6. I will dress and groom in a way that is appropriate for this company and position. 5 4 3 2 1
7. I know how to arrive at the interview site. 5 4 3 2 1

During the Interview

8. I can handle the small talk that arises in the opening phase of the interview. 5 4 3 2 1
9. I nonverbally communicate my interest and enthusiasm for the job. 5 4 3 2 1
10. I am prepared to answer the kinds of questions likely to be asked (see Table 7–3) in a way that shows how I can meet the employer's needs. 5 4 3 2 1
11. I back up all my answers with examples that help clarify and prove what I'm saying. 5 4 3 2 1
12. I give concise answers to the interviewer's questions. 5 4 3 2 1
13. I present myself confidently and with enthusiasm. 5 4 3 2 1
14. I am prepared to respond to illegal questions the interviewer might ask. 5 4 3 2 1
15. I know when and how to deal with salary questions. 5 4 3 2 1
16. I have prepared a list of references. 5 4 3 2 1
17. I am prepared to ask questions of my own about the job and organization. 5 4 3 2 1
18. I practiced asking and answering questions until I am comfortable and articulate. 5 4 3 2 1

After the Interview

19. I know how to write an effective thank-you letter. 5 4 3 2 1
20. I am prepared to follow up with the interviewer to determine my status, if necessary. 5 4 3 2 1

Scoring

Total the numbers you have circled. If your score is between 80 and 100, you appear to be well-prepared for interviews. If your score is between 60 and 80, you are moderately prepared. If your score is below 60, you would do well to make additional preparations before any employment interviews.

Source: After Ron and Caryl Krannich, *Interview for Success: A Practical Guide to Increasing Job Interviews, Offers, and Salaries*, 8th ed. (Manassas Park, VA: Impact Publications, 2003), pp. 12–17.

Post-Interview Follow-up

Without exception, every employment interview should be followed immediately by a thank-you letter to the person who interviewed you. As Figure 7–4 shows, this letter serves several purposes:

- It demonstrates common courtesy.
- It reminds the employer of you.
- It gives you a chance to remind the interviewer of important information about you that came up in the interview and to provide facts you may have omitted then.
- It can tactfully remind the interviewer of promises made, such as a second interview or a response by a certain date.
- It can correct any misunderstandings that may have occurred during the interview.[37]

If you don't get the job, consider contacting the person who interviewed you and asking what shortcomings kept you from being chosen. Even if the interviewer isn't comfortable sharing this information with you (it might not have anything to do with your personal qualifications), your sincere desire to improve yourself can leave a positive impression that could help you in the future.

Unlike most business correspondence, a thank-you letter doesn't have to be type-written. Because it is a personal expression of gratitude, handwriting is considered acceptable. Depending on the formality of your relationship and the image you want to create, you may still choose to use a regular business-letter format. Whatever style you choose, the letter should be neat, error-free, and carefully composed.

FIGURE 7–4
Sample Thank-You Message

From: Susan Mineta [stm@comnet.net]
Sent: Tuesday, March 30, 2010 9:14 AM
To: Leslie Thoresen [lesthor@blogsite.com]
Subject: Thank you!
Attached: S Mineta articles.pdf

Dear Mr. Thoresen:

I left our meeting yesterday full of excitement. Your remarks about the value of my experience as a student journalist and blogger were very encouraging. I also appreciate your suggestion that I speak with Mr. Leo Benadides. Thank you for promising to tell him that I'll be calling within the next week.

Since you expressed interest in the series I wrote on how Asian women are breaking cultural stereotypes, I am attaching copies to this e-mail. I hope you find them interesting.

Your remarks about the dangers of being typecast exclusively as a writer on women's issues were very helpful. Just after we spoke I received an assignment to write a series on identity theft and the elderly. I'll be sure to let you know when these articles appear online.

Thank you again for taking time from your busy day. I will look forward to hearing from you when the job we discussed is officially created.

Sincerely,

Susan Mineta
8975 Santa Clarita Lane
Glendale, CA 90099
(818) 214-0987

Interviewing and the Law

Many laws govern which questions are and are not legal in employment interviews, but the general principle that underlies them all is simple: Questions may not be asked for the purpose of discriminating on the basis of race, color, religion, sex, disabilities, national origin, or age. Employers may still ask about these areas, but the U.S. government's Equal Employment Opportunity Commission (EEOC) permits only questions that investigate a **bona fide occupational qualification (BFOQ** in bureaucratic jargon) for a particular job. This means any question asked should be job-related. The Supreme Court has said that "the touchstone is business necessity."[38] Table 7-4 on pages 214–215 lists questions that are generally not considered BFOQs as well as those that are legitimate.

The Americans with Disabilities Act of 1990 (ADA) requires equal access to employment and provision of "reasonable accommodations" for persons with disabilities. It defines *disability* as a "physical" or "mental impairment" that "substantially limits" one or more "major life activities." As with any other job-related issue, the key question is what is "reasonable." The law clearly states, however, that disabled candidates can be questioned only about their ability to perform "essential functions" of a job and that employers are obligated to provide accommodations for disabled candidates and employees. If a person indicates a need for reasonable accommodation during the application process, the company is required to provide it. For example, a person who is deaf can request an interpreter at company expense for the interview.[39]

There are several ways to answer an unlawful question:[40]

1. *Answer without objection.* Answer the question, even though you know it is probably unlawful: "I'm 47."

2. *Seek explanation.* Ask the interviewer firmly and respectfully to explain why this question is a BFOQ: "I'm having a hard time seeing how my age relates to my ability to do this job. Can you explain?"

3. *Redirection.* Shift the focus of the interview away from a question that isn't job-related and toward the requirements of the position itself: "What you've said so far suggests that age is not as important for this position as is willingness to travel. Can you tell me more about the travel requirement?"

4. *Refusal.* Explain politely but firmly that you will not provide the information requested: "I'd rather not talk about my religion. That's a personal matter for me." If you are sure you aren't interested in the job, you could even end the interview immediately: "I'm very uncomfortable with these questions about my personal life, and I don't see a good fit between me and this organization."

Choosing the best response style depends on several factors.[41] First, it is important to consider the probable intent of the interviewer. The question may indeed be aimed at collecting information that will allow the employer to discriminate, but it may just as well be a naive inquiry with no harm intended. Some interviewers are unsophisticated at their job. A study reported in *The Wall Street Journal* revealed that over 70 percent of 200 interviewers in Fortune 500 corporations thought that at least 5 of 12 unlawful questions were safe to ask.[42] In another survey, employers at 100 small businesses were presented with five illegal interview questions. All of the respondents said they either would ask or had asked at least one of them.[43] Results like these suggest that an illegal question may be the result of ignorance rather than malice. The interviewer who discusses family, nationality, or religion may simply be trying to make conversation. Be careful not to introduce these topics yourself as it may open the door to conversations and questions you would rather not deal with.

Table 7–4	Questions Interviewers Can and Cannot Legally Ask

Federal law restricts employer interviewer questions and other practices to areas clearly related to job requirements. The following are some questions and practices that are generally considered legitimate and others that are not.

Subject	Unacceptable	Acceptable
Name	What is your maiden name? Have you ever changed your name?	Name "Is there another name I'd need to check on your work and education record?"
Residence	"Do you own or rent your home?"	Place of residence
Age	Age Birth date Dates of attendance or completion of elementry or high school Questions that tend to identify applicants over age 40	Statement that hire is subject to verification that applicant meets legal age requirements "If hired, can you show proof of age?" "Are you over 18 years of age?" "If under 18, can you, after employment, submit a work permit?"
Birthplace, citizenship	Birthplace of applicant, applicant's parents, spouse, or other relatives "Are you a U.S. citizen?" *or* citizenship of applicant, applicant's parents, spouse, or other relatives Requirement that applicant produce naturalization, first papers, or alien card *prior to employment*	"Can you, after employment, submit verification of your legal right to work in the United States?" *or* statement that such proof may be required after employment
National origin	Questions as to nationality, lineage, ancestry, national origin, descent, or parentage of applicant, applicant's parents, or spouse "What is your mother tongue?" *or* language commonly used by applicant How applicant acquired ability to read, write, or speak a foreign language	Languages applicant reads, speaks, or writes, if use of a language other than English is relevant to the job for which applicant is applying
Sex, marital status, family	Questions that indicate applicant's sex Questions that indicate applicant's marital status Number and/or ages of children or dependents Provisions for child care Questions regarding pregnancy, childbearing, or birth control Name or address of relative, spouse, or children of adult applicant "With whom do you reside?" or "Do you live with your parents?"	Name and address of parent or guardian if applicant is a minor, statement of company policy regarding work assignment of employees who are related
Race, color	Questions as to applicant's race or color Questions regarding applicant's complexion or color of skin, eyes, hair	

Subject	Unacceptable	Acceptable
Religion	Questions regarding applicant's religion Religious days observed *or* "Does your religion prevent you from working weekends or holidays?"	Statement by employer of regular days, hours, or shifts to be worked
Arrest, criminal record	Arrest record *or* "Have you ever been arrested?"	"Have you ever been convicted of a felony?" Such a question must be accompanied by a statement that a conviction will not necessarily disqualify an applicant from employment
Military service	General questions regarding military service such as dates and type of discharge Questions regarding service in a foreign military	Questions regarding relevant skills acquired during applicant's U.S. military service
Organizations	"List all organizations, clubs, societies to which you belong."	"Please list job-related organizations or professional associations to which you belong that you believe enhance your job performance."
References	Questions of applicant's former employers or acquaintances that elicit information specifying the applicant's race, color, religious creed, national origin, ancestry, physical handicap, medical condition, marital status, age, or sex	"By whom were you referred for a position here?" Names of persons willing to provide professional and/or character references for applicant
Physical description, photograph	Questions as to applicant's height and weight Requirement that applicant affix a photograph to application Request that asks applicant, at his or her option, to submit a photograph Requirement that calls for a photograph after interview but before employment	Statement that photograph may be required after employment
Physical condition, handicap	Questions regarding applicant's general medical condition, state of health, or illnesses Questions regarding receipt of workers' compensation "Do you have any physical disabilities or handicaps?"	Statement by employer that offer may be made contingent on applicant's passing a job-related physical examination "Do you have any physical condition or handicap that may limit your ability to perform the job applied for? If yes, what can be done to accommodate your limitation?"

For further information about illegal questions consult these online sources:
http://jobsearchtech.about.com/od/interview/l/aa022403_2.htm
www.collegegrad.com/ezine/23illega.shtml
www.usatoday.com/careers/resources/interviewillegal.htm

A second factor when considering how to respond to an illegal question is your desire for the job at hand. You may be more willing to challenge the interviewer when a position isn't critical to your future. On the other hand, if your career rides on succeeding in a particular interview, you may be willing to swallow your objections. A third factor to consider is your feeling of comfort with the interviewer. For example, a female candidate with school-age children might welcome the chance to discuss child care issues with an interviewer who has identified herself as a single mother who faces the same challenges. A fourth item to consider is your own personal style. If you are comfortable asserting yourself, you may be willing to address an illegal question head-on. If you are less comfortable speaking up, especially to authority figures, you may prefer to respond less directly.

Being interviewed does not mean you are at the mercy of the interviewer; laws do govern your rights as a candidate. If you choose to take a more assertive approach to illegal questioning that you believe resulted in discrimination, you have the right to file a charge with the EEOC and your state Fair Employment Practices Commission within 180 days of the interview. In practice, the EEOC will withhold its investigation until the state commission has completed its inquiry. Federal and state agencies have a backlog of cases, however, so it may take years to complete an investigation. The commission may mediate the case, file a suit, or issue you a letter to sue.[44] Keep in mind that just because you can file a lawsuit doesn't mean this will always be the best course of action: A suit can take many months, or even years, to be settled and a ruling in your favor may not result in a large settlement. Furthermore, knowledge that you've filed a suit is not likely to make you an attractive candidate to other employers who hear of your action. Seeking professional counsel can help you make a decision that balances your personal values and practical considerations.

Sample Employment Interview

The following transcript is based on a real interview. As you read it, pay attention to both the interviewer's questions and the applicant's responses. In both cases, notice the strengths and the areas needing improvement. What parts of this interview would you like to incorporate in your style? What parts would you handle differently?

[The interview begins with an exchange of pleasantries]	**Interviewer:**	Monica Hansen? I'm Chris Van Dyke. Welcome.
	Applicant:	It's good to meet you.
[. . . and small talk.]	**Interviewer:**	Did you have any trouble finding us?
	Applicant:	The directions were perfect. And thanks for the parking pass.
[The interviewer briefly previews the approach of the interview and the anticipated amount of time.]	**Interviewer:**	Oh, yes. That's a necessity. The garage costs $12 per day if you don't have one.
		We'll have about a half-hour this morning to talk about the personnel administrator's position you've applied for. I'd like to learn about you. And, of course, I want to answer any questions you have about us.
	Applicant:	Great. I'm looking forward to it.

Cleaning Up Your Digital Dirt

In spite of your best efforts to create a résumé and present yourself as a qualified job applicant, prospective employers have other ways of forming impressions of you, including all of the information available online. To discover what others can easily see about you, try these options:

1. Google yourself by typing your name into the search engine at **www.google.com.** Employers do it and so can you. The only hits may be advice you gave about training your Jack Russell terrier or a review you wrote about a great restaurant. On the other hand, you may find comments you made at meetings you attended, information about you in newspaper articles, public hearings, or court actions. You may be able to get site owners to remove things you would rather not have on record. Learn how to "un-Google" yourself at **www.wikihow.com/Ungoogle-Yourself.**

2. Review your profile on Web sites like Facebook (**www.facebook.com**) or MySpace (**www.myspace.com**), and/or Web sites you have created. Imagine the impression your profiles would make on prospective employers and consider editing references and photos you no longer want to share with the world—or at least change your privacy settings. The photo of you from the Halloween party your sophomore year or the comments others wrote about you might not create the best impression.

Source: Mike Hargis, "Social Networking Dos and Don'ts," available at www.careerbuilder.com/Article/CB-964-The-Workplace-Social -Networking-Dos-and-Donts/?ArticleID=964&cbRecursionCnt=1 &cbsid=316e44f43ea14225975e2c4d365bc009-283878043-JA-5 &ns_siteid=ns_us_g_Mike_Hargis%2C_%E2%80. Retrieved on December 29, 2008.

[Body of interview begins with an open question about employment history.]	**Interviewer:**	Good. Let's begin by having you tell me about your most recent position. Your résumé says you were at ITC in Springfield. Is that right?
[Interviewee uses question to showcase the skills acquired in past job that could help in the one being offered here.]	**Applicant:**	That's right. My official job title was personnel assistant, but that really doesn't describe very well the work I did. I recruited nonexempt employees, processed the payroll, oriented new employees, and maintained the files.
[Follow-up questions explore areas of interest in the new job.]	**Interviewer:**	Were you involved with insurance?
[The applicant uses this answer to point out another skill that she brings to the job.]	**Applicant:**	Yes. I processed workers' compensation claims and maintained the insurance reports for our health care plans. I learned a lot about dealing with government regulations.
	Interviewer:	And you said you were involved in hiring?
	Applicant:	Yes. I was responsible for recruiting and interviewing all clerical and administrative support people.
[Another open question, this time exploring the applicant's ability to analyze her own performance.]	**Interviewer:**	How did that go?

217

[The applicant fails to use this answer to showcase her abilities . . .]	**Applicant:**	It was tough in Springfield. There's actually a shortage of talented support people there. It's an expensive town to live in, and there aren't a lot of people who can afford living there on an administrative assistant's salary. It's not like Atlanta, where there's plenty of good help.
[so the interviewer follows up with another question.]	**Interviewer:**	What did you learn about hiring from your experiences at ITC?
[This answer is better, since it describes insights and skills the applicant brings to this job.]	**Applicant:**	I learned to look further than the résumé. Some people seem great on paper, but you find there's something wrong when you hire them. Other people don't have much experience on paper, but they have a lot of potential.
	Interviewer:	How did you get beyond paper screening?
	Applicant:	Well, if someone looked at all promising, I would phone the former employers and talk to the people the applicant actually worked for. Of course a lot of former employers are pretty noncommittal, but they usually would give clues about what they really thought about the person I was investigating—giving an indirect opinion without saying it outright.
	Interviewer:	What would you do if this was the person's first job?
[The applicant demonstrates resourcefulness here, spelling out her skill in the last sentence of her answer.]	**Applicant:**	I found that almost everyone had done some kind of work—part-time or vacation. And I could check up on that. Or I would even ask for the names of a few teachers and phone them up, if the person was just graduating. I learned that there's almost always a way to find what you're looking for, if you get creative.
	Interviewer:	Didn't that take a lot of time?
[This is a subtle way of saying, "I have good judgment."]	**Applicant:**	Yes, it did. But it was worth it in the long run, since we got much better employees that way. We almost never had to dismiss someone whom we'd done a phone check on.
	Interviewer:	You were promoted after a year. Why?
[Again, the applicant's answer introduces a trait that would be valuable in the new job: The desire for self-improvement.]	**Applicant:**	I was lucky to be in the right place. The company was growing, and we were very busy. I tried to take advantage of the situation by offering to do more and by taking classes at night.

Interviewer: What classes did you take?

[Presumably the skills acquired in these courses would be useful if the applicant is hired. In any case, she demonstrates the desire to learn skills useful in the business world.]

Applicant: I took an applied human relations class last spring. And before that, a couple of computer classes: one in database management and one in desktop publishing. Our department was thinking about starting an employee newsletter, and I wanted to see if we could produce it in-house.

Interviewer: It sounds like you've done very well at ITC. Why do you want to leave?

[The response begins with a provocative statement, and then goes on to supply a solid reason for seeking a new job.]

Applicant: In some ways I *don't* want to leave. The people are great—most of them—and I've enjoyed the work. But I'm looking for more challenges, and there isn't much chance for me to take on more responsibility there.

Interviewer: Why not?

Applicant: Well, my boss, the personnel director, is very happy in her job and has no plans to leave. She's young, and there's very little chance I'll be able to advance.

[The interviewer seeks specifics to elaborate on the broad statement "I'm looking for more challenges"]

[. . . and the candidate supplies answers.]

Interviewer: I see. Well, that is a problem. And what kind of responsibilities are you looking for?

Applicant: I'd say the biggest one is the chance to help make policy. In my past jobs, I've been carrying out policies that other people—management—have made. That's been fine, but I'd like to be involved in setting some policies myself.

[Again, the interviewer follows up by seeking more specifics]

[. . . and the candidate is prepared with detailed responses.]

Interviewer: What kinds of policies?

Applicant: Oh, there are several. Designing benefits packages. Coming up with a performance review system that people will take seriously. Teaching our supervisors how to interview and hire more systematically.

[The interviewer makes a smooth transition to a new topic.]

Interviewer: I see. Well, the position you've applied for certainly does have those sorts of responsibilities. Let me ask you another question. What do you enjoy most about personnel work?

[The stock answer "I like to work with people" is so broad that it has little meaning]

Applicant: Well, I really enjoy the chance to work so much with people. Of course, there's a lot of paperwork, too, but I especially like the chance to work with people.

[. . . so the interviewer seeks clarification.]

Interviewer: When you say "people," what kinds of work are you thinking of?

Applicant: I guess the common denominator is making people happy. Lots of employees get involved with the personnel department—once they've been hired, that is—because they have problems. Maybe it's an insurance claim or a problem with their performance review. It makes me feel good to see them leave feeling satisfied, or at least feeling better after they've come in so upset.

Interviewer: Are you always able to help them?

Applicant: No, of course not. Sometimes a person will want the impossible, and sometimes there just won't be any answer.

[Again, the interviewer uses a situational approach, seeking specifics.]

Interviewer: Can you give examples of these times?

[The applicant does a good job of describing a situation that illustrates her previous answer.]

Applicant: Well, one example of an impossible request comes up a lot with health insurance. At ITC we could choose from two plans. With one plan you could use any doctor you wanted. You had to make a co-payment with that one. With the other plan, you had to choose a doctor from a list of preferred providers, but there was no co-payment. If an employee chose the preferred-provider plan and later decided he or she wanted to use a doctor that wasn't on the list, we just couldn't do anything about it.

Interviewer: We've had that problem here, too. How did you handle it?

Applicant: Being sympathetic helped a little. Even if I couldn't give them what they wanted, at least saying I was sorry might have made it seem less like a total rejection. I also pointed out that they *could* switch plans during the open-enrollment period, which comes every year. I've also suggested to my boss that we do a better job of informing people about the restrictions of the preferred-provider plan before they sign up and maybe even get them to sign a statement that says they understand them. I think that would reduce the surprises that come up later.

[With this new topic, the interviewer shifts from fact to opinion questions.]

Interviewer: That's a good idea. Monica, what qualities do you think are important for a personnel officer?

Applicant: Knowing the job is definitely important, but I'd say getting along with people might be even more important.

Interviewer: And how would you describe your ability to get along?

Applicant: Sometimes I think I deserve an Academy Award for acting the opposite of the way I feel.

Interviewer: Really? Tell me about it.

[The applicant offers a specific example to illustrate her provocative statement about acting the opposite of the way she feels.]

Applicant: Every so often people will come in with an attitude problem, and I try to calm them down by acting more pleasant than I feel. For example, we've had people who think they're entitled to take 6 months off for a workers' compensation claim, when the doctor has said they're ready to come back after a few weeks. They come in and yell at us, and it's tough to be pleasant at times like those. But I don't think there's any point in being blunt or rude. It just makes them more angry.

[This indirect question really asks, "What kind of manager might you be?"]

Interviewer: I see what you mean. Let's shift gears, Monica. If you were to pick a boss, what are the important traits that he or she should have?

Applicant: Let me see . . . certainly lots of follow-up—letting people know where they stand. The ability to give criticism constructively and to compliment good work. Giving people a task and then leaving them alone, without nagging.

Interviewer: But still being there to help if it's needed, right?

Applicant: Sure. But also giving me the space to finish a job without staying *too* close.

Interviewer: Anything else?

Applicant: Being available for help, as you said. Being consistent. And being willing to train employees in new jobs, letting them grow. And considering the personal goals of employees.

[The interviewer turns to a new topic area.]

Interviewer: In personnel work, there's a need for confidentiality. What does that mean to you?

Applicant: That's an important area. You see lots of personal information, and it's easy to make offhand remarks that could upset someone.

Interviewer: What kinds of things do you have to be careful about?

Applicant: Oh, even something as simple as a person's birthday. Most people wouldn't care, but some people might be offended if their birthdays got out. I've learned to be constantly on guard, to watch what I say. I'm a private person anyway, so that helps.

[This question explores the candidate's personal attitudes.]

Interviewer: Monica, I've been asking you a lot of questions. Let me ask just one more; then it can be your turn. What are the factors that motivate you?

Applicant: Well, I like to be busy. If things aren't busy, I still work, but I like to be stimulated. I seem to get more work done when I'm busy than when there's plenty of time. It's crazy, but true. I'm also motivated by the chance to grow and take on as much responsibility as I can handle.

[Almost every employment interview includes a chance for the interviewee to ask questions.]

Interviewer: Monica, what questions do you have for me? What can I tell you about the job or the company?

[The applicant wisely begins by asking about the company, not focusing on personal questions such as compensations.]

Applicant: What kind of growth do you see for the company?

Interviewer: Well, we have 155 employees now. As I think you know, we're 5 years old, and we started with five employees. Our sales were up 14 percent last year, and it looks like we'll be expanding more.

Applicant: How many employees do you think will be added?

Interviewer: Well, we hired 20 new people last year, and we expect to hire almost the same number this year.

Applicant: And what's the turnover like?

Interviewer: That's a good question for a personnel person to ask! We've been growing so much, and people have been able to move into more responsible jobs, so they've been satisfied for the most part. Our turnover has been pretty low—about 15 percent annually.

[This question focuses on responsibilities of the job.]	**Applicant:**	Will the person you hire be involved in making policy?
	Interviewer:	Yes, definitely. We're still trying to catch up with ourselves after growing so fast. A big project for this year is to put together an employee handbook. Too many of our policies are verbal now, and that's not good. Developing that handbook would mean working directly with the president of the company, and that definitely involves developing policy.
[Finally, the applicant asks about compensation and benefits.]	**Applicant:**	Of course, I'm interested in learning about the benefits and salary.
[The interviewer appropriately defers a complete answer until the company has a clearer idea of the candidate's desirability.]	**Interviewer:**	Of course. Here's a copy of our benefits summary for you to study. We can talk about salary later. Right now I'd like you to meet a couple of our managers. After you've spoken with them, we can get back together to discuss salary and other matters.
[The interviewer wraps up the conversation by describing when the hiring decision will be made.]		We will definitely be making our decision within the next 10 days, so I promise you you'll have an answer before the first of next month. It's been a real pleasure talking to you, Monica. You certainly express yourself well. I'll talk with you again soon.
	Applicant:	Thanks. I've enjoyed the talk, too. I'll look forward to hearing from you.

The Performance Appraisal Interview

A working group is like an athletic team: Even the best players need the guidance of a coach to help them do their individual best and work with other members. Managers are the coaches in most organizations, and the performance appraisal interview is one way they help their team members.

Definition and Importance

Performance appraisal interviews are scheduled regularly between superior and subordinate to discuss the quality of the subordinate's performance. More specifically, these interviews have several functions, including the following:

- *Letting the employee know where he or she stands.* This kind of feedback includes praising good work, communicating areas that need improvement, and conveying to the employee his or her prospects for advancement.
- *Developing employee skills.* The review can be a chance for the employee to learn new skills. Among their other roles, managers and supervisors should be teachers. The performance appraisal interview can be a chance to show an employee how to do a better job.

- *Improving employment relationship.* Performance reviews should improve superior–subordinate relationships and give employees a sense of participation in the job. Ideally, employees will leave the interview feeling better about themselves and the organization.

- *Helping management learn the employee's point of view.* A performance appraisal should include upward as well as downward communication. It provides a chance for subordinates to explain their perspective to managers.

- *Counseling the employee.* An appraisal interview provides the chance for managers to learn about personal problems that may be affecting an employee's performance and to offer advice and support.

- *Setting goals for the future.* One result of every performance appraisal interview should be a clear idea of how both the superior and the subordinate will behave in the future.

Some bosses and employees complain that performance reviews are a nuisance. Management guru Robert Townsend agrees—to a point. "Printed forms for performance appraisal and MBOs are used by incompetent bosses in badly managed companies," he claims.[45] Performance appraisals appear to be increasingly unpopular and a recent survey of human resources professionals found that 32 percent were unsatisfied with their company's process.[46] Despite criticisms of this sort, authorities on communication agree that most managers and supervisors need to give employees *more* feedback, not less. "Day-to-day coaching is the most overlooked step of the performance process," says *One Minute Manager* co-author Kenneth Blanchard.[47] Townsend agrees. "Real managers manage by frequent eyeball contact," he insists, quoting one good boss's description of the process: "Half our meetings are held in the hall, the other half in the washroom."

Perhaps these management experts have a point. If bosses spent more time giving employees informal feedback and setting goals on a day-to-day basis, there might be less

Dilbert: © Scott Adams/Dist. by United Feature Syndicate, Inc. Reprinted by permission.

FIGURE 7–5

The Performance Appraisal Process

Review previously set goals ⟶ Define new goals ⟶ Discuss successes, problems, and needs

need for quarterly or semiannual formal meetings. But one way or the other, performance review is one of the most important responsibilities a manager has.

Despite the potential threat of being evaluated, performance appraisals can be welcomed by employees. One of the greatest hungers that workers have is to know where they stand with management. Researchers have found that receiving personal feedback correlates highly with job satisfaction,[48] and appraisal interviews offer a periodic session dedicated to providing just that feedback. Despite this fact, 40 percent of all employees report that they don't receive a regular performance review.[49]

Just because employees want feedback doesn't mean that they are always satisfied with the performance appraisals they do receive. Sometimes performance reviews can be contaminated by organizational politics, generating resentment and undermining morale.[50] This sort of bias isn't new: Over 18 centuries ago in 3rd-century China, a member of the Wei dynasty's court complained about a manager: "The Imperial Rater of Nine Grades seldom rates men according to their merits but always according to his likes and dislikes."[51] Intentionally or not, many unskilled managers turn appraisal sessions into criticisms of past shortcomings that do little besides arouse resentment and defensiveness in employees. The interviewing skills outlined in this section can help make sure that a performance review meets the needs of both management and employees.

Performance review should be an ongoing process, not something that happens only at infrequent intervals during a scheduled interview.[52] The functions of performance appraisal listed on pages 223–224 can and should be performed constantly in the kind of process pictured in Figure 7–5. This doesn't mean that formal interviews are useless, for they provide a chance to focus on how well the ongoing job of judging and improving performance is proceeding. The value of a formal review is captured by former Chrysler chairman Lee Iacocca, who describes how the procedure works in his company:

> *Every three months, each manager sits down with his immediate superior to review the manager's past accomplishments and to chart his goals for the next term. Once there is agreement on these goals, the manager puts them in writing and the supervisor signs off on it. . . . The discipline of writing something down is the first step toward making it happen. In conversation, you can get away with all kinds of vagueness and nonsense, often without even realizing it. But there's something about putting your thoughts on paper that forces you to get down to specifics. That way, it's harder to deceive yourself—or anybody else.*[53]

Steps in the Appraisal Process

After an initial exchange of pleasantries—usually brief—the manager should provide a rationale for the interview, an outline of what information will be covered and how it will be used, and a preview of the interview's probable length. After the preliminaries, the body of an appraisal interview should go on to cover three areas: a review of the criteria established in past meetings, a discussion of the employee's performance, and a setting of goals for the future.

Review Progress   The first step in the body of any appraisal interview should be to identify the criteria by which the employee is being evaluated. Ideally, these criteria

will already be clear to both the manager and the employee, but it is wise to restate them. A manager might say,

> Bill, as I'm sure you remember, we decided at our last meeting to focus on several targets. We agreed that if you could reach them, you'd be doing your present job very well and you'd be setting yourself up for an assistant sales manager's position. Here's the list of targets we developed last time [shows employee list]. So these are the areas we need to look at today.

Discuss Successes, Problems, and Needs   After the criteria have been defined, the discussion can focus on how well the employee has satisfied them. Discussion will be easiest when the goals are measurable: Are sales up 15 percent? Have jobs been completed on time? If the employee has explanations for why targets were not reached, it is the manager's job to consider these fairly. Some goals are subjective, so the evaluation of their performance will be a matter of judgment as well. Even seemingly vague goals like "being more patient with customers" can be at least partially clarified by turning them into simple behavioral descriptions such as "letting customers talk without interrupting them."

When evaluating past performance, it is important to maintain a balance among the points under consideration. Without meaning to let it happen, a manager and employee can become involved in discussing (or debating) a relatively unimportant point at length, throwing the overall look at the employee's performance out of perspective. A skillful interviewer will focus only on the most important criteria, usually dealing with no more than three areas that need work. Even the most demanding manager will realize upon reflection that changing old habits is difficult and that it is unrealistic to expect dramatic improvement in too many areas within a short time.

Even when an appraisal is conducted with the best of intentions, its evaluative nature raises the odds of a defensive response. Feedback will be best received when it meets several criteria. Observing these guidelines can boost the chances of keeping the interview's tone constructive:

- *Feedback should be accurate.* Perhaps the worst mistake an evaluator can make is to get the facts wrong. Before you judge an employee, be sure you have an accurate picture of his or her performance and all the factors that affected it. A tell-and-listen approach can help the manager understand an employee's performance more fully.

- *Feedback should be relevant to the job.* For example, it may be legitimate to comment on an employee's appearance in a job that involves contact with the public, but it is out of line to be critical about the way he or she handles personal matters after business hours.

The best chances of success occur when the review offers a balance of praise and constructive suggestions for improvement. Both everyday experience and research have demonstrated the power of positive reinforcement. One study revealed that the commitment level of employees dropped when their behavior was identified as only "satisfactory."[54] A manager who uses praise in appraisal interviews should remember the tips for praising outlined in Chapter 5 (pages 131–133).

Sooner or later, even the most outstanding employee will need to hear criticism about his or her work. Delivering negative information is one of the biggest challenges a manager or supervisor can face. The guidelines in Chapter 5 (pages 133–135) offer tips on how to offer negative feedback supportively. Handling critical situations well isn't just the boss's responsibility; the subordinate needs to behave responsibly too. The guidelines for coping nondefensively with criticism outlined on pages 135–137 should

Table 7–5	Checklist for Performance Appraisal Interviewing

a. Interview covers key areas
    i. Orients employee
    ii. Establishes positive climate
    iii. Reviews past achievement of goals
    iv. Identifies successes, problems, and needs in employee's area of responsibility
    v. Establishes new goals with employee

b. Feedback delivered constructively
    i. Information accurate
    ii. Feedback appropriate to critic's role
    iii. Balance of praise and constructive criticism

c. Praise delivered effectively
    i. Praise sincere
    ii. Specific behaviors identified
    iii. Emphasis on progress, not perfection
    iv. Praise communicated by deeds as well as by words

d. Criticism expressed constructively
    i. Criticism limited to key areas
    ii. Criticism delivered in face-saving manner
    iii. Criticism accompanied by offer to help
    iv. Benefits of cooperating emphasized

e. Interview accomplishes all necessary functions
    i. Lets employee know where he or she stands
    ii. Develops employee skills
    iii. Improves communication climate, boosts morale
    iv. Helps management understand employee's point of view
    v. Counsels employee as appropriate
    vi. Sets goals for future

be helpful when it is your turn to receive critical messages. While following these guidelines won't guarantee a successful performance review, it can increase the chances that the meeting will be genuinely constructive and serve the interests of both the superior and the subordinate.

Set Goals   Once the employee and manager have discussed past successes, problems, and needs, the task becomes defining goals for the future. The goals should meet several criteria:

● They should focus on the most important aspects of the job. The tried-and-true 80:20 rule applies here: Changing 20 percent of a worker's behavior will usually solve 80 percent of the problems.

● They should be described as specifically as possible so that both manager and employee will know what actions constitute the target.

- A time period should be stated for each target. People often work best when faced with a deadline, and setting dates lets both parties know when the results are due.

- The targets ought to provide some challenge to the worker, requiring effort yet being attainable. A manageable challenge will produce the greatest growth and leave workers and managers feeling pleased with the changes that occur.

Review and Respond to the Written Record   The appraisal process commonly has a written dimension in addition to the interview itself. Before the meeting, the manager often completes an evaluation form listing characteristics or behaviors important to the job. Ideally, the information on this form is taken from the goals set at the previous interview. In some organizations, the subordinate also fills out a self-rating form covering similar areas. In most companies, a performance review is summarized and documented with a written evaluation. In most cases, the manager completes a final report that summarizes the results of the session. The employee usually has the option of adding his or her own response to the manager's report. This document then becomes part of the employee's records and is used as a basis for future evaluations and as a source of information for decisions about promotions. (See Table 7–5.)

review points

- Information-gathering interviews conduct research by collecting background information to define goals and create specific questions and to identify the best interviewee.

- A career research interview helps the interviewer research a career field, be remembered by the interviewee, and gain referrals to assist in beginning and shaping one's career.

- Personal contacts are vital to choosing interviewees and professionalism in written and oral communication are essential while contacting an interviewee, conducting the interview, and following up after the interview.

- Performing well in an employment interview is usually necessary for being hired. Many positions are never advertised, so job-seekers must begin long before an interview to conduct background research, then contact potential employers appropriately, usually with a cover letter and résumé.

- Candidates should rehearse for panel, behavioral, and audition interview formats and in all cases, think constructively, make contact professionally, and dress appropriately. Interviewees need to be prepared for key questions and constantly focus on how they can help the organization reach its goals by responding to the employer's needs and concerns. Answers should be honest, positive, brief, and enthusiastic. Support answers with evidence and ask pertinent questions. Always follow up with a letter of thanks to the interviewer(s).

- Federal and state laws restrict interviewers from asking questions that are not related to the bona fide occupational qualifications of a job. Interviewees can know what questions are acceptable and unacceptable and be prepared with several strategies for responding to illegal questions.

- Performance appraisal interviews are a structured way for superiors and their subordinates to look at the quality of the subordinate's performance and how employees are viewed by management, and to jointly set goals.

- Appraisal interviews begin with a clear statement of criteria and a review of the employee's performance, citing successes and problems, and conclude with both the manager and employee setting goals for the next evaluation period.

key terms

 Test your understanding of these key terms by visiting the Online Learning Center Web site at www.mhhe.com/adler10e.

audition interview 197
behavioral interview 197
bona fide occupational qualification (BFOQ) 213
career research interview 190
diagnostic interview 187
employment interview 194
exit interview 187
gatekeeper 191

investigative interview 187
panel interview 197
performance appraisal interview 223
research interview 187
scannable résumé 197
stress interview 197
survey interview 187

activities

 Go to the self-quizzes at the Online Learning Center at **www.mhhe.com/adler10e** to test your knowledge of chapter concepts.

1. Invitation to Insight

Consider the four types of interviews common to most occupations. For each type:

a. Identify a specific interview you have taken part in or will encounter.

b. Describe the goal of the interviewee and the interviewer in each situation. Is it similar or conflicting? If conflicting, what extra preparations would be advisable?

c. For the past interviews, describe how satisfied you were with your behavior. For future interviews, predict how satisfied you expect to be with your behavior, given your present level of interviewing skill.

d. Use concepts you have learned in this chapter to suggest at least two improvements you can enact in your next interview.

2. Invitation to Insight

Select a person in your chosen career who plays a role in hiring new employees. Conduct an information-gathering interview to discover the following:

a. What methods are used to identify job candidates?

b. What format is used to interview applicants?

c. What formal and informal criteria are used to hire applicants?

d. What personal qualities of applicants make a positive or negative impression?

3. Invitation to Insight

Brainstorm 5 to 10 specific actions you have taken (in classes, on the job, or in volunteer activities) that demonstrate your ability to perform well. Include specific evidence for each. Recall the positive results of your actions.

For added practice, team up with a classmate. Use the PAR approach (see p. 208) to role-play asking and answering interview questions. As your classmate asks questions, answer with actions and results. Then switch roles.

4. Skill Builder

For each of the following topics identify at least two people you could interview to gather information and write one or more specific objectives for each interview:

a.   Learning more about a potential employer. (Name a specific organization.)
b.   Deciding whether to enroll in a specific class. (You choose which one.)
c.   Deciding which type of personal computer or software application to purchase.
d.   Exploring career opportunities in a city of your choice.
e.   Determining the best savings or investment vehicle for you at this time.
f.   Comparing health insurance plans available to students.

5. Skill Builder

You can develop your skill and gain appreciation for the value of the informational interview by doing one of the following activities:

a.   Conducting an informational interview with a professional in a career field that interests you. Possible goals are to learn more about the field, to learn how to advance in your current job, or to learn what it would take to switch fields. Follow these steps:
1.   Identify a promising interviewee.
2.   Write a letter requesting an interview.
3.   Follow up your letter with a phone call to arrange a date.
4.   Develop a list of questions that will achieve your stated purpose. Be sure that these questions follow the guidelines in Chapter 6.
5.   Conduct the interview and report your results. Analyze how well you performed and suggest how you could improve in conducting future interviews.
6.   Write a thank-you letter to your interviewee.

b. Identifying a specific organization you would like to work for, and completing the following pre-interview steps:

1. Identify the person—by title and name, if possible—who has the power to hire you.
2. Using research and the results of informational interviews, analyze the requirements for the position you would like to hold.
3. Develop a list of questions a potential boss might ask in a selection interview.
4. Prepare answers to those questions.

c. Role-playing an actual interview, with a companion filling the role of your potential employer.

6. Skill Builder

Imagine that a supervisor or instructor is preparing an evaluation of your performance. Four areas will be covered:

a. Quality of work.
b. Productivity.
c. Communication skill.
d. Attitude.

1. For each area, write one or two measurable objectives that could be used as assessments in your area of work.
2. Based on your actual behavior on the job, prepare a verbal explanation describing how well you have met these assessments during the last month.
3. Identify several areas in which you could improve. From this information compose several measurable behavioral objectives for the coming month.

resources

 For extensive readings and Web sites on types of interviews, see the Online Learning Center Web site at www.mhhe.com/adler10e.

Museum of Springfield

Paul Georgakis is the new media coordinator at the Museum of Springfield. He is working on the biggest assignment of his career: developing the Web site for the museum's forthcoming new show "Images of Springfield." The exhibit is being underwritten by Midwestern Industries, and museum curator Mary Weston has told Paul that the board of trustees is counting on the exhibit's success to open the door to more corporate support. "If that happens we'll have a shot at becoming a top-quality regional museum," Mary tells Paul. "I don't have to tell you how important that is to the board of trustees." Mary might as well have said, "I don't have to tell you how important this is to your career."

Along with Paul, the project team for the Web site includes four other members:

Elaine Dorsch is the site's designer. Bringing San Francisco–based Elaine onboard was a coup for Paul. She has created sites for several world-class organizations, and she took the museum job for a deeply discounted fee because she grew up in Springfield and wants to give something back to the community.

Roger Chilton, a history professor at the local branch of the state university, is the content expert on the exhibit and the accompanying Web site. His specialty is the influence of business and government institutions on underprivileged groups in 19th-century U.S. society.

Julia Winger is the corporate liaison with Midwestern Industries. She has made it clear that her company is glad to support the museum and that it expects to be recognized for doing so. "Doing good can help Midwestern Industries do well," she told Paul.

Mary Weston, Paul's boss, represents the museum's administration and board of trustees.

The Web site project got off to a good start. But lately, several problems have developed. On a practical level, it has proved almost impossible to get all members to attend the last few meetings. Because Elaine is based in San Francisco and Julia's office is in Minneapolis, it has proved difficult for both of them to squeeze in visits to Springfield.

Even more disturbing has been the growing tension, as it has become clear that Roger's exhibit includes some disturbing images and stories. Julia recently sent the team an e-mail saying, "Midwestern Industries isn't contributing several hundred thousand dollars to upset the community." Roger replied, "It isn't a historian's job to make people happy." Paul is growing worried that either Roger or Julia may pull out of the project, and either scenario would be a disaster.

Finally, it has become clear that Elaine views any suggestion for revising her design as an assault on her artistic talent. "I don't tell you how to run your museum or Midwestern Industries," she says. "You're the experts in your own fields, and I am in mine. I know what I'm doing, and you just have to trust me."

Paul's boss Mary has made it clear that she is counting on him to keep the team together and the project on track.

As you read the chapters in this unit, consider how answers to the following questions might help Paul manage this difficult job:

1. What types of power listed in Chapter 8 does each team member have? How can the members use their power to help the group achieve its goal?

2. What approach to leadership outlined in Chapter 8 can Paul use to keep the group functioning well?

3. What are the personal goals of each member? How do these goals contribute to and/or interfere with the group's job?

4. How can the group use the systematic problem-solving method outlined in Chapter 8 to overcome the challenges it faces?

5. What decision-making method(s) should the members use in deciding how to resolve their disagreements?

6. Are there ways the team can handle some of its tasks without meeting in person?

7. What might an agenda for the team's next meeting look like?

8. What techniques outlined in Chapter 9 can Paul use when he chairs face-to-face meetings?

8

Working in Teams

chapter outline

The Nature of Teams
  Teams Are Essential
  Characteristics of Work Groups
  What Makes a Group a Team?
  Virtual Teams

Leadership and Influence in Groups and Teams
  Centralized Leadership
  Becoming a Leader
  Power and Influence of Members

Problem-Solving Communication
  Systematic Problem Solving
  Stages in Group Problem Solving
  Functional Role Analysis
  Decision-Making Methods

Effective Communication in Groups and Teams
  Recognize Both Group and Personal Goals
  Promote Desirable Norms
  Promote an Optimal Level of Cohesiveness
  Avoid Excessive Conformity
  Encourage Creativity

Review Points
Key Terms
Activities
Resources

chapter objectives

After reading this chapter, you should be able to

1. Diagnose a group and identify the kind of communication that can transform it into a team.
2. Analyze the advantages and drawbacks of working both face-to-face and as a virtual team.
3. Compare various approaches to centralized leadership, self-directed teams, and power distribution.
4. Identify the stages and characteristics of each stage of group problem solving and the roles that help groups function.
5. Explain various decision-making methods and the circumstances in which each is most appropriate.
6. Apply the guidelines for effective communication in groups and teams (goals, norms, cohesion, conformity, creativity) to a group to which you belong.

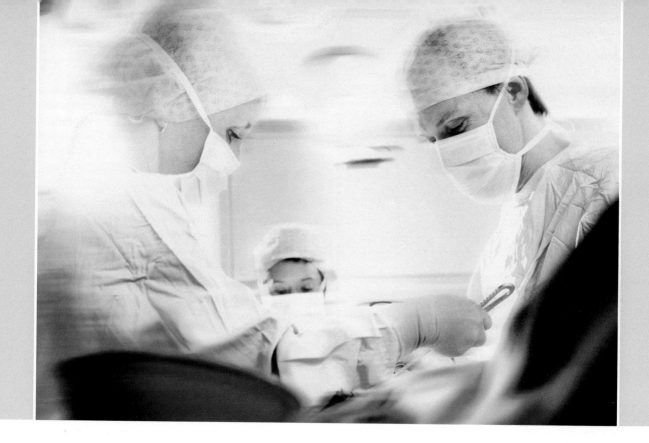

In his book *Tales of a New America*, Robert Reich describes the importance of teamwork in an increasingly technological age:

> Rarely do even Big Ideas emerge any longer from the solitary labors of genius. Modern science and technology is too complicated for one brain. It requires groups of astronomers, physicists, and computer programmers to discover new dimensions of the universe: teams of microbiologists, oncologists, and chemists to unravel the mysteries of cancer. With ever more frequency, Nobel prizes are awarded to collections of people. Scientific papers are authored by small platoons of researchers.[1]

Experts from across the world of work echo the importance of teamwork. As legendary baseball manager Casey Stengel put it, "Gettin' good players is easy. Getting 'em to play together is the hard part." Benjamin Franklin made the case even more dramatically: "We must indeed all hang together, or most assuredly, we shall all hang separately."

The Nature of Teams

Working with others is a vital part of virtually every job.[2] In a national survey of architects and landscape architects, over 75 percent of these professionals reported that they "always" or "often" worked in teams.[3] In the burgeoning field of multimedia, the ability to work as a team member has been identified as the top nontechnical job skill.[4] Motorola, Ford, USAA Insurance, and 3M Corp. have used teams to become leaders in their fields.[5]

Teams take many forms in the world of business and the professions. *Project teams* work on a specific task, usually for a finite period of time; for example, a group of marketing experts design a publicity program to accompany the rollout of a new software product. *Service teams* support customers or employees; for example, public utilities have service agents available around to clock to help customers. *Management teams* work collaboratively on a daily basis within organizations to help them perform their missions. At a university, for example, top officials meet regulary to coordinate their divisons: academic, student support, financial, physical facilities, and so on. *Action teams* offer immediate responses activated in (typically) emergency situations; for example, community health workers form teams to deal with public health threats.[6]

Teams Are Essential

No matter how brilliant you are, being a solo player is not an option in today's business world. Gary Kaplan, owner of a Pasadena, California, executive recruiting firm, offers one explanation of why team players are valued over rugged individualists: "The single-combat warrior, that bright, purposeful worker, tends to suck up a lot of oxygen in an organization. And now they're often seen as too innovative and too difficult."[7]

Just because groups *can* be effective doesn't guarantee that they always *will* succeed. Table 8–1 lists the conditions where groups are superior to individuals working alone, as well as those where groups are not the best approach. You can see that, in the right circumstances, groups have several advantages over the same number of individuals working alone.[8] One of these advantages is *productivity*. Research shows that the old saying "Two heads are better than one" can be true: Well-conceived and efficiently operating groups produce more solutions than individuals working alone, and the solutions are

Table 8–1	Group vs. Individual Performance

Group Superior to Individuals	Individuals Superior to Group
Task requires broad range of talents and knowledge	Task requires limited knowledge, information (which individuals possess)
Complicated task (requires division, coordination of labor)	Simple task (can be done by one person or individuals working separately)
Time available for deliberation	Little time available
Members are motivated to succeed	Members don't care about job
High standards of performance	"Social loafing" is the norm

Source: Adapted from J. D. Rothwell, *In Mixed Company*, 5th ed. (Belmont, CA: Wadsworth, 2004), p. 76; and A. P. Hare, "Roles, Relationships, and Groups in Organizations: Some Conclusions and Recommendations," *Small Group Research* 34 (April 2003), pp. 123–154.

likely to be better. Social scientists use the term *synergy* to describe how the capability of a group can be greater than the output all of its members could produce individually.[9]

Along with greater productivity, the *accuracy* of an effective group's work is higher than that of individuals. Consider the task of creating a new product. A group of people from sales, marketing, design, engineering, and manufacturing is likely to consider all the important angles, whereas one or two people without this breadth of perspective would probably miss some important ideas.

Teams not only produce better products but also generate more *commitment* and *enthusiasm* from the members who created them. People are usually more committed to a decision if they have had a part in making it. Recognizing this principle, many American companies create participatory management programs and quality circles that involve employees in important decisions. For example, William Deardon, chief executive officer of Hershey Foods Corporation, established a corporate planning committee to make the major plans and decisions for the company. "I figured that if we worked it out together," he explained, "the members of the group would feel that it was their plan and our plan—not my plan—and they'd work harder to implement it."[10]

Working effectively in groups calls for many of the skills described in earlier chapters of *Communicating at Work*. Chapter 1 discussed when to meet face-to-face and when to use other communication channels—telephone, electronic mail, and so on. Chapter 2 emphasized the importance of adapting to cultural norms when working with others. The listening skills outlined in Chapter 3 are essential when working in teams, as are the interpersonal skills described later in Chapter 5. Chapter 4 offered tips on using language effectively and being sensitive to nonverbal cues. The fundamental communication skills described so far in this book are important, but there are also special characteristics that distinguish communication in groups. In the following pages you will learn about those characteristics and how to apply them when you work in groups and teams.

Characteristics of Work Groups

The word *group* is often used to refer to any assembly of people—the commuters on the morning train, the sightseers gathering for a walking tour of the downtown area, the rock band at a local nightspot. When we talk about people interacting at work, we use the label differently. But not all collections of people—even people who come together in working settings—are groups.

For our purposes, a **work group** is a small, interdependent collection of people with a common identity who interact with one another, usually face-to-face over time, to reach a goal. Using this definition, we can single out several significant characteristics of work-centered groups that can help you develop ways to work more effectively with others on the job.

Size   Most experts say that a twosome is not a group because the partners do not interact in the same way that three or more people do. For instance, two people working together can resolve disputes only by persuading each other, giving in, or compromising. In groups, however, members can form alliances and outvote or pressure the minority.

Although less agreement exists about when a collection of people becomes too large to be considered a group, virtually every small-group expert argues that any collection much larger than 20 people loses many of the properties that define groups—at least effective ones.[11] Research on a number of companies has found that 10-person teams often produce better results at a quicker rate and with higher profits than do groups of several hundred.[12] There are several reasons why size doesn't translate into effectiveness: People begin to act in formal ways. Members have fewer chances to participate, since a few talkative members are likely to dominate the group; quieter members lose their identity and become less committed to the team. Coalitions can form, leading members to become more concerned with having their side win than with tackling the challenge at hand.

Most communication experts suggest that the optimal size for small decision-making groups is either five or seven members.[13] The odd number of participants eliminates the risk of tie votes. Teams with fewer than five members lack the resources to come up with good ideas and to carry them out, while larger groups suffer from the problems of anonymity, domination, and lack of commitment. Recent research suggests 5 to 12 members can succeed, provided the type of task and the team composition are given primary consideration.[14]

Interaction   A collection of people studying in a library or working out at the gym is merely co-acting. Likewise a roomful of trainees at a seminar isn't a group unless and until the individuals start interacting.

Shared Purpose   Guests at a reception or attendees at a convention might talk with one another, but unless they share a collective goal, they won't collectively accomplish anything. One challenge facing anyone leading a newly created group is to give members a clear sense of shared purpose.

Interdependence   Group members don't just interact; they depend on one another. Consider the workers in a restaurant: If the kitchen crew fails to prepare orders promptly or correctly, the servers' tips will decline. If the employees who clear tables don't do their jobs quickly and thoroughly, the servers will hear complaints from their customers. If the waiters fail to take orders accurately, the cooks will have to fix some meals twice. In a restaurant, as in any real team, the employees are part of an interdependent system.

One manager let employees know how valuable they are with the following memo:

```
          You Arx a Kxy Pxrson
My kxyboard works vxry wxll—xxcxpt for onx kxy. You would
think that with all thx othxr kxys functioning propxrly, onx
kxy not working would hardly bx noticxd; but just onx kxy out
of whack sxxms to ruin thx wholx xffort.
     You may say to yoursxlf—Wxll I'm only onx pxrson. No onx
will noticx if I don't do my bxst. But it doxs makx a diffxrxncx
bxcausx to bx xffxctivx an organization nxxds activx partici-
pation by xvxry onx to thx bxst of his or hxr ability.
     So thx nxxt timx you think you arx not important, rxmxmbxr
my kxyboard. You arx a kxy pxrson.
```

Regular Interaction and Communication   A group that interacts over a period of time develops particular characteristics. For example, a group will tend to develop shared standards of appropriate behavior that members are expected to meet. Typical expectations involve how promptly meetings begin, what contribution each member is expected to make to certain routine tasks, what kind of humor is appropriate, and so on.

Identity   Both members and outsiders view groups as distinct entities. Some groups have a formal title such as "benefits committee" or "accounting department." Others

The Redeem Team

In the 1992 Olympic Games in Barcelona, the U.S. men's basketball team earned a place in sports history. This group proved to be one of the most illustrious collections of athletes in the history of the game, soundly defeating every opponent on the way to a gold medal and earning the label of the "Dream Team."

By the 2004 Olympic Games in Athens, the fortunes of Team USA had declined. The group suffered a string of humiliating losses. These defeats were due in part to the refusal of several American top-tier athletes to join the team, and to a lack of enthusiasm and teamwork.

Determined to recapture their lost honor, Team USA took a different approach in preparing for the 2008 games in Beijing. Rather than simply recruiting superstars, the focus was on building cohesion. Said managing director Jerry Colangelo, "Basketball is the ultimate team game, and we wanted to put together a roster that would play with a team concept."

Toward this end, Colangelo emphasized the importance of teamwork over ego when recruiting players. "This was not about them," he said. "This was about representing their country with the pride that other Olympians have represented their country."

Along with attitude, the team invested time in working together. Breaking with the past, Coach Mike Krzyzewski was hired three years in advance. Most of the players were involved with the team for two years before the Olympic competition. Members grew as a unit by practicing intensively together—over 42 days in 2006, and even more in 2007 and 2008.

These practices paid dividends in the 2008 Beijing games. The team dominated even its strongest opponents, playing undefeated and earning a gold medal. For this performance the Americans earned the title "The Redeem Team."

Superstar Kobe Bryant captured the shared sense of purpose after the team's championship victory: "Everybody wants to talk about NBA players being selfish, being arrogant, being individuals. Well, what you saw today was a team bonding together, facing adversity and coming out of here with a big win."

CRITICAL ANALYSIS: Explore how the "Redeem Team" approach illustrates group effectiveness by considering these questions.

1. Which elements of team effectiveness listed on pages 239–240 characterized the U.S. Olympic basketball team? Think about a team to which you currently belong or have belonged in the past. How well does this group embody the elements on pages 239–240?

2. How could your team become more effective by adopting additional characteristics described on pages 239–240?

Sources: A. Bagnato, "US Golden Again," United States Olympic Committee, August 24, 2008, **http://basketball.teamusa.org/news/article/6514;** and M. Sappenfeld, "'Redeem Team' Wants More than Olympic Gold," *Christian Science Monitor*, August 19, 2008, **http://features.csmonitor.com/olympics08/2008/08/19/%E2%80%98redeem-team%E2%80%99-wants-more-than-olympic-gold.**

have an informal identity like "lunchtime power walkers" or "those guys who carpool together." In either case, the fact that the group is seen as distinct has important consequences. To a greater or lesser extent, members feel their own image is tied to the way the group is regarded. In addition, the group's identity means that the addition or loss of a member feels significant to the people involved, whether the change in membership is cause for celebration or disappointment.

What Makes a Group a Team?

The term **team** appears everywhere in the business world. The positive connotations of a team—spirit, cooperation, hard work—lead some managers to give every collection of workers the team label. You don't have to be an athlete to appreciate the value of teams, and you don't need to be a cynic to know that calling a group of people a team doesn't make them one.[15] True teams have all the attributes of a group, but they have other qualities that distinguish them and make them more satisfying to work in and more productive.[16] Communication researchers Carl Larson and Frank LaFasto spent nearly 3 years interviewing members of over 75 teams that were clearly winners. The groups came from a wide range of enterprises, including a Mount Everest expedition, a cardiac surgery team, the presidential commission that studied the space shuttle *Challenger* accident, the group that developed the IBM personal computer, and two championship football teams. Although the groups pursued widely different goals, they all shared eight important characteristics. You can understand both why your team functions as it does and how to improve its effectiveness by analyzing how well your group fits the profile of these winning teams.

- *Clear and inspiring shared goals.* Members of a winning team know why their group exists, and they believe that purpose is important and worthwhile. Ineffective groups have either lost sight of their purpose or do not believe that the goal is truly important.

- *A results-driven structure.* Members of winning teams focus on getting the job done in the most effective manner. They do whatever is necessary to accomplish the task. Less effective groups either are not organized at all or are structured in an inefficient manner, and their members don't care enough about the results to do what is necessary to get the job done.

- *Competent team members.* Members of winning teams have the skill necessary to accomplish their goals. Less effective groups lack people possessing one or more key skills.

- *Unified commitment.* People in successful teams put the group's goals above their personal interests. While this commitment might seem like a sacrifice to others, for members of winning teams the personal rewards are worth the effort.

- *Collaborative climate.* Another word for collaboration is *teamwork*. People in successful groups trust and support one another.

- *Standards of excellence.* In winning teams, doing outstanding work is an important norm. Each member is expected to do his or her personal best. In less successful groups, getting by with the minimum amount of effort is the standard.

- *External support and recognition.* Successful teams need an appreciative audience that recognizes their effort and provides the resources necessary to get the job done. The audience may be a boss, or it may be the public the group is created to serve.

- *Principled leadership.* Winning teams usually have leaders who can create a vision of the group's purpose and challenge members to get the job done. Finally, they have the ability to unleash the talent of group members.

You may not be able to single-handedly transform your entire organization into a team-friendly environment, but it is still possible to influence the group of people with whom you work. Examine the characteristics of teams listed above and ask yourself whether you are communicating in a manner that makes that small but important leap possible.

Virtual Teams

Virtual teams interact and function as groups without being in the same place at the same time.[17] Technology permits virtual groups to transcend boundaries of location

Working in Virtual Teams

1. *Strive for some "face time," especially during the group's formation.* Virtual teams are most cohesive, trusting, and successful when members have had a chance to spend time together in person, especially during the group's development.

2. *Put communication on the agenda.* Agree up front on when and how members should communicate with one another. Consider which channels are most appropriate and agree on response times.

3. *Be mindful of time zone differences.* When members of a virtual team are dispersed across time zones, it's especially important to schedule meetings so no members are inconvenienced. Time differences can be especially challenging when groups span several continents. For example, if some members are in California and others in India are time shifted by a half day, the only times that may work for people with normal schedules are early morning and early evening. Remember Asia is a day *ahead* of the United States; Europe is a half to a full day *behind*.

4. *Use time zones to your advantage.* Consider handing off tasks that members in other time zones can tackle while you are off work. For example, a member in Seattle can request information at the end of the workday, and teammates in Florida can respond at the start of their next workday, so an answer will be in the sender's in-box when s/he logs on 3 hours later.

5. *Keep a personal touch.* Express some of the same emotions and personal thoughts that you would in face-to-face communication. Doing so can build camaraderie and the human feeling that virtual teams may lack without face-to-face communication.

6. *Consider using "back channels."* Use telephone, personal e-mail, and instant messaging to confer directly with one or more team members when you need to deal with issues and relationships personally in a way that will save the group time and effort.

7. *Do a trial run of technology.* Make sure in advance of meetings that all the technology upon which your team relies is working. It can be frustrating and discouraging to waste meeting time dealing with glitches.

8. *Seek input from all team members.* Sometimes members who are more comfortable with the technology of the virtual team will "speak" more than those who have more expertise in the team area, but not with the technology being used.

9. *Be aware of cultural differences in communication style.* These exist in cyberspace as well as in face-to-face communication. Remind yourself of style differences in high- and low-context cultures, expectations of leaders and team members, preferences for direct and indirect means of expression. Learn to read between the lines of those who may not directly criticize your ideas or offer advice.

Sources: D. L. Duarte and N. T. Snyder, *Mastering Virtual Teams: Strategies, Tools and Techniques That Succeed,* 3rd ed. (San Francisco: Josey-Bass, 2006); M. E. Guffey, *Business Communication: Process and Product,* 6th ed. (Florence, KY: Southwestern/Cengage, 2008); and J. D. Rothwell, *In Mixed Company: Communicating in Small Groups and Teams,* 7th ed. (Boston: Cengage, 2010), pp. 378–380.

and time. Barry Caldwell, supervisor of computer-aided industrial design technologies at Ford Motor Company's Corporate Design division, concurs, explaining how Ford's virtual teams span the globe: "We can't change the fact that Europe is five or six hours ahead [of Michigan]," he says. "But virtual teams can be extremely effective if you can have people working in Italy or Germany—five hours ahead of you—and they can hand work off to Dearborn at the end of their day, and you can carry it further and then pass it back. Instead of an eight-hour day, you can get 14 hours."[18]

Besides being more efficient, in some circumstances virtual teams can be at least as effective as those who meet face-to-face. While newly formed teams do best when members can meet in person, established groups work equally well in cyberspace.[19] In one study, teams that worked by exchanging e-mails produced better results than individuals and in-person groups.[20]

Virtual teamwork can be just as valuable for busy people who work near one another. Some human resources experts claim that when people work more than 50 feet apart, their likelihood of collaborating more than once a week is less than 10 percent.[21] Given this fact, virtual meetings can boost the efficiency of people who work under the same roof.

Another advantage of virtual teams is the leveling of status differences. On networked teams, rank is much less prominent than in face-to-face groups.[22] In e-mail, the ideas of a new or mid-level worker look identical to those of a senior manager. Back-and-forth dialogue is much less intimidating in mediated format than it might be when you have to face the boss in person.

Sometimes a virtual group needs to communicate in real time. Teleconferencing and instant messaging (IMing) make it easy and inexpensive to conduct synchronous virtual meetings. In other cases, working asynchronously can be more effective. Michael Charnow, vice president at California software developer Ontek Corp., describes the value of asynchronous conferencing for his staff: "We wanted telecommunications capabilities because work such as programming and research is done at all hours of the day and night, and we don't feel that people have to be physically present to do their best work."[23] For asynchronous meetings, Web-based discussion tools provided by Google, Yahoo, and others are simple to set up and manage.

Despite the advantages of virtual teamwork, computer networking can't replace all of the functions of personal contacts. Frank Carrubba, executive vice president and chief technical officer of Philips Electronics NV in the Netherlands, explains the need for what some wags have called "face time": "You have to figure out how to deal with people other than in the terminal of a computer and keep them spirited over long distances, especially when failures arise. And you have to know how to use the brief times when people are brought together."[24]

Leadership and Influence in Groups and Teams

Throughout most of the history of organizations, the importance of centralized leadership in groups went unquestioned. The common thinking was that one ingredient in effective group functioning was the presence of a leader who could motivate members and make final decisions. Recently, however, experts in business and professional communication have come to recognize another approach to group functioning that puts most or all of the power into the hands of members. Since both of these approaches—centralized and decentralized—are common in today's workplace, the following pages will look at how communication operates in each one.

Centralized Leadership

The difference between effective and ineffective leaders can be dramatic: A losing team gets a new coach and, with the same players, begins winning against the same opponents; a demoralized division gets a new sales manager, and orders increase; a production crew gets a new supervisor, and workers who once spent their time complaining find new enjoyment and productivity. Whatever the nature of the organization, we count on the person in charge to make the enterprise work.

What qualities make leaders effective? Business tycoon T. Boone Pickens emphasized the role of communication: "A good team leader should make communication his No. 1 priority."[25] Sometimes, however, the question is difficult to answer. Many effective leaders seem to perform their role effortlessly, and people seem to follow them naturally; others seem to rule by sheer force. Scholars and researchers have studied leadership from many perspectives. Following are some leadership approaches.

Trait Approach

The **trait approach** is based on the belief that all leaders possess common traits that lead to their effectiveness. The earliest research sought to identify these traits, and by the mid-1930s scores of studies pursued this goal. Conclusions were contradictory. Certain traits did seem common in most leaders, including physical attractiveness, sociability, desire for leadership, originality, and intelligence.[26] Despite these similarities, the research also showed that these traits were not *predictive* of leadership. In other words, a person possessing these characteristics would not necessarily become a leader. Another research approach was necessary.

Style Approach

Beginning in the 1940s, researchers began to consider the **style approach.** They asked whether the designated leader could *choose* a way of communicating that would increase effectiveness. This research identified three managerial styles. Some leaders are **authoritarian,** using legitimate, coercive, and reward power at their disposal to control members. Others are more **democratic,** inviting members to help make decisions. A third leadership style is **laissez-faire:** The designated leader gives up the power of that position and transforms the group into a leaderless collection of equals.

Early research seemed to suggest that the democratic style produced the best results,[27] and contemporary studies suggest that members of groups with democratic leadership are slightly more satisfied than those run by autocratic leaders.[28] Still, it is an oversimplification to say that a democratic approach always works best. For instance, groups with autocratic leaders were more productive in stressful situations, while democratically led groups did better when the conditions were nonstressful.[29]

One of the best-known stylistic approaches is the *Leadership Grid*® by Robert Blake and Jane Mouton (see Figure 8–1),[30] which shows that good leadership depends on skillful management of the task and the relationships among group members. The horizontal axis of the grid measures a manager's concern for task or production—getting the job done. The vertical axis measures the leader's concern for people and relationships. Blake and Mouton's grid counteracts the tendency in some naive managers to assume that if they focus solely on the task, good results will follow. They argue that the most effective leader is one who adopts a 9,9 style, showing high concern for both product *and* people.

Contingency Approaches

Unlike the style approach, **contingency approaches** are based on the idea that the "best" leadership style is flexible—it changes from one situation to the next. For instance, a manager who successfully guides a project team developing an advertising campaign might flop as a trainer or personnel officer.

Psychologist Fred Fiedler conducted extensive research in an attempt to discover when a task-oriented approach works best and when a relationship-oriented style is most effective.[31] He found that a decision about whether to emphasize task or relationship issues in a situation depends on three factors: (1) *leader–member relations,* including the

FIGURE 8–1

The Leadership Grid®

Source: From *Leadership Dilemmas–Grid Solutions* by Robert R. Blake and Anne Adams McCanse (formerly the *Managerial Grid* by Robert R. Blake and Jane S. Mouton). Houston: Gulf Publishing Company, p. 29. Copyright 1991 by Scientific Methods, Inc. Reproduced by permission of Grid International Inc.

attractiveness of the manager and the loyalty of the followers; (2) *task structure*, involving the degree of simplicity or complexity of the job; and (3) *the leader's power*, including job title and the ability to coerce and reward.

Generally, Fiedler's research suggests that a task-oriented approach works best when circumstances are extremely favorable (good leader–member relations, highly structured tasks) or extremely unfavorable (poor leader–member relations, unstructured task, weak leader power). In moderately favorable or unfavorable circumstances, a relationship-oriented approach works best. While these findings are useful, it is important not to overstate them. In most cases, good leadership requires a mixture of relationship and task concerns. The question is not which dimension to choose, but which one to *emphasize*.

Another model of situational leadership is the life-cycle approach developed by Paul Hersey and Kenneth Blanchard.[32] The **life-cycle theory** suggests that a leader's concern for tasks and relationships ought to vary, depending on the readiness of the subordinate or subordinates to work independently. According to the life-cycle theory, a worker with a low level of readiness needs a style of leadership that is highly directive and task-related. As the group member becomes more competent and motivated, the manager ought to offer rewards in terms of social reinforcement. As the subordinate becomes able to perform the task without the guidance of the boss, the manager ought to withdraw the task-related supervision even more, while encouraging the employee's new ability. Finally, when the worker's ability to handle a task is superior, the boss can cut back the amount of socioemotional support, knowing that the worker is functioning at the highest level and that any reinforcements are now primarily internal.

Becoming a Leader

Sometimes leaders are appointed by higher-ups, but in many cases they emerge from a group. **Emergent leaders** may be chosen by the members of a group either officially or informally. An athletic team may elect a captain. The owners' association of a condominium chooses a head. Union members pick a team to represent them in contract negotiations with management.

Emergent leaders don't always have official titles. A group of disgruntled employees might urge one person to approach the boss and ask for a change, for example. A team of students assigned to develop a class project might agree that one person is best suited to take the lead in organizing and presenting their work. Sometimes emergent leaders are officially recognized, but other times their role is never acknowledged overtly. In fact, there are often cases where the designated leader may be the titular head, while an emergent leader really runs the show. Fans of late-night movies recall how the young, inexperienced lieutenant learns to defer to the grizzled, wise sergeant. This pattern often repeats itself in everyday working situations, when new managers or supervisors recognize the greater knowledge of old-timers who are subordinates on the organizational chart. In cases like these, the new manager is smart to defer to the unofficial, emergent leader—at least until he or she gains some experience and wisdom.

Communication researcher Ernest Bormann has studied how emergent leaders gain influence, especially in newly formed groups.[33] According to Bormann, a group selects a leader by the *method of residues*—a process of elimination in which potential candidates are gradually rejected for one reason or another until only one remains. This process of elimination occurs in two phases. In the first, members who are clearly unsuitable are rejected. The surest path to rejection is being quiet: Untalkative members were never chosen as leaders in the groups Bormann studied. Failing to participate verbally in a group's work leaves the impression of indifference and lack of commitment. Another ticket to early rejection is dogmatism: Members who express their opinions in strong, unqualified terms are usually perceived as being too extreme and inflexible to take a leading role. A third cause of elimination as leader is a lack of skill or intelligence: Competence is obviously a necessary condition for successful leadership, and members who lack this quality are rejected early.

Quietness, dogmatism, and incompetence are almost always grounds for disqualification. Beyond these factors, a communication style that members find irritating or disturbing is likely to knock a member out of consideration as a leader. A variety of behaviors fall into this category, depending on the composition of the group. In one case being too serious might be grounds for rejection, while in a different situation a joker would earn disapproval. Using inappropriate language could be a disqualifier. In a group with biased members, gender or ethnicity might be grounds for rejection.

After clearly unsuitable members have been eliminated, roughly half of the group's members may still be candidates for leadership. This can be a tense time, since the jockeying for a role of influence may pit the remaining candidates against one another. In some groups, the contenders for leader acquire what Bormann calls "lieutenants," who support their advancement. If only one candidate has a lieutenant, his or her chances of becoming leader are strong. If two or more contenders have supporters, the process of leader emergence can drag out or even reach a stalemate. The Career Tip box on page 246 offers advice for the times when you want to take on leadership of a group.

How to Emerge as a Group Leader

If you are interested in seeking a leadership position— and you almost certainly will be at one time or another— research has demonstrated that the following types of behavior will help you assert your influence.

- *Participate early and often.* Talking won't guarantee that you will be recognized as a leader, but failing to speak up will almost certainly knock you out of the running.

- *Demonstrate your competence.* Make sure your comments identify you as someone who can help the group succeed. Demonstrate the kinds of expert, connection, and information power described later in this chapter.

- *Don't push too hard.* It's fine to be assertive, but don't try to overpower other members. Even if you are right, your dogmatism is likely to alienate others.

- *Provide a solution in a time of crisis.* How can the group meet a deadline? Gain the sale? Get the necessary equipment? Members who find answers to problems like these are likely to rise to a position of authority.

Sources: Reprinted by permission of Waveland Press, Inc., from M. Z. Hackman and C. E. Johnson, *Leadership: A Communication Perspective*, Long Grove, IL: Waveland Press, Inc., 2004. All rights reserved. See also C. Anderson and G. J. Kilduff, "Why Do Dominant Personalities Attain Influence in Face-to-Face Groups? The Competence-Signaling Effects of Trait Dominance," *Journal of Personality and Social Psychology* 96 (2009), pp. 491–503.

In their book *Getting It Done: How to Lead When You're Not in Charge*, Roger Fisher and Alan Sharp describe "lateral leadership" as a way to avoid the extremes of doing nothing or taking charge and bossing others. They suggest that a group member can lead others by doing three things: *asking* thoughtful, sincere questions to get others to think creatively and contribute their ideas; *offering* ideas to help the group while inviting others to challenge your thoughts; and *doing* something constructive needed by the group and modeling the behavior needed.[34]

Power and Influence of Members

Most working groups have what social scientists call a **designated leader**—the boss, chairperson, coach, or manager who has formal authority and responsibility to supervise the task at hand. Other groups, called **self-directed work teams** are responsible for managing their own behavior to get a task done.[35] For example, at one General Mills cereal plant, teams schedule, operate, and maintain machinery so effectively that the plant runs with no managers present during night shifts. The company reports that productivity at plants that rely on self-managed teams is as much as 40 percent higher than at traditional factories. At Federal Express, a group of clerks spotted and solved a billing problem, saving the company $2.1 million in just 1 year. Harley-Davidson successfully organizes operations at its Kansas City, Missouri, motorcycle assembly plant using self-directed teams.[36]

Whether or not a group has a designated leader, every member has the power to shape events. Over a half century ago, John French and Bertram Raven identified several forms of power that are usually possessed by one or more members of a group—not necessarily just the designated leader.[37] Depending on how they are used, these forms of power can make or break the success of a working group.

Position Power

Position power is the ability to influence that comes from the position one holds. We often do things for the boss precisely because he or she holds that title. While legitimate power usually belongs to designated leaders, people in lesser positions sometimes have jobs that involve telling higher-ups what to do. For example, a media expert might tell the CEO or board chairman what will and won't work in a presentation to stockholders.

"Now that you've all put in your two cent' worth, I should like to interject my fifty-one per cent controlling inerest."

Coercive Power

The power to punish is known as **coercive power,** since we often follow another's bidding when failure to do so would lead to unpleasant consequences. Designated leaders have coercive power: They can assign unpleasant tasks, deny pay raises, and even fire us. Other members have coercive power, too, though it is usually subtle. A committee member or officemate who acts as a blocker when things don't go his way is coercing others to take his views into account, implying, "If you don't follow at least some of my suggestions, I'll punish the group by continuing to object to your ideas and refusing to cooperate with you."

Reward Power

The flip side of coercive power is **reward power**—the ability to reward. Designated leaders control the most obvious rewards: pay raises, improved working conditions, and the ability to promote. But, again, other members can give their own rewards. These come in the form of social payoffs, such as increased goodwill, and task-related benefits, like voluntary assistance on a job.

Expert Power

Expert power comes from the group's recognition of a member's expertise in a certain area. There are times when one expert is better suited to make a decision than is an entire team. Designated leaders aren't always the experts in a group. In a manufacturing firm, for example, a relatively low-ranking engineer could influence management to alter a project by using her knowledge to declare that a new product won't work. Problems can arise either when management doesn't recognize a knowledgeable member as an expert or when unqualified people are granted expert status.

Referent Power

The term **referent power** alludes to the influence members hold due to the way others in the group feel about them: their respect, attraction, or liking. It is here that the greatest difference between designated leaders and members with true influence occurs. An unpopular boss might have to resort to his or her job title and the power to coerce and reward that comes with it to gain compliance, whereas a popular person, with or without a leadership title, can get others to cooperate without threatening or promising.[38] Mike Zugsmith, co-owner of a commercial real-estate brokerage, captures the importance of referent power, even for a boss: "When I started this company in 1979, I was 28. I was supervising salespeople who were 20 to 30 years my senior. It readily became apparent that simply because your name is on the door doesn't mean you'll get respect. You have to earn it."[39]

Information Power

Information power is the ability of some members to influence a group because of the information they possess. This information is different from the kind of knowledge that gives rise to expert power. Whereas an expert possesses some form of talent based on training or education, an information-rich group member has access to otherwise obscure knowledge that is valuable to others in the group. A new employee who was hired away from a competitor, for example, is likely to play a key role in the decisions of how his new company will compete against the old one. Likewise, a member who is well connected to the organizational grapevine can exert a major influence on how the group operates: "Don't bring that up now. Smith is going through a divorce and he's saying no to everything." "I just heard there's plenty of money in the travel and entertainment budget. Maybe this is the time to propose that reception for the out-of-town distributors we've been thinking about."

Connection Power   In the business world, a member's influence can often come from the connections he or she has with influential or important people inside or outside the organization—hence the term **connection power.** The classic example of connection power is the son or daughter of the boss. While the official word from the top may be "Treat my kid just like any other employee," this is easier said than done. Not all connection power is harmful. If one member sees a potential customer socially, he is in a good position to help the business. If another one knows a government official, she can get off-the-record advice about how to handle a government regulation.

If we recognize the influence that comes with connection power, the old saying "It isn't what you know that counts, it's who you know" seems true. If we look at all the types of power described in this section, we can see that a more accurate statement is "What counts is whom you know [connection power], what you know [information and expert power], who respects you [referent power], and who you are [legitimate power]." This range of power bases makes it clear that the power to influence a group is truly shared among members, all of whom have the ability to affect how well a group works as a unit and the quality of the product it turns out.

Problem-Solving Communication

In the past decades, researchers have developed several methods for helping groups solve problems and make decisions effectively. By taking advantage of these methods, groups can come up with the highest-quality work possible.

Systematic Problem Solving

The range of problems that groups face on the job is almost endless. How can we cut expenses? Increase market share? Reduce customer complaints? Offer a better employee-benefits program? Not all groups approach problems like these systematically,[40] but most researchers agree that groups have the best chance of developing high-quality solutions to problems like these when they follow a systematic method for solving problems.[41]

The best-known problem-solving approach is the **reflective-thinking sequence,** developed over 80 years ago by John Dewey and used in many forms since then.[42] In its most useful form, the reflective-thinking sequence is a seven-step process.

1. *Define the problem.* A group that doesn't understand the problem will have trouble finding a solution. Sometimes the problem facing a group is clear. It doesn't take much deliberation to understand what's necessary when the boss tells you to work out a vacation schedule for the next 6 months. On the other hand, some problems need rewording because they are too broad as originally presented. The

Dilbert: © Scott Adams/Dist. by United Feature Syndicate, Inc. Reprinted by permission.

best problem statements are phrased as probative questions, ones that encourage exploratory thinking:

Too Broad	Better
How can we reduce employee turnover?	How can we reduce turnover among new employees? (This suggests where to look for the nature of the problem and solutions.)
How can we boost the morale of the office staff?	How can we reduce the complaints about too much work?

2. *Analyze the problem.* At this stage, the group tries to discover the causes and extent of the problem, probably by doing some research between meetings. Questions that are usually appropriate in this stage include (a) How bad is that problem? (b) Why does it need to be resolved? and (c) What are its causes? It can be just as useful to focus on the positive aspects of the situation during this phase to consider how they can be strengthened. Questions in this area include (a) What forces are on our side? (b) How do they help us? and (c) How can we strengthen them?

    A group analyzing the question "How can we reduce complaints about too much work?" might find that the problem is especially bad for certain staffers. It might discover that the problem is worst when staffers have to type long reports at the last minute. It might learn that the major complaint doesn't involve hard work as much as it does resentment at seeing other people apparently having a lighter load. Positive research findings might be that the staffers understand the importance of their role, that they view being chosen to do important jobs as a sign of respect for the quality of their work, and that they don't mind occasional periods of scrambling to meet a deadline.

3. *Establish criteria for a solution.* Rather than rushing to solve the problem, it's best to spend some time identifying the characteristics of a good solution. Who would it have to satisfy? What are the cost constraints? What schedule needs to be met? Sometimes criteria like these are imposed from outside the group. Other requirements come from the members themselves. Regardless of the source of these requirements, the group needs to make them clear before considering possible

solutions. Without defining the criteria of a satisfactory solution, the group may waste time arguing over proposals that have no chance of being accepted.

4. *Consider possible solutions to the problem.* This is the time for using the creative thinking techniques described later in this chapter. A major hazard of group problem solving is that it may get bogged down in arguing over the merits of one or two proposals without considering other solutions that might exist. Besides limiting the quality of the solution, such squabbling also leads to personal battles among members.[43]

    The most valuable feature of brainstorming is the emphasis on generating many ideas before judging any of them. This sort of criticism-free atmosphere encourages people to volunteer solutions that, in turn, lead to other ideas. A brainstorming list for the overworked staffers might include the following:

    - Cut down on the number of jobs that have to be done over; create a company style book that shows how letters are to be set up, how contract clauses should be phrased, and so on.

    - Have staffers help each other out—someone with too much work to do can ask someone else to take over a project.

    - Establish a typing pool: Instead of assigning a staffer to a specific person or group, turn over all typing tasks to a group leader who will distribute them. Since the typists will be working as a group, they can train new typists themselves.

5. *Decide on a solution.* Once the group has considered all possible solutions to a problem, it can go back and find the best answer to the problem. This is done by comparing each idea to the list of criteria developed earlier by the group. In addition to measuring the solution against its own criteria, the group should judge any potential solutions by asking three questions: First, will the proposal bring about all the desired changes? If it solves only part of the problem, it isn't adequate without some changes. Second, can the solution be implemented by the group? If the idea is good but is beyond the power of this group to achieve, it needs to be modified or discarded. Finally, does the idea have any serious disadvantages? A plan that solves one set of problems while generating another probably isn't worth adopting.

6. *Implement the solution.* Inventing a solution isn't enough. The group also has to put the plan into action. This probably involves several steps. First, it's necessary to identify the specific tasks that must be accomplished. Second, the group must identify the resources necessary to make the plan work. Third, individual responsibilities must be defined: Who will do what, and when? Finally, the group should plan for emergencies. What will happen if someone is sick? If the project runs over budget? If a job takes longer than expected? Anticipating problems early is far better than being caught by surprise.

7. *Follow up on the solution.* Even the best ideas don't always work out perfectly in practice. For this reason, the group should check up on the implementation of the solution to see whether any adjustments are needed.

Stages in Group Problem Solving

The systematic problem-solving approach described above is certainly sensible, but it doesn't consider how the relationships among individual members can make it difficult for them to follow this kind of rational approach faithfully.[44] As groups conduct business, their discussions are likely to move more or less regularly through several phases characterized by different types of communication. Aubrey Fisher identified four of these stages: orientation, conflict, emergence, and reinforcement.[45]

The first stage in a group's development is the **orientation phase,** sometimes called **forming.**[46] This is a time of testing the waters. Members may not know one another very well and so are cautious about making statements that might offend. For this reason, during the orientation stage team members aren't likely to take strong positions even on issues they regard as important. It is easy to mistake the lack of conflict during this phase as harmony and assume that the task will proceed smoothly. Peace and quiet are often a sign of caution, not agreement. Despite the tentative nature of communication, the orientation stage is important because the norms that can govern the group's communication throughout its life are often formed at this time.

After the team members understand the problem and have a feel for one another, the group typically moves to the **conflict phase,** which has been called **storming.** This is the time when members take a strong stand on the issue and defend their positions against others. Disagreement is likely to be greatest during this phase, and the potential for bruised egos is strongest. The norms of politeness that were formed during orientation may weaken as members debate with one another, and there is a real risk that personal feelings will interfere with the kind of rational decision making described in the preceding section. Conflict does not have to be negative, however. If members adopt the kinds of constructive approaches outlined in Chapter 5, they can come up with high-quality solutions that have the potential to get the job done and leave everyone satisfied.[47]

Some groups never escape from the conflict stage. Their interaction—at least about the problem at hand—may end when time pressures force a solution that almost no one finds satisfactory. The boss may impose a decision from above, or a majority might overrule the minority. Time may even run out without any decision being made. Not all groups suffer from such unhappy outcomes, however. Productive teams manage to work through the conflict phase and move on to the next stage of development.

The **emergence phase** of problem solving, sometimes called **norming,** occurs when the members end their disagreement and solve the problem. The final decision may be enthusiastically supported by every member. In some cases, though, members may compromise or settle for a proposal they didn't originally prefer. In any case, the key to emergence is acceptance of a decision that members can support (even if reluctantly). Communication during the emergence phase is less polarized. Members back off from their previously held firm positions. Comments like "I can live with that" and "Let's give it a try" are common at this point. Even if some people have doubts about the decision, there is a greater likelihood that they will keep their concerns to themselves. Harmony is the theme.[48]

The fourth stage of discussion is the **reinforcement phase.** This stage has also been called **performing** because members not only accept the decision but also actively endorse it. Members who found arguments against the decision during the conflict stage now present evidence to support it. In school, the reinforcement stage is apparent when students presenting a group project defend it against any complaints the instructor might have. On the job, the same principle applies: If the boss finds fault with a team's proposals, the tendency is to band together to support them.

In real life, groups don't necessarily follow this four-step process (summarized in Table 8-2) neatly. In an ongoing team, the patterns of communication in the past can influence present and future communication.[49] Teams with a high degree of conflict might have trouble reaching emergence, for example, whereas a group that is highly cohesive might experience little disagreement.

Sometimes a group can become stuck in one phase, never progressing to the phases that follow. Members might never get beyond the superficial, polite interaction of

Table 8–2 — Characteristics and Guidelines for Problem-Solving Stages

	Member Behaviors	Member Concerns	For Higher Performance
Forming	Most comments directed to designated leader. Direction and clarification frequently sought. Status accorded to members based on their roles outside the group. Issues discussed superficially.	Why am I in this group? Why are the others here? Will I be accepted? What is my role? What jobs will I have? Will I be able to handle them? Who is the leader? Is s/he competent?	Provide structure. Clarify tasks, roles, and responsibilities. Encourage balanced participation, discourage domination by any. Identify one another's expertise, needs, values, and preferences.
Storming	Some members try to gain disproportionate share of influence. Subgroups and coalitions form. Designated leader may be challenged. Members overzealously judge one another's ideas and personalities.	How much autonomy will I have? Will I be able to influence others? What is my place in the pecking order? Who are my friends and allies? Who are my enemies? Do my ideas get any support here? Who don't some of the others see things my way? Is this aggravation worth the effort?	Use joint problem-solving. Discuss group's problem-solving ideas. Have members explain how others' ideas are useful and how to improve them. Establish norm supporting expression of different viewpoints.

orientation. If they do, they might become mired down in conflict. Ongoing groups might move through some or all of the stages each time they tackle a new problem, as pictured in Figure 8–2 on page 254. In fact, a group that deals with several issues at one time might be in different stages for each problem.

Knowing that a group to which you belong is likely to pass through these stages can be reassuring. Your urge to get down to business and quit wasting time during the orientation phase might be tempered if you realize that the cautious communication is probably temporary. Likewise, you might be less distressed about conflict if you know that the possibility of emergence may be just around the corner.

Functional Role Analysis

Another way every member can shape the way a group operates is by acting in whatever way is necessary to help get the job done. This approach has been labeled the "functional perspective" because it defines influence in terms of fulfilling essential functions, not

	Member Behaviors	Member Concerns	For Higher Performance
Norming	The group establishes and follows rules and procedures.	How can we get organized well enough to stay on top of our tasks?	Challenge the team, fight complacency.
	Members sometimes openly disagree.	How close should I get to other members?	Establish norms of high performance.
	The group laughs together, has fun.	How can we work in harmony?	Request and provide both positive and constructive feedback on individual and team actions.
	Members have a sense of "we-ness."	How do we compare to other groups?	
	The group feels superior to other groups.	What is my relationship to the leader?	Encourage open discussions about individual ideas and concerns.
	Groupthink may be a risk.	How do we keep conflicts and differences under control?	
		How can we structure things to run smoothly?	
High Performing	Members seek honest feedback from one another.	How can we continue at this pace?	Jointly set challenging goals.
	Roles are clear, yet members cover for one another as needed.	How might we share our learnings with one another?	Look for opportunities to increase group's scope.
	Members openly discuss and accept differences.	What will I do when this process is over?	Question assumptions, norms, and traditional approaches.
	Members encourage one another to do better.	How will I find another team as good as this one?	Develop mechanism for ongoing self- and group assessment.

Source: After Ed Kur, "The Faces Model of High Performing Team Development," *Management Development Review* 9, no. 6 (1996), pp. 32–41.

formal titles. These essential contributions have earned the name **functional roles** because they involve functions that are necessary for the group to do its job. Table 8–3 on page 255 lists these functional roles and notes some dysfunctional behaviors that reduce the effectiveness of a group. As the table shows, there are two types of functional roles. **Task roles** play an important part in accomplishing the job at hand. **Relational roles** help keep the interaction between members running smoothly.[50]

Table 8–3 is a valuable diagnostic tool. When a group isn't operating effectively, you must determine which functions are lacking. For instance, you might note that the group has several good ideas but that no one is summarizing and coordinating them. Or perhaps the group lacks a crucial piece of information, but no one realizes this fact.

In some cases, your diagnosis of a troubled group might show that all the necessary task functions are being filled but that the social needs of members aren't being met. Perhaps members need to have their good ideas supported ("That's a terrific idea, Neil!").

FIGURE 8–2
Cyclical Stages in an Ongoing Group

Source: From G. J. Galanes, K. Adams, and J. K. Brilhart, *Effective Group Discussion*, 11th ed. (New York: McGraw-Hill, 2004).

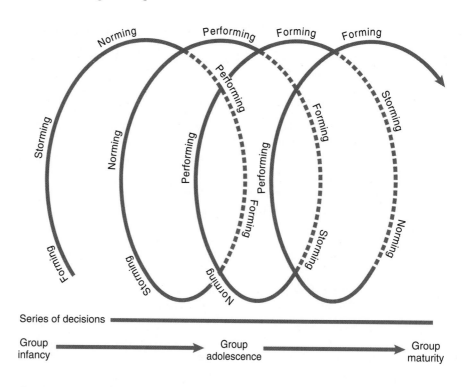

Maybe personal conflicts need to be acknowledged and resolved ("I know I sound defensive about this. I've worked on this idea for a month, and I hate to see it dismissed in 5 minutes."). When social needs like these go unfilled, even the best knowledge and talent often aren't enough to guarantee a group's smooth functioning.

Sometimes a group will transform important functional roles into formal ones. For example, at financial services giant Charles Schwab, one person in every meeting serves as an observer–diagnoser.[51] This person doesn't take part in the discussion; instead, he or she creates a list of what went right (e.g., "Good creativity," "Excellent use of time") and what went wrong (e.g., "Lots of digressions," "Personal criticism created defensiveness") in the meeting. This list gets included in the minutes, which are reviewed by management. It's easy to imagine how the observer's comments can help a group work effectively.

Having too many people fill a functional role can be just as troublesome as having nobody fill it. For example, you might discover that several people are acting as opinion givers but that no one is serving as an opinion seeker—like a series of radio stations broadcasting but no one receiving. If two or more people compete for the role of direction giver, the results can be confusing. Even social roles can be overdone. Too much tension relieving or praise giving can become annoying.

Once you have identified the missing functions, you can fill them. Supplying these missing roles often transforms a stalled, frustrated group into a productive team.[52] Other members probably won't recognize what you're doing, but they will realize that you somehow know how to say the right thing at the right time.

Decision-Making Methods

Disagreement may be a healthy, normal part of solving problems on the job, but sooner or later it becomes necessary to make a decision as a group. Whether the issue is who will work over the weekend, how to split the year-end bonus money among members, or which approach to advertising is best, there usually has to be only one answer to a

Table 8–3	Functional Roles of Group Members

Task Functions

1. *Information or opinion giver.* Offers facts or opinions relevant to group task.
2. *Information or opinion seeker.* Asks others for task-related information or opinions.
3. *Starter or energizer.* Initiates or encourages task-related behavior (e.g., "We'd better get going on this").
4. *Direction giver.* Provides instructions regarding how to perform task at hand.
5. *Summarizer.* Reviews what has been said, identifying common themes or progress.
6. *Diagnoser.* Offers observations about task-related behavior of group (e.g., "We seem to be spending all of our time discussing the problem without proposing any solutions").
7. *Gatekeeper.* Regulates participation of members.
8. *Reality tester.* Checks feasibility of group ideas against real-world contingencies.

Relational Functions

1. *Participation encourager.* Encourages reticent members to speak, letting them know that their contribution will be valued.
2. *Harmonizer.* Resolves interpersonal conflicts between members.
3. *Tension reliever.* Uses humor or other devices to release anxiety and frustration of members.
4. *Evaluator of emotional climate.* Offers observations about socioemotional relationships between members (e.g., "I think we're all feeling a little defensive now," or "It sounds like you think nobody trusts you, Bill").
5. *Praise giver.* Reinforces accomplishments and contributions of group members.
6. *Empathic listener.* Listens without evaluation to personal concerns of members.

Dysfunctional Roles

1. *Blocker.* Prevents progress by constantly raising objections.
2. *Attacker.* Aggressively questions the competence or motives of others.
3. *Recognition seeker.* Repeatedly and unnecessarily calls attention to self by relating irrelevant experiences, boasting, and seeking sympathy.
4. *Joker.* Engages in joking behavior in excess of tension-relieving needs, distracting members.
5. *Withdrawer.* Refuses to take stand on social or task issues; covers up feelings; does not respond to others' comments.

problem. As business instructor Joel Baum puts it, "*How* you decide is just as important as *what* you decide. The process you use has a direct impact on how members feel about the decision. It can influence commitment, excitement, and buy-in; or it can create feelings of resentment and exclusion."[53] There are a number of ways to make business decisions like these.

Functional Roles in Action

Either individually or in a group,

1. Identify a task that would likely be addressed in a group discussion (e.g., planning a fund-raising event, developing a policy on personal use of computers). Or, choose a task that you are already working on in a group.

2. Present examples of how each of the functional roles (task and relational) listed in Table 8–3 could be performed in the group's discussion. Explain how each role can lead to higher-quality solutions.

3. Present examples of how each of the dysfunctional roles in Table 8–3 might be enacted in the group's discussion. Describe the consequences of each of these roles.

Consensus Consensus is a collective group decision that every member is willing to support. The purest form of consensus is unanimous, unequivocal support: the belief of every member that the decision reached is the best possible one. An entire employee search committee might, for instance, agree that a particular candidate is perfect for a job. This state of unanimity isn't always possible, however, and it isn't necessary for consensus. Members may support a decision that isn't their first choice, accepting the fact that it is the best one possible for the group at that time. In the case of the new employee, the committee members might agree on a candidate who is the second choice of some members since the people who will actually be working with her are her most enthusiastic supporters.

Consensus is valued more highly in some cultures than others. For example, British and Dutch businesspeople value the "team must be aboard" approach. On the other hand, Germans, French, and Spanish communicators depend more on the decision of a strong leader and view a desire for consensus as somewhat wishy-washy.[54]

Cultural norms aside, consensus has both advantages and drawbacks. While it has the broadest base of support from members, reaching consensus takes time. It requires a spirit of cooperation among group members, a willingness to experience temporary disagreements, a commitment to listening carefully to other ideas, and a win–win attitude. Given these challenges, it's wise to limit consensus decisions to important issues when the need for agreement is high, and when the group can dedicate the time and effort necessary to reach agreement.[55]

Majority Vote Whereas consensus requires the agreement of the entire group, deciding by a **majority vote** needs only the support of a plurality of the members. Thus, majority voting decisions are much quicker and easier to reach. A 10-person

THE FAR SIDE® BY GARY LARSON

"Okay, Williams, we'll just vote. ... How many here say the heart has four chambers?"

staff choosing a decorating scheme for the new office might talk almost endlessly before reaching consensus, but with a majority vote, the decision would require the agreement of only 6 members. While majority vote works well on relatively minor issues, it is usually not the best approach for more important decisions (at least not in small groups), since it can leave a substantial minority unsatisfied and resentful about being railroaded into accepting a plan they don't support.

Minority Decision

In a **minority decision,** a few members make a decision affecting the entire group. This is frequently the case in business situations. For instance, the executive committee of a corporation often acts on behalf of the board of directors, which, in turn, represents the shareholders. Minority decisions are also made in less exalted circumstances. A steering group responsible for planning the company picnic might delegate tasks like publicity, entertainment, and food to smaller collections of members. As long as the minority has the confidence of the larger group, this method works well for many decisions. While it doesn't take advantage of the entire group's creative thinking, the talents of the subgroup are often perfectly adequate for a task.

Expert Opinion

When a single person has the knowledge or skill to make an informed decision, the group may be best served by relying on his or her **expert opinion.** As one observer puts it, "If you want a track team to win the high jump, you find one person who can jump seven feet, not seven people who can jump one foot." Some group members are experts because of specialized training: a structural engineer working with a design team on a new building, a senior airline mechanic who decides whether a flight can depart safely, or a systems analyst involved in the development of a new data control system. Other people gain their expertise by experience: the purchasing agent who knows how to get the best deals or a labor negotiator seasoned by years of contract deliberations.

Despite the obvious advantages, following an expert's suggestions isn't always as wise an approach as it might seem. First, it isn't always easy to tell who the expert is. Length of experience isn't necessarily a guarantee, since the business world abounds with old fools. Even when a member clearly is the expert, the other members must *recognize* this fact before they will willingly give their support. Unfortunately, some people who are regarded as experts don't deserve the title, while some geniuses may be ignored.

Authority Rule

In many business groups, decision making is often a matter of **authority rule:** The designated leader makes the final decision. This doesn't mean that such leaders must be autocratic: They often listen to the ideas and suggestions of members before making the decisions themselves. The owner of a family business might invite employees to help choose a new company logo, while selecting the final design after hearing their opinions. A store manager might consult with employees about scheduling work hours, while reserving the final decisions for herself. The input from group members can help an authority to make higher-quality decisions than would otherwise be possible. One major risk of inviting suggestions from subordinates, however, is the disappointment that might follow if these suggestions aren't accepted.

Choice of a Decision-Making Method

Each decision-making method has its advantages and disadvantages. The choice of which one to use depends on several factors.

ethical challenge

What type of decision is being made? If the decision can best be made by one or more experts, or if it needs to be made by the authorities in charge, then involving other group members isn't appropriate. If, however, the task at hand calls for creativity or requires a large amount of information from many sources, then input from the entire group can make a big difference.

How important is the decision? Trivial decisions don't require the involvement of the entire group. It's a waste of time and money to bring everyone together to make decisions that can easily be made by one or two people.

How much time is available? If time is short, it simply may not be possible to consult everyone in the group. This is especially true if the members are not all available—if some are away from the office or out of town, for example. Even if everyone is available, the time-consuming deliberations that come with a group discussion may be a luxury you can't afford.

What are the personal relationships among members? Even important decisions might best be made without convening the whole group if members are on bad terms. If talking things out will improve matters, then a meeting may be worth the emotional wear and tear that it will generate. But if a face-to-face discussion will just make matters worse, then the decision might best be made in some other way.

Effective Communication in Groups and Teams

Whether you are in a group with centralized leadership or one with shared decision-making power, you can communicate in ways that help the group work effectively and make the experience satisfying. For the group to function well, each member must take into account the issues and problems that may arise whenever people try to communicate.

Recognize Both Group and Personal Goals

Every business and professional group operates to achieve some specific goal: selling a product, providing a service, getting a job done, and so on. In addition to pursuing a group's goals, members usually also have their own *individual* goals. Sometimes an individual's goal in a group is identical (or nearly identical) to the shared goal of the group. For example, a retailer might join the community Christmas fund-raising campaign out of a sincere desire to help the needy. In most cases, however, people also have more personal motives for joining a group. The retailer, for instance, might realize that working on the fund-raising campaign will improve both his visibility and his image in

Use the inventory below to identify how well your group is performing these important communication practices.

As a Group, How Well Did You	Not Well				Very Well
Define or clarify the task	1	2	3	4	5
Exchange and share information	1	2	3	4	5
Encourage expression of various points of view	1	2	3	4	5
Evaluate and analyze data	1	2	3	4	5
Use the best decision-making approach (consensus, majority rule, etc.)	1	2	3	4	5
Focus on tasks, not individuals	1	2	3	4	5
Demonstrate respect for all	1	2	3	4	5
Encourage feedback	1	2	3	4	5
Encourage expression of opinion	1	2	3	4	5
Build on others' ideas	1	2	3	4	5
Ask for clarification of ideas	1	2	3	4	5
Demonstrate equality	1	2	3	4	5
Address disagreements or misunderstandings	1	2	3	4	5
Stay on task	1	2	3	4	5

the community—and ultimately lead to more business. Notice the relationships between some common group and individual goals:

Group Goal	Individual Goal
Sales department wants to meet annual sales target.	Sales representative wants to earn bonus.
Retailer wants to expand hours to attract new business.	Employees want to avoid working nights and weekends.
Company wants employee to attend a seminar in Minneapolis.	Employee wants to visit family in Minneapolis.

As some of these examples show, personal goals aren't necessarily harmful to a group or an organization if they are compatible with the group's objectives. In fact, under these circumstances they can actually help the group to achieve its goals. For instance, sales representatives who want to increase their commissions will try to sell more of the company's products. Similarly, an otherwise reluctant employee might volunteer to attend a January seminar in Minneapolis to see her family during the visit.

Only when an individual's goals conflict with the organization's or group's goals do problems occur. If Lou and Marian hate each other, their arguments could keep the group from getting much done in meetings. If Bill is afraid of losing his job because of a mistake that has been made, he may concentrate on trying to avoid being blamed rather than on solving the problem.

The range of personal goals that can interfere with group effectiveness is surprisingly broad. One or more team members might be concerned with finishing the job quickly and getting away to take care of personal business. Others might be more concerned with being liked or appearing smart than with doing the job as quickly or effectively as possible. Someone else might want to impress the boss. All these goals, as well as dozens of others, can sidetrack or derail a group from doing its job.

As Table 8-4 shows, groups will be harmonious and most efficient when the members are also reaching their personal goals. You can boost the effectiveness of your group by doing everything possible to help members satisfy those goals. If the people in your group are looking for fun and companionship, consider ways to tackle the job at hand that also give them what they want. On the other hand, if they are in a hurry because of busy schedules, concentrate on keeping meetings to a minimum. If some

Table 8-4	Group Process Variables Associated with Productivity

1. Members are clear about and agree with group goals.
2. Tasks are appropriate for group versus individual solutions.
3. Members are clear about and accept their formal roles.
4. Role assignments match member abilities.
5. Level of leader's direction matches the group's skill level.
6. All group members are free to participate.
7. Group gets, gives, and uses feedback about its effectiveness and productivity.
8. Group spends time defining and discussing problems it must solve or decisions it must make. Members also spend time planning how they will solve problems and make decisions.
9. Group uses effective decision-making strategies that were outlined in advance.
10. Group evaluates its solutions and decisions.
11. Norms encourage high performance and quality, success, and innovation.
12. Subgroups are integrated into the group as a whole.
13. The group contains the smallest number of members necessary to accomplish its goals.
14. Group has enough time to develop cohesiveness and accomplish its goals.
15. Group has cooperative orientation.
16. Periods of conflict are frequent but brief and the group has effective ways of dealing with conflict.

Source: Research summarized in S. A. Wheelan et al., "Member Perceptions of Internal Group Dynamics and Productivity," *Small Group Research 29* (1998), pp. 371–393.

members like recognition, stroke their egos by offering compliments whenever you can sincerely do so. The extra effort that you spend attending to the individual needs of members will pay dividends in terms of the energy and loyalty that the group gains from happy members.

In some cases, group members announce their personal goals. In other cases, though, stating a personal goal outright could be embarrassing or counterproductive. A committee member wouldn't confess, "I volunteered to serve on this committee so I could find new people to date." An employee would never say openly, "I'm planning to learn everything I can here and then quit the firm and open my own business." Personal goals that are not made public are called **hidden agendas.**

Hidden agendas are not necessarily harmful. The dating goals of a member needn't interfere with group functions. Similarly, many other personal motives are not threatening or even relevant to a group's business. Some hidden agendas are even beneficial. For instance, an up-and-coming young worker's desire to communicate competence to the boss by volunteering for difficult jobs might well help the group. International team consultant Frank Heckman sees that the "bottom line is that we all have personal agendas and to some degree, some are hidden even to us."[56] Other hidden agendas, however, are harmful, and Heckman adds that "the problem will come in if the individual is duplicitous and undermines what the team is trying to achieve."[57] Two feuding members who use meetings to disparage each other can only harm the group, and the person collecting ideas to go into business himself will most likely hurt the organization when he takes its ideas elsewhere.

There is no single best way to deal with harmful hidden agendas. Sometimes the best course is to bring the goal out into the open. For example, a manager might speak to feuding subordinates one at a time, let them know she recognizes their problem, and work with them to solve it directly and constructively (probably using the conflict management skills described in Chapter 5). When you do decide to bring a hidden personal goal into the open, it's almost always better to confront the member privately. The embarrassment of being unveiled publicly is usually so great that the person becomes defensive and denies that the hidden goal exists.

At other times, it is best to treat a hidden personal goal indirectly. For example, if a member's excessive talking in meetings seems to be a bid for recognition, the best approach might be to make a point of praising his valid contributions more frequently. If two feuding subordinates continue to have trouble working together, the manager can assign them to different projects or transfer one or both of them to different groups.

Promote Desirable Norms

Norms are informal, often unstated rules about what behavior is appropriate in a group.[58] Some norms govern the way tasks are handled, while others shape the social interaction of the group. A group's norms are often shaped by the culture of the organization to which it belongs. For example, 3M's success has been attributed to its "bias for yes": When in doubt, employees are encouraged to take a chance instead of avoiding action for fear of failure.[59] Likewise, Motorola's turnaround has been attributed to its changing norms for conflict. The company's culture now makes it acceptable to disagree strongly (and loudly) in meetings, instead of keeping quiet or being overly diplomatic.[60] As Table 8–5 on page 262 shows, the norms in some groups are constructive, while other groups have equally powerful rules that damage their effectiveness.[61]

The challenge of establishing norms is especially great when members come from different cultural backgrounds.[62] For example, group members from a low-context culture

Table 8–5	Typical Constructive (and Destructive) Norms for a Working Group

- Handle (Ignore) business for co-workers who are away from their desks.
- Be willing (Refuse) to admit your mistakes.
- Occasional time off from work for personal reasons is (isn't) okay, as long as the absence won't harm the company.
- Do (Don't) be willing to work overtime without complaining when big, important deadlines approach.
- Say so (Keep quiet) if you disagree. Don't (Do) hint or go behind others' backs.
- Avoid (Hold) side conversations during meetings.
- Don't (Do) interrupt or ignore others' ideas.
- Arrive on time (Be late) for meetings.
- Celebrate (Don't celebrate) successes.
- Honor (Shirk) your commitments.

Source: After Joel A. C. Baum, "Avoiding Common Team Problems," HomePage for Game Theory and Competitive Strategy MGT 2056–Fall 2003, retrieved August 26, 2003, from **www.rotman .utoronto.ca/~baum/mgt2003/avoid.html.**

(such as the U.S. or Canada) would be more likely to address conflicts directly, whereas those from high-context backgrounds (East Asia or the Middle East, for example) would be inclined to use indirect approaches. Likewise, members from a background where high power distance is the norm would be less likely to challenge a group's leader than those from a background where low power distance is the norm.

Once norms are established, members who violate them create a crisis for the rest of the team, who respond in a series of escalating steps.[63] Consider, for example, a worker who violates the norm of not following up on her obligations between group meetings. Her teammates might react with increasing pressure:

- *Delaying action.* Members talk among themselves but do not approach the deviant, hoping that she will change without pressure.

- *Hinting about the violation.* Members tease the violator about being a "flake" or about being lazy, hoping that the message behind the humor will cause her to do her share of work.

- *Discussing the problem openly.* Members confront the nonconformist, explaining their concerns about her behavior.

- *Ridiculing and deriding the violator.* Persuasion shifts to demands for a change in behavior; the group's pressure tactics may well trigger a defensive response in the nonconforming member.

- *Rejecting or isolating the deviant.* If all other measures fail, the team member who doesn't conform to group norms is asked to leave the group. If she cannot be expelled, other members can effectively excommunicate her by not inviting her to meetings and by disregarding any attempts at communicating she might make.

There are two ways in which an understanding of norms can help you to function more effectively in a group.

The Unproductive Teammate

You are a member of what was once a dream team of productive workers. Until recently, everyone worked well together to meet the team's goals. When one member took time off to care for a child in the hospital a few months ago, everyone was happy to cover for him. Over the next months the same member began missing more work because of other problems—a spouse needing care, a sports injury, and moving to a new home. The rest of the group has begun to doubt that their unproductive colleague will ever contribute his fair share to the group again, and they agree that it's time to raise this issue.

Describe how the team can deal with this issue in a way that acknowledges both the unproductive member's legitimate problems and the group's need for the member to do his share.

Create Desirable Norms Early   Norms are established early in a group; and once they exist, they are difficult to change. This means that when you participate in a group that is just being established, you should do whatever you can to create norms that you think will be desirable. For example, if you expect members of a committee to be punctual at meetings, it's important to begin each session at the appointed time. If you want others to be candid about their feelings, it's important to be frank yourself and encourage honesty in others at the outset.

Comply with Established Norms Whenever Possible   In an established group, you have the best chance of reaching your goals if you handle the task and social relationships in the group's customary manner. If your co-workers are in the habit of exchanging good-natured insults, you shouldn't be offended when you are the target—and you will be accepted as one of them if you dish out a few yourself. In a group in which the norm is never to criticize another member's ideas directly, a blunt approach probably won't get you very far. When you are entering an established group, it's wise to learn the norms by personal observation and by asking knowledgeable members before plunging in.

A national or regional culture can also shape the way group members communicate with one another. Differences in managing conflict are a good example. The straight-talking low-context style that is accepted in many parts of the English-speaking world is not the norm in other places.[64] It may not always be possible to follow established norms. If a group is in the habit of cracking racist jokes, doing shabby work, or stealing company property, for example, you would probably be unwilling to go along just to be accepted. This sort of conflict between personal values and group norms can lead to a major crisis in values. If the potential for conflict is great enough and the issue is sufficiently important, you may decide to do whatever you can to join a different, more compatible group.

Promote an Optimal Level of Cohesiveness

Cohesiveness can be defined as the degree to which members feel themselves part of a group and want to remain with that group. You can think of cohesiveness as a magnetic force that attracts members to one another, giving them a collective identity. As you might suspect, highly cohesive groups have happier members than less closely knit groups. Workers who belong to cohesive groups are likely to have higher rates of job satisfaction and lower rates of tension, absenteeism, and turnover than those who belong to less cohesive groups.[65] They also make better decisions.[66]

Not all cohesive work groups are productive—at least not in terms of the organization's goals. In strikes and slowdowns, for example, highly cohesive workers can actually shut down operations. (Of course, the workers' cohesiveness in such cases may help them to accomplish other group goals, such as higher pay or safer working conditions.) In less dramatic cases, cohesiveness in observing anti-organization norms ("Don't work too hard," "Go ahead and report our lunch as a business expense—we always do that," "If you need some art supplies for your kids, just take them from the supply closet") can leave group members feeling good about each other but raise ethical issues and harm the interests of the organization. Finally, too much cohesiveness can lead to the kinds of "groupthink" described on pages 265–267.

Cohesiveness develops when certain conditions exist in a group. Once you understand these conditions, you can apply them to groups on or off the job. You can also use them to analyze why a group's cohesiveness is high or low and choose ways to reach and maintain a desirable level of cohesiveness. Here are seven factors that promote an optimal level of cohesiveness.[67]

Shared or Compatible Goals   Group members draw closer together when they have a similar aim or when their goals can be mutually satisfied. For instance, the members of a construction crew might have little cohesiveness when their pay is based on individual efforts, but if the entire crew receives a bonus for completing stages of the building ahead of schedule, the members are likely to work together better.

Progress toward Goals   When a group makes progress toward its target, members are drawn together; when progress stops, cohesiveness decreases. Members of the construction crew just mentioned will feel good about each other when they reach their target dates or can reasonably expect to do so. But if they consistently fall short, they are likely to get discouraged and feel less attraction to the group; when talking to their families or friends, there will be less talk about "us" and more about "me."

Shared Norms or Values   Although successful groups tolerate or even thrive on some differences in members' expressed attitudes and behaviors, wide variation in what members consider appropriate behavior reduces cohesiveness. For example, a person who insists on wearing conservative clothes in a business where everyone else dresses casually probably won't fit in with the rest of the group.

Minimal Feelings of Threat among Members   In a cohesive group, members usually feel secure about their status, dignity, and material and social well-being. When conflict arises over these issues, however, the results can be destructive. If all of the junior executives in a division are competing for the same senior position—especially if senior positions rarely open—the cohesiveness of the group is likely to suffer, at least until the job is filled.

Interdependence among Members   Groups become more cohesive when members need one another to satisfy group goals. When a job can be done by one person alone, the need for unity decreases. An office team in which each member performs a different aspect or stage of a process will be less cohesive than one in which members rely on one another.

Competition from Outside the Group   When members perceive an external threat to their existence or dignity, they draw closer together. Almost everyone knows of a family whose members seem to fight constantly among themselves until an outsider criticizes one of them. The internal bickering stops for the moment, and the group unites against the common enemy. An uncohesive work group could draw together in a similar way when another group competes with it for such things as use of limited company resources or desirable space in a new office building. Many wise managers deliberately set up situations of competition between groups to get tasks accomplished more quickly or to generate more sales dollars.

Shared Group Experiences   When members have been through an experience together, especially an unusual or trying one, they draw closer together. This is why soldiers who have gone through combat together often feel close for the rest of their lives. Work groups that have accomplished difficult tasks are also likely to be more cohesive. Some organizations also provide social events such as annual "retreats" for their executives; retreats might include workshops to discuss particular aspects or problems of members' jobs, sports events, and parties. Annual sales meetings are often partially intended to increase group cohesiveness, since these meetings are not the most cost-efficient way to distribute sales information.

Avoid Excessive Conformity

Bad group decisions can also come about through too much agreement among members. Irving Janis calls this phenomenon **groupthink,** an unwillingness, for the sake of harmony, to examine ideas critically.[68] Janis describes several characteristics of groups that succumb to groupthink:

- *Illusion that the group is invulnerable:* "We can afford to raise the price on our deluxe-model kitchen appliances because they're so much better than anything else on the market. Even if our competitors could develop comparable models, we'd still outdo them on style."

career tip

Devil's Advocate and Other Anti-conformity Tools

Since medieval times, the Catholic Church has appointed a "Devil's Advocate" to present all possible arguments—even seemingly slight ones—against promoting a candidate toward sainthood. The Church recognizes the danger of one-sided enthusiasm and relies on the advocate to make sure that decision makers consider all sides of the issue. This approach can serve nonreligious groups just as well, especially when there is an undisputed consensus toward making an important decision. If your group doesn't have the foresight to appoint a devil's advocate, you can take on this role by challenging the majority's thinking.

Other approaches can serve as antidotes to groupthink. If the group has enough members, it can be helpful to set up two (or more) subgroups to consider approaches independently. Another approach is to request the opinions of respected outsiders who haven't been influenced by the collective enthusiasm of members.

- *Tendency to rationalize or discount negative information:* "I know the market research says people will buy other brands if our prices go up any more, but you know how unreliable market research is about things like that."

- *Willingness to ignore ethical or moral consequences of the group's decision:* "The waste we're dumping in the river may kill a few fish, but look, this company provides jobs and a living for all the people who live in this town."

- *Stereotyped views of other groups:* "The only thing those people at the head office care about is the bottom line. They don't give a damn about what we think or what we need."

- *Group pressure to conform:* "Come on, none of the rest of us is interested in direct-mail marketing. Why don't you forget that stuff?"

- *Self-censorship:* "Every time I push for an innovative ad campaign, everybody fights it. I might as well drop it."

- *Illusion of unanimity:* "Then we all agree: cutting prices is the only way to stay competitive."

- *"Mindguards" against threatening information:* "They're talking about running the machines around the clock to meet the schedule. I'd better not bring up what the supervisor said about how her staff feels about working more overtime."

Diversity of voices can serve as an antidote to groupthink by broadening outlooks and enriching discussions. However, one study found that multicultural groups might be inclined toward groupthink if their awareness of cultural differences creates a desire to avoid conflict.[69]

A second type of harmful conformity has been labeled **risky shift:** the likelihood of a group to take positions that are more extreme than the members would choose on their own.[70] A risky shift can work in two directions. When members are conservative, their collective decisions are likely to be more cautious than their individual positions. More commonly, groups are prone to taking positions that are riskier than the choices members would have taken had they been acting separately. Thus, risky shift results either in taking risks that aren't justified and suffering the costs or in avoiding necessary steps that the team needs to take to survive and prosper.

Paradoxically, cohesive teams are most prone to groupthink and risky shift. When members like and respect one another, the tendency to agree is great. The best way to guard against this sort of collective blindness—especially in very cohesive groups—is to seek the opinions of outsiders who may see things differently. In addition, leaders who are highly influential should avoid stating their opinions early in the discussion.[71]

"My team is having trouble thinking outside the box. We can't agree on the size of the box, what materials the box should be constructed from, a reasonable budget for the box, or our first choice of box vendors."

Encourage Creativity

One advantage of broadly based participation in groups is the greater chance for creativity.[72] As more members bring their different perspectives to a task, the chances of coming up with a winning solution increase. As one executive put it, "innovation is a team sport."[73]

As the cartoon on this page suggests, the quantity of people involved doesn't guarantee the quality of their contributions. One way to boost the creativity of the group is through **brainstorming**—an approach that encourages free thinking and minimizes conformity. The term was coined by advertising executive Alex Osborn, who noticed that groups were most creative when they let their imaginations run free.[74] As Nobel Prize winner Linus Pauling put it, "The key to creativity is to have lots and lots of ideas, then throw away the bad ones."[75]

Out of these observations came a series of steps that, with variations, are now used widely. The cardinal rules of brainstorming include

- All evaluation and criticism of ideas is forbidden during the early phases of the process.
- Quantity—not quality—of ideas is the goal.
- New combinations of ideas are sought.

One expert offers several other tips for healthy brainstorming:

- Don't let the boss speak first.
- Encourage members to speak whenever they have an idea. Don't follow a set speaking order.
- Include a variety of members in a session, not just experts.
- Don't write down each and every word idea.[76]

With these rules in mind, the group follows the basic approach outlined below.

Generate Possible Solutions
During this stage, a recorder lists all the ideas generated by the group on a chalkboard or flip chart that everyone can see. The leader encourages "hitchhiking" on previous ideas, so that one suggestion leads to variations. The leader should also keep the level of enthusiasm high to spur more contributions.

Eliminate Duplicate Ideas
After the brainstorming session is completed, duplicate suggestions are eliminated. No evaluation of ideas is made at this stage; the group simply clarifies and simplifies the list of ideas it has developed.

Evaluate Ideas   Once the group has generated all the ideas it can think of, it can begin to decide which are worth considering seriously. Unless only one or two ideas stand out as winners, it's usually best to prune the unworkable ones in several passes. Begin by scratching the clearly unworkable ideas, leaving any that have even some merit. After discussing the remainder, the group can pick the top two or three ideas for serious consideration and then decide which one is best.

Brainstorming can be even more effective in virtual groups than in face-to-face meetings.[77] Furthermore, more ideas are generated when brainstorming is anonymous than when members know who is contributing suggestions.

review points

- Effective small groups are productive and accurate, and their decisions are supported by members.

- Small groups share characteristics of size, interaction, shared purpose, interdependence, regular interaction and communication, and identity. Virtual teams transcend time and space boundaries and present both advantages and challenges.

- The best approach to group leadership depends on the circumstances. In groups with a designated leader, the optimal style depends on leader–member relations, the structure of the task, and the leader's power. In groups with no designated leader, a predictable process occurs in which a single leader often emerges.

- In many groups leadership is shared among members, who may each possess one or more types of power (position, coercion, reward, expert, referent, information, connections).

- Groups often solve problems in a systematic way, moving in and out of stages (forming, storming, norming, and performing).

- Members contribute to the effectiveness of groups by enacting various functional roles, both task and relational, while dysfunctional roles detract from group effectiveness.

- Choosing the best decision-making method (consensus, majority vote, minority decision, expert opinion, or authority rule) ensures that the group uses time effectively and generates an outcome that members support.

- Groups can be more successful when members recognize and try to fulfill both personal and group goals, promote desirable norms, promote an optimal level of cohesiveness, avoid excessive conformity (groupthink and risky shift), and boost creativity.

key terms

Test your understanding of these key terms by visiting the Online Learning Center Web site at www.mhhe.com/adler10e.

authoritarian leadership style   243
authority rule   257
brainstorming   267
coercive power   247

cohesiveness   263
conflict phase   251
connection power   248
consensus   256

contingency approaches to leadership   243
democratic leadership style   243
designated leader   246
emergence phase   251
emergent leader   245
expert opinion   257
expert power   247
forming stage   251
functional roles   253
groupthink   265
hidden agenda   261
information power   247
laissez-faire leadership style   243
life-cycle theory of leadership   244
majority vote   256
minority decision   257
norming stage   251
norms   261

orientation phase   251
performing stage   251
position power   247
referent power   247
reflective-thinking sequence   248
reinforcement phase   251
relational roles   253
reward power   247
risky shift   266
self-directed work teams   246
storming stage   251
style approach to leadership   243
task roles   253
team   239
trait approach to leadership   243
virtual team   240
work group   237

activities

→ Go to the self-quizzes at the Online Learning Center at www.mhhe.com/adler10e to test your knowledge of chapter concepts.

1. Invitation to Insight

Consider an effective team you have observed or participated in. Identify the characteristics that contributed to this team's productivity. Provide an example of each. Then use concepts from this chapter to suggest at least one way the team could have improved.

2. Invitation to Insight

Analyze the types of power that exist in your class or some other working group. Which members use each type of power? Who exerts the most influence? What kinds of power do you possess?

3. Skill Builder

Using Table 8–3, identify the role each of these statements represents.

    a. "Debby, could you hold on and let Martin speak first?"
    b. "So far we have discussed six funding sources . . ."

    c. "Although you seem to disagree, both of you are concerned with . . ."
    d. "I think you're really on to something. That seems like the information we need."
    e. "What else do you think we should consider?"

4. Skill Builder

With three to six of your classmates, decide which method of decision making would be most effective for your group in each of the following situations:

    a. Choosing the safest course of action if you were lost in a dangerous area near your city or town.
    b. Deciding whether and how to approach your instructor to propose a change in the grading system of your course.
    c. Designing the most effective campaign for your school to recruit minority students.
    d. Duplicating for distribution to your instructor and classmates the solutions to this exercise that your group developed.

e. Hiring an instructor for your department.
f. Choosing the name for a new brand of breakfast cereal.
g. Selecting a new computer system.
h. Deciding which of three employees gets the desirable vacant office.
i. Planning the weekend work schedule for the upcoming month.
j. Deciding whether the employees should affiliate with a labor union.

5. Invitation to Insight

Although it may be larger than most of the groups discussed in this chapter, your class is a good model of the principles described here. Answer the following questions about your class or about a group that you participate in:

a. What are the stated goals of the class or group? Does the group have any unstated, shared goals?
b. What are your individual goals? Which of these goals are compatible with the group's goals, and which are not compatible? Are any of your individual goals hidden agendas?
c. What are your instructor's or the group leader's individual goals? Were these goals stated? If not, how did you deduce them?

How compatible are these goals with the official goals of the class or group?
d. How do the individual goals of other members affect the functioning of the group as a whole?

6. Skill Builder

Suggest several norms that would be desirable for each of the following groups. In your list, include norms that address tasks, relationships, and procedures. How could you promote development of these norms as the group's leader? As a member?

a. A student fund-raising committee to develop scholarships for your major or department.
b. The employees at a new fast-food restaurant.
c. A group of new bank tellers.
d. A company softball team.

7. Invitation to Insight

Which of the functional roles in Table 8–3 do you generally fill in groups? Do you fill the same role in most groups at most times, or do you switch roles as circumstances require? Do you tend to fill task roles or relational roles? How could you improve the functioning of one group you belong to by changing your role-related behavior?

8. Skill Builder

Use the skills you learned in Chapters 6 and 7 to interview one member of a work-related group. Identify the following:

   a. What is the level of the group's cohesiveness? Is this level desirable, too high, or too low?

   b. Which of the factors on pages 263–265 contribute to the level of cohesiveness in this group?

   c. On the basis of your findings, develop a report outlining specific steps that might be taken to improve the degree of cohesiveness in this group.

9. Skill Builder

Recall a group you've participated in that demonstrated an excessive level of conformity. Identify negative outcomes that resulted from the excessive conformity. Which characteristics of groupthink did the group exhibit? What allowed these characteristics to exist? Write at least three suggestions that might have helped the group prevent overconformity.

resources

 For extensive readings and Web sites on working in teams, see the Online Learning Center Web site at **www.mhhe.com/adler10e.**

9

Effective Meetings

chapter outline

Types of Meetings
Information-Sharing Meetings
Problem-Solving or Decision-Making Meetings
Ritual Activities
Virtual Meetings

Planning a Problem-Solving Meeting
When to Hold a Meeting
Setting an Agenda

Conducting the Meeting
Beginning the Meeting
Conducting Business
Concluding the Meeting
Following Up the Meeting

Review Points
Key Terms
Activities
Resources

chapter objectives

After reading this chapter you should be able to

1. Describe various types and purposes of meetings.
2. Identify reasons to hold a meeting and determine when a meeting is not necessary.
3. Construct a complete meeting agenda.
4. Analyze participant behavior at meetings and identify several methods to encourage full participation of all members, keep discussion on track, create a positive atmosphere, and promote understanding.
5. Effectively bring a meeting to a close and follow up appropriately.

As they do every week, the agents of a real estate firm meet to discuss the latest trends in the market and to share information that will help them increase their sales.

The tenants in an apartment building gather to discuss the need for better maintenance and security.

A group of employees meets with top management to discuss a list of important issues, including the need for child care, a potential series of layoffs, and health benefits.

Examples like these show that meetings are a fact of life on the job. In this chapter, we focus specifically on how groups operate in meetings, that is, on those occasions when their members communicate simultaneously to deal with common concerns.

Meetings really are ubiquitous. The number of times people meet as they do business is staggering: Between 11 million and 20 million business meetings take place each day in the United States, and businesspeople spend an average of half their time attending them.[1] In one corporation alone, managers spend an astonishing 4.4 million hours per year in meetings.[2] As Table 9–1 on page 274 shows, the cost of meetings—even for small organizations—is considerable. If you include the time spent planning and following up on face-to-face interaction, the costs are even higher. For example, the Dow Jones Travel Index indicates that the average cost of an overnight business trip is $1,250 to $1,400.[3]

Just because meetings are common doesn't mean that they are always productive.[4] Surveys show that employees consider at least one-third of the gatherings they attend to be unnecessary and/or conducted poorly.[5] Another study found that unproductive meetings cost U.S. businesses as much as $37 billion annually.[6] While unambitious

Table 9–1	Hourly Costs of Meetings*				
Average Annual Salary of Attendees	**Number of People Attending Meeting**				
	2	**4**	**6**	**8**	**10**
$100,000	$112	$224	$236	$448	$560
75,000	84	168	252	336	420
62,500	70	140	210	280	350
50,000	56	112	168	224	280
37,500	42	84	126	168	210
25,000	28	56	84	112	140

Figures do not include cost of employee benefits, lost productivity, facility, and equipment.

workers may find that meetings break up a busy workday, more-focused employees view unnecessary and inefficient meetings as a frustrating waste of time.[7]

Organizations in which this cynicism is justified are in trouble. Beyond wasting precious time, pervasively inefficient meetings contribute to an overall atmosphere that isn't in anybody's best interests. "Meetings matter because that's where an organization's culture perpetuates itself," says William R. Daniels, senior consultant at American Consulting & Training.[8] Meetings—whether they are good or bad—are a sign of an organization's health.

Since meetings are so common and so important, this chapter takes a closer look at them. By the time you have finished reading these pages, you should understand some methods for planning and participating in meetings that will produce efficient, satisfying results.

Types of Meetings

People meet for many reasons. In most business and professional settings, meetings fall into three categories: information-sharing, problem-solving, and ritual activities. Of course, some meetings may serve more than one purpose.

Information-Sharing Meetings

In many organizations, people meet regularly to exchange information. Police officers and nurses, for example, begin every shift with a meeting in which the people going off duty brief their replacements on what has been happening recently. Members of a medical research team experimenting with a new drug may meet regularly to compare notes on their results. In many office groups, the Monday morning meeting is an important tool for informing group members about new developments, emerging trends, and the coming week's tasks. Perkin Elmer Corporation, a producer of scientific measuring instruments and precision optical equipment, is a typical example. The firm schedules a weekly meeting of all corporate and top executives to keep them up-to-date on the activities of the more than 20 divisions the company has around the world.

Problem-Solving or Decision-Making Meetings

In other meetings, a group may decide to take some action or make a change in existing policies or procedures. Which supplier should we contract? Should we introduce a new product line? Should we delay production so we can work out a design flaw in our new keyboard? Where can we cut costs if sales don't improve this year? How can we best schedule vacations?

Problem solving of one sort or another is the most common reason for a business meeting. Because problem-solving and decision-making meetings are the most challenging types of group activity, the bulk of this chapter discusses how to conduct them effectively.

Ritual Activities

In still other meetings, the social function is far more important than any specific task. In one firm, Friday afternoon "progress review sessions" are a regular fixture. Their apparently serious title is really an insider's tongue-in-cheek joke: The meetings take place in a local bar and to an outsider look like little more than a TGIF party. Despite the setting and apparently unbusinesslike activity, however, these meetings serve several important purposes.[9] First, they reaffirm the members' commitment to one another and to the company. Choosing to socialize with one another instead of rushing home is a sign of belonging and caring. Second, the sessions provide a chance to swap useful ideas and stories that might not be appropriate in the office. Who's in trouble? What does the boss really want? As you read in Chapter 1, this sort of informal communication can be invaluable, and the meetings provide a good setting for it. Finally, ritual meetings can be a kind of perk that confers status on the members. "Progress review committee" members charge expenses to the company and leave work early to attend. Thus, being invited to join the sessions is a sign of having arrived in the company.

Virtual Meetings

The term *meeting* conjures up images of people seated around a table, transacting business. But technology has made meetings possible even when the participants are half a world apart. *Virtual meetings* can take several forms.

Teleconferences are essentially multiparty telephone conferences. Intraorganization phone systems usually have a teleconferencing capability, and most telephone companies

career tip

Reframing Complaints in Meetings

Problem-solving meetings can generate complaints, defensiveness, and even outright hostility. Reframing members' complaints can nudge the discussion toward constructive solutions. Here are some reframing strategies:

Reframe complaints about the past as hopes for the future

Statement: "Why do we always have to drive across town for these meetings?"

Reframe: "From now on, you'd like to find a way to keep everybody's travel time equal, right?"

Reframe negative statements as positive desires or visions

Statement: "I've got work to do! All this long range planning is a waste of time."

Reframe: "You want to be sure the time we spend planning makes a difference in the long run, right?"

Reframe personal attacks as issues

Statement: "Jaclyn is always butting in when I have a customer, stealing my commissions."

Reframe: "So, we need to make sure we have clear lines about communicating with customers."

Reframe individual concerns as community or group interests

Statement: "I've got kids at home and no child care! I can't keep working weekends on short notice."

Reframe: "All of us have lives outside of work. Let's talk about how we can handle rush jobs without creating personal emergencies or burning out."

Sources: S. Littlejohn and K. Domenici, *Communication, Conflict and the Management of Difference* (Long Grove, IL: Waveland Press, 2007) pp. 282–283; see also K. Domenici and S. Littlejohn, "The Affirmative Turn in Strategic Planning," *OD Practitioner* 39 (1) (2007), pp. 36–39.

provide a similar feature for a modest monthly fee. With this approach, the person who calls the meeting dials the first participant, then briefly taps the hang-up button and calls other numbers. When all parties have come on the line, the caller sends another signal and everyone is able to talk freely with one another. Even though teleconferences are affordable and easy to use, many communicators overlook them as a useful way for distant parties to meet and hash out details that would take much longer via e-mail or a chain of two-person phone conversations.

Videoconferences allow users in distant locations to see one another while they talk. Videoconferencing is especially valuable in organizations with widespread operations. For example, CKE Restaurants of Santa Barbara, California, operates over 3,400 restaurants, including Hardee's, Carl's Jr., La Salsa, and Timber Lodge Steakhouse. The company uses Web-based conferencing to link members spread across the U.S., saving thousands of dollars over the cost of face-to-face meetings.[10]

You don't need an elaborate organizational network to hold a videoconference. With low-cost Webcams and microphones, free software, and a high-speed Internet connection, you can hold virtual meetings with people anywhere on Earth. Chapter 13 describes Webinars, which are a special kind of videoconference in which a host presents a product or idea to a group of participants who can comment and ask questions.

Collaboration in Cyberspace: Geography Makes a Difference

How important is communication when members from across the country and around the world meet in cyberspace? To answer this question, corporate giants Verizon and Microsoft commissioned a study to determine how virtual teams in a variety of industries and countries collaborate.

The study revealed that the importance of collaboration on performance was consistent across various industries (e.g., health care, government, financial services, manufacturing) and around the world. As one member of the Verizon/Microsoft study remarked, ". . . global companies that collaborate better, perform better. Those that collaborate less, do not perform as well. It's just that simple."

Researchers discovered geograpic differences in the communication preferences of workers. For example, Americans were more likely to enjoy working alone. They expressed a preference for using e-mail rather than the telephone. They were more comfortable with audio, video, and Web conferencing technologies than people of other regions of the world, and were more likely to multitask when on conference calls.

As a group, Europeans expressed a preference for communicating in real time with colleagues. They felt more obligated to answer the phone, and they expected others to call them back rather than leave a voicemail message.

Professionals in the Asia-Pacific region, more than anywhere else, expressed a desire to keep in touch constantly during the workday. As a result they found the phone to be an indispensable tool and preferred instant messaging to e-mail.

Differences like these show that teams are more productive when members take cultural differences into account when planning to communicate.

Sources: "Meetings around the World: The Impact of Collaboration on Business Performance" (Palo Alto, CA: Frost & Sullivan, 2006). Online at **http://newscenter.verizon.com/kit/collaboration/ MAW_WP.pdf**; "New Research Reveals Collaboration Is a Key Driver of Business Performance Around the World," Microsoft Corp., June 2006. **www.microsoft.com/presspass/press/2006/ jun06/06-05VerizonBusinessCollaborationPR.mspx**.

Whether you are having a teleconference or videoconference, following some basic guidelines will help the meeting run smoothly:

- Before the meeting, send your agenda and copies of any documents that will be discussed to all participants. Number pages of longer documents to avoid unnecessary paper shuffling.

- At the beginning of the meeting, have participants introduce themselves and state their location.

- In phone conversations, parties should identify themselves whenever necessary to avoid confusion. ("Ted talking here: I agree with Melissa. . . .")

- Avoid interrupting others or leaving out persons simply because you can't see them.

- Keep distractions (ringing phones, slamming doors, etc.) to a minimum.

- Use the best equipment possible. Cheap speakerphones and computer cameras may make it difficult to understand one another.[11]

Planning a Problem-Solving Meeting

Successful meetings are just like interviews, presentations, letters, and memos: They must be planned.

ethical challenge

Dealing with Opposing Viewpoints

Your manager has asked you to provide suggestions from your department with regard to the company's policy on flex time. These suggestions will be taken seriously and have a strong chance of being adopted.

You are in a position to call a meeting of key people in your department to discuss the issue.

Two of the most vocal members of the department have diametrically opposed positions on flex time. One of them (whose position on the issue is different from yours) will be out of the office for a week, and you could call the meeting while he is gone. What do you do?

When to Hold a Meeting

Given the costs of bringing people together, the most fundamental question is whether to hold a meeting at all. In one survey, middle and upper managers reported that over 25 percent of the meetings they attended could have been replaced by a memo, e-mail, or phone call.[12] Other experts report that roughly half of all business meetings are unproductive.[13] Not surprisingly, workers believe they attend too many meetings.[14]

There are many times when a meeting probably isn't justified:[15]

- The matter could be handled just as well over the phone.
- You could send a memo, an e-mail, or a fax to achieve the same goal.
- Key people are not available to attend.
- The subject would be considered trivial by many of the participants.
- There isn't enough time to handle the business at hand.
- Members aren't prepared.
- The meeting is routine, and there is no compelling reason to meet.
- The job can be handled just as well by one or more people without the need to consult others.
- Your mind is made up or you've already made the decision.

Keeping these points in mind, a planner should call a meeting (or appoint a committee) only when the following questions can be answered "yes."[16]

Is the Job beyond the Capacity of One Person? A job might be too much for one person to handle for two reasons: First, it might call for more *information* than any single person possesses. For example, the job of improving health conditions in a food-processing plant would probably require the medical background of a health professional, the experience of employees, and a manager who knows the resources.

Second, a job might take more *time* than one person has available. For instance, even if one employee were capable of writing and publishing an employee handbook, it's unlikely that the person would be able to handle the task and have much time for other duties.

Are Individuals' Tasks Interdependent? Each member at a committee meeting should have a different role. If each member's share of the task can be completed without input from other members, it's better to have the members co-acting under the supervision of a manager.

Consider the job of preparing the employee handbook that we just mentioned. If each person on the handbook team is responsible for a separate section, there is little need for the group to meet frequently to discuss the task.

There are times when people who do the same job can profit by sharing ideas in a group. Members of the handbook team, for example, might get new ideas about how the book could be made better from talking to one another. Similarly, sales representatives, industrial designers, physicians, or attorneys who work independently might profit by exchanging experiences and ideas. This is part of the purpose of professional conventions. Also, many companies schedule quarterly or annual meetings of people who do similar but independent work. While this may seem to contradict the requirement for interdependence of members' tasks, there is no real conflict. A group of people who do the same kind of work can often improve their individual performance through meetings by performing some of the complementary *functional roles*. For example, one colleague might serve as reality tester. ("Writing individual notes to each potential customer in your territory sounds like a good idea, but do you really have time to do that?") Another might take the job of being information giver. ("You know, there's a printer just outside Boston who can do large jobs like that just as well as your regular printer, but he's cheaper. Call me, and I'll give you the name and address.") Others serve as diagnosers. ("Have you checked the feed mechanism? Sometimes a problem there can throw the whole machine out of whack.") Some can just serve as empathic listeners. ("Yeah, I know. It's tough to get people who can do that kind of work right.")

Is There More than One Decision or Solution?

Questions that have only one right answer aren't well suited to discussion in meetings. Whether the sales force made its quota last year and whether the budget will accommodate paying overtime to meet a schedule, for instance, are questions answered by checking the figures, not by getting the regional sales managers or the department members to reach an agreement.

Tasks that don't have fixed outcomes, however, are appropriate for committee discussion. Consider the job facing the members of an advertising agency who are planning a campaign for a client. There is no obvious best way to sell products or ideas such as yearly physical examinations, office equipment, or clothing. Tasks such as these call for the kind of creativity that a talented, well-chosen group can generate.

Are Misunderstandings or Reservations Likely?

It's easy to see how meetings can be useful when the goal is to generate ideas or solve problems. But meetings are often necessary when confusing or controversial information is being communicated. Suppose, for instance, that changing federal rules and company policy require employees to document their use of company cars in far more detail than was ever required before. It's easy to imagine how this sort of change would be met with grumbling and resistance. In this sort of situation, simply issuing a memo outlining the new rules might not gain the kind of compliance that is necessary. Only by talking out their complaints and hearing why the new policy is being instituted will employees see a need to go along with the new procedure. "I can write down the vision of the company a thousand times and send it out to people," says Dennis Stamp, chairman of Vancouver's Priority Management Systems, Inc. "But when I sit with them face-to-face and give them the vision, for some reason it is much more accepted."[17]

Agenda for Your "Dream Team" Meeting

Imagine you could assemble a meeting with several of the people who would be best equipped to help you advance in your career. This group could include people from organizations that interest you, experts you have seen in the media, academics, and people in your community. Use the guidelines in these pages to create an agenda for this hypothetical meeting. To your class group, present

- A description of your career goals.
- A list of the people you want to include in your hypothetical meeting, and why you chose them.
- An agenda for the meeting that follows the format in Figure 9–1.

Setting an Agenda

An **agenda** is a list of topics to be covered in a meeting. A meeting without an agenda is like a ship at sea without a destination or compass: No one aboard knows where it is or where it's headed. Smart organizations appreciate the importance of establishing agendas. At computer chip giant Intel, company policy requires meeting planners to circulate. You can start building an agenda by asking three questions:

1. What do we need to do in the meeting to achieve our objective?
2. What conversations will be important to the people who attend?
3. What information will we need to begin?[18]

Agenda items can come from many sources: the group leader, minutes from previous meetings, group members, or standing items (e.g., committee reports).[19]

As Figure 9–1 illustrates, a complete agenda contains this information: a list of the attendees (and whoever else needs to see the agenda), the meeting's time and location, necessary background information, and a brief explanation of each item. You might argue that such a detailed agenda would take too much time to prepare. But once you realize that preparing the attendees with this sort of information will produce better results, you will realize that the advance work is well worth the effort. In fact, it's probably wise to follow up your detailed memo with another e-mail or phone call to make sure members are prepared to deal thoughtfully with important items.

Time, Length, and Location   To avoid problems, all three of these details need to be present on an agenda. Without the *starting time*, you can expect to hear such comments as "I thought you said 10, not 9," or "We always started at 3 before." Unless you announce the *length*, expect some members to leave early. Failure to note the *location* results in members' stumbling in late after waiting in the "usual place," wondering why no one showed up.

If your group needs to meet regularly, the best way to schedule meetings may be to build the time and place into everyone's schedule. At the Ritz-Carlton chain of luxury hotels, everyone in the organization starts the workday with a briefing. At company headquarters, top managers meet with the president of the company. Around the world, local employees start their daily shifts by covering the same points addressed in the headquarters meeting.[20]

FIGURE 9–1

Format for a
Comprehensive
Agenda

AGENDA

Date: December 19, 2007

To: Pat Rivera, Fred Brady, Kevin Jessup, Monica
             Flores, Dave Cohn

CC: Ellen Tibbits, Louisville Design Group
             (invited presenter)

From: Ted Gross

Subject: Planning meeting for new Louisville office

Meeting time: Tuesday, April 2, 9:30-11:30 a.m.

Location: Third-floor conference room.

Background: We are still on target for an August 10
                 opening date for the Louisville office.
                 Completing the tasks below will keep us on
                 schedule—vital if we're to be ready for the
                 fall season.

We will discuss the following items:

1. **Office Equipment**   15 minutes
   *Please come with a list of equipment you think will be
   needed for the office.* At the meeting we'll refine this
   list to standardize our purchases as much as possible.
   Let's try to start out with compatible equipment!

2. **Office Decoration**   20 minutes
   Ellen Tibbits of the Louisville Design Group will present
   a preliminary design for our reaction. She will come up
   with a final plan based on our suggestions.

3. **Promotion**   15 minutes
   Kevin wants to prepare a series of press releases for
   distribution to Louisville media a month or so before the
   office opens. *Please come with suggestions of items that
   should be mentioned in these releases.*

Participants   The overall size of the group is important: When attendance grows beyond seven members, the likelihood of some members' falling silent increases. If the agenda includes one or more problem-solving items, it's best to keep the size small so that everyone can participate in discussions. If the meeting is primarily informational, a larger group may be acceptable.

Be sure to identify on the agenda the people who will be attending. By listing who will attend, you alert all members about whom to expect in the meeting. If you have overlooked someone who ought to attend, a member who received the agenda can tell you. It is frustrating and a waste of time to call a meeting and then discover that the person with key information isn't there.

Background Information   Sometimes participants will need background information to give them new details or to remind them of things they may have

career tip

Members Can Be Leaders, Too

Good leadership promotes successful meetings, but members can also play an important role in making a meeting successful. The following tips can be used by every person involved in a meeting:

- Ask that an agenda be sent out before the meeting or agree on an agenda at the beginning of the meeting.

- Ask for help at the beginning of the meeting. Seek clarification on the meeting's goal. Is it to present information? To make a decision?

- Be tactfully bold and suggest canceling an unnecessary or badly planned meeting. Convene it when there is a need and an agenda.

- Volunteer to be a record keeper. A written set of minutes reduces the chance for misunderstandings, and keeping notes yourself leads to a record that reflects your perception of events.

- Suggest that a timekeeper be appointed, or volunteer yourself. This person advises the group when time for addressing each issue—and the meeting itself—is nearly over and alerts the group when time runs out.

- Ask for help before the meeting closes: "Exactly what have we decided today?" "What do we need to do before our next meeting?"

Source: Adapted from A. M. Keep, *Moving Meetings* (New York: Irwin, 1994).

---

forgotten. Background information can also provide a description of the meeting's significance.

Items and Goals   A good agenda goes beyond just listing topics and describes the goal for the discussion. "Meetings should be outcome- rather than process-driven," says Anita Underwood, Dun and Bradstreet's vice president of organizational management.[21] Most people have at least a vague idea of why they are meeting. Vague ideas, however, often lead to vague meetings. A clear list of topics and goals like the ones in Figure 9–1 will result in better-informed members and more productive, satisfying meetings.

The best goals are *result-oriented*, *specific*, and *realistic*. Notice the difference between goals that do and don't meet these criteria:

Poorly Worded	Better
Let's talk about how we can solve the sales problems in the northwestern region.	We will brainstorm and create a list of specific ways our product can be shown to be useful in the special climate conditions of the Northwest.
We're going to talk about the new income-savings plan.	We will explain the advantages and disadvantages of our two income-savings plans so employees can decide which best suits their needs.
Joe Fishman will tell you about his trip to the new supplier's plant.	Joe will explain the facilities of our new supplier and how we can use them to cut costs.

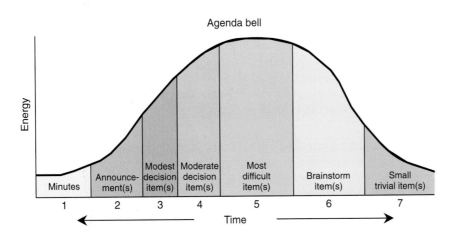

Agenda bell

FIGURE 9–2
A Bell-Shaped Agenda Structure

Source: From John E. Tropman, "The Agenda Bell." Copyright © John E. Tropman. Used with permission.

Goals like these are useful in at least two ways: First, they help to identify those who ought to attend the meeting. Second, specific goals also help the people who do attend to prepare for the meeting, and they help to keep the discussion on track once it begins.

The person who calls the meeting isn't the only one who can or should set goals. There are many times when other members have important business. The planner is often wise to use an "expectations check" to identify members' concerns.[22] Members can be polled before the meeting, so that their issues can be included in the agenda or at the start of the meeting. The fact that a member wants to discuss something, however, does not mean that the topic should automatically be considered. If the issue is inappropriate, the planner may choose to postpone it or handle it outside the meeting.

Pre-meeting Work   The best meetings occur when people have done all the necessary advance work. The agenda is a good place to tell members how to prepare for the meeting by reading information, developing reports, preparing or duplicating documents, or locating facts or figures. If all members need to prepare in the same way (for example, by reading an article), adding that fact to the agenda is advised. If certain members have specific jobs to do, the meeting organizer can jot these tasks on their individual copies: "Sarah, be sure to bring last year's sales figures"; "Wes, please duplicate copies of the annual report for everyone."

The order of agenda items is important. Some experts suggest that the difficulty of items should form a bell-shaped curve, with items arranged in order of ascending and descending difficulty (see Figure 9–2). The meeting ought to begin with relatively simple business: minutes, announcements, and the easiest decisions. Once members have hit their stride and a good climate has developed, the group can move on to the most difficult items. Ideally, these should occupy the middle third of the session. Then the final third of the meeting can focus on easier items to allow a period of decompression and goodwill.

Conducting the Meeting

To the uninitiated observer, a well-run meeting seems almost effortless. Time is used efficiently, the tone is constructive, and the quality of ideas is good. Despite their apparent simplicity, results like this usually don't just happen: They grow from some important communication skills.

Beginning the Meeting

Effective openings get the meeting off to a good start. First, they give everyone a clear picture of what is to be accomplished. Second, they define how the group will try to reach its goal. Finally, they set the stage for good teamwork and, thus, good results. The first few remarks by the person who called the meeting can set the stage for a constructive session. They should cover the following points.[23]

Identify the Goals of the Meeting
This means repeating the information listed in the agenda, but mentioning it here will remind everyone of the meeting's goals and help to focus the discussion. For example:

> "We're faced with a serious problem. Inventory losses have almost doubled in the last year, from 5 to 9 percent. We need to decide what's causing these losses and come up with some ideas about how to reduce them."

Provide Necessary Background Information
Background information explains the context of the meeting and gives everyone the same picture of the subject being discussed. It prevents misunderstandings and helps members to understand the nature of the information the group will consider. Clarifying key terms is often helpful:

> "By 'inventory losses,' we mean materials that are missing or damaged after we receive them. These losses might occur in the main warehouse, en route to the stores, or within the stores themselves."

Show How the Group Can Help
Outline the contributions that members can make during the meeting. Some of these contributions will come from specific people:

> "Tom's going to compare our losses with industry figures, so we can get an idea of how much of the problem is an unavoidable cost of doing business. Chris will talk about his experiences with the problem at Sterling, where he worked until last year. That firm had some good ideas we may be able to use."

Other contributions can be made by everyone present. This is the time to define specifically how each member can help make the meeting a success:

> "We're counting on everybody here to suggest areas where we can cut losses. Once we've come up with ideas, I'll ask each of you to work out a schedule for putting the ideas to work in your department."

Preview the Meeting
If you have not already done so, outline how the meeting will run. For instance:

> "We'll begin by hearing the reports from Tom and Chris. Then we'll all work together to brainstorm a list of ways to cut losses. The goal here will be to get as many ideas as possible. Once we've come up with a list, we can decide which ideas to use and how to make them work."

Identify Time Constraints
Clarify how much time is available to prevent wasting time. In some cases, it's only necessary to remind the group of how much time can be spent in the meeting as a whole ("We can develop this list between now and 11 o'clock

Dilbert © Scott Adams/Dist. by United Feature Syndicate, Inc. Reprinted by permission.

if we keep on track"). In other cases, it can be useful to preview the time available for each agenda item:

> "Tom and Chris have promised to keep their remarks brief, so by 10 o'clock we should be ready to start brainstorming. If we get our list put together by 10:30, we'll still have a half hour to talk about which ideas to try and how to put them into action."

Following these guidelines will get your meeting off to a good start. Even if you are not in charge of the meeting, you can still make sure that the opening is a good one by asking questions that will get the leader to share the kind of information just listed:

> "How much time do you expect we'll need?"

> "How far do you expect we'll get today?"

> "What can we do to help solve the problem?"

And so on.

Conducting Business

No meeting will be successful without committed, talented participants. But even the best attendees do not guarantee success. Someone—either the leader or a responsible member—has to be sure that all important business is covered in a way that takes advantage of the talents of everyone present.

Parliamentary Procedure   **Parliamentary procedure** is a set of rules that governs the way groups conduct business and make decisions in meetings. The term may bring up images of legislators using obscure rules to achieve political goals. ("Madam Chairperson, I move we set aside the order of business and refer this motion to the committee of the whole. . . .")

While parliamentary procedure can be a form of gamesmanship, when used sensibly it can be a useful tool for managing group meetings. This approach can keep discussions clear and efficient while safeguarding the rights of everyone involved in deliberations.

When to use parliamentary procedure   There are several situations when parliamentary procedure is an appropriate way to operate a meeting:

- *When a group's decisions will be of interest to an external audience.* This approach provides a record of the group's operations (the "minutes" of meetings), so interested

career tip

Seating Arrangements, Power, and Conflict

To a naïve communicator, where people sit around a meeting table might not seem important. But several decades of research have demonstrated that position can matter. Consider some possible dynamics in the seating arrangement pictured here.

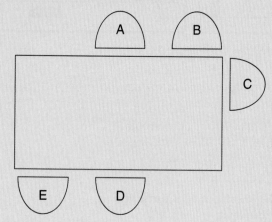

Research shows that high-power individuals typically choose the most focal position in a group—usually opposite the door, at the end of the table. If B's lieutenants occupy seats A and C and the door is near E, then B is sitting in the most powerful position. Several studies show that even if B is sitting in this position only accidentally, he or she is still likely to be perceived by others as being more powerful than other members. Conversely, people who wish to avoid interaction choose the least focal positions such as A, D, and E.

Seating opposite another member increases the potential for disagreement. The seating arrangement pictured here increases the chances that A, B, and C will disagree with D and E.

Given findings like these, where you sit in a meeting can have consequences. One way to minimize these effects—if you want to do so—is to sit in a circle. And, of course, meetings in cyberspace don't provide opportunities for power differences and conflicts due to seating arrangements.

Sources: L. D. Bjorseth, "The Language of Seating," **www.hodu .com/sit.shtml**; Y. Chu, W. F. Strong, J. Ma, and W. E. Greene, "Silent Messages in Negotiations: The Role of Nonverbal Communication in Cross-Cultural Business Negotiations," *Journal of Organizational Culture, Communications and Conflict* (2005); M. Hickson, *Nonverbal Communication: Studies and Applications,* 4th ed. (New York: Oxford University Press, 2007).

observers can learn about the input of each member and the decisions made by the group as a whole.

- *When haste may obscure critical thinking.* Because it slows down the pace of discussions, parliamentary procedure can help groups deliberate before making decisions. Of course, there is no guarantee that this approach will help a group avoid making bad decisions, but it might.

- *When emotions are likely to be strong.* Parliamentary procedure gives members with minority viewpoints a chance to speak, and its rules (when properly enforced) discourage uncivil behavior.

Order of business   It's always a good idea to have an agenda. Under the rules of parliamentary procedure, the agenda provides a plan to handle business in a logical manner. The standard meeting agenda has the following parts:

1. *Reading of the minutes.* A good set of minutes is more than a formality: It gives everyone involved a chance to make sure the record describes what *really* happened and helps future groups learn from the decisions of this group.

2. *Reports.* Smart groups use committees to handle tasks. This is the time when these groups, as well as individual members, share information with the rest of the group.

3. *Unfinished business.* The group now addresses matters that haven't yet been settled.

4. *New business.* This is the time when members can bring up new issues for the group to discuss and decide on.

Motions   When a member wants the group to deliberate, he or she introduces a **motion:** a specific proposal for action.

> "I move we redirect 10 percent of contributions to the Annual Fund to the endowment."

> "I move that we send two delegates to the annual convention in Chicago, with the goal of interviewing candidates for the position of associate director."

> "I move we go on record opposing the city's proposal to convert open parkland into parking."

Good motions address a single issue in a brief, clear way. Once introduced, a motion must be seconded by someone other than its sponsor. This procedure ensures that only those motions deemed worthy by at least two members are discussed by the group. Motions can be discussed and amended by other members. Once discussion is complete, a motion is decided by a public vote.

Using parliamentary procedure isn't an all-or-nothing proposition. Many groups use some of its elements without binding themselves to learning and using the full set of rules. See the Resources on the Online Learning Center at **www.mhhe.com/adler10e** for more detailed advice on using this approach.

Participation

Loosely structured, informal meetings may appear to give everyone an equal chance to speak out, but because of gender, culture, and style differences, every member may not have the same access.[24] Group members' relative status or rank, ages, gender, and cultural backgrounds all influence interaction patterns in groups. Unbalanced participation can cause two sorts of problems: First, it discourages people who don't get a chance to talk. Second, it prevents the group from considering potentially useful ideas. There are several ways to improve participation at meetings.

Use the nominal group technique   One method for giving every member's ideas an equal chance to be considered is the **nominal group technique (NGT).**[25] (The method's name comes from the fact that, for much of this process, the participants are a group in name only, since they are working independently.) The NGT method consists of five phases:

1. Each member writes down his or her ideas, which are then collected by a discussion leader. This method ensures that good ideas from quiet members will have a chance for consideration.

2. All ideas are posted for every member to see. By keeping the authorship of ideas private at this point, consideration is less likely to be based on personal factors such as authority or popularity.

3. Members discuss the ideas to better understand them, but criticism is prohibited. The goal here is to clarify the possibilities, not to evaluate them.

4. Each member privately rank-orders the ideas from most to least promising. Individual ranking again prevents domination by a few talkative or influential members.

5. Items that receive the greatest number of votes are discussed critically and thoroughly by the group. At this point, a decision can be made, using whichever decision-making method described in Chapter 8 (e.g., consensus, majority rule) is most appropriate.

This approach lends itself nicely to computer-mediated meetings. With most groupware packages, members can anonymously input ideas via computer and have their contributions displayed for consideration by everyone. This anonymity can empower quiet group members, who might otherwise be too intimidated to speak up.

The NGT method is too elaborate for relatively unimportant matters but works well for important issues. Besides reducing the tendency for more talkative members to dominate the discussion, the anonymity of the process lessens the potential for harmful conflicts.

Have members take turns   Another approach is to give every member a turn to speak. While it probably isn't wise to conduct an entire meeting this way, the technique can be useful at the beginning of a meeting to start members off on an equal footing, or in the middle if a few people are dominating the discussion, or at the end if some people have not been heard.

Use questions   Questions that draw out listeners are another way to encourage participation. Four types of questions can balance the contributions of members.

Overhead questions are directed toward the group as a whole, and anyone is free to answer:

"Sales have flattened out in the western region. Can anybody suggest what's going on?"

"We need to find some way of rewarding our top producers. I'd like to hear your ideas."

As long as overhead questions draw a response from all members, it's wise to continue using them. When a few people begin to dominate, however, it's time to switch to one of the following types.

Direct questions are aimed at a particular individual, who is addressed by name:

"How would that suggestion work for you, Kim?"

"Greg, how's the new plan working in your department?"

Direct questions are a useful way to draw out quiet members, but they must be used skillfully. Never start a discussion with a direct question. This creates a schoolroom atmosphere and suggests the rule "Don't speak until you're called on"—hardly a desirable norm in most meetings. It's also important to give respondents a way out of potentially embarrassing questions. For example, a chairperson might ask, "Tony, can you give us the figures for your department now, or will you need to check them and get back to us?"

Reverse questions occur when a member asks the leader a question and the leader refers the question back to the person who originally phrased it:

"Suppose the decision were up to you, Gary. What would you do?"

"That's a good question, Laurie. Do you think it's a practical idea?"

Reverse questions work well when the leader senses that a member really wants to make a statement but is unwilling to do so directly. It's important to use reverse questions with care: The member could be asking for information, in which case a direct answer is appropriate.

Relay questions occur when the leader refers a question asked by one member to the entire group:

> "Cynthia has just raised a good question. Who can respond to it?"

> "Can anyone offer a suggestion for Les?"

Relay questions are especially useful when the leader wants to avoid disclosing his or her opinion for fear of inhibiting or influencing the group. Relays should usually be rephrased as overhead questions directed at the entire group. This avoids the suggestion that one member is smarter than the others. Of course, if a particular person does have special expertise, it is appropriate to direct the inquiry to him or her:

> "Didn't you have a problem like that once with a distributor, Britt? How did you work things out?"

Keeping Discussions on Track

Sometimes the problem isn't too little discussion but too much. Groups often talk on and on without moving any closer to accomplishing the group's goal. When this happens, the leader or some other member needs to get the discussion back on track by using one of the following techniques.

Remind the group of time pressures   When the group is handling an urgent topic in a leisurely manner, you can remind everyone about the importance of moving quickly. But when doing so, it is important to acknowledge the value of the comments being made:

> "Radio ads sound good, but for now we'd better stick to the newspaper program. John wanted copy from us by noon, and we'll never make it if we don't get going."

Summarize and redirect the discussion   When members ramble on about a topic after the job is done, you can get the discussion moving again by tactfully summarizing what has been accomplished and mentioning the next task:

> "It seems we've come up with a good list of the factors that might be contributing to absenteeism. Can anybody think of more causes? If not, maybe we should move on and try to think of as many solutions as we can."

Use relevancy challenges   When a discussion wanders from the business at hand, summarizing won't help. Sometimes the unrelated ideas are good, but just don't apply to the group's immediate job. In other cases, they are not only irrelevant but also worthless. In either situation, you can get the group back on track by questioning the idea's relevancy. In a **relevancy challenge,** the questioner tactfully asks a member to explain how an apparently off-the-track idea relates. Typical relevancy challenges sound like this:

> "I'm confused, Tom. How will leasing new equipment instead of buying it help us to boost productivity?"

> "Fran asked us to decide which word-processing package to buy. Does the graphics package you mentioned have something to do with the word-processing decision?"

case study

(Lap)topless Meetings

It's no surprise that meeting-goers in high-tech environments like California's Silicon Valley often bring along and use digital communication devices—laptops, Blackberries, iPhones, Sidekicks, and a host of other gadgets.

Multitasking device users suffer from what one observer calls "continual partial attention." An industry insider describes the problem: "One of my biggest frustrations when I was an engineer at Google was being summoned to an executive meeting only to find three-quarters of the executives too busy with their laptops. I'd spend hours preparing a summary of my project status, a briefing on a new strategy area, or a review of staffing assignments. Nothing communicates disrespect to your reports like ignoring them when they're with you."

In an effort to stem this problem, a growing number of firms in the information economy and beyond have declared a ban on mobile devices in meetings. For example, San Francisco design firm Adaptive Path encourages staffers to leave their laptops and other devices behind when they attend meetings. John Vars, co-founder of San Francisco's Dogster.com, explains the logic of his company's policy on device-free meetings: "Even if people are just taking notes, they are not giving the natural human signals that they are listening to the person who is speaking. It builds up resentment. It can become something that inhibits good teamwork."

The results of what one wag called "topless meetings" are encouraging. Dogster's Vars reports, "Meetings go quicker and there is also just a shared experience. People are communicating better, the flow is faster."

CRITICAL ANALYSIS: Explore the impact of technology on meetings by considering these questions:

1. Some critics of the "no laptop" policy argue that people are most likely to retreat into technology when meetings are worthless. They claim that if meetings were called only for good reasons and were managed well, attendees would pay attention. How valid do you think this observation is?

2. If you think there is at least some value in bringing mobile communication devices to meetings, can you suggest an alternative to the "no laptop" policy that still minimizes distractions?

3. When members do bring mobile devices to meetings, how can you use the tips on pages 289–292 to keep them focused on the discussion at hand?

Sources: J. Guynn, "Silicon Meetings Go 'Topless'," *Los Angeles Times*, March 31, 2008, p. A1; "The Laptop Herring," *Rands in Response*, August 21, 2007, accessed February 2, 2009, at http://articles.latimes.com/2008/mar/31/business/fi-nolaptops31.

At this point the member who made the original remark can either explain its relevance or acknowledge that it wasn't germane. In either case, the advantage of this sort of challenge is that it isn't personal. It focuses on the *remark* and not on the *person* and thus reduces the chance of a defensive response.

Promise to deal with good ideas later   Another way to keep the goodwill of a member who has brought up an irrelevant idea is to suggest a way of dealing with it at the appropriate time:

> "That equipment-leasing idea sounds promising. Let's bring it up to Jeff after the meeting and see what he thinks of it."

> "A graphics package seems important to you, Lee. Why don't you look into what's available, and we can decide whether the change would be worth the cost."

As with relevancy challenges, your suggestion about dealing with an idea later has to be sincere if the other person is going to accept it. One way to show your sincerity is to mention exactly when you would like to discuss the matter. This might be a specific time ("after lunch"), or it might be when certain conditions are met ("after you've worked up the cost"). Another way to show your sincerity is to inquire about the idea after the meeting: "How's the research going on the graphics package?"

Keeping a Positive Tone   Almost everyone would agree that getting along with people is a vital ingredient in a successful career. In meetings, getting along can be especially tough when others don't cooperate with your efforts to keep the meeting on track—or, even worse, attack your ideas. The following suggestions can help you handle these irritating situations in a way that gets the job done and keeps potential enemies as allies.

Ask questions and paraphrase to clarify understanding

Criticizing an idea—even an apparently stupid one—can result in a defensive reaction that will waste time and generate ill will. It's also important to remember that even a seemingly idiotic remark can have some merit. Given these facts, it's often wise to handle apparently bad ideas by asking for some clarification. And the most obvious way to clarify an idea is to ask questions:

> "Why do you think we ought to let Marcia go?"
>
> "Who would cover the store if you went skiing next week?"
>
> "What makes you think we shouldn't have a Christmas party this year?"

You can also paraphrase to get more information about an apparently hostile or foolish remark:

> "It sounds as if you're saying Marcia's doing a bad job."
>
> "So you think we could cover the store if you went skiing?"
>
> "Sounds as if you think a Christmas party would be a waste of money."

This sort of paraphrasing accomplishes two things: First, it provides a way to double-check your understanding. If your replay of the speaker's ideas isn't accurate, he or she can correct you: "I don't think Marcia's doing a bad job. I just don't think we need so many people up front." Second, even if your understanding is accurate, paraphrasing is an invitation for the other person to explain the idea in more detail: "If we could find somebody to work a double shift while I am skiing, I'd be willing to do the same thing for him or her later."

Enhance the value of members' comments

It's obvious that you should acknowledge the value of good ideas by praising or thanking the people who contribute them. Surprisingly, you can use the same method with apparently bad ideas. Most comments have *some* merit. You can take advantage of such merits by using a three-part response:[26]

1. Acknowledge the merits of the idea.
2. Explain any concerns you have.
3. Improve the usefulness of the idea by building on it or asking others for suggestions.

Notice how this sort of response can enhance the value of apparently worthless comments:

> "I'm glad you're so concerned about the parking problem, Craig [acknowledges merit of comment]. But wouldn't requiring people to carpool generate a lot of

career tip

Opting Out of Meetings

What should you do when you are expected to attend a meeting that you know will be a waste of time? There are some occasions when you can't escape worthless meetings: when you are formally obligated to attend, when your absence would damage your reputation, or when your boss insists that you show up.

On other occasions, though, you may consider using one of the following strategies to make your nonattendance acceptable:

- Provide written input. If your sole reason for showing up is to provide information, a memo or written report may be a good substitute for your physical presence.

- Suggest a productive alternative. There may be other ways for you—and maybe even other attendees—to achieve objectives without actually having a face-to-face meeting: an exchange of e-mails, teleconferencing, or delegating the job to a smaller group. Suggesting these alternatives may earn you the gratitude of others who don't want to attend the meeting any more than you do.

- Tell the truth. In some cases you may choose to explain your reasons for not wanting to attend. Of course, you should do so diplomatically. Instead of saying, "These meetings are always a waste of time," you might say, "I'm not sure my attendance would serve any useful purpose."

Source: Adapted from S. M. Lippincott, *Meetings: Do's, Don'ts, and Donuts,* 2nd ed. (Pittsburgh, PA: Lighthouse Point Press, 1999).

---

resentment [balancing concern]? How could we encourage people to carpool voluntarily [builds on original idea]?"

"You're right, Pat. Your department could use another person [acknowledges merit of comment]. But Mr. Peters is really serious about this hiring freeze [balancing concern]. Let's try to come up with some ways we can get you more help without having to hire a new person [builds on original idea]."

Pay attention to cultural factors Like every other type of communication, the "rules" for conducting productive, harmonious meetings vary from one culture to another. For example, in Japan problem-solving meetings are usually preceded by a series of one-to-one sessions between participants to iron out issues, a process called *nemawashi.*[27] The practice arises from the Japanese cultural practice that two people may speak candidly to each other, but when a third person enters the discussion, they become a group, requiring communicators to speak indirectly to maintain harmony. By contrast, in countries where emotional expressiveness is the norm, volatile exchanges in meetings are as much the rule as the exception. "I've just come back from a meeting in Milan," stated Canadian management consultant Dennis Stamp. "If people acted the same way in North American meetings you'd think they were coming to blows."[28]

Concluding the Meeting

The way a meeting ends can have a strong influence on how members feel about the group and how well they follow up on any decisions that have been made or instructions that have been given.[29]

When to Close the Meeting   There are three times when a meeting should be closed.

When the scheduled closing time has arrived   Even if the discussion has been a good one, it's often best to close on schedule to prevent members from drifting off to other commitments one by one or losing attention and becoming resentful. It's wise to press on only if the subject is important and the members indicate willingness to keep working.

When the group lacks resources to continue   If the group lacks the necessary person or facts to continue, adjourn until the resources are available. If you need to get cost figures for a new purchase or someone's approval for a new idea, for example, it is probably a waste of time to proceed until the data or go-ahead has been secured. In these cases, be sure to identify who is responsible for getting the needed information, and set a new meeting date.

When the agenda has been covered   It seems obvious that a meeting should adjourn when its business is finished. Nonetheless, any veteran of meetings will testify that some discussions drag on because no one is willing to call a halt. Unless everyone is willing to socialize, it's best to use the techniques that follow to wrap up a meeting when the job is completed.

How to Conclude a Meeting   A good conclusion has three parts. In many discussions, the leader will be responsible for taking these steps. In leaderless groups or in groups with a weak leader, one or more members can take the initiative.

Signal when time is almost up   A warning allows the group to wrap up business and gives everyone a chance to have a final say:

> "We have about 15 minutes before we adjourn. We still need to hear Bob's report on the Kansas City conference, so let's devote the rest of our time to that."

> "It's almost time for some of you to leave for the airport. I'd like to wrap up our meeting by putting the list of suggestions Mr. Moss has asked us to send him into its final form."

Summarize the meeting's accomplishments and future actions   For the sake of understanding, review what information has been conveyed and what decisions have been made. Just as important is reminding members of their responsibilities:

> "It looks like we won't have to meet again until the sales conference next Tuesday in San Juan. We'll follow the revised schedule that we worked up today. Chris will have copies to everyone first thing tomorrow morning. Nick will call the hotel to book the larger meeting room, and Pat will take care of having the awards made up. Let's all plan to meet over dinner at the hotel next Tuesday night."

Thank the group   Acknowledging the group's good work is more than just good manners. This sort of reinforcement shows that you appreciate the group's efforts and encourages good performance in the future. Besides acknowledging the group as a whole, be sure to give credit to any members who deserve special mention:

> "We really got a lot done today. Thanks to all of you, we're back on schedule. Bruce, I appreciate the work you did on the specifications. We never would have made it without you."

Evaluate the effectiveness of your meetings by using this format:

0 = Never; 1 = Rarely; 2 = Sometimes; 3 = Usually; 4 = Often; 5 = Always.

Planning the Meeting

_____ 1. Are meetings held when (and only when) necessary?

_____ 2. Is membership well chosen (appropriate size and necessary knowledge and skills)?

_____ 3. Is enough time allotted for tasks, and is the meeting time convenient for most members?

_____ 4. Is the location adequate (size, facilities, free from distractions)?

_____ 5. Is a complete agenda created (date, time, length, location, attendees, background information, goals) and circulated far enough in advance of the meeting?

During the Meeting

_____ 6. Opening the meeting

    a. Are goals, necessary background information, and expectations for members' contributions clear?

    b. Are the sequence of events and time constraints previewed?

_____ 7. Encouraging balanced participation

    a. Do leader and members use questions to draw out quiet members?

    b. Are off-track comments redirected with agenda references and relevancy challenges?

    c. Do leader and members suggest moving on when an agenda item has been dealt with adequately?

"You were all great about coming in early this morning. The extra rehearsal will make a big difference in the presentation. Those charts are terrific, Julie. And your suggestion about using the slide projector will make a big difference, Lou. Let's all celebrate after we get the contract."

Following Up the Meeting

It's a mistake to assume that even a satisfying meeting is a success until you follow up to make sure that the desired results have really been obtained. A thorough follow-up involves three steps.

Build an Agenda for the Next Meeting
Most groups meet frequently, and they rarely conclude their business in one sitting. A smart leader plans the next meeting by noting which items need to be carried over from the preceding one. What unfinished business must be addressed? What progress reports must be shared? What new information should members hear?

Follow Up on Other Members
You can be sure that the promised outcomes of a meeting actually occur if you check up on other members. If the meeting provided

_____ 8. Maintaining a positive tone

    a. Are questioning and paraphrasing used as nondefensive responses to hostile remarks?

    b. Are dubious comments enhanced as much as possible?

    c. Does the meeting reflect the cultural norms of attendees?

_____ 9. Solving problems creatively

    a. Is the problem defined clearly (versus too narrowly or broadly)?

    b. Are the causes and effects of the problem analyzed?

    c. Are clear criteria for resolving the problem established?

    d. Are possible solutions brainstormed without being evaluated?

    e. Is a decision made based on the previously established criteria?

    f. Are methods of implementing the solution developed?

Concluding and Follow-up

_____ 10. Concluding the meeting

    a. Does the meeting run the proper length of time with a warning given shortly before conclusion to allow wrap-up of business?

    b. Are a summary of the meeting's results and a preview of future actions given?

    c. Does the leader acknowledge member's contributions and clarify assignments?

_____ 11. Follow-up activities

    a. Does the leader build an agenda for the next meeting upon results of the previous one?

    b. Do members follow through, and does the leader follow up with member assignments?

instructions—such as how to use the new long-distance phone service—see whether the people who attended are actually following the steps that were outlined. If tasks were assigned, check on whether they're being performed. You don't have to be demanding or snoopy to do this sort of checking. A friendly phone call or personal remark can do the trick: "Is the new phone system working for you?" "How's it going on those sales figures?" "Did you manage to get ahold of Williams yet?"

Take Care of Your Own Assignments   Most homework that arises out of meetings needs continued attention. If you wait until the last minute before tackling it, the results are likely to be sloppy and embarrassing.

review points

- Meetings are common, often time-consuming, and costly.

- Meetings serve one of these purposes: sharing information; problem-solving or ritual (confer status, build cohesion, provide informal communication channels).

- Virtual meetings present advantages and challenges for leaders and participants.

- Meetings should be held only when the job at hand is more than one person can handle, requires a division of labor, and has more than one right answer. If misunderstanding or resistance to a decision is likely, it is also wise to hold a meeting to overcome those hazards.

- Well in advance of each meeting, members should receive an agenda that announces the time, length, and location of the session; those who will attend; background information on the topic; goals for the meeting; and any advance work members need to do.

- After a meeting is called to order, the chair announces the goals of the session, reviews necessary background information, shows how members can help, previews how the session will proceed, and identifies any time constraints.

- The participation of quiet members is encouraged by using the nominal group technique, giving everyone a chance to speak, and using questions.

- The chair and members keep discussion on track by referring to time pressures, summarizing and redirecting remarks of members who have digressed, using relevancy challenges, and promising to deal with tangential issues after the meeting.

- The tone of meetings stays positive if members make an attempt to understand one another by asking questions and paraphrasing, enhancing the value of one another's comments, and being culturally aware.

- A meeting should close at its scheduled time, when the group lacks resources to continue, or when the agenda has been completed—whichever comes first. The chair gives notice that time is almost up, summarizes accomplishments and future actions, and thanks group members for their contributions.

- Chairs' duties after a meeting include building agendas for next sessions, following up with other members, and honoring their own commitments.

key terms

→ Test your understanding of these key terms by visiting the Online Learning Center Web site at www.mhhe.com/ader10e.

agenda   280
direct question   288
motion   287
nominal group technique (NGT)   287
overhead questions   288
parliamentary procedure   285

relay questions   289
relevancy challenge   289
reverse questions   288
teleconference   275
videoconference   276

activities

 Go to the self-quizzes at the Online Learning Center at www.mhhe.com/adler10e to test your knowledge of chapter concepts.

1. Invitation to Insight

You can gain an appreciation for the importance of meetings by interviewing one or more people in a career field that is of interest to you.

   a. Ask questions such as
      1. How frequent are meetings in your work?
      2. How long do these meetings typically take?
      3. What kinds of topics are covered in your meetings?
      4. What formats are used (parliamentary procedure, following agenda, open-ended discussions with no clear agenda, virtual versus face-to-face)?
      5. How effective are meetings? What factors contribute to their effectiveness or ineffectiveness?

   b. Compare your findings with your classmates' findings.

      1. Which types of meetings occur most frequently (informational, problem-solving, ritual)?
      2. Which types of formats occur most frequently?
      3. Are the advantages mentioned by interviewees similar to those identified in the text?
      4. Based on concepts from the text, suggest remedies for the challenges identified by the interviewees.

2. Skill Builder

Use the information in this chapter to decide which of the following tasks would best be handled by a problem-solving group and which should be handled by one or more individuals working separately. Be prepared to explain the reasons for each choice.

   a. Developing procedures for interviewing prospective employees.

   b. Tabulating responses to a customer survey.
   c. Investigating several brands of office machines for possible purchase.
   d. Choosing the most desirable employee health insurance program.
   e. Organizing the company picnic.
   f. Researching the existence and cost of training programs for improving communication among staff members.

3. Skill Builder

With a group of your classmates, simulate a group decision-making process using the nominal group technique. Use one of the following scenarios or create one of your own:

   a. Choosing a topic from this class about which you could deliver a group oral presentation.
   b. Deciding where you and your classmates might go for a field trip.
   c. Selecting the next novel your book club will read and discuss.

After you complete the role play, discuss advantages and disadvantages of the nominal group technique as a decision-making procedure.

4. Invitation to Insight

Ask someone you know to provide you with a copy of an agenda from a workplace meeting, or provide one of your own from a meeting you have attended. With a group of classmates, analyze the agenda.

   a. Which elements of an effective agenda are present? Which are absent?
   b. To what degree does the agenda illustrate *result-oriented, specific,* and *realistic* goals?
   c. Suggest improvements for future agendas. If result-oriented goals are missing, write some examples.

5. Skill Builder

You are chairing a meeting in which one member whom everyone dislikes is aggressively promoting an idea. Time is short, and everyone in the group is ready to make a decision that will go against the disliked member's position. You realize that the unpopular idea does have real merit, but lending your support and urging further discussion will put the group further behind and leave the other members annoyed with you.

Suggest three different ways you could handle the situation. For each, write out the specific comments you would make. Using concepts and vocabulary from this chapter, discuss advantages and disadvantages of each scenario.

6. Skill Builder

Use the skills introduced on pages 287–289 to describe how you would respond to the following comments in a meeting. Identify which skill you are using:

  a. "There's no way people will work Sundays without being paid double overtime."
  b. "No consultant is going to tell me how to be a better manager!"
  c. "I don't think this brainstorming is worth the time. Most of the ideas we come up with are crazy."
  d. "Talking about interest rates reminds me of a time in the 1980s when this story about President Carter was going around. . . ."
  e. "Sorry, but I don't have any ideas about how to cut costs."

resources

For extensive readings and Web sites on productive meetings, see the Online Learning Center Web site at **www.mhhe.com/adler10e.**

Fresh Air Sports

Fresh Air Sports Rentals began 8 years ago in a southern California beachfront hut where Woody and Sandy Belmont rented out fat-tired cruiser bikes to tourists. Business was good, and within a year Fresh Air customers could also rent a variety of other outdoor gear including surfboards, mountain bikes, and paddleboats.

Over the years Fresh Air has grown into a network of 18 locations throughout the western United States and Canada. The company is big enough now that name recognition is feeding the business: Customers who have rented from Fresh Air in one location look for it in other vacation spots. Woody and Sandy are thinking seriously of expanding the business to resorts on the East Coast, in Mexico, and in Central America.

Next month, Fresh Air is having its first-ever associates' meeting in San Diego. Woody and Sandy need to develop several presentations for that conference:

- A keynote speech, welcoming the employees and building enthusiasm for the company and for the upcoming meeting. During this speech, Sandy and Woody will also introduce Fresh Air's new management team.

- An informative program on how to avoid sexual harassment claims. Fresh Air's new human relations director will deliver this talk, but Sandy wants to play a close role in its development.

- A session introducing the company's new incentive plan, in which employees will receive bonuses for increasing sales. While the potential for greater compensation is good, base salaries will decline under this arrangement. Woody knows that it's important to sell the plan to employees if it has a chance of succeeding.

- A series of awards presentations at the closing dinner. At this session, employees will be honored for their exceptional service. Woody and Sandy want to include enough employees to boost morale, without creating so many awards that they appear meaningless.

As you read the chapters in this unit, consider the following questions for each presentation:

1. What is the general goal for each presentation? Create a specific goal for each one.
2. What factors outlined in Chapter 10 (audience, occasion, speaker) should Sandy and Woody consider for each presentation?
3. Construct an outline for at least one of the presentations, based on your analysis in question 2 above. Include material for the introduction and conclusion and the main points in the body.
4. For each main point in the body of the presentation you developed in question 3 above, identify one type of supporting material that you could use to make the point clearer, more interesting, and/or more persuasive.
5. Describe the style of delivery that would be most effective for each of the presentations to be delivered at the San Diego meeting. Besides the speaker's style, discuss ways in which the speaking environment could be arranged to help achieve the presentation's goal.

10

Developing and Organizing the Presentation

chapter outline

Analyzing the Situation
Analyzing the Audience
Analyzing Yourself as the Speaker
Analyzing the Occasion

Setting Your Goal and Developing the Thesis
General and Specific Goals
Developing the Thesis

Organizing the Body
Brainstorming Ideas
Basic Organizational Plan
Identify Main Points and Subpoints
Choose the Best Organizational Pattern
Rules for Main Points

Planning the Introduction and Conclusion
Functions of the Introduction
Types of Opening Statements
Functions of the Conclusion
Types of Closing Statements

Adding Transitions
Functions of Transitions
Characteristics of Effective Transitions

Review Points
Key Terms
Activities
Resources

chapter objectives

After reading this chapter, you should be able to

1. Develop an effective strategy for a specific presentation based on a complete analysis of the situation.
2. Identify general and specific goals for a given speaking situation.
3. Construct a clear thesis based on an analysis of a specific speaking situation.
4. Choose and develop an organizational plan for the body of a presentation that best suits its goal and the audience.
5. Create an effective introduction and conclusion for a presentation, following the guidelines in this chapter.
6. Design a presentation that contains effective transitions between the introduction and body, between points in the body, and between the body and conclusion.

Whatever your field, whatever your job, speaking to an audience is a fact of life. Sales representatives and account executives deliver presentations to potential customers. Brand managers propose ideas to management and explain new product lines to the sales force. Department heads and supervisors brief superiors on recent developments and subordinates on new company policies. Computer specialists explain new systems and software to the people who will use them. Presentations are so pervasive that some experts have estimated that speakers address audiences an astonishing 33 million times each day.[1] According to one survey, businesspeople give an average of 26 presentations a year.[2] Table 10–1 on page 304 offers a sample of the kinds of presentations that most people deliver sooner or later in their careers. Chapter 13 offers specific advice on planning and delivering various types of business presentations.

While some business and professional presentations are formal, full-dress performances before large audiences, most are comparatively informal talks to a few people or even a single person. If you drop into your boss's office and say, "Do you have a few minutes? I have some information that may help us cut down our travel expenses," you're arranging a presentation. You're also delivering a presentation when you teach the office staff how to use the new database, explain the structure of your department to a new employee, or explain to management why you need a larger budget.

Even when you create a written report, you will often introduce its contents in an oral presentation, and the quality of your spoken remarks may be the measure of your success. In fact, the quality of your presentation may determine whether anyone ever reads your documents. Furthermore, the highly public nature of presentations means that your reputation can rest or fall on how you handle yourself in front of an audience.

| Table 10–1 | Common Types of Presentational Speaking |

Type of Presentation	Example
Briefing and informational announcements	Announcing new health insurance procedure
Orientation sessions	Conducting new-employee orientation
Training programs	Explaining how to operate new computer software
Research and technical reports	Describing a market research survey
Progress reports	Giving a status report on monthly sales
Civic and social presentations	Making a speech at a local service club
Convention and conference presentations	Reporting on company's technological breakthroughs
Television and radio interviews	Describing company's position on industrial accident or injury
Introductions	Introducing new employee to other workers
Sales presentations	Presenting product to potential customer
Project and policy proposals	Proposing new travel policy to management
Seeking resources	Making loan request to commercial lender
Ceremonial occasions	Speaking at retirement celebration for longtime employee

As your career progresses, presentational speaking skills become even more important.[3] One automobile executive explained,

As an executive rose in management, he had to rely less on his technical training and more on his ability to sell his ideas and programs to the next level of management. When I was just an engineer somewhere down the line working on a technical problem, everything affecting me was in my grasp. All I had to do was solve this particular problem, and I was doing my job. But now, as head of advanced engineering, I have to anticipate and predict product trends and then sell my programs for capitalizing on those trends.[4]

Most people who work in organizations eventually find that their effectiveness and success depend on their ability to organize their ideas and present them effectively. Sometimes a written memo or report will do the job, but there are often important reasons for presenting your ideas personally. For example, if people don't understand a point in a proposal, they may put it aside for weeks or simply veto it. Delivering your message personally provides immediate feedback that helps you clarify points and answer questions. Oral presentations are often more persuasive as well. A speaker's knowledge, enthusiasm, and apparent confidence can influence people to accept or reject an idea in a way that a written document cannot.

In practice, you'll rarely get approval for an important idea without explaining it personally. As one executive put it,

The people who have the power and responsibility to say yes or no want a chance to consider and question the proposal in the flesh. Documents merely set up a meeting and record what the meeting decided. Anyone serious about an idea welcomes the chance to present it himself–in person. We wisely discount proposals whose authors are unwilling to be present at the launching.[5]

How Much Time Does It Take to Plan a Presentation?

Mark Twain once said, "It usually takes more than 3 weeks to prepare a good impromptu speech." This humorous observation highlights a truth about virtually every presentation: Success comes from careful planning, and planning takes time.

Almost every inexperienced speaker underestimates the amount of time necessary to create an effective presentation. Most experts use the hour-per-minute principle: Expect to spend about 1 hour of preparation time for every minute you will be speaking. Some professionals suggest a more modest 10-to-1 ratio between preparation and speaking time. "If I'm building a new presentation from scratch, you're probably talking about at least 10 hours of research and development for 1 hour of delivery time," says corporate trainer Bob Pike.

Experts agree that the way you spend preparation time is more important than the actual number of hours you spend. Most suggest that analyzing your audience is essential. Even for 1-hour speeches he has delivered many times before, Pike spends at least 2 to 3 hours researching the specific audience he will be addressing. He often asks key clients to fill out questionnaires that identify their specific interests, level of knowledge, any topics, or even specific words he should avoid.

Speakers are like athletes: Time spent planning and practicing is an investment that produces winning results.

Note: For more information on presentation planning, see Dave Zielinski, "Clock Work: How to Make the Most of Your Preparation Time," *Presentations*, February 2002, pp. 32–40.

Presentations aren't delivered only to internal audiences. Many people also give work-related addresses to listeners outside their organizations. Realizing that effective speakers carry their message to the public in ways that print and electronic media can't match, companies send representatives into the community to deliver speeches in a wide variety of settings.[6] Some of the world's biggest corporations sponsor training. Toastmasters International, a group dedicated to helping businesspeople present their ideas effectively, now has nearly 235,000 members in 11,700 clubs in 92 countries.[7] Research confirms that speakers can become more effective with training.[8] Even people who seem to work in fairly solitary jobs give speeches to clubs, professional organizations, and community groups.

Different kinds of presentations make different demands on the speaker. For example, a sales presentation to one customer may often seem more like a conversation because the customer may interrupt with questions, while a speaker addressing an audience of several hundred people may delay questions until the end. In spite of the differences, all presentations make many of the same demands on the speaker. The planning, structure, support, and strategy of each of them are very important, and a good speaker follows approximately the same steps in planning and developing almost any presentation. The material in Chapters 10–13 applies to almost any presentation you will give in your career or profession.

Analyzing the Situation

Before you plan even one sentence of the actual presentation, you have to think about the situation in which you'll speak. A presentation that might fascinate you could bore or irritate the audience. You can make sure that your approach is on target by considering three factors: the audience, yourself as the speaker, and the occasion.

case study

Selling to Seniors: Audience Analysis or Audience Deception?

For over 13 years, entrepreneur Tyrone M. Clark operated "Annuity University." This two-day workshop trained over 7,000 people to sell annuities to senior citizens. In late 2002, the state of Massachusetts slapped Clark with a cease-and-desist order, accusing his firm of tricking seniors into trading in their investments for expensive and complicated annuity policies.

According to *The Wall Street Journal*, here are some of the practices Clark advocated:

- Oversimplifying the nature of the investments being sold. Clark says it, "You'll waste time if you think you can impress them with charts, graphs, printouts or use sophisticated words." Instead, he recommends, "Tell them it's like a CD—it's safe, it's guaranteed."

- Using fear appeals. "[Seniors] thrive on fear, anger, and greed," says Clark. "Show them their finances are all screwed up so that they think, 'Oh, no, I've done it all wrong.'"

- Enticing retirees to attend sales seminars by offering free meals.

- Learning about investors' concerns. At seminars, seniors note their concerns from a list of topics including taxes, Social Security, insurance, and protection of assets. Salespeople are encouraged to refer to these concerns when they call customers to set up a sales appointment.

CRITICAL ANALYSIS: Many of the strategies listed above are based on the kind of audience analysis described in this chapter. To understand their implications, consider the following questions:

1. Identify the principle of audience analysis behind each of the strategies listed above.

2. Describe how each principle could be abused to make unethical pitches to potential investors.

3. As appropriate, describe how each principle could be used ethically.

Sources: "Annuities 101: How to Sell to Senior Citizens," *The Wall Street Journal*, July 2, 2002, p. C1, and "Complaint Is Filed in Annuity Case," *The Wall Street Journal*, September 26, 2002, p. C3.

Analyzing the Audience

The saying "Different strokes for different folks" is never more true than when you are delivering a presentation. Having good ideas isn't enough. You have to present those ideas in a way that your listeners will understand and appreciate. One corporate communication expert declared, "Designing a presentation without an audience in mind is like writing a love letter and addressing it 'To Whom It May Concern.'"[9] Former Chrysler president Lee Iacocca pinpointed the value of audience analysis:

> It's important to be able to talk to people in their own language. If you do it well, they'll say "God, he said exactly what I was thinking." And when they begin to respect you, they'll follow you to the death. The reason they're following you is not because you're providing some mysterious leadership. It's because you're following them.[10]

Asking yourself a number of questions about your listeners will shape the way you adapt your material to fit their interests, needs, and backgrounds.

Who Are the Key Audience Members?

Not all audience members are equally important. Sometimes one or two listeners has the power to approve or reject your appeal. Abraham Lincoln made this point clearly when his cabinet unanimously opposed one of his ideas. "The vote is eight to one against the plan," the president stated. "The motion carries." In cases such as this, you need to identify the interests, needs, attitudes, and prejudices of the key decision makers and then focus your appeal toward them.

Sometimes it's easy to identify the key members. You don't have to be a communications expert to figure out that your boss has more power than the interns who are listening in on your presentation. There are times, though, when you will need to do some prespeaking investigation to identify the opinion leaders and decision makers in your audience.

How Much Do They Know?
A group of experts doesn't need the background information that less informed audiences would require. In fact, these people would probably be bored and offended by your basic explanation. Likewise, people who are familiar with a project don't need to be brought up-to-date—unless they have missed some late-breaking developments.

It's also important to ask yourself what your listeners do *not* know: Uninformed people or non-experts will be mystified (as well as bored and resentful) unless you give them background information.

What Do They *Want* to Know?
People will listen to you if you address *their* interests, not yours. Asking for a promotion because you need the money isn't nearly as effective as demonstrating that you can help the company better in the new position. Asking for an assistant because you feel overworked isn't as likely to impress your boss as showing how the help will increase productivity or allow you to take on more business. Perhaps the most important key to effective selling is identifying the prospect's needs and showing how the product can satisfy them.

The job titles of your listeners can give you clues about what they want to know. If audience members are specialists—in engineering, finance, or marketing, for example—they'll probably be interested in the more technical aspects of your talk that pertain to their specialties. On the other hand, an audience of non-experts would probably be bored by a detailed talk on a subject they don't understand. Surprisingly, most managers fall into this category. "Just give me a quick description, a schedule, and the dollar figures" is a common managerial attitude.

What Are Their Personal Preferences?
The personal idiosyncrasies of your listeners can make all the difference in how your message is received. Does your audience prefer that a presentation be formal or casual? Humorous or straitlaced? Fast-paced or leisurely? Knowing these preferences can make the difference between success and failure in a presentation. One business consultant described how attitudes can vary from one set of listeners to another:

> We found . . . that in the same corporation engineers giving reports to different department heads were required to go about it in a totally different manner. One department head wanted every detail covered in the report. He wanted analyses of why the report was being done, complete background on the subject under discussion, and a review of the literature, and he expected the report to run twenty or thirty written pages. In addition, he wanted

Always tailor your presentation to your audience

an oral presentation that covered almost every detail of the report. The man who ran the department right down the hall wanted just the opposite. He wanted short, comprehensive reports discussing only the elements that were new. He said he already knew what was going on in his department. He didn't want an analysis of the situation, and he didn't want any young engineer wasting his time. The reports that got an A in one department got an F in another and vice versa. Therefore, the first rule for anyone giving a report is to ask those who requested the report what form they would like it to take.[11]

Audience attitudes can be hard to anticipate. One architect describes how he had to disguise the use of cost-saving technology to suit the mistaken assumptions of some clients.

When I [used to] prepare a preliminary design for a client, I often sketch[ed] a floor plan "free-hand": meaning that I quickly [drew] the design idea without a lot of detailed measurements. . . . With the advent of computer aided design (CAD), we can produce the same design on the computer . . . faster, more accurately, and at the same cost as before.

Although this approach seems like a win–win scenario for the architect and the client, experience proves that this isn't the case.

Some of our clients have complained that we are spending too much time and money on these preliminaries . . . they want something fast and cheap. They assume that because of how the product looks, we are spending more time (and more of their money) too early in the process. No amount of explanation will appease them.

So, what to do? We just purchased a new software product. It is called Squiggle. It takes the very accurate, crisp, straight lines of a computer design and actually makes it look hand-drawn. Now, the clients will look at a computer drawing, but see hand-drawn.[12]

Which Demographic Characteristics Are Significant?

A number of measurable characteristics of your listeners might suggest ways to develop your remarks. One such characteristic is gender. What is the distribution of men and women? Even in this age of relative enlightenment, some topics must be approached differently, depending on your audience's gender.

A second demographic characteristic is *age*. A life insurance salesperson might emphasize retirement benefits to older customers and support for dependent children to younger ones with families.

Cultural background is often an important audience factor. You would use a different approach with blue-collar workers than you would with a group of white-collar professionals. Likewise, the ethnic mix of a group might affect your remarks. The points you make, the examples you use, and even the language you speak will probably be shaped by the cultural makeup of your audience. At the most basic level, you need to be respectful of your audience. For example, when speaking to people from other countries, avoid chauvinistic remarks like "That's the way we do it back home."[13]

Another demographic factor is the *economic status* of your audience. This factor is especially important in sales, where financial resources "qualify" potential customers as prospects for a product or service as well as suggest which features are likely to interest them.

Not every variable is important in planning every speech. For instance, an engineer speaking about recent advances in the field should consider her audience's level of knowledge (about engineering and those advances) and occupations (that is, what those advances have to do with her listeners' work), but matters such as gender, age, and economic status probably wouldn't be as important. On the other hand, a representative

Speaking to International Audiences

Developing a presentation for any audience takes careful planning. When your listeners come from a background different from yours, extra thought is required. The following tips will boost the odds of achieving your goal with a diverse audience.

1. *If in doubt, address listeners more formally than usual.* As a rule, business is conducted more informally in the United States and Canada than in many other parts of the world. What seems friendly in much of North America may be perceived as disrespectful elsewhere.

2. *Make your presentation highly structured.* Be sure to follow the guidelines in this chapter for organizing a presentation. Have a clear introduction in which you identify your thesis and preview your remarks. Highlight key points during the body of your presentation, using a clear organizational pattern. Conclude with a summary of your main ideas.

3. *Use standard English.* Most non-native speakers learned English in school, so avoid idioms and jargon that may be unfamiliar. Whenever possible, use simple words and sentences. Also, use nouns instead of pronouns whenever possible to minimize confusion.

4. *Speak slightly more slowly than usual.* Don't, however, raise the volume of your voice: Shouting won't make you easier to understand.

5. *Use handouts.* Most non-native audience members will have higher reading than listening comprehension, so printed supporting materials will help them understand and remember your points. Providing listeners with printed information in advance of your presentation will make it easier for them to follow your remarks.

6. *Consult with a local coach.* Share your remarks with someone familiar with your audience before the presentation to make sure your ideas are clear and free of blunders that will undermine your credibility. When U.S. president John F. Kennedy announced his solidarity with the citizens of Germany's historic capital by proclaiming "*Ich bin ein Berliner*," any resident of the city could have told him the words translated as "I am a jelly doughnut."

Sources: Adapted from La.Tresa Pearson, "Think Globally, Present Locally," *Presentations*, April 1996, pp. 20–27, 68; K. Schmidt, "How to Speak So You're Open to Interpretation," *Presentations*, December 1999, p. 126; and "Speaking Globally," retrieved February 10, 2009, from **www.toastmasters.org**.

---

from Planned Parenthood speaking to a community organization would have to consider gender, age, and economic status as well as listeners' religious backgrounds and their attitudes toward pregnancy planning and the medical profession. The first step to good audience analysis is to recognize which dimensions of your listeners' background are important and to profile those dimensions accurately.

What Size Is the Group? The number of listeners will govern some very basic speaking plans. How many copies of a handout should you prepare? How large must your visuals be to be seen by everyone? How much time should you plan for a question-and-answer session? With a large audience, you usually need to take a wider range of audience concerns into account; your delivery and choice of language will tend to be more formal; and your listeners are less likely to interrupt with questions or comments. A progress report on your current assignment would look ridiculous if you delivered it from behind a podium to four or five people. You would look just as foolish speaking to a hundred listeners while reclining in a chair.

What Are the Listeners' Attitudes?   You need to consider two sets of attitudes when planning your presentation. The first is your audience's attitude toward *you as the speaker.* If listeners feel hostile or indifferent ("Charlie is such a bore"), your approach won't be the same as the one taken if they are excited to hear from you ("I'm glad he says he's going to simplify the paperwork; last year, he did a great job of speeding up the process for getting repairs done").

In addition to listeners' feelings about you, the audience's attitude about *your subject* should influence your approach. Do your employees think the benefits of the new pension plan are too far in the future to be important? Does the sales force think the new product line is exciting or just the same old line in a new package? Do the workers think the new vice president is a genius or just another figurehead? Attitudes such as these should govern your approach.

One way to discover the attitudes of your audience—and to gain the audience's approval of your idea—is to meet with listeners before your presentation. One experienced professional explained how he applies this principle:

> *Whenever I'm going to make a proposal—to clients or to my own bosses—I make it a practice to sit down with them in advance and test my approach with them. Then I go back and design a presentation that either supports their positive attitudes or provides answers to their questions and objections.*

In addition to making personal contacts, you often can research your audience's attitudes online. With almost instant access to a wealth of sources including news stories, blogs, social networking sites, and comments on company Web sites, you often can find out what your key listeners think about you and your topic before you speak to them. One trial consultant uses this approach to research potential jurors before a big case:

> *If a juror has an attitude about something, I want to know what that is. . . . Anyone who doesn't make use of [Internet searches] is bordering on malpractice.*[14]

Analyzing Yourself as the Speaker

No two presentations are alike. While you can learn to speak better by listening to other speakers, a good presentation is rather like a good hairstyle or sense of humor: What suits someone else might not work for you. One of the biggest mistakes you can make is to try to be a carbon copy of some other effective speaker. When developing your presentation, be sure to consider several factors.

Your Goal   The very first question to ask yourself is why you are speaking. Are you especially interested in reaching one person or one subgroup in the audience? What do you want your key listeners to think or do after hearing you? How will you know when you've succeeded?

Your Knowledge   It's best to speak on a subject about which you have considerable knowledge. This is usually the case, since you generally speak on a subject precisely because you *are* an authority. Regardless of how well you know your subject, you may need to do some research—on the last 3 years' sales figures, the number of companies that have used the flexible-hours program you're proposing, the actual maintenance costs of the new equipment your company is buying, and so on.

If you do need to gain more information, don't fool yourself into a false sense of security by thinking you know enough. It's better to overprepare now than to look like a fool later. Kenneth Clarke, Britain's finance minister, embarrassed himself due to faulty knowledge. While visiting the town of Consett in northern England, he praised its success as an industrial center, saying it had "one of the best steelworks in Europe." But the steel mill had closed down 15 years earlier, putting 3,000 employees out of work. To redeem himself for that gaffe, Clarke cited another Consett factory as a major competitor in the world of disposable diapers. The town's diaper plant had closed down 2 years before.[15]

Your Feelings about the Topic   An old sales axiom says, You can't sell a product you don't believe in. Research shows that sincerity is one of the greatest assets a speaker can have.[16] When you are excited about a topic, your delivery improves: Your voice becomes more expressive, your movements are more natural, and your face reflects your enthusiasm. On the other hand, if you don't care much about your topic—whether it's a report on your department's sales, a proposal for a new program, a product you're selling, or a new method you're explaining—the audience will know it and think, If the speaker doesn't believe in it, why should I? A good test for your enthusiasm and sincerity is to ask yourself if you really care whether your audience understands or believes what you have to say. If you feel indifferent or only mildly enthusiastic, it's best to search for a new idea for your proposal or a new approach to your subject.

Analyzing the Occasion

Even a complete understanding of your audience won't give you everything you need to plan an effective presentation. You also need to adapt your remarks to fit the circumstances of your presentation. Several factors contribute to the occasion.

Facilities   Figure 10–1 on page 312 shows how you can adapt the layout of a room to suit the speaking situation. Whatever arrangement you choose, you need to consider some important issues. Will there be enough seating for all the listeners? What type of equipment is available for you to use? Will there be distracting background noises?

Questions like these are critical, and failure to anticipate facility problems can trip you up. For example, the absence of an easel to hold your charts can turn your well-rehearsed presentation into a fiasco. Lack of a convenient electrical outlet can replace your PowerPoint show with an embarrassing blackout. Even the placement of doorways can make a difference. Most experienced speakers won't settle for others' assurances about facilities; they check out the room in advance and come prepared for every possible disaster.

Time   There are two considerations here. The first is the time of day you'll be speaking. A straightforward, factual speech that would work well with an alert, rested audience at 10:00 A.M. might need to be more entertaining or emphatic to hold everyone's attention just before quitting time.

Besides taking the hour of day into account, you also need to consider the length of time you have to speak. Most business presentations are brief. One director of a Los Angeles shopping mall typically gives prospective vendors 20 minutes to make their pitch: "I automatically x-out anyone who is late or exceeds their time allotment. My experience has shown that people who have trouble adhering to parameters and deadlines are unreliable."[17] Alan Brawn, national sales manager for Hughes-JCC, reinforces the importance of keeping your remarks within the preset time limit: "Typically, if major points aren't made in about six minutes, a person's time in the sun is done."[18]

FIGURE 10–1

Room Arrangement Options

Source: After G. L. Morrisey, T. L. Sechrest, and W. B. Warman, *Loud and Clear: How to Prepare and Deliver Effective Business and Technical Presentations*, 4th ed. (Cambridge, MA: Perseus Books, 1997), pp. 146-147.

When you control the room arrangement where you will speak, consider these options:

Conference
Accommodates smaller groups (10 or fewer)
Allows audience viewing and writing
Promotes audience interaction and discussion
Allows sharing of materials or viewing models

Horseshoe
Accommodates groups of 10–30
Allows eye contact with all of audience
Allows audience viewing and writing
Promotes informal discussion

Classroom
Accommodates formal groups (around 20)
Allows audience viewing and writing
Limits audience interaction
Limits participation to Q & A

Herringbone
Accommodates groups of 20–30
Less formal than classroom
Useful to intersperse presentation and small group discussions
Allows ready switch from lecture to discussion

Auditorium
Accommodates large groups (over 20)
Limits audience writing and interacting
Limits audience participation to Q & A

Sometimes the length of your talk won't be explicitly dictated, but that doesn't mean you should talk as long as you like. Usually, factors in the situation suggest how long it's wise for you to speak. Notice, for example, how well speaker Hugh Marsh adapted his remarks to the after-dinner setting of his summary business report to a group of association members:

> Good evening, ladies and gentlemen. Whenever I get on a podium this late, after a long day at the office, I remind myself of several immutable laws.
>
> First, there is Marsh's First Law of Oratory—on any platform, any speech will grow in length to fill the time available for its delivery. Well, take heart. I only have fifteen minutes.
>
> Then there is Marsh's Second Law of Oratory—the farthest distance between two points is a speech. Or, as we used to say in Texas, speeches too often are like a Longhorn steer—a point here and a point there and a lot of bull in between. Well, again, take heart. I will try to keep my two points close together.
>
> Another law I remind myself of is Marsh's Third Law of Oratory—no speech ever sounds as good at 7:00 P.M. as it did at noon.
>
> And, finally, there is Marsh's First Law of Meeting Attendance—everybody's gotta be someplace. As long as we're here, let's be friends. I'll be brief. You be attentive. I'll make my few points and get off so we can get back to the fun part of the meeting—socializing.[19]

Context   As Chapter 1 explained, the context of your presentation also influences what you say or how you say it. For example, if others are speaking as part of your

Adapting to the Situation

Share with your group examples from your experience of excellent and/or terrible business and professional communication. Share the lessons you learned from each experience. Be prepared to explain how the examples and lessons you chose will be appropriate and useful for the members of your group.

Here are a few examples to get you started:

- "I once had a professor who was blind. After one day of class, he had memorized the names of all 30 students, and he could recognize them by voice and their position in the classroom. This experience reminded me how it's possible to do almost anything with enough focus and that I have no business complaining when things get a little hard for me. It also reminded me how much people like being remembered by name. Now I try to apply that lesson to people I meet."

- "I work at a local golf course. After being there for almost a year and getting lots of good feedback from our customers, I asked my boss for a small raise. He replied, Are you kidding? I could train a monkey to do your job. Even though I knew the comment wasn't fair, it hurt. I hope I remember never to toss off thoughtless comments without thinking about their potential to hurt others. The experience also taught me a lesson about how *not* to manage employees!"

program, you need to take them into account. ("I had originally planned to discuss the technical aspects of our new express delivery system, but I think Carol has covered them pretty thoroughly. Let me just bring your attention to two things.") Preceding speakers may have left your audience feeling bored or stimulated, receptive or angry, thoughtful or jovial. Since that state of affairs will affect how the audience receives your presentation, you should try to adjust to it.

Current events could also affect what you say or how you say it. For example, if you're presenting your new budget proposal just after the company has suffered a major financial loss, you should be prepared to show how your budget will cut costs.

Setting Your Goal and Developing the Thesis

An absolutely essential step in planning any presentation is to define your goal—what you want to accomplish. Speaking without a clear goal is a recipe for failure. As speaking coach Sandy Linver put it,

> Giving a presentation without recognizing, focusing on, and remembering your objective is the equivalent of dumping the contents of your briefcase all over your boss's desk. You don't speak to fill time by reeling off fact after unorganized fact, nor to show beautiful pictures that take the breath away, nor to impress the audience with your wit and skill as a dramatic speaker. You don't give speeches to win speech-making awards. You are there to make the best of an opportunity, just as you do in every other aspect of your business activities.[20]

There are two kinds of goals to consider: general and specific.

General and Specific Goals

As the name implies, a **general goal** (sometimes called a *general purpose*) is a broad indication of what you're trying to accomplish. There are three general speaking goals: to inform, persuade, and entertain. While one type of goal may be primary, a speaker often attempts to accomplish more than one. For example, a human resources officer

Keeping Your Goals Private

Sometimes it can be ethical to withhold your goal from an audience, while doing so at other times is unethical. Check your ability to distinguish the difference by identifying three situations for each of the following:

1. When it is legitimate to withhold your goal.
2. When withholding your goal would be unethical.

might be smart to make an informative session on filing insurance claims as entertaining as possible to keep the audience's attention.

The goal of an *informative* presentation is either to expand your listeners' knowledge or to help them acquire a specific skill. Teaching a group of product managers about new developments in technology, training a new sales representative, or giving a progress report on regional sales to a senior sales manager are all typical examples of informative talks.

Persuasive presentations focus on trying to change what an audience thinks or does. Selling is the most obvious example, but there are others as well. A union organizer will try to persuade a group of employees to vote for a union. An accountant might try to convince management to adopt a different procedure for reporting expenditures. A marketing manager might try to convince sales representatives to be more enthusiastic about a product that has not sold well.

Sometimes a speaker's goal is to *entertain* the audience. The welcoming speaker at a convention might concentrate on getting the participants to relax and look forward to the coming events. After-dinner speakers at company gatherings or awards dinners usually consider themselves successful if their remarks leave the group in a jovial mood.

The **specific goal** (sometimes called the *specific purpose*) of your presentation describes the outcome you are seeking. If you think of a speech as a journey, your specific goal is your destination. Stating the specific goal tells you what you will have accomplished when you have "arrived." A good specific-goal statement usually describes *whom* you want to influence; *what* you want them to think or do; and *how, when,* and *where* you want them to do it. Your goal statement should combine the answers to these questions into a single statement: "I want (whom) to (do what) (how, when, where)." Here are some good examples of goal statements:

"I want the people who haven't been participating in the United Way campaign to sign up."

"I want at least five people in the audience to ask me for my business card after my talk and at least one person to schedule an appointment with me to discuss my company's services."

"I want at least five people in the department to consider transferring to the new Fort Worth office."

"I want the boss to tell the committee that he's in favor of my proposal when they discuss it after my presentation."

Like these examples, your goal statements should do three things: describe the reaction you are seeking, be as specific as possible, and make your goal realistic.

Describe the Reaction You Are Seeking

Your goal should be worded in terms of the *desired outcome*: the reaction you want from your audience. You can appreciate the importance of specifying the outcome when you consider a statement that doesn't meet this criterion: "I want to show each person in this office how to operate the new voice mail system correctly."

What's wrong with this statement? Most important, it says nothing about the desired audience response. With a goal such as this, you could give a detailed explanation of the whole system without knowing whether anyone learned a thing! Notice the improvement in this statement: "I want everyone in this group to show me that he or she can operate the voice mail system correctly after my talk." With this goal, you can get an idea of how well you've done after delivering your presentation.

Be as Specific as Possible   A good goal statement identifies the who, what, how, when, and where of your goal as precisely as possible. For instance, your target audience—the who—may not include every listener in the audience. Take one of the statements we mentioned earlier: "I want the boss to tell the committee that he's in favor of my proposal when they discuss it after my presentation." This statement correctly recognizes the boss as the key decision maker. If you've convinced him, your proposal is as good as approved; if not, the support of less influential committee members may not help you. Once you identify your target audience, you can focus your energy on the people who truly count.

The best goal statements describe your goals in *measurable terms*. Consider these examples:

Vague	Specific
I want to collect some donations in this meeting.	I want to collect at least $15 from each person in this meeting.
I want to get my manager's support for my idea.	I want my manager to give me 1 day per week and the help of a secretary to develop my idea.

Knowing exactly what you want to accomplish dramatically increases the chances that you will reach your goal. Suppose you need to convince a group of subordinates to stay within budget. You already know that the following statement is no good: "I want to talk about the importance of our new budget limitations." (If you're not sure why, take another look at the preceding section on describing reactions.) A more result-oriented goal would be "I want this group to stay within budget." But even this goal statement has problems. Whom are you going to encourage: people who are already holding the line on expenses or those who look like they might overspend? How many people do you hope to persuade? How will you appeal to them? When do you want them to do it: beginning immediately or when they get around to it? The latter may not be until after the fiscal year is over—too late to save this year's profits in your department. A comprehensive specific-goal statement can take care of questions such as these: "I want to convince the four people who had spent more than half their year's budgets by May 1 that the department's solvency depends on their cutting expenses and have them show me a revised plan by the end of the week that demonstrates how they intend to trim costs for the rest of the year." This statement gives you several ideas about how to plan your presentation. Imagine how much more difficult your task would be if you had settled for the first vague goal statement.

career tip

Invitational Rhetoric: Presentations as Dialogue

Informing, entertaining, and persuading are all goals that suggest speaking is a one-way affair—something that a presenter does *to* an audience. In recent years, some scholars have suggested a fundamentally different "invitational" approach. As its name suggests, invitational speaking involves a dialogue in which speaker and audience clarify positions and explore issues without trying to persuade one another.

Invitational speaking works best in a climate of equality and mutual respect. Both speaker and audience members recognize each other's perspectives as valuable and worthy of exploration. An invitational speaker also recognizes that listeners ultimately have the right and power to decide for themselves whether and how to accept the speaker's ideas.

At first an invitational approach might seem too weak for a hard-headed business world. In fact, its open-minded approach can be very effective in a variety of business and professional settings. As Chapter 3 explained, most sales professionals emphasize the importance of listening and responding to the customer's concerns. Chapter 7 described how employment and performance appraisal interviews can be more successful if you present yourself as willing to speak to and learn from an interviewer instead of just selling your position. In Chapter 13 you will learn the importance of responding thoughtfully and respectfully in question-and-answer sessions.

Note: For more information on invitational speaking, see J. E. Bone, C. L. Griffin, and T. M. L. Scholz, "Beyond Traditional Conceptualizations of Rhetoric: Invitational Rhetoric and a Move Toward Civility," *Western Journal of Communication* 72 (2008), pp. 434–462; and S. K. Foss and K. A. Foss, *Inviting Transformation: Presentational Speaking for a Changing World,* 2nd ed. (Prospect Heights, IL: Waveland Press, Inc., 2003).

Developing the Thesis

The **thesis statement**—sometimes called the *central idea* or *key idea*—is a single sentence that summarizes your message. Some communication coaches even advise boiling down your thesis to two words.[21] Table 10-2 offers some tips for formulating this sort of statement. Once you have a thesis, every other part of your talk should support it. The thesis gives your listeners a clear idea of what you are trying to tell them:

"We're behind schedule, but we can catch up and finish the job on time."

"The credit rating you earn now can help—or hurt—you for decades."

"Investing now in a new system will save us money in the long run."

Table 10–2	Methods for Defining a Thesis Statement

1. Imagine that you met a member of your audience at the elevator and had only a few seconds to explain your idea before the doors closed.
2. Imagine that you had to send a one- or two-sentence e-mail that communicated your main ideas.
3. Ask yourself, it my listeners heard only a small portion of my remarks, what is the minimum they should have learned?
4. Suppose that a friend asked one of your listeners what you were driving at in your presentation. What would you want the audience member to say?

Presentations without a clear thesis leave the audience asking, What's this person getting at? And while listeners are trying to figure out the answer, they'll be missing much of what you're saying.

The thesis is so important that you will repeat it several times during your presentation: at least once in the introduction, probably several times during the body, and again in the conclusion.

Beginning speakers often confuse the thesis of a presentation with its goal. Whereas a goal statement is a note to *yourself* outlining what you hope to accomplish, a thesis statement tells your *audience* your main idea. Sometimes the two can be virtually identical. There are other cases, however, where goal and thesis differ. Consider a few examples:

Goal	Thesis
I want this client to advertise on our Web site.	Advertising on our Web site will boost your sales.
Parents will be confident that their children are being prepared for later schooling.	Our preschool curriculum is based on sound educational theory and research.
Workers will be more careful about conserving.	Energy conservation cuts expenses, which leaves energy money for salaries.
Audience members will be able to respond to sexual harassment instead of accepting it.	You don't have to accept sexual harassment.
I want to acquire new customers seeking this state-of-the-art technology.	Recent advances have dramatically changed industry in the past few years.

It may seem unethical to avoid mentioning your goal to an audience, but sometimes the omission is a matter of common sense and not deception. Mr. Krakos already knows the Sun Valley representative wants to sell him bread, but he's most interested in hearing *why* he should change suppliers. Similarly, an after-dinner speaker at a local service club might have the goal of getting the audience to relax, but sharing that goal would probably seem out of place.

There are other times, however, when hiding your goal would clearly be unethical. A speaker who began his presentation by saying, "I don't want to sell you anything; I just want to show you some aspects of home safety that every homeowner should know," and then went on to make a hard-sell pitch for his company's home fire alarms would clearly be stepping out of bounds. It usually isn't necessary to state your goal as long as you are willing to share it with your audience, if asked. It's very rare, however, not to state the thesis at the beginning of a presentation.

Organizing the Body

Inexperienced speakers make the mistake of starting to plan a talk by beginning at the beginning, by first writing an introduction. This is like trying to landscape a piece of property before you've put up a building. Even though it doesn't come first

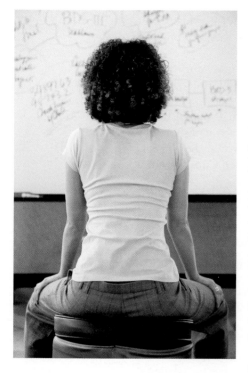

in a presentation, the body is the place to start your organizing. Organizing the body of a talk consists of two steps: identifying the key points that support your thesis, and then deciding what organizational plan best develops those points.

Brainstorming Ideas

Once you have figured out your thesis, you are ready to start gathering research to support your presentation. The first step is to pull together a list of all the information you might want to include. You'll probably already have some ideas in mind, but finding other possibilities will usually require further research. If, for example, you want to sell potential customers on your product, you'll want to find out which competing products they are using now and how they feel about them. You'll also want to discover whether they are familiar with your product and what attitudes they have about it. In other cases, the material you'll need to discuss may appear to be obvious. If you're giving a report on last month's sales, the figures might form the bulk of your remarks. If you are explaining how to use a new piece of equipment, the operating steps appear to be the obvious body of your talk.

Your brainstorming and research will produce a list of material from which you'll build your presentation. For example, suppose that you have been asked to address a group of employees about why you want them to use Mercury Overnight for letters and packages that need to be delivered quickly. Using your research on Mercury Overnight, you might make up a list that looks something like the one in Figure 10-2.

Notice that this list is a random assortment of points. In fact, your own collection of ideas probably won't even be neatly listed on a single piece of paper. More likely it will be scribbled on an assortment of index cards, check stubs, message pads, or whatever you had at hand when you came across a piece of promising information. Once you've assembled what seems like enough raw material, you're ready to organize it.

Basic Organizational Plan

Once you have a list of possible ideas, you are ready to organize them in a clear form that helps achieve your speaking goal. Most people will agree that clarity is important, but few realize just how critical it is. A substantial body of research indicates that organizing your remarks clearly can make your messages more understandable, keep your audience happy, and boost your image as a speaker.[22] Despite the benefits of good organization, most presentations suffer from a variety of problems in this area:

- Taking too long to get to the point.
- Including irrelevant material.
- Leaving out necessary information.
- Getting ideas mixed up.[23]

Problems like those above can lead to organizational chaos. Even experienced speakers can get into trouble when they speak without preparing their ideas. U.S. president George W. Bush was a more effective speaker when working from prepared

- Mercury Overnight will pick up the package at your office instead of you having to go through the mailroom.

- It will also deliver right to your office if the label is marked properly, so you don't have to wait for the mailroom to process and deliver it to you.

- When we experimented with different delivery services, Mercury delivered every single package we gave it within 24 hours.

- Some of the companies we tried took 2 days or more about 25 percent of the time.

- One company we tried got the package in on time about 90 percent of the time.

- Other companies we've tried have held up packages for as much as a week for no good reason.

- Mercury will deliver into the rural areas where many of our customers are, while some of the other companies only deliver in the urban areas.

- Mercury will bill the departmental accounts, saving bookkeeping time.

- Some companies charge a lot of extra money for the odd-sized packages we send sometimes, but Mercury just charges by weight.

- Because we can't always count on overnight delivery with the delivery service we're using now, we often have to take time off to run a package across town.

- Mercury charges less than its competitors for heavy packages.

- If we send several things at once to the same place, Mercury will give us a lower "group rate."

- Mercury will come out at any time to pick up a package.

- Other companies will only make a regular daily stop, which doesn't do you much good if your package isn't ready when they come.

- Mercury will make pickups from 7 in the morning until midnight, which is nice if you're working early or late.

- If you send the package through the post office and don't put enough postage on it, the post office sends it back and the package won't get there in time.

- The packages that we've sent through some other shippers sometimes get so badly damaged that the contents have to be replaced. The shipper will pay for the contents if you insure the package, but that doesn't get it there on time.

- Sometimes you have to ship a one-of-a-kind item, like a prototype for an advertisement, and if it gets lost or damaged it can take weeks to make a new one.

- Mercury's best shipping fee includes insurance.

- It isn't easy to figure out which delivery service is best.

- When the company was smaller, we used to just send things by mail.

- We researched the idea of setting up our own delivery service, but management vetoed it because it cost too much.

FIGURE 10–2

Selling Points Produced by a Brainstorming Session

notes than when speaking off the cuff. His answer to a question about his proposed Social Security plan illustrates the problem:

> Because the—all which is on the table begins to address the big cost drivers. For example, how benefits are calculated, for example, is on the table; whether or not benefits rise based

upon wage increases or price increases. There's a series of parts of the formula that are being considered. And when you couple that, those different cost drivers, affecting those—changing those with personal accounts, the idea is to get what has been promised more likely to be—or closer delivered to what has been promised.[24]

Most speakers would find that some of their own remarks would look almost as disjointed. The key to avoiding a meaningless stream of ideas is to organize your ideas before speaking.

No matter what the subject or the goal, most effective presentations follow a well-known pattern: First, tell them what you're going to tell them; then, tell them; then, tell them what you told them. The format looks like this:

Introduction
- Attention getter
- Thesis
- Preview

Body (two to five main points)
    I.
    II.
    III.
    IV.
    V.

Conclusion
- Review
- Closing statement

This linear, logical approach to organization isn't the only way to structure a presentation. Researchers have found that it works best with Euro-American audiences or listeners receptive to the Euro-American cultural standard. Listeners from other backgrounds may use less linear patterns, which have been given labels including "star," "wave," and "spiral."[25] Despite the value of these patterns in certain situations, the standard format is probably the safest approach with most business audiences who are part of Euro-American culture.

You have probably encountered this format many times. Despite its familiarity, many speakers act as if they have never heard of it. They launch into their subjects without any prefatory remarks about what they're about to say. Some finish their main ideas and then stop speaking without any summation or closing. Still others deliver what seems to be a model three-part talk but don't stop there; they continue tacking on new information after you have closed your mental files: "Did I mention that. . . ," "We had the same problem, by the way, last year when. . . ," or "Oh, another thing I should have mentioned . . ." Even worse, many speakers don't seem to have *any* organizational plan in mind. Their remarks sound as if the speakers had dropped their note cards and shuffled them together in random order before addressing the group.

Identify Main Points and Subpoints

The list of ideas you've compiled by brainstorming and research probably contains more material than you'll want to use in your talk. So the next step is to figure out which key points best support your thesis and help you achieve your purpose. Your analysis of the speaking situation will also help you to pinpoint your key ideas.

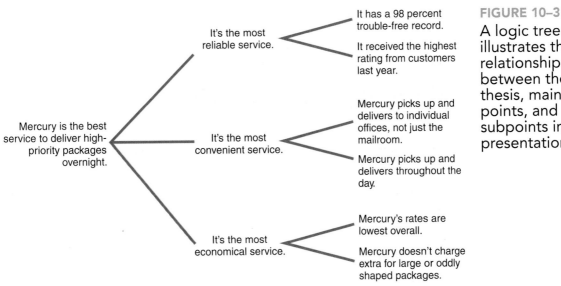

FIGURE 10–3

A logic tree illustrates the relationship between the thesis, main points, and subpoints in a presentation.

On the basis of this analysis, you might decide these are the major reasons that would convince listeners to sign up to use Mercury:

I.   Mercury is more reliable.

II. Mercury is more convenient.

III. Mercury is more economical.

None of these points was on the brainstorming list in Figure 10-2, but they emerge as themes from that list. Each of the points that did appear on that list will fit into one of these categories, so the speech can be organized around these three points.

How do you identify your main points? One way is by applying the "1-week-later" test: Ask yourself what main points you want people to remember 1 week after the presentation. Since most listeners won't recall much more than a few ideas, your 1-week-later points logically should be emphasized during your talk.

The basic ideas that grow out of your audience analysis or brainstorming list might work well as the main points of your talk, but this doesn't always happen. As with the Mercury delivery service example, there may be better ways to organize your material. Before you can decide, you need to think about the different ways the body of a presentation can be organized.

Once you have identified main points, you can fill in your plan with the subpoints that expand on each of them. These subpoints can be added to a standard outline like the one in Figure 10-4 on page 339. A more visual way to represent the relationship between a thesis, main points, and subpoints is by drawing a logic tree like the one in Figure 10-3.[26]

Choose the Best Organizational Pattern

There are many ways to organize the body of a presentation. Some work best for fundamentally informative subjects, and others are more effective when you want to persuade your listeners. You should choose the one that best develops your thesis and thus helps you to achieve your goal.

Chronological

A **chronological pattern** arranges your points according to their sequence in time. You can use it to explain a process, such as the steps in putting an order through the order-fulfillment and shipping departments or the schedule for developing a new product. One of its most common uses is to give instructions:

Thesis: Downloading the software program is easy.

   I.   Click *Manual Download.*

  II.   When the *File Download* box appears, choose a folder location.

 III.   Close all applications including your Web browser.

 IV.   Double-click on the saved file icon to start the installation process.

Chronological patterns are also useful for discussing events that develop over time:

Thesis: We need to stay on schedule if we're to get the catalog out in time for the holidays.

   I.   A product list must be ready by March 1.

  II.   Photography and catalog copy have to be completed by May 6.

 III.   Page proofs have to be read and corrected by July 30.

 IV.   Final proofs have to be reviewed by department heads by August 30.

  V.   Catalogs have to be shipped no later than October 5.

Chronological patterns may be used for discussing history:

Thesis: A review of the past 5 years shows that we've been moving toward empowering our entire workforce to make decisions.

   I.   Five years ago, management introduced the Employee Advisory Council.

  II.   Four years ago, we started project teams with people from every division.

 III.   Two years ago, the company started allowing department supervisors to approve purchases.

 IV.   Over the past year, the company has made changes in our billing process.

Spatial

A **spatial pattern** organizes material according to how it is put together or where it is physically located. You might use a spatial pattern to show the parts in a model for a new product, the location of various departments in your building, or the safety requirements of a piece of equipment—where safety shields should be placed, the support required in the floor, and so on. You might sell a piece of real estate with a spatially organized presentation like this:

Thesis: This home provides all the space you need.

I.   The upstairs has enough bedrooms for every member of the family, plus a private study.

II.   The main floor is spacious, with a large living room, a formal dining room, and an eat-in kitchen.

III.   The basement has a finished playroom for the children and a utility room.

IV.   The yard has large trees and lots of space for a garden.

You can also show the geographical nature of a subject by citing examples from many places:

Thesis: Business is better in some areas than in others.

I.   Northeast regional sales are 50 percent ahead of last year's.

II.   Mid-Atlantic regional sales are 10 percent ahead of last year's.

III.   Southern regional sales are about the same as last year's.

IV.   Midwest regional sales are down about 25 percent from last year's.

Topical   A **topical pattern** groups your ideas around some logical themes or divisions in your subject. For example, you might organize a proposal for simplifying the expense-accounting procedures around the reasons for the change or a sales presentation for photocopiers around the three major types of copiers you think a customer might be interested in. An accountant might organize a proposal for a new inventory system this way:

Thesis: A just-in-time inventory system has three major benefits.

I.   It eliminates excess inventory that may result from long-term ordering.

II.   It cuts down on waste resulting from supplies becoming outdated or shopworn.

III.   It saves on storage and computer-records costs.

The topical approach is sometimes termed a *catchall approach* because people occasionally describe a list of points as *topical* if they can't think of another pattern that will work. However, a jumbled list of ideas isn't organized just because you call it topical. A genuine topical approach has elements logically related according to some scheme an audience can easily recognize.

Cause–Effect   A **cause–effect pattern** shows that certain events have happened or will happen as a result of certain circumstances. For example, you might show prospective life insurance customers how certain clauses will provide extra coverage if they are hospitalized or demonstrate how a new advertising program will help a product reach a wider market. You might also use it to demonstrate how certain circumstances are creating a problem:

Thesis: Redecorating the offices before raising salaries [*cause*] will damage morale and affect productivity [*effect*].

I.   When employees see the offices being redecorated without having received a cost-of-living raise over the past year, they'll be discouraged.

II. Discouraged employees aren't as likely to give the company their best efforts during the upcoming season.

An alternative form of the cause–effect structure is an *effect–cause* structure. When you use this structure, you focus more on results: You begin with the result and how it came to pass or how you think it can be made to happen. For example, you might use an effect-cause pattern to explain why a company has a strict policy about absenteeism or to explain how you expect to accomplish a sales goal you have set. It may also be used to explain how a problem has been created:

Thesis: The decline in our profits [*effect*] is the result of several problems [*cause*].

I.   Our profits have decreased 15 percent.

II. Several factors are responsible.
    A.   Our competitors are offering better service at lower prices.
    B.   Our maintenance costs have nearly doubled.
    C.   Our advertising is not effective.

As Table 10-3 shows, chronological, spatial, topical, and cause–effect plans are best suited to informative presentations. While they can be used when your goal is to persuade an audience, you will have better results if you use whichever of the following organizational plans best matches your topic and the speaking situation.

Problem–Solution   A **problem-solution pattern** is the simplest persuasive scheme. As its name suggests, you begin by showing the audience that something is wrong with the present situation and then suggest how to remedy the situation.

Table 10–3   Presentation Styles and Their Corresponding Organizational Patterns

Informative	Persuasive
Chronological	Problem–Solution
Spatial	Criteria Satisfaction
Topical	Comparative Advantages
Cause–Effect	Motivated Sequence

This plan works especially well when your audience doesn't feel a strong need to change from the status quo. Since listeners have to recognize that a problem exists before they will be interested in a solution, showing them that the present situation is not satisfactory is essential before you present your idea. For example:

Thesis: Establishing a system of employee incentives can boost productivity.

I.   Our level of productivity has been flat for over 2 years while the industrywide rate has climbed steadily in that period. [*Problem*]

II. Establishing an incentive system will give employees a reason to work harder. [*Solution*]

A problem-solution pattern might also be used to show how updating a computer system will solve problems with inventory monitoring, why a potential customer needs a personal financial advisor, or why a department needs additional staff.

The problem-solution approach can be effective, but it isn't the best strategy for every persuasive situation. If your listeners already recognize that a problem exists, you may not need to spend much time proving the obvious. In such circumstances, you might do better to use one of the following three strategies.

Criteria Satisfaction

A **criteria satisfaction** organizational strategy sets up criteria that the audience will accept and then shows how your idea or product meets them.

A venture capitalist used a criteria satisfaction plan when seeking investors for a business project. Notice that he introduced each criterion and then showed how his project would satisfy it:

Introduction: Being in the right place at the right time can be the key to financial success. I'm here to offer you a chance to reap substantial benefits from an extremely promising project. Like any investment, this project needs to be based on the sound foundation of a solid business plan, a talented management team, and adequate financing. Let me show you how the project meets all of these important requirements.

Body:

I.   The first criterion is that the business plan must be solid. Extensive market research shows the need for this product. . . .

II. The second criterion is a talented management team. Let me introduce the key members of this management team and describe their qualifications. . . .

III. The third criterion is a solid, realistic financial plan. The following plan is very conservative yet shows strong potential for a substantial profit. . . .

Conclusion: Because it meets the conditions of a solid business plan, this project is worth your serious consideration.

In this example, the speaker introduced each criterion and then immediately showed how his plan satisfied it. A different approach is to present all the criteria first and then present your proposal. The strategy here is to gain the audience's acceptance first and boost your credibility. Having done this, you go on to show how your plan meets the criteria presented. With this approach, the thesis is deferred—which is especially smart when the audience may not be inclined to accept it without some powerful arguments.

A manager used a criteria satisfaction plan with a deferred thesis to announce a wage freeze to employees—hardly a popular idea. If she had announced her thesis first ("A wage freeze is in your best interest"), the employees probably would have been too upset to listen thoughtfully to her arguments. By leading her audience through the reasons leading up to the freeze, she increased the chances that the employees would understand management's reasoning. Notice how the thesis is first presented in the middle of the body and is restated in the conclusion:

Introduction: You know that we've faced declining revenues for the past year. During these hard times, we need a policy that is best both for the company and for you, the employees. That's the only way we will be able to survive.

Body:

I. There are three important criteria for selecting a policy. [*Introduces criteria first*]
   A. It should be fair.
   B. It should cause the least harm to employees.
   C. It should allow the company to survive this difficult period without suffering permanent damage.

II. A wage freeze is the best plan to satisfy these criteria. [*Satisfaction of criteria*]
   A. It's fair.
      1.
      2.
   B. It causes minimal harm to employees.
      1.
      2.
   C. It will enable the company to survive.
      1.
      2.

Conclusion: A wage freeze is the best plan at this difficult time.

Comparative Advantages   A **comparative advantages** organizational plan puts several alternatives side-by-side to show why yours is the best. This strategy is especially useful when the audience is considering an idea that competes with the one you're advocating. In many such cases a head-on comparison that supports your case is far more effective than ignoring alternative plans. A purchasing agent made the case to her boss for leasing office equipment instead of borrowing to buy it outright:

Thesis: When we remodel the offices, we can use our budget far more efficiently by leasing equipment and furnishings instead of buying them.

Body:

I.   Our up-front costs will be dramatically lower because there's no down payment.

II. The application process will be easier. To qualify for a loan, we have to give the bank 2–3 years of financial records. A lease requires us to furnish only 6 months of records.

III. We can keep pace with technology. Short-term leases will cost us less than buying new equipment every few years. We couldn't afford to do that if we buy equipment outright.

IV. We can buy more. Because lease costs are lower, we can get better quality equipment that will improve our productivity.

Conclusion: When it comes to value for our dollar, leasing is definitely the way to go.

Motivated Sequence

The **motivated sequence** organizational plan is a five-step scheme designed to boost the involvement and interest of the audience.[27] Regardless of the topic, the sequence of steps is the same:

1. *Attention.* Capture the attention of the audience by introducing the problem in an interesting manner. (This functions as an introduction.)
2. *Need.* Explain the problem clearly and completely. Use a variety of supporting material to back up your claim, proving that the problem is serious. Ideally, make your listeners feel that the problem affects them in some way. Make them eager to hear a solution.
3. *Satisfaction.* Present your solution to the problem. Provide enough support to prove that the solution is workable and that it will, indeed, solve the problem.
4. *Visualization.* Describe clearly what will happen if your proposal is adopted so that the audience has a clear mental picture of how your proposal will solve the problem. You may also paint a verbal picture of what will happen if your proposal is *not* adopted. In either case, the key to success in this step is to paint a vivid picture of the outcomes, showing how your proposal will make a real difference.
5. *Action.* Call for a response by your audience. Explain what listeners can do to solve the problem. (This functions as the conclusion.)

The motivated sequence plan provides a step-by-step approach for organizing a speech. It builds on the basic problem–solution plan: Step 1 arouses the interest of listeners so that they will be more receptive to the topic. Step 4 goes beyond simply providing a solution and helps the audience picture what a difference it will make. Step 5 guides the audience on how to bring the solution about, making it easier for listeners to take the necessary steps and arousing them to act. Unlike most presentations, this approach usually won't require a preview in the opening of your remarks.

The motivated sequence approach works best when the problem that you present and the solution that you propose are easy to visualize. If your listeners can imagine the problem and see themselves solving it by following your plan, they'll be motivated to accept your reasoning. And because the motivated sequence approach closes with an appeal to action, it is especially well suited to getting an immediate response to your proposal. Recognizing this fact, a fund-raiser used it to generate pledges for an urgent appeal:

[Attention]	Here's a picture of the Myer family. Ted, the father, is a trained stonemason and proud of it. Anne, the mom, is a registered nurse. Little Chris is a normal kid who loves baseball and pizza. His teachers say he has a gift for math and languages.
[Need]	Since this photo was taken, the Myers have had a run of terrible luck. Last year, Ted fell at work and wrenched his back. He's been unable to work ever since, and his disability insurance has almost run out. Three months after Ted's accident, Anne was diagnosed as having leukemia. She's undergoing treatment, and the doctors are optimistic; but she can't work now, and there's no telling when she will be able to return to her job. The Myers lived on their savings for 6 months, but now all the money is gone. Last week they had to move out of their apartment, and they have nowhere else to go. Nowhere, that is, except Transition House.
[Satisfaction]	You can help provide temporary housing for the Myers and other neighbors who are in trouble by contributing to Transition House. Your donations will give these people a safe place to stay while they get back on their feet and save them from life on the street.
[Visualization]	We're hoping to raise enough money tonight to give the Myer family a month at Transition House. During that time, Ted can finish training for a new career as a book-keeper and get back to work. He hopes to become a CPA. Once he's on the job, the Myers will be able to find a new apartment so that Anne can fight for her health and Chris can stay in his same school, where he's doing so well.
[Action]	What we need from you tonight is a donation. We're asking for anything you can afford: the price of an evening on the town or maybe a postponement of that new outfit you were thinking of buying. In just a moment, I'll be passing out pledge cards. . . .

At first glance, the motivated sequence approach seems to depart from the basic introduction-body-conclusion pattern of organizing a presentation. A closer look shows that the plan does follow the same pattern:

Introduction
- Attention

Concept Mapping Software

Sometimes the best way to organize ideas is visually. Until recently, the best approach was to write ideas on index cards, spread them out on the table or floor, and rearrange them until a clear plan emerged. Now, computer software makes the task quicker and easier. While no program can substitute for critically analyzing your organizational strategy, "concept mapping" software programs are a useful tool for visualizing your options.

The *Communicating at Work* Online Learning Center at **www.mhhe.com/adler10e** provides some outlining software. More elaborate programs available on the Web offer free trials so you can see how well they work for you. Here are some notable examples:

"Inspiration" (**www.inspiration.com**) is a visual tool for developing ideas. The program's diagram view provides an easy-to-use equivalent of the index card approach. Each idea you type into the computer appears onscreen inside its own box or circle. You can rearrange these ideas with your mouse until they fall into patterns that seem clear and effective. Then, with a simple command, the visual map is turned into a traditional outline, suitable for conversion into speaker's notes, handouts, or visual aids. Besides serving as an outlining tool, Inspiration makes it easy to create concept maps, process flows, knowledge maps, flowcharts, and other visual diagrams.

Other concept-mapping software programs include Decision Explorer (**www.banxia.com/dexplore/index.html**), MindManager (**www.mindjet.com**), IHMC's Concept Map (**http://cmap.ihmc.us/conceptmap.html**), and VisiMap (**www.visimap.com**). Additional resources to try include ActionOutline (**www.canadiancontent.net/tech/download/ActionOutline.html**) and B-liner (**www.bliner.com**).

Body

I. Need

II. Satisfaction

III. Visualization

Conclusion
- Action

Each has an introduction that captures the attention of your audience and gives members reasons to listen. Each has a body that is arranged in a pattern that is easy to follow and helps achieve the purpose of the presentation. Each has a conclusion that reinforces the thesis of the talk and leaves the audience motivated to accept it.

Rules for Main Points

Whichever pattern of organization you use, your main points should meet the following criteria.

Main Points Should Be Stated as Claims
A **claim** is a statement asserting a fact or belief. If you state your claims in full, grammatical sentences, they will probably satisfy the 1-week-later test and be remembered by your listeners. Notice how describing main points as claims in complete sentences is clearer and far more effective than using simple three- or four-word statements.

Fragment	Claim
Choosing a physician	It's essential to choose a health care provider from the list of approved doctors.
Sexual and ethnic discrimination	Allowing sexual or ethnic considerations to intrude into our hiring decisions isn't just bad judgment, it's illegal.
Demographic changes in the market	Due to demographic changes, we can expect our market to shrink in the next 10 years.

All Points Should Develop the Thesis   Consider the following outline:

Thesis: Allowing employees more latitude in choosing their work hours is good for the company and for the workers.

I.   Flexible scheduling can work in several ways.

II.   Flexible scheduling improves morale.

III.   Flexible scheduling reduces absenteeism.

The first point may be true but doesn't say anything about flexible scheduling's value and, therefore, ought to be dropped.

A Presentation Should Contain No More than Five Main Points
Your main points are, after all, what you want your listeners to remember, and people have difficulty recalling more than five pieces of information when they are presented orally.[28] For that reason, it is imperative that your presentation contain no more than five main points. This requires some discipline. Consider the advice of David Dempsey, a trial attorney and professor of public speaking at Oglethorpe University in Atlanta, about the need to ruthlessly edit your ideas:

> *Make three points that stick, rather than 10 quick points that leave no lasting impression. Constantly ask yourself, "Is this the most important issue, the best example, the most compelling way to illustrate my point?"*[29]

Even when you have a large amount of material, it's usually possible to organize it into five categories or fewer. For example, if you were preparing an analysis of ways to lower operating expenses in your organization, your brainstorming list might include these ideas:

- Reduce wattage in lighting fixtures.
- Hire outside data processing firm to handle seasonal billing rather than expand permanent in-house staff.
- Sell surplus equipment.
- Reduce nonbusiness use of copying machines.

- Reduce temperature in less-used parts of the building.
- Pay overtime rather than add new employees.
- Retrofit old equipment instead of buying new machinery.

Your outline could consolidate this list into three areas:

Thesis: We can reduce operating costs in three areas: energy, personnel, and equipment.

   I.   We can reduce our energy costs.
      A. Reduce wattage in lighting fixtures
      B. Reduce temperature in less-used parts of the building

  II.   We can reduce money spent on new personnel.
      A. Hire outside data processing firm for seasonal billing
      B. Encourage overtime instead of adding employees

 III.   We can reduce our purchase and maintenance costs on equipment.
      A. Retrofit old equipment
      B. Sell surplus equipment
      C. Reduce personal use of copying machines

This outline contains all the items in your list, but organizing them into three broad categories makes your presentation much easier to comprehend than a seven-point presentation would be.

Main Points Should Be Parallel in Structure Whenever Possible

Parallel wording can reflect your organization and dramatize your points. Consider how the repetition of "We can reduce . . ." in the outline above helps drive the point home far more forcefully than does the following, less effective wording of your main points:

   I.   Managing energy costs can save us money.

  II.   Careful hiring practices will reduce overhead.

 III.   Equipment purchase and maintenance are controllable costs.

You won't always be able to state your main points using parallel construction, but a look at many of the examples in this chapter shows you that it can be used often.

Each Main Point Should Contain Only One Idea   Combining ideas or overlapping them will confuse audiences. Consider this outline:

Thesis: Many local businesses boost their effectiveness and serve their communities by seeking a diverse workforce.

   I.   Employees from diverse ethnic backgrounds can reach multiple audiences.

  II.   Employees with disabilities can function as effectively as other workers.

 III.   Age diversity provides a variety of points of view that can help sales, marketing, and operations.

Planning the Introduction and Conclusion

The body of a presentation is important, but the introduction that precedes it needs just as much attention. Your introduction should take between 10 and 15 percent of the speaking time. During this short time—less than 1 minute of a 5-minute talk—your listeners form their initial impression of you and your topic. That impression, favorable or not, will affect how they react to the rest of your remarks. To be most effective, an introduction should accomplish several purposes.

Functions of the Introduction

As you have already learned, an introduction should have two parts: an attention getter and a thesis statement and preview. These two parts should accomplish five things.

Capture the Listeners' Attention
As you learned in Chapter 4, audiences don't always approach a presentation ready to listen. The topic may not seem important or interesting to them. Your listeners may have been ordered to attend your presentation. Even when the presentation is obviously important, your listeners will usually have other matters on their minds. It's vital, therefore, to begin by focusing attention on you and your topic if there is any chance that the listeners' minds are elsewhere.

Give Your Audience a Reason to Listen
The best way to grab and hold your listeners' attention is to convince them that your message will be important or interesting to them. For example, if company employees are generally satisfied with the insurance program the company has been using, they won't be interested in hearing about a new health plan that will be cheaper for the company unless you can begin by enumerating its advantages to them—for instance, that it will provide them with better emergency services. Similarly, management will be more interested in hearing your new ideas if you first say that the plans you're proposing will yield higher profits.

Set the Proper Tone for the Topic and Setting
If you want potential customers to buy more fire insurance, your opening remarks should prepare them to think seriously about the problems they would encounter if they had a fire in the house. If you want to congratulate your subordinates about their recent performance and encourage them to perform even better on the next assignment, your opening remarks should put them in a good mood—not focus on the problems you must face. In any case, your introduction should establish rapport with your listeners. Robert Moran accomplished this goal when he began his remarks to a Japanese audience:

> If I were an American and you were an American audience, I would probably begin my speech with a joke. If I were Japanese speaking to a Japanese audience, I would probably begin with an apology. Since I am neither American nor Japanese, I will begin with an apology for not telling a joke.[30]

Establish Your Qualifications
If the audience already knows that you are an expert on the subject, if a previous speaker has given you an impressive introduction, or if your authority makes it clear that you're qualified to talk, establishing credibility isn't necessary. In other cases, however, you need to demonstrate your competence quickly so that the listeners will take your remarks seriously. Nonverbal behaviors will also help boost (or diminish) your credibility. Recall the information on nonverbal communication in Chapter 4, and see additional advice on building credibility through nonverbal behavior in Chapters 12 and 13.

Introduce Your Thesis and Preview Your Presentation   In most cases, you need to state your main idea clearly at the beginning of your remarks so that your listeners know exactly what you're trying to say. In addition to your thesis statement, a preview of your main points tells your listeners where you're headed.

Accomplishing these five goals in less than 1 minute isn't as difficult as it might seem because you can accomplish several functions at the same time. For example, notice how an insurance agent introduced a 30-minute talk on an admittedly difficult topic:

> *Being an insurance agent gives me a lot of sympathy for tax collectors and dog catchers. None of us has an especially popular job. After all, it seems that with life insurance you lose either way: If the policy pays off, you won't be around to enjoy the money. On the other hand, if you don't need the policy, you've spent your hard-earned savings for nothing. Besides, insurance isn't cheap. I'm sure you have plenty of other things you could use your money for: catching up on bills, fixing up your house, buying a new car, or even taking a vacation.*
>
> *With all those negatives, why should you care about insurance? For that matter, why am I devoting my career to it? For me, the answer is easy: Over the years, I've seen literally hundreds of people–people just like you and me–learn what a difference the right kind of insurance coverage can make. And I've seen hundreds more suffer from learning too late that insurance is necessary.*
>
> *Well, tonight I want to give you some good news. I'll show you that you can win by buying insurance. You can win by gaining peace of mind, and you can even win by buying insurance that works like an investment, paying dividends that you can use here and now.*

Types of Opening Statements

Of all parts of a presentation, the opening words are the hardest for many speakers. You have to be interesting. You have to establish the right tone. Your remarks have to relate to the topic that's being discussed. And, finally, the opening statement has to feel right for you.

The kind of opening you choose will depend on your analysis of the speaking situation. With familiar topics and audiences, you may even decide to skip the preliminaries and give just a brief background before launching into the thesis and preview:

> "We've made good progress on Mr. Boynton's request to look into cost cutting steps. We've found that it is possible to reduce operating expenses by almost 10 percent without cutting efficiency. We'll be introducing six steps this morning."

In most cases, you will want to preface your remarks with some sort of opening statement. Following are seven of the most common and effective ways to begin a presentation.

Ask a Question   Asking the right question is a good way to involve your listeners in your topic and establish its importance to them.

Many speakers try to capture attention by asking the audience a **rhetorical question:** one to which the answer is obvious, and which does not really call for a response. For example, a manager who wants to whip up employee enthusiasm for a proposal that will reduce paperwork might ask, "Is it just me, or does anybody else feel like we've spent too much time filling in forms?" Rhetorical questions work well when you can be sure the audience's reaction is the one you want.

When used poorly, rhetorical questions can be risky. Beware of asking questions that listeners won't care about ("Have you ever wondered what the Sherman Antitrust Act means to you?"). Other rhetorical questions can be so thought-provoking that your

Dilbert © Scott Adams/Dist. by United Feature Syndicate, Inc. Reprinted by permission.

audience will stop listening to you: "If you had to fire three of the people who report to you, how would you decide which ones to let go?" When you decide to begin with a rhetorical question, be sure to avoid mistakes like these.

Other questions call for an overt response: "How many people here are from out of state?" "Who has had trouble meeting deadlines for sales reports?" "What do you see as the biggest threat facing the company?" If you *are* seeking an overt reaction from your listeners, be sure to let them know: "Let me see a show of hands by the people who . . ." "Hold up your program if you're among those who . . ." If you want them to respond mentally, let them know: "Answer this question for yourself. Are you sure that all of your expense reports would pass an Internal Revenue audit?"

Tell a Story   Since most people enjoy a good story, beginning with one can be an effective way to get the audience's attention, set the tone, and lead into the topic. James C. May, CEO of the Air Transport Association of America, used the story of *Apollo 13* to help his audience appreciate the dangers of global climate change, and to suggest that a solution is possible:

> With all of the turmoil we are seeing in financial markets and the world economy, it may be useful, and perhaps inspirational, to recall an event that could have been one of the great disasters in human exploration. But which instead stands as a classic example of human ingenuity and cooperation in times of crisis: the Apollo 13 mission to the moon.
>
> As the Apollo 13 spacecraft was hurtling toward the moon on April 14, 1970, it was rocked by an onboard explosion, which caused Commander Jim Lovell to utter the famous words, "Houston, we have a problem."
>
> Some problem! The blast caused a sudden loss of oxygen, power and water . . . Then, as the world watched, a new danger arose: Rapidly rising levels of carbon dioxide–CO_2–inside their tiny cabin were putting the astronauts in imminent danger of dying.
>
> With only two hours to find a solution, experts at Mission Control frantically set about building a crude but workable air filtration system. Apollo 13 never did make it to the moon. Against long odds, however, it did circle the moon and find its way home.
>
> We–meaning all of us who are inhabitants of the spaceship Earth–are looking for the same kind of safe deliverance for our planet and ourselves. On a vastly larger scale, the earth's atmosphere really is comparable to the pocket of air inside the lunar module.[31]

Present a Quotation   Quotations have two advantages: First, someone else has probably already said what you want to say in a very clever way. Second, quotations let you use a source with high credibility to back up your message.

Not every quotation has to come from a distinguished person. As long as the character you quote is appropriate for the audience and the topic, he or she can be almost anyone—even a fictional character:

> "The comic strip character Pogo once said, 'We have met the enemy, and it's us.' If you think about all the paperwork that keeps us from being more productive, that comment could describe us."

Make a Startling Statement
An excellent way to get listeners' attention is to surprise them. Sales presentations often include startling facts in their openings: "Do you know that half of all business calls never reach the intended party?" This approach will work only if your startling statement bears a clear relationship to your topic. Stephen Gardner, the assistant attorney general of Texas, used this approach in an exposé of the abuses of credit bureaus:

> *The whole credit system is frighteningly out of control. Not only are your financial matters virtually an open book, but it is an open book with a couple of pages missing, some lines crossed out, and some pieces in backwards!*[32]

Refer to the Audience
Mentioning your listeners' needs, concerns, or interests clarifies the relevance of your topic immediately and shows that you understand your listeners. For example: "I know you're all worried by rumors of cutbacks in staff. I called you here today to explain just what the budget cuts will mean to this department."

Former California governor George Deukmejian used the technique of referring to the audience in a talk to the Los Angeles Rotary Club. Deukmejian acknowledged the fact that people who listen to after-lunch speakers—even famous ones—appreciate brevity:

> *I promise not to speak for too long this afternoon. It's worth noting that the Lord's Prayer is only 56 words long. The Gettysburg Address is 226. The Ten Commandments are 297. But the U.S. Department of Agriculture's order on the price of cabbage is 15,269 words. I'll try to finish somewhere in between.*[33]

Refer to the Occasion
Sometimes the event itself provides a good starting point: "We're here today to recognize some very important people."

Sometimes you can begin by referring to some other aspect of the situation, for example, by relating your remarks to those of a previous speaker: "I was very interested in what Larry had to say about the way our expenses will rise in the next couple of years. Let's look at one way we can keep that increase as small as possible."

In a speech to employees at the U.S. Department of Justice, Attorney General Eric Holder referred to the occasion that prompted his remarks: "Every year, in February, we attempt to recognize and to appreciate black history. It is a worthwhile endeavor, for the contributions of African Americans to this great nation are numerous and significant."[34]

By referring to the occasion of Black History Month, Holder prepared his audience for the message that Americans reach out to those from different racial backgrounds:

> *Black History month is a perfect vehicle for the beginnings of such a dialogue. And so I urge all of you to use the opportunity of this month to talk with your friends and co-workers on the other side of the divide about racial matters. In this way we can hasten the day when we truly become one America.*[35]

Use Humor   The right joke can be an effective way to get attention, make a point, and increase your audience's liking for you. The vice president of an advertising agency, for example, might begin an orientation session for new management trainees with the following tale:

> *Maybe you've heard the story about the guy who smells awful all the time. When asked the reason for this he explains that it's because of his job—working in a circus giving enemas to elephants. The listener asks, "Why don't you get another job?" and the guy replies hotly, "What! And get out of show business?"*
>
> *Well, that story has some truth in our business too. Lots of people view advertising as glamorous: three-hour expense-account lunches and big commissions. Advertising is certainly a kind of show business, but along with all the glamor comes a lot of hard, messy work. I want to begin this orientation program by telling you about both the clean, easy parts and the tough, grubby ones. Then you'll have a better idea what to expect in the next months and years.*

Jokes aren't the only kind of humorous opener. Sometimes you can make an amusing remark that will set the tone perfectly for your message. For instance:

> *Some people say that problems are not problems, but rather, they are opportunities. If that's the case, then given the present situation, we are faced with a hell of a lot of opportunities.*[36]

Any humor you use should be appropriate to your topic and to the occasion. Telling a few knock-knock jokes before you launch into your financial report will draw attention—but not to your topic. The tone of your presentation could be ruined by a joke. For instance, you probably shouldn't tell a few jokes about smog and then say, "But seriously, folks, I want to talk about what we're doing to curb air pollution from our own factories."

Your jokes should also be appropriate for your audience. The inside jokes that work well with your office staff, for example, are likely to alienate clients at a contract negotiation because outsiders won't understand them. Jokes that are off-color or in any way make light of sexism, racism, or disabilities are likely to offend or embarrass someone in your audience. The risks of telling them aren't worth the laughs they might generate.

Functions of the Conclusion

With the end of your presentation in sight, it can be tempting to wrap things up with a lame comment like "That's about it." Resist the temptation to close quickly and weakly: Experts agree that your final words may create a lasting impression.[37] The conclusion of your presentation should be even shorter than the introduction: not much more than 5 percent of your total speaking time. Within those few moments, though, you must accomplish two important things: review and close. Let's look at each of these parts in detail.

The Review   Your review should contain a restatement of your thesis and a summary of your main points. Sometimes these two elements will be presented almost exactly as they appear on your outline:

> "This afternoon, I've suggested that our merchandising approach needs changing to become more profitable. I've suggested three such changes: first, to increase our newspaper advertising; second, to feature higher-quality merchandise; and third, to expand our product line in all areas."

Your review can also be a subtler rewording of the same information:

> "By now I hope you agree with me that some basic merchandising changes can improve our balance sheet. When people find out that we have a broad range of

high-quality products, I'm convinced that we'll have more customers who will spend more money."

The Closing Statement   A strong closing will help your listeners to remember you favorably; a weak ending can nullify many of your previous gains. Besides creating a favorable impression, the closing statement will give your remarks a sense of completion. You shouldn't leave your audience wondering whether you've finished. Finally, a closing statement ought to incite your listeners, encouraging them to act or think in a way that accomplishes your purpose. Let's look at several varieties of closing statements.

Types of Closing Statements

Several of the techniques used for getting attention in your introduction will also work well as closing statements:

"Will your presentation have a bloopers part at the end?"

© 2003 Ted Goff. Reprinted by permission.

> Ask a question.
>
> Tell a story.
>
> Give a quotation.
>
> Make a startling statement.
>
> Refer to the audience.
>
> Refer to the occasion.
>
> Use humor.

In addition, there are several other types of closing statements you might use.

Return to the Theme of Your Opening Statement   Coming back to where you started gives a sense of completeness to your presentation. With this approach, you should refer to your opening statement but add a new insight, further details, or a different ending:

> "At the beginning of my talk, I asked whether you might not be paying more tax than you need to. I suspect you discovered that you've been overly generous with Uncle Sam. I hope I have helped you to understand your real liability and to take advantage of some of the tax shelters available to you."

One way to capture your audience's attention is to split your story. Start, but don't finish it in your introduction. Cut off your narrative at a key point, perhaps just before the climactic finish, promising your audience that you will wrap it up in the course of your remarks.

Appeal for Action   When your goal involves getting the audience to act in a certain way, you can sometimes close your presentation by asking for your desired result:

> "So now that you know what these workshops can do, the only question is when you ought to enroll. We have openings on August 19 and on September 23. I'll be available in a moment to sign you up for either date. I'm looking forward to seeing you soon."

End with a Challenge   Whereas an appeal asks for some action, a challenge almost demands it:

> "You can go on as before, not failing completely but not doing the best possible job. Or you can use the ideas you've heard this morning to become more creative, more productive, and more successful. Why be average when you can be superior? Why settle for a few hopes when you can reach your dreams? It's up to you."

Adding Transitions

Transitions are words or sentences that connect the segments of a presentation. As Figure 10-4 shows, they work like bridges between the major parts of your remarks and tell your listeners how these parts are related. Transitions should occur between the introduction and the body, between the main points within the body, and between the body and the conclusion. The examples below illustrate each of these instances:

> "Those are big promises. Let me talk about how we can deliver on them."

> "Not all the news is bad, however. Let me tell you about some good things that happened at the conference."

> "After hearing about so many features, you may have trouble remembering them all. Let's review them briefly."

Functions of Transitions

Transitions like the preceding examples serve three important purposes.

They Promote Clarity   Clarity in speech—especially one-way speech like presentations—is more difficult to achieve than clarity in writing. The format of a letter, memo, book, or report makes its organization of ideas clear. Paragraphs, lists, different typefaces, and underlining can all emphasize how ideas are related to one another. In a presentation, however, listeners don't have the benefit of any of these aids to figure out how your ideas are put together. They have only what the verbal cues—transitional words and phrases—provide.

They Emphasize Important Ideas   Transitions within presentations highlight important information the way italics and bold type emphasize it in print:

> "Now let's turn to a third reason—perhaps the most important of all—for equipping your field representatives with electronic pagers."

> "That's what company policy says about the use of expense accounts. Now let's take a look at how things *really* work."

They Keep Listeners Interested   Transitions give momentum to a presentation. They make listeners want to find out what comes next:

> "So we gave them the best dog-and-pony show you've ever seen. And it was perfect—just like we planned. What do you think they said when we were finished?"

> "By now you're probably asking yourself what a product like this will cost. And that's the best news of all. . . ."

Purpose: After hearing this talk, the prospective customer will sign up to use Mercury as its exclusive overnight delivery service.

Thesis: Mercury is the best service to deliver your high-priority packages on time.

INTRODUCTION

    A. Overnight delivery services aren't cheap, but they are worth the expense *if* they do the job of getting important materials into the right hands quickly. [*Attention getter*]

    B. After comparing Mercury with the other delivery services, you'll see that it is the best one to do the job. [*Thesis*]

    C. As I'll explain in the next few minutes, Mercury is more reliable, convenient, and economical than the competition. [*Preview*]

Transition: Let me start by explaining why Mercury is best with the most important feature of any delivery service: reliability.

BODY

    I. Mercury is more reliable than other services.

        A. Mercury's 98 percent trouble-free record beats every other service.

        B. Other services have held up deliveries for as much as 1 week.

        C. Other services have damaged packages.

        D. In some cases, other services have even lost packages.

Transition: Besides being reliable, Mercury is the best service in another important way ...

    II. Mercury is more convenient than other services.

        A. Mercury picks up and delivers items to individual offices, not just to the mailroom like ABC Overnight.

        B. Mercury picks up or delivers packages any time between 7:00 A.M. and midnight, instead of only coming by once a day like International Air Freight.

        C. Mercury is the only service that will bill departmental accounts separately, saving you bookkeeping time.

Transition: Because it's so convenient and reliable, you might think that Mercury is more expensive than other services, but it's not.

    III. Mercury is more economical than other services.

        A. It doesn't charge extra for oddly shaped packages.

        B. It charges less than every other service for heavy packages.

        C. The shipping fee includes insurance.

Transition: By now you can see why it's worth considering Mercury as the provider of your overnight mail service ...

CONCLUSION

    A. Mercury is reliable, convenient, and economical. [*Thesis/Review*].

    B. With Mercury you won't just pay for the best service ... you'll get it.

FIGURE 10–4

A Complete Presentation Outline

Use this list to check how well your presentation is organized.

Does the **introduction**

_____ 1. Capture the attention of your audience?

_____ 2. Give your audience reasons to listen?

_____ 3. Set an appropriate tone?

_____ 4. Establish your qualifications, if necessary?

_____ 5. Introduce your thesis and preview the content?

Does the **body**

_____ 1. Use the most effective organizational pattern?

    a. Chronological

    b. Spatial

    c. Topical

    d. Cause–effect

    e. Problem–solution

    f. Criteria satisfaction

    g. Comparative advantages

    h. Motivated sequence

_____ 2. State your main points in complete sentences?

_____ 3. Use your main points to develop your thesis?

_____ 4. Contain no more than five main points?

_____ 5. Express only one idea in each main point?

_____ 6. State your main points in parallel structure if possible?

Do you have **transitions** that

_____ 1. Refer to both recent and upcoming material, showing relationships between the two?

_____ 2. Emphasize your important ideas?

_____ 3. Clarify the structure of your ideas?

_____ 4. Exist in all necessary parts of presentation?

    a. Between introduction and body

    b. Between main points within body

    c. Between body and conclusion

Does the **conclusion**

_____ 1. Review your thesis and your main points?

_____ 2. Conclude with an effective closing statement?

Characteristics of Effective Transitions

Transitions that promote clarity, emphasize important ideas, and keep listeners interested possess two characteristics. First, they refer to both preceding and upcoming ideas. A transition is like a bridge: To get listeners from one point to another, it must be anchored at both ends. By referring to what you just said and to what you'll say next, you are showing the logical relationship among those ideas. Notice the smooth connections between the ideas in these transitions:

> "Those are the problems. Now let's see what can be done about solving them."

> "Now you see that the change makes sense financially. But how will it be received by the people who have to live with it?"

If you have trouble planning a transition that links preceding and upcoming material smoothly, the reason may be that the ideas aren't logically related or the organizational plan you've chosen is flawed. Review the organizing patterns on pages 321–327 and the rules for main points on pages 329–331 to be sure that the structure of your presentation's body is logically suited to the topic.

Transitions should also call attention to themselves. You should let listeners know that you're moving from one point to another so that they will be able to follow the structure of your ideas easily. Notice how the examples you have read so far all make it clear that the presentation is shifting gears. This sort of highlighting is often due to the use of keywords:

> "The *next* important idea is . . ."

> "*Another* reason we want to make the change . . ."

> "*Finally*, we need to consider . . ."

> "To *wrap things up* . . ."

Phrases like these are not in themselves good transitions, since they do not refer to both previous and upcoming material strongly enough. But when used as part of a transition like the ones illustrated in these pages, they do signal listeners that you are moving to a new part of your presentation. A presentation checklist, covering transitions and the other organizational concepts discussed in this chapter, is presented in the Self-Assessment on page 340.

review points

- Almost everyone makes on-the-job presentations, formal and informal, for external and internal audiences. Career direction and success may depend on a speaker's reputation.
- Speakers should use a three-part analysis: First, analyze the audience. Who are the key listeners; what do they already know; what do they want to know; and what are their preferences, significant demographics, size, reason for being there, and attitudes?
- Second, speakers should analyze themselves as speakers by considering their goal for speaking, their knowledge of the subject, and the sincerity they bring to the topic.

- Finally, speakers should analyze the speaking occasion by considering the facility, the time of day and length of time they will speak, and the context in which their remarks will occur.

- A speaker's next steps are to define both general and specific goals and to create the thesis. Is the general goal to inform or persuade? The specific goal identifies who the speakers want to reach, what they want them to do, and how, when, and where they want them to act. Clear goal statements define the desired audience reaction in a specific and attainable manner.

- After defining the goal, speakers must clearly structure the thesis as a single sentence. It is the central idea and will be repeated throughout the presentation, so it is essential to design it carefully.

- Clearly organized presentations increase audience comprehension and speaker credibility by following a basic structure of introduction, body, and conclusion.

- While brainstorming for ideas, the goal statement and audience analysis serve as devices for choosing items that are appropriate for this specific presentation. These items are then arranged into main points and subpoints and into the most appropropriate organizational pattern.

- Common organizational patterns are chronological, spatial, topical, cause–effect, problem–solution, criteria satisfaction, comparative advantages, and motivated sequence.

- After the body of the presentation has been developed, an introduction is created to capture the attention of the audience, give a reason to listen, and state the thesis. The conclusion reviews the thesis and main points and closes with a strong statement.

- Finally, transitions connect the introduction to the body, the main points of the body, and the body to the conclusion. They call attention to themselves to keep listeners oriented and highlight the preceding and following material.

key terms

→ Test your understanding of these key terms by visiting the Online Learning Center Web site at www.mhhe.com/adler10e.

cause–effect pattern   323
chronological pattern   322
claim   329
comparative advantages pattern   326
criteria satisfaction pattern   325
general goal   313
motivated sequence pattern   327

problem–solution pattern   324
rhetorical question   333
spatial pattern   322
specific goal   314
thesis statement   316
topical pattern   323
transition   338

activities

Go to the self-quizzes at the Online Learning Center at www.mhhe.com/adler10e to test your knowledge of chapter concepts.

1. Invitation to Insight

Gain insights about occasion and audience analysis by interviewing a professional who frequently delivers presentations to a variety of audiences in the workplace. Ask your interviewee questions such as

a. How do you gather information about your potential audience? About the expectations of the occasion?
b. Compare the expectations of some of the various audiences you address.
c. In what ways do you adjust your presentations for these audiences?
d. What do you do if you discover that your audience members' knowledge level about your topic will vary widely?
e. How do you appeal to an audience who will probably be bored by or opposed to your topic?
f. What are some strategies for tweaking your presentation so it's appropriate to the occasion?

In class, share answers gleaned from various interviews.

2. Skill Builder

Identify the most important factors about your audience, the occasion, and yourself as a speaker that you should consider when planning a presentation to

a. Ask your boss for a raise.
b. Give instructions to a trainee.
c. Interview for a job.
d. Announce a cost increase in employee health care benefits.
e. Brief a new supervisor on the key operating procedures within your group.

3. Skill Builder

Imagine that you have been asked to give a 15-minute description of your department's functions. How would your goal and approach differ for each of the following audiences?

a. A group of new employees from all over the company.
b. New employees within the department.
c. A group of managers from other departments.
d. Several of your superiors.
e. A supplier who is helping you update equipment.
f. A group of customers touring the company.

4. Skill Builder

Write a specific-goal statement for each of the following situations. Then translate your goal into an effective thesis:

a. A farewell speech honoring a not-too-popular manager at his retirement dinner.
b. A training session introducing a new emergency evacuation plan.
c. A kickoff speech for the United Way payroll deduction campaign.
d. An appeal to the boss to hire an additional employee in your department.
e. A proposal to your department head for changing course requirements for the major.
f. A banker's speech to an economics class on the topic "The Changing Banking Industry."
g. A request to your landlord for new office carpeting.

5. Skill Builder

Write a specific goal and thesis statement for a presentation about the value of learning communication skills introduced in this book. Imagine you will be addressing your presentation to an organization you work for or a college class you're taking. What demographic information would be important to know about your audience? Which demographic information would not be relevant to your presentation? Next, identify three to five key points you would cover in your presentation.

6. Invitation to Insight

How would you enhance your credibility if you were delivering a presentation to various businesses in your community, asking them to establish internships for communications students?

7. Skill Builder

What kinds of material would you gather for a presentation on each of the following topics? Where would you find your information?

a. How changes in the cellular telephone industry will affect consumers.
b. How to begin an investment program.
c. Changing trends in the popularity of various academic courses over the last 10 years.
d. Why students should (should not) buy a personal computer.
e. Career opportunities for women in the field of your choice.

8. Skill Builder

Which organizational plan (chronological, spatial, and so on) would you use for each of the following presentations?

a. Instructions on how to file a health insurance claim form.
b. A request for time and money to attend an important convention in your field.
c. A comparison of products or services between your organization and a competitor.
d. A report on an industrial accident.
e. Suggestions on reducing employee turnover.

9. Skill Builder

Develop outlines for three of the following topics or for a topic that you are knowledgeable about, applying the rules for main points given in this chapter:

  a.   When to use small claims court.
  b.   The importance of creativity in advertising.
  c.   Renting versus leasing a car.
  d.   The proper format for a business letter.
  e.   Types of sexual harassment.
  f.   The fastest-growing jobs in the 21st century.

10. Skill Builder

Prepare an introduction and a conclusion for each of the following presentations:

  a.   A talk to employees announcing personnel layoffs.
  b.   The last in a day-long series of talks to a tired audience on maintaining and operating equipment.
  c.   An appeal to co-workers for donations to the Community Holiday Relief Fund.
  d.   A talk, the topic of which is "What Employers Look for in a College Graduate," to your class by the president of the local chamber of commerce. (Plan your concluding remarks to follow a question-and-answer period.)

resources

For extensive readings and Web sites on developing and organizing presentations, see the Online Learning Center Web site at **www.mhhe.com/adler10e.**

11

Verbal and Visual Support in Presentations

chapter outline

Functions of Supporting Material
 Clarity
 Interest
 Proof

Verbal Support
 Definitions
 Examples
 Stories
 Statistics
 Comparisons
 Quotations
 Citing Your Sources

Visual Aids
 Types of Visual Aids
 Media for Presenting Visual Aids
 Presentation Software
 Guidelines for Using Visual Aids
 Review Points
 Key Terms
 Activities
 Resources

chapter objectives

After reading this chapter, you should be able to

1. Develop and use each type of verbal aid as appropriate to add interest, clarity, and/or proof to a main point.
2. Design a visual aid appropriate for a given situation.
3. Choose the most appropriate and effective medium for presenting visual aids in a specific context.
4. Design and critique a presentation using PowerPoint or similar software.

Tom Sutcliffe was frustrated. "I know I deserve that raise," he said firmly to his friend and co-worker Tina Agapito. "I laid out all the reasons to the boss as clear as day. I've been doing the work of two people ever since Van left. My productivity is higher than anybody else's in the place. My salary is way behind the industry average. And all my clients are happy. What else does he want?"

Tina tried to be supportive. "I know you deserve the raise, Tom. And I just can't believe the boss doesn't see that too. Did you back up your claims?"

"What do you mean?" Tom replied.

"Did you give him evidence about your productivity or about how your salary compares with the industry? And did you give him some proof about all your happy clients?"

"I guess not," said Tom. "But I shouldn't have to sell myself around here. The boss ought to appreciate a good employee when he has one!"

"Maybe so," Tina answered. "But the boss hears a lot of requests for money and resources. And he's really busy. Maybe if you can make your case clearer and more interesting, you've still got a chance."

Tina's advice to Tom was good. Solid ideas won't always impress an audience. Most listeners are busy and preoccupied, and they usually don't care nearly as much about your message as you do. The kind of clear organization described in Chapter 10 will help make your presentations a success, but you often need to back up your well-organized points in a way that makes your audience take notice, understand you, and accept your message. In other words, you need to use plenty of supporting material.

Functions of Supporting Material

Supporting material is anything that backs up the claims in a presentation. You can see the relationship between these claims and supporting material in the following examples:

Claim	Support
We could increase sales by staying open until 10 P.M. on weekday evenings.	An article in *Modern Retailing* cites statistics showing that stores with extended evening hours boost profits by more than 20 percent of the direct overhead involved with the longer business day.
Replacing the ink cartridge on the printer isn't as complicated as it seems.	Here's a diagram that shows how to do it.
Taking the time to help customers will boost their loyalty and increase your commissions.	Let me read you a letter written just last week by one satisfied customer.

As these examples show, a presentation without supporting material would still be logical if it followed the organizational guidelines in Chapter 10. But it probably wouldn't achieve its goal because it would lack the information necessary to develop the ideas in a way that the audience would understand or appreciate. Carefully selected supporting material can make a presentation more effective by adding three things: clarity, interest, and proof.

Clarity

Supporting material can make abstract or complicated ideas more understandable. Notice how the following analogy clarifies how computers with point-and-click user interfaces were such a revolutionary improvement over earlier generations that relied on arcane keyboard commands:

"And that's our plan.
Any questions?"

Imagine driving a car that has no steering wheel, accelerator, brake pedal, turn signal lever, or gear selector. In place of all the familiar manual controls, you have only a typewriter keyboard.

Any time you want to turn a corner, change lanes, slow down, speed up, honk your horn, or back up, you have to type a command sequence on the keyboard. Unfortunately, the car can't understand English sentences. Instead, you must hold down a special key with one finger and type in some letters and numbers, such as "S20:TL:A35," which means, "Slow to 20, turn left, and accelerate to 35."

If you make typing mistakes, one of three things will happen. If you type an unknown command, the car radio will bleat and you will have to type the command again. If what you type happens to be wrong but is nevertheless a valid command, the car will blindly obey. (Imagine typing A95 instead of A35.) If you type something the manufacturer didn't anticipate, the car will screech to a halt and shut itself off.[1]

Interest

Supporting material can enliven a presentation by making your main points more vivid or meaningful to the audience. Notice how one attorney added interest to a summary aimed at discrediting his opponent's restatement of evidence:

> It seems that when Abe Lincoln was a young trial lawyer in Sangamon County, Illinois, he was arguing a case with a lawyer whose version of the facts came more from his imagination than the testimony. Lincoln, in his argument, turned on him and said:
>
> "Tell me, sir, how many legs has a sheep got?" "Why, four, of course," the fellow answered. "And if I called his tail a leg, then how many legs would that sheep have?" Lincoln asked. The answer came, "Then he'd have five." "No!" Lincoln roared, pounding the jury rail, "he'd still have just four legs. Calling his tail a leg won't make it a leg. Now let's look at the actual testimony and see how many tails you've been calling legs."[2]

Proof

Besides adding clarity and interest, supporting material can provide evidence for your claims and make your presentation more convincing. A speaker might use supporting materials this way to back up the claim "Employer-sponsored day care can boost productivity as well as help parents":

> A survey of Union Bank employees in California showed the value of on-site, employer-sponsored day care. Turnover of employees using the bank's on-site center was only 2.2 percent, less than one quarter of the 9.9 percent turnover for workers who used other forms of day care. And that's not all: Employees using the day care center were absent from work an average of 1.7 days a year less than other parents of young children.[3]

Whenever you use work of others to back up your claims, be sure to cite the source. Some sources, of course, are more credible than others. In the preceding paragraph, for example, the claim that employer-sponsored day care is good for employers is strengthened by citing a survey done by a respected bank. The same claim wouldn't be as persuasive coming from a survey of employees who were seeking day care, since their motives would be more self-serving.

Verbal Support

As Table 11–1 shows, many kinds of verbal supporting material can be used to add interest, clarity, or proof to a presentation. The most common supports for business and professional presentations are definitions, examples, stories, statistics, comparisons, and quotations. Consider the preferences of your audience when choosing the types of support you'll present.

Definitions

You can appreciate the need for a speaker to define unclear terms by recalling times when someone began using unfamiliar language, leaving you confused and unable to understand:

> "SQLite is a software library that implements a self-contained, serverless, zero-configuration, transactional SQL database engine. Content can be stored as INTEGER, REAL, TEXT, BLOB, or as NULL"

| Table 11–1 | Types of Verbal Support |

Type	Definition	Use	Comments
Definition	Explains meaning of a term	Clarify	Important when terms are unfamiliar to an audience or used in an uncommon way
Example	Brief reference that illustrates a point	Clarify Add interest (if sufficient number given)	Usually best in groups of two or more, if brief
Story	Detailed account of an incident	Clarify Add interest Prove (factual only)	Adapt to audience Must clearly support thesis Tell at appropriate length
Statistics	Numerical representations of point	Clarify Prove Add interest (when combined with other form of support)	Link to audience's frame of reference Use sparingly Round off Supplement with visuals, handouts
Comparisons	Examinations or processes that show how one idea resembles another	Clarify Add interest (figurative) Prove (literal)	Tailor familiar item to audience Make sure comparison is valid
Quotations	Opinion of expert or articulate source	Clarify Add interest (sometimes) Prove	May be paraphrased or read verbatim Cite source Use sources credible to audience Follow up with restatement or explanation

Definitions remove this sort of confusion by explaining the meaning of terms that are unfamiliar to an audience or are used in a specialized or uncommon way: Words can be defined by denotation, connotation, etymology (history or origin of the word), or negation (stating what it is not).

"A *smart electrical meter* doesn't just measure how much energy a customer uses. It identifies when you used it, and sends that information back to the local utility for monitoring and billing purposes."

"In the tax code, *a capital gain* is not the same as ordinary income. It is the profit that results when you sell assets like real estate or shares of stock for more than you paid for them. A *capital gains tax* is the amount government charges on that profit." (negation)

"*Bollywood* is the informal name of the Hindi language film industry based in Mumbai, India. The term is a combination of the words 'Bombay' (the old name for Mumbai) and 'Hollywood." (etymology)

Examples

Examples are brief illustrations that back up or explain a point. A speaker arguing for an enhanced package of employee benefits could cite examples of companies that already provide a variety of perks:

- Gasket maker Fel-Pro of Skokie, Illinois, contributes $3,500 annually for up to 4 years of college tuition for employees' children.
- Anheuser-Busch employees take home two free cases of beer a month.
- Employees of Ben & Jerry's take home three free pints of ice cream a day.
- Apple Computer gives its employees 6-week paid sabbaticals every 5 years.[4]

Likewise, a marketing consultant explaining how the name of a business can attract customers could back up the claim by citing examples of clever names:

- Totally Twisted, a Maryland pretzel company.
- Now Showing, a movie theater turned lingerie shop in Oklahoma.
- Access/Abilities, a California firm that helps people with disabilities.[5]

The same consultant could show how poor names can discourage business:

- Coffin Air Service.
- Big Bill's Plumbing.
- Bland Farms, a mail-order food company.[6]

In many cases you don't need to look outside your own experience for examples to back up a point. Union members claiming that "management cares more about buildings and grounds than employees" might back up their claim by offering examples:

We keep hearing that "employees are our most important asset," yet we don't see dollars reflecting that philosophy. In the 2.5 years since our last pay raise, we have seen the following physical improvements at this site alone: a new irrigation system for the landscaping, renovation of the corporate offices, expansion of the data processing wing, resurfacing of all the parking lots, and a new entrance to the building. Now all those improvements are helpful, but they show that buildings and grounds are more important than people.

When they are used to prove a point, examples are most effective when several are given together. If you are supporting the claim that you are capable of taking on a more challenging job, it is best to remind your boss of several tasks you have handled well. After all, a single example could be an isolated instance or a lucky fluke.

Stories

Stories illustrate a point by describing an incident in some detail. Almost everyone loves to hear a good story. It adds interest and, when well chosen, it can drive home a point better than logic and reasoning alone.[7]

This account of a farmer and his children shows how stories can make a powerful point—in this case, a farmer's contrast between conventional agriculture and an organic approach:

When I worked for a conventional farm, I would come home and my kids would want to hug me. They couldn't because I had to shower first and my clothes had to be removed and disinfected. Today, I can walk right off the field into the waiting arms of my kids because there's nothing toxic on my body to harm them.[8]

Storytelling to Make a Point

Well-chosen and well-told stories can help you make a point in an interesting and compelling way. In a brief presentation of 2 minutes or less, use a story to illustrate an important lesson regarding professional communication. The story you tell may be based on your personal experience, something you observed, or something you read or heard about from others.

Organize your presentation in one of two ways: Either state your thesis first and then show how the story supports it or tell the story first, and then show how it illustrates your thesis. In either case, conclude by showing audience members how your thesis and the story that illustrates it relate to their professional lives.

As the consultant who retold this story explained, "While data are obviously important and must support your story, you have to touch hearts before you can influence minds."[9]

Research bears out the power of stories to reach an audience. In a study exploring effective ways to persuade listeners, one group of subjects was presented with statistical information like "Food shortages in Malawi are affecting more than 3 million children." A second group was shown the photo of a 7-year-old Malian girl named Rokia, and told that she is desperately poor, and that "her life will be changed for the better by your gift." People in the second group gave significantly more.[10]

Stories come in three categories: fictional, hypothetical, and factual. *Fictional stories* allow you to create material that perfectly illustrates the point you want to make. This fictional story uses humor to help listeners understand the importance of being proactive in business:

In Greece there is an old monastery perched on top of a high mountain, with steep cliffs on every side. The only way to visit it is to get in a wicker basket and have a monk pull you up by ropes.

One visitor noticed that this rope—the one his life depended on—was old and quite frayed. He asked the monk, "When do you change the rope?" The monk replied, "Whenever it breaks."

After the laughter died down, the speaker used this story to make his point:

In this company we don't wait until the rope breaks. We don't even let it fray. We fix things before they become hazards.[11]

Other stories are *hypothetical:* "Imagine yourself. . . ," "Think about a typical customer . . . ," and "What would you do if . . ." Besides being involving, hypothetical stories allow you to create a situation that illustrates exactly the point you are trying to make. You can adjust details, create dialogue, and use figures that support your case. But your account will be effective only if it is believable.

A representative explaining the concept of "Guaranteed Account Value" in a variable annuity investment might use a hypothetical example like this:

Suppose you were unlucky enough to have a nasty accident that kept you from working for 6 months. Imagine dealing with the pain and inconvenience of your injuries. Then imagine yourself trying to cope with your loss of income. Would you have enough money saved to support yourself and the people who are counting on you? Would you have enough insurance coverage to make up for your lost income?

Factual stories can also add interest and clarity. The story below, from a frustrated consumer, illustrates the thesis that many businesses are more interested in making a sale than in supporting their products after the deal is closed. Notice how the last sentence restates the main idea so that the point of the story is clear:

> *Last Tuesday I decided to call the automobile dealership. There were two numbers listed in the phone book, one for "Sales," the other for "Service." I asked the service manager if I could bring my car in the following Saturday. Service managers always have a way of making you feel unwanted, and he seemed pleased to be able to tell me that they were closed Saturday and wouldn't be able to take me until a week from Thursday.*
>
> *I didn't make a date. Instead I called the other number, under "Sales." "Are you open Saturday?" I asked. "Yes, sir," the cheery voice said at the other end of the phone. "We're here Saturdays from eight in the morning till nine in the evening, and Sundays from noon until six."*
>
> *Now, if I can buy a car on Saturday, why can't I get one fixed on Saturday? What's going on here anyway? I think I know what's going on, of course. We're selling things better than we're making them, that's what's going on.*[12]

While both factual and fictional stories can make a presentation clearer and more interesting, only the factual type can prove a point:

> "Cutting the payroll by using temporary employees sounds like a good idea, but it has problems. Listen to what happened when we tried it at the place I used to work. . . ."

> "I'm sure Wes can handle the job. Let me tell you what happened last year when we assigned him to manage the Westco account. . . ."

> "You might think life insurance isn't necessary for a young, healthy person like you, but remember Dale Crandall, the linebacker from State? Well, he was about as healthy as they come, but . . ."

Whether they are fictional, or factual, effective stories possess several characteristics.[13] First, they should be relatively brief: Don't spin out a 5-minute yarn to make a minor point. They should also be interesting and appropriate for your audience: A story that offends your listeners will be memorable, but not in the desired way. Most important, a story must support the point you are trying to make. An amusing story that doesn't support your thesis will just distract your listeners.[14]

Dilbert: © Scott Adams/Dist. by United Feature Syndicate, Inc. Reprinted by permission.

Statistics

Statistics are numbers used to represent an idea. Most statistics are collections of examples reduced to numerical form for clarity. If you were arguing that there was a serious manu-facturing problem with a new product line, describing one or two dissatisfied customers would not prove that the problem went beyond the usual "acceptable" rate of error in manufacturing. The following statement, though, would constitute proof: "Our return rate on the new line is just over 40 percent—as opposed to the usual rate of 5 percent—and of all those returns, four-fifths are related to a flaw in the gear assembly." Statistics are a common form of support in business presentations. They are used to measure the size of market segments, sales trends, decreasing or increasing profits, changes in costs, and many other aspects of business.

When handled well, statistics are especially strong proof because they are firmly grounded in fact and because they show that the speaker is well informed.[15] Consider this example:

> The U.S. Census Bureau reports that people with a bachelor's degree earn an average of 62 percent more than those with only a high school diploma. Over a lifetime, the gap in earning potential between a high school grad and someone with a B.A. is more than a million dollars. These figures show that whatever sacrifices you make for a college education in the short term are worth it in the long term.

Despite their potential effectiveness, poorly used statistics can spoil a presentation. One common mistake is to bury an audience under an avalanche of numbers like this speaker did at an annual stockholders' meeting:

> Last year was an exciting one for our company. We earned $6.02 per share on a net income of $450 million, up from $4.63 per share on income of $412 million in the preceding year. This increase came in part from a one-time gain of $13 million from the sale of common stock to New Ventures group, our research and development subsidiary. Excluding this one-time gain, we increased our earnings per share 5.8 percent in the recent year, and we increased our net income 6.5 percent.

These numbers would be very appropriate in a printed annual report, but when a speaker rattles them off one after another, there is little chance that audience members will follow them. Rather than smothering your listeners with detail, you can provide a few key numbers in your presentation, if necessary backed up by accompanying written materials.

> As the report you're holding details, last year was a good one for us. Earnings per share were up almost 6 percent, our net income grew by 6.5 percent, on top of a $13 million one-time gain.

As this example shows, it's usually best to simplify information by rounding off numbers. It's easier to understand "almost two-thirds" than it is to absorb "64.3 percent," and "almost twice the cost" is easier to grasp than is "Item A costs $65.18, while item B runs $127.15."

Besides having too many numbers, statistic-laden presentations are too dry for all but the most dedicated and involved audiences to handle. When you are speaking to a group of nonspecialists, it's important to link your figures to a frame of reference the group will understand. Notice how the following statistics (presented in the form of examples) give new impact to the old principle that time is money:

> For a manager who is earning $30,000 a year, wasting one hour a day costs the company $3,750 a year. . . . And for a $100,000-a-year executive, a two-hour lunch costs the company an extra $12,500 annually.[16]

When a presentation contains more than a few statistics, you will probably need to use visual aids to explain them: Numbers alone are simply too confusing to understand. The material on pages 360–364 offers guidelines about how to present statistical data graphically.

Comparisons

Comparisons can make a point by showing how one idea resembles another. Some comparisons—called analogies—are *figurative*. They compare items from an unfamiliar area with items from a familiar one. By considering a few examples, you can appreciate the value of figurative comparisons to add clarity and interest to a presentation:

> "The cheap special fares advertised by some airlines are misleading, since the 'mouse print' at the bottom of the page lists so many restrictions. No food chain could get away with advertising prime rib at $3 a pound, limited to six roasts per store, available only when bought in pairs Tuesday through Thursday afternoons."[17]

> U.S. senator Mitch McConnell used a comparison to illustrate the magnitude of spending in a multi-trillion-dollar bill before Congress: ". . . if you had spent a million dollars every day since Jesus was born, you still wouldn't have spent a trillion."[18]

By linking the familiar with the unfamiliar, figurative analogies can also help listeners understand concepts that would otherwise be mystifying. One speaker used a figurative comparison to explain a limitation of cable modem Internet connections in terms easily understandable by non-experts:

> *Remember what happens when you're taking a shower and someone turns on another faucet or flushes the toilet? The flow of water drops for everybody. A similar thing happens with the flow of data over an Internet connection: When more people are using the system, the speed at which data flows is slower.*

Management consultants and authors have used a wide variety of comparisons to suggest how organizations can be more effective. For example, a book called *Judo Strategy* suggests that small organizations can out-compete giant competitors just like a lightweight judo master can defeat a larger opponent.[19] Other writers have shown how businesses can be more effective by resembling winning sports teams, military strategists, and even ant colonies.[20] It's easy to imagine how each of these comparisons helps clarify the concept being explained.

Other comparisons are *literal*, linking similar items from two categories. An account executive might use this sort of comparison to argue, "We need to spend more of our advertising budget on direct mail. That approach worked wonders on the NBT campaign, and I think it can do the same for us here."

After an explosion killed 12 in a West Virginia coal mine, some observers used a comparison to argue that weak federal laws make it financially worthwhile for mine owners to break safety rules:

> *Driving solo in a California carpool lane carries a bigger fine than allowing combustible materials to accumulate in a coal mine.*[21]

Whenever you propose adopting a policy or using an idea because it worked well somewhere else, you are also using comparisons as proof. The strength of this proof will depend on how clearly you can establish the similarity between the items you are comparing.

Cherrypicking Support?

Imagine you are planning a sales presentation to a prospective client. To back up your claims that the product or service you are offering is outstanding, you know you need to use examples of outstanding service and testimonials of satisfied customers. You do have a few good examples of each, but sadly they aren't representative of the kind of feedback your organization usually receives. It would be easier to come up with examples and complaints that reflect unhappy clients.

How can you reconcile the need to be honest with the desire to sign up a new customer?

Whether their purpose is to add clarity, interest, or proof, comparisons should possess two characteristics: First, the familiar part of comparisons should be well known to the audience. For instance, it would be a mistake to say "Jumbo certificates of deposit are similar to Treasury bills in several ways" if your listeners don't know anything about Treasury bills. Second, you should be sure your comparisons are valid. You would be stretching a point if you tried to discourage employee abuse of the copying machine by claiming, "Using the machine for personal papers is a crime, just as much as robbery or assault." A closer match is both more valid and effective: "You wouldn't help yourself to spare change from a cash register; everybody with a conscience knows that would be a case of petty theft. But using the copying machine for personal papers costs the company, just as surely as if the money came out of the cash register."

Quotations

Quotations use the words of others who are authoritative or articulate to help you make a point more effectively than you could on your own. Some quotations add clarity and impact. You might, for example, add punch to a talk on the importance of listening to customer complaints by citing a successful businessperson like Bill Gates, founder of Microsoft: "Your most unhappy customers are your greatest source of learning." Likewise, you could emphasize the importance of getting agreements in writing by quoting movie producer Sam Goldwyn: "A verbal contract isn't worth the paper it's written on." Or you might repeat the words of Oprah Winfrey about taking responsibility for your own success:

> I don't think of myself as a poor deprived ghetto girl who made good. I think of myself as somebody who from an early age knew I was responsible for myself, and I had to make good.[22]

Some quotations are too long, boring, or confusing to read word-for-word. In these cases, you can still take advantage of the material by paraphrasing it, as in this example:

> Before we go overboard on the idea of flexible scheduling, it's important to consider the research conducted recently by Professors Graham Staines of Rutgers University and Joseph Pleck of Wellesley College. In a survey of over 1,000 employees, they found that people who worked modified schedules were not as happy with their family lives as were people who worked a traditional Monday through Friday, 9-to-5 shift.

Citing Your Sources

Whether you are quoting someone or using a statistic, it's both proper and effective to cite the source. Showing that your ideas are based on authoritative sources boosts your credibility.

Here is a simple four-step method for citing sources without interrupting the flow of your presentation:

1. *State your point:* "The trend of working from home is growing."

2. *Identify the source of your citation:* "In the March 12 edition of *USA Today* columnist Stephanie Armour states that . . ."

3. *State the content of your citation:* "Just about anyone with a high-speed Internet connection and a telephone can become a virtual free agent, handling customer service calls for major corporations."

4. *Explain how and why the material is important for members of your audience:* "That means almost everybody in this room has the potential to work from home, whether while you are going to school, raising a child, or have limited mobility."

Use the following guidelines to cite sources.

Cite the Source in a Way That Adds to the Credibility of Your Presentation
Notice how the citations in this section introduce their source, and consider how much less effective they would be without this sort of introduction.

Cite Sources That Have Credibility with Your Audience
Citing Karl Marx about the abuse of workers won't impress an audience of Republican manufacturers, whereas a similar message from an article in *The Wall Street Journal* might be effective.

Restate the Point of Long Citations
If your citation takes a long time to deliver, summarize the point it makes before moving on:

"After hearing Roberta's figures, you can see that our advertising dollars are well spent."

"You can see from this research that there are hidden costs in this proposal."

"Customer letters like those make it clear that we need to improve our service."

Visual Aids

The old cliché is true: A picture often *is* worth a thousand words. That is why charts, diagrams, and other graphic aids are part of most business presentations.

Researchers have verified what good speakers have always known intuitively: Using visual aids makes a presentation more effective. In one study, two groups of business students watched videotaped presentations describing upcoming time-management seminars. One group saw a version of the talk with no visual support, while the other saw the same talk with a number of high-quality visuals. After the presentation, audience members were asked about their willingness to enroll in the time-management course and about their opinion of the speaker they had just viewed.

Audience members who saw the presentation with visuals were clearly more impressed than those who saw the same talk with no visual support. They planned to spend 16.4 percent more time and 26.4 percent more money on the time-management seminar being promoted. They also viewed the speaker as more clear, concise, professional, persuasive, and interesting.[23]

Well-designed graphics are also easier to understand than words alone. A chart listing a point-by-point comparison of two products is easier to follow than a detailed narrative. A plummeting sales curve tells the story more eloquently than any words. You can appreciate

Mosquitoes Create a Buzz over Bill Gates' Speech

Microsoft founder Bill Gates is passionate about eliminating the scourge of malaria from the world. The disease kills millions of people each year, but Gates told an elite California audience that it's hard for Westerners to appreciate the impact of the disease because the majority of deaths occur in the developing world.

Then Gates used a unique strategy to show his listeners the risk faced by so many less fortunate people in tropical parts of the world. "There's no reason only poor people should have the experience," he calmly remarked as he opened a jar and released a swarm of mosquitoes. Nervous laughter erupted as the tiny insects flew into the audience.

The stir caused by the mosquito stunt was immediate and widespread. Audience members tweeted the news into cyberspace, where it spread around the world faster than any infectious disease.

Gates' simple strategy of using mosquitoes as props dramatized his point far more effectively than would otherwise have been possible.

CRITICAL ANALYSIS:

1. Gates' mosquito stunt obviously made his speech more interesting. Did it also make his material more clear? How well did it help prove his thesis? Did it further his goal of advancing the cause of malaria prevention?

2. Imagine that Gates had not reassured his audience immediately that the mosquitoes were malaria-free. What (if any) responsibility does a speaker have to protect an audience from becoming disturbed or upset?

Source: Bill Gates, "How I'm trying to change the world now." Speech delivered at the TED conference, Long Beach, California, February 4, 2009. Retrieved March 10, 2009 from **www.ted.com/talks/bill_gates_unplugged.html.**

the value of visuals to make a point quickly and clearly by reading the text below alone and then sketching out a chart that would make the point much more vividly:

> *The power of tax-free accumulation is tremendous. Suppose you invested $10,000 at 10 percent. If you were taxed at a rate of 33 percent, your investment would grow to $35,236 over 20 years. If you were in the 28 percent tax bracket, your original nest egg would grow to $40,169. But with a tax-free investment, the original $10,000 would appreciate to a value of $67,275.*

Visuals can help make complicated statistics easier for you to explain and easier for your listeners to understand. Besides increasing the clarity of your material, visuals will make your presentations more interesting. For example, investment brokers often use an array of well-prepared charts, tables, models, and so on to add variety to information that would be deadly dull without it.

Visuals can also boost your image in ways that extend beyond the presentation itself. A professional display of visuals labels you as a professional person—a candidate for recognition in the future by superiors and the public. Finally, visuals can make your information more memorable. Researchers have discovered that audiences recall far more information when it is presented both verbally and visually than when it is presented in only one way:[24]

Visual aids perform many useful functions:

- They can *show how things look*. An architect might use a model or an artist's sketch to describe a project to potential clients, and an advertising director could use photographs of a new product as part of a campaign.

- They can *show how things work*. An engineer could include diagrams as part of the instructions for a piece of equipment, and a sales representative could use a model to show how a boat is designed for speed and safety.

- They can *show how things relate to one another*. An organizational chart provides a clear picture of the reporting relationships in a company; a flowchart pictures the steps necessary to get a job done.

- They can *emphasize important points*. You might use a chart to show customers the features of a new product or develop a graph to show the performance of a stock.

Types of Visual Aids

As a speaker, you can choose from a wide array of visual aids to make your presentations more effective. You won't use them all every time you speak, but sooner or later you will, in your presentations, use almost every type described in the following pages.

Objects and Models   As the Case Study on page 358 shows, there are times when objects can add interest, clarity and proof to your topic. This is certainly true in training sessions and in some types of selling, where hands-on experience is essential. It's difficult to imagine learning how to operate a piece of equipment without actually giving it a try, and few customers would buy an expensive, unfamiliar piece of merchandise without seeing it demonstrated.

When you do use an object or model for instructional purposes, be sure the item is large enough for everyone to see. Small items like a microchip or a piece of jewelery can work in a one-on-one presentation, but this approach will only frustrate a larger group of listeners. It is almost always a bad idea to pass an object around for the audience to examine. Doing so will probably distract both the person who has the object at a given moment and the other people who are craning their necks to get a preview.

Photographs   Photographs can be the most effective means of illustrating a variety of images that need literal representation: an architectural firm's best work, a corporation's management team, or a stylish new product. Photographs also provide an

FIGURE 11–1
Floor Plan

FIGURE 11–2
Drawing

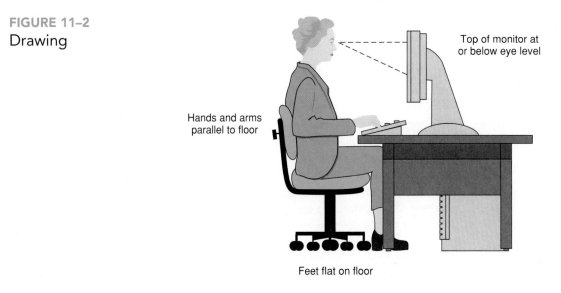

Top of monitor at
or below eye level

Hands and arms
parallel to floor

Feet flat on floor

excellent form of proof. For instance, an insurance investigator's picture of a wrecked auto may be all that exists of a car months later, when a claim is argued in court.

Diagrams   Diagrams are abstract, two-dimensional drawings that show the important properties of objects without being completely representational. Types of diagrams you might use in presentations include floor plans (see Figure 11–1 on page 359), drawings (see Figure 11–2), and maps (see Figure 11–3). Diagrams are excellent for conveying information about size, shape, and structure.

Lists and Tables   Lists and tables are effective means of highlighting key facts and figures. They are especially effective when you list steps, highlight features, or compare

FIGURE 11–3
Map

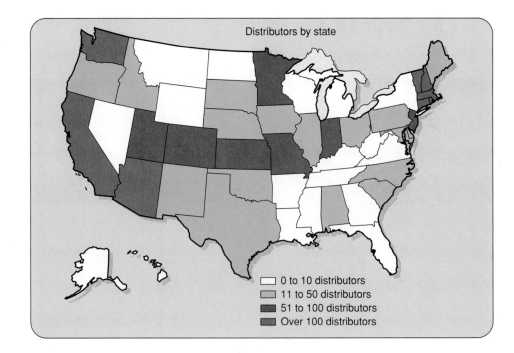

Distributors by state

☐ 0 to 10 distributors
☐ 11 to 50 distributors
☐ 51 to 100 distributors
☐ Over 100 distributors

College Costs, 1996–2009

	Private 4-Year	Public 4-Year	Public 2-Year
1996–97	$12,994	$2,975	$1,465
1999–2000	$15,518	$3,362	$1,649
2002–03	$18,060	$4,098	$1,674
2005–06	$21,235	$5,491	$2,191
2008–09	$25,143	$6,585	$2,402

FIGURE 11–4

Table

related facts: advantages and disadvantages, current and past performance, your product versus a competitor's, and so on. The table in Figure 11–4 shows how the cost of a college education has increased over time. A sales manager might use a similar chart to compare this year's sales performance and last year's in several regions.

Amateur speakers often assume they need only enlarge tables from a written report for an oral presentation. In practice, this approach rarely works. Most written tables are far too detailed and difficult to understand to be useful to a group of listeners. As you design lists and tables for presentation, remember the following points:

- *Keep the visual aid simple.* List only highlights. Use only keywords or phrases, never full sentences.

- *Use numbered and/or bulleted lists to emphasize key points.* Numbered lists suggest ranking or steps in a process, while bulleted lists work best for items that are equally important.

- *Use text sparingly.* If you need more than eight lines of text, create two or more tables. Lines of text should never exceed 25 characters across, including spaces.

- *Use large type.* Make sure that the words and numbers are large enough to be read by everyone in the audience.

- *Enhance the list's or table's readability.* Careful layout and generous use of white space will make it easy to read.

Pie Charts

Pie charts like the one in Figure 11–5 illustrate component percentages of a single item. Frequently, they are used to show how money is spent. They also can illustrate the allocation of resources. For example, a personnel director might use a pie chart to show the percentage of employees who work in each division of the company.

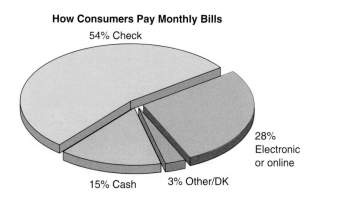

How Consumers Pay Monthly Bills

54% Check

28% Electronic or online

15% Cash

3% Other/DK

FIGURE 11–5

Pie Chart

FIGURE 11–6
Bar Chart

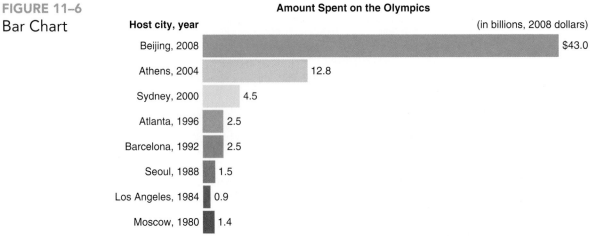

FIGURE 11–6
Bar Chart

Follow these guidelines when constructing pie charts:

- *Place the segment you want to emphasize at the top-center* (12 o'clock) *position* on the circle. When you are not emphasizing any segments, organize the wedges from largest to smallest, beginning at 12 o'clock with the largest one.
- *Label each segment,* either inside or outside the figure.
- *List the percentage for each segment* as well as its label.

Bar and Column Charts   **Bar charts** like the one shown in Figure 11–6 compare the value of several items: the productivity of several employees, the relative amount of advertising money spent on different media, and so on. Simple **column charts** reflect changes in a single item over time. Multiple-column charts like the one in Figure 11–7 compare several items over time.

FIGURE 11–7
Multiple-Column
Chart

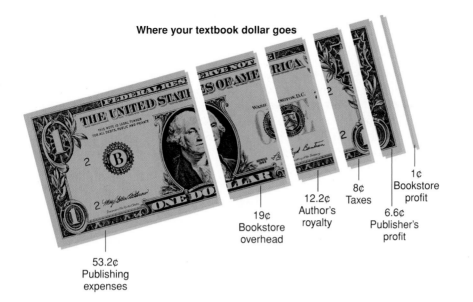

Where your textbook dollar goes

53.2¢
Publishing
expenses

19¢
Bookstore
overhead

12.2¢
Author's
royalty

8¢
Taxes

6.6¢
Publisher's
profit

1¢
Bookstore
profit

FIGURE 11–8
Pictogram

Several tips will help you design effective bar and column charts:

- *Always represent time on the horizontal axis* of your chart, running from left to right.

- *Arrange the bars in a sequence* that best suits your purpose. You might choose to order them from high to low, from low to high, in alphabetical order, or in order of importance.

- *Make sure the numerical values represented are clear.* This may mean putting the numbers next to bars or columns. In other cases, the figures will fit inside the bars. In a few instances, the scale on the axes will make numbering each bar unnecessary.

Pictograms   **Pictograms** are artistic variations of bar, column, or pie charts. As Figure 11–8 shows, pictograms are more interesting than ordinary bars. This makes them useful in presentations aimed at lay audiences such as the general public. Pictograms are often not mathematically exact, however, which makes them less suited for reports that require precise data.

Graphs   **Graphs** show the correlation between two quantities. They are ideally suited to showing trends, such as growth or decline in sales over time. They can also represent a large amount of data without becoming cluttered. Graphs can chart a single trend, or show relationships among two or more trends like the one in Figure 11–9. Notice in

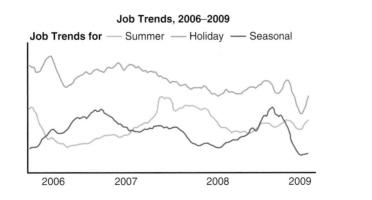

Job Trends, 2006–2009

Job Trends for —— Summer —— Holiday —— Seasonal

2006   2007   2008   2009

FIGURE 11–9
Multiple-Line
Graph

Figure 11-10 how identical data can be manipulated by adjusting the horizontal and vertical axes.

Video   There are times when video support is a plus. If you are illustrating action—the performance of an athletic team or the gestures of a speaker, for example—video may do the job better than any other medium.

Despite the benefits of video, including footage that you pull off Web sites like YouTube or create yourself can be risky. Problems with amateur work include segments that last too long and lack continuity, casting the rest of your message in an unprofessional light.

Media for Presenting Visual Aids

Choosing the most advantageous way to present your visual aids is just as important as picking the right type. The best photograph, chart, or diagram will flop if it isn't displayed effectively.

Chalk- and Dry-Erase Marker Boards   When these boards are available in a presentation room, they can be useful for recording information that comes up on the spot, such as brainstorming ideas or a tally of audience responses to your questions. When you're presenting preplanned visuals, though, it's usually best to use a medium that doesn't require you to turn your back on the audience and write or draw freehand.

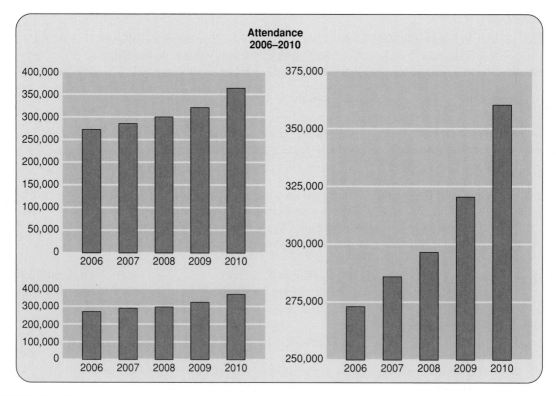

FIGURE 11–10

The same data can be distorted by varying the horizontal and vertical size and axes of a graph. These graphs were created using Microsoft PowerPoint.

Instead of using a chalk or whiteboard, consider large-size Post-it notes. This makes it easy for you (or other participants) to recategorize the ideas without having to erase and rewrite them. Also, you can take the sticky notes with you at the end of your talk as a record of the points.

Flip Charts and Poster Board
Flip charts consist of a large pad of paper attached to an easel. You reveal visuals on a flip chart one at a time by turning the pages. You can also produce visuals on rigid poster board, which you can display on the same sort of easel.

A major advantage of flip charts and poster displays is that they are relatively simple to prepare and easy to use. Their low-tech nature eliminates the risk of equipment problems. Also, you can create them with familiar materials: pens, rulers, and so on. Most copy shops can also turn computer-generated files into high-quality posters. In addition, flip charts and poster boards are relatively portable (most easels collapse into a carrying case) and easy to set up. Despite these advantages, the size of flip charts and poster boards is a problem: They may be too small for easy viewing and too large to transport easily.

Transparencies and Photographic Slides
Transparencies are clear sheets, usually the size of standard business paper, that are used with an overhead projector to cast an image on a screen. Transparencies can be produced quickly in a copy machine or printer, are visible in a lighted room, and you can draw on them as you speak. But in the digital age, transparencies may seem old-fashioned and they require a bulky projector that may not even be available.

Photographic **slides** are projected on a screen like overhead transparencies. They work best when you want to show an actual photographic image. You can add, delete, and rearrange them to suit the needs of a particular presentation. On the other hand, viewing slides requires a bulky projector and a darkened room. While the projector is on, the speaker is only a shadowy figure to the audience. You are probably better off displaying photographic images via a computer and data projector, as described below.

Computer Displays
With a computer and data projector you can present a wealth of material: text photos, charts, graphs, and video. With the right setup, you can even use a computer to create visuals during your presentation: a Web site demonstration, for example, or a brainstorming list. It's easy to transport the data you want to project on a flash drive or other portable storage device.

With all computer-supported presentations keep Murphy's Law in mind: Whatever can go wrong with the system probably will. Beware of compatibility problems. Test all parts of the system together, just as you plan to use it, ideally in the place where you will speak. A sophisticated display is useless if it doesn't work when you are standing in front of an expectant audience.

Handouts
Handouts provide a permanent record of your ideas. Intricate features of a product, names and phone numbers, or "do's and don'ts" are easier to recall when your listeners have a printed record of them. Handouts also enable you to give your audience more details than you want to talk about in your presentation. You might, for instance, mention the highlights of a sales period or briefly outline the technical features of a new product and then refer your listeners to a handout for further information.[25]

You can use handouts to reduce or eliminate your listeners' need to take notes. If you put key ideas and figures on a handout, listeners' attention will be focused on you instead of on their notebooks—and you'll be sure their notes are accurate. Some speakers

Finding Photographs and Videos

Anyone with an Internet connection and Web browser can search among millions of online photos and videos quickly and easily by using Google, YouTube, and other Web sites. Once on Google's home page, type in a description of the photo or drawing you are seeking and click on "Images" or "Video" right above the search box. To refine your search, click on "Advanced" and enter the criteria into the on-screen form. Once you activate your search, your screen will display a list of thumbnail photos of the images or video stills. Click on any images that you want to view more closely and a larger version will appear.

When you have found an image you want to use in your presentation, you can copy and paste it into PowerPoint or another presentation program, or you can save it for future use.

Be sure to give credit to the source for any photos or videos you use, and honor any restrictions that are posted on the Web site where you find an image or footage.

use an "electronic blackboard," a plastic write-and-wipe board that can produce hand-out-sized copies of what you've written on the board. Environmentally astute presenters may save paper and boost portability by e-mailing handouts after the presentation or posting them online.

The biggest problem with handouts is that they can be distracting. The activity that accompanies passing around papers interrupts the flow of your presentation. Once the handout is distributed, you'll have to compete with it for your audience's attention. For this reason, it's better to distribute handouts *after* you've finished speaking. If printed material has to be introduced during your presentation, tell your listeners when to begin referring to it and when to stop: "Let's take a look at the budget on the pink sheet in your folders. . . . Now that we've examined the budget, let me direct your attention to the chart up here."

Presentation Software

Presentation software such as Microsoft PowerPoint and Apple's Keynote allow anyone with a computer to create and deliver a professional-looking presentation with text and visuals.

Advantages of Presentation Software

Presentation software helps speakers in many ways by enabling them to generate customized materials on an as-needed basis. Listed below are some of the things you can do with a good software program:

- Deliver an on-screen show with special effects such as smooth transitions between screens, animation, and synchronized timing that reveals each point as you raise it.
- Organize a set of speaker's notes for yourself.
- Prepare a variety of handouts for your audience, based on your speaking notes or displays.
- Create "run-time" versions of your displays so that you can distribute copies of your presentation to people who may not have seen you speak.
- Create charts, graphs, and tables.

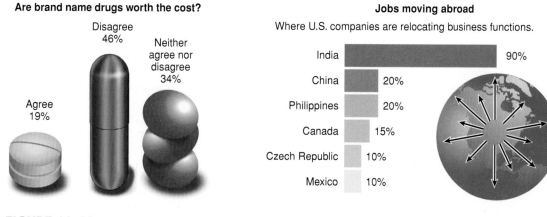

FIGURE 11–11

Spicing Up PowerPoint Slides

Source: In "MARS 2003 OTC/DTC survey," *USA Today*, June 11, 2003, pp. A1, B1.

Microsoft PowerPoint is the dominant program in this field, chosen by over 90 percent of the speakers who use presentation software.[26] According to Microsoft's estimate, over 30 million PowerPoint presentations are made every day.[27] Like all presentation software programs, PowerPoint allows you to create and display information in both outline and slide formats. Figure 11–11 illustrates how presentation software can enhance the display of information by importing and manipulating art from the Internet or other sources.

Although computer-assisted design can be very effective, it isn't foolproof. Even basic presentation software programs—like their word processing and spreadsheet cousins—take time to learn. If you are using such a program for the first time, prepare to invest an hour or two of study and practice before turning out a finished product. It's even better to get the help of a friend or co-worker who is already skilled with a design program. Such help can save you a great deal of the time and frustration you would otherwise experience in trial-and-error experimenting or leafing through an instruction book.

Once you have mastered a program, it is important to resist the temptation to overuse it. In most presentations, simplicity is a virtue. Just because it is *possible* to produce an elaborate visual full of detail doesn't mean that this sort of display will communicate your message effectively. For example, the three-dimensional chart in Figure 11–12 is probably as complex as a visual display should be—at least in an oral presentation. If it were any more complex, the figure would be hard to understand in the limited time available for viewing. Detailed visuals may be appropriate for written reports, but in oral talks simplicity is usually the best approach.

Dangers of Presentation Software   Every competent speaker should be able to use presentation software when the need arises. But, like any form of technology, PowerPoint and its cousins can cause new problems at the same time they solve old ones.[28] You should avoid several pitfalls of computerized design programs.

Poorly conceived messages   Presentation software makes it relatively easy to create charts and graphs, import images, integrate snappy animation, and wrap them all up in a handsome design; but if the structure of your presentation isn't clear, listeners won't understand your message or believe what you say. For this reason, it is essential

FIGURE 11–12

Displaying Data

Most presentational software programs can display data in a variety of formats. The best exhibits illustrate a point clearly without becoming too complex.

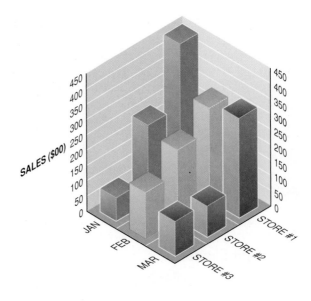

that you organize your points clearly and back up your claims before you begin transferring your message to software. Resist the temptation to format your ideas with presentation software before you have a structure that follows one of the organizational plans in Chapter 10 and make sure your points are backed up with the kinds of supporting material described earlier in this chapter.

Design over content   A common mistake is to spend more time on the design of a presentation than its content. Even the most handsome slides won't make up for weak ideas. Design expert Edward Tufte says,

> If your numbers are boring, then you've got the wrong numbers. If your words or images are not on point, making them dance in color won't make them relevant. Audience boredom is usually a content failure, not a decoration failure.[29]

There is something seductive about the ease with which you can tinker with fonts, backgrounds, and transitions. Before you know it, you will have spent far too much time without much additional return. As one expert put it:

> We've got highly paid people sitting there formatting slides—spending hours formatting slides—because it's more fun to do that than concentrate on what you're going to say. . . . Millions of executives around the world are sitting there going "Arial? Times Roman? Twenty-four point? Eighteen point?"[30]

Again, the best way to avoid the seduction of favoring form over content is to create at least a rough outline of your material before you start using your presentation software.

Overly complex presentations   Just because you *can* use presentation software to create elaborate computer productions doesn't mean you always *should*

"My presentation lacks power and it has no point. I assumed the software would take care of that!"

use it. A digital display may dazzle your audience, but the spectacle might actually draw attention away from you and your message. It's hardly a success if listeners remember your terrific graphics and elaborate animation, but can't recall the points you made.

Another danger of overly elaborate presentations is the possibility that they will make material more confusing than it would have been if presented in a simpler way. This has been a problem in the U.S. armed forces, where overzealous presenters are known as "PowerPoint Rangers." Secretary of the Army Louis Caldera acknowledged that some military brass have alienated lawmakers by staging overly elaborate presentations. "People are not listening to us, because they are spending so much time trying to understand these incredibly complex slides," he says.[31]

Guidelines for Using Visual Aids

Whether you are using handouts, poster boards, flip charts, transparencies, slides, chalkboard, or computer displays, be sure to follow the basic rules discussed in this section.[32]

Selection   As with any part of your presentation, visual exhibits must be chosen with care. Use a visual only when it makes a point better than you could alone.

Be sure you have a reason for using a visual aid   If your image doesn't explain a point better than words alone, don't use it. One professional described the common mistake of using too many visuals:

> The biggest mistake people make is in expecting the visuals to be the presentation when, in reality, you should be the presentation. If the audience is too involved in looking at the screen, they're not looking at you, so your words have less of an impact. The goal of any visual presentation should be to enhance what the speaker says, not distract from it.[33]

Visuals used for their own sake will distract your audience from the point you're trying to make. Douglas Vogel, a professor of management information systems at the University of Arizona, cites an example of how using animation without any purpose can backfire: "If the animation is improperly focused or too clever, people may only remember 'dancing cows' and not 'how milk may be good for you.'"[34]

Keep your slide shows brief   Keep in mind the rule that "less is more." The chances of listeners recalling your points is inversely proportional to the number of slides you show.

Match the sophistication of your visuals to the audience   Presentations to important audiences—top bosses, key customers, and so on—usually require polished graphics. There are exceptions, however. For example, financial and scientific professionals are usually receptive to a no-frills approach. Amy Ofsthun, product manager of Polaroid's Digital Palette film recorder, explains: "If they see color and exciting visuals, people feel the data is being massaged somehow. They don't trust the results."[35]

For routine talks, you can probably produce perfectly adequate exhibits on your own. Thanks to advances in computer graphics, you may even be spared the trouble of having to create figures from scratch. In any case, you shouldn't mix informal images with more formal ones any more than you would wear tennis shoes with a business suit.

Design   Confusing or sloppy exhibits will be counterproductive. The simple guidelines below will help you create clear, neat images.[36]

technology tip

Avoiding Computer Catastrophes in Presentations

When you use computers as presentational aids, you can count on an equipment failure sooner or later. The following tips can minimize the chances that hardware or software glitches will scuttle your performance.

- *Set up in advance.* Give yourself lots of time to set up and test your equipment before the presentation is scheduled to begin. The last thing you want your audience to see is you frantically rebooting the computer, swapping cables, and trying to troubleshoot software.
- *Always bring two of everything.* Assume your equipment will fail, because it certainly will at some time. Borrow backups for laptop computers, display panels or projectors, modems, and any other hardware you plan to use.
- *Back up your programs.* Having your work saved on a CD-ROM, flash drive, or some other storage medium can salvage a catastrophe.
- *Have backup technical support available.* Line up an expert who you can call if something doesn't work.
- *Beware of the Web.* Real-time use of the Internet is an invitation to disaster. Connections can be slow, and Web sites can go down without notice. Whenever possible, it's best to store images of sites you will use on your hard drive, and/or a backup medium: CD, DVD, or thumb drive.
- *Have a contingency plan.* Be prepared for the possibility that your equipment will fail. Have copies of key exhibits prepared as handouts. They may not be as glamorous as high-tech displays, but they're far better than nothing.

Make sure the visual is large enough to see   The visual that looks so clear on the desktop in front of you might be almost microscopic from where your listeners are seated. Avoid using items, drawings, or photographs that are so small you have to describe them or pass them around. Remember, a distracting or unclear visual is worse than no support at all.

Keep the design of your visuals simple   Show only one idea per exhibit and avoid unnecessary details. Use simple typefaces.[37]

Use only a few words   Most exhibits are visual images, so you should avoid excessive text. Captions should contain only keywords or phrases, not sentences. Omit subtitles. Follow the "Rule of Seven": Each slide should contain no more than seven lines, and each line should have no more than seven words. If an exhibit needs further explanation, supply it verbally. Remember that you are giving an oral presentation, not showing your audience a written report.

Use only horizontal printing   Avoid vertical or diagonal wording. If necessary, place captions in margins to allow you to use a horizontal format.

Label all items for clear identification   Make sure each exhibit has a descriptive title. Label each axis of a chart, each part of a diagram, and so on.

Presentation   The way you present your exhibits is as important as their design.

Display a visual only while you are discussing it   Putting up a visual before discussing it or leaving it up after you've finished talking about it is confusing and

Use the scale below to answer each item. Then focus your efforts on improving your use of supporting material in areas you identified as needing work.

	Excellent 3	Competent 2	Needs Work 1
1. Each point (claim) contains at least one piece of verbal and/or visual support.	3	2	1
2. Each piece of supporting material makes my claims more			
a. Clear	3	2	1
b. Interesting	3	2	1
c. Persuasive	3	2	1
3. I used a variety of verbal support (definitions, examples, stories, statistics, and comparisons) to add impact to my presentation.	3	2	1
4. My visuals (charts, graphs, photos, video, etc.) make my points more clear, interesting, and persuasive.	3	2	1
5. I present visuals in a way that contributes to my effectiveness:			
a. I look at my audience, not the at visuals, while speaking.	3	2	1
b. I display visuals only when discussing them.	3	2	1
c. I practiced using all technology (e.g., computers, projectors) to make sure it operates smoothly in the venue where I will speak.	3	2	1
6. I present information honestly and accurately to support my claims.	3	2	1
7. The complexity and sophistication of the materials I cite are appropriate for my audience and topic.	3	2	1
8. I cite the sources of my supporting material when appropriate. (You don't always cite sources: e.g., for hypothetical examples, some definitions, stories you've created, etc.)	3	2	1

distracting. In PowerPoint, you can blank out the screen by pushing either the "B" or period (.) keys. Pushing a second time makes the screen visible again.

Make sure your visuals will work in the meeting room   Double-check the availability of easels, screens, and other equipment you'll need. Be sure that electrical outlets are in the right locations and extension cords are available if you will need them. Check sight lines from all audience seats. Be sure you can easily control lighting levels as necessary.

Practice using your visuals   Rehearse setting up and removing visuals smoothly and quickly. Review the comments you'll make with each one. Be sure exhibits are arranged in the right order and lined up properly so that you can avoid the embarrassment of mixed-up charts or upside-down slides.

review points

- Supporting material is vital in any presentation and serves three purposes: to clarify ideas, to make material more interesting, and to offer proof.
- Definitions, examples, stories (fictional, hypothetical, and factual), statistics, comparisons (figurative and literal), and quotations all serve as verbal support.
- Speakers create ethical and credible presentations by knowing when and how to cite their sources.
- In business presentations, visual aids can make a point more quickly and clearly than words alone, add variety and interest, and boost a speaker's professional image.
- Visuals serve several functions: They highlight important information, show how things look, how they work, or how they relate to one another.
- Speakers can use several types of visual aids: objects, models, photographs, diagrams, lists and tables, pie charts, bar and column charts, pictograms, graphs, and videos.
- Visuals can be presented via a number of media: flip charts and poster-board displays, transparencies, photographic slides, computer displays, videoplayers, and handouts.
- Presentation software such as PowerPoint allows presenters to develop professional-looking visual exhibits quickly and easily; however, it is important not to overuse features that result in cluttered and overstimulating, but unclear, aids.
- Successful speakers plan their messages carefully, emphasize content over design, and strive for simplicity and clarity.
- Whatever the medium, all visuals should follow the same basic rules. They should be easy to understand, purposeful, well suited to the point they illustrate and to the audience, and workable in the presentational setting.
- Speakers need to be familiar with their visuals to avoid unpleasant surprises during delivery.

key terms

→ Test your understanding of these key terms by visiting the Online Learning Center Web site at www.mhhe.com/adler10e.

bar charts   362
column charts 362
comparisons   355
definitions   349
examples   351
flip charts   365
graphs   363
handouts   365
pictograms   363

pie charts   361
presentation software   366
quotations   356
slides   365
statistics   354
stories   351
supporting material   348
transparencies   365

activities

→ Go to the self-quizzes at the Online Learning Center at **www.mhhe.com/adler10e** to test your knowledge of chapter concepts.

1. Invitation to Insight

Read a printed version of a speech. You can find sample speeches in your college library or at online sites such as Federal Observer (**www.federalobserver.com/words.php.**) or Newsmax (**http://archive.newsmax.com/hottopics/Great_Speeches.shtml**).

Find examples of at least three types of supporting material. For each item, categorize which type of support it is. How well does it follow the guidelines in the text (for example, if it's a citation, does it follow the four-step method?). Then analyze whether the supporting material provides clarity, interest, and/or proof of the thesis. In your analysis, consider the interests and knowledge level of the intended audience. Does this support appeal most to auditory, visual, or tactile learners?

2. Skill Builder

Which types of support introduced in this chapter (definition, statistics, etc.) would you use to add interest, clarity, and proof to the following points? Provide specific examples.

a.   Tuition costs are keeping promising students out of college.

b.   Textbooks are (are not) overpriced.
c.   Timely payment of bills is in the customer's best interest.
d.   Companies are helping themselves as well as employees by sponsoring and subsidizing exercise programs during work hours.
e.   A liberal arts education can benefit one's career—better in many ways than technical training.

3. Skill Builder

Construct a brief speech about one of the types of supporting material identified in the text. In your mini-speech, present a brief attention-getter, a definition, and a visual aid that illustrates this type of support. Explain potential uses and misuses of this type of support. Close your speech effectively by using one of the types of conclusions discussed in the previous chapter.

4. Skill Builder

Practice your skill at developing visual aids by doing one of the following activities:

a.   Develop a chart or graph showing the overall changes in the demographic characteristics (age, sex, and so on) of your student body over the past 10 years.

b. The local chamber of commerce has hired you to compile graphic exhibits that will be used in presentations to encourage people to visit and settle in your area.

Design materials reflecting the following information:

1. Average monthly rainfall.
2. Month-to-month variations in temperature.
3. Days with sunshine.

If you believe that these figures would *discourage* an audience, choose data that paint an appealing picture of your area.

c. Develop three visual aids that could be used to introduce new students to registration procedures used in your school.

5. Skill Builder

Choose a fact or statistic you can illustrate with visual aids. Develop two different versions of your visual aid that would be effective for two different audiences or occasions (e.g., a group of interns, a workshop at a scientific conference, a formal company dinner, a weekly staff meeting).

6. Skill Builder

Collect examples of each type of verbal and visual support described in this chapter. Comment on how effectively each example follows the guidelines in the text. Describe how each one should be adapted for use in an oral presentation.

7. Invitation to Insight

You can get a sense of how visual aids are used, ignored, overused, or misused by attending a presentation of your choice in the community. Identify the visual support the speaker uses and evaluate its effectiveness for the intended audience and occasion. If you had been hired as a consultant, what advice would you give the speaker about the effectiveness of his or her visual exhibits?

resources

For extensive readings and Web sites on verbal and visual support for presentations see the Online Learning Center Web site at **www.mhhe.com/adler10e.**

Delivering the Presentation

chapter outline

Types of Delivery
Manuscript Presentations
Memorized Presentations
Extemporaneous Presentations
Impromptu Presentations

Guidelines for Delivery
Visual Elements
Verbal Elements
Vocal Elements

Question-and-Answer Sessions
When to Answer Questions
How to Manage Questions

Speaking with Confidence
Accept a Moderate Amount of
Nervousness
Speak More Often
Rehearse Your Presentation
Focus on Your Topic and Audience,
Not on Yourself
Think Rationally about Your Presentation

Review Points
Key Terms
Activities
Resources

chapter objectives

After reading this chapter, you should be able to

1. Choose and use the delivery type best suited for a given presentation.
2. Create and deliver effective extemporaneous and impromptu presentations.
3. Conduct an effective question-and-answer session following suggested guidelines.
4. Apply knowledge about speaker anxiety to speak effectively to others with minimal negative effects.

No matter how well designed, a presentation has to be well delivered in order to succeed. If you look sloppy, speak in a way that is hard to understand, or seem unenthusiastic, listeners are likely to doubt or even reject your ideas. As communication consultant Roger Ailes puts it, "You become the message. People cannot distinguish between the words and who speaks them."[1]

The following pages offer suggestions that can help you deliver your remarks in a way that makes your message clearer, more interesting, and more persuasive. They describe the various styles of delivery, offer tips for improving your visual and vocal performance, explain how to deal with questions from the audience, and give advice for dealing with the nervousness that often accompanies an important presentation.

Types of Delivery

The word "presentation" may conjure up images of a speaker standing behind a lectern delivering information to a passive audience. While some business and professional presentations follow this model, many of them are far more interactive.

When it comes to presentation style, there are three patterns:[2] *Monologues* are one-way speeches, delivered without interruption. These are most appropriate in large settings and on formal occasions. In smaller groups they can feel artificial and create the impression that the speaker doesn't care much about the audience. *Guided discussions* are more interactive. A speaker presents information and has a preset idea of what material to cover, but listeners are encouraged to speak up with questions and comments. Managing a guided discussion is more challenging, but the potential for more audience buy-in can be worth the effort. *Interactive presentations*, as their name implies, involve the audience even more: Although the speaker still controls the program, an interactive presentation feels more like a conversation than a speech. Interactive presentations are common in sales settings, where the interests of the customer should drive the communication.

When it comes to actually delivering material, speakers have four options, though two of them—extemporaneous and impromptu—will serve you best in most situations.

Manuscript Presentations

In **manuscript presentations,** speakers read their remarks word-for-word from a prepared statement. Manuscript speaking is common at annual companywide meetings, conventions, and press conferences. Yet few experiences are as boring as the average manuscript presentation.

Naive speakers often try to conceal their nervousness at facing a large audience by reading from a script—and they turn into lifeless drones. Since most speakers are not trained at reading aloud, their delivery is halting and jerky. Even worse, a nervous speaker who relies too heavily on a manuscript can make serious mistakes without even knowing it. Management consultant Marilyn Landis describes one such disaster:

> I remember the president of a large corporation who followed his usual pattern of asking his public relations director to write a speech for him. Due to a collating error, the script contained two copies of page five. You guessed it. The president read page five twice—and didn't even realize it.[3]

In legal or legislative testimony, diplomatic speeches, or other situations in which a slight misstatement could have serious consequences, manuscript speaking may be your best means of delivery. Most presentations, however, do not fall into this category. A simple but important rule for most cases, then, is *don't read your presentation.*

"I think it's safe to say Charlie, himself, was aware of what was proving to be a tedious and uneven presentation..."

Memorized Presentations

If speaking from a script is bad, trying to memorize that script is even worse. You have probably been subjected to a memorized sales pitch from a telemarketer or door-to-door salesperson. If so, you know that the biggest problem of a **memorized presentation**—one recited word-for-word from memory—is that it *sounds* memorized.

It might seem that memorizing a presentation would help with your nervousness, but memorizing almost guarantees that stage fright will become a serious problem. Speakers who spend great amounts of time simply learning the words of a talk are asking for trouble. During the presentation, they must focus on remembering what comes next instead of getting involved in the meaning of their remarks.

Sometimes it's necessary to memorize parts of a presentation since referring to notes at a critical moment can diminish your credibility. A salesperson is usually expected to know the major features of the product—how much horsepower it has, how much it costs, or how many copies per minute it delivers. A personnel manager might be expected to know, without referring to a brochure, the value of the employee's life insurance (if each employee's is the same) and how much the employee contributes to the premium. A co-worker would look foolish at a retirement dinner if she said, "Everybody knows about Charlie's contributions . . ." and then had to pause to refer to her notes. For such situations, you can memorize essential *parts* of a presentation.

Extemporaneous Presentations

An **extemporaneous presentation** is planned and rehearsed, but not word-for-word. If you prepare carefully and practice your presentation several times with a friend, a family member, or even a group of co-workers or subordinates, you have a good chance of delivering an extemporaneous talk that seems spontaneous and even effortless. Virtually every presentation you plan—a sales presentation, a talk at the local high school, a progress report to a management review board, a training lecture, an annual report to employees or the board of directors—should be delivered extemporaneously.

A good extemporaneous presentation should be carefully rehearsed, but it will never be exactly the same twice because you will be speaking *with* the audience, not *at* them. One speaking coach explained:

> I tell presenters to strive for dialogue behavior in a monologue setting. Dialogue behavior is two people talking across a kitchen table—it's comfortable and natural, and you don't have to think much about it. Monologue behavior is a presenter talking stiffly to his slides.[4]

Extemporaneous speakers use notes for reminders of the order and content of ideas. There is no single best format for these notes. Some speakers prefer abbreviated outlines, while others find that index cards with keywords or phrases work best. One hint if you do use note cards: It is a good idea to have them punched and on a ring, so they can't scatter if dropped.

Whatever form you use, your speaking notes should possess the following characteristics.

Notes Should Be Brief
Overly detailed notes tempt a speaker to read them. Inexperienced salespeople who rely on a brochure, for instance, often wind up reading to their prospective customers. More experienced salespeople might be able to use the brochure's boldface headings as a guide. If you are using presentation software such as PowerPoint, the points on your slides may be all that you need to guide you.

Notes Should Be Legible
Your words shouldn't turn into meaningless scribbles when you need them. The writing on your notes should be neat and large enough to be read at a glance. Better yet, print them out in an easy-to-read typeface and size.

Notes Should Be Unobtrusive
Most audiences won't be offended if you speak from notes, as long as the notes aren't distracting. A sheet of paper flapping in your hand can become a noisy irritation, as can shuffling several sheets of paper on a lectern. Some speakers avoid such problems by providing their listeners with a guide and then using the guide for their own notes.

on your feet

Impromptu Presentations

Sooner or later you will be asked to give an **impromptu presentation**–an unexpected, off-the-cuff talk. A customer might stop in your office and ask you to describe the new model you'll have next spring. At a celebration dinner, you may be asked to "say a few words." A manager might ask you to "give us some background on the problem" or to "fill us in on your progress." You may suddenly discover at a weekly meeting that your subordinates are unaware of a process they need to know about in order to understand the project you are about to explain.

Giving an impromptu talk needn't be as threatening as it seems. Most of the time, you will be asked to speak about a subject within your expertise–such as a current project, a problem you've solved, or a technical aspect of your training–which means you have thought about it before. Another reassuring fact is that most listeners won't expect perfection in unrehearsed remarks.

Your impromptu presentations will be most effective if you follow these guidelines.[5]

Anticipate When You May Be Asked to Speak   Most impromptu speaking situations won't come as a complete surprise. You may be an "expert" on the subject under discussion or at least one of the people most involved in a situation. Or perhaps your knowledge of the person in charge suggests that impromptu remarks are to be expected. In any case, if you prepare yourself just in case you're asked to speak, your remarks will be better planned and delivered.

Focus on Your Audience and the Situation   Think about your audience and the situation in which you'll be speaking. What is on your listeners' minds? What are their attitudes? What are the circumstances in which you are speaking? The more you can ground your remarks in the context, the better.

Accept the Invitation with Assurance   Try to look confident, even if you're less than delighted about speaking. If you stammer, stall, or look unhappy, your audience will doubt the value of your remarks before you say a word. Once asked, you're going to speak whether or not you want to. You might as well handle the situation well.

Organize Your Thoughts   The safest way to avoid rambling is to use the few moments before you speak to sketch an outline–mental if necessary, jotted down if possible. It can follow the introduction-body-conclusion format described in Chapter 10. When you speak, state your thesis in the first moments you are addressing the audience: "I see several problems with that idea," or "From my experience with the Digitech project, I think our cost projections are low." If you aren't sure what your opinion is, present that thesis: "I'm not sure which approach we ought to take. I think we need to look at both of them closely before we decide."

Label each of your main points as you cover it in the body of your remarks: "My first point is that . . ." Then conclude by restating your thesis.

Present Reasons, Logic, or Facts to Support Your Viewpoint　As with any presentation, your points will be clearer and more persuasive when you back them up with supporting material: statistics, examples, comparisons, and so forth. Of course, this information won't be as detailed as it would be if you had been able to prepare it in advance, but provide some evidence or explanation to support your points: "As I recall, the Digitech job ran 10 percent over estimate on materials and 15 percent over on labor."

Don't Apologize　Nobody expects a set of impromptu remarks to be perfectly polished, so it is a mistake to highlight your lack of knowledge or preparation. Remarks like "You caught me off guard" or "I'm not sure whether this is right" are unnecessary. If you really don't have anything to contribute, say so.

Don't Ramble　Many novice speakers make the mistake of delivering their message and then continuing to talk: "So that's my point: I think the potential gains make the risk worthwhile. Sure, we'll be taking a chance, but look what we stand to win. That's why I think it's not just a matter of chance, but a calculated risk, and one that makes sense. We'll never know unless we try, and . . ." The speaker needed only one sentence to conclude: "I think the risk is worth taking."

Guidelines for Delivery

Choosing the best method of delivery will help make your presentations effective, but it is no guarantee of total effectiveness. Your speeches will be better if you also consider the visual and vocal elements of delivery: how you look, what words you use, and how you sound.

Visual Elements

A major part of good delivery is how a speaker looks. You can improve your visual effectiveness by following several guidelines.

Dress Effectively　Appearance is important in any setting. How you dress is even more important when you get up to speak, however. You may be able to hide a rumpled suit behind your desk sometimes or get away with wearing clothes more casual than usual office norms dictate the day you move your office furniture—but not when you get up to give your financial report at the annual meeting or present your latest proposal to top management.

Dressing effectively doesn't always mean dressing up. If the occasion calls for casual attire, an overly formal appearance can be just as harmful as underdressing. Automotive consultant Barry Isenberg found that an informal appearance contributed to his success as a leading speaker. While waiting to speak to an audience of hundreds of auto wreckers at a day-long seminar, Isenberg looked on as an attorney dressed impeccably in a

career tip

Stand or Sit?

The decision whether to sit or stand during any presentation will be based on your goals for that presentation. Certainly, in a large room without amplification, you'll need to stand to be seen and heard. It would seem awkward and unnecessary to stand when presenting to one other person over coffee. There are other times, however, when the decision to sit or stand could go either way.

Consider standing when you want to

- Be perceived as taking charge.
- Be able to breathe and project better.

- See and be seen by the audience and maintain eye contact.
- Stand out from other speakers, who may be seated.

Consider sitting when you want to

- Be seen as building rapport with the group.
- Be considered part of the team.
- Avoid being labeled arrogant or show-stealing.

Source: After J. A. Daly and I. N. Engleberg, *Presentations in Everyday Life,* 3rd ed. (Boston: Allyn & Bacon, 2008), p. 337.

---

three-piece suit gave an organized talk on warranties. Despite the importance of the topic, the audience was obviously bored silly. Isenberg rushed upstairs to his hotel room and changed out of his business suit and into the attire of his listeners—casual pants and an open-neck shirt. When his turn to speak arrived, Isenberg moved out from behind the lectern and adopted a casual speaking style that matched his outfit. Afterward, a number of listeners told Isenberg he was the first speaker who seemed to understand their business.[6]

Step Up to Speak with Confidence and Authority

Employees are often surprised to discover that their forceful, personable superiors completely lose their effectiveness when they have to address a group of people—and show this before they say a word. Speakers who fidget with their hands or their clothing while waiting to speak, approach the podium as if they were about to face a firing squad, and then fumble with their notes and the microphone send the nonverbal message "I'm not sure about myself or what I have to say." An audience will discount even the best remarks with such a powerful nonverbal preface.

Your presentation begins the moment you come into the view of your listeners. Act as if you are a person whose remarks are worth listening to.

Get Set before Speaking

If you need an easel or projection screen, move it into position before you begin. If a lectern needs repositioning, do it before you begin your talk. The same goes for the other details that come with so many presentations: Adjust the microphone, close the door, reset the air conditioner, rearrange the seating.

Just as important, be sure to position yourself physically before beginning. Usually out of nervousness, some speakers blurt out their opening remarks before they are set in their speaking position. A far better approach is to stand or walk to the position from which you will talk, get set, wait a brief moment (a "power pause") while you connect with your audience, and then begin speaking.

Begin without Looking at Your Notes

Make contact with the audience as you begin speaking. You can't establish a connection if you are reading from notes. You can memorize the precise wording of your opening statement, but it isn't really necessary. Whether you say "I have a new process that will give you more reliable results at a lower cost" or "My new process is more reliable and costs less" isn't critical: The important thing is to make your point while speaking directly to your listeners.

Establish and Maintain Eye Contact

A speaker who talks directly to an audience will be seen as more involved and sincere. Whether you're proposing an innovative new product line, reassuring your employees about the effects of recent budget cuts, or trying to convince a group of local citizens that your company is interested in curbing pollution, your impression on the audience can ultimately determine your success.

This kind of immediacy comes in great part from the degree of eye contact between speaker and listeners. Use the moment before you speak to establish a relationship with your audience. Look around the room. Get in touch with the fact that you are talking to real human beings: the people you work with, the potential customers who have real problems and concerns you can help with, and so on. Let them know by your glance that you are interested in them. Be sure your glance covers virtually everyone in the room. Look about randomly: A mechanical right-to-left sweep of the group will make you look like a robot. Many speech consultants recommend taking in the whole room as you speak. If the audience is too large for you to make eye contact with each person, choose a few people in different parts of the room, making eye contact with each one for a few seconds.

Stand and Move Effectively

Table 12-1 on page 384 describes some effective and ineffective ways to stand and move when you are speaking. The best stance for delivering a presentation is relaxed but firm. The speaker's feet are planted firmly on the ground and spaced at shoulder width. The body faces the audience. The head is upright, turning naturally to look at the audience.

Having good posture doesn't mean standing rooted to the ground. Moving about can add life to your presentation and help release nervous energy. You can approach and refer to your visual aids, walk away from and return to your original position, and approach the audience. Your actions should always be purposeful, though. Nervous pacing might make a speaker feel better, but it will turn listeners into distracted wrecks.

If you're addressing a small group, such as four or five employees or potential customers, it may be more appropriate to sit when you're delivering a presentation. Generally, the same rules apply in such cases. You should sit up straight and lean forward—lounging back in your chair or putting a foot up on the desk indicates indifference or even contempt. Sit naturally; your behavior should be as direct and animated as it would be if you were conversing with these people—which, in a way, you are.

Don't Pack Up Early

Gathering your notes or starting for your seat before concluding is a nonverbal statement that you're anxious to get your presentation finished. Even if you are, advertising the fact will only make your audience see the presentation as less valuable. Keep your attention focused on your topic and the audience until you are actually finished.

Pause, then Move Out Confidently

Be certain that you drop your pitch to end your remarks so you clearly indicate that you are finished. A raised pitch sounds questioning, unsure, and leaves the audience wondering whether you are finished. When you end your remarks (or finish answering questions and recapping your

Table 12–1	Common Interpretations of Speaker's Body Language

Viewed as dictatorial or arrogant:
- Crossed arms
- Pounding fists
- Hands on hips
- Pointing index finger
- Hands behind back
- Hands in "steeple" position
- Hands on lapel or hem of jacket
- Preening gestures

Viewed as insecure or nervous:
- Gripping the lectern
- Chewing on objects, cuticles, fingernails, lips
- Constant throat clearing
- Playing with hair, beard, jewelry
- Rocking back and forth
- Rubbing or picking at clothes or body
- Clenched fists
- Jingling coins or keys in pockets or hands
- Repeatedly putting glasses on and off
- Slouching
- Standing extremely rigidly

Viewed as open and confident:
- Open hands
- Expansive gestures
- Stepping out from behind the lectern
- Walking toward and into the audience
- Animated facial expressions
- Dramatic pauses
- Confident and consistent eye contact

Source: After D. Bocher, *Speak with Confidence: Powerful Presentations That Inform, Inspire and Persuade* (New York: McGraw-Hill, 2003).

thesis), pause, then move out smartly. Even if you are unhappy with yourself, don't shuffle off dejectedly or stomp away angrily. Most speakers are their own greatest critics, and there is a good chance the audience rated you more favorably than you did. If you advertise your disappointment, however, you might persuade them that you really were a flop.

Verbal Elements

The words you choose are an important part of your delivery. As you practice your presentation, keep the following points in mind.

Cheerleader Sales Reps

Anyone who has spent time in a physician's waiting room has probably noticed pharmaceutical sales representatives seeking the attention of the doctor. Observation is likely to show that many, if not most, of those reps are young, attractive women. One physician noted, "There's a saying that you'll never meet an ugly drug rep."

A *New York Times* story revealed that many of these good-looking salespeople are former university cheerleaders. A Memphis, Tennessee, employment agency named Spirited Sales Leaders (SSL) specializes in providing former cheerleaders to organizations.

Recruiters and industry officials, however, insist that attractiveness isn't the main criterion for choosing good-looking sales reps. "It's the personality," says Lamberto Andreotti, president of worldwide pharmaceuticals for Bristol-Myers Squibb.

CRITICAL ANALYSIS: Reflect on the role of appearance in business presentations by considering the following questions:

1. In your opinion, is it ethical for employers to favor physically attractive people to represent their organizations?

2. If appearance is a fact of life, what can you do to enhance your effectiveness when representing yourself and your organization?

Sources: S. Saul, "Gimme an Rx! Cheerleaders Pep Up Drug Sales," *The New York Times*, November 28, 2005, p. A1. Spirited Sales Leaders www.spiritedsales.com.

Use an Oral-Speaking Style   Spoken ideas differ in structure and content from written messages. The difference helps explain why speakers who read from a manuscript sound so stuffy and artificial. When addressing your audience, your speech will sound normal and pleasing if it follows some simple guidelines:

- *Keep most sentences short.* Long, complicated sentences may be fine in a written document, where readers can study them until the meaning is clear, but in an oral presentation your ideas will be easiest to understand if they are phrased in brief statements. Complicated sentences can leave your listeners confused: "Members of field staff, who are isolated from one another and work alone most of the time, need better technology for keeping in touch with one another while in the field as well as with the home office." The ideas are much clearer when delivered in briefer chunks: "Members of the field staff work alone most of the time. This makes it hard for them to keep in touch with one another and with the home office. They need better means of technology to stay in contact."

- *Use personal pronouns freely.* Speech that contains first-person and second-person pronouns sounds more personal and immediate. Instead of saying "People often ask," say "You might ask." Likewise, say "Our sales staff found," not "The sales staff found."

- *Use the active voice.* The active voice sounds more personal and less stuffy than passive use of verbs. Saying "It was decided" isn't as effective as saying "We decided." Do not say "The meeting was attended by 10 people"; say "Ten people attended the meeting."

- *Use contractions often.* Unless you need the complete word for emphasis, contractions sound much more natural. Instead of saying "We do not expect many changes," say "We don't expect many changes." Rather than saying "I do not know; I will find out and give you an answer as soon as possible," say "I don't know; I'll find out and give you an answer as soon as possible."

Using Video to Analyze Your Delivery

Seeing yourself from the audience's point of view can be an effective way to analyze and improve your delivery in presentations. A simple video recorder or webcam, televison or computer, and a notepad are all you need.

After recording your presentation, view it with a notepad and pen in hand. Divide the page into two columns labeled "Liked" and "Didn't Like." Then jot down both your strengths and the areas to improve as you screen the video four times:

- **As Is** Replay the video in its original form, just as it would appear to an audience.

- **Muted** Now watch yourself with no audio. Pay attention to your physical presence: posture, gestures, facial expressions, and so on.

- **Audio Only** Listen to your voice without any video. Are you easy to understand? Fluent? Enthusiastic?

- **Fast Forward** Finally, speed up the video and see whether any important expressions, mannerisms, or other movements become apparent.

This simple exercise should give you both a sense of your delivery strengths and a list of areas to work on.

Source: T. Zaun, "There's More Than One Way to Use Video," *Presentations*, December 2003, p. 78.

- *Address your listeners by name.* Using direct forms of address makes it clear that you are really speaking to your listeners and not just reading from a set of notes. Personalized statements will help build rapport and keep an audience listening: "Frank, you and your colleagues in the payroll office are probably wondering how these changes will affect you"; "Ms. Diaz, it's a pleasure to have the chance to describe our ideas to you this morning."

Don't Emphasize Mistakes   Even the best speakers forget or bungle a line occasionally. The difference between professionals and amateurs is the way they handle such mistakes. The experts simply go on, adjusting their remarks to make the error less noticeable.

Usually, an audience won't even be aware of a mistake. If listeners don't have a copy of your speaking outline, they won't know about the missing parts; even if they notice that you have skipped a section in a brochure you're going over with them or in a prepared outline you've distributed after your speech for their reference, they'll assume you did it on purpose, perhaps to save time. If you lose your place in your notes, a brief pause will be almost unnoticeable—as long as you don't emphasize it by frantically pawing through your notes.

What about obvious mistakes—citing the wrong figures, mispronouncing a name, or trying to use equipment that doesn't work, for example? The best response here is again the least noticeable. "Let me correct that. The totals are for the first quarter of the year, not just for March," you might say and then move on. When equipment fails, adapt and move on: "The chart with those figures seems to be missing. Let me summarize it for you."

Finally, don't emphasize what you *didn't* do ("I didn't have time to create a chart like I wanted to"); instead, emphasize what you *did* do ("I researched the sales figures for the past 5 years").

Use Proper Vocabulary, Enunciation, and Pronunciation   The language of a board of directors' meeting or a formal press conference is different from that of a factory workers' meeting or an informal gathering of sales

Using a Microphone

Sooner or later you are likely to face a speaking situation where you'll need to use a microphone. Microphones are generally one of two types: a stationary one that is attached to a podium, or a lavaliere model that clips onto your clothing and requires you to wear a transmitter (about the size of a pack of cigarettes).

When using a stationary microphone, try to keep about 6 to 8 inches between your lips and the mouthpiece to avoid a very nasal or very thin-sounding voice. Keep the microphone about an inch below your lip level to avoid the "popping" sound that can accompany puffs of breath used in sounds like "p" and "t." Maintain a consistent distance for uniform volume. A one-directional microphone has only one spot that picks up sound, so even turning your head can prevent your voice from being picked up. A multidirectional mike allows more animated movement, since it can pick up your voice even if you move slightly to one side or the other of the mouthpiece.

With a lavaliere microphone, you have greater range of body motion and can walk around more freely; however, you'll need to plan your dress more carefully. Ideally, choose an outfit with a sturdy lapel or collar to clip the microphone onto. Turtlenecks or collarless tops may not allow the proper distance from lips to microphone; the microphone might flop around on very flimsy fabrics like soft silks or thin knits. When you turn, turn your whole body, not just your head, so that you are always speaking into the microphone. You'll also need to consider the "transmitter bulge." The transmitter might fit easily into pants with front pockets and pleats, in a jacket's inside pocket, or clip onto a belt under a loose-fitting jacket. Avoid tight-fitting pants and jackets that won't accommodate the transmitter without an unsightly hump.

Whatever type of microphone you use, test it in advance. If there is someone in charge of the sound system, introduce yourself and ask for any advice with regard to the particular equipment and room. Practice by asking someone to check your volume while sitting in various parts of the room. Move around with a lavaliere microphone to see if any areas of the room produce interference, buzzing, or high-pitched sounds. Be sure your movements don't dislodge the microphone, and be certain that you switch it off before and after speaking so that any private conversations remain private.

Sources: From T. Antion, *Great Speaking* 4, no. 6 (April 24, 2002), retrieved from **www.antion.com/ezine/v4n6.txt;** S. Berkley, "Microphone Tips," *Great Speaking* 4, no. 7 (May 14, 2002), retrieved from **www.antion.com/ezine/v4n7.txt;** and R. Grant-Williams, "Speak Up!" *Women in Business* 54, no. 2 (March/April 2002), p. 38.

representatives at a resort. It is important to choose language that is appropriate to the particular setting.

It is also important to pronounce your words correctly. Few mistakes will erode your credibility or irritate an audience as quickly as will mispronouncing an important term or name: The word is *scenario*, not "screenario," and the author of this book likes to be called "Adler," not "Alder." Enunciation—articulating words clearly and distinctly—is also important. "We are comin' out with a new data processin' system" makes the speaker sound ignorant to many people, even if the ideas are good.

Vocal Elements

How you sound is just as important as what you say and how you look. Speakers' voices are especially effective at communicating their attitudes about themselves, their topics, and their listeners: enthusiasm or disinterest, confidence or nervousness, friendliness or hostility, respect or disdain. The following guidelines are important elements in effective communication.

Speak with Enthusiasm and Sincerity

If you don't appear to feel strongly about the importance of your topic, there's little chance your audience will. Yet professionals often seem indifferent when they present ideas they're deeply committed to.[7]

The best way to generate enthusiasm is to think of your presentation as sharing ideas you truly believe in and speak with conviction, in your own style. Consultant Roger Ailes makes this point emphatically:

> The truth is, no one can manufacture an image for anyone. If you want to improve or enhance yourself in some way, the only thing a consultant can do for you is to advise and guide you. We can point out assets and liabilities in your style and we then offer substitutions and suggestions to aid you. You have to want to improve and work at it. Most importantly, whatever changes you make have to conform to who you really are—at your best. All the grooming suggestions, all the speech coaching, all the knowledge about lighting, staging, and media training—everything popularly associated with "image-making"—won't work if the improvements don't fit comfortably with who you essentially are.[8]

In the stress of making a presentation, you might forget how important your remarks are. To prevent this, remind yourself of why you are speaking in the moments before you speak. Thinking about what you want to say can put life back into your delivery.

Speak Loudly Enough to Be Heard

At the very least, a quiet voice makes it likely that listeners won't hear important information. In addition, listeners often interpret an overly soft voice as a sign of timidity or lack of conviction. ("She just didn't sound very sure of herself.") Shouting is offensive, too ("Does he think he can force his product down our throats?"), but a speaker ought to project enough to be heard clearly and to sound confident.

Avoid Disfluencies

Disfluencies are those stammers and stutters ("eh," "um," and so forth) that creep into everyone's language at one time or another. Other "filler words" are "ya know," "like," "so," "OK," and so on. A few disfluencies will be virtually unnoticeable in a presentation; in fact, without them, the talk might seem overly rehearsed and stilted. An excess of jumbles, stumbles, and fillers, however, makes a speaker sound disorganized, nervous, and uncertain.

Vary Your Speech

Just as in your best everyday speaking style, the rate, pitch, and volume of your speech in a presentation should vary. Let your genuine enthusiasm for the topic and situation drive your speaking style, just as it does in your everyday conversations. Be sure to slow down and speak slightly louder when you are stating your thesis and your main points, however. Your audience understands such cues to mean "This is important."

Use Pauses Effectively

Don't be afraid of silence; it can be used for emphasis, to give your audience time to consider what you've presented, to formulate an answer to a question you've posed, or to indicate the importance of what you've just said. Being comfortable with pauses indicates you're comfortable in the role of speaker; every second does not have to be filled in with words.

Either on campus or using other resources, use a camcorder to capture a rehearsal of a presentation you are planning. If possible, present your remarks to at least one or two listeners, who will represent your real audience.

After your presentation, review the recording and note the effectiveness of your delivery in each of the following areas.

Visual Elements

____ I dressed effectively.

____ I stepped up with confidence and authority.

____ I got set before speaking.

____ I began speaking without looking at notes.

____ I maintained eye contact throughout my presentation.

____ I stood and moved effectively.

____ I didn't pack up before concluding.

____ Upon conclusion, I paused and then moved out confidently.

Verbal Elements

____ I used an oral-speaking style.

____ I didn't emphasize my mistakes.

____ I used proper vocabulary, enunciation, and pronunciation.

Vocal Elements

____ I spoke with enthusiasm and sincerity.

____ I spoke loudly enough to be heard.

____ I avoided disfluencies.

____ I varied the rate, pitch, and volume of my voice.

____ I used pauses effectively.

Your first rehearsal will probably reveal things you want to change about your delivery. After noting areas you want to improve, record and review the presentation again. Repeat this process until you are satisfied with the results.

Question-and-Answer Sessions

The chance to answer questions on the spot is one of the biggest advantages of oral presentations. Whereas a written report might leave readers confused or unimpressed, your on-the-spot response to questions and concerns can win over an audience.

Audience questions are a part of almost every business and professional talk from sales presentations and training sessions to boardroom meetings. Sometimes question-and-answer sessions are a separate part of the presentation. Other times, they are mingled with the speaker's remarks. In any case, a skillful response to questions is essential.

career tip

Minimizing Audience Interruptions

A few interruptions can rattle even confident speakers. The following tips can help minimize the chances that deliberate or unintentional interruptions throw you off:

- Post a sign outside the room warning that a presentation is in progress, and close the doors to the room before you begin speaking.

- Program telephones in the room to ring elsewhere, or activate voice mail to prevent them from ringing during your talk.

- Ask that questions and comments be held until the end of your presentation (if you won't be comfortable responding to them during your talk).

- Let the audience know when there will be a break in the presentation.

- Ask your audience to turn off beepers and cell phones for the duration of the presentation.

- Check with service personnel or post notices outside the room to be sure refreshments aren't delivered in the middle of your presentation.

- Be certain that setup for another event isn't about to begin in your room before you are finished. (This is especially important if you are the last speaker in a program.)

When to Answer Questions

The first issue to consider is whether you should entertain questions at all. Sometimes you have no choice, of course. If the boss interrupts your talk to ask for some facts or figures, you're not likely to rule the question out of order. But there may be cases when time or the risk of being distracted will lead you to say something like "Because we only have 10 minutes on the agenda, I won't have time for questions. If any of you do have questions, see me after my presentation or during the break or lunch."[9] If your presentation does call for questions from the audience, you can pretty much control when they are asked.

During the Presentation   Speakers often encourage their listeners to ask questions during a talk. This approach lets you respond immediately to the concerns of your listeners. If people are confused, you can set them straight by expanding on a point; if they have objections, you can respond to them on the spot.

Dealing with your listeners' questions during a talk does have its drawbacks. Some questions are premature, raising points you plan to discuss later in your talk. Others are irrelevant and waste both your time and your listeners'. If you decide to handle questions during a talk, follow the guidelines below.

Allow for extra time   Answering questions sometimes occupies as much time as your planned talk. A 15-minute report can run a half-hour or longer with questions. If your time is limited, keep your remarks brief enough to leave time for the audience to respond.

Promise to answer premature questions later   Don't feel obligated to give detailed responses to every question. If you plan to discuss the information requested by a questioner later in your talk, say, "That's a good question; I'll get to that in a moment."

After the Presentation   Postponing questions until after your prepared remarks lets you control the way your information is revealed. You don't have to worry about someone distracting you with an irrelevant remark or raising an objection you plan to answer. You also have much better control over the length of your talk, lessening the risk that you'll run out of time before you run out of information.

On the other hand, when you deny listeners the chance to speak up, they may be so preoccupied with questions or concerns that they miss much of what you say. For instance, you might spend half your time talking about the benefits of a product while your listeners keep wondering whether they can afford it. In addition, since most of the information people recall is from the beginning and the end of presentations, you risk having your audience remember the high price you mentioned during the question-and-answer session or the sticky question you couldn't answer rather than the high quality you proved in your presentation.

How to Manage Questions

Whether you handle them during or after a presentation, questions from the audience can be a challenge. Some are confusing. Others are thinly veiled attacks on your position: "How much time have you New York folks spent out here in the Midwest?" Still other questions are off the topic you're discussing: "Your talk about film projectors was very interesting. I wonder, do you ever teach classes on making films?" You can handle questions most effectively by following the suggestions below.

Start the Ball Rolling   Sometimes listeners may be reluctant to ask the first question. You can get a question-and-answer session rolling with your own remarks: "One question you might have is . . . ," or "The other day someone asked whether . . ." You can also encourage questions nonverbally by leaning forward as you invite the audience to speak up. You might even raise your hand as you ask for questions.

Anticipate Likely Questions   Put yourself in the position of your listeners. What questions are they likely to ask? Is there a chance that they will find parts of your topic hard to understand? Might some points antagonize them? Just as you prepare for an important exam by anticipating the questions that are likely to be asked, you should try to prepare responses to the inquiries you're likely to receive.

Clarify Complicated or Confusing Questions
Make sure you understand the question by rephrasing it in your own words: "If I understand you correctly, Tom, you're asking why we can't handle this problem with our present staff. Is that right?" Besides helping you understand what a questioner wants, clarification gives you a few precious moments to frame an answer. Finally, it helps other audience members to understand the question. If the audience is large, rephrase every question to make sure that it has been heard: "The gentleman asked whether we have financing terms for the equipment."

Treat Questioners with Respect   There's little to gain by antagonizing or embarrassing even the most hostile questioner. You can keep your dignity and gain the support of other listeners by taking every question seriously or even complimenting the person who asks it: "I don't blame you for thinking the plan is farfetched, Nora. We thought it was strange at first, too, then the more we examined it, the better it looked."

Even when you are certain you are right, you can't win by arguing with audience members. A "yes-but" reply ("Yes, we did exceed the budget, but it wasn't our fault . . .") is likely to make you sound argumentative or defensive and antagonize the questioner. Instead,

ethical challenge

Faking Your Feelings

Every speaker wants to appear confident and enthusiastic. But sometime during the course of your speaking career you are likely to face an audience when you do not feel self-assured or enthusiastic about your topic. How can you reconcile the ethical demand to be honest with the pragmatic reality that business communicators are sometimes asked to present ideas they do not personally like?

Suppose, for instance, that you have been asked to introduce a colleague who you dislike and believe is unqualified for his/her job to a group of new employees or customers. How would you handle this challenge?

Or imagine that your supervisor created a proposal for your department to share certain equipment with another department. You do not favor the proposal because you foresee conflicts in completing work on time. Because you are enthusiastic and well liked in all departments, your supervisor asks you to present the proposal to the other department "with your usual enthusiasm and persuasion." What do you do?

You may choose to use the interviewing skills described in Chapters 6 and 7 of this book to ask experienced communicators how they face these challenges. On the basis of their answers and your own thoughts, develop a policy on how accurately your public demeanor should reflect your private misgivings.

---

you can use a "yes-and" response: "Yes, we did exceed the budget, and that bothers us too. And that's why we included an explanation of the problems in our report."[10]

Keep Answers Focused on Your Goal

Don't let questions draw you off track. Try to frame answers in ways that promote your goal: "This certainly is different from the way we did things in the old days when you and I started out, Steve. For instance, the computerized system we have now will cut both our costs and our errors. Let me review the figures once more."

You can avoid offending questioners by promising to discuss the matter with them in detail after your presentation or to send them further information: "I'd be happy to show you the electrical plans, Peggy. Let's get together this afternoon and go over them."

Buy Time When Necessary

Sometimes you need a few moments to plan an answer to a surprise question. You can buy time in several ways. First, *wait for the questioner to finish speaking*. Besides being courteous, this gives you time to mentally compose an answer. Next, you can *reflect the question back to the person who asked it*: "How would you deal with the situation and still go ahead with the project, Mary?" You can also *turn the question to another audience member*: "Chris, you're the best technical person we have. What's the best way to save energy costs?"

Address Your Answer to the Entire Audience

Look at the person asking the question while he or she is asking it, but address your answer to everybody. This approach is effective for two reasons: First, it keeps all the audience members involved instead of making them feel like bystanders. Second, it can save you from getting trapped into a debate with hostile questioners. Most critics are likely to keep quiet if you address your response to the entire group. You may not persuade the person who has made a critical remark, but you can use your answer to gain credibility with everybody else.

Follow the Last Question with a Summary

Since listeners are likely to remember especially well the last words they hear you speak, always follow the question-and-answer session with a brief restatement of your thesis and perhaps a call for your

Confidence-Building Strategies

Sooner or later, even the most confident speakers encounter a situation that generates anxiety. When this happens to you, the following tips can help you keep your feelings under control.

- Before the presentation, walk around or stretch to relieve stress and burn off excess nervous energy. Avoid alcohol and caffeine before speaking.

- Rehearse your presentation in front of friends or colleagues. Make sure your test audience tells you honestly about what works and what doesn't. It's better to learn while there is still time to adjust your approach.

- Before speaking, walk around the room and talk with people who will be listening to your presentation. This will help bridge the speaker–listener gap, and help you think of audience members as real people.

- Remember: A presentation isn't brain surgery. You are sharing what you know with people who want to know it too. Keep the presentation in perspective and you will do better.

- Wear clothing that is familiar and makes you look good. Dressing in a new outfit can contribute to discomfort and feelings like "this isn't the real me."

- During the presentation, seek out friendly faces and establish and maintain eye contact. Once you see that people are on your side, your self-confidence will grow.

- Don't try to be like anyone else. It's fine to observe speakers you admire for pointers, but develop your own approach. Recall how effective you are when you are speaking at your best, and use that as the basis of your speaking style.

---

audience to act in a way that accomplishes your purpose for speaking. A typical summary might sound like this:

> I'm grateful for the chance to answer your questions. Now that we've gone over the cost projections, I think you can see why we're convinced that this proposal can help boost productivity and cut overhead by almost 10 percent overnight. We're ready to make these changes immediately. The sooner we hear from you, the sooner we can get started.

Speaking with Confidence

If the thought of making a presentation leaves you feeling anxious, you are in good company. According to Irving Wallace and David Wallechinsky's *Book of Lists*, a sample of 3,000 Americans identified "speaking before a group" as their greatest fear, greater even than death.[11] This doesn't mean most people would rather die than give a speech, but it does suggest which event makes them more anxious.

Stage fright—or *communication apprehension*, as communication specialists call it—is just as much a problem for businesspeople as it is for the general population. Communispond, a New York communications consulting firm, surveyed 500 executives and found that nearly 80 percent listed stage fright as their greatest problem in speaking before a group, putting it ahead of such items as "handling hostile interrogators."[12] Another survey found that roughly a third of the population in one city suffered from more-than-normal anxiety about speaking to an audience.[13]

When the demands of a job include presentational speaking, career success can be jeopardized by speech anxiety.[14] If you get butterflies in your stomach at the thought of giving a speech, if your hands sweat and your mouth gets dry, if you feel faint or nauseated or have trouble thinking clearly, you might be comforted to know that most people, including famous performers, politicians, and business executives who frequently appear

Dilbert © Scott Adams/Dist. by United Feature Syndicate, Inc. Reprinted by permission.

before audiences, experience some degree of nervousness about speaking. Although it is common, communication apprehension doesn't have to present a serious problem.

It is reassuring to know that, however anxious you feel, your apprehension isn't as visible as you might fear. In several studies, communicators have been asked to rate their own level of anxiety.[15] At the same time, other people gave their impression of the speaker's level of nervousness. In every case, the speakers rated themselves as looking much more nervous than the observers thought they were. Even when the anxiety is noticeable, it doesn't result in significantly lower evaluations of the speaker's effectiveness.

These research findings are good news for anxious speakers. It's reassuring to know that, even if you are frightened, your listeners aren't likely to recognize the fact or find it distracting. And knowing that the audience isn't bothered by your anxiety can actually reduce a major source of nervousness, leading you to feel more confident.

Accept a Moderate Amount of Nervousness

A certain amount of anxiety is not just normal, it's even desirable. One consultant says, "If I had a way to remove all fear of speaking for you, I wouldn't do it. The day you become casual about speaking is the day you risk falling on your face."[16] The threat of botching your presentation can lead to what Edward R. Murrow once called "the sweat of perfection," spurring you to do your best. And the adrenaline rush that comes as you stand up—your body's response to a threatening situation—can make you appear more energetic, enthusiastic, and forceful than would be the case if you were more relaxed and casual.

A proper goal, then, is not to eliminate nervousness but to *control* it. As one experienced speaker put it, "The butterflies never go away; it's just that after a while they begin to fly in formation."

The time of greatest nervousness for most speakers is before they even begin speaking, when they are thinking about an upcoming presentation.[17] Once you get under way, it is likely that your anxiety will decrease. Keeping this fact in mind ("It will only get better once I start speaking") may even help reduce your prespeech nervousness.

Speak More Often

Like many unfamiliar activities—ice skating, learning to drive a car, and interviewing for a job, to mention a few—the first attempts at speaking before a group can be unnerving. One source of anxiety is lack of skill and experience. In addition, the very newness of the act is frightening.[18]

Since newness generates anxiety, one way to become a more confident speaker is to speak more. As with other skills, your first attempts should involve modest challenges with relatively low stakes. Speech courses and workshops taught in colleges, corporations, and some community organizations provide opportunities for a group of novices to practice before one another and a supportive instructor. Once on the job, it's a good idea to make a number of beginning presentations to small, familiar audiences about noncritical matters.

Rehearse Your Presentation

Many presentational catastrophes come from inadequate rehearsal. Missing note cards, excessive length, clumsy wording, and confusing material can all be remedied if you practice in advance. As you add more and more technological aids to your presentation, the need for complete and careful rehearsal increases dramatically. Projector bulbs can burn out, extension cords can be too short, slides can be upside down or mixed up, and microphones can fail. It's better to find out these facts before you face a real audience.

Computer-assisted presentations can create the ultimate presentational nightmare, as these two examples illustrate:

> Multimedia producer Dave Mandala was scheduled to deliver a sophisticated presentation in Hungary. Just to be safe, he shipped himself 12 monitors instead of the 8 he needed. He was horrified to open his metal-framed, cushioned packing cases to find that each one was filled with water.

> Craig O'Connor, a telecommuting consultant, used his own equipment to deliver an important talk. Halfway through the presentation, O'Connor's personal calendar program flashed a message onto the two huge projection screens he was using, reminding him of his wife's request to pick up a package of feminine hygiene products on the way home.[19]

Rehearsals can minimize catastrophes like these. They will also ensure that you are familiar with your material by the time you face your audience. As you practice your talk, follow the guidelines below.

Rehearse on Your Feet, before an Audience
Mental rehearsal has its place, but you won't know if your ideas sound good or if they fit into the available time until you say them aloud. Rehearse several times in front of real live listeners. In fact, the more closely the size of your practice audience resembles the number of people you will face in your real presentation, the more confident you will feel.[20] David Green, a curriculum director for Dale Carnegie & Associates, explains: "That's what rehearsal is for—to get your mind off the content and onto connecting with an audience. . . ."[21]

Expect Your Talk to Run 20 Percent Longer
Presentations almost always run longer in real time than during rehearsals. If you are speaking for 10 minutes, rehearse for about 8. Even if your talk ultimately runs a bit short, nobody will mind.

Pay Special Attention to Your Introduction and Conclusion
Audiences remember the opening and closing of a talk most clearly. The first and last moments of your presentation have special importance, so make sure you deliver them effectively in a way that makes every word count.

Rehearse in a Real Setting
If possible, rehearse in the room where you will actually speak. Make sure that you have all the equipment you will need and that it all works.

Focus on Your Topic and Audience, Not on Yourself

Thinking about your feelings—especially difficult ones like anxiety—is understandable. But obsessing about your nervousness will only make you more anxious. It's far more productive to focus your energy on the message you are delivering and on the audience to whom you are delivering it. If you believe in what you're saying and you have a genuine desire to have your audience understand and accept your message, then your natural enthusiasm will take over and your nervousness will shrink to manageable size.

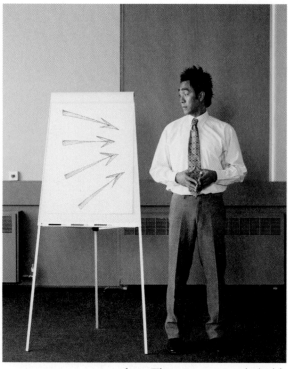

Think Rationally about Your Presentation

Some speakers feel more apprehensive because of the way they *think* about the speech than because of the act of speaking.[22] Researchers have identified a number of irrational but powerful beliefs that lead to unnecessary apprehension.[23] Among these mistaken beliefs are the following three myths.

Myth: A Presentation Must Be Perfect

Whether you're addressing a meeting of potential clients worth millions of dollars to your company or a small group of trainees, your presentation must be clearly organized, well documented, and effectively delivered. Expecting it to be perfect, though, is a surefire prescription for nervousness and depression. "Practice only makes you better," says Otis Williams Jr., founder of a professional development and training firm in Cincinnati, "but perfection doesn't exist. The goal is to become so comfortable with what you're saying, it'll roll off your tongue with minimum effort."[24] A talk can be effective without being flawless. The same principle holds for other types of speaking errors. Most listeners won't notice if you omit a point or rearrange an idea or two.

Myth: It Is Possible to Persuade the Entire Audience

Even the best products don't sell to everyone, and even the most talented people don't win the full support of their audiences. It is unrealistic to expect one presentation will achieve everything you are seeking. If you think of your remarks as one step in a campaign to achieve your long-term goals, you will feel less pressure. Chapter 13 offers more tips on how to gradually move your audience toward your ultimate goal.

Myth: The Worst Will Probably Happen

Some pessimistic speakers make themselves unnecessarily nervous by dwelling on the worst possible outcomes. They imagine themselves tripping on the way to the podium, going blank, or mixing up their ideas. They picture the audience asking unanswerable questions, responding with hostility, or even laughing. Even though such disasters are unlikely, these daydreams take on a life of their own and may create a self-fulfilling prophecy: The fearful thoughts themselves can cause the speaker to bungle a presentation.

Replacing this type of self-defeating thinking with more rational beliefs can result in dramatically increased confidence when you face an audience.[25] One way to overcome the irrational fear of failure is to indulge your catastrophic fantasies. Picture yourself fainting from terror, everyone falling asleep, or the boss firing you on the spot. Then consider the slim likelihood that these worst-case scenarios are likely to happen. Next, consider the possibility that you will encounter minor problems, such as being interrupted or encountering a technology glitch. Consider how you can manage these challenges, and how little they are likely to affect the success of your presentation. Now imagine the best possible outcome, such as receiving a standing ovation or an immediate promotion to the vice presidency. And consider more probable positive outcomes such as keeping the audience's attention and achieving your goal. Realize that catastrophes are unlikely and that, to a great extent, you have the power to determine the outcome of your presentation.

review points

- An extemporaneous style of delivery is usually the most effective of the four types (manuscript, memorized, extemporaneous, impromptu) as it combines the enthusiasm of spontaneity with the accuracy of rehearsal. Manuscript delivery may be necessary for legal or diplomatic reasons.

- A speaker's notes should be brief, legible, and inconspicuous.

- When an impromptu talk is necessary, it is most effective if the speaker presents a clear thesis; supports it with reasons, logic, or facts; speaks without apologizing; and does not ramble on.

- Good delivery involves visual, verbal, and vocal elements. Visually, a speaker needs to look enthusiastic and confident by getting set physically and making eye contact before beginning; by maintaining eye contact and moving naturally; and by ending without rushing away.

- Verbally, a speaker should use an oral style, avoid calling attention to mistakes, and use appropriate vocabulary and pronunciation.

- Vocally, a speaker sounds well rehearsed and committed to both the topic and the audience by using enough volume, variety, and pauses without disfluencies.

- Question-and-answer sessions are part of almost every presentation. They allow a speaker to respond to an audience quickly. Decide whether to invite questions during or after your prepared presentation. Handling questions during a talk permits you to clarify points as they arise, although there is a risk of getting sidetracked. Responding to questions after the talk lets you control the timing of information.

- Speakers can improve Q&A sessions by asking a question if no one else does, anticipating potential questions, clarifying complex questions, focusing on and addressing the audience with respect, and providing a summary.

- Anxiety about speaking is common and a manageable amount of anxiety even contributes to an energetic presentation. Successful speakers keep anxiety within tolerable limits by accepting it as normal, speaking often, rehearsing, being audience-centered (not self-centered), and thinking rationally.

- Rational thought dispels the myths that the speech needs to be perfect to be effective, that everyone in a single presentation can be persuaded, and that catastrophes are certain.

key terms

Test your understanding of these key terms by visiting the Online Learning Center Web site at www.mhhe.com/adler10e.

disfluencies   388
extemporaneous presentation   379
impromptu presentation   380

manuscript presentation   378
memorized presentation   378

activities

Go to the self-quizzes at the Online Learning Center at www.mhhe.com/adler10e to test your knowledge of chapter concepts.

1. Invitation to Insight

With two or more classmates, try the various styles of delivery for yourself. Follow these steps:

a. Begin by choosing a paragraph of text on an appropriate business or professional topic. You can write the copy yourself or select an article from a newspaper, magazine, or some other publication.

b. Read the text to your listeners verbatim. Pay attention to your feelings as you deliver the comments. Do you feel comfortable and enthusiastic? How do your listeners describe your delivery?

c. Try to memorize and then deliver the segment. How difficult is it to recall the remarks? How effective is your delivery?

d. Now deliver the same remarks extemporaneously, rephrasing them in your own words. See whether this approach leaves you more comfortable and your listeners more favorably impressed.

2. Skill Builder

Locate a section of written material from a basic text. Prepare to present the information from this section as an extemporaneous speech. Create a set of speaking notes, written as key phrases rather than as complete sentences. Your notes should be arranged in outline format with an introduction (with an attention-getter, thesis, and preview), a body (organized according to main points and supporting points), and a conclusion.

Then use these notes to present the ideas extemporaneously.

3. Invitation to Insight

Scan a current television guide and select a program in which a speaker is making some sort of oral presentation. The subject matter is not important: The show can be educational, religious, political, or news-related.

a. Turn down the volume, and observe the speaker's visual delivery. Notice the effects of dress, posture, gesture, facial expression, and eye contact.

b. What do these aspects of delivery suggest about the speaker's status, enthusiasm, sincerity, and competence?

4. Invitation to Insight

Locate a television or radio program that involves an oral presentation on some subject. The content is not important. Interview shows are fine, but don't choose shows in which the characters are acting roles other than themselves. Use the criteria in the Self-Assessment on page 389 to evaluate the quality of delivery. What lessons can you apply to your speaking from your analysis of this speaker?

5. Skill Builder

Practice using an oral-speaking style. Fill in the empty boxes below with examples of effective oral language. A few examples have been completed for you.

Advice	Poor	Better
Keep most sentences short.	"Members of field staff, who are isolated from one another and work alone most of the time, need better technology for keeping in touch with one another while in the field as well as with the home office."	"Members of the field staff work alone most of the time. This makes it hard for them to keep in touch with one another and with the home office. They need better means of technology to stay in contact."
	"The idea I'd like to explain to you is that, although avoiding and accommodating seem like polite ways of interacting, it can sometimes be preferable to employ an assertive linguistic style."	

	"A substantial body of research indicates that organizing your remarks clearly can make your messages more understandable, keep your audience happy, and boost your image as a speaker."	
Use personal pronouns freely.	"People often ask . . ."	"You might ask . . ."
	"Those who attempt to use this strategy don't always succeed at first."	
	"Students would be well advised to learn strategies of effective communication."	
Use the active voice.	"It was decided that . . ."	"We decided."
	"It has been pointed out that . . ."	
	"Memorization was tried by some of the most apprehensive student speakers in the class."	
Use contractions often.	"We do not expect many changes."	"We don't expect many changes."
	"I will describe the strategies that I have found to be most effective in conducting interviews."	
	"It is important to ponder how often you have been in this situation."	
Address your listeners by name.	"We're pleased to present our ideas this morning."	"Ms. Diaz, it's a pleasure to describe our ideas to you this morning."
	"Members of the audience might like to try this idea."	
	"Last week someone gave a speech about wearing seat belts. Tonight I'll build on that theme."	

6. Invitation to Insight

You can gain useful insights about managing communication apprehension by interviewing several professionals who frequently deliver presentations. Inquire whether they have ever felt anxiety about speaking in front of others. If so, how have they managed their stage fright?

resources

 For extensive readings and Web sites on delivering presentations, see the Online Learning Center Web site at **www.mhhe.com/adler10e.**

13

Types of Business Presentations

chapter outline

Informative Presentations
  Briefings
  Reports
  Training

Persuasive Presentations
  Organizing Persuasive Messages
  Types of Persuasive Presentations
  Strategies for Ethical Persuasion

Group Presentations
  Approaches to Organizing a Group Presentation
  Planning Introductions, Conclusions, and Transitions in Group Presentations
  Delivering a Group Presentation

Special-Occasion Speaking
  Welcoming a Guest or Group
  Introducing Another Speaker
  Honoring a Person or an Institution
  Giving a Toast
  Presenting an Award
  Accepting an Award
Review Points
Key Terms
Activities
Resources

chapter objectives

After reading this chapter, you should be able to

1. Prepare and deliver the following types of informative presentations: briefing, feasibility report, status report, final report, training session.
2. Choose the most persuasive organization plan for your topic, audience, and situation.
3. Understand the elements of and be able to construct motivational speeches, goodwill speeches, proposals, and sales presentations.
4. Design a persuasive appeal that is ethical and effective.
5. Distinguish persuasive strategies (problem–solution, comparative advantage, criteria satisfaction, and motivated sequence) and use each in appropriate presentations.
6. Work with others to plan and deliver a group presentation.
7. Prepare and deliver remarks for these special occasions: welcoming remarks, introducing another speaker, honoring a person or institution, giving a toast, and presenting and accepting an award.

After reading this far, you know how to deliver an effective presentation. The information in Chapters 10 through 12 will serve you well, but specific situations call for specific approaches. This chapter offers guidelines for delivering a variety of presentations: informative talks (briefings, reports, training), persuasive talks in various forms, group presentations, and remarks you will make on special occasions (welcoming remarks, introductions, giving and accepting awards, honoring special guests, and celebratory toasts).

This chapter builds on the skills you have already learned, helping you gain the extra margin of effectiveness that can make your presentations interesting and effective—even outstanding.

Informative Presentations

Briefings, reports, training, and explanations are certainly informative, but there is also a persuasive element to most, if not all, good informative talks. Unless your audience is already motivated to hear what you have to say—whether management will be giving end-of-year bonuses in December, for example—you'll need to convince them that your remarks are worth listening to. Furthermore, you will almost always be trying to create a good impression about yourself—a persuasive goal. Despite the overlap between informative and persuasive speaking, it's worthwhile to focus on how to proceed when your primary goal is "teaching," not "preaching."

Briefings

Briefings are short talks that give already interested and knowledgeable audience members the specific information they need to do their jobs. Some briefings update listeners on what has happened in the past. For example, nurses and police officers attend briefings before each shift to learn what has been happening since their last watch. Other briefings focus on the future. The executive chef of a restaurant might brief waiters about the details of the day's menu specials, and the account representative handling an advertising account might brief the agency's team about a client's interests and quirks before an important meeting. Although used for many purposes, briefings share the following characteristics:

- *Length.* As the name suggests, most briefings are short—usually no more than 2 or 3 minutes on a given subject.

- *Organization.* Because of their brevity, briefings usually don't require the kinds of attention-grabbing introductions or conclusions described in Chapter 10. They are organized in a simple way, usually topically or chronologically.

- *Content.* Briefings may summarize a position ("As you know, we're committed to answering every phone call within 1 minute"), but they usually don't make complex arguments in its favor. Most briefing attendees already know why they are there, and the main focus should be getting them ready to do the job at hand.

- *Presentation aids.* Some briefings may include simple visual aids ("Here's what our new employee ID badges will look like"), but they rarely contain the kind of detail found in longer and more complex presentations.

- *Language and delivery.* Because of their informal nature, briefings are usually quite conversational. Delivery is more matter-of-fact than dramatic.

Here is a sample briefing for a group of representatives who are preparing to staff a start-up company's exhibit booth at a trade show. Notice that the remarks are concise and well organized. They briefly state a thesis ("How we handle ourselves will make a huge difference") and then lay out clear instructions for the sales team.

> *This is our first chance to show the public what we've got. The way we handle ourselves the next 3 days can make a huge difference in our initial year. I know you're up to the job. Here are a few last-minute items before we get going.*
>
> *First, about the brochures: They were supposed to show up today via overnight mail, but they haven't arrived yet. Casey will keep checking with the mail room, and if they aren't here*

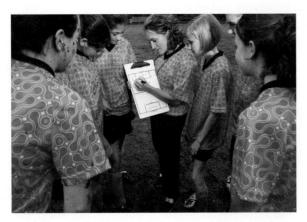

> *by 9:00 he will head over to the copy shop across the street and print out 500 fact sheets that we can use until the brochures arrive. So if the brochures are here, we'll use them. If they're not here, we hand out the fact sheets.*
>
> *It's going to get very busy, especially midmorning and midafternoon. You may not have as much time as you'd like to chat with visitors. At the very least, be sure to do three things. First, be sure each person is signed up for the drawing for our free Caribbean vacation. The information they give us on the sign-up sheets will help us track who visited our booth.*
>
> *Second, be sure to invite each person to the reception we're giving tomorrow night. Give them one of our printed invitations so they know where and when it is.*

Finally—and this is the most important thing—ask them what product they're using and how they like it. If they are happy with their current product, find out what they like about it and show them ways in which they might find ours even easier to use. If they don't like the product they're using, show them the features of ours.

Remember—stay upbeat and never criticize our competitors. Listen to the customers, and show them how our product can meet their needs. Any questions?

Reports

In a **report,** you give your audience an account of what you or someone you represent has learned or done. Reports come in an almost endless variety. Table 13–1 lists some common types. Some are internal, given to audiences within your organization. Others are external, delivered to outsiders such as clients, agencies, or the general public. Some reports are written, and others are oral. Even written reports are often presented orally. Some reports are extremely long and detailed, while others are quite brief. Finally, some reports are formal and others are presented informally.

An organization's culture determines the manner in which you present a report: brief or elaborate, with or without visual aids and question-and-answer sessions, and so on. Learn the conventions for your audience by watching accomplished colleagues and asking experienced (and successful) co-workers.

Status Reports
Probably the most common type of informative presentation is the **status report,** sometimes called a *progress report.* In many meetings, you can expect to hear someone ask, "How's the project going?"

The person asking this question usually doesn't want a long-winded blow-by-blow account of everything that has happened since your last report. You will gain the appreciation of your audience and boost your credibility by presenting a brief, clear summary of the situation. The following format will almost always serve you well. Cover each of the points briefly, and expect your listeners to pose questions when they want more information.

Table 13–1	Common Report Types

Progress/Status
- Contractor or architect's report to client
- Quarterly financial report to board of directors
- Monthly marketing report to marketing manager
- Annual report to public

Investigative
- Was a customer's complaint justified?
- Why has our overhead increased 15 percent in the last year?
- Is there gender bias in our hiring and promotions?

Feasibility
- Will staying open 24/7 be profitable?
- Can we afford to offer health insurance to part-time staff?

1. *Review the project's purpose.*

2. *State the current status of the project.* When relevant, include the people involved (giving credit for their contributions) and the methods you have used.

3. *Identify any obstacles you have encountered and attempts you have made to overcome those obstacles.* If appropriate, ask for assistance.

4. *Describe your next milestone.* Explain what steps you will take, and when they will happen.

5. *Forecast the future of the project.* Focus on your ability to finish the job as planned by the scheduled completion date.

A brief progress report would sound something like this:

On February 3, we were told to come up with an improved Web site for the company. [Reviews the project's purpose.] *Paul and I have been exploring the sites of other companies in the field, and we've developed a list of features that our site should have. We'll be happy to share it with anybody who is interested.* [Describes the current status of the project. In a longer progress report, the speaker might identify the features, and even give examples of them.]

We know we'll need a Web site designer soon, and we haven't found anybody locally whose work we like. [Identifies issues and problems. In a longer report, the speaker might list the shortcomings.] *We would welcome any suggestions you might have. If you have some names and contact information, please e-mail them to me so we'll have them in writing.*

We plan to pick a designer and have sketches ready by the end of next month. [Describes next milestone.] *If we can do that, we should be able to have the new Web site up by the end of March, right on schedule.* [Forecasts the future of the project.]

Final Reports   As its name suggests, a **final report** is delivered upon completion of an undertaking. The length and formality of a final report will depend on the scope of that undertaking. If you are describing a weekend conference to your colleagues it would most likely be quite short and informal. On the other hand, a task force reporting to top management or the general public on a year-long project would most likely deliver a detailed and much more formal report. You can adjust the following guidelines to fit your situation:

1. *Introduce the report.* State your name and your role unless everyone in the audience already knows you. Briefly describe the undertaking you are reporting on.

2. *Provide necessary background.* Tell your listeners what they need to know to understand why the project was undertaken, why you and others became involved, and any other factors that affected your approach.

3. *Describe what happened.* Explain what happened during the undertaking. Aim this discussion at the level of interest appropriate for your audience. For example, if others will be following in your footsteps, give details of challenges and how you dealt with them. If other persons were involved, mention them and offer your thanks.

4. *Describe the results.* Report on the outcomes of the undertaking. Include a discussion of successes and failures. Describe any future events related to your topic.

5. *Tell listeners how to get more information.*

A very abbreviated final report might sound like this:

Hi everybody. My name is Betsy Lane, and I'm the chair of our county's United Way campaign. [Self-introduction.]

Technical Reports

There are two types of technical reports: those given to technical audiences (colleagues in your workplace or at technical conferences) and those given to nontechnical audiences (clients and customers with varying levels of expertise or officials in charge of money or decision making who don't share your level of mastery). Follow these guidelines for both types:

- Use language appropriate for your audience. For a nontechnical audience, use language that is understandable and teach technical terms that are essential to understanding the presentation. Jargon is useful for a technical audience that will understand it; use jargon with absolute precision.

- Use analogies to clarify concepts for a nontechnical audience, being certain to point out limits of an analogy.

- Adapt visual aids to the audience. The nontechnical audience needs visuals that make sense to non-experts; have extra visuals in even simpler formats to use if the audience seems unclear. Knowledgeable audiences appreciate precise data presented in formats common to your field; have extra visuals with more technical data if the audience requires it.

- Watch your audience carefully. If they seem puzzled, try to slow down, reiterate key points, use additional examples, or in a small, interactive group, stop and ask about the puzzled looks. If an audience seems bored or is losing interest, try to become more animated with greater vocal variety and movement.

Note: For more information on technical reports, see L. Gurak, *Oral Presentations for Technical Communication* (Boston: Allyn & Bacon, 2000); and M. Alley, *The Craft of Scientific Presentations* (New York: Springer-Verlag, 2002), p. 437. See also "Technical Briefings," Toastmasters International, **www.toastmasters.org/ MainMenuCategories/FreeResources/NeedHelpGivingaSpeech/ BusinessPresentations/TechnicalBriefings.aspx**.

As you know, United Way is dedicated to helping people in our community to help themselves develop healthier, more productive lives. We support over 50 agencies that provide a multitude of services: Promoting wellness for all ages and abilities, making sure that all children enter school ready to learn, helping people toward lifetime independence, sustaining safe neighborhoods, and educating young people for responsible adulthood. The need and the opportunities are great, and we set the bar high this year: $3 million. [Provides necessary background.]

This has been an especially challenging year for local nonprofits: The economy has been on the weak side, and there are more deserving causes and people needing support than ever. Rather than letting this situation discourage us, it energized the United Way team. This year we were fueled by the efforts of almost 2,500 volunteers at over 400 organizations, large and small. Every one of them gave generously of their time and talents. [Describes what happened.]

I am delighted to tell you that, as of last Friday, we met our goal. The campaign has raised over $3,125,000 in donations and pledges for the coming year. This means we won't have to say "no" to a single organization. [Describes results.]

There is so much to tell you about this campaign and the work of so many terrific people. We do hope you'll read more about the effort that led to this year's success. Our report will be available in about 3 weeks, and in the meantime you can read the highlights on the United Way Web site. [Tells listeners how to get more information.]

For now, though, let's celebrate!

Feasibility Reports A **feasibility report** evaluates one or more potential action steps and recommends how the organization should proceed. Would a bonus system increase profitability and retain employees? Is job sharing a good idea? Would subsidizing employees who use public transportation solve the parking problem? Feasibility studies help answer questions like these.

Most feasibility reports should contain the following elements.

1. *Introduction.* Briefly define the problem and explain its consequences. Explain why it is important to consider the alternatives you will be discussing. Briefly show the audience that you have approached this problem methodically. Consider explaining your conclusions, if the audience won't object strongly. If listeners are likely to object to your recommendation, consider postponing it until later in your presentation.

2. *Criteria.* Introduce the standards you used to evaluate alternative courses of action. For example,

   - Will the course of action really do what's wanted?
   - Can we implement it?
   - Will implementation fit within time constraints?
   - Can we afford it?

   Explaining your criteria is especially important if your recommendations are likely to be controversial. It's hard for anyone to argue with criteria like those above, so getting listeners to accept them before they hear your recommendations can be an effective way of selling your conclusions. (See the criteria satisfaction organization plan in Chapter 10.)

3. *Methodology.* Describe the process you used to identify and evaluate the plan(s) under consideration. The amount of detail you supply will depend on the audience and situation. For a relatively minor project, your explanation will probably be brief. For a major feasibility study—especially when it's controversial or when your credibility is in question—you will probably need to describe your approach in detail.

4. *Possible solutions.* Provide a detailed explanation of each solution you considered.

5. *Evaluation of the solutions.* Measure the suitability of each solution against the criteria you listed earlier. Offer whatever supporting material is necessary to show how you arrived at your conclusions.

6. *Recommendations.* Describe the solution that best fits the criteria provided earlier. If you have done a good job evaluating solutions using the criteria already introduced, the recommendation should be relatively brief and straightforward.

7. *Conclusion.* Briefly summarize your findings, showing how they can help solve the problem at hand.

Training

Training teaches listeners how to *do* something: operate a piece of equipment or use software, relate effectively with the public, avoid or deal with sexual harassment—the range of training topics is almost endless. Training can be informal, such as the simple advice an experienced employee gives a newcomer about how to transfer a telephone call. At the other end of the spectrum, some training is extensive and highly organized. Corporations including Disney, Anheuser-Busch, Dell Computer, Harley-Davidson, and General Electric have full-blown institutes dedicated to training their employees.[1]

Successful businesses recognize the value of training. One measure of its importance is the amount of time and money that firms invest in training their employees. For example, at McDonald's, every person who takes an order or prepares food has

Adult Learning Styles

Adults in the workplace learn in ways that are different from methods used in educational institutions from primary school through university.

Adults learn best when

- Material is clearly relevant to their personal lives. Show them what personal value the training program will have for them. Encourage learners to explore and explain how they can use the material you present.

- Taking an active role in the training process. Don't just lecture. Give them a chance to experience the principles you are introducing.

- Training is aimed at their level of experience. Go over their heads and you will lose them; approach the topic too simplistically and you will insult and bore them.

- Given some control over the pace of learning. Be prepared to speed up or slow down your coverage in response to feedback from your audience.

- E-Learning is as enjoyable and engaging for the boomer generation as it is for Gen Y.

Sources: Based on information in M. S. Knowles, "Adult Learning," in *The ASTD Training and Development Handbook*, ed. R. L. Craig (New York: McGraw-Hill, 1996), pp. 553–565; M. Scullard and J. Sugeman, "Everything DiSC Pulse: Challenging Your Assumptions About E-Learning," *Presentations* (March 5, 2009). Retrieved April 4, 2009, from **www.presentations.com/msg/search/article_display .jsp?vnu_content_id=1003947907**.

received 80 hours of instruction.[2] On any given day, International Business Machines Corporation is training 22,000 of its employees somewhere in the world. This sort of training doesn't come cheap. The annual cost of this training for IBM is $1.5 billion, not counting the participants' time.[3]

Some training is done by experts. Large organizations have staffers who design and deliver instructional programs. There are also firms and freelancers who create and deliver training on a fee-for-service basis. (See the Online Learning Center Web site at **www.mhhe.com/adler10e** for more information about professional trainers.) Despite the existence of a training industry, the U.S. Bureau of Labor Statistics says that almost 75 percent of all work-related training is delivered informally on the job.[4] This fact suggests that, sooner or later, you will be responsible for designing and delivering training no matter what your job may be. The information here will help you do a good job.

Planning a Training Program A successful training presentation begins long before you face your audience, when you use the guidelines in Chapter 10 (pp. 305–313) to analyze the audience, the occasion, and your own goals and knowledge about the topic. Most training experts agree about the importance of each of the following steps.[5]

Define the training goal Training always aims to change the way your audience acts, so the place to begin is to identify who you want to teach and the results you want to bring about. The more specifically you can identify the target audience and the desired outcome, the more successful your training will be. You can see the difference between vague and specific goals in these examples:

Vague: Train employees to deal more effectively with customer complaints.

Better: Everyone in the Sales and Customer Service departments will know how to use the tactics of listening, asking questions, and agreeing to deal more effectively with customer complaints.

Vague: Train the staff to use our new online purchasing system.

Better: Employees who are authorized to buy new and replacement equipment will know how to use the new online purchasing system to locate vendors, place orders, track shipments, and check their department's purchasing budget.

See the discussion of "Setting Your Goal and Developing the Thesis" in Chapter 10 for more guidelines on defining goals.

Develop a schedule and list of resources   Once you have defined your goals and identified the target audience, you are ready to design the training. This step includes

- Figuring how much time you will need to plan and publicize the training, and the steps you need to take between now and the time you deliver it.

- Identifying the staffing and physical resources you need, and making sure they are available. Line up the facility, and make sure its furnishings and layout suit your design. Identify the materials participants will need (pens, pencils, folders, name tags; or tents, refreshments, etc.) and the equipment you will use (computer, projection system, lectern, charts, etc.).

- Creating and/or purchasing any necessary training materials.

Involve the audience   Lecturing to a passive audience has its place, but it isn't the only way to train an audience. Figure 13–1 lists several ways you can present new information. It shows that listeners who are actively involved in a presentation will understand and remember the material far better than a passive audience.[6] People will learn how to operate a particular machine, fill in a certain form, or perform a specified procedure much better with hands-on experience than they will if they are only told what to do. For example, Lever Corporation trains its representatives to sell industrial cleaning equipment by teaching them to operate the machines themselves.[7]

FIGURE 13–1

Average Retention Rates of Various Training Methods

An important learning principle, supported by extensive research, is that people learn best when they are actively involved in the learning process. The "lower down the cone" you go, the more you learn and retain.

Source: Reprinted by permission of NTL® Institute for Behavioral Sciences.

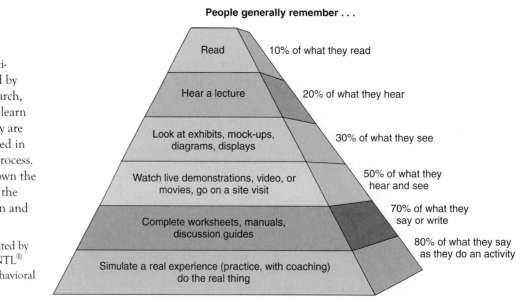

People generally remember . . .

- Read — 10% of what they read
- Hear a lecture — 20% of what they hear
- Look at exhibits, mock-ups, diagrams, displays — 30% of what they see
- Watch live demonstrations, video, or movies, go on a site visit — 50% of what they hear and see
- Complete worksheets, manuals, discussion guides — 70% of what they say or write
- Simulate a real experience (practice, with coaching) do the real thing — 80% of what they say as they do an activity

technology tip

Podcasting

A **podcast** is an audio (or sometimes video) program that is available for download to subscribers who use "podcatching" applications like Apple's iTunes. Subscribers can listen to podcasts when and where they choose, on either a computer or a portable device like a smart cell phone or MP3 player.

Podcasts can serve a number of useful functions:

- **Customer support** Providers can deliver updates and guidelines to their customers and clients.

- **Marketing** Podcasts can disseminate news about your product or service to media outlets and other interested parties. For example, realtors can give their clients a virtual tour of properties.

- **Self-promotion** You can talk about your latest work. (Be sure to present this information in ways that have value for listeners!)

- **Internal communication** Keep subscribers informed about developments that affect their organization: product updates, staffing changes, legislation, trends in the field, etc.

- **Training and teaching** Faculty can make lectures available to students. Health care providers can deliver news to practitioners and the public.

- **Advocacy** Encourage subscribers to support your point of view and agenda. (Write your legislator about pending legislation.)

Content and Delivery Tips

- **Provide value to listeners** Put yourself in the position of subscribers: Think about what information would be valuable to them, and make sure your podcasts provide it.

- **Keep your message brief** Busy people with short attention spans want information that's concise.

As with any good presentation, design with length in mind. Edit ruthlessly. If your material still takes a long time to present, break it into several short episodes.

- **Prepare, but don't script** Speak extemporaneously, as with most effective presentations. Use the best combination of coherence and conversational style.

- **Make it engaging and interactive** Use software to spice up the broadcast: Add theme music and create transitional sound effects between show segments. Add interest by using the kinds of stories, examples, comparisons, and other forms of support described in Chapter 11. Encourage feedback from subscribers and share listener response in future podcasts.

Production and Delivery Tips

- **Reduce distracting noise** Nobody wants to hear your ringing phone or barking dog. Microphones can be sensitive, so be aware of ambient noise such as the hum of a ventilation system or the buzz of fluorescent lights.

- **Use a good microphone and speaking technique** Practice microphone technique by recording and listening to yourself. Don't publish a podcast until its audio quality is professional.

- **Link podcasts to a blog or Web site** A Web site or blog provides a single location where you can compile all your podcasts. Users can bookmark this location and embed a link to it in their postings and correspondence. Your blog or Web site also makes it easy for listeners to comment. Software like blogspot (www.blogspot.com) makes it easy for you to create an online repository of all your material.

Sources: Podcasting Tools, **www.podcasting-tools.com;** A. D. Detrick, "Is Your Culture Podcast-Ready?" Training Day, February 8, 2007, **http://vnutravel.typepad.com/trainingday/2007/02/is _your_culture.html;** and J. VanOrden, "7 Tips for Podcast Success," **http://jasonvanorden.com/7-tips-for-podcast-success-in-2007**.

A variety of other tools involve the audience in a way that boosts both understanding and interest: quizzes, contests, and having trainees teach one another. For example, if you plan to give the audience statistics such as the ethnic makeup of the U.S., first present them with blank charts listing major ethnic groups and have them try to fill in the correct percentages. This way, when you present the information, they will be more eager to hear the statistics and see how accurate or inaccurate their estimates were. The few minutes you take to let an audience fill in the blanks measurably enhances interest in your figures. Similarly, you can create worksheets and surveys that mirror information you'll present. You can also involve the audience by letting them practice the skill you are teaching, having volunteers demonstrate a skill, or pausing for an audience to read a passage silently. You can let the whole audience brainstorm or form small groups to brainstorm and then let each group report back.[8]

Listeners are likely to understand and remember a message when you use more than one approach. You can show a diagram, for example, while you describe it. If you're discussing a physical object, you might display photos of it on slides or even bring in the object itself to show your listeners. If you are illustrating a process, you might decide to play a brief video of it. Talking about a new line of clothing or a new food product isn't nearly as effective as giving your audience a firsthand look or taste, for example. Likewise, telling listeners in a training session how to deal with customer objections isn't nearly as effective as demonstrating the procedure for them or letting them handle a situation themselves.

Organize your presentation   Use the tips in this section and see Chapter 10 for methods of organizing the overall presentation. The most reliable format is probably a problem–solution approach, since listeners are most likely to pay attention to the information you provide when they view it as solving a problem that they face.

Delivering the Training   When you finally are ready to deliver the training, several tips can help make it most effective.

Link the topic to the audience   Sometimes the intrinsic interest of the subject is reason enough to listen; for instance, most people would pay close attention to a session on employee benefits because they know these benefits are worth something to them personally.

What can you do with a subject that isn't intrinsically interesting? One way to boost interest is to show that listening will help the audience avoid punishment. ("Don't try to charge the company for anything you're not entitled to. If you do, you could lose your job.") A more pleasant and effective alternative involves demonstrating the payoffs that come from listening. A financial officer explaining new expense account procedures, for instance, might begin by saying, "We want to make sure you get the company to reimburse you for all expenses you're entitled to. I also don't want you to spend your own money, thinking the company will pay you back, and then find out it won't." Expense reporting might be a tedious subject to many people, but the chance to save money (or to avoid losing money) would interest most listeners.

Start with an overall picture   Every presentation needs an introduction. But when the goal is to inform listeners, a clear preview is especially important. Without an overview, your listeners can become so confused by your information trees that they won't be able to see the conceptual forest. Orient the audience by sketching the highlights of your message in enough detail to help listeners see what they are expected to know and how you will explain it to them:

> *This morning, we're going to learn about the new e-mail system. I'll start by spending a little time explaining how the system works. Then we'll talk about the four ways you can use the system. First I'll show you how you can send messages to any person or group of people in*

the company—instantly. Then we'll talk about how you can get messages others have sent you. After that you will learn how you can put items on the companywide bulletin board. Finally, I'll show you how you can take part in companywide electronic conversations about topics that interest you.

I'll spend about 10 minutes describing each of these steps in detail, and after each description you'll get a chance to try out the system yourself. By the time we break for lunch, you should be able to use the system in a way that will save you time and hassles and keep you better informed about what you need to know to get your job done. You won't be an expert, but you'll know enough to make the system work.

Emphasize the organization of your material   You can use a number of devices to help listeners understand the structure of your material:

- *Number items:* "The first advantage of the new plan is . . ." or "A second benefit the plan will give us is . . ."

- *Use signposts:* "We've talked about the benefits of our new health care plan. Now let's talk about who will provide them"; "*Another* important cost to consider is our overhead"; "*Next*, let's look at the production figures"; and "*Finally*, we need to consider changes in customer demand."

- *Use interjections:* "So what we've learned—and this is important—is that it's impossible to control personal use of office telephones."

- *Use repetition and redundancy:* "Under the old system it took 3 weeks—that's 15 working days—to get the monthly sales figures. Now we can get the numbers in just 2 days. That's right, 2 days."

- *Add internal summaries and previews:* "You can see that we've made great progress in switching to the new inventory system. As I've said, the costs were about 10 percent more than we anticipated, but we see that as a one-time expense. I wish I could be as positive about the next item on the agenda—the customer service problems we've been having. Complaints have increased. We do believe we've finally identified the problem, so let me explain it and show you how we plan to deal with it."

Cover only necessary information   You will usually be far more knowledgeable about the topic than is the audience to whom you speak. This knowledge is both a blessing and a potential curse. On the one hand, your command of the subject means

Dilbert © Scott Adams/Dist. by United Feature Syndicate, Inc. Reprinted by permission.

on your feet

Poster Presentations

Most presentations have a clearly defined beginning and ending and are delivered to a fixed group of listeners. Poster sessions are different: They present work to conference attendees who are walking around an exhibit area, choosing the topics that interest them. The presenter usually stands next to the poster, allowing for passersby to engage in one-on-one discussions.

Unlike most presentations where visual aids support the words, in poster sessions a few words support the visuals. At their best, posters are visual representations of ideas, not just papers or slides tacked on a board. Clear titles allow the viewer to locate sections of interest: goals, methods, conclusions.

Practice your skill in this unique form of communication by preparing a brief poster presentation on a topic about which you are familiar. For example, presentations in a typical group might include "How to choose an Internet Service Provider," "How restaurant menus manipulate customers," or "How to choose an internship."

Some guidelines will help you conduct effective poster sessions:

- Design your display for eye-catching viewing at arm's length. Use large type to highlight your key points rather than trying to cover everything you would put in a longer paper. Use display elements—bullets, enumeration, tables, clip art, graphs, figures, photos—rather than paragraph style, to convey your points clearly and concisely.

- Prepare a brief (less than 1 minute) explanation of your topic that expands on the information your poster describes. You can deliver this explanation to listeners who ask general questions like "Tell me more about your work."

- Be prepared to speak louder than you usually would to a small audience. Posters are often displayed in noisy, crowded environments without good acoustics.

- Keep your enthusiasm high, remembering that each new person will be hearing your explanation for the first time.

- Be prepared to give interested listeners more information on your work. A handout with more details and/or a Web site or your e-mail address can let them follow up.

Sources: Adapted from C. Coffin, "Planning and Preparing an Effective Scientific Poster," in *The Health Care Communication Group, Writing, Speaking, & Communication Skills for Health Professionals* (New Haven: Yale University Press, 2001), pp. 118–132. See also "Interactive Paper Session Tips," International Communication Association, **www.icahdq.org/conferences/interactive.asp**.

that you can explain the topic thoroughly. On the other hand, you may be tempted to give listeners more information than they want or need.

If you cover your topic in too much detail, you are likely to bore—or even antagonize—your listeners. One personnel specialist made this mistake when briefing a group of staffers about how to file claims with a new health insurance carrier. Instead of simply explaining what steps to take when they needed care, he launched into a 20-minute explanation of why the company chose the present carrier, how that company processed claims at its home office, and where each copy of the four-part claims form was directed after it was filed. By the time he got to the part of his talk that was truly important to the audience—how to get reimbursed for out-of-pocket expenses—the staffers were so bored and restless that they had a hard time sitting still for the information. Don't make a mistake like this in your presentations: As you plan your remarks, ask yourself what your listeners need to know, and tell them just that much. If they want more information, they will probably ask for it.

Avoid Jargon   Sometimes you will be introducing trainees to specialized terms and language. This may be as simple as introducing new employees to your company jargon for departments ("If you need help with your computer, call IRD") or locations ("This is what we call the Annex"). Some jargon is necessary, but don't use any more than necessary. If you overwhelm your listeners with too much specialized terminology, you will probably bore them and leave them so confused that they'll give up trying to understand the material you are explaining. Don't be a techno-snob: Tell people what they need to know in language they will understand.

Link the Familiar to the Unfamiliar   Research has shown that people have the best chance of understanding new material when it bears some relationship to information they already know.[9] Without a familiar reference point, listeners may have trouble understanding even a clear definition. Two examples illustrate how comparisons and contrasts with familiar information help make new ideas more understandable:

Confusing:	Money-market funds are mutual funds that buy corporate and government short-term investments. [In order to understand this definition, the audience needs to be familiar with money-market funds and with corporate and government short-term investments.]
More Familiar:	Money-market funds are like a collection of IOUs held by a middleman. The funds take cash from investors and lend it to corporations and the government, usually for between 30 and 90 days. These borrowers pay the fund interest on the loan, and that interest is passed along to the investors. [If the listeners understand IOUs and interest, they can follow this definition.]

Persuasive Presentations

Sooner or later, everyone needs to influence the thinking or actions of others. When an issue is especially important, persuasion frequently takes place in a presentation. Even when you have made your case in writing, a good presentation is often essential. Business consultant James Lukaszewski explains:

> We live in a "tell me" world. The last time you presented a plan to your boss to accomplish something—you know—that beautiful 2-inch-thick, tabbed notebook with 150 pages, 31 tabs, and 5,000 well-chosen words? Was it actually read? Or did your boss simply put his hand on it, look you in the eye, and say, "Show me what's in here and tell me how it's going to help us achieve our objectives."[10]

The following pages show you how to create presentations that change minds and produce the results you are seeking.

Organizing Persuasive Messages

Credibility may be important, but the way you structure your message also plays a major role in determining how successful you will be at persuading an audience. Chapter 10 discussed several patterns for organizing the body of a presentation. Here we recap the use of problem–solution, comparative advantages, criteria satisfaction, and motivated sequence patterns as they apply to persuasive situations. As Table 13-2 on page 414 shows, there is no single best plan. The one you choose will depend on the topic and your audience's attitude toward it.

Table 13–2	Considerations for Choosing a Persuasive Organization Pattern

Organization Plan	Considerations
Problem–solution	Most basic persuasive pattern. Most helpful when audience needs convincing that a problem exists.
Comparative advantages	Use when audience is considering alternatives to your proposal. Show how your plan is superior to others. Defer thesis if audience will object to idea before hearing your reasoning.
Criteria satisfaction	Use when audience is not likely to consider alternative plans. Choose criteria important to your audience, and show how your plan meets them. If audience may be hostile to your plan, introduce criteria before discussing the plan.
Motivated sequence	Use when problem and solution are easy to visualize. Effective when seeking immediate audience reaction.

Problem–Solution   As its name suggests, a **problem–solution** plan first persuades the audience that something is wrong with the present situation and then suggests how to remedy the situation. This plan works especially well when your audience does not feel a strong need to change from the status quo. Since listeners have to recognize that a problem exists before they will be interested in a solution, showing them that the present situation is not satisfactory is essential before you present your idea. For example:

Problem	Solution
Many employees are arriving late due to increasing congestion.	Offer flexible working hours.
Cost of travel is skyrocketing.	Increase capability to hold some meetings via videoconference.

A problem–solution pattern might also be used to show how updating a computer system will solve problems with inventory monitoring, why a potential customer needs a personal financial advisor, or why a department needs additional staff.

If your listeners already recognize that a problem exists, you may not need to spend much time proving the obvious. In such circumstances, you might touch on the problem in the introduction to your talk and devote the entire body to suggesting a solution. If you are competing against other ideas, however, a comparative advantages plan may be a better organization strategy.

Comparative Advantages   A **comparative advantages** approach puts several alternatives side by side and shows why yours is the best. This strategy is especially useful when the audience is considering an idea that competes with the one you're advocating. Under this circumstance, ignoring alternative plans is a bad idea. A head-on comparison that supports your case is a far more effective plan. The manager of a health club used a comparative advantages approach to encourage new members:

Introduction: When you decide to join a health club, you have several choices in the area. You might be tempted by the special introductory rates at some other clubs in town, but a feature-by-feature look shows that Millennium is your best choice.

Body:
I.   The club is open longer every day than any other club in town.
II. The club has more exercise machines than any other in town.
III. The club has a wider variety of activities than any other in town: aerobics classes, swimming, saunas, massage, racquetball, and a snack bar.
IV. The club's staff are all licensed fitness counselors—a claim that no other club in town can make.

Conclusion: When it comes to value for your dollar, Millennium is your best health-club choice.

In the preceding example, the speaker made her thesis clear at the beginning of her presentation. A comparative advantages approach also works well when you choose to defer your thesis. In this instance, you can build a case showing how your proposal is superior to the alternatives and then present your thesis as a conclusion. An insurance agent used this strategy to convince an audience to buy coverage:

Introduction: How should you spend your discretionary income?

Body: There are several alternatives.
I.   You can spend it all on recreation, but that won't buy financial security for your family if anything happens to you.
II. You can make investments to plan for the future, but there is always the risk of losing that money.
III. More expensive housing is an option, but it risks placing you even more in debt.
IV. Insurance guarantees your family an income if you die or are disabled.

Conclusion: At least some of your disposable income ought to be devoted to insurance.
[*Deferred thesis*]

In this situation, deferring the thesis was a smart idea. If the speaker had started by praising the virtues of buying insurance, most listeners would have tuned out. Since very few people relish the thought of spending their discretionary income on something as intangible as more insurance coverage, they'd probably reject the idea unless they were led to the conclusion that it is the best choice.

Criteria Satisfaction

A **criteria satisfaction** strategy sets up criteria for a plan that the audience will accept and then shows how your idea or product meets them.

"When you look for a long-distance phone carrier, you want one that has low rates. You also want one that has a strong signal and allows you to make calls when you're away from home."

After establishing your criteria, you show how the product, service, or idea you are presenting will meet the criteria.

on your feet

Public Service Announcement

Public service announcements (PSAs) are short pieces aimed at persuading audiences to support nonprofit organizations, issues, or causes.

Develop your persuasive skills by creating and presenting to your group a 30-second or 1-minute PSA that supports the good cause of your choice. This may be an on-campus service (e.g., counseling, job placement, health services, fitness center) or a community cause (United Way, open space, recycling, child care).

Organize your PSA using the motivated sequence approach described on this page and pages 327–329 in Chapter 10. Create an outline that follows this plan, labeling each step (attention, need, satisfaction, visualization, action).

"Let me show you how TeleCall offers you low rates from anywhere, with quality that meets or beats the big carriers."

It can be even more effective to invite the audience to supply the criteria. If you have researched your audience, you should know in advance what they are likely to want, and your appeal will be even more effective:

"I'd like you to tell me, What are the things that you want in a long-distance phone carrier?"

Once your listeners have identified what will satisfy them, you can show how your product or service will meet their needs. Organize criteria in the order of importance to the client, not to you.

Unlike a comparative advantages approach, a criteria satisfaction plan does not consider alternative ideas. For this reason, it is a good approach when your audience isn't likely to think of alternative plans.

Motivated Sequence As you read in Chapter 10, the **motivated sequence organization plan** has five steps:

1. Attention
2. Need
3. Satisfaction
4. Visualization
5. Action

The need and satisfaction steps are similar to those in a problem–solution approach, but the visualization and action steps add a new element. The visualization step allows listeners to picture how your solution could work for them. An event planner proposing to organize a wedding or a business meeting might show clients photos of similar occasions she planned or describe in vivid detail the way she proposes to create a memorable occasion for this client. As its name implies, the action step calls for the listeners to go beyond just agreeing with the presenter to take a step toward adopting his or her plan. Salespeople sometimes call this step "closing," because it cements the deal.

Rate your presentation on the following items using this scale: 3 = accomplished excellently, 2 = accomplished competently, 1 = needs improvement.

1. I maximized my credibility by

   a. Demonstrating my competence through knowledge of the topic and sharing my credentials.   3   2   1

   b. Earning the trust of my audience via honesty and impartiality.   3   2   1

2. I structured my arguments logically by

   a. Using the most effective organization plan for my goal and audience (problem–solution, criteria satisfaction, comparative advantages, motivated sequence).   3   2   1

   b. Avoiding the use of logical fallacies (*ad hominem, post hoc*, etc.).   3   2   1

3. I used appropriate psychological strategies such as

   a. Appealing to the needs of my audience.   3   2   1

   b. Structuring a realistic goal.   3   2   1

   c. Focusing my appeals on my critical audience segment.   3   2   1

   d. Deferring my thesis with a hostile audience.   3   2   1

   e. Presenting ample evidence to support my claims.   3   2   1

   f. Citing opposing ideas when appropriate.   3   2   1

   g. Adapting to the cultural style of my audience.   3   2   1

4. I took an ethical approach by relying on genuine persuasion, not coercion or manipulation.   3   2   1

Types of Persuasive Presentations

Unlike purely informative presentations that don't advocate a position, persuasive presentations aim to change the way an audience thinks, feels, or acts. The most common types of persuasive presentations are motivational and goodwill speeches, proposals, and sales presentations.

Consider these examples to see how common persuasion is on the job:

- Two partners are convinced that they have a winning idea for a new restaurant. They meet with a commercial loan officer from a local bank to seek financing for their project.

- Faced with a wave of injuries, the foreman of a construction crew convinces his team members that they need to observe safety practices more carefully.

- As part of a community-relations program, the electric company has started a community speakers' bureau. The bureau's director is speaking to a group of employees to recruit them as volunteers for the service.

- A group of employees has grown increasingly disgruntled with the boss's policy on vacation scheduling. They have chosen a three-person delegation to present their grievances.

Motivational Speeches

A **motivational speech** attempts to generate enthusiasm for the topic being presented. At their worst, motivational speeches can combine the most oppressive elements of a bad sermon and a high school pep rally. On the other hand, when delivered effectively and at the proper time, such presentations can produce good results. For example, the organizers of a fund-raising event need to generate enthusiasm to recruit and motivate volunteers. Likewise, a manager trying to persuade her subordinates to fill out lengthy reports or work extra hard to cut costs will succeed only if she can sell her ideas to a potentially skeptical workforce.

Goodwill Speeches

As its name implies, a **goodwill speech** aims to create a favorable image of the speaker's cause in the minds of the audience. Representatives of organizations frequently speak to audiences to promote interest or support for their organizations. A corporate recruiter addressing graduating seniors and a bank economist explaining economic forecasts are making speeches of goodwill. So is the company's representative addressing the press after an oil spill.

These goodwill speeches may seem informative, but they also try to change the attitudes or behavior of their listeners. The corporate recruiter is trying to encourage some students to apply for jobs with his company; the economist is trying to build the image of her institution as a leading business bank; and the utility company representative is trying to soften negative reactions.

Proposals

In a **proposal** you advocate that your audience take specific action. Some proposals are aimed at external audiences. Other proposals are focused on internal audiences. You might, for example, try to persuade management to support a ride-sharing program or reimburse employees for education costs, or you might try to convince your boss to give you more staffing support or a raise in pay. (See the Career Tip on page 419 for advice on requesting a raise.)

Whatever the topic and audience, the most straightforward approach for a proposal is the problem–solution approach described in Chapter 10. While the particulars will vary, each section of this two-part approach is likely to include information listed here:

1. *Introduce the problem*
   a. Demonstrate the nature of the problem in terms the audience will understand.
   b. Show undesirable consequences of the problem.
   c. Highlight ethical dimensions of the situation if the current situation is morally wrong.
   d. Provide causal analysis of the situation. (How did this problem develop?)
2. *Provide a solution (with supporting evidence)*
   a. Describe the positive consequences of your proposal.
   b. Show how your proposal will avoid bad consequences.
   c. Highlight the ethical reasons for your approach. Show why it's the right thing to do.
   d. Address the feasibility of your proposal. Show that it can be done: cost, time, motivation, etc. Include an operation timeline to strengthen the proposal.

How to Request a Raise

Asking for a raise is a kind of proposal, even though you typically will present your arguments informally to your boss. Here are tips that can increase your chances for success:

The best time to seek a raise

- When you or your department have been recognized for doing a good job.
- After you have volunteered to take on additional responsibilities (and have handled them successfully).
- If the organization can't easily replace you or do without your services.
- After you have contributed directly to the company's profitability and success (and you can demonstrate this connection).
- When the organization is in strong financial shape.
- When your relationship with your boss is good.

What to ask for

- Research the compensation range for jobs like yours in the industry. Check with professional associations in your field or Web-based salary surveys such as **www.jobstar.org.** Demonstrate that your request is reasonable by providing comparative figures.
- Consider asking for noncash benefits. For many people, pay isn't the only kind of compensation. For example, you might also seek more vacation time, a more flexible schedule, discounts on company products, or use of a company vehicle.

Don'ts

- Don't get emotional. Losing your temper is unlikely to be persuasive, and it can damage your long-term relationship with your boss.
- Don't confuse effort with contribution. Working hard is admirable, but effort alone probably won't be enough to earn you a raise. Show your boss that the *results* you produce justify better compensation.
- Don't rely on longevity ("I've been here for 8 years") or personal need ("My rent just went up 20 percent"). It's better to demonstrate that you *deserve* a raise.

Here, in outline form, is how the problem–solution plan would look in the body of a presentation proposing an employee wellness program:

I. Health-related problems are hurting our company [*Problem*]
    A. Health costs are increasing
        1. Insurance premiums are increasing
        2. Out-of-pocket expenses for employees are growing
    B. Productivity is declining due to employee health problems
        1. Absenteeism is growing
        2. Workers who stay on the job are less productive
        3. Some employees are leaving us due to health problems

II. A wellness program could reduce the impact of these problems [*Solution*]
    A. Elements of a program
        1. Nutrition education
        2. Exercise education
        3. Substance-abuse counseling
    B. Benefits
        1. Healthier employees
        2. More-productive employees
        3. Lower health costs (insurance and out-of-pocket)

technology tip

Making the Most of Webinars

A webinar is a hybrid form of online communication, part meeting and part presentation. The host presents a product or idea to a group of participants who can comment and ask questions. Some Webinars are supported by dedicated software such as GoToWebinar, which allows audience polling and gives attendees a chance to exchange instant messages during the event. Others consist of a one-way Web feed, with members phoning in to establish an audio connection. Webinars may be offered live or in an on-demand format.

Regardless of the format, hosting a Webinar calls for all the skills you would use in any presentation, plus a few unique ones. The following tips can help make your Webinar experience a success:

Tips for the Host

- **Plan your technology** Make sure your hosting setup is absolutely reliable. Test to see that participants can log on, view your Web feed, and both talk and hear you. Make sure you can track their attendance and hear their remarks. You can't afford to antagonize participants with connection problems.

- **Start professionally** Create a welcome screen with instructions and an agenda for attendees to see when attendees log on. Make sure you welcome callers individually as each one checks in. If possible, mute the voices of participants until you are ready to invite comments.

- **Plan your time** An hour or less is long enough. Midweek and midday can work well if you are reaching across time zones and to large audiences. Be sure your material will fit into the allotted time so you don't end early or run out of time. Practice, practice, practice!

- **Keep the audience engaged** Unlike in a face-to-face session, you can't see whether participants are listening. You typically risk losing people's interest when one topic lasts longer than 10 minutes, so create variety to maintain interest. Consider inviting questions at several points instead of waiting until the end of your talk.

Tips for Attendees

- **Test your connection in advance** Most Webinars provide an e-mail with the URL to join. Test this link well before the Web meeting starts. You won't be able to join the conference, but you should get an idea of whether you'll need other software like an ActiveX component.

- **Mute your phone** Put your phone on mute if possible. Background noise such as typing, music, and eating will distract and annoy attendees, especially those who wear headsets.

- **Don't hog the session** Webinars aren't the time to challenge presenters or try to show how much you know. Be respectful of others when asking questions. Ask the presenter if it's okay to ask another question so you don't use all the available time.

- **Inquire about a session archive** Many Webinars are recorded, and others are accompanied by informational files you can save for future referral. Be sure to ask the host about these.

Sources: "10 Great Webinar Tips." Retrieved March 23, 2009 from **www.powerwebresults.com/webinar-tips.html;** "Tips for Conducting a Successful Webinar," *Tech Soup,* February 3, 2009. Retrieved March 23, 2009, from **www.techsoup.org/learningcenter/training/page11265.cfm;** and W. W. Turmel, *6 Weeks to a Great Webinar* (Glen Ellyn, IL: Achis Marketing Service, 2008).

When circumstances warrant, you might consider organizing your proposal by using one of the other persuasive strategies originally discussed in Chapter 10 and revisited later in this chapter: criteria satisfaction, comparative advantages, or motivated sequence.

Sales Presentations

In a **sales presentation,** one party presents remarks aimed at persuading another to purchase a product or service. Unlike the communication in retail settings, sales presentations are planned in advance. Sales presentations range from platform speeches in front of large audiences to less formal sit-down talks with small groups of decision makers.

Whatever their size, sales presentations will adhere to the guidelines that follow.

Establish client relationships before your presentation   Whenever possible, establish relationships with your audience before you make your presentation. Getting to know the people you hope to persuade will give you valuable information on what they want, and suggest how you can satisfy their needs. Just as important, preexisting relationships will make your listeners more comfortable with you.

Just before speaking, try to talk informally with the people to whom you'll present. This sort of conversation can help build rapport, and it can also give you ideas about how to fine-tune your remarks to address what's on their minds.

Put your clients' needs first   Your clients don't want to hear about you or what you have to offer. They want to hear how to solve their problems. Don't focus on your products, company, services, or needs, but on the buyer's problems and concerns. What isn't working well for the client right now? What does he or she want to happen? Once you know what's missing, you can find out how your product or service can fill that need. As business expert and educator Robert Kiyosaki puts it, "True selling means being *passionate* about your company's product or service and *compassionate* with the wants, dreams, needs of your fellow human beings." He adds that "manipulation, deception, pressure, false sincerity, and phony smiles is *not* selling. *Selling is communication.* True selling is caring, listening, solving problems and serving your fellow human being."[11]

Listen to your clients   Unlike most other presentations, sales-oriented talks call for greater audience involvement. One study of salespeople found that the difference between top and average performers was the willingness to listen. The prospective buyers of top performers spoke between 30 and 70 percent of the time.[12] Rather than viewing questions and comments as interruptions, welcome them as a chance for you to learn what the client wants. Once you hear what's on your listeners' minds, you have the chance to speak directly to their concerns. Remain flexible: If you are interrupted, address the concerns. Then review your last points before moving on. Trainer Kevin Hogan captures this approach: "The great salespeople ask questions and have great listening skills. Poor salespeople get locked into script mode. They focus on the product they have to sell rather than the client who has a need."[13]

Emphasize benefits, not features   Features are qualities of a product or service that make it desirable and distinguish it from the competition. Salespeople can understandably get excited about features, and they are often tempted to promote these features to prospective customers. But it really isn't features that will impress customers—it's the **benefits** that will flow from those features. So you must "sell the benefit, not the feature."[14]

Here is an example of the difference between some features and benefits of a Web-based customer service product. It's obviously important to describe the features, but the benefits are what will motivate customers to sign on.

Feature	Benefit
100% Web-based	You don't have to host the product on your server or maintain it.

"Knowledge base" gives customers answers to frequently asked questions (FAQs)	Your telephone support costs are substantially reduced.
	Your support personnel are relieved from the drudgery of repeatedly answering the same questions.
	Your staff can add new solutions with a single mouse click.
Fully customizable	Lets you create the content, look, and feel just right for your business.

Use an effective closing strategy   In closing, a presenter must be upbeat and optimistic. Clear and realistic goals from the outset help you determine how best to close. An effective close summarizes the primary benefits and the ways in which the benefits meet or exceed clients' needs. It then calls for action. The action might be any action that moves the sale along: agreement to a test or trial run, agreement to another meeting, agreement to attend a demonstration or arrange for your presentation to higher-level decision makers. Think long term. As consultant Hans Stennek states, "I've never been a believer in closing because my objective is not to close the sale but to open a relationship."[15]

Strategies for Ethical Persuasion

Since persuasion often conjures up images of unscrupulous hucksters peddling worthless products to gullible consumers, it is important to begin our discussion with a definition of persuasion as an ethical and honorable form of communication. **Persuasion** is the act of motivating an audience, through communication, to voluntarily change a particular belief, attitude, or behavior.[16] This definition helps distinguish persuasion from other ways of influencing an audience.

To understand the nature of persuasion, imagine that the city council has announced its intention to turn a local athletic field and playground into a parking lot. The area's residents are understandably upset. Faced with this situation, the residents have four choices. First, they could accept the decision and do nothing to change it. This alternative is neither persuasive nor satisfying.

A second alternative would be to use *coercion*—forcing the council against its will to reverse its decision. The group could try to coerce a change by invading and disrupting a council meeting, demanding that the council promise to keep the park or face more demonstrations. Threatening to mount a recall campaign against any members who insist on supporting the parking lot would be another coercive approach. Although threats and force can change behavior, they usually aren't the best approach. The recipient of the threats can counterattack, leading to an escalating cycle of hostility. Threatened parties often dig in their heels and resist changing to save face or as a matter of principle, responding, "I'll be damned if I'll change just because you threaten me." Coercion also makes the instigator look bad.

A different approach to getting someone to change his or her mind involves *manipulation*—tricking the other party into thinking or acting in the desired way. A deceptive approach to the park-versus-parking lot problem might be to present the council with a petition against the lot containing forged signatures that inflate the petition's size or to gain public sympathy by exaggerating the adverse effects of the project on certain groups—children, the elderly, and small-business owners, for example.

It is reassuring to know that besides being ethical, honesty is also the best effective policy when it comes to changing the mind of an audience. Social judgment theory (explored in detail later in this chapter) reveals that a "boomerang effect" often occurs when receivers learn that they have been the target of manipulative communication. Faced with this discovery, they will often change their attitudes in the direction opposite that advocated by a speaker.[17] In other cases, speakers are viewed as more credible when they openly admit that they are trying to persuade an audience.

A final way to achieve change is persuasion—communication that convinces the other person to act voluntarily in the desired way. The citizens' group could organize an appeal showing that the community sees keeping the park as more important than increasing the amount of available parking. It could describe the benefits of the park, bringing in local residents to testify about its importance to the community. What you'll learn in the following pages is how to make the best possible case for your position so that others will voluntarily choose to accept it.

Manipulation, persuasion, and coercion don't fall into three distinct categories. Rather, they blend into one another, like colors of the spectrum:

Coercion	Persuasion	Manipulation

Consider the example of the city park: Speakers could remind the council that unhappy voters might remember the decision to close the park and choose other candidates in the next election. Approaches like this seem to have a coercive element even if they give the other party a choice of whether to comply. The boundary between persuasion and manipulation is also fuzzy. If speakers compliment council members on their past concern for the environment and responsiveness to the voters before trying to persuade them to cancel the parking facility, are the speakers being persuasive or deceitful? If they stage an emotional but accurate series of pleas by children who will be forced to play in the street if the lot is built, are they being manipulative or merely smart?

The point where one method of gaining compliance stops and another begins will vary from situation to situation. Perhaps the best measures of whether a particular message is genuinely persuasive are (1) whether the recipient feels truly free to make a choice and (2) whether the originator would feel comfortable if he or she were the recipient of the message instead of its sender.

Maximize Your Credibility
Winston Churchill once said that when it comes to public speaking, what matters most is who you are, then how you say what you want to say, and, finally, what you say. Even without taking this assertion literally, it is true that credibility is a powerful factor in persuasion. **Credibility** is the persuasive force that comes from the audience's belief in and respect for the speaker. When your audience has little time or inclination to examine your evidence and reasoning in detail, it will rely almost exclusively on your credibility to decide whether to accept your claims.[18] Research shows that you can enhance your credibility in a variety of ways.[19]

ethical challenge

Demonstrate your competence Listeners will be most influenced by a speaker whom they believe is qualified on the subject. You are more likely to believe career advice from a self-made millionaire than from your neighbor who has been fired from four jobs in 3 years. Similarly, the department staff is more likely to accept the direction of a new manager who seems knowledgeable about the specific work of that department. Management is more likely to agree to take a risk on a new manufacturing material if the product manager seems to know the market very well. These are all examples of trusting someone's competence.

There are three ways to boost your competence. The first is by demonstrating your *knowledge of the subject*. For example, the product manager might help to establish her credibility by citing statistics ("Our market research showed that 85 percent of the potential market is more concerned with maintenance costs than the initial cost of the product. A study published in the trade journal last month demonstrated that maintenance costs are often 80 percent of the cost of the equipment"). She could also remember facts ("Dorwald Associates tried something like this, although only in government markets, and it was pretty successful") and recent appropriate examples ("I was checking the records last week, and I realized that we could afford to replace the machines every 5 years on what we'd save on maintenance if we used plastic instead of metal").

A second way to demonstrate competence is by making your *credentials* known. These credentials could be academic degrees, awards and honors, or successful experiences ("I helped set up Hinkley's very profitable system a few years ago, and I think the same approach we took there could help us now"). To avoid the appearance of egotism, it can be best to have others talk about your credentials ("Clara has a degree in accounting, so her ideas have special value here").

A third way to show your competence is through *demonstration of your ability*. This means speaking effectively during your presentation, of course. But with an audience who already knows you, the reputation you have acquired over time will be even more powerful. If you have a reputation for being talented and hardworking, listeners will be disposed to accept what you have to say. If they regard you as incompetent, you will have a hard time persuading them to accept the ideas in your presentation.

Earn the trust of your audience The most important ingredient of trustworthiness is *honesty*. If listeners suspect you aren't telling the truth, even the most impressive credentials or grasp of the subject will mean little. For instance, a union leader gets little support from union members if they think that he's made a private agreement with management. If your motives will ever be suspect, confess them before others can raise doubts ("I know the compensation plan in this proposal will benefit me, but I hope you can see how it will boost productivity and cut turnover"). Of course, you should never say *anything* that can be considered dishonest.

Impartiality is a second element of trustworthiness. We are more likely to accept the beliefs of impartial speakers than of those who have a vested interest in persuading us. If you have a vested interest in the position you are presenting (e.g., asking for a pay raise or a desired assignment), you can boost your credibility by citing impartial third parties who support your position. With the pay raise, for example, you might cite salary surveys showing that the compensation you are seeking is in line with industry standards. If you are asking for a plum assignment, you could get the people with whom you would be working to endorse your request.

Emphasize your similarity to the audience
Audiences are most willing to accept the ideas of a speaker whose attitudes and behaviors are similar to their own. This persuasive ability exists even when the similarities are not directly related to the subject at hand. Thus, a subordinate may get a better hearing from the boss when both are golfers, have children of the same age, come from the same part of the country, or dress similarly. Customer-service representatives for farm machinery generally wear casual clothing and open-necked shirts to fit in with the people they visit. Many sales representatives begin conversations with prospects by mentioning a common interest—gardening, baseball, or a recent event that affects the customer's business.

Similarity in areas related to the speaker's topic is even more persuasive. This fact has led to the strategy of establishing *common ground* between speaker and listeners early in a presentation. A speaker who shows that he and the audience have similar beliefs will create goodwill that can make listeners willing to consider more controversial ideas later on. Notice, for example, how a business owner seeking a zoning variance based her appeal to the local architectural review board:

> *Like you, I'm a strong believer in preserving the character of our town. As a businesswoman and a long-time resident, I realize beauty and lack of crowding are our greatest assets. Without them, our home would become just another overgrown collection of shopping malls and condominiums.*
>
> *Also, like you, I believe that change isn't always bad. Thanks to your efforts, our downtown is a more interesting and beautiful place now than it was even a few years ago. I think we share the philosophy that we ought to preserve what is worth saving and improve the town in whatever ways we can. I appreciate the chance to show you how this project will make the kind of positive change we all seek.*

This speaker's chances of gaining acceptance for her proposal were increased by her demonstrated support for the principles the board promotes. Of course, the board has to believe that the speaker is sincere. If members suspect she is just telling them what they want to hear, her credibility will shrink, not grow.

career tip

Balancing Logic and Emotion

Some presentations are based on highly reasoned arguments backed up by plenty of fact-based supporting material. Others appeal more to the listeners' emotions. What support they offer may have more entertainment value than logical force. Well-told jokes or dramatic stories may not pass a careful analysis, although they can capture the attention of some audiences.

Which type of support—logical or emotional—is better? According to the *elaboration likelihood model of persuasion*, the answer depends on your audience. Listeners who are highly involved in a subject and care deeply about it are most likely to look for strong arguments backed up by a wealth of supporting material. By contrast, listeners who are less involved with the subject are more easily persuaded by an engaging speaker who delivers easy-to-digest stories and examples. They also rely more heavily on the credibility and likability of a speaker than the content of his or her arguments.

Fortunately, choosing logic vs. emotion isn't an either–or matter: Most presentations will contain elements of each approach.

Note: For a more detailed discussion of the elaboration likelihood model, see E. Griffin, A First Look at Communication Theory, 7th ed. (New York: McGraw-Hill, 2009).

Use Logical Arguments An organized presentation isn't necessarily a logical one. Many arguments that sound logical at first are actually flawed by errors in reasoning, or **fallacies.**[20] Fallacious reasoning isn't always intentional: The person making the case might not be aware that his or her thinking is flawed. Whether or not they are deliberate, fallacies can weaken your case by casting doubt on the merits of your position. The following pages describe the most common fallacies (by both English and Latin names), so you can avoid using them.[21]

Personal attack (*ad hominem*) An ad hominem fallacy attacks the integrity of a person in order to weaken the argument he or she is making. Some ad hominem arguments are easy to spot: Calling someone an "idiot" isn't very persuasive. Other ad hominem arguments aren't so obvious, though.

Reduction to the absurd (*reductio ad absurdum*) A reductio ad absurdum fallacy attacks an argument by extending it to such extreme lengths that it looks ridiculous. "If we allow developers to build homes in one section of this area, soon we will have no open spaces left." Or, "If we have our after-hours customer service handled by an offshore company, pretty soon we won't have any employees here at home." Far-fetched projections like these call for a closer look: Developing one area doesn't necessarily mean that other areas have to be developed, and hiring some employees from overseas won't necessarily lead to widespread layoffs at home. Either of these policies might be unwise, but the ad absurdum reasoning doesn't prove it.

Either—Or An either—or fallacy sets up false alternatives, suggesting that if the inferior one must be rejected, then the other must be accepted. "If you believe that the arts in this community are important, you'll contribute to our fund-raising campaign." This sort of argument ignores the fact that it's possible to support the arts in other ways besides donating to a particular cause.

False cause (*post hoc ergo propter hoc*) A post hoc fallacy mistakenly assumes that one event causes another because they occur sequentially. Post hoc fallacies aren't

Standing in Your Audience's Shoes

Many persuasive attempts fail because communicators fail to understand how their appeals look to the people they are trying to reach. You can overcome this sort of blindness by imagining yourself to be a member of your prospective audience. What would you know? What would your attitudes be toward the topic? Your level of interest? How would you regard the speaker? By walking a mile in your listeners' shoes, you can learn how to construct messages that focus on them, not on yourself.

always easy to detect without careful research. For example, a critic might blame the policy of letting some employees work from home for a drop in productivity, noting that output began to drop shortly after telecommuting was introduced. A casual link in this case *may* exist, but there might be other reasons for the decline—a change in the nature of work, for example.

Bandwagon appeal (*argumentum ad populum*)   An *argumentum ad populum* fallacy is based on the often dubious notion that just because many people favor an idea, you should too. Sometimes, of course, the mass appeal of an idea can be a sign of its merit. If leading companies have adopted a product, then there's a good chance it will work for yours. But in other cases widespread acceptance of an idea is no guarantee of its validity. The majority of employees in your company might invest the bulk of their retirement plan dollars in the company's stock, but almost every financial advisor will tell you that this is a dangerous idea. The lesson here is simple to comprehend but often difficult to follow: Don't just follow the crowd; consider the facts carefully and make up your own mind.

Use Psychological Appeals   Logical arguments and your own credibility are both strong assets when you're trying to persuade others. In addition, though, a number of strategies for presenting your arguments will boost the odds that you can achieve your goal.

Appeal to the needs of your audience   Perhaps the key to effective selling is identifying the prospect's needs and showing how the product can satisfy them. One organization's success at implementing this principle was featured in *Fortune* magazine:

> [At Lanier] a salesman does not merely sell hardware. He goes into an office, asks to see how the paperwork is handled, makes himself an overnight expert about the business involved, then prepares a plan for increasing its productivity by using a specific Lanier machine. When he gives a demonstration, he programs the machine to churn out that prospect's actual paperwork.[22]

Even if the audience is not interested in or is unsympathetic to an idea, there is usually some way to link a proposal to the listeners' needs or values. A representative of an oil company speaking to residents of a coastal town where offshore drilling is being proposed could defend the move by showing how the local economy would benefit and how drilling platforms increase the abundance of marine life in the oceans, which in turn improves fishing.

Whenever possible, base your appeal on several needs. Listeners who are not reached by one appeal can still be persuaded by another. If you were trying to persuade your fellow workers to use public transportation instead of driving their own cars to work, you could identify several needs and show how your proposal would satisfy each one:

Need	Satisfaction
Save money	Getting out of your car, even for a few days each week, means you'll spend less on gas, parking, wear, and auto maintenance.
More time	On the bus or train, you can read and/or work instead of having to drive yourself.
Less stress	You won't have to deal with the aggravation of traffic congestion and annoying drivers.

Make your goal realistic   Presentational speaking is like most other aspects of life: You usually don't get everything you want. Even the best presentation can't accomplish miracles. Asking audience members to accept an idea that they strongly oppose can backfire. Social scientists have refined this commonsense principle into *social judgment theory.*[23]

This theory helps speakers decide how to craft their arguments by identifying the range of possible opinions listeners might have about a speaker's arguments. (See Figure 13-2.) A listener's preexisting position is termed an **anchor.** All the arguments a persuader might use to change the listener's mind cluster around this anchor point in three zones. The first area is the listener's **latitude of acceptance.** As its name implies, this zone contains positions the listener would accept with little or no persuasion. By contrast, the **latitude of rejection** contains arguments that the listener opposes. Between these areas lies the **latitude of noncommitment,** containing arguments that the listener neither accepts nor rejects.

Social judgment theory teaches a very practical lesson about how much to ask from your audience. Arguments in the listeners' latitude of noncommitment may not impress them, and those in the latitude of rejection will just strengthen their opposition. The best chance for success comes when your plea is at the outer edge of the audience's latitude of acceptance. Communication scholar Em Griffin offers a perfect example of this principle:

> *A striking story of social judgment theory in action comes from a university development director I know who was making a call on a rich alumnus. He anticipated that the prospective donor would give as much as $10,000. He made his pitch and asked what the wealthy*

FIGURE 13-2

Range of Responses to a Persuasive Appeal

| Latitude of noncommitment | Latitude of acceptance | Latitude of noncommitment | Latitude of rejection |

businessman would do. The man protested that it had been a lean year and that times were tough—he couldn't possibly contribute more than $20,000.

> *The fund-raiser figured that he had seriously underestimated the giver's latitude of acceptance and that $20,000 was on the low end of that range. Without missing a beat he replied, "Trevor, do you really think that's enough?" The alumnus wrote a check for $25,000.*[24]

Social judgment theory teaches that persuasion isn't a one-shot affair. In many cases your persuasive campaign will consist of many messages delivered over time, each one aimed at expanding your listeners' latitude of acceptance. An oil company representative defending his company's proposal to start offshore drilling shouldn't expect his arguments about promoting business growth and increasing marine life to turn opponents into enthusiastic supporters. Rather than asking for their endorsement, his goal might simply be to have them recognize that offshore drilling is "not all that bad." Similarly, a sales representative trying to sell furnishings for a new office building should not expect to make a $2 million sale on her first call; she might try only to make an appointment to present her proposal to a planning committee.

A human resources assistant at a medium-sized company used the lessons of social judgment theory to choose a realistic goal in her campaign to persuade the corporation to set up a day care center for the preschool-aged children of employees. Rather than ask her boss to authorize funds for the center—a goal she knew was unrealistic—she requested approval to conduct a feasibility study in which she would explore the ways that similar companies provided for child care. If the boss responded favorably to the center after seeing the results of this survey, she would present a full-blown proposal. If he still had doubts, her backup proposal was to suggest that the company subsidize tuition at a nearby child care center—a plan closer to the boss's anchor point.

Focus appeals on critical audience segments   Sometimes one or two listeners have the power to approve or reject your appeal. In cases such as this, it is important to identify the interests, needs, attitudes, and prejudices of the key decision makers and then focus your appeal toward them. For instance, if the office-furnishings sales representative finds that most of the members of the planning committee vote with the president, her presentation to the committee will be aimed at his apparent needs and interests. If she finds that the president doesn't meet with the planning committee, she might try to get an appointment to speak with the president.

Defer thesis with hostile audience   Usually, you state your thesis during the introduction of a presentation, but this rule may not be effective with skeptical or hostile listeners. If a manager seeking acceptance of changes in staffing thinks that the audience will respond favorably to her thesis ("Increased business has led us to open up several new positions, and we'd like you to apply for them"), she'll put the idea in the introduction of the speech. If she believes the thesis will not be received enthusiastically ("Employee contributions to health care premiums will have to increase") or if she believes an audience that hears the news too early will be too upset to accept—or even hear—the rationale behind the decision, she will present the thesis later in the speech.

A presentation with a deferred thesis still needs an introduction to capture the attention of the audience, demonstrate the importance of the topic, and orient the listeners to what will follow. In talks with a deferred thesis, the part of the introduction containing the preview carries the extra burden of setting up the thesis without stating it directly:

> *It's no secret that increasing health care costs, combined with an industrywide slump, have hurt the company. Today I want to tell you how management has tried to cope with these problems in a way that will protect our jobs as much as possible.*

After the preview, the body of the presentation leads the audience members, step by step, to the point at which they are ready to understand and accept the speaker's thesis:

> *Given the problems we've faced, management's choice has been to either lay off personnel, cut wages, or ask all of us to help pay for our own health care. We hope you agree that our decision to ask us to chip in on health costs is the best one under the circumstances and that you'll realize we still consider you valuable members of our team.*

Present ample evidence to support claims   Chapter 11 outlined the types of support that can help you prove your claims: examples, stories, statistics, comparisons, and quotations. When your goal is to persuade an audience, the generous use of support is especially important.

Research demonstrates that when an audience hears persuasive evidence backing up a persuasive claim, the chances increase that the influence of the message will last long after the presentation has concluded.[25] Furthermore, evidence supporting a claim makes listeners less likely to accept opposing viewpoints that they may hear after you have finished speaking.

The best evidence comes from credible sources. If your credibility on the subject is not high, be sure to cite others whose expertise and impartiality your listeners respect. For example, a prospective customer would expect a sales representative to praise a product he or she is trying to sell. But if the salesperson cites others who know the product and who don't have an interest in its sale, the message ("This product is excellent") becomes more persuasive. In this case, the testimony of other customers or of an independent testing service such as Consumers Union would be excellent evidence.

Consider citing opposing ideas   Research indicates that it is generally better to mention and then refute ideas that oppose yours than to ignore them.[26] There are three situations when it is especially important to forewarn listeners about opposing ideas.

When the audience disagrees with your position   With hostile listeners, it's wise to compare their position and yours, showing the desirability of your thesis. If management has previously opposed products similar to the one you are about to propose, for instance, you'll need to bring up the managers' objections ("It's too risky, the capital outlay is too big, and the sales force can't sell it") and show how your proposal will meet their objections ("We can minimize the risk and the initial costs by limiting the first production run; if we put extra emphasis on advertising and show the salespeople how other companies have sold similar products very successfully in the last few years, they'll be more enthusiastic and more effective"). Similarly, if you're trying to sell an out-of-the-way plant location to a company that is planning to build its new plant in a more central location, you might show that transportation is as cheap and available in your location as in the central one or that savings on real estate taxes and labor will allow the company to pay higher transportation costs. If you don't mention arguments that are already on their minds, your listeners may consider you uninformed.

When the audience knows both sides of the issue   Well-informed listeners, even if they haven't made up their minds about an issue, will find a one-sided appeal less persuasive than a presentation that considers opposing arguments. Discussing these ideas shows that you are not trying to avoid them. Even if you refute the competition, considering it at all is more evenhanded than focusing exclusively on your plan and never acknowledging that alternatives exist.

An account executive at a full-service stock brokerage showed that he respected the knowledge and judgment of his listeners at an investment seminar when he discussed the alternatives to using the services of his firm:

> I know that most of you are familiar enough with the financial marketplace to be asking yourself "Why don't I save money and use a discount brokerage?" And that's a fair question. After all, discount firms charge you a much smaller commission for each transaction than full-service houses like mine. I'd like to suggest that the answer to the question of which kind of brokerage to use lies in the old saying "You get what you pay for." If you use a discount firm, you'll get limited service. Now, that may be all you want and all you need. But if you're looking for a source of financial support and attention, you'll get it at a full-service brokerage. Let me explain.

When the audience will soon hear your viewpoint criticized or another one promoted   You will be better off defusing the opponents' thesis by bringing up and refuting their arguments than by letting them attack your position and build up theirs in its place. For example, a union organizer speaking to a group of plant workers might anticipate an argument from management this way:

> The company representative will tell you that after we organized the Oregon plant, the people were out of work, on strike, for 4 months the next year. That's true. What the company probably won't tell you is that the people got strike pay from the union. The company also won't tell you that the people there were losing money every year before that because their wages weren't keeping up with inflation, and the strike got them guaranteed cost-of-living raises, plus life, health, and disability benefits and improved safety conditions.

Adapt to the cultural style of your audience   The cultural background of your listeners may affect the way they respond to various types of persuasive appeals.[27] The intensity of emotional appeals is a good example. The traditional Euro-American ideal is to communicate without becoming too excited. By contrast, cultures in Latin America and the Middle East are generally more expressive, and their members respond more favorably to displays of emotion. An approach that would seem logical and calm to an audience in Seattle or Toronto might seem cold and lifeless to a group in Mexico City or Istanbul. Conversely, a Mexican or Turk speaker might seem overly excitable to a group in the United States or Canada.

The types of supporting material that are regarded as most persuasive also differ from one culture to another. Euro-American culture places a high value on data that can be observed and counted. Statistical data and eyewitness testimony are considered strong evidence. Communicators from other backgrounds are less impressed by these sorts of proofs. Arab speakers commonly rely on religious and national identification. They are more likely to use elaborate language, which would be considered flowery by other cultural standards. In some parts of Africa, for example, the words of a witness would be regarded with suspicion because members of that culture believe that people who speak out about a topic have a particular agenda in mind.

As Chapter 10 suggested, acceptable ways of organizing a message also vary. U.S. presenters are used to straightforward messages that introduce a thesis early in the presentation, develop it in the body, and summarize it in the conclusion. Japanese presenters rely less on a strong, direct close. Instead, they stress harmony with the audience, relying on this climate to generate acceptance of an idea.

Differences like these make it important to know the cultural preferences of your audience. Just because listeners come from a particular country or belong to a particular ethnic group doesn't mean they can be stereotyped, especially in a shrinking world where communication and travel blur national boundaries. Nonetheless, being sensitive to the attitudes of your listeners can help you avoid delivering a message that antagonizes, rather than persuades, them.

Group Presentations

Group presentations are common in the working world. Sometimes the members of a group may be asked (or told) to present their information together. Other times team members choose to speak collectively, realizing that several presenters can be more effective than a single person.

Group presentations can be effective for a variety of reasons. Hearing from several speakers can provide the variety that will keep audience members tuned in. In addition, the skills and perspectives of several people can give a more complete message than any single speaker could provide. For example, a sales pitch to a potential client would probably be strengthened by the contributions of experts in marketing, customer support, and product design. Finally, team presentations can boost audience receptivity by providing a balance of gender, ethnicity, age, and other factors.

Approaches to Organizing a Group Presentation

There are two ways to decide who will say what in a group presentation: by topic and by task. The approach you take will depend on an analysis of the situation.

Organizing by Topic
In some cases, it makes sense to break the presentation into separate segments, with each speaker addressing one or more topics. Organizing by topic is a logical approach when different parts of the material call for special expertise. For instance, a press conference in which county department heads announce new approaches to cost cutting almost demands separate information from each person. Likewise, a sales presentation would profit from having topics like customer support, engineering, and production discussed by representatives from each of those departments.

Organizing by Task
Sometimes a presentation doesn't fall neatly into separate topics. In this case, it may make sense to assign speakers separate roles within the discussion of a topic. One role might be "spokesperson," whose job it is to introduce the main points. Other members might take the role of "example givers," offering details to support the spokesperson's claims. For example, a neighborhood association urging the city council to install a new traffic signal at a busy intersection might use a problem-solution plan. One person's job would be to describe

the overall problem and the group's solution. After making each of these main points, that speaker would introduce several individuals to back up the points with a range of supporting details. This plan organizes the material clearly and provides an impressive array of speakers who are more likely to convince the council than a single presenter. A rough outline for this approach would look something like this:

1. *Spokesperson describes the problem:* "Lack of a traffic signal encourages speeding traffic, leading to several accidents and near misses. This situation risks lives and exposes the city to liability suits."

2. *Other speakers offer support:* Neighbor 1 cites police reports on the number of speeding tickets issued in the past year. Neighbor 2 describes hospital reports on injuries from accidents at the intersection. Neighbor 3 describes recent near misses. Neighbor 4 (an attorney) explains the city's exposure to lawsuits.

3. *Spokesperson suggests a solution:* "Installation of a new traffic signal will reduce or eliminate the problem in a cost-effective way."

4. *Other speakers offer support:* Person 1 compares the cost of a new signal to the cost of settling lawsuits arising out of future accidents at the intersection. Person 2 shows that funds are available in the city's street improvement fund. Person 3 presents a petition of neighbors requesting traffic control at the intersection (suggesting voter support for the signal).

Planning Introductions, Conclusions and Transitions in Group Presentations

Along with an introduction and conclusion to the entire presentation, each speaker should provide a mini-introduction and conclusion to his or her segment. These help listeners follow the overall plan and prevent confusion that can come when several speakers share the stage.

This mini-introduction is part of a group presentation by members of an architectural firm seeking to make the short list of candidates for a corporate design job:

> Good morning, everybody. As David told you in his introduction, I'm Diana Salazar. I think you'll agree my colleges have shown you a beautiful design. But beauty alone isn't enough: You need a building that can be constructed on time and on budget. That's why I want to spend a few minutes showing you how we can deliver just that.

Like the introduction, transitions are an especially important way to help listeners follow the structure of a group presentation. Clear transitions help smooth the adjustment listeners need to make as they shift their attention from one speaker to another. There are two ways to handle transitions: A single master of ceremonies (probably the person who introduced the presentation) can make them, or each speaker can introduce the next person after summarizing his or her own section. Whichever method you choose, make sure the relationship between the preceding and following sections is clear.

The conclusion can be given by the same emcee or by the final speaker. If you choose the latter approach, be certain that the wrap-up restates the group's overall thesis and main points and doesn't just review the most recent remarks.

Delivering a Group Presentation

The potential for mix-ups and mistakes is especially great in group presentations. The key to minimizing problems is extensive rehearsal. Consider issues like the setup and position of speakers in advance to avoid last-minute bumbling. Will members speak

Whether you prepare a group presentation in class, at work, or in your community, use this form to evaluate your group's preparation and delivery. Score each item as 1 = needs improvement, 2 = adequate, or 3 = more than adequate, and pay special attention to those you identified as needing improvement:

Planning and Organizing the Group Presentation

1. Meeting time is used for brainstorming and discussing items that require everyone's participation.

   a. Topic is chosen (if this is the group's prerogative).   1   2   3

   b. Overall approach and roles are determined   1   2   3
      (setup, logistics, research, timekeeper).

2. Group members work independently outside meeting time.   1   2   3

3. Members decide whether to organize by task or by topic.   1   2   3

4. Organizing creates a coherent whole.

   a. Introduction helps orient audience to topic, divisions, and speakers.   1   2   3

   b. Transitions create smooth changeovers from one speaker to another   1   2   3
      and show the audience the relationship of one part to another.

   c. Conclusion reviews and summarizes all main points made by all   1   2   3
      speakers.

Delivering the Group Presentation

5. Speakers are positioned for quick access and minimal time between   1   2   3
   speakers.

6. Speakers transition without fumbling, bumping, or disruption.   1   2   3

7. Group members can easily see each person who speaks.   1   2   3

8. Group members give their full attention to the current speaker.   1   2   3

9. Speakers' words reinforce, review, and connect to previous and   1   2   3
   following speakers' presentations.

10. Speakers do not contradict each other.   1   2   3

while seated around a table? Will they sit in a row until it is each one's turn? Or will they come up from the audience? Choose the format that helps you make the best possible impression and avoid delays. Waiting for speakers to get from their chairs to the lectern greatly increases lag time, and the larger the room, the greater the distance. Sitting together at a table may provide a better and more cohesive look, as well as minimize delays. If the group does sit around a table, try to angle it so that the members of the team can comfortably see speakers as they present. However you set up the presentation, be sure speakers can rise and sit as necessary without bumping, banging, and clanging into equipment, the table, and each other.

In considering where to position team members when they are not speaking, think about how they will look to the audience. Remember that they will make an impression even when they aren't the principal focus of attention. When it is your turn to speak, be sure to talk to the audience, not your teammates. When you're not speaking, look at the speaker and listen with undivided attention. Even if you are bored because you've heard the remarks so often during rehearsal, or you are nervous about your upcoming turn, act like the ideas are fresh or interesting. Don't review your notes or let your eyes wander from the speaker, or you will encourage the audience to do the same.

Special-Occasion Speaking

In business settings, there are many special speaking occasions and events, some of which you will quite likely be asked to participate in or be given a chance to volunteer for. You may be asked to give a welcome to guests touring your facility, introduce a speaker at a staff meeting or annual banquet, present an award to a retiring employee, or accept an award you've won. Perhaps you'll present a tribute to a member of a civic organization you belong to or bid farewell to a supervisor who was promoted out of your department. Keep in mind that every context is unique; you will want to adjust to the physical, social, chronological, and cultural context of each occasion. The following guidelines will help you feel confident and achieve your goals when delivering special-occasion remarks.

Welcoming a Guest or Group

When you are **welcoming** someone, your remarks often set the tone for the whole event. Warmth and sincerity in words and behavior are important. Whether you are welcoming a special guest for a 2-hour banquet or a group of permanent new employees, try to follow these guidelines:

- Say who you are (if the audience doesn't know) or on whose behalf you are speaking.
- Identify the person or people you are welcoming (unless you are welcoming the entire audience).
- Thank the guest or group for coming (if they had a choice).
- Tell why the occasion is especially important or significant.

As you deliver your remarks, be sure to speak to the person or group you are welcoming. If appropriate, turn to the audience and invite your listeners to participate in the welcome by clearly stating or showing them how you want them to behave. The example below illustrates how this technique can be used with the guidelines to produce effective welcoming remarks:

All of us at Sizetec USA welcome members of our Japanese plant's team to the ribbon cutting of our new facility. We are honored that you took time to travel so far to be with us today. We have a great deal to learn from one another, and your visit will help all of us make Sizetec an industry leader. This is an exciting day for us, and we extend a warm welcome to you. [Turn to audience.] Please join me in a round of applause to welcome our Japanese guests.

ethical challenge

Honoring a Less-than-Honorable Person

Imagine your job is to speak briefly to welcome, introduce, toast, or give an award to someone who you know is undeserving of respect. For example, the person about whom you must speak might be manipulative, racist, or lazy. (Feel free to think of a specific person who fits this description, and imagine the circumstances under which you might be required to publicly honor him or her.)

Describe how you would proceed in these circumstances. How could you be true to yourself while dealing with the obligations that often operate in business and professional situations?

Introducing Another Speaker

When handled well, your **introduction of another speaker** will help make his or her remarks a success. Here are some guidelines that will help you deliver an effective introduction. You may choose to switch the order of the information here, but you will almost always need to include it in some way, unless the audience is aware of it already.

- *Briefly preview the topic about which the person will speak.* If the speaker's topic is very familiar, you may need only to mention it. If the audience is unfamiliar with the topic, you may need to include more background information about the topic and explain why it is significant for the group.

- *Give the audience reasons to listen to the person you are introducing.* Share interesting and relevant parts of the speaker's background. Whenever possible, show how his or her remarks will have value for the audience.

- *Enhance the credibility of the person you are introducing.* Share information that will showcase his or her qualifications. Select the most interesting biographical information for your audience to describe the person you are introducing. It is best to give some general information and a few specifics, rather than rattling off long lists: "John has done training with many groups, including the Air Force, IBM, and Baxter Healthcare." Don't be vague ("John has done a lot of training for big groups"), but don't burden the audience with too much time-consuming detail either ("John has done training for . . ." followed by a list of 20 companies).

A good introduction requires that you learn about the person you are introducing in advance. If you can, meet in person or interview the speaker over the phone. If possible, obtain a résumé or biographical information in writing ahead of time. The more you know, the better you can make your introduction.

Make sure all the information in your introduction is accurate. Check and practice the pronunciation of names, cities, and companies that you are unsure of. Ask the person how he or she would like to be referred to (title and last name, first and last name, or first name only).

As you plan your introduction, be sensitive to culture and gender differences. For example, members of many cultures prefer to be identified by formal titles (such as "director") that are not commonly used in the U.S. or Canada. Likewise, the humor that may be appreciated in the U.S. could easily offend listeners—or the persons being introduced—if they are from cultures with more formal styles of communication. Strive for consistency if you are introducing more than one person. A common faux pas is referring to men as "Mr." or "Dr." while calling women by their first names.

Notice how these points have been incorporated in this informative introduction:

For the last 9 months you've heard a great deal about how we will be expanding operations into Mexico. This is a big step for us, and I'm sure everybody has a lot of questions and maybe some concerns.

Today I'm pleased to introduce you to Mr. Dante Gutierrez, who will be managing our Mexican operations. Mr. Gutierrez comes to us with a great amount of experience on both sides of the border. After founding and operating one of northern Mexico's foremost import-export firms, Mr. Gutierrez became executive director of Baja California's Asociación de la Industria, a leading business group. He has lived and worked in both Mexico and the U.S. His experience in manufacturing and cross-border trade will be a tremendous help as we expand our operation in Mexico and Central America.

Along with his professional credentials, you'll find that Mr. Gutierrez is a great guy. He's friendly and helpful, and very approachable. I'm sure you will find that Mr. Gutierrez is a terrific resource as we learn more about our new market and its customers.

Please join me in giving Mr. Gutierrez a warm welcome!

The following tips will help your introduction be a success:[28]

- Plan your remarks carefully in advance. Don't take an impromptu approach.
- Your introduction should *appear* spontaneous and natural, even though it is planned. Practice your delivery so you won't have to rely on notes.
- When making your introduction, look at the audience, not at the person being introduced.
- Keep the introduction short. You aren't the main attraction. In most cases a 1- or 2-minute introduction will be enough. If the audience already knows the person you are introducing, it can be even shorter.

Honoring a Person or an Institution

When you are asked to give a speech of **tribute**, both chronological and topical approaches can be effective. You can follow the person's life or career chronologically and pay tribute to achievements and characteristics along the way, or you might choose some themes or traits from the person's life and organize around those topics. If you do choose to pay tribute along theme lines (bravery and commitment, for example), anecdotes and examples can illustrate your points.

Many of the guidelines for tributes parallel those for introductions: accuracy of names and details and sensitivity to culture, gender, and personal desires. Check your information with the person to whom tribute is being paid if possible or practical; if not, check with an extremely authoritative source. A sample tribute to an accountant who is leaving a firm is presented below. Of course, if the speaker had more time, each of the traits selected could be illustrated with more anecdotes that the audience would be familiar with.

Today is a day of celebration as we pay tribute to Joseph Begay. It is a privilege to speak for the management team here at Contrast Accounts and to honor Joe.

In thinking about Joe's accomplishments here, two words come to mind: commitment and community. Joseph is committed to doing a job well. He commands a tremendous measure of respect and esteem from colleagues in all of our departments. From Betty Murphy in Costs Analysis to Mike Burroughs in Media Relations, Joseph has earned our admiration for his commitment to quality work for our clients. Who else could have persuaded us to redo the entire Simpson account in less than 2 months? Who else could have enticed us with pizzas

Steve Jobs Speaks to Graduates

In 2005 Steve Jobs, legendary co-founder and CEO of Apple Computer, delivered a memorable speech at Stanford University's commencement ceremony.

The address was a masterpiece of audience analysis. Since most Stanford grads are ambitious and career-oriented, Jobs wisely concluded that they didn't need traditional advice on how to succeed. Instead, he focused on how apparent hardships can help create a meaningful life.

Jobs recounted personal stories about how major setbacks turned out to be blessings. He told listeners how following his passions after dropping out of college led to the design of the Macintosh computer. He described how the devastation of losing his job at Apple in 1985 challenged and reinvigorated him to make new breakthroughs. Finally, he told his audience how a cancer diagnosis reminded him that every day is a precious gift that must be used to do what one loves.

Jobs's status as a Silicon Valley legend gave him the credibility to tell ambitious Stanford graduates to follow their dreams instead of slavishly focusing on the most obvious career path. It's safe to assume that his listeners will remember the point of this speech long after many particulars of their education are forgotten.

Sources: "'You've Got to Find What You Love,' Jobs Says," *Stanford Report,* June 14, 2005. **http://news.stanford.edu/news/2005/june15/jobs-061505.html**. To watch the speech, type "Jobs Stanford Speech" into your favorite video search engine.

---

to get us to stay late and finish? Joe is committed to our clients and to our colleagues. The focal point of his work has been to help us all better understand the needs of members from various departments who populate our company. Joseph has helped us come together to look at specific ways we could meet the needs of diverse departments, and he has provided us with opportunities to give expression to our common frustrations and concerns which revolve around quality products for our clients.

Second only to his commitment is Joe's unique way of building community among us. It is because of Joe that over the past 6 years many of us first discovered our shared interests and commonalities across departments. The collective tasks he assigned to us created a bond and a basis for our common union. He showed us how to let our collective interests rise above our differences and then how to respect and work with our differences. I speak for many of us in saying I have increased admiration and regard for the wisdom and the work of our colleagues and for the intricate web of talents that contribute to Contrast Accounts' success. Through shared endeavors initiated by Joe we realized that we are not interchangeable parts but unique professionals with vision and expertise. Joe helped us all catch a glimpse of what community and connection can mean and how they can be achieved cross-departmentally.

I believe that because of Joe's commitment and creation of community, we are all richer, and Joe, I'd like to have you stand as we pay tribute to you and your endeavors here with a last round of applause.

Giving a Toast

Sooner or later you are likely to be asked to deliver a special type of tribute—a **toast.** Besides honoring the person to whom it refers, a well-crafted toast can boost your visibility and notability in any organization. Remember that toasts usually express appreciation and recognize accomplishments as well as hopes and wishes for the future. Here are some hints to help you choose the right words.

- *Choose the time wisely.* If it is up to you to choose the moment, be sure everyone is present. At a dinner, choose the moment when the group has just been seated or wait until just before dessert. At a stand-around cocktail party or outdoor barbecue, wait until most people have drinks.

- *Be prepared.* Think ahead about the occasion, the attendees, and the person or people you are toasting. Delivering an impromptu toast can be risky. Use some inside information or little-known facts that compliment the person.

- *Look spontaneous.* Even though you have planned your remarks in advance, try to avoid reading notes or sounding memorized.

- *Be brief.* A 30- to 60-second toast is the norm; a 2-minute one is the maximum. If in doubt, say less, not more. End by raising your glass and gently clinking the glass of a person near you and saying, "Cheers," "Salud," or a similar expression.

- *Be visible and audible.* Be sure to stand. If it is an unorganized mill-around affair, look for an elevation: a hillside, a stair (not a chair) to stand on, the step to the stage, the back porch. Be certain you have everyone's attention before speaking and begin loudly enough to be effective.

- *Be inclusive.* Alternate your gaze between the audience and the person or people you are honoring.

- *Be sober.* Beware of your consumption of alcohol beforehand. You may pay the price for a slurred or inappropriate toast for a long time. The beverage need not be alcoholic; club soda and water are also used for toasts.

- *Be appropriate.* If you are debating whether a remark or story would be humorous or offensive, leave it out. If you think something is funny but aren't sure that the humor will be appreciated by the honoree and guests, leave it unsaid.

Go to the Advanced Public Speaking Institute Web site at **www.public-speaking.org** and click on "Humor Techniques" for more suggestions for toasts.

Presenting an Award

Sometimes persons may know they are recipients of awards, and at other times your announcement may come as a surprise. Depending on the situation, you will choose whether to let the audience (and winner) know who is receiving the award at the beginning of the speech or save that information until the end. For an effective **award presentation**, follow these tips:

- If everyone knows who is receiving the award, mention the person's name early in your remarks. If the audience doesn't know who is receiving the award, you might want to build suspense by withholding his or her name until the end.

- State the name and nature of the award.

- State the criteria for selection.
- Relate the way (or ways) in which the recipient meets the criteria, using specific examples.
- Make the presentation.
- Be sure that the person receiving the award—not you, the presenter—is the center of attention and focus.

As the example below illustrates, this approach can serve as a framework for creating interesting, enthusiastic presentations:

"Success isn't measured by where you are, but by how far you've come from where you started." These words exemplify the spirit of the Most Improved Player award. Each year, players have the privilege and difficult task of voting for the player they believe is the most improved. The winner of this award must have demonstrated to her teammates spirit and commitment and must have shown improvement and refinement in skills. This is not an easy task. Always spurring others on and never giving up even when we were down 14–7 against the Bulldogs, this year's winner went from being unable to stop a goal to stopping six goals in our last championship game. So, Mary Lee, it is with gratitude and delight that I present to you from your teammates the Most Improved Player award.

Accepting an Award

When you accept an award, a few brief remarks are usually all that's necessary. Recalling the long-winded speeches at the annual Academy Awards ceremony will help you appreciate the sentiment behind Marlene Dietrich's advice to Mikhail Baryshnikov when she sent him to accept her award from the Council of Fashion Designers: "Take the thing, look at it, thank them, and go."[29] This approach is probably too extreme, but brevity is certainly an important element of most acceptances. So, too, is gratitude. The following plan can help you organize your sincere gratitude in an effective way:[30]

1. Express your sincere gratitude (and surprise, if appropriate).
2. Acknowledge and show appreciation to contributors.
3. Describe how the reward will make a difference.
4. Say thank you again.

The following thank-you remarks, given by the head of a volunteer committee that had staged a profitable fund-raiser, illustrate how this simple approach can be sincere, easy, and effective:

You have really surprised me today. When I said I'd help plan the auction, the last thing on my mind was an award. Raising scholarship money was our goal, and breaking last year's fund-raising record was the only reward I'd hoped for. Getting this special thank-you is more than I had ever expected, and I am deeply honored.

I'm also a little embarrassed to be singled out like this. We couldn't have broken that record without a tremendous amount of hard work by everybody. Chris and her committee rounded up an incredible bunch of auction items. Ben and his gang provided food and entertainment that we'll be talking about for years. Darnelle's publicity team brought in the donors. And Leo's talents as an auctioneer squeezed every last dollar out of those items. With wonderful people like this, how could we have gone wrong?

I'm going to put this plaque in my office, right above my desk. Whenever I'm feeling tired and discouraged about human nature, it will remind me how generous and hard working people can be for a good cause. It will also remind me how lucky I am to know you all and to have worked with you.

So thanks again for this wonderful award. You're a great bunch of people, and I can hardly wait until we do it all again next year!

review points

- Informative presentations include briefings, reports (status, feasibility, and final), and training sessions.

- Unlike reports, briefings are short and give the minimum information needed. Status reports review the project's purpose; describe its current state, its obstacles and the efforts to overcome them; the next milestone; and the project's future. Final reports require introductions, background information, a description of events, results, and directions to get more information. A feasibility report includes an introduction, criteria, methodology, possible solutions, an evaluation of solutions, recommendations, and a conclusion.

- Training sessions necessitate careful planning by defining the desired outcome, scheduling the needed time and resources, choosing the best training method, and organizing all training elements. Effective trainers link the topic to the audience, create an overall picture, emphasize their organization plan, cover only required information, avoid jargon, and link the familiar to the unfamiliar.

- Many business occasions call for persuasive presentations such as motivational and goodwill speeches, proposals, or sales presentations.

- Ethical persuasion differs from both manipulation and coercion. It encourages listeners to make free choices after hearing sound reasoning and accurate information.

- Persuasive presentations may follow several organization plans: problem–solution, comparative advantage, criteria satisfaction, or motivated sequence. The audience, topic, and goal will determine which of these plans will be the most effective.

- Proposals advocate a specific action and consist of two parts: the problem and the solution. Sales presentations are most successful in the long term when they establish client relationships, consider client needs, listen to and welcome clients' participation, focus on benefits not features, and use effective closings.

- Speakers heighten their credibility by demonstrating competence, trustworthiness, and similarity to the audience. Speakers earn the trust of their audience through honesty and impartiality. Successful speakers avoid fallacies or errors in reasoning such as personal attacks, reduction to the absurd, either–or, false cause, and bandwagon appeals.

- Group presentations require special planning and can be organized by topic or by task. Careful analysis of the topic and situation often reveals the best approach. Group presentations need effective introductions and conclusions, and especially well planned transitions to connect main points and avoid confusion from multiple speakers. Attention to nonverbal communication helps speakers enhance the presentation's flow and create unity and cohesion.

- Business contexts often require special-occasion presentations such as speeches of welcome and introductions, toasts, honoring persons or institutions, and presenting and accepting awards. Effective business communicators know the basics of each of these special presentations.

key terms

Test your understanding of these key terms by visiting the Online Learning Center Web site at www.mhhe.com/adler10e.

anchor   428
award presentation   439
benefits   421
briefing   402
comparative advantages organization plan   414
credibility   423
criteria satisfaction organization plan   415
fallacy   426
feasibility report   405
features   421
final report   404
goodwill speech   418
latitude of acceptance   428
latitude of noncommitment   428
latitude of rejection   428

motivated sequence organization plan   416
motivational speech   418
persuasion   422
podcast   409
problem–solution organization plan   414
proposal   418
report   403
sales presentation   420
speech of introduction   436
status report   403
toast   438
training   406
tribute   437
welcoming remarks   435

activities

Go to the self-quizzes at the Online Learning Center at www.mhhe.com/adler10e to test your knowledge of chapter concepts.

1. Skill Builder

Create an approach that will involve the audience in each of the following trainings. Use ideas from this chapter and the Online Learning Center at **www.mhhe.com/adler10e.** Demonstrate your technique in class.

a. How to handle phone customer complaints nondefensively.
b. How to use digital photos to update your Web site.
c. How to use a particular campus system (registration, student job placement) or fill out a widely used form (financial, graduation, or internship application).

2. Skill Builder

Define a specific training goal and a method to link the information to the audience for the following training sessions.

a. Listening skills for student service employees.
b. Presenting a "Dress for Success" seminar for a specific industry or employer (sales, marketing, law).
c. Training volunteer students to lead campus tours for visiting high school students.
d. Using *APA* style to cite sources in term papers for nontraditional students.
e. Understanding diversity in our state (or company) for all new employees.

3. Invitation to Insight

Increase your understanding of adult learning styles by conducting one of the following exercises.

a. Interview a professional who conducts trainings in the workplace. Ask your interviewee to describe successful strategies for motivation, direct involvement, and retention.
b. Attend a workplace training or explanation session. Analyze the presenter's use of goals, motivation, direct involvement of the learners, and techniques to enhance retention.

4. Invitation to Insight

Attend a professional persuasive presentation. Based on the descriptions in this text of various types of persuasive presentations, would you consider the presentation successful? Which of the speaker's strategies did you find effective? Which strategies did you find to be ineffective? Did the presentation illustrate ethical persuasion? How did the speaker establish credibility? Explain your answers and provide examples.

5. Skill Builder

Choose a product or service that you are familiar with, or choose one of these: off-site archiving of computer files; cell phone pricing plan; deli delivery service for employees; company-supported memberships at a health club.

a. Identify an audience to whom you could sell this product.
b. Create a chart with two columns: features and benefits. List and differentiate between the features and benefits of the product.

6. Skill Builder

What organizational plan would be best suited to the message in each of the following situations?

a. Showing a customer why leasing a car is a better choice than buying one.
b. Convincing a charitable foundation to grant money to your job-training program for disadvantaged teenagers.
c. Demonstrating the features of an expensive computer system.
d. Persuading the loan officer at a local bank to lend you money for your proposed business venture.
e. Encouraging local businesspeople to join a service club to which you belong.

7. Invitation to Insight

Read a persuasive article in a magazine or newspaper. Try to determine which organizational pattern the article follows. Why do you think the author chose this pattern? Is it effective for the intended audience?

8. Skill Builder

With a small group of your classmates, plan a group presentation in which you (a) review the meaning of a communication concept you've learned about in this class, (b) provide examples to illustrate the concept, and (c) explain how students can apply this concept in their own lives.

Decide whether you will organize your presentation by topic or by task. Assign speaking roles, and plan your introduction, transitions, and conclusion. Agree on a set of unobtrusive signals you can use to regulate teammates' delivery. Conduct at least one dress rehearsal of your presentation. When you are ready, videotape the presentation.

Watch your video. Evaluate your presentation, using the Self-Assessment form found on page 434. Discuss your evaluation with your teammates.

9. Skill Builder

Prepare the following special-occasion speeches.

a. Welcome. Prepare a speech of welcome for a guest from the community who is visiting your class to better understand your college's opportunities.
b. Introduction. Create an introduction for a guest from a prominent community business who is invited to speak to your class about job interview strategies.
c. Speech to honor. Construct and present a speech (3 minutes) that honors one of your classmates or a person or institution in your community whom you believe deserves recognition.
d. Award. Create an award for a classmate (best team member, best listener, best speaker, most improved speaker) that reflects some achievement or activity during the semester.
e. Celebration dinner. Your work team has just met a very important project deadline and your work received rave reviews from your supervisor.

resources

For extensive readings and Web sites on the types of business presentations, see the Online Learning Center Web site at **www.mhhe.com/adler10e.**

appendix I
Sample Presentations

Sample Informative Presentation

The following presentation is typical of informative talks given every business day. The personnel specialist in a medium-sized company has gathered a group of staff members together to describe the features of a tax-reduction plan explaining employee benefits. Notice how the speaker uses most of the strategies covered in Chapter 13 to make her ideas clearer and to increase the attention of her audience.

The speaker's goal here is to help listeners decide whether they're interested enough in the benefits plan to attend a much longer meeting on the subject. She wisely chose this approach to avoid going into detail about the plan when some people might not be interested. By giving a short description of how the plan works, she can keep this introductory talk brief and simple.

[The promise of increasing take-home pay is a guaranteed attention-getter.]

I know you're busy, but I don't think you'll mind taking a few minutes away from work this morning. You see, I'm here today to show you a way that you can increase the amount of money you take home each month.

[This opening illustrates the persuasive element that is called for in many informative presentations.]

No, I'm not going to announce an across-the-board raise. But increasing your salary isn't the only way to boost your income. Another way that works just as well is to reduce your taxes. After all, every dollar less you pay in taxes is like having a dollar more in your pocket.

[An overall view of the plan is presented here.]

In the next few minutes, I'll explain the company's Flexible Benefits Plan. It's a perfectly legal option that lets you increase your real income by cutting the amount of taxes you pay, so that your income will grow even without a raise. I know this sounds too good to be true, but it really works! I've already signed up, and figure it will save me almost $2,000 a year. It can probably save you a lot, too.

[A brief transition alerts listeners to the first main point in the body of the presentation: the difference between before- and after-tax dollars.]

Before you can appreciate how the Flexible Benefits Plan works, you have to understand the difference between before-tax and after-tax dollars. *[The speaker shows Exhibit 1 here.]* Before-tax dollars are the amount that shows up every month in the "Gross Amount" box on our paychecks. But we don't get to spend our full salaries. There are several deductions: federal income tax withholding, Social Security (the amount in the "F.I.C.A." box), state tax withholding, and disability insurance premiums (the amount in the "S.D.I." box). What's left in the "Net Amount" box is our pay in after-tax dollars.

[The enlarged display of a familiar paycheck stub clarifies the unfamiliar concepts of before- and after-tax dollars.]

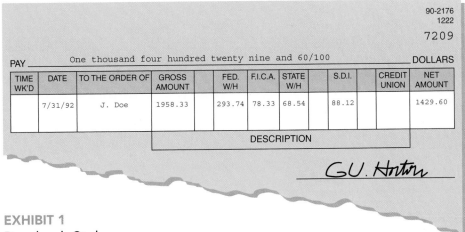

										90-2176
										1222
										7209

PAY ___ One thousand four hundred twenty nine and 60/100 ___ DOLLARS

TIME WK'D	DATE	TO THE ORDER OF	GROSS AMOUNT		FED. W/H	F.I.C.A.	STATE W/H		S.D.I.		CREDIT UNION	NET AMOUNT
	7/31/92	J. Doe	1958.33		293.74	78.33	68.54		88.12			1429.60

DESCRIPTION

GU. Horton

EXHIBIT 1

Paycheck Stub

[The speaker wisely avoids a complicated discussion of before- and after-tax dollars in different tax brackets.]

Once all those deductions are taken away from our pay, every before-tax dollar shrinks in value to about 73 cents. *[The speaker shows Exhibit 2 here.]* And that's in a low tax bracket. If your income is higher, then the difference between before- and after-tax dollars is even bigger. This means that it takes at least $136.33 in after-tax dollars to buy something that costs $100 in before-tax dollars.

[The visual display increases the clarity and impact of the difference between before- and after-tax dollars.]

$1.00

73 cents

Before tax   After tax

EXHIBIT 2

Value of Before- and After-Tax Dollars

[The transition here makes movement to the second part of the body clear.]

You can probably see now that it's better to buy things in before-tax dollars whenever you can. And that's what the Flexible Benefits Plan lets you do. Let me explain how it works.

[An internal preview orients the audience to the next two points.]

The Flexible Benefits Plan is so great because it allows you to pay for some important items in before-tax dollars. The plan lets you set aside pay in two categories: medical costs and dependent care. Let's cover each of these in detail so you can see which expenses are covered.

[The speaker generates audience involvement by inviting listeners to consider their own expenses in the following areas.]

A look at the chart entitled "Allowable Medical Expenses" shows which items you can use under the Flexible Benefits Plan. *[The speaker points to each item in Exhibit 3 as she discusses it.]* As I cover these expenses, think about how much you spend in each area.

[The chart helps listeners understand which expenses are covered.]

- Health insurance deductibles
- Health insurance co-payments
- Drugs and prescriptions
- Vision care and equipment
- Psychologists and psychiatrists
- Dental care and orthodontia

EXHIBIT 3
Allowable Medical Expenses

[The hypothetical example helps show how the plan works in real life.]

First we'll talk about health-insurance deductibles and co-payments. Under our company's policy, you pay the first $300 of expenses for yourself and each dependent. You also make a $10 co-payment for each visit to a doctor. Let's say that you and one dependent have to pay the $300 deductible each year, and that you made five visits to the doctor. That's a total of $650 per year you could have covered under the plan.

[A citation helps prove that the cost of medicines is considerable.]

Drugs and prescriptions include every kind of medicine you buy, even if you buy it over the counter without a prescription. And, don't forget, the plan covers payments you make for everyone you claim as a dependent: your kids, maybe your spouse, and maybe even an older parent whom you're caring for. Here's an article from *Changing Times* magazine that says a family of three spends an average of $240 per year on drugs. Maybe you spend even more. Whatever you do spend on medicine can be included in the plan, which means you will pay less for it than if you used after-tax dollars.

[Examples of typical vision-care fees illustrate the potential costs in this area.]

Vision care and equipment include eyeglasses and contact lenses as well as any fees you or your dependents pay to optometrists or ophthalmologists. With a pair of reading glasses costing at least $45 and a new set of contact lenses costing over $80, the money could really mount up.

Psychologists and psychiatrists are also covered, which means that any counseling you receive will cost a lot less.

Dental care and orthodontia are covered, too. If you or your dependents need major dental work, this can mean a lot. And if you're paying for your kids' braces, you can really save a bundle. We did some checking, and the average orthodontic treatment today runs about $3,500 over 3 years—or over $1,000 per year.

[Comparing the unfamiliar benefits plan to the familiar notion of a discount helps make the advantages clear.]

Nobody likes to spend money for medical expenses like these, but paying for them with before-tax dollars under the Flexible Benefits Plan is like getting a discount of 20 percent or more—clearly, a great deal.

[The transition here uses signposting to mark a shift to the second type of expense covered by the plan.]

But medical costs aren't the only expenses you can include in the Flexible Benefits Plan. There's a second way you can boost your take-home pay: by including dependent care in the plan.

[The example of potential savings under the plan is a guaranteed attention-getter for working parents.]

For most people, dependents are children. Any costs of caring for your kids can be paid for in before-tax dollars, meaning you'll pay a lot less. You can include day care services, preschool fees, even in-home care for your child. We did some checking and found that keeping a child in preschool or day care in this area from 8:30 in the morning until 5 P.M. averages about $5,000 per year. By shifting this amount into the Flexible Benefits Plan, the real cost drops by over $1,000. Not bad for filling out a few forms!

[A restatement of the thesis is combined with the introduction of an example to support its claim.]

When you combine the savings on health care and dependents, the potential savings that come from joining the Flexible Benefits Plan are impressive. Let's take a look at a typical example of just how much money the Flexible Benefits Plan can save. Your personal situation probably won't be exactly like this one, but you can still get a feeling for how good the plan is. *[The speaker shows Exhibit 4.]*

[The chart provides a visual outline of the example. Without the exhibit, the dollar amounts would be too confusing to follow.]

	WITHOUT PLAN	WITH PLAN
GROSS SALARY	$23,500	$23,500
SALARY REDUCTIONS		
Health Care	0	650
Prescriptions and Drugs	0	240
Vision Care	0	60
Dental Care	0	180
Dependent Care	0	1,800
	$23,500	$20,570
TAXES		
Federal Income Tax @ 15%	3,525	3,085
State Income Tax @ 3.5%	764	720
FICA and SDI @ 8.15%	1,915	1,676
	$6,204	$5,481
AFTER-TAX EXPENSES		
Health Care	650	0
Prescriptions and Drugs	240	0
Vision Care	60	0
Dental Care	180	0
Dependent Care	1,800	0
Net Pay	$14,366	$15,089
ANNUAL SAVINGS $723		

EXHIBIT 4

Savings with Flexible Benefits Plan

Let's suppose your salary is $23,500 and you have a spouse and one child. Let's say that your health and dependent expenses are pretty much like the ones we've been discussing here today. [*The speaker points to "Salary Reductions" section of chart.*] Your health insurance deductibles and co-payments amount to $650, and you spend $240 over the year on prescriptions and drugs. Let's say that one person in your family needs one set of eyeglasses. You all get dental check-ups, and you don't even have cavities! You spend $1,800 on child care—not bad these days.

If we look at the top third of the chart, it might seem that following the plan costs you more. After all, your salary would be $23,500 without the plan but only $20,570 with your expenses deducted from the plan.

[*As the speaker points to the "Annual Savings" line on the chart, the audience sees in real dollars the potential advantage of the plan.*]

But look what happens once we start to figure taxes. [*The speaker points to "Taxes" section of chart.*] Since your pay with the plan is less, you pay less in taxes. A little subtraction shows that the difference between the $6,204 you'd pay without the plan and the $5,481 you'd pay with it amounts to a savings of $723.

This is just a small example of how much you can save. If your expenses are higher—if you have more medical costs, for example—the advantage is even greater. As your salary goes up and you move into a higher tax bracket, the advantages grow, too. And don't forget that the savings I've been talking about are just for 1 year. As time goes by, your earning power will grow even more.

[*In a restatement of the thesis the speaker returns to the main advantage of the plan.*]

Now you can see why we're so glad to offer the Flexible Benefits Plan. It can boost your take-home pay even before you get a raise. It costs you nothing.

[*Listeners are told what to do next if they are interested in the plan.*]

If you're interested in learning more, we encourage you to read the booklet I'll hand out in a moment. It contains a worksheet that will help you estimate how much you stand to save under the plan. If the idea still interests you, please attend the workshop we'll be holding next Friday during the lunch hour in the third-floor meeting room. At that time, we can answer your questions and make an appointment for each of you to sign up at the personnel office. In the meantime, I'll be happy to answer any questions you have now.

Sample Sales Presentation

The following presentation (outlined Figure A1-1) demonstrates most of the persuasive principles covered in Chapter 13 as well as the general guidelines about speaking to an audience introduced in Chapters 10 through 12. The purpose and approach are based on a sound audience analysis. As you will see, the talk has a clear thesis and a clear, logical organizational structure. A variety of verbal and visual supports add interest, clarity, and proof.

The speaker's company, Ablex Technologies, manufactures sophisticated electronic components. One of its best customers is BioMedical Instruments (BMI), which produces a wide variety of sophisticated medical diagnostic instruments. The company's biggest contracts with BMI are for kidney-dialysis and blood-analyzer parts, which total almost $1 million per year.

Under a much smaller and older contract, Ablex also supplies BMI with parts for an X-ray unit. BMI doesn't make the unit anymore but is committed to furnishing current users with replacement parts until the machines drop out of use, and Ablex is obliged to supply BMI. Producing these X-ray parts is usually a problem: Orders are small and sporadic, leading to delays and headaches for everyone concerned. The speaker is presenting a plan that offers a better way to handle replenishment of the X-ray parts.

The audience is Mary Ann Hirsch, the buyer at BMI, and two production engineers. Although the purchasing director and the chief project engineer are not at the presentation, they will rely on the information gathered by their subordinates and, ultimately, will be the ones to approve or reject this idea—so in a way, they're part of the audience, too.

[*Introduction emphasizes the positive aspects of the relationship with the customer. Brief sketch of the problem establishes common ground. "We're in this together, and it's no good for either of us."*]

We've been involved in a long, positive relationship with BMI. The only troubles we've ever encountered have come from the X-ray parts. Even though they are only a small part of our business with you, they seem to involve the greatest headaches for you and us. The timing

Thesis: The proposed forecasting and purchasing agreement will allow both BMI and Ablex to better supply X-ray parts in a timely, affordable, and trouble-free manner.

Introduction
    I. Our basically positive relationship with BMI has only one
       problem: the X-ray parts.
   II. While a problem does exist, there is a solution
       A. The problem involves erratic orders for X-ray parts.
       B. Our solution has several benefits.

Body
    I. Supplying X-ray parts has been a continuing headache.
       A. Orders for X-ray parts are irregular and unpredictable.
          [*line graph*]
       B. These irregular orders make it tough to ship orders to
          BMI in a timely way. [*example*]
   II. Fortunately, there is a solution to the X-ray problem.
       A. Here's an outline of our plan.
       B. The plan has several advantages.
          1. Orders can be delivered more quickly.
             [*comparison chart*]
          2. Order is more flexible. [*examples*]
          3. Time can be saved in ordering and follow-up.
             [*example*]
          4. The unit cost is less than under current plan.
             [*column chart, comparison chart*]

Conclusion: By now you can see that there's a solution to the X-ray
  problem.
    I. The plan has advantages for everyone involved.
   II. We look forward to putting it into action soon.

FIGURE A-1
Outline of Sample Presentation

[*Preview lists the main advantages of the plan that will be proposed.*]

of these orders is impossible for you to predict, which makes it hard for us to get parts from our suppliers and deliver the product to you quickly. This leads to all sorts of problems: unhappy customers who have to wait for the equipment they ordered and time spent by people at both of our companies keeping in touch.

We think there's a better way to handle the X-ray problem. It'll reduce frustration, cut costs, and let all of us spend our time on more productive parts of our jobs. But before we talk about this new plan, let me review why the present arrangement for handling X-ray orders is such a headache.

[Transition leads to the "problem" section of the presentation.]

The main problem we face is irregular orders. A look at the order history for the last year shows that there's no pattern—and no way to predict when customers will order replacement parts for their X-ray units. *[The speaker shows Exhibit 5 here.]*

[Visual exhibit clearly demonstrates the unpredictable nature of customer orders.]

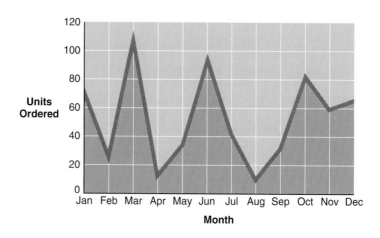

EXHIBIT 5

X-Ray Ordering Pattern

[Example shows the problems flowing from irregular orders.]

This unpredictable pattern makes it tough for us to serve you quickly. We have to order parts from our suppliers, which often can take a long time. For instance, in the February 17 order, it took 6 weeks for our suppliers to get us the parts we needed to manufacture the X-ray components you needed. Once we had the parts, it took us the usual 4 weeks to assemble them. As you said at the time, this delay kept your customer waiting almost 3 months for the components needed to get their equipment up and running, and that's poison for customer relations.

[Example highlights amount of time wasted.]

Delays like this aren't just bad for your relationship with customers, they also waste time—yours and ours. Mary Ann, do you remember how many phone calls and letters it took to keep track of that February order? In fact, every year we spend more time on these X-ray orders that involve a few thousand dollars than we do on the dialysis and blood-analyzer parts that involve around a million dollars annually. That's just not a good use of time.

[Transition leads to the second consequence of irregular orders: wasted time. "Solution" part of the presentation then introduced.]

So we clearly have a situation that's bad for everybody. Fortunately, we believe there's a better way—better for you, us, and your customers. The plan involves your giving us an annual purchasing forecast for X-ray parts. Instead of waiting for your customers to place individual orders, you'd estimate the total sales likely to occur in a year. Then we would acquire enough parts from our suppliers to assemble those items so that we could have them ready quickly as your customers place orders.

[Advantages of solution are previewed in the chart.]

This simple plan has several advantages. They're summarized on this chart, but let me explain them in a little more detail. [*The speaker shows Exhibit 6 here.*]

- Quicker delivery
- Flexible ordering
- Fewer problems
- Lower cost

EXHIBIT 6
Advantages of Annual Forecasting for X-Ray Parts

[Strongest advantage to listeners is introduced first to get positive impression early.]

The first advantage is that advance purchasing will speed up delivery of your orders. Instead of waiting for our suppliers to ship parts, we can begin to assemble your order as soon as you send it. You can get an idea of the time savings by looking at how much time this plan would have saved on the order you placed in February. [*The speaker shows Exhibit 7.*]

[Bar chart graphically demonstrates time saved.]

WITH ANNUAL FORECASTING SYSTEM	PARTS FABRICATED	4 WEEKS
CURRENT SYSTEM	PARTS ON ORDER FROM SUPPLIER PARTS FABRICATED	10 WEEKS

17   24   3   10   17   24   31   7   14   21   28
FEB.   MARCH   APRIL

EXHIBIT 7

Annual Forecasting Speeds Delivery Time

[Transition leads to the second advantage of the plan: flexibility. Hypothetical example helps audience visualize this advantage.]

Besides being quick, the plan is flexible. If you wind up receiving more orders than you anticipated when you made your original forecast, you can update the plan every 6 months. That means we'll never run out of parts for the X-ray units. Suppose you projected 1,400 units in your original forecast. If you've already ordered 1,000 six months later, you could update your forecast at that point to 2,000 units and we'd have the parts on hand when you needed them.

[Transition leads to anticipation of a possible listener objection: What if orders decrease? Credible authority is cited to support this point.]

This semiannual revision of the forecast takes care of increases in orders, but you might be wondering about the opposite situation—what would happen if orders are less than you expected. The plan anticipates that possibility, too. We're willing to extend the date by which you're obliged to use your annual estimate of parts to 18 months. In other words, with this plan you'd have 18 months to use the parts you expected to use in 12. That's pretty safe, since Ted Forester [BMI's vice president of sales and marketing] predicts that the existing X-ray machines will be in use for at least the next 6 or 7 years before they're replaced with newer models.

[Internal review reminds listeners of previously introduced advantages and leads to identification of a third benefit: less wasted time.]

Flexibility and speed are two good advantages, but there are other benefits of the plan as well. It can save time for both you and us. You know how much time we spend on the phone every time there's a surprise X-ray order, and I imagine you have to deal with impatient customers, too. Talking about delays is certainly no fun, and with this annual purchasing plan it won't be necessary since we can guarantee delivery within 3 weeks of receiving your order. Think of the aggravation that will avoid!

[Second most important advantage is introduced last, where it is likely to be remembered by listeners.]

By now, you can see why we're excited about this plan. But there's one final benefit as well: The plan will save you money. When we order our parts in larger quantities, the unit price is less than the one we face with smaller orders. We're willing to pass along the savings to you, which means that you'll be paying less under this plan than you are now. Notice how ordering a year's supply of parts drops the unit price considerably. *[The speaker shows Exhibit 8.]*

[Chart visually highlights cost savings.]

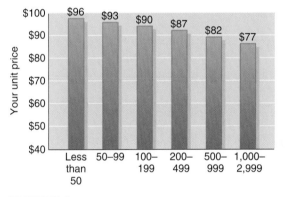

EXHIBIT 8

Annual Forecasting Reduces Unit Price

You can see that this plan is a real money saver. Compare the savings you could have realized on last year's order of 597 units if this plan had been in effect. *[The speaker shows Exhibit 9.]*

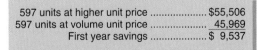

597 units at higher unit price	$55,506
597 units at volume unit price	45,969
First year savings	$ 9,537

EXHIBIT 9

One Year's Saving with Annual Forecasting Plan

[Conclusion reviews the plan's advantages and makes appeal to adopt it.]

So that's the plan. It's simple. It's risk-free. It's convenient. It's flexible. And along with all these advantages, it can cut your costs. We're prepared to start working with you immediately to put this plan into action. If we start soon, we'll never have to deal with X-ray headaches again. Then we can put our energy into the larger, more satisfying projects that are more rewarding for both of us.

appendix II
Business Writing

Entire books and academic courses are devoted to the study of business writing. This appendix is no substitute for a thorough study of this important topic. It does, however, provide some guidelines about creating the most common types of written business messages. Many organizations have their own styles, which may vary in one or more ways from these basic rules. When you are writing on behalf of an organization, you will want to learn and follow its conventions.

Writing Well

Just as your style of dress and grooming creates a first impression when you meet others in person, the appearance of your written messages makes a powerful statement to readers, who are likely to consider them a reflection of your other qualities. Besides creating a good impression of yourself, well-designed and well-executed business writing makes your message easier to understand. Likewise, a shabby e-mail, report, letter, or memo has the same effect as stained clothes, bad breath, mumbling, or rambling on disjointedly.

Get the Fundamentals Correct

The appearance of your message will determine the reaction it creates as much as its content. One consultant put it this way: "In memos and reports, intonation and body language aren't available to you. That's what formatting is for—to substitute for them."[1]

The first decision when formatting a business document is whether to type it or write it longhand. The culture of an organization usually offers clues about when handwritten notes are acceptable, so pay attention to how the successful people around you communicate.

Three occasions when handwritten notes are definitely appropriate—even preferable—are for thank-yous and personal messages of congratulations or condolence. In addition, it may be acceptable to jot a quick note to a colleague or boss in longhand. In virtually every other situation, though, it's professional to type.

Documents should be laid out on the page or screen so that they are easy to read and understand. Margins should be wide enough to keep the document from looking cramped—at least an inch all around on a printed page. Position the copy on the page so it is not crammed toward the top, bottom, or one side. A left-aligned document with a ragged right edge is easier to read than a justified document that has a straight right margin.

For most documents, choose a font size between 9 and 12 points. The font you use also sends a message. The most common fonts used in business are Times Roman (called a serif font because its "feet" make the letters appear to flow together and is easy to read) and Helvetica or Arial (sans serif fonts with no "feet"). Sans serif fonts work well for titles and headings, as they are sharp and clear. In business documents, avoid shadow, script, outline, or radically different fonts, as they can be difficult to read and may call more attention to the medium than the message. Keep fonts consistent for easier reading. Spelling and grammar indicate how careful or sloppy you are, so they should be impeccable. Don't count on your spell-checker to catch your misspelling of *principle* when you meant *principal* or *it's* when you meant *its*. Spell-checking is no help with most names, so you will have to be sure that the letter to Ms. MacGregor doesn't leave your desk addressed to Ms. McGregor.

Adapt to Your Audience

Put yourself in the shoes of the person or people who will read your message, and write in a way that addresses their concerns, knowledge, and interests. Ask yourself questions such as "What do they want or need to know? How much detail is necessary? Why should they care about my topic? What will motivate them to do what I'm asking?"

Once you have identified what your readers care about, write in a way that demonstrates your concern. Make the receiver's needs the subject of your first sentences. Instead of writing "We received your request for a refund and will begin working on it," write "You should receive your refund within 4 days." When responding to a complaint, don't say, "The long wait you experienced was due to a temporary staffing shortage." (The reader isn't likely to care about your staffing problems.) Instead, say, "You are absolutely right: Customers shouldn't have to wait for service."

Organize Carefully

Business writing must first and foremost be organized. Start by listing all of the items you need to cover and then group the items into logical categories. Finally, arrange the categories into a clear organizational pattern according to your purpose. One general rule is to list items from most to least important. Another is to consider what the reader needs to know first in order to understand what comes next. The organizational patterns in Chapter 10 can also be used in many written messages.

Writing experts recommend putting good news first whenever possible: "Your order will be shipped today." If you are delivering bad news, try to begin by expressing agreement, appreciation, or explanation: "I was very pleased with the quality of your crew's work on the recent job. The only question I have is about the $250 listed as 'extra charges.'"

Your message will be clearest if you build coherence into each paragraph as well as into the overall design by using parallel structure and transitions as demonstrated in Chapter 10.

Be Concise

Time is precious for most businesspeople. There are several ways to tighten up your writing:

- *Omit needless words and phrases.* If one word will do, use it and eliminate the others. Some phrases are too cumbersome for business writing. For instance, "at the present time" can more succinctly be stated "now." Other common phrases can be shortened:[2]

Lengthy Phrase	Shortened Version
The question as to whether	Whether
In the month of May	In May
We are in receipt of	We received

Lengthy Phrase	Shortened Version
Please do not hesitate to call	Please call
Please be advised that I will arrive at 8:00.	I will arrive at 8:00.
A distance of 3 feet	3 feet

- *Eliminate "who is" and "that are."*[3] The sentence "Jeannette, who is the paralegal, declined to comment on the case" could be stated more simply: "The paralegal Jeannette declined comment on the case," or "Jeanette, the paralegal, . . ."
- *Don't overuse intensifiers* ("really," "very," "so") *and superlatives* ("fantastic," "best"). Avoid excessive and unnecessary adverbs ("absolutely," "positively").
- *Avoid "fumblers."* Phrases like "what I mean is" and "what I'm trying to get at is" imply "I don't think I'm being clear" or "I don't think you can understand what I mean from what I wrote."[4]

Be Clear and Professional

Whenever possible, use precise terms, describe in details, and quantify facts rather than give opinion or evaluations. Use concrete statements rather than abstract ones and avoid jargon, slang, clichés, and idioms.

- *Use precise terms that give specific details.* "We will contact you soon" leaves the reader asking, Who will contact me? How will contact be made? Letter, phone, in person? When will I be contacted? Next week? Next month? Instead, write "Our sales manager, Nahid Ravi, will phone you by June 6."
- *Use the active voice.* "The memo was sent by the director" is passive. "The director sent a memo" uses active voice. The active voice creates more lively and direct writing.
- *Use names and titles consistently.* If you are referring to everyone in a group by first and last name, don't add a title (Mrs. or Dr.) to only one person. If you are referring to everyone with a title and a last name, don't refer to lower-ranking, female, or minority participants by first name. Stay fair and consistent. Use "Ms." to refer to all women, unless you are certain there is a personal preference for Mrs. or Miss.
- *Refer to the age, race, or different ability of an individual only if it is necessary.* If you need to refer to ethnicity or race, use the term preferred by the group or the individual (see discussion of ethnicities and disabilities in Chapter 2). Always refer to a person before a condition. Use "persons with HIV," not "HIV patients or victims." Use "persons who use wheelchairs," not "crippled persons" or "persons *confined* to wheelchairs." Don't label groups of people by a condition (epileptics, amputees). Use the additional guidelines for avoiding bias in your writing found at **www.apastyle.org/disabilities.html.**
- *Avoid jargon.* When writing for external audiences, avoid jargon and acronyms that your readers might not understand.
- *Avoid slang and pop culture terms.* Using slang ("dude," "awesome") will make you seem more adolescent than professional. Save informality for nonbusiness messages.

Build Goodwill

The best way to build goodwill is to demonstrate that you have the reader's best interests in mind.

- *Emphasize positive concepts rather than negative ones.* State what can be done rather than what can't be or hasn't been done. For example, when proposing a meeting, don't say that you are busy next Tuesday. Instead, say "I can meet anytime next Monday, Wednesday, Thursday, or Friday."

- *Adopt a helpful and respectful approach.* Blaming others and using "you" statements often create defensiveness. "You didn't turn in your time sheet before the June 1 deadline" is an accusatory "you" statement that blames the reader. You minimize the chance of a defensive reaction by saying the same thing just as clearly and less aggressively: "Since we received your time sheet on June 4, your check will be processed with others submitted that week and will be ready June 15."

Routine Business Messages

Along with the writing practices described so far, various forms of business writing each call for specific considerations.

E-Mail Messages and Memos

Memos—e-mails and the printed variety—are the most common form for internal business correspondence. They range from short messages to longer documents. Regardless of their subject or length, the same considerations will shape these messages.

Paper or Electronic Format?   For centuries, paper was the only medium for memoranda. Now, however, you can choose whether to deliver your message electronically, in hard copy, or both. Here are some factors to consider when deciding which format is most appropriate.
Choose e-mail when

- The message is informal.
- You want the message delivered immediately.
- There are multiple recipients, especially when they are geographically distributed.
- You want a record that can be stored electronically and circulated easily.

Use paper when

- You want to make a formal impression.
- Legal requirements demand a printed format.
- You want your message to stand out from a flood of e-mails.
- The recipient prefers hard copy.

The proper format for printed memos (like the one here) differs slightly from those sent as e-mails (see Figure 7-2, page 193.).

Memo Tips

- Don't include a salutation ("Dear Joe") or complimentary close ("Sincerely,").

- Don't sign the memo at the bottom. You may write your initials next to your name on the "FROM" line.

- The body of a memo is single-spaced, with blank lines separating paragraphs.

Style for Memos and E-mails   As the example in Figure A2–1 shows, how you express a message can be as important as the ideas behind it. Keep these factors in mind as you compose your thoughts.

- *"Keep it short"* is the most important stylistic guideline in crafting a useful e-mail message or memo. Whenever possible, limit your message to what can be seen in two or three paragraphs—one screenful of text.

- *Make the essence of your message clear in the opening paragraph.* For example, "We need to decide on a logo for the new product within the next week," or "I'm writing to see whether you would be interested in serving on a community outreach committee."

- *Use formatting to make your points clear.* Single-space your message with a double space between paragraphs. Use bullets and numbered lists to make information more readable and accessible.

- *Be wary of using the informal style you might use outside of work.* Shortcuts ("wanna," "sorta"), emoticons, and chat acronyms (LOL "laughing out loud") can create problems, especially with strangers. Don't use all capital letters since this creates the effect of shouting. All lowercase is unprofessional and inappropriate. Capitalization, grammar, and spelling are important. Profanity, off-color remarks, and gossip never belong in company e-mail.

FIGURE A2–1

Memorandum format

MEMO

Date: June 17, 2010
To: Halim Eby, Director of Human Resources
From: Daniel Goldstein *DG*
Re: Notification of FMLA

I am requesting Family Medical Leave to assist in our family readjustment following my wife's return from deployment with the National Guard.

I am requesting that my leave

   1. begin August 1, 2010, and extend to December 1, 2010.

   2. be intermittent up to 12 hours per week.

   3. be paid from my accrued sick leave.

Attached is the Department of Labor form "Certification of Health Care Provider," signed by our physician.

Elements of E-mail Messages and Memos
Every e-mail and paper memo should include the date, your name, other people receiving the message (usually labeled "cc"), and a subject line. Beyond these basics, consider the following:

- Make your subject line brief and descriptive (e.g., "Agenda change for Friday's meeting") to help the receiver identify your topic. Messages with vague subject lines (e.g., "Update" or "Hi") run the risk of being ignored, misfiled, or deleted.

- If you need to correspond about several topics, consider separate messages for each one. This makes it easier for the recipient to keep track of and respond to each one.

- Consider sending a blind copy ("bcc") if you don't want the primary recipients to know that others are seeing the correspondence. This approach isn't necessarily devious. For example, you might send your boss a blind copy of your e-mail to an irate customer, saying, "This is how I resolved the problem we discussed last week."

Best Practices for E-Mail Messages and Memos
When composing and sending memos and e-mails, follow this advice:

- *Don't use company channels for personal business.* Use your own personal e-mail account for private correspondence, chatting with friends, and other nonbusiness exchanges. One expert advised thinking of e-mails as "giant, moving billboards, exposing our every thought to the cyberworld."[5] Your personal e-mails most likely would not be the best advertising for your company.

- *Don't impose on others.* Most businesspeople are already overwhelmed with e-mail and paperwork, so only send messages on a "need to know" basis. Avoid the temptation to send unnecessary messages to others or forward ones that the recipient won't appreciate.

- *Be cautious about putting delicate topics in writing.* Don't write about topics that would better be handled by phone or in person. Written channels usually aren't the best way to initiate difficult messages like negative appraisals, firings, and resignations. E-mail has the potential to be misunderstood, so avoid using it in a hurry or to convey sarcasm or humor if the receiver is likely to misunderstand.

- *Think before sending problematic messages.* Stop, think, and wait *before* you send a message if you are angry or frustrated. The scathing note you wrote in anger to one person may be forwarded to many colleagues. Once a message is sent, it is irretrievable and the impact on your career could be disastrous. Never send information you are not sure is accurate (e.g., canceled meetings, changed deadlines, budget figures).

- *Treat every message as a public, permanent document.* Despite what you might assume, e-mail is not private: It has the potential to be forwarded (purposely or accidently) without your permission or knowledge. Even if you delete a message, it can remain available to employers, other businesses, and courts for years. In fact, e-mail has the same weight as a letter or memo sent on company letterhead.[6]

- *Double-check your addressee list.* A misaddressed message can lead to embarrassment and humiliation.

- *Use "cc" when others need and expect copies and when you want the recipient to know that you are sending them.* In reply to a customer's complaint, you might want that customer to see that you are sending your response regarding safety to all technicians who were part of the problem.

- *Include relevant copy from earlier messages when you forward them or reply to the sender.* This provides all the relevant information in a single document.

- *Be mindful about using special formatting.* The fancy fonts and images you use may appear differently on the screen of your recipient's computer or portable device.

- *Honor the chain of command.* E-mail can be a way to level hierarchies and reach important people, expedite projects, and reduce time otherwise spent in meetings. Despite these advantages, it is often important to follow the regular chain of command. Pay attention to your organization's culture and your communication goals. Sending an e-mail to your CEO suggesting a new procedure for your division without first checking with your immediate supervisor could spell disaster for your career.

- Salutations ("Dear Mr. Nakayama," "Hi Gina") are an optional, but often useful, element of e-mail messages. As one expert pointed out, "Blunt is not businesslike."[7] (Salutations typically aren't used in printed memos.) Bulk or broadcast e-mails or those to groups can begin with salutations like "Good morning" or "Dear Computer Policy Committee Members."

- *Consider including a signature block at the end of each e-mail* listing your name, organization, phone, fax, e-mail and physical addresses, and Web site link. This information allows others to reach you easily, regardless of where they are picking up your message. Cute quotations and graphics in your signature are not advisable for business, unless it is your company slogan or a tagline indicating the work you do.

Letters

Even in an age of electronic communication, there is still a place for traditional letters. They are used for formal occasions, when the correspondence may be displayed, when a signature on paper is a legal requirement, or when the recipient prefers to have a paper version.

Perhaps the most common layout for business letters is the block format. For an example, see Figure A2–2. As this name suggests, each element and paragraph is set flush with the left margin.

Beyond the elements in Figure A2–2, some letters need to contain additional information. This might include status (e.g., Urgent, Confidential), attention line, recipients receiving copies, a postscript, and second page headers. For correct use of these items, see the "Business Writing Resources" in the *Communicating at Work* Online Learning Center Web site at **www.mhhe.com/adler10e.**

Writing for Employment

Chapter 7 describes several paths to seeking employment. At some point most job seekers will send a job application letter and a résumé. The résumé remains a mainstay of the employment process, and now Internet options can enhance both the résumé process and product.

Résumés

A résumé is a marketing document—an advertisement in which you sell yourself to potential employers. A résumé summarizes your background and qualifications for employment. Résumés serve as a screening device, helping prospective employers decide which candidates' applications are worth further consideration.

A résumé won't get you hired, but it can put you on the short list of candidates to be considered or cause you to be dropped from the running. As you read in Chapter 7, in competitive hiring situations, screening candidates is a process of elimination as

Heading	**TAMARA J. BUTTON** **1111 W. Stanton Rd.** **Andover, KS 67002** **(241) 264-1411 tjb@teacom.com**
Date *Don't abbreviate.*	March 11, 2010
Addressee *Unless writing a friend,* *include courtesy title* *(Mr., Ms., Dr., etc.).*	Mr. Jacob Bruneau Franco-American Electrical Specialists 300 W. Burton Street Wichita, KS 67202
Salutation	Dear Mr. Bruneau:
Body of letter	
Set paragraphs flush with left margin.	After six years as an electrician in the U.S. Air Force, I am prepared to take the skills I developed in the military into the civilian sector. I hope you will find that the wide range of abilities and the work habits I developed in the military provide strong qualifications for the position of field manager that is currently posted on the Franco-American Web site.
Separate paragraphs with a single vertical space.	As the enclosed résumé indicates, I bring to the field manager's job a wide range of skills. I have worked on commercial, industrial, and residential projects. I learned the trade from the bottom up, starting as an apprentice and progressing until I supervised a crew of 40 subordinates on complex multimillion-dollar projects, both in the U.S. and abroad.
	My experience in the Air Force has also helped to develop the personal skills necessary to work in this demanding field. I have worked successfully with a wide range of "customers," including military commanders and civilian contractors. As I gained more responsibilities, I learned how to manage subordinates to get jobs done error-free and on schedule. I'm proud to say that, in my final assignment with the Air Force, I was recognized as "Noncommissioned Officer of the Year."
	I also bring to Franco-American a strong work ethic. I have tackled jobs under a variety of demanding conditions, ranging from the frozen arctic cold to triple-digit desert heat. Many of the jobs for which I was responsible required 24-hour availability.
	I would welcome the chance to meet with you in person to explore how I might help Franco-American Electric as a field manager. Thank you in advance for your time and consideration.
Complimentary close	Sincerely,
Signature	*Tamara J. Button*
Enclosure line	Enclosure: Résumé

FIGURE A2–2
Letter Format

much as selection. The people doing the hiring have more applications than they can handle, so they naturally look for ways of narrowing down the candidates to a manageable number. A good résumé can keep you in the running. A résumé can also be useful for presenting yourself to potential employers who might hire you for a job that hasn't yet been announced or even created.

Besides listing your qualifications, a résumé offers tangible clues about the type of person you are. Are you organized and thorough? How well can you present your ideas? Is your work accurate? After you have left the interview, your résumé will remain behind as a reminder of the way you tackle a job and of the kind of employee that you are likely to be.

Résumé Fundamentals No matter what the job or field, all good résumés follow the same fundamentals.

Customize to fit a particular position You may keep a generic resume on hand when a new networking contact unexpectedly asks for your resume or to use as a template to adapt when specific openings occur, but the most effective résumés are tailored to the interests and needs of a particular position and employer. For example, a medical technician should stress laboratory skills when applying for a job in a lab; but when a job opening is in a clinic, the same technician should emphasize experience that involves working with people. A résumé that encourages job offers focuses on the employer's needs and how you can help the employer.

Be sure your résumé looks professional Like every important business document, your résumé should be impeccable. Any mistakes or sloppiness here could cost you the job by raising doubts in an employer's mind. Even small errors can be fatal: According to the Society for Human Resource Management, more than 75 percent of employers reject applicants whose résumés contain spelling errors or are grammatically sloppy.[8]

Because the design of résumés can be complicated and the stakes are high, many candidates hire professional services to create them. Whether you create the résumé yourself or have it professionally done, the final product should reflect the professional image you want to create.

Although you want to make yourself stand out from the crowd, be cautious about using unusual fonts or paper. A novel approach may capture the fancy of a prospective boss, or it may be a turn-off. The more you know about the field and the organization itself, the better your decisions will be about the best approach.

In companies and positions looking for creativity, some novel ideas may work. A third-place winner of an Enterprise Rent-A-Car creative résumé contest had submitted a pizza box résumé to a pizza corporation and her photo on a milk carton (to alert the company of its "missing" worker) to another.[9] You may be remembered with a creative and unusual résumé, but these gimmicks won't work in most traditional employment situations. The résumé is a business document and needs to look professional.

Be positive, dynamic, and specific Figures A2–3 and A2–4 illustrate several characteristics of effective resumes. Use the word "I" sparingly. The words "fired" and "unemployed" do not belong on your résumé.[10] Begin sentences with positive verbs (created, developed, analyzed), as in Table A2–1 on page 466. And, of course, be absolutely honest about everything you include.

Be specific about accomplishments, including numbers whenever possible. For example, don't say "Designed training for large groups" when you can say "Designed training for groups of over 100 employees." It's less effective to say "Helped cut costs" than to say "Reduced costs by 21 percent in 3 years."

Your résumé should almost never exceed two pages in length, and one is usually better. Employers are often unimpressed with longer résumés, which are hard to read and can seem padded, especially when they come from people with comparatively little job experience.

Table A2–1   Dynamic Verbs in Résumés Demonstrate Accomplishments

Communication/People Skills	Technical Skills	Organizational Skills
Collaborated	Assembled	Arranged
Communicated	Calculated	Compiled
Consulted	Constructed	Executed
Directed	Engineered	Maintained
Drafted	Fabricated	Monitored
Interviewed	Installed	Processed
Marketed	Maintained	Purchased
Moderated	Operated	Screened
Negotiated	Overhauled	Standardized
Presented	Programmed	Systematized
Publicized	Solved	Updated
Translated	Upgraded	Verified

Source: Adapted from Quintessential Careers. Retrieved April 17, 2009, from **www.quintcareers.com/action_skills.html.** This Web site also lists action verbs to describe skills in each of these areas: creative, data/financial, helping, management/ leadership, research, and teaching.

Résumé Elements   While résumés can be organized in more than one way, they almost always contain the same basic information. Résumés are not autobiographies: The purpose is to get an interview, not tell your life history. Personal information like age, height, weight, religion, race, marital status, and children does not belong in a résumé. The following elements appear in most, if not all, résumés.

Name and contact information   This usually includes your name, address, phone numbers, e-mail address, and Web site. Make sure that the information allows an interested employer to reach you easily. Listing a personal e-mail address and home or cell phone number is preferable to listing a current employer's. Be certain to check these frequently and respond speedily. Be certain your voice mail message and e-mail address are not offensive or do not create an impression you wouldn't want. "Devilgirl" or "Lazyboy" does not convey the impression of a serious job candidate. You might set up a separate e-mail account expressly for seeking employment. If you will not be at your school or other current address long, you will want to list both a permanent home address and a school address. Indicate how long (i.e., "until May 31") an address will be valid.

Objective or summary of qualifications   Some career advisers say that a statement of your career objectives can help identify the fit between you and a job. An effective objective consists of two parts. The first part should announce your general goal and mention some important demonstrated skills—talents that will qualify you for the job. The second should detail one or more specific areas in which you want to work. For example,

"A position in public relations using proven skills in writing, researching, and motivating. Special interests in radio and television programming."

An even more effective strategy is to begin your résumé with a summary of the assets you bring to a job. For example,

- Demonstrated skills as a self-starter who builds strong relationships with clients.
- Consistently met sales goals while working independently in satellite office.
- Had highest client retention rate of all sales representatives in Western Division.
- Earned "Certificate of Mastery" from TCE Institute while working full-time.

Although you will probably describe this information in the body of your résumé, leading with your strengths in a summary highlights your strengths and motivates a prospective employer to examine the rest of your application more carefully.

Education   Employers are usually interested in learning about your post–high school education and training, degrees earned, major and minor fields of study, and dates of attendance and/or graduation. If you attended college, it is unnecessary to include high school. Begin with your most recent education and work backward. If the information is helpful and space permits, list notable courses you have taken. If your grade-point average is impressive, include it. Finally, note any honors or awards you have earned. If they are numerous, list them in a separate "Awards and Honors" section.

Experience   Every employer wants to know what kinds of work you have performed. By using the general title "Work Experience" instead of the more limited "Employment History," you can highlight a summer internship, delete a dishwashing job, group minor or similar jobs together, and include volunteer work or club activities that taught you marketable skills.

Employers are more interested in the duties you performed than in job titles. They search for the answers to two questions: What can you do? What are your attributes as an employee? You can provide answers to these questions by accompanying your job title, name of employer, and city with a list of the duties you performed. There is no need to use complete sentences—phrases will do. Be sure to use very concrete language, including technical terminology, to describe the work you performed. Place this section either before or following the section on education, depending on which will be most important to an employer. For an extensive list of words that might help you accurately describe the transferable skills you have, see **http://owl.english.purdue.edu/handouts/ pwp_skillinv.html.**

Special interests and aptitudes   This is the place to showcase any unique talents or experiences that you bring to the job. This section might include community-service activities (cite offices you have held), languages you can write or speak, special equipment you can operate, relevant hobbies, and so on. The key here is to include only information that the employer will find useful and that casts you in a favorable light.

Memberships   Include this section only if you belong to organizations that are related to the career field or position you are seeking. Include any offices or significant committee appointments you have held. Membership in service and civic groups is usually less important, so include it only if you have held a major office.

Certifications   If you are certified or licensed in any occupational field, either create a category in which to display that fact, or include it in the "Special Interests and Aptitudes" section described above. For instance, if you are a Microsoft Certified Systems Engineer, list your MCSE certification. If your Notary Public or CPR certification could benefit an employer, include it.

Reference list   Don't list references on a résumé unless specifically requested. Instead, create a reference list separate from your résumé and bring it to an interview. This list can include three to five persons (not family members) who know your work and character. Be certain that you ask each potential reference in advance for permission to use his or her name.

Give each reference a copy of your résumé and keep each informed of the places and positions you are applying for. You might remind a college professor of the term project you completed or remind a past employer of an accomplishment you'd like mentioned.

Types of Résumés   There are three common approaches to organizing a résumé: chronological, functional, and hybrid (also called modified chronological or combination). Each has its own advantages, and the one you choose will probably depend on the specific job description you are applying for and your past accomplishments.

The **chronological approach** emphasizes your education and work experience and is most effective when such experience clearly relates to the job you are seeking, when you have worked within the field. Within the categories "Education," "Work Experience," and "Related Experience" (if you have such a section), list entries in reverse order, beginning with your most recent experience. Under each position, describe your responsibilities and accomplishments, emphasizing ways in which they prepared you for the job you are now seeking. If you are a recent graduate, you may want to list your education first. (See Figure A2–3.) Cite your grades only if they are especially strong.

The **functional approach** features the skills you bring to the job (organizer, researcher, manager, etc.), and as Figure A2–4 illustrates, it provides examples of the most significant experiences that demonstrate these abilities. This approach is especially appropriate in the following instances:

- When you are first entering the job market or reentering it after an absence.
- When you have held a variety of apparently unrelated jobs.
- When you are changing careers or specialties.
- When your work history has been interrupted.
- When your past job titles don't clearly show how you are qualified for the position you are seeking.

When you write a functional résumé, follow the "Skills" category immediately with a chronological "Work History" and a scaled-down "Education" section that lists only institutions, degrees, and dates. Either of the latter two categories may come first, depending on whether you gained most of your skills and experience in school or on the job.

Whatever format you choose, experts agree that strong résumés possess the same qualities:

- *They focus on the employer's needs.* If you understand what qualities (perseverance, innovation, ability to learn quickly) and skills (e.g., mastery of software, selling) an employer needs, you can focus your résumé to show how you fit the job.

ANTHONY TOLIVAR

e-mail: a.tolivar@connectnet.org   phone: 223-705-6596

Home address   University address
1716 S. Hacienda Rd.   3211 Coit Rd.
La Habra, CA 90631   Dallas, TX 75254

SUMMARY OF QUALIFICATIONS

- Academic background in political and economic dimensions of food policy
- Experience working in commercial and nonprofit organizations related to international food security
- Strong work ethic and ability to work independently as necessary

EDUCATION

Current: University of Texas at Dallas
Graduating (Bachelor of Science degree) in May 2011
Major in International Relations, Asian Studies emphasis

Fall 2008: Shanghai International Studies University (Rotary International Ambassadorial Scholar)
Mandarin language program, ethnographic study of contemporary Chinese culture.

RELATED EXPERIENCE

August 2009–January 2010: Undergraduate Research Fellow, University of Texas at Dallas
In Asia, analyzed the effectiveness of Rotary International programs in promoting international trade. Interviewed officials from municipal government, business, and nonprofit sectors in Philippines, Taiwan, Japan and China.

September 2009–February 2010: Correspondent, Food Policy blog (http://foodpolicy.org)
Published dispatches on insights gained from travels in East Asia for the award-winning Web site.

September 2007–present: Assistant Coordinator, International Food Security Treaty, Southwest Division
Assisted in coordinating media and fundraising events to educate public and recruited volunteers for this campaign to guarantee nutrition rights around the world.

May 2009–August 2009: International Trade Research Intern, Southern California World Trade Center
Conducted individualized, in-depth sales and marketing research for the Trade Center's members.

Fall 2008: Intern, The American Chamber of Commerce, Shanghai
Developed marketing materials, publications, and grant proposals to promote U.S. economic interests in China.

Summer 2007: Intern, Center for Food Safety, San Francisco, California
Conducted research to identify and remediate threats to food safety; helped develop funding proposals for major donors.

LANGUAGES

Fluency in Spanish
Competence in *biao zhun* (standard pronunciation) Mandarin Chinese

FIGURE A2–3
Chronological Résumé Featuring Education and Work Experience

- *They are concise.* A long-winded résumé sends the wrong message in a business environment where time is money and clarity is essential. Use simple, brief statements to describe yourself, and avoid verbose language.

- *They are honest.* Outright lies are obvious grounds for disqualification, of course. But getting caught exaggerating your qualifications will raise serious doubts about your honesty in other areas. As one expert put it, "Be aggressive, be bold, but be honest."[11]

Amy Matthews

Harvard University
Box C-23123
Cambridge, MA 02138
617-555-0392
amatthews@harvard.edu

OBJECTIVE

To contribute my education and health management skills in a position with a growing and dynamic firm.

EDUCATION

BACHELOR OF SCIENCE
Harvard University, Cambridge, Massachusetts, May 2008
Major: Health Sciences
Minor: Management

RELEVANT COURSES

- Human Anatomy & Physiology I
- Human Anatomy & Physiology II
- Health Policy
- Organizational Analysis and Health Care
- Health Care Management
- Human Resource Management

Health Management Skills

- Served as Assistant to the Director of the Stacey G. Houndly Breast Cancer Foundation.
- Functioned as Public Health Representative for the Cambridge Area Public Health Administration.
- Coordinated, Harvard University Public Health Awareness Week, 2006, 2007.

Communications Skills

- Served as a phone-a-thon caller on several occasions, soliciting donations from Harvard alumni and parents for Harvard University.
- Volunteered for a political campaign, distributing literature door to door, fielding questions and making phone calls to local constituents.

Management Skills

- Handled all back-office management functions, including employee relations and accounting.
- Oversaw client relations, order processing and routine upkeep of the business.
- Coordinated efforts between customer needs and group personnel.
- Designed all market research analysis and projects for our client.
- Delegated suggestions and duties to other team members.
- Presented market research results to client with suggestions of implementation.
- Participated in Youth Leadership Boston, a group dedicated to developing leadership skills through diverse programming.

Leadership Skills

- Served as formal/social coordinator for my sorority program council.

- Elected Vice President of Risk Management for Panhellenic, a group that oversees and coordinates educational programming for Harvard's Greek system.

Systems Abilities

- Windows 7, Macintosh OS, and Linux operating systems
- Microsoft Office (all applications and versions)
- HTML/XML Web Publishing: Multiple authoring tools. Microsoft SQL, Oracle, and FileMaker Pro database management systems

FIGURE A2–4
Functional Résumé Focusing on Demonstrated Skills

Source: Adapted from Quintessential Careers Toolkit, **www.quintcareers.com/resume_sample_1.html.**

Electronic Résumés   Electronic résumés are an increasingly widespread alternative to the paper-and-ink variety. Since many employers look for—and sometimes even require—applicants to submit information electronically, it is important to know how this part of the hiring system operates. The most common types of electronic résumés are e-mail attachments, scannable format, and Web-based documents.[12]

E-mail résumés   Submitting an e-mail résumé involves attaching a computer file of the résumé to an e-mail message and sending it to one or more prospective employers. You will probably create your résumé is in a word processing format, but it is usually wise to convert and submit it in PDF format so it will look the way you want it to on any computer, and so it can't be modified. A résumé might also consist of a Web page (HTML) file or, in some cases, even an audio or video format. The most important consideration when crafting a résumé you plan to submit as an e-mail attachment is to be sure the recipient will be able to open and read it after downloading.

Online résumés and job banks   If you have your own Web site, you can post your résumé there; but there is another alternative. Web-based job banks are services where job seekers can post information about themselves for potential employers to review. Résumés posted on some job banks are open to anyone who wants to see them, while other banks allow you to store a résumé and send it to employers you select. More information on résumé banks is available at **http://jobstar.org/internet/res-main.htm**.

Web-based résumés have several advantages. Literally thousands of employers worldwide can access your materials as quickly as you post them. You can update and change your résumé readily. You can include portfolios with accessible graphics and sound that demonstrate your experience and showcase your expertise in displaying your work on the Internet.[13]

Despite these advantages, online résumés have a unique set of drawbacks. Once your résumé is posted on the Web, you may have no control over who sees it and where it is transferred. Many currently employed job seekers have been chagrined to learn that their current boss has found their postings in job banks. Check the privacy policies of sites before posting, but be aware that those policies may change. The bottom line is that privacy is not assured once a résumé is posted. Be sure to date your résumé in case it becomes a permanent irretrievable fixture in cyberspace. For résumés posted online, you may choose to protect at least some of your privacy by listing only an e-mail address for contact. Before posting a résumé for a specific employer, check the employer's existence and legitimacy. You may want to leave out your current employer, listing only the type of position or the industry you are currently employed in so unscrupulous headhunters don't contact you at your present job. For more information on confidentiality and privacy online, go to **http://featuredreports.monster.com/privacy/intro**.

Scannable résumés   A scannable is a paper résumé that is formatted so that prospective employers can enter its contents into a database. The use of scannable résumés has grown because human resource personnel are unable to review all the materials they receive from job applicants, so they use OCR (optical character recognition) software to enter the content of résumés into their databases. Once the content is digitized, employers can sort it according to a variety of criteria, including applicants' employment experience and skills.

Employers program their software to search scanned résumés for keywords, so be sure to identify and include terms commonly used in the field where you are seeking work. For example, industrial engineers might include "Kaizen" and "time studies," whereas a pharmacist might list "compounding." Include any industry-related jargon and acronyms that the scanning software may be programmed to recognize. For example, OCP (Oracle Certified Professional) and CCNA (Cisco Certified Networking Associate) are recognized in the Information Technology sector. For examples of skill keywords (by job categories) and personal trait keywords, see **www.eresumes.com/eresumes.html**. Use the *Occupational Outlook Handbook* (**www.bls.gov/oco**) and other career resources online for lists of keywords specific to your career field. Note any keywords used in the job description. Since length and details don't faze a computer, scannable résumés may be longer than paper ones, giving you the best chance of including everything that might impress a prospective employer.

A résumé has the best chance of being scanned accurately if you follow these guidelines:[14]

- Create and save the document in ASCII plain text formatting, unless instructed to do otherwise by the source to which you'll be sending your résumé.

- Be sure only your name is on the top line. An address on the same line will confuse the software.

- Send only digital or a high-quality laser printed copy, not a photocopy. The scanning device is better able to get all of your information from a high-quality printer.

- Use only simple fonts in standard sizes and only white paper. The scanner is unable to recognize large fonts, patterned paper, script, graphics, boxes, and vertical or horizontal lines.

- Do not fold or staple the résumé.

- Be certain your name is on each page.

It is prudent to keep an updated scannable copy of your résumé handy. If you are sending a résumé, call ahead and ask whether the résumé will be scanned. If it will, consider sending two résumés, the scannable version and one for human eyes (be sure to indicate which is which).[15] Or you might send the scannable résumé and take the (better-looking) one-page résumé to the interview.

Strategies for electronic résumés   Résumé preparation and delivery are changing, but a basic principle holds: Adapt to your audience. Customize the content and method of transmission of your résumé for individual companies, positions, and, when possible, the people who will read it.

Compared to paper résumés, electronic ones have both advantages and drawbacks. When you send a paper résumé, the recipient sees exactly what you created, although receiving and forwarding it to others may take time. With electronic résumés, there is a greater risk that your reader may not be able to view the document for technical reasons or may not want to open the file because of the additional time it takes and the potential for a virus. Furthermore, some companies automatically delete unsolicited e-mails with attachments, so find out before you attach.

When you do submit a résumé electronically, follow these guidelines:[16]

- Don't bombard employers with résumés for positions that don't exist or for which you are not qualified.

- Be sure to include a cover letter that tells the employer what position you are applying for.

- Although plain text files and e-mail limit your formatting, you can still use bullets to make your cover letter more readable by using plus signs (+) or asterisks (*).

Employment-Seeking Letters

Letters give you the chance to present yourself to prospective employers in a favorable light. Here is advice about how to use this correspondence to your best advantage.

Job Application Letters   Whenever you send your résumé to a prospective employer in print or electronically, accompany it with a job application letter (also called a cover letter) that is personalized for the particular job you are applying for and the organization to which you are applying. As one expert put it, a cover letter is "an introduction, a sales pitch and a proposal for further action all in one."[17]

Cover letters should be sent to a specific individual. If you do not know the appropriate person, call the company and ask for the individual's name, being certain that you get the spelling and title correct.

As Figure A2–2 (page 464) illustrates, cover letters include the following information:

- The first lines should let the reader know what position you are applying for, how you know of the position, and any connection you have to the company. If you are responding to an advertisement, mention the job title, number, and publication. You might be writing at the suggestion of a mutual acquaintance or as a result of your research.

- An introduction (or reintroduction) of yourself if the reader doesn't know (or remember) who you are.

- A brief description of the most impressive accomplishments that are relevant to the job at hand. Remember: Don't just say you can help the organization. Offer some objective evidence that backs up your claim. Show knowledge of the company through personal experience or positive news articles.

- A statement regarding the next step you hope to take—usually a request for an interview. Detail any information about limits on your availability, but keep these to an absolute minimum.

- A final, cordial expression of appreciation to the reader for considering you.

Follow-up Letters   Always follow up an interview by sending a thank-you to the interviewer(s). As with other correspondence, the decision about whether to convey it in print or via the Internet depends on the preferences of the person to whom you'll be writing. In any case, make sure your thank-you arrives within a day or two following your interview. Besides showing your good manners, a follow-up letter is an opportunity to remind the interviewer of your uniqueness and the strengths you will bring to the company.

Your follow-up letter should thank the interviewer for the opportunity to meet and the chance to have learned more about the position and the company. Also offer thanks for the chance to have met any other people to whom you were introduced. Use the letter to assert why you believe you are well qualified for the job, and how you can serve the company's needs. Address any concerns the interviewer may have had, and add information about yourself that you did not have an opportunity to state during the interview. Be certain the letter concludes on a positive note and expresses goodwill. Be absolutely positive that you have correctly spelled every name you use and that your letter is free of any other mistakes. Errors are likely to raise doubts about the quality of work that you might do after you are hired.

Thank-you letters are also appropriate for someone who has referred you to an employer, given a recommendation (phone or written) for you, or given job-search information to you.

Reports

Reports are a part of business life. They vary in size and frequency from two-paragraph weekly memos on the number of new hires to an occasional 20-page report complete with graphs, analysis, and recommendations on the feasibility of some new office space. The readers' needs and the corporate culture will determine the size, format, and frequency of reports.

Types of Reports

Reports, like presentations, may be informative or persuasive. Some reports present information, some may propose solutions to problems, and others analyze a problem and propose a course of action. Common reports include trip, progress, incident, feasibility, and minutes of meetings.

Trip

Trip reports often justify the money organizations spend on them. Know why the report is being written and for whom. Is it for your manager to justify the type of workshop you attended or for accounting to withstand an audit? Usually trip reports answer these questions: Where did you go? With whom? Why? When? What did you learn? Whom did you meet? State the name of the conference or meeting, city and location, and your purpose for attending.

In the body of your narrative, emphasize two or three key points. If your job is to report to all employees, select information employees need and will find interesting on safety, legal issues, or changes in policy. If your conference covered new products or new prices for old products, you may want to detail those. If your report goes only to your supervisor, you may want to include a section on needs or ideas for change that you learned on the trip.

Progress

Progress reports (also called periodic operating reports) occur at fixed intervals: weekly sales reports, monthly customer complaints, yearly safety reports. These reports may be largely statistical, but most will require some description of regular events and any unusual events (special sales, emergency closures, power outages). Answer the question, What is our status? If appropriate, indicate any hurdles you have overcome or have yet to overcome and then describe the next objective.

Incident

Incident reports (also called situational reports) report on nonroutine occurrences such as accidents or special events. They may be required in the form of memos. Some organizations have special forms for these reports with very precise requirements for legal or human resource concerns. Before beginning an incident report be sure you know who is asking for the report and the level of detail required. Always ask if you aren't sure. When describing the incident, use precise facts such as numbers, dates, times, and quotations. Rather than report, "An employee fell on a staircase," write "Jane Winthrop, an employee in the Claims Department, reported that she fell on the north staircase inside the building at 4:00 P.M., Tuesday, June 26, 2010."

Feasibility Reports

Feasibility reports address the questions of whether projects are possible, practical, advantageous, safe, or advisable. They use data to analyze the advantages and disadvantages of a particular project or to determine whether something can or should be done.

Begin by knowing what the main question is: How can we improve employee accessibility to supplies without loss of supplies? How can we improve training on new equipment in a timely manner to minimize repairs caused by improper use of new equipment? Then describe the problem or need, the criteria for comparing solutions, the possible solutions, and how well each solution meets the criteria. Tables, graphs, and other visuals are effective ways to add to this analysis section. Be certain you understand whether your assignment is to report information only or to draw conclusions and make recommendations. If the latter is part of your assignment, you'll want a section in which you give your recommendations.

Minutes of Meetings   Minutes are a record of a group's meeting. They are especially useful when the events of a meeting will be of interest to people who were not present. Minutes are also helpful when a group needs to determine what happened at an earlier point in time.

Minutes should have a heading that indicates the name of the organization, the name of the group that met (Parking Task Force or Quality Assessment Team), "Minutes of (date)," and the place and time of the meeting. List the meeting facilitator and members present. If people other than regular members are present, indicate their position after their names (Salvadora Rojas, advisor; Arthur Urlin, guest). Minutes will usually include these sections: Agenda, Announcements, Old Business, New Business, and Action Items. Use numbers or bullets to identify separate items; under old and new business, use bullets or boldfaced headings to organize topics. Under Action Items, identify who is responsible for completing an item and the completion date.

Report Basics

Regardless of the report's contents and size, the following guidelines will help you produce a top-quality document on schedule.

Understand the Purpose   Begin by knowing the purpose of the report. A specific goal statement for reports should follow the same format for presentations explained in Chapter 10:

> "After reviewing this report, the Operations Manager will have a clear idea of how the cost of electricity has changed over the past 3 years, and how costs are likely to change in the next 2 years."

> "After reading this report, my boss will see that giving traveling staff laptop computers will increase their productivity enough to pay for the equipment."

You can define the purpose of a report by asking yourself what it will be used for, who will read it, and what amount of detail is required. A routine one-paged expense report isn't the place to present your ideas for reforming the company's accounting policy. By contrast, if you have been asked to analyze a problem of high employee turnover, simply presenting data without including your analysis of causes and proposing solutions would make the report incomplete. If you have any doubts about the purpose of the report, ask the person or people who have requested it for clarification.

Create a Schedule for a Longer Report   Once you understand the purpose of the report, list all of the tasks necessary to complete the report and devise a workable schedule. Allot time for researching (Internet, library visits, studies, surveys, interviews), outlining, writing a draft, getting any preliminary approvals needed, creating exhibits, and editing and writing the final copy.

Organize for Comprehension   Determine what organizational pattern will help readers understand your report. The organizational patterns discussed in Chapter 10 can be used for written reports, also. Chronological patterns are often used for progress reports. Topical patterns work for reports that need to cover several areas. For example, a report on a possible location for a new factory might be organized by topics such as natural resources, transportation, workforce availability, and tax base. Another common organizational pattern for reports is by level of importance. A report on the growing loss of quality personnel might focus on the most important features first and move to less important ones. Create an outline to work from; it will help you clarify the organizational pattern.

Format for Readability   Break your report into logical divisions and indicate these with formatting: boldface, boxes, horizontal lines, headings, bullets, numbers, and white space. All of these can help the reader see what goes together and which are the important features. If it is permissible in your organization, use the templates for reports that are included in most word processing programs.

Document Carefully   The purpose of documentation is to give credit to your sources and allow the reader to identify and find the source if more information is needed. Citing your sources avoids plagiarism. In longer reports to scientific and academic organizations, use MLA or APA style. In business, use the style of documentation that is accepted within your organization or industry.

Determine the Preferred Medium   Some organizations prefer reports to be submitted eletronically, while others except printed documents. Follow the protocol of the organization to which you'll be presenting the report.

Report Elements

Not every report should include all of the following elements. The amount of information covered, its nature, the conventions of the organization, and the needs of your readers will help you decide which parts to include.

Title Page   Every report needs a descriptive title. If the document is a long one, the first page should include the title; "Submitted by . . ." or "Prepared by . . ." with the author(s) name; and "Submitted to . . ." or "Prepared for . . ." with the name of the intended audience or person requesting the report. The last item on the page is the date of submission.

Letter of Transmittal   If the report is presented to persons inside the company, use a memo (instead of letter) of transmittal. The letter or memo will include a short history of the report (who assigned or authorized it and why), a brief summary of significant findings, conclusions, expression of thanks and acknowledgment of assistance from others, and clear instructions regarding how the reader is to respond. It is also appropriate to offer to answer questions and indicate how best to contact you.

Table of Contents   If the report is a long one with several sections, a table of contents will help readers locate material. Show the major sections of the report and the page each begins on.

Abstract or Executive Summary   This section provides readers with a quick overview of the report's key sections. In most cases the summary should be no longer than one page or 10 percent of the full report.

Exhibits and Appendixes   Many reports include tables, charts, graphs, and other visuals that illustrate points made in the body of the document. If there are several, a list of each exhibit and page number helps readers locate them. Depending on the accepted style in your field, these items can be listed as exhibits either within the body of the report or in appendixes at the back of the document.

Bibliography or References   Depending on the accepted practices in your occupation and the formality of the report, you might include only sources you cited or those you cited plus others you used but didn't cite. Some reports will include not only those sources cited and used but also additional sources of information.

resources

→ For extensive readings and Web sites on business and employment writing, including writing for social media, see the Online Learning Center Web site at **www.mhhe.com/adler10e.**

glossary

Note: The number in parentheses at the end of each definition refers to the chapter in which the term is first discussed.

A

action-oriented listening style A listening style in which the listener's primary concern is understanding and organizing facts to accomplish a task or get a job done. *See also* Content-oriented listening style, People-oriented listening style, Time-oriented listening style. (3)

agenda A list of topics to be covered in a meeting. Agendas also usually note the meeting's time, length, and location and the members who will attend. Complete agendas provide background information and outcome goals. (9)

anchor A listener's preexisting position on an issue being advocated. (13)

audition interview A type of interview in which a prospective employer asks the candidate to demonstrate (rather than describe) his/her ability to perform a job-related task. (7)

authoritarian leadership style A leadership style in which the designated leader uses legitimate, coercive, and reward power to control members. (8)

authority rule A group decision-making method in which a designated leader makes a final decision, either with or without consulting group members. (8)

award presentation A type of presentation in which the speaker describes an award and explains the reasons the recipient is receiving it. (13)

B

bar chart A chart consisting of horizontal or vertical bars that depict the values of several items in comparative terms. (11)

behavioral interview An employment interview in which the candidate is asked to give concrete examples of past behaviors that show how he or she behaved in certain situations. (7)

benefits As used in a sales presentation, advantages that the target audience will gain from the features of a product or service. (13)

biased language Any statement that seems to be objective but actually conceals the speaker's emotional attitude. (4)

bona fide occupational qualification (BFOQ) A job requirement that is deemed reasonably necessary for the performance of a particular job. In employment interviewing, only questions exploring BFOQs are lawful. (7)

boomers The generation born between 1946 and 1964, whose lives were shaped by the social reforms of the 1960s. (1)

brainstorming An approach to idea generation that encourages free thinking and minimizes conformity. (8)

C

career research interview An informational interview to help a candidate define and achieve career goals. (7)

cause–effect pattern An organizational arrangement that shows that events happened or will happen as a result of certain circumstances. (10)

channel The method or medium used to deliver a message (e.g., face-to-face communication, written memos, or the telephone). (1)

chronological pattern An organizational arrangement that presents points according to their sequence in time. (10)

claim A statement asserting a fact or belief. (10)

closed questions Questions that restrict the interviewee's responses, usually to yes or no, a number or an item from preselected items, or an either–or response. (6)

co-culture A group that has a clear identity within the encompassing culture. (2)

coercive power The ability to influence others that arises because one can impose punishment or unpleasant consequences. (8)

cohesiveness The degree to which group members feel part of and want to remain with the group. (8)

collectivist culture A culture with strong social frameworks in which members of a group (such as an organization) are socialized to care for one another and for the group. (2)

column chart A visual exhibit consisting of vertical columns that depict the quantity of one or more items at different times; used to show changes in quantity over time. (11)

communication climate A metaphor used to describe the quality of relationships in an organization. (5)

communication networks Regular patterns or paths along which information flows in an organization. *See also* Formal communication networks, Informal communication networks. (1)

comparative advantages organization plan An organizational strategy that puts several alternatives side by side and shows why one is the best. (10, 13)

comparisons A type of support in which the speaker shows how one idea is similar to another; may be figurative or literal. (11)

compromise An orientation toward negotiation that assumes that each side needs to lose at least some of what it was seeking. (5)

briefing An informative presentation that succinctly informs listeners about a specific task at hand. (13)

computer conferencing   A form of technology that allows individuals to work on a single document via computer, making changes that can be viewed by other participants. (1)

confirming messages   Messages that express value toward other persons. (5)

conflict phase   The second of Aubrey Fisher's four group problem-solving phases; characterized by members' taking strong stands that result in conflict within the group. (8)

connection power   The ability to influence that arises because of one's connections and associations inside and outside the organization. (8)

consensus   A decision-making method in which the group as a whole makes a decision that each member is willing to support. (8)

content messages   The dimension of messages that focus on the topic under discussion. *See also* Relational messages. (1)

content-oriented listening style   A listening style in which the listener hears details and analyzes and evaluates what is said. *See also* Action-oriented listening style, People-oriented listening style, Time-oriented listening style. (3)

context   The environment of physical, social, chronological, and cultural variables that surrounds any process of communication. (1)

contingency approaches to leadership   Leadership theories that assert that the most effective leadership style is flexible, changing as needed with the context. (8)

counterfeit questions   Utterances that appear to be questions but are actually statements, forms of advice, traps, or attacks on the speaker. (3)

credibility   The persuasive force that comes from the audience's belief in and respect for the speaker. (13)

criteria satisfaction organization plan   An organizational strategy that sets up standards (criteria) that the audience accepts and then shows how the speaker's idea or product meets the criteria. (10, 13)

critical incident questions   Interview questions that ask the interviewee about a specific situation rather than a hypothetical one. (6)

culture   The set of values, beliefs, norms, customs, rules, and codes that leads people to define themselves as a distinct group, giving them a sense of commonality. (2)

D

decoding   The process of attaching meaning to words, symbols, or behaviors. (1)

definition   A form of support that explains the meaning of terms that are unfamiliar to an audience or are used in a specialized or uncommon way. (11)

democratic leadership style   A leadership style in which the designated leader encourages members to share decision making. (8)

descriptive statements   Statements that describe the speaker's perspective instead of evaluating the sender's behavior or motives. *See also* "I" language, "You" language. (5)

designated leader   A leader whose title indicates a leadership role, either by appointment or by group selection. (8)

diagnostic interview   An interview in which professionals (e.g., doctors and lawyers) gather information on their patients' or clients' needs. (7)

direct question (in a group)   A question addressed (by name) to a particular individual. (9)

direct questions (in an interview)   Straightforward questions that ask exactly what the interviewer wants to know. (6)

disconfirming messages   Messages that show a lack of valuing for other persons. (5)

disfluencies   Vocal disruptions such as stammers (uh, um) or filler words (ya know, like, OK) that distract audiences and interfere with understanding. (12)

downward communication   Communication that flows from superiors to subordinates. (1)

E

emergence phase   The third of Aubrey Fisher's four group problem-solving phases; characterized by an end to conflict and emergence of harmony within the group. (8)

emergent leader   A leader chosen by the group, either officially or informally. (8)

emotional intelligence (EQ)   Aptitude and skills needed for interacting well with others. Refers to interpersonal communication skills rather than cognitive or intellectual abilities. (5)

employment interview   An interview designed to judge the qualifications and desirability of a candidate for a job. (7)

encoding   The intentional process of creating a message. (1)

equivocal terms   Words with more than one meaning. Equivocation can lead to unintentional misunderstandings. In contrast, *strategic ambiguity* is often used in business to promote harmony and soften the blow of unpleasant messages. (4)

ethnocentrism   The inclination to see all events from the perspective of one's own culture and to evaluate one's own culture as superior and other persons or cultures as inferior. (2)

examples   Brief illustrations that back up or explain a claim. (11)

exit interview   An interview designed to discover why an employee is leaving an organization. (7)

expert opinion   A decision-making method in which a single person perceived as an expert makes a decision for the group. (8)

expert power   The ability to influence that arises because of one's knowledge, ability, and expertise in a particular area. (8)

explanation   An informative presentation that increases listeners' understanding of a subject. (13)

extemporaneous presentation A type of delivery in which the major ideas are planned and rehearsed but the speech is given spontaneously from notes. (12)

F

factual questions Questions that ask for verifiable, factual information rather than opinion. (6)

fallacy An error in the logic of an argument. (13)

feasibility report A type of presentation that evaluates potential action steps and makes recommendations about how to proceed. (13)

features Qualities of a product or service that make it desirable and distinguish it from the competition. (13)

feedback The recognizable response of a receiver to a sender's message. (1)

feminine style of speech Culturally influenced style of speaking motivated by a concern for creating connections, establishing goodwill, showing support, and building community. *See also* Masculine style of speech, Rapport talk. (4)

final report Report delivered upon completion of an undertaking. (13)

flip chart A large pad of paper, attached to an easel, that is used to create and/or display visuals. (11)

formal communication networks Officially designated paths of communication designed by management to indicate who should communicate with whom. (1)

forming stage A phase in problem-solving groups characterized by tentative statements and getting-acquainted types of communication; also called *orientation phase*. (8)

functional roles Types of behavior that are necessary if a group is to do its job effectively. *See also* Relational roles, Task roles. (8)

G

gatekeeper A person, such as a personal assistant or a receptionist, who manages access to another person. (7)

genderlects Distinct and different styles of speaking that characterize masculine and feminine speech. (4)

general goal A broad indication of the purpose of a speech, generally to inform, persuade, or entertain. (10)

generation X The generation born between 1965 and 1982 that is comfortable with technology, seeks work–life balance, and values performance over length of service. (1)

generation Y The generation born between 1982 and 1991 (also called the Why Generation or First Globals) that has an international worldview, is proficient with technology and multitasking, and has high career expectations. (1)

goodwill speech A speech with the primary aim of creating a favorable image of the speaker's cause in the minds of the audience. (13)

graph A visual display that shows the correlation between two quantities. (11)

groupthink A condition in which group members are unwilling to critically examine ideas because of their desire to maintain harmony. (8)

H

handout Document(s) distributed during or after a presentation. (11)

hidden agenda A group member's personal goal that is not made public. (8)

high-context culture A culture that relies heavily on subtle, often nonverbal cues to convey meaning and maintain social harmony. (2)

high-level abstractions Terms that cover a broad range of possible objects or events without describing them in much detail. (4)

highly structured interview An interview that consists of a standardized list of questions, sometimes in precise order and wording, as in research interviews. (6)

horizontal (lateral) communication Communication in which messages flow between members of an organization who have equal power or responsibility. (1)

hostile work environment Verbal or nonverbal behavior that has the intention or effect of interfering with someone's work or creating an environment that is intimidating, offensive, or hostile. (4)

hypothetical questions Questions that ask an interviewee how he or she might respond under certain circumstances. (6)

I

"I" language Language in which the communicator describes his or her feelings, needs, and behaviors without accusing others. (5)

immediacy Verbal and nonverbal behaviors that indicate closeness and liking. (4)

impromptu presentation A type of delivery in which the speaker has little or no preparation time before presenting his or her remarks. (12)

indirect questions Questions that get at information the interviewer wants to know without asking for it directly. (6)

individualistic culture A culture whose members are inclined to put their own interests and those of their immediate families ahead of social concerns. (2)

informal communication networks Patterns of interaction that are based on proximity, friendships, and shared interests. (1)

information power The ability to influence that arises because of one's access to otherwise obscure information. (8)

interview A two-party, somewhat structured conversation in which at least one person has a specific purpose. (6)

investigative interview   An interview designed to discover the causes of an incident or problem. (7)

J

jargon   Specialized terminology used by members of a particular group. The word is used in a derogatory sense when applied to language that is overly obscure. (4)

L

laissez-faire leadership style   A leadership style in which the leader gives up power and transforms a group into a leaderless collection of equals. (8)

lateral communication   *See* Horizontal communication.

latitude of acceptance   The range of positions or arguments a person would accept with little or no persuasion. (13)

latitude of noncommitment   The range of positions or arguments a person neither accepts nor rejects. (13)

latitude of rejection   The range of positions or arguments a person opposes. (13)

leading questions   Questions that direct the interviewee to answer in a certain way, often by indicating the answer the interviewer wants to hear. (6)

life-cycle theory of leadership   An approach to understanding leadership that suggests that a leader's attention to tasks and relationships should vary depending on the organizational maturity of subordinates. (8)

long-term orientation   Cultural orientation that defers gratification in pursuit of long-range goals. *See also* Short-term orientation. (2)

lose–lose orientation   An approach to negotiation in which one party's perceived loss leads to an outcome with negative consequences for the other parties. (5)

low-context culture   A culture that uses language primarily to express thoughts, feelings, and ideas as clearly and logically as possible. (2)

low-level abstractions   Highly specific statements that refer directly to objects or events that can be observed. (4)

M

majority vote   A decision-making method in which a vote is taken and the item with the most votes is the one accepted. (8)

manuscript presentation   A type of delivery in which the speaker reads word-for-word from prepared remarks. (12)

masculine style of speech   Culturally influenced style of speaking that focuses less on feelings and relationships and more on information, facts, knowledge, and competence. *See also* Feminine style of speech, Report talk. (4)

matures   The generation born between 1900 and 1945 (also called the Greatest Generation), whose lives were shaped by the Depression and World Wars I and II. They value workplace loyalty, authority, punctuality, and productivity. (1)

memorized presentation   A type of delivery in which the speech is memorized and recited word-for-word from memory. (12)

message   Any symbol or behavior from which others create meaning or that triggers a response. (1)

mindful listening   A manner of listening by being fully present, attentive and thoughtful to the messages we receive. (3)

mindless listening   Listening to others' messages routinely and automatically without much mental investment. (3)

minority decision   A decision-making method in which a few members make a decision for the whole group. (8)

moderately structured interview   A flexible interview in which major topics, their order, questions, and probes are planned but not rigidly adhered to. (6)

monochronic time orientation   Cultural orientation in efficiency in accomplishing tasks is generally a higher priority than addressing personal relationships. *See also* Polychronic time orientation. (2, 4)

motion   In a meeting conducted according to parliamentary procedure, a specific proposal for action that must be seconded in order to be discussed by the group. (9)

motivated sequence organization plan   An organizational strategy that presents a topic in terms of five sequential concepts: attention, need, satisfaction, visualization, and action. (10, 13)

motivational speech   A speech aimed primarily at generating enthusiasm for the topic being presented. (13)

N

negotiation   Discussion of specific proposals for the purpose of finding a mutually acceptable agreement or settlement. (5)

networking   The process of meeting people and maintaining contacts to get career information, advice, and job leads. (1)

noise   Any factor that interferes with a message. Such factors are also called *barriers* or *interference*. (1)

nominal group technique (NGT)   A five-phase method for giving group members' ideas equal chance at consideration. (9)

nonstructured interview   An interview that consists of a topical agenda but no planned, specific questions. (6)

nonverbal communication   Communication that consists of messages sent by nonlinguistic means, whether visually, physically, or vocally. (4)

norming stage   A phase in problem-solving groups characterized by an end to conflict and emergence of harmony within the group. Also termed *emergence phase*. (8)

norms   Informal rules about what behavior is appropriate in a group. Explicit norms are made clear by speaking about them or writing them out. Implicit norms are not openly discussed but are known and understood by group members. (8)

O

online meeting   A type of virtual meeting in which computer users create a chat room and exchange typed messages in real time. (9)

open questions   Questions that invite a broad, detailed response. *See also* Closed questions. (6)

opinion questions   Questions that seek the respondent's judgment about a topic. (6)

organizational chart   A drawing or model that shows the levels of authority and reporting relationships in an organization. (1)

organizational culture   A relatively stable picture of an organization that is shared by its members. (2)

orientation phase   The first of Aubrey Fisher's four problem-solving phases of groups; characterized by tentative statements and getting-acquainted types of communication. (8)

overhead question   A question directed at all members of a group, inviting a response from any member. (9)

P

panel interview   An interview conducted by a group of questioners with whom the candidate will work, who are commonly from different levels within an organization. (7)

paralanguage   Nonlinguistic vocal qualities such as rate, pitch, volume, and pauses. (4)

paraphrasing   Listening to another and restating what has been said in your own words. Both feelings and factual content can be paraphrased. (3)

parliamentary procedure   An established set of rules that govern the process of conducting meetings. Codified in *Robert's Rules of Order.* (9)

people-oriented listening style   A style of listening in which the listener is most concerned with creating and maintaining positive interpersonal relationships. *See also* Action-oriented listening style, Content-oriented listening style, Time-oriented listening style. (3)

performance appraisal interview   An interview, usually conducted by a superior, in which the quality of a subordinate's work is discussed. (7)

performing stage   A phase in problem-solving groups characterized by members' active endorsement of group decisions. Also termed *reinforcement phase.* (8)

persuasion   The act of motivating an audience, through communication, to voluntarily change a particular belief. (13)

pictogram   A visual support that employs an artistic or a pictorial variation of a bar, column, or pie chart. (11)

pie chart   A round chart that is divided into segments to illustrate percentages of a whole. (11)

podcast   An audio (or sometimes video) program that is available for download to subscribers who use "podcatching" applications. (13)

polychronic time orientation   Cultural orientation in which personal relationships are generally a higher priority than efficient use of time. *See also* Monochronic time orientation. (2, 4)

position power   The ability to influence that comes from the position one holds. (8)

power distance   A measure of a culture's acceptance (high or low) of differences in authority. (2)

presentation software   Computer software programs (e.g., Microsoft PowerPoint) that create displays used in presentations. Such programs typically include capabilities for creating special audio, visual, and transition effects, speaker notes, and handouts. (11)

primary questions   Interview questions that introduce a new topic or a new area within a topic. *See also* Secondary questions. (6)

problem-oriented messages   Messages that aim at meeting the needs of both the sender and the other party. (5)

problem–solution pattern (organization plan)   An organizational arrangement in which the speaker first convinces the audience that a problem exists and then presents a plan to solve it. (10, 13)

proposal   A type of presentation that advocates for a particular position or action. (13)

Q

quid pro quo sexual harassment   A form of sexual harassment that implies a job benefit is tied to an employee submitting to unwelcome sexual advances. (4)

quotation   A form of support that uses the words of others who are authoritative or articulate to make a point more effectively than the speaker could on his or her own. (11)

R

rapport talk   Language that creates connections, establishes goodwill, and builds community; more typically used by women. (4)

receiver   Any person who perceives a message and attaches meaning to it, whether the message was intended for that person or not. (1)

referent power   The ability to influence because one is respected or liked by the group. (8)

reflective-thinking sequence   A seven-step problem-solving approach developed by John Dewey. (8)

reinforcement phase   The fourth of Aubrey Fisher's four group problem-solving phases; characterized by members' active endorsement of group decisions. (8)

relational messages   The dimension of messages that focus on how communicators feel about one another. *See also* Content messages. (1)

relational roles   Functional roles that help facilitate smooth interaction among members. (8)

relative words   Terms that only have meaning in relationship to other (unspecified) terms. (4)

relay question   In groups, a question asked by one member and which the leader then addresses to the entire group. (9)

relevancy challenge   A request that asks a group member to explain how his or her seemingly off-track idea relates to the group task. (9)

report   An informative presentation that describes the state of an operation. (13)

report talk   Language that conveys information, facts, knowledge, and competence; more typically used by men. (4)

research interview   An interview designed to gather data on which to base a decision. (7)

reverse question   In groups, a question asked of the leader and which the leader refers back to the person who asked it. (9)

reward power   The ability to influence that arises because one can induce desirable consequences or rewards. (8)

rhetorical question   A question with an obvious answer, which does not call for an overt response. (10)

risky shift   A type of harmful conformity in which groups take positions that are more extreme (on the side of either caution or risk) than the positions of individual members. (8)

S

sales presentation   A type of presentation aimed at persuading others to purchase a product or service. (13)

scannable résumé   A résumé prepared in plain text format with clear keywords and phrases to be "read" and evaluated by software to screen potential job candidates. (7)

secondary questions   Interview questions that seek additional information about a topic that is under discussion. *See also* Primary questions. (6)

self-directed work teams   Groups that manage their own behavior to accomplish a task. (8)

self-monitoring   The process of paying close attention to one's own behavior and using these observations to shape the way one behaves. (4)

sender   Any person who sends a message, whether intentionally or unintentionally. (1)

short-term orientation   Cultural orientation that seeks quick payoffs for effort rather than deferred gratification in pursuit of long-range goals. *See also* Long-term orientation. (2)

sincere questions   Requests for information that are genuinely meant to help the listener understand. *See also* Counterfeit questions. (3)

slides   Color transparencies that are projected onto a screen. (11)

social intelligence   The ability and skills of interacting well with other persons. *See also* Emotional intelligence. (5)

social orientation   Cultural orientation that places a greater priority on personal relationships than on accomplishing tasks. *See also* Task orientation. (2)

spatial pattern   An organizational arrangement that presents material according to its physical location. (10)

specific goal   A concrete statement of what response a speaker is seeking as the result of his or her remarks. (10)

speech of introduction   A type of presentation that prepares the audience to listen to another speaker by emphasizing the upcoming speaker's qualifications or importance of the topic. (13)

statistics   Numbers used to represent an idea. (11)

status report   A type of informative presentation that reviews the purpose, progress, obstacles, and milestones of a project. Also called a *progress report*. (13)

stories   Detailed descriptions of incidents that illustrate a point; may be factual or hypothetical. (11)

storming stage   A phase in problem-solving groups characterized by members' taking strong stands that result in conflict within the group. Also termed *conflict stage*. (8)

stress interview   An employment interview in which the candidate is subjected to the pressures typically encountered on the job. (7)

style approach to leadership   An approach to studying leadership based on the assumption that the designated leader's style of communication affects the group's effectiveness. (8)

supporting   A type of listening in which the listener responds with reassurance or comfort.

supporting material   Material that backs up claims in a presentation. (11)

survey interview   An interview conducted with a number of people to gather information for conclusions, interpretations, or future action. (7)

T

task orientation   Cultural orientation that places a greater priority on accomplishing tasks than on managing personal relationships. *See also* Social orientation. (2)

task roles   Functional roles that are needed to accomplish a group's mission. (8)

team   A group that is especially cohesive and effective because of clear and inspiring goals, a results-driven structure, competent members, unified commitment, a collaborative climate, standards of excellence, external support and recognition, and principled leadership. (8)

teleconferencing   A technology that allows participants in two or more locations to see and speak with each other. (1, 9)

text messaging (texting)   A method of communicating by sending short typed messages usually to one other person via a mobile phone or PDA. (1)

theory X   Theory of human motivation that assumes employees are inherently lazy and will avoid work if they can. Organizations that operate on theory X typically have close supervision of workers and comprehensive systems of controls. *See also* Theory Y. (2)

theory Y   Theory of human motivation that assumes employees, under optimal conditions, are self-motivated, anxious to accept greater responsibility, and capable of self-control and self-direction. *See also* Theory X. (2)

thesis statement   A single sentence that summarizes the central idea of a presentation. (10)

time-oriented listening style   A listening style in which the listener thinks most about efficiency and prefers a fast pace. Such listeners often appear impatient. *See also* Action-oriented listening style, Content-oriented listening style, People-oriented listening style. (3)

toast   A type of tribute that expresses appreciation and/or honors the accomplishments of an individual or a group. (13)

topical pattern   An organizational arrangement in which ideas are grouped around logical themes or divisions of the subject. (10)

training   An informative presentation that teaches listeners how to perform a task. (13)

trait approach to leadership   A leadership theory based on the belief that all leaders possess common traits that make them effective. (8)

transition   A statement used between parts of a presentation to help listeners understand the relationship of the parts to one another and to the thesis. (10)

transparency   A clear sheet used with an overhead projector to cast an image on a screen. (11)

triangle of meaning   A model illustrating the indirect relationship between an object, idea, process, or other referent and the word (or other symbol) used to represent it. (4)

tribute   A type of special-occasion presentation that honors a person's or group's achievements or characteristics. (13)

trigger words   Terms that have such strong emotional associations that they set off an intense emotional reaction in certain listeners. (4)

Twitter   A social networking communication channel in which individuals or companies send short messages (tweets) to persons who have signed up to receive their messages and can read and reply to them via cell phone or the Internet. (1)

U

uncertainty avoidance   A measure of how accepting a culture is of a lack of predictability. (2)

upward communication   Communication that flows from subordinates to superiors. (1)

V

videoconferencing   The holding of a meeting or conference by means of audio and visual transmissions that enable two or more geographically separated persons to see, hear, and talk to each other. (1, 9)

virtual team   A team that conducts most or all of its work via electronic channels. (8)

W

welcoming remarks   A type of special-occasion presentation in which the speaker welcomes an individual or group, indicating the significance of the visit and setting the tone for the occasion. (13)

win–lose orientation   An approach to negotiation that assumes that any gain by one party is possible only at the expense of the other party. (5)

win–win orientation   A collaborative approach to negotiation that assumes that solutions can be reached that meet the needs of all parties. (5)

work group   A small, interdependent collection of people with a common identity who interact with one another, usually face-to-face over time, to reach a goal. (8)

Y

"you" language   Language that often begins with the word *you* and accuses or evaluates the other person. (5)

notes

Chapter 1

1. *Job Outlook 2008* (Bethlehem, PA: National Association of Colleges and Employers), retrieved August 28, 2009 from **www.jobweb.com/studentarticles.aspx?id=1219**.

2. B. W. Bowman, "What Helps or Harms Promotability?" *Harvard Business Review* 42 (January–February 1964), p. 14.

3. S. P. Morreale and J. C. Pearson, Why Communication Education Is Important: The Centrality of the Discipline in the 21st Century, *Communication Education* 57:2 (2008), pp. 224-40.

4. D. A. Nellermoe, T. R. Weirich, and A. Reinstein, "Using Practitioners' Viewpoints to Improve Accounting Students' Communications Skills," *Business Communication Quarterly* 62 (1999), pp. 41-60.

5. See, for example, A. L. Darling and D. P. Dannels, "Practicing Engineers Talk about the Importance of Talk: A Report on the Role of Oral Communication in the Workplace," *Communication Education* 52 (2003), pp. 1-16.

6. L. B. Mauksch, D. C. Dugdale, S. Dodson, and R. Epstein, "Relationship, Communication, and Efficiency in the Medical Encounter," *Archives of Internal Medicine* 168:13 (2008), pp. 1387-95; and Frederick Holmes, "If You Listen, the Patient Will Tell You the Diagnosis," *International Journal of Listening* 21:2 (2007), pp. 156-61.

7. B. Calandra, "Toward a Silver-Tongued Scientist." *The Scientist* 16 (September 16, 2002), p. 42.

8. *Santa Barbara News-Press*, August 22, 1999, p. J1.

9. J. Richman, "The News Journal of the Life Scientist," *The Scientist* 16 (September 16, 2002), p. 42.

10. "Harper's Index," *Harper's*, December 1994, p. 13.

11. Joint Commission on Accreditation of Healthcare Organizations, "Sentinel Event Statistics," accessed August 7, 2006, from **www.jointcommission.org/SentinelEvents/Statistics**.

12. W. Levinson, D. Roter, and J. P. Mullooly, "Physician-Patient Communication: The Relationship with Malpractice Claims Among Primary Care Physicians and Surgeons," *Journal of American Medical Association* 277 (1997), pp. 553-59. See also H. P. Rodriguez, A. C. Rodday, R. E. Marshall, K. L. Nelson, W. H. Rogers, and D. G. Safran, "Relation of Patients' Experiences with Individual Physicians to Malpractice Risk," *International Journal for Quality in Health Care* 20(1) (2008), pp. 5-12.

13. S. Ginsberg, "So Many Messages and So Little Time," *Business Outlook*, May 5, 1997, p. C1.

14. See, for example, A. Petofi, "The Graphic Revolution in Computers," in *Careers Tomorrow: The Outlook for Work in a Changing World*, E. Cornish, ed. (Bethesda, MD: World Future Society, 1988), pp. 62-66.

15. G. Lorge, "Virtual Lessons, Real Productivity," retrieved August 28, 2009 from **www.stanfordalumni.org/news/magazine/2008/janfeb/features/seriosity.html**.

16. W. G. Powers and P. L. Witt, "Expanding the Theoretical Framework of Communication Fidelity," *Communication Quarterly* 56:3 (2008), pp. 247-67.

17. Cited in V. V. Weldon, "The Power of Changing the Context," *Vital Speeches of the Day* 60 (1994), pp. 217-19.

18. For a discussion of content and relational messages, see R. Adler and N. Towne, *Looking Out/Looking In*, 11th ed. (Belmont, CA: Wadsworth, 2005), pp. 27-28.

19. See, for example, K. Byron, "Carrying Too Heavy a Load? The Communication and Miscommunication of Emotion by Email," *Academy of Management Review* 33 (2008), pp. 309-27.

20. D. M. Driscoll, et al., "Who Says Ethics Are Nice?" *Across the Board* 34 (June 1997), pp. 47-50.

21. M. D. Montgomery and C. Ramus, "Corporate Social Responsibility Reputation Effects on MBA Job Choice," *Graduate School of Business Research Paper #1805*, May 2003, Stanford, CA. Retrieved September 26, 2005, from **https://gsbapps.stanford.edu/researchpapers/library/RP1805.pdf**.

22. C. R. Roberts, "He Argues for Ethics," *Tacoma News Tribune*, May 16, 2005. Retrieved October 1, 2005, from **http://elibrary.bigchalk.com**.

23. M. Velasquez, C. Ande, T. Shanks, S.J., and M. J. Meyer, "Thinking Ethically: A Framework for Moral Decision Making" in *Business Ethics 07/08*, J. E. Richardson, ed., (Dubuque, IA: McGraw-Hill/Dushkin, 2008), pp. 2-4.

24. P. J. O'Connor and S. H. Godar, "How Not to Make Ethical Decisions: Guidelines from Management Textbooks," *Teaching Business Ethics* 3 (1999), pp. 69-86. See also D. B. Tinsley, "Ethics Can Be Gauged by Three Key Rules," in *Business Ethics 05/06*, J. E. Richardson, ed. (Dubuque, IA: McGraw-Hill/Dushkin, 2005), pp. 11-12.

25. For a discussion of the characteristics of networks, see P. R. Monge, "The Network Level of Analysis," in *Handbook of Communication Science*, C. R. Berger and S. H. Chafee, eds. (Newbury Park, CA: Sage, 1987), pp. 239-70.

26. For a review of research on formal networks, see F. M. Jablin, "Formal Organization Structure," in *Handbook of Organizational Communication*, F. Jablin, L. Putnam, K. Roberts, and L. Porter, eds. (Newbury Park, CA: Sage, 1987), pp. 389-419.

27. "Managers' Shoptalk," *Working Woman*, February 1985, p. 22.

28. D. Katz and R. Kahn, *The Social Psychology of Organizations*, 2nd ed. (New York: Wiley, 1978), p. 239.

29. T. J. Peters and R. H. Waterman, Jr., *In Search of Excellence: Lessons from America's Best-Run Companies* (New York: Harper & Row 1982), p. 267.

30. S. Silverstein, "Corporate Communications Gap Keeps Executives, Lower Ranks in the Dark," *Los Angeles Times*, January 10, 1999, p. C5.

31. See, for example, J. W. Kassing, "Investigating the Relationship between Superior-Subordinate Relationship Quality and Employee Dissent," *Communication Research Reports* 17 (2000), pp. 58–70.

32. L. Schuster, "Wal-Mart Chief's Enthusiastic Approach Infects Employees, Keeps Retailer Growing," *The Wall Street Journal*, April 20, 1982, p. 21.

33. F. Rice, "Champions of Communication," *Fortune*, June 3, 1991, pp. 111–20.

34. Adapted from Katz and Kahn, *The Social Psychology of Organizations*, p. 245.

35. J. W. Kassing, op. cit.

36. W. G. Bennis, *An Invented Life: Reflections on Leadership and Change* (Reading, MA: Addison-Wesley, 1993).

37. L. P. Stewart, A. D. Stewart, S. A. Friedley, and P. J. Cooper, *Communication between the Sexes: Sex Differences and Sex-Role Stereotypes*, 2nd ed. (Scottsdale, AZ: Gorsuch Scarisbrick, 1990), p. 226.

38. F. Dansereau and S. E. Markham, "Superior-Subordinate Communication: Multiple Levels of Analysis," in *Handbook of Organizational Communication*, F. M. Jablin, L. L. Putnam, K. H. Roberts, and L. W. Porter, eds. (Newbury Park, CA: Sage, 1987).

39. T. Petzinger, Jr., "Two Executives Cook Up Way to Make Pillsbury Listen," *The Wall Street Journal*, September 27, 1996, p. B1.

40. J. E. Spillan, M. Mino, and M. S. Rowles, "Sharing Organizational Messages Through Effective Lateral Communication," *Qualitative Research Reports in Communication* (Fall 2002), pp. 96–104.

41. G. Goldhaber, *Organizational Communication*, 6th ed. (Dubuque, IA: Wm. C. Brown, 1993), pp. 163–64.

42. D. O. Wilson, "Diagonal Communication Links within Organizations," *Journal of Business Communication* 29 (Spring 1992), pp. 129–43.

43. K. Mieszkowski, "Change—Barbara Waugh," *Fast Company* 20 (December 1998), p. 146.

44. Adapted from Goldhaber, *Organizational Communication*, pp. 174–75.

45. T. W. Ferguson, "Who's Mentoring Whom?" *Forbes*, May 19, 1997, p. 252.

46. See, for example, P. G. Doloff, "Beyond the Org Chart," *Across the Board*, February 1999, pp. 43–47.

47. J. E. Lukaszewski, "You Can Become a Verbal Visionary," *Executive Speeches* 12 (August–September 1997), pp. 23–30.

48. "Did You Hear It Through the Grapevine?" *Training & Development*, October 1994, p. 20.

49. See R. Cross and A. Parker, *The Hidden Power of Social Networks: Understanding How Work Really Gets Done in Organizations* (Boston: Harvard Business School Press, 2004), p. 11.

50. T. E. Deal and A. A. Kennedy, *Corporate Cultures: The Rites and Rituals of Corporate Life* (Reading, MA: Addison-Wesley, 1982), p. 86.

51. D. Krackhardt and J. R. Hanson, "Informal Networks: The Company Behind the Chart," *Harvard Business Review* 71 (1993), pp. 104–11.

52. R. M. Kanter, "The New Managerial Work," *Harvard Business Review* 67 (1989), pp. 85–92.

53. J. B. Bush, Jr., and A. L. Frohman, "Communication in a 'Network' Organization," *Organizational Dynamics* 20 (Autumn 1991), pp. 23–36.

54. E. M. Eisenberg and H. L. Goodall, Jr., *Organizational Communication: Balancing Creativity and Constraint* (New York: St. Martin's, 1993), p. 9.

55. T. J. Murray, "How to Stay Lean and Mean," *Business Month*, August 1987, pp. 29–32.

56. M. Jackson, "Study Shows Workplace Goofing Off Often Pays Off for the Employer," *Santa Barbara News-Press*, January 7, 1998, p. B8.

57. K. Roane, "Nuances of Networking: A Savvy Approach for the Next Century," retrieved October 1, 2005, from **www.susanroane.com/articles/nuance.html**.

58. For more advice on networking, see R. E. Kelley interviewed by A. M. Webber, "Are You a Star at Work?" *Fast Company Career Guide* (New York: Fast Company Media Group, 2000), pp. 46–50.

59. T. H. Feely, "Testing a Communication Network Model of Employee Turnover Based on Centrality," *Journal of Applied Communication Research* (2000), pp. 262–77. See also "Network Inside Your Organization," *Fast Company Career Guide* (New York: Fast Company Media Group, 2000), p. 13.

60. P. S. Dodds, R. Muhamad, and D. J. Watts, "An Experimental Study of Search in Global Social Networks," *Science* 301 (2003), pp. 827–29.

61. K. S. Lyness and D. E. Thompson, "Climbing the Corporate Ladder: Do Female and Male Executives Follow the Same Route?" *Journal of Applied Psychology* 85 (2000), pp. 86–101. See also K. Miller, *Organizational Communication: Approaches and Processes*, 4th ed. (Belmont, CA: Wadsworth, 2006), pp. 265–67.

62. K. E. Kram, "Phases of the Mentoring Relationship," *Academy of Management Journal* 12 (1983), pp. 608–25.

63. L. Gardenswartz and A. Rowe, "Starting a Mentoring Program?" *Managing Diversity* 6 (January 1997), pp. 1–2. See also *Mentoring Process*, retrieved January 25, 2006, from **www.advancingwomen.com/wk_mentprocess.html**.

64. See, for example, L. M. Flaherty, K. J. Pearce, and R. B. Rubin, "Internet and Face-to-Face Communication: Not Functional Alternatives," *Communication*

Quarterly 46 (1998), pp. 250–68; V. C. Sheer and L. Chen, "Improving Media Richness Theory: A Study of Interaction Goals, Message Valence, and Task Complexity in Manager-Subordinate Communication," *Management Communication Quarterly* 18 (2004), pp. 76–93; and J. W. Turner and N. L. Reinsch, "The Business Communicator as Presence Allocator: Multicommunicating, Equivocality, and Status at Work," *Journal of Business Communication* 44 (2007), pp. 36–58.

65. K. Byron, "Carrying Too Heavy a Load? The Communication and Miscommunication of Emotion by Email," *Academy of Management Review* 33:2 (2008), 309–27.

66. A. Bryant, "Fare Rage," *Newsweek*, October 23, 2000, p. 46.

67. R. K. Garrett and J. N. Danziger, "IM=Interruption Management? Instant Messaging and Disruption in the Workplace," *Journal of Computer-Mediated Communication* 13:1 (2007), article 2. Retrieved August 28, 2009 from **http://jcmc.indiana.edu/vol13/issue1/garrett.html**. See also J. W. Turner, J. Grube, C. Tinsley, C. Lee, and C. O'Pell, "Exploring the Dominant Media: How Does Media Use Reflect Organizational Norms and Affect Performance?" *Journal of Business Communication* 43:3 (2006), pp. 220–50.

68. A. Harmon, "Clique of Instant Messagers Expands into the Workplace," *The New York Times*, March 11, 2003, p. C1.

69. C. Biggs, "Instant Messaging," *Enterprise Systems Journal* 16 (January 2001), p. 42.

70. Harmon, op. cit.

71. F. Thorsberg, "Ten Tips for Proper IM Manners," AOL Computer Center, August 12, 2002, and from K. Lorenz, *Six Rules for IM-ing at Work*, retrieved August 28, 2009 from **http://jobs.aol.com/article?id=2005080 8184709990048**.

72. "'We Never Talk Anymore': Survey Reveals Few Executives Use Telephone or Meet in Person at Work," retrieved February 9, 2006, from **www.officeteam.com/ PressRoom;jsessionid=CwZX1nzn5DxDdnY3LYsphb xRPS4JQ22ftzKJXHcyMT0d4Gp8H4S0**.

73. Y. M. Kalman, G. Ravid, D. R. Raban, and S. Rafaeli, "Pauses and Response Latencies: A Chronemic Analysis of Asynchronous CMC," *Journal of Computer-Mediated Communication* 12:1 (2006). Retrieved August 28, 2009 from **http://jcmc.indiana.edu/vol12/issue1/kalman.html**.

74. J. Waldvogel, "Greetings and Closings in Workplace Email," *Journal of Computer-Mediated Communication* 12:2 (2007). Retrieved August 28, 2009 from **http://jcmc. indiana.edu/vol12/issue2/waldvogel.html**.

75. L. Garton and B. Wellman, "Social Impacts of Electronic Mail in Organizations: A Review of the Research Literature," *Communication Yearbook* 18 (Newbury Park, CA: Sage, 1995), pp. 434–53. See also M. Parks and L. Roberts, "Making MOOsic: The Development of Personal Relationships On-line and a Comparison to Their Off-line Counterparts," presented at the annual conference of the Western Speech Communication Association, Monterey, CA, February 1997.

76. "Are You Connected?" *Training & Development*, November 1994, p. 18.

77. A. Overholt, "Intel's Got (Too Much) Mail," *Fast Company*, March 2001, p. 44.

78. N. L. Renisch and J. W. Turner, "Ari, R U There? Reorienting Business Communication for a Technological Era," *Journal of Business and Technical Communication* 20:3 (July 2006), pp. 339–56.

79. R. H. Lengel and R. L. Daft, "The Selection of Communication Media as an Executive Skill." *Academy of Management Executive*, 2 (1998), p. 229.

80. J. Montague, "When E-Mail Just Won't Do," *Hospitals & Health Networks* 70 (October 20, 1996), pp. 10–11.

81. See, for example, L. A. Baxter, "'Talking Things Through' and 'Putting It in Writing': Two Codes of Communication in an Academic Institution," *Journal of Applied Communication Research* 21 (1993), pp. 313–23.

82. J. J. Mitchell, "Why Can't We All Get Along? E-mail vs. Voice Mail Culture Should Provide a Clue," *San Jose Mercury News*, July 21, 1996, p. 6E. For a discussion of the importance of personal contact in an increasingly technological world, see S. R. Herndon, "Theory and Practice: Implications for the Implementation of Communication Technology in Organizations," *Journal of Business Communication* 34 (1997), pp. 121–29.

83. J. W. Turner, J. Grube, C. Tinsley, C. Lee, and C. O'Pell, "Exploring the Dominant Media: How Does Media Use Reflect Organizational Norms and Affect Performance?" *Journal of Business Communication* 43:3 (2006), pp. 220–50.

Chapter 2

1. While many Hispanics prefer to be identified with their country of origin and some prefer Latino/a to Hispanic, we generally use the term Hispanic while acknowledging the ongoing discussion. See N. Chong and F. Baez, *Latino Culture: A Dynamic Force in the Changing American Workplace* (Yarmouth, ME: Intercultural Press, 2005), pp. 4–5.

2. J. F. Kikoski and C. K. Kikoski, *Reflexive Communication in the Culturally Diverse Workplace* (Westport, CT: Quorum, 1996), p. 3.

3. "Tripling of Hispanic and Asian Populations in 50 Years; Non-Hispanic Whites May Drop to Half of Total Population," U.S. Census Bureau publication CB04-44. Retrieved September 11, 2008, from **www .census.gov/Press-Release/www/releases/archives/ population/001720.html**.

4. *Directory of Foreign Firms Operating in the U.S.*, 18th ed. (Millis, MA: Uniworld Business Publications, 2005).

5. U.S. Census Bureau, *Population Profile of the United States: 2000.* Retrieved October 15, 2005, from **www.census.gov/hhes/www/laborfor/laborforce.html**.

6. Kiplinger Letter 79 (December 27, 2002).

7. "Employment at U.S.-Based Global Companies," *Workforce Management,* July 2005, pp. 36–46.

8. *Directory of Foreign Firms,* op cit.

9. K. H. Hammonds, "Fast Forward," *Fast Company* 44 (March 2001), p. 113.

10. DuPont advertisement, reprinted in L. E. Boone, D. L. Kurtz, and J. R. Block, *Contemporary Business Communication,* 2nd ed. (Englewood Cliffs, NJ: Prentice-Hall, 1996), p. 637.

11. L. Copeland, "Making the Most of Cultural Differences at the Workplace," *Personnel,* June 1988, p. 53.

12. N. Bartrum, "Diversity for All," *Association Management,* July 2003, p. 58.

13. M. W. Lustig and J. Koester, *Intercultural Competence: Interpersonal Communication Across Cultures,* 4th ed. (Boston: Allyn & Bacon, 2003), p. 27.

14. E. Hall, *The Silent Language* (Greenwich, CT: Fawcett, 1959), p. 169.

15. J. A. Barker, *Future Edge: Discovering the New Paradigms of Success* (New York: William Morrow, 1992), p. 124.

16. Ibid., p. 125.

17. See, for example, Y. Zhu, "Comparing English and Chinese Persuasive Strategies in Trade Fair Invitations: A Sociocognitive Approach," *Document Design* 2:1 (2001), pp. 2–17.

18. Boone, Kurtz, and Block, *Contemporary Business Communication,* p. 603.

19. C. J. Williams, "Not All Ways Wal-Mart as Chain Takes on Germany," *Los Angeles Times,* August 15, 1999, p. C1.

20. K. M. Glover, "Do's and Taboos," *Business America* 111 (August 13, 1990), p. 5.

21. F. H. Katayama, "How to Act Once You Get There," *Fortune's Pacific Rim Guide,* 1989, p. 87.

22. R. Falkoff, "The Karaoke Business Meeting." Retrieved August 16, 2006, from **http://workabroad.monster.com/articles/karaoke/**.

23. "UPS: From Local Startup to Global Titan," *Business Week,* June 27, 2007. Retrieved May 3, 2009, at **www.businessweek.com/smallbiz/content/jun2007/sb20070627_827624.htm**.

24. T. Padgett and C. S. Lee, "Go South, Young Yanquis," *Newsweek,* September 19, 1994, p. 48.

25. F. Trompenaars, *Riding the Waves of Culture* (Burr Ridge, IL: Irwin, 1994), p. 123.

26. M. Chen, *Inside Chinese Business: A Guide for Managers Worldwide* (Boston: Harvard Business School Press, 2001), p. 209.

27. M. Miller, "A Clash of Corporate Cultures," *Los Angeles Times,* August 15, 1992, pp. A1, A8.

28. E. Hall, *Beyond Culture* (New York: Doubleday, 1959).

29. Chen, *Inside Chinese Business,* p. 137.

30. K. Melymuka, "Tips for Teams," *Computerworld* 31 (April 28, 1997), p. 72.

31. M. Morris, *Saying and Meaning in Puerto Rico: Some Problems in the Ethnology of Discourse* (Oxford: Pergamon, 1981).

32. D. Locke, *Increasing Multicultural Understanding: A Comprehensive Model* (Newbury Park, CA: Sage, 1992), p. 140.

33. G. Hofstede, *Cultures and Organizations: Software of the Mind* (New York: McGraw-Hill, 1997).

34. See, for example, M. Nishishiba and L. D. Ritchie, "The Concept of Trustworthiness: A Cross-Cultural Comparison between Japanese and U.S. Business People," *Journal of Applied Communication Research* 28 (2000), pp. 347–67. See also S. Witteborn, "Conceptualization and Study of Collective Identities: Implications for Research in Culture and Communication." Paper presented at the annual meeting of the International Communication Association, Dresden International Congress Centre, Dresden, Germany, June 16, 2006. **www.allacademic.com/meta/p91318_index.html**.

35. D. Taub, "Global Recruiting: Richard Ferry Helped Take Korn/Ferry International from Two-Man Office to World's No. 1 Executive Search Firm," *Los Angeles Business Journal,* December 16, 1996, p. 1.

36. "Formula for Success," *Financial World,* December 8, 1992, p. 40.

37. Hofstede, *Cultures and Organizations,* pp. 189–210.

38. S. Roll and M. Irwin, *The Invisible Border: Latinos in America* (Boston: Intercultural press, 2008), pp. 91–98.

39. For a summary of research on this subject, see J. J. Bradac, "Language Attitudes and Impression Formation," in H. Giles and W. P. Robinson, eds., *The Handbook of Language and Social Psychology* (Chichester, England: Wiley, 1990), pp. 387–412. See also S. H. Ng and J. J. Bradac, *Power in Language: Verbal Communication and Social Influence* (Newbury Park, CA: Sage, 1993).

40. E. D. Markley, *Regional Accent Discrimination in the Hiring Process: A Language Attitude Study* (University of North Texas, 2000). Online at **www.library.unt.edu/theses/open/20002/markley_e_dianne/thesis.pdf**.

41. R. L. Birdwhistell, *Kinesics and Context* (Philadelphia: University of Philadelphia Press, 1970), pp. 30–31.

42. See B. J. Hall, *Among Cultures* (Fort Worth: Harcourt College Publishers, 2002), p. 239, for a discussion of Greek and Israeli conflict styles.

43. Lustig and Koester, *Intercultural Competence,* p. 267.

44. E. C. Condon, "Cross-Cultural Interferences Affecting Teacher–Pupil Communication in American Schools," *International and Intercultural Communication Annual* 3 (1976), pp. 108–120.

45. L. A. Samovar and R. E. Porter, *Communication between Cultures,* 5th ed. (Belmont, CA: Wadsworth, 2004), p. 199.

46. For information on generational differences, see K. Auby, "A Boomers Guide to Communicating with Gen X and Gen Y." Retrieved September 11, 2008, from **www.businessweek.com/magazine/content/08_34/b4097063805619.htm**; S. P. Eisner, "Managing 'Generation Y,'" *Advanced Management Journal* 70 (2005), pp. 13–17; T. Erickson, "When Boomers Work for Gen X and Gen Y," *Harvard Business Online*, September 9, 2008. Retrieved September 11, 2008, from **www.businessweek.com/managing/content/sep2008/ca2008099_258565.htm**. See also S. Lyons, L. Duxbury, and C. Higgins, "Are Gender Differences in Basic Human Values a Generational Phenomenon?" *Sex Roles: A Journal of Research* 53 (2005), pp. 763–79.

47. J. Zogby, *The Way We'll Be: The Transformation of the American Dream* (New York: Random House, 2008), and John Zogby, "The Evolving American Dream," *AARP Bulletin* (October 2008), p. 37.

48. K. G. Stone, "Disability Act Everyone's Responsibility in America," *Albuquerque Journal*, February 19, 1995, p. H2.

49. D. O. Braithwaite and D. Labrecque, "Responding to the Americans with Disabilities Act: Contributions of Interpersonal Communication Research and Training," *Journal of Applied Communication Research* 22 (1994), pp. 285–94. See also D. O. Braithwaite, "'Just How Much Did That Wheelchair Cost?': Management of Privacy Boundaries by Persons with Disabilities," *Western Journal of Speech Communication* 55 (1991), pp. 254–75.

50. "Communicating with People with Disabilities," *Business First* 11 (October 9, 1995), p. 14B. See also A. L. Colvert and J. Smith, "What Is Reasonable? Workplace Communication and People Who Are Disabled," in *Handbook of Communication and People with Disabilities: Research and Application*, eds. D. O. Braithwaite and T. L. Thompson (Mahwah, NJ: Erlbaum, 2000).

51. See J. Skelly, "The Rise of International Ethics," *Business Ethics*, March–April 1995, pp. 2–5. Reprinted in J. E. Richardson, ed., *Business Ethics 97–98* (Guilford, CT: Dushkin/McGraw-Hill, 1997), pp. 164–68.

52. P. F. Buller, J. J. Kohls, and K. S. Anderson, "A Model for Addressing Cross-Cultural Ethical Conflicts," *Business & Society* 36 (June 1997), pp. 169–93.

53. See T. Donaldson, "Values in Tension: Ethics Away from Home," *Harvard Business Review*, September–October 1996, pp. 48–62.

54. Ibid.

55. J. F. Kiboski, "Effective Communication in the Performance Appraisal Interview: Face-to-Face Communication for Public Managers in the Culturally Diverse Workplace," *Public Personnel Management* 28, no. 2 (Summer 1999), pp. 301–23.

56. M. Marby, "Pin a Label on a Manager—and Watch What Happens," *Newsweek*, May 14, 1990, p. 43.

57. Copeland, "Making the Most of Cultural Differences," p. 60.

58. T. Weiss, "Reading Culture: Professional Communication as Translation," *Journal of Business & Technical Communication* 11 (1997), pp. 321–38.

59. L. M. Millhous, "The Experience of Culture in Multicultural Groups," *Small Group Research* 30 (1999), pp. 280–308.

60. J. C. Pearson, L. Turner, and W. Todd-Mancillas, *Gender and Communication*, 3rd ed. (Madison, WI: Brown & Benchmark, 1995), pp. 153–57.

61. Q. Dong, K. D. Day, and C. M. Collaço, "Overcoming Ethnocentrism through Developing Intercultural Communication Sensitivity and Multiculturalism," *Human Communication* 11: 1 (2008), pp. 27–38.

62. M. Houston, "When Black Women Talk with White Women: Why Dialogues Are Difficult," in *Our Voices*, eds. Gonzalez, Houston, and Chen, p. 137.

63. J. N. Martin and T. K. Nakayama, *Intercultural Communication in Contexts* (Boston: McGraw-Hill, 2004), pp. 420–21.

64. C. M. Kelly, *The Destructive Achiever: Power and Ethics in the American Corporation* (Reading, MA: Addison-Wesley, 1988), p. 159.

65. E. Cose, *The Rage of a Privileged Class: Why Are Middle-Class Blacks So Angry? Why Should America Care?* (New York: HarperCollins, 1993), p. 9.

66. Presentation by Ann Rhoades. Anderson School of Management, University of New Mexico, Albuquerque, NM, October 2, 2008.

67. S. F. Gale, "The Bookstore Battle," *Workforce Management Online*, August 2003. Retrieved October 30, 2005, from **www.workforce.com/archive/feature/23/49/48/index.php?ht=bookstore%20battle%20bookstore%20battle**.

68. E. C. Ravlin and C. L. Adkins, "A Work Values Approach to Corporate Culture: A Field Test of the Value of Congruence Process and Its Relationship to Individual Outcomes," *Journal of Applied Psychology* 74 (June 1989), pp. 424–33.

69. J. Kotter and J. Heskett, *Corporate Culture and Performance* (New York: Free Press, 1992), p. 7.

70. J. Keyton, *Communication and Organizational Culture* (Thousand Oaks, CA: Sage, 2005).

71. J. W. Gilsdorf, "Organizational Rules on Communicating: How Employees Are—and Are Not—Learning the Ropes," *Journal of Business Communication* 39 (April 1998), pp. 173–201.

72. R. D. Ireland, "Corporate Culture Best Conveyed by Mid-level Managers," *Baylor Business Review* 10 (Spring 1992), pp. 18–19.

73. Gilsdorf, op. cit.

74. *Workforce Week*, May 25–29, 2003; retrieved May 27, 2003, from **www.workforce.com/section/09/article/23/44/64.html#values#values**.

75. R. S. Hansen, "Uncovering a Company's Corporate Culture Is a Critical Task for Job-Seekers," retrieved November 26, 2001, from **www.quintcareers.com/ employer_corporate_culture.html**.

76. D. McGregor, *The Human Side of Enterprise* (New York: McGraw-Hill, 1960).

77. See M. W. Kramer and J. A. Hess, "Communication Rules for the Display of Emotions in Organizational Settings," *Management Communication Quarterly* 16 (2002), pp. 66–80.

78. M. H. Brown, "Defining Stories in Organizations: Characteristics and Functions," in *Communication Yearbook 13*, ed. J. A. Anderson (Newbury Park, CA: Sage, 1990), pp. 162–90. See also J. Meyer, "Tell Me a Story: Eliciting Organizational Values from Narratives," *Communication Quarterly* 43 (1995), pp. 210–24.

79. J. K. Barge, "Memorable Messages and Newcomer Socialization," *Western Journal of Communication* 68 (2004), pp. 233–56.

80. E. Gustkey, "A Team of Cut-Ups," *Los Angeles Times*, June 21, 1996, pp. C1, C7.

81. T. J. Peters and R. H. Waterman, *In Search of Excellence: Lessons from America's Best-Run Companies* (New York: Harper & Row, 1982), p. 240. See also J. M. Byer and H. M. Trice, "How an Organization's Rites Reveal Its Culture," *Organizational Dynamics*, Spring 1987, p. 15.

82. B. Filipczak, "Corporate Body Language," *Training* 33 (November 1996), p. 8.

83. The following sections are adapted from T. E. Deal and A. A. Kennedy, *Corporate Cultures: The Rites and Rituals of Corporate Life* (Reading, MA: Addison-Wesley, 1982), pp. 129–33.

84. J. Waldvogel, "Greetings and Closings in Workplace Email," *Journal of Computer-Mediated Communication* 12:2 (2007), article 6. Accessed May 3, 2009, from **http:// jcmc.indiana.edu/vol12/issue2/waldvogel.html**.

85. J. K. Barge, "Why Communication?" *Communication Currents* 3:4 (August 2008). Accessed September 17, 2008, at **www.communicationcurrents.com/**.

Chapter 3

1. S. Covey, *The Seven Habits of Highly Effective People* (New York: Simon & Schuster, 1989).

2. T. Peters, "Leadership Is Confusing as Hell," *Fast Company*, March 2001. Online at **www.fastcompany.com/ online/44/rules.html**.

3. J. Franzen, "The Listener," *New Yorker*, October 6, 2003, p. 85.

4. J. L. Winsor, D. B. Curtis, and R. D. Stephens, "National Preferences in Business and Communication Education: An Update," *Journal of the Association for Communication Administration* 3 (1997), pp. 170–79.

5. V. Marchant, "Listen Up!" *Time*, June 28, 1999, p. 74. See also K. W. Hawkins and B. P. Fillion, "Perceived Communication Skill Needs for Work Groups," *Communication Research Reports* 2 (1999), pp. 167–74.

6. T. Rankin, "The Measurement of the Ability to Understand Spoken Language," *Dissertation Abstracts* 12 (1952), pp. 847–48.

7. J. D. Weinrauch and J. R. Swanda Jr., "Examining the Significance of Listening: An Exploratory Study of Contemporary Management," *Journal of Business Communication* 13 (February 1975), pp. 25–32.

8. J. P. Kotter, "What Effective General Managers Really Do," *Harvard Business Review* 60 (1982), pp. 156–67; and R. G. Nichols and L. A. Stevens, "Listening to People," *Harvard Business Review* 68 (1990), pp. 95–102.

9. H. Mintzberg, "The Manager's Job: Folklore and Fact," *Harvard Business Review* 53 (July–August 1975), pp. 49–61.

10. S. L. Becker and L. R. V. Ekdom, "That Forgotten Basic Skill: Oral Communication," *Association for Communication Administration Bulletin* 33 (1980), pp. 12–15.

11. V. DiSalvo, D. C. Larsen, and W. J. Seiler, "Communication Skills Needed by Persons in Business Organizations," *Communication Education* 25 (1976), pp. 269–75.

12. *U.S. News & World Report*, May 26, 1980, p. 65.

13. D. H. Sweet, "Successful Job Hunters Are All Ears," *Managing Your Career* (New York: Dow Jones, 1993).

14. A. J. Sutcliffe, *First-Job Survival Guide* (New York: Henry Holt, 1997).

15. B. D. Sypher, R. N. Bostrom, and J. H. Siebert, "Listening, Communication Abilities, and Success at Work," *Journal of Business Communication* 26 (1989), pp. 293–303.

16. S. D. Johnson and C. Bechler, "Examining the Relationship between Listening Effectiveness and Leadership Emergence," *Small Group Research* 29 (1998), pp. 452–71.

17. E. R. Alexander, L. E. Penley, and I. E. Jerigan, "The Relationship of Basic Decoding Skills to Managerial Effectiveness," *Management Communication Quarterly* 6 (1992), pp. 58–73.

18. L. O. Cooper, D. R. Seibold, and R. Suchner, "Listening in Organizations: An Analysis of Error Structures in Models of Listening Competency," *Communication Research Reports* 14 (1997), pp. 312–20.

19. Ibid.

20. V. Alonzo, "5 Steps to Bigger Sales," *Incentive* 174, no. 10 (October 2000), pp. 117–19.

21. "General Interactional Skills," National Breast Cancer Centre, accessed March 10, 2003, from **www.nbcc.org .au/pages/subsections/skills.htm**.

22. USMLE Web site, **www.usmle.org/news/cse/harris .asp**, accessed July 28, 2003.

23. Ibid.; and R. K. Sobel, "The Art of Listening," *U.S. News & World Report*, June 9, 2003, p. 58.

24. J. Brownell, "Listening in the Service Industries," in *Listening in Everyday Life: A Personal and Professional Approach*, eds. D. Borisoff and M. Purdy (Lanham, MD: University Press of America, 1991), pp. 229, 256.

25. P. LaBarre, "Leader-Feargal Quinn," *Fast Company* 52 (November 2001), p. 88. Accessed July 28, 2003, from **www.fastcompany.com/magazine/52/quinn.html**.

26. B. H. Spitzberg, "The Dark Side of Incompetence," in *The Dark Side of Interpersonal Communication* (Hillsdale, NJ: Erlbaum, 1994), pp. 27–28.

27. R. G. Nichols, *Are You Listening?* (New York: McGraw-Hill, 1957), pp. 1–17.

28. See, for example, S. Golan, "A Factor Analysis of Barriers to Effective Listening," *Journal of Business Communication* 27 (1990), pp. 25–36; and J. E. Hulbert, "Barriers to Effective Listening," *Bulletin for the Association for Business Communication* 52 (1989), pp. 3–5.

29. Peter Senge quoted in "Listening Quotations," January 20, 2003. Received from **webmaster@listen.org** (International Listening Association).

30. J. W. Turner, and N. L. Reinsch, "The Business Communicator as Presence Allocator: Multicommunicating, Equivocality, and Status at Work," *Journal of Business Communication* 44: 1 (2007), pp. 36–58.

31. "McDonald's Listens—Finally!" *Listening Leader*, March 9, 1998. Online at **www.listencoach.com**.

32. A. Arsenault, "Too much information?: Gatekeeping and Information Dissemination in a Networked World." Paper presented at the annual meeting of the International Communication Association, San Francisco, CA, May 2007.

33. A. Vangelisti, M. L. Knapp, and J. A. Daly, "Conversational Narcissism," *Communication Monographs* 57 (1990), pp. 251–74.

34. T. Peters, *Thriving on Chaos: Handbook for a Management Revolution* (New York: Knopf, 1987), p. 117.

35. P. F. Drucker, "Management Communications," in *Management—Tasks, Responsibilities, Practices* (New York: Harper & Row, 1974).

36. *Industrial Marketing*, April 1982, p. 108.

37. D. Borisoff and M. Purdy, eds., *Listening in Everyday Life: A Personal and Professional Approach* (Lanham, MD: University Press of America, 1991), p. xiii.

38. S. H. McDaniel, H. B. Beckman, D. S. Morse, J. Silberman, D. B. Seaburn, and R. M. Epstein, "Physician Self-disclosure in Primary Care Visits: Enough About You, What About Me?" *Archives of Internal Medicine* 167 (2007), pp. 1321–26.

39. E. Cooper, "Are You in the Listening Zone?" *On Wall Street* 11, no. 7 (July 2001).

40. S. Peterson, "Managing Your Communication: The Year 2000 and Beyond," in *Vital Speeches of the Day*, January 1, 1995.

41. T. D. Thomlison, "Intercultural Listening," in *Listening in Everyday Life: A Personal and Professional Approach*, eds. D. Borisoff and M. Purdy (Lanham, MD: University Press of America, 1991), p. 119.

42. M. Houston, "When Black Women Talk with White Women: Why Dialogues Are Difficult," in *Our Voices: Essays in Culture, Ethnicity, and Communication: An Intercultural Anthology*, eds. A. Gonzalez, M. Houston, and V. Chen (Los Angeles: Roxbury, 1994), pp. 133–39.

43. Thomlison, "Intercultural Listening," p. 117.

44. M. L. Lusting and J. Koester, *Intercultural Competence: Interpersonal Communication across Cultures*, 3rd ed. (New York: Longman, 1999), p. 250.

45. L. D. Mare, "Ma and Japan," *Southern Speech Communication Journal* 55 (Spring 1990), pp. 319–28.

46. J. C. Pearson, R. L. West, and L. H. Turner, *Gender and Communication*, 3rd ed. (Madison, WI: Brown & Benchmark, 1995), pp. 35–36.

47. D. Tannen, *You Just Don't Understand: Women and Men in Conversation* (New York: Morrow, 1990), p. 142.

48. C. A. Rategan, "He Said, She Said," *Current Health* 2 (September 1993), p. 6.

49. M. Booth-Butterfield, "She Hears . . . He Hears: What They Hear and Why," *Personnel Journal,* May 1984, pp. 36–42.

50. D. Tannen, *Talking from 9 to 5* (New York: Morrow, 1994), p. 284.

51. L. Iacocca and W. Novak, *Iacocca: An Autobiography* (New York: Bantam, 1984), p. 74.

52. D. J. McNerney, "Improve Your Communication Skills," *HR Focus* 71 (1994), p. 22. See also J. Procter, "You Haven't Heard a Word I Said: Getting Managers to Listen," *IEEE Transactions on Professional Communication* 37 (1994).

53. A. D. Wolvin and C. G. Coakley, "A Survey of the Status of Listening Training in Some Fortune 500 Companies," *Communication Education* 40 (1991), pp. 152–65.

54. L. L. Barker and K. W. Watson, *Listen Up* (New York: St. Martin's Press, 2000).

55. K. W. Watson, L. L. Barker, and J. B. Weaver, *The Listening Styles Profiles* (New Orleans: SPECTRA, 1995).

56. E. Langer, *Mindfulness* (Reading, MA: Addison-Wesley, 1990); and C. Hajek and H. Giles, (2003), "New Directions in Intercultural Communication Competence: The Process Model," in *Handbook of Communication and Social Interaction Skills*, J. O. Greene and B. R. Burleson eds. (Mahwah, NJ: Lawrence Erlbaum, 2003), pp. 935–58.

57. J. K. Burgoon, C. R. Berger, and V. R. Waldron, "Mindfulness and Interpersonal Communication," *Journal of Social Issues* 56 (2000), pp. 105–27.

58. A. Miller, "The Mindful Society," *Shambhala Sun*, September 2008, pp. 56–62, 106. Retrieved May 13, 2009 from **www.shambhalasun.com/index.php?option=com_content&task=view&id=3253&Itemid=244**.

59. Covey, *The Seven Habits*, p. 235.

60. Tyena Dollinger, "Listen Using the 20/80 Rule," *Listening Leader* newsletter, March 29, 2004.

61. D. Carnoy, "Rick Pitino," *Success* 45 (October 1998), pp. 68–71.

62. D. Borisoff and D. A. Victor, *Conflict Management: A Communication Skills Approach* (Englewood Cliffs, NJ: Prentice-Hall, 1989), p. 45.

63. R. S. Wyer, Jr. and R. Adaval, "Message Reception Skills in Social Communication," in *Handbook of Communication and Social Interaction Skills*, eds. J. O. Greene and B. R. Burleson (Mahwah, NJ: Erlbaum, 2003), pp. 291–355.

64. M. J. Marquardt, *Leading with Questions: How Leaders Find the Right Solutions by Knowing What to Ask* (Hoboken, NJ: Jossey-Bass, 2005), p. 92.

Chapter 4

1. B. Keysar and A. S. Henly, "Speakers' Overestimation of Their Effectiveness," *Psychological Science* 13 (2002). See also R. S. Wyer and R. Adaval, "Message Reception Skills in Social Communication," in *Handbook of Communication and Social Interaction Skills*, eds. J. O. Greene and B. R. Burleson (Mahwah, NJ: Erlbaum, 2003), pp. 291–355.

2. C. K. Ogden and I. A. Richards, *The Meaning of Meaning* (New York: Harcourt Brace, 1923).

3. R. Bello, "Determinants of Equivocation," *Communication Research* 27 (2000), pp. 161–94.

4. M. Meyer and C. Fleming, "Silicon Screenings: The Marriage of Hollywood and Silicon Valley Gets Off to a Rocky Start," *Newsweek*, August 15, 1994, p. 63.

5. M. Miller, "A Clash of Corporate Cultures," *Los Angeles Times*, August 15, 1992, pp. A1, A8.

6. J. S. Armstrong, "Unintelligible Management Research and Academic Prestige," *Interfaces* 10 (1980), pp. 80–86.

7. D. Legard, "IT Vendors Worst for Jargon, Deloitte Says," IDG News Service, June 17, 2003, at **www.idg .net/idgns/2003/06/17/ITVendorsWorstForJargon Deloitte.shtml**.

8. "Up in Smoke," *Accountant's Journal* 66 (April 1987), p. 10.

9. T. Simmons, "Are You a Buzzword Abuser?" *Presentations*, April 2003, pp. 31–34.

10. T. Terez, "Eager for a Paradigm Shift? Not So Fast!" *Workforce*, February 2002, p. 26.

11. C. Quinn, "Lose the Office Jargon, It May Sunset You," *The Age* (September 1, 2007). Retrieved May 12, 2009, from **www.theage.com.au/news/in-depth/ bjobsb-lose-the-office-jargon-it-may-sunset-your- career/2007/08/31/1188067363016.html**.

12. T. Weiss, "Translation in a Borderless World," *Technical Communication Quarterly* 4 (1995), pp. 407–25.

13. See, for example, J. B. Bavelas, A. Black, N. Chovil, and J. Mullett, *Equivocal Communication* (Newbury Park, CA: Sage, 1990); and E. M. Eisenberg, H. L. Goodall Jr., and A. Tretheway, *Organizational Communication: Balancing Creativity and Constraint*, 6th ed. (New York: St. Martin's, 2007), pp. 23–36.

14. A. Schneider, "Why You Can't Trust Letters of Recommendation," *The Chronicle of Higher Education* online, June 30, 2000, at **http://chronicle.com**; and C. Conrad and M. S. Poole, *Strategic Organizational Communication in a Global Economy*, 6th ed. (Belmont, CA: Thomson Wadsworth, 2005), p. 265.

15. "Litigation-Proof Letters of Recommendation," accessed February 16, 2001, at **www.wildcowpublishing.com/ other/letter.html**.

16. R. Rubin, "Doctor–Patient Language Gap Isn't Healthy," *USA Today*, May 1, 2003, p. 9D.

17. Conrad and Poole, op. cit.

18. J. J. Bradac, J. M. Wiemann, and K. Schaefer, "The Language of Control in Interpersonal Communication," in *Strategic Interpersonal Communication*, eds. J. A. Daly and J. M. Wiemann (Hillsdale, NJ: Erlbaum, 1994), pp. 102–4. See also S. H. Ng and J. J. Bradac, *Power in Language: Verbal Communication and Social Influence* (Newbury Park, CA: Sage, 1993), p. 27.

19. L. A. Hosman, "The Evaluative Consequences of Hedges, Hesitations, and Intensifiers: Powerful and Powerless Speech Styles," *Human Communication Research* 15 (1989), pp. 383–406.

20. J. Bradac and A. Mulac, "Attributional Consequences of Powerful and Powerless Speech Styles in a Crisis-Intervention Context," *Journal of Language and Social Psychology* 3 (1984), pp. 1–19.

21. J. J. Bradac, "The Language of Lovers, Flovers [sic], and Friends: Communicating in Social and Personal Relationships," *Journal of Language and Social Psychology* 2 (1983), pp. 141–62.

22. D. Geddes, "Sex Roles in Management: The Impact of Varying Power of Speech Style on Union Members' Perception of Satisfaction and Effectiveness," *Journal of Psychology* 126 (1992), pp. 589–607.

23. D. Tannen, *You Just Don't Understand: Women and Men in Conversation* (New York: Morrow, 1990), p. 47. For a detailed summary of masculine and feminine language, see D. Canary and T. Emmers-Sommer, *Sex and Gender Differences in Personal Relationships* (New York: Guilford, 1997); D. Tannen, *Talking from 9 to 5: How Women's and Men's Conversational Styles Affect Who Gets Heard, Who Gets Credit, and What Gets Done at Work* (New York: Morrow, 1994); and J. T. Wood, *Gendered Lives: Communication, Gender, and Culture*, 4th ed. (Belmont, CA: Wadsworth, 2001).

24. D. Tannen, *Talking from 9 to 5*, pp. 45–46.

25. L. Mullany, *Gendered Discourse in the Professional Workplace* (Houndmills, UK: Palgrave Macmillan, 2007), pp. 47–48, 204–5.

26. K. Byron, "Male and Female Managers' Ability to Read Emotions: Relationships with Supervisor's Performance

Ratings and Subordinates' Satisfaction Ratings," *Journal of Occupational and Organizational Psychology* 80:4 (2007), pp. 713–33.

27. M. R. Mell, S. Vazire, N. Ramirez-Esparza, R. B. Slatcher, and J. W. Pennebaker, "Are Women Really More Talkative Than Men?" *Science* 6:317 (July 2007), p. 82. See also D. Tannen, "Who Does The Talking Here?" *The Washington Post*, July 15, 2007, p. B07. Retrieved from **www9.georgetown.edu/faculty/tannend/post071507.htm**.

28. L. Mullany, *Gendered Discourse*, pp. 47–48, 204–5.

29. See, for example, D. Geddes, "Sex Roles in Management: The Impact of Varying Power of Speech Style on Union Members' Perception of Satisfaction and Effectiveness," *Journal of Psychology* 126 (1992), pp. 589–607.

30. For a discussion of the principle "You can't not communicate nonverbally," see T. Clevenger Jr., "Can One Not Communicate? A Conflict of Models," *Communication Studies* 42 (1991), pp. 340–53.

31. Y. M. Kalman, G. Ravid, D. R. Raban, and S. Rafaeli, "Pauses and Response Latencies: A Chronemic Analysis of Asynchronous CMC," *Journal of Computer-Mediated Communication* 12:1 (2006). Retrieved May 12, 2009, from **http://jcmc.indiana.edu/vol12/issue1/kalman.html**.

32. L. McCoy, "First Impressions," *Canadian Banker* 10 (September/October 1996), pp. 32–36.

33. J. B. Stiff, J. L. Hale, R. Garlick, and R. G. Rogan, "Effect of Cue Incongruence and Social Normative Influences on Individual Judgments of Honesty and Deceit," *Southern Speech Communication Journal* 55 (1990), pp. 206–29.

34. H. S. Friedman, "Paradoxes of Nonverbal Detection, Expression, and Responding: Points to PONDER," in *Interpersonal Sensitivity: Theory and Measurement*, eds. J. A. Hall and F. J. Bernieri (Mahwah, NJ: Erlbaum, 2001), pp. 351–62.

35. K. Byron, S. Terranova, and S. Nowicki, "Nonverbal Emotion Recognition and Salespersons: Linking Ability to Perceived and Actual Success," *Journal of Applied Social Psychology* 37:11 (2007), 2600–19.

36. R. A. Baron, and G. D. Markman, "Beyond Social Capital: The Role Of Entrepreneurs' Social Competence In Their Financial Success," *Journal of Business Venturing* 18:1 (2003), pp. 41–60.

37. K. Byron, "Male and Female Managers' Ability to Read Emotions," pp. 713–33.

38. P. Ekman, "Cross-Cultural Studies of Facial Expression," in *Darwin and Facial Expression*, ed. P. Ekman (New York: Academic Press, 1973).

39. N. Sussman and H. Rosenfeld, "Influence of Culture, Language and Sex on Conversational Distance," *Journal of Personality and Social Psychology* 42 (1982), pp. 67–74.

40. N. Ambady, D. LaPlante, T. Nguyen, R. Rosenthal, N. Chaumeton, and W. Levinson, "Surgeons' Tone of Voice: A Clue to Malpractice History," *Surgery* 132 (2002), pp. 5–9.

41. "Word Up." *The Guardian*, September 21, 2001. Retrieved May 12, 2009, from **www.guardian.co.uk/g2/story/0,3604,555379,00.html.%22**.

42. See, for example, J. K. Burgoon, T. Birk, and M. Pfau, "Nonverbal Behaviors, Persuasion, and Credibility," *Human Communication Research* 17 (1990), pp. 140–69.

43. See J. D. Rothwell, *In Mixed Company*, 3rd ed. (Ft. Worth, TX: Harcourt Brace Jovanovich, 1998), pp. 246–48.

44. S. Roan, "Overweight and Under Pressure," *Los Angeles Times*, December 18, 1990, pp. E1, E4.

45. "Philip Condit, CEO, Boeing/McDonnell Douglas: A True Listening Leader," *Listening Leader*, November 24, 1997, **www.listencoach.com/SiteFrameSet.html**.

46. J. Matthews, "In Offices across America, Attire Is Changing," *Washington Post*, January 31, 1994, p. 26.

47. K. H. Hammonds, "All the Right Moves: Meanwhile, Back at the Office," *Fast Company* 72 (July 2003), p. 70. Retrieved December 5, 2005, from **www.fastcompany.com/magazine/72/backattheoffice.html**.

48. J. H. Laabs, "Mixing Business with Passion," accessed January 22, 2001, from **www.workforce.com/archive/article/000/77/84.xci?topicname5business_issues_and_trends**.

49. I. Amiel, "A Nationwide Survey on Business Casual Conducted by a Team of AICI Professionals," Association of Image Consultants International, accessed February 14, 2001, from **www.aici.org/dec99p5.html**.

50. Ibid.

51. Dana May Casperson quoted in M. Marchetti, "Barbarians at the Buffet," *Successful Meetings*, May 2003, p. 57.

52. L. T. Cullen, "What (Not) to Wear to Work," *Time* (May 29, 2008), p. 49.

53. W. Wells and B. Siegel, "Stereotyped Somatypes," *Psychological Reports* 8 (1961), pp. 1175–78.

54. V. Reitman, "Learning to Grin—and Bear It," *Los Angeles Times*, February 22, 1999, p. A1.

55. B. Hunter, "Are You Ready to Face '60 Minutes'?" *Industry Week*, March 8, 1982, p. 74.

56. "Memos," *Industry Week*, January 11, 1982, p. 11.

57. A. Mehrabian, *Silent Messages*, 2nd ed. (Belmont, CA: Wadsworth, 1981).

58. D. Borisoff and L. Merrill, *The Power to Communicate: Gender Differences as Barriers*, 2nd ed. (Prospect Heights, IL: Waveland, 1992), p. 48.

59. E. Hall, *The Hidden Dimension* (New York: Doubleday, 1969), pp. 113–25.

60. M. L. Knapp and J. A. Hall, *Nonverbal Behavior in Human Interaction*, 3rd ed. (Ft. Worth, TX: Harcourt Brace Jovanovich, 1992), pp. 127–30.

61. Ibid., p. 129.

62. Mehrabian, *Silent Messages*, p. 51.

63. D. Ogilvy, *Principles of Management* (New York: Ogilvy & Mather, 1968), p. 2.

64. T. Allen, "Meeting the Technical Information Needs of Research and Development Projects," M.I.T. Industrial Liaison Program Report No. 13-314, Cambridge, MA, November 1969.

65. P. Manning, *Office Design: A Study of Environment* (Liverpool: Pilkington Research Unit, 1965), p. 474.

66. Research summarized in P. A. Andersen and L. L. Bowman, "Positions of Power: Nonverbal Influence in Organizational Communication," *The Nonverbal Communication Reader* (Prospect Heights, IL: Waveland, 1990), pp. 404–5.

67. Steele, *Physical Settings and Organizational Development*, p. 38.

68. J. E. McGrath and J. R. Kelly, *Time and Human Interaction* (New York: Guilford, 1989). See also D. I. Ballard and D. R. Seibold, "Time Orientation and Temporal Variation across Work Groups: Implications for Group and Organizational Communication," *Western Journal of Communication* 64 (2000), pp. 218–42.

69. "Are You Really Ready to Change Jobs?" in "Fall Job Market," advertising supplement to the *Washington Post*, September 28, 1986, p. 22.

70. "Coaching Football–Italian Style," *Thousand Oaks (CA) News Chronicle*, January 4, 1990, pp. 1, 20.

71. Research summarized in D. E. Hamachek, *Encounters with the Self*, 2nd ed. (Ft. Worth, TX: Holt, Rinehart and Winston, 1987), p. 8. See also J. A. Daly, A. L. Vangelisti, and S. M. Daughton, "The Nature and Correlates of Conversational Sensitivity," in *Interpersonal Communication: Readings in Theory and Research*, ed. M. V. Redmond (Ft. Worth, TX: Harcourt Brace, 1995).

72. D. A. Dunning and J. Kruger, "Unskilled and Unaware of It: How Difficulties in Recognizing One's Own Incompetence Lead to Inflated Self-Assessments," *Journal of Personality and Social Psychology* 77 (1999), pp. 1121–34.

73. A. Mehrabian, *Nonverbal Communication* (Chicago: Aldine/Atherton, 1972).

74. Research summarized by V. P. Richmond and J. C. McCroskey, *Nonverbal Behavior in Interpersonal Relations*, 5th ed. (Boston: Allyn & Bacon, 2004).

75. H. S. Friedman, R. E. Riggio, and D. F. Casella, "Nonverbal Skill, Personal Charisma, and Initial Attraction," *Personality & Social Psychology Bulletin* 14 (1988), pp. 203–11.

76. D. Goleman, *Emotional Intelligence: Why It Can Matter More Than I.Q.* (New York: Bantam, 1995), p. 115.

77. E. S. Sullins, "Emotional Contagion Revisited: Effects of Social Comparison and Expressive Style on Mood Convergence," *Personality and Social Psychology Bulletin* 17 (1991), pp. 166–74.

78. See E. Griffin, "Expectancy Violations Theory," in *A First Look at Communication Theory*, 6th ed. (New York: McGraw-Hill, 2006).

79. L. Jansma, "Sexual Harassment Research: Integration, Reformulation, and Implications for Mitigation Efforts," in *Communication Yearbook 23* (Thousand Oaks, CA: Sage, 2000).

80. From **http://www.de.psu.edu/harassment/legal**.

81. From **http://www.eeoc.gov/stats/harass.html**.

82. U.S. EEOC Press Release, "EEOC and Ford Sign Multimillion Dollar Settlement of Sexual Harassment Case." Accessed July 29, 2003, from **www.eeoc.gov/press/9-7-99.html**.

83. MSPB, 1995, xi, cited in M. A. Newman et al., "Sexual Harassment in the Federal Workplace," *Public Administration Review* 63, no. 4 (July/August 2003).

84. New Mexico Commission on the Status of Women, *Dealing with Sexual Harassment* (2002). Retrieved December 6, 2005, from **www.state.nm.us/womenscommission/Publications/sexhbrochre.pdf**, p. 5.

Chapter 5

1. D. B. Curtis, J. L. Winsor, and R. D. Stephens, "National Preferences in Business and Communication Education," *Communication Education* 38 (1989), pp. 6–14.

2. L. Goodspeed, "'People Skills' Stressed over Experience for Tech CEOs," *Boston Business Journal* 19 (April 23, 1999), p. 46.

3. R. H. Hersh, "Intentions and Perceptions: A National Survey of Public Attitudes toward Liberal Arts Education," *Change* 29 (1997), pp. 16–23. For more information on the importance of communication skills for managers, see D. St. John, "Forget the Global Communication Climate for a Minute: How's the Weather inside Your Own Organization?" *Communication World* 12 (March 1996), p. 24.

4. See, for example, R. Bellinger, "It Takes More than Tech," *Electronic Engineering Times* (August 30, 1999), pp. 91–96; and J. M. Napolitano, "Learning to Really Communicate," *Journal of Property Management* (March/April 2000), p. 12. See also L. B. Mauksch, D. C. Dugdale, S. Dodson, and R. Epstein, "Relationship, Communication, and Efficiency in the Medical Encounter: Creating a Clinical Model from a Literature Review," *Archives of Internal Medicine* 168:13 (2008), pp. 1387–95.

5. L. Iacocca and W. Novak, *Iacocca: An Autobiography* (New York: Bantam, 1984), p. 58.

6. D. Goleman, *Emotional Intelligence: Why It Can Matter More than I.Q.* (New York: Bantam, 1995). See also H. Weisinger, *Emotional Intelligence at Work: The Untapped Edge for Success* (San Francisco: Jossey-Bass, 1997); and D. Goleman, *Social Intelligence: The New Science of Human Relationships* (New York: Random House, 2006).

7. D. Goleman, *Working with Emotional Intelligence* (New York: Bantam, 2000), p. 211. See also A. M. Suliman, and F. N. Al-Shaikh, "Emotional Intelligence at Work: Links to Conflict and Innovation," *Employee Relations* 29:2 (2007), pp. 208–220.

8. R. L. Dilenschneider, "Social Intelligence," *Executive Excellence* 14 (March 1997), p. 8.

9. R. M. Guzley, "Organizational Climate and Communication Climate: Predictors of Commitment to the Organization," *Management Communication Quarterly* 5 (1992), pp. 379–402. See also D. T. Bastien, R. D. McPhee, and K. A. Bolton, "A Study and Extended Theory of the Structuration of Climate," *Communication Monographs* 62 (1995), pp. 87–109; and T. J. Houghton, "A Study of Communication among Supervisors: The Influence of Supervisor/Supervisee Verbal Aggressiveness on Communication Climate and Organizational Commitment," *Dissertation Abstracts International* 61 (2001), p. 3826.

10. Pamela Shockley-Zalabak, *Fundamentals of Organizational Communication: Knowledge, Sensitivity, Skills, Values*, 3rd ed. (New York: Longman, 1995), pp. 249–52.

11. R. Fisher and S. Brown, *Getting Together: Building Relationships as We Negotiate* (Boston: Houghton Mifflin, 1988).

12. "Nineteen Eighty-Nine Turkeys of the Year," *San Jose Mercury News*, November 23, 1989, p. 1D.

13. K. Patterson, *Crucial Skills* 3, no. 28 (July 20, 2005). This is an e-newsletter from and copyright by VitalSmarts, L.C., **www.vitalsmarts.com**.

14. K. Patterson, "Creating a Culture of Accountability," *Crucial Skills 3*, no. 39. This is an e-newsletter from and copyright by VitalSmarts, L.C., **www.vitalsmarts.com**, 2005.

15. C. Carson and W. R. Cupach, "Facing Corrections in the Workplace: The Influence of Perceived Face Threat on the Consequences of Managerial Reproaches," *Journal of Applied Communication Research* 28 (2000), pp. 215–34.

16. R. Korobkin and C. Guthrie, "Psychological Barriers to Litigation Settlement and Experimental Approach," *Michigan Law Review* 107 (1994), pp. 107–92.

17. K. Anderson, "Handling Criticism with Honesty and Grace," *Public Management* 82 (May 2000), pp. 30–34.

18. For more information about this survey, see R. Zupek, "Fight the Good Fight: Six Tips to Managing Workplace Conflict." Available at **http://msn.careerbuilder.com/ custom/msn/careeradvice/viewarticle.aspx?articleid= 1202&SiteId=cbmsnhp41202&sc_extcmp=JS_1202_ home&GT1=10563&cbRecursionCnt=1&cbsid=ee90 ae37f14e40e8b4ae5ad806a33652-250077808-JT-5**.

19. J. Slaton, "Hoteliers Say Hiring Is Their Toughest Job," *New Orleans City Business*, November 25, 1996.

20. S. Berglos, "Harmony Is Death: Let Conflict Reign," *Inc.*, May 1995, pp. 56–58.

21. L. Coser, *The Functions of Social Conflict* (New York: Free Press, 1956).

22. For a detailed account of these conflict types, see W. W. Wilmot and J. L. Hocker, *Interpersonal Conflict*, 7th ed. (New York: McGraw-Hill, 2007), pp. 62–75, 138–65.

23. J. P. Folger, M. S. Poole, and R. K. Sturtman, *Working through Conflict: Strategies for Relationships, Groups, and Organizations*, 5th ed. (Boston: Allyn & Bacon, 2004).

24. For more detailed descriptions of the approaches to conflict discussed in the text, see Wilmot and Hocker, op. cit., pp. 138–65.

25. D. Starkey, "Finding Common Ground," *Sacramento Business Journal*, February 20, 1998, pp. 12–13.

26. D. Tannen, *Talking from 9 to 5* (New York: Morrow, 1994), p. 91.

27. M. H. McCormack, *What They Don't Teach You at Harvard Business School* (New York: Bantam, 1984), pp. 152–53.

28. T. O'Neill, "Here's the Church, Here's the (Fake) Steeple," *Cincinnati Enquirer*, January 20, 1996, pp. B1, B6.

29. C. Pavitt and B. Kemp, "Contextual and Relational Factors in Interpersonal Negotiation Strategy Choice," *Communication Quarterly* 47 (1999), pp. 133–50. See also S. D. Friedman, P. Christensen, and J. DeGroot, "Work and Life: The End of the Zero-Sum Game," *Harvard Business Review*, November–December 1998, pp. 119–29.

30. R. J. Burke, "Methods of Resolving Superior–Subordinate Conflict: The Constructive Use of Subordinate Differences and Disagreements," *Organizational Behavior and Human Performance* 5 (1970), pp. 393–411.

31. R. Fisher and W. Ury, *Getting to Yes: Negotiating Agreement without Giving In* (Boston: Houghton Mifflin, 1981), pp. 41–57.

Chapter 6

1. C. J. Stewart and W. B. Cash Jr., *Interviewing: Principles and Practices*, 12th ed. (New York: McGraw-Hill, 2008), p. 1.

2. Ibid.

3. M. H. McCormack, *What They Don't Teach You at Harvard Business School* (New York: Bantam, 1984), p. 87.

4. D. Harper, "Strictly for Salesmen," in a review of G. Gard, "Championship Selling," *Industrial Distribution*, May 1987, p. 122.

5. L. B. Andrews, "Mind Control in the Courtroom," *Psychology Today* 16 (March 1982), p. 70.

6. K. O. Locker, *Business and Administrative Communication* (New York: Irwin/McGraw-Hill, 2003), p. 371.

7. W. G. Kirkwood and S. M. Ralston, "Inviting Meaningful Applicant Performances in Employment Interviews," *Journal of Business Communication* 36 (1999), pp. 55–76.

8. D. Deaver, in Shirley J. Shepherd, "How to Get That Job in 60 Minutes or Less," *Working Woman*, March 1986, p. 118.

9. Adapted from G. L. Wilson and H. L. Goodall Jr., *Interviewing in Context* (New York: McGraw-Hill, 1991), p. 291.

Chapter 7

1. S. Walton and J. Huey, *Made in America* (New York: Bantam, 1993), pp. 104–5.

2. M. Hopkins, "The Anti-Hero's Guide to the New Economy," *Inc.*, January 1998, pp. 37–48.

3. M. Granovetter, *Getting a Job: A Study of Contacts and Careers*, 2nd ed. (Chicago: University of Chicago Press, 1995).

4. R. N. Bolles, *What Color Is Your Parachute? A Practical Manual for Job-Hunters and Career-Changers* (Berkeley, CA: Ten Speed Press, 2009), pp. 27–40.

5. G. Crispin and M. Mehler, "Impact of the Internet on Source of Hires," at **www.careerxroads.com/news/ IMPACTOFTHEINTERNET.doc**.

6. Quintessential Career & Job Tips, *Quint-Zine* 3 (2002), p. 1. Accessed January 4, 2009, at **www.quintcareers .com/QuintZine/archives/20021014.html**.

7. W. Baker, *Achieving Success through Social Capital* (San Francisco: Josey-Bass, 2000), p. 10.

8. A. Tugend, "Readers Weigh In with Tips on Jobs and Money." *New York Times*, December 19, 2008. Accessed December 3, 2009, at **www.nytimes.com**.

9. M. S. Granovetter, "The Strength of Weak Ties," *American Journal of Sociology* 78 (1973), pp. 1360–80.

10. E. M. Rogers, *Diffusion of Innovations*, 3rd ed. (New York: Free Press, 1983), p. 297.

11. K. Dobbs, "Knowing How to Keep the Best and Brightest," *Workforce*, April 2001, pp. 57–60.

12. M. S. Peterson, "Personnel Interviewers' Perceptions of the Importance and Adequacy of Applicants' Communication Skills," *Communication Education* 46 (1997), pp. 287–91.

13. H. D. Tschirgi, "What Do Recruiters Really Look For in Candidates?" *Journal of College Placement*, December 1972–January 1973, pp. 75–79.

14. For an assessment of interview effectiveness, see W. G. Kirkwood and S. M. Ralston, "Inviting Meaningful Applicant Performance in Employment Interviews," *Journal of Business Communication* 66 (1999), pp. 55–76.

15. "The Hidden Hurdle: Executive Recruiters Say Firms Tend to Hire 'Our Kind of Person,'" *The Wall Street Journal*, May 12, 1979, p. 1.

16. R. N. Bolles, *What Color Is Your Parachute? A Practical Manual for Job-Hunters and Career-Changers* (Berkeley, CA: Ten Speed Press, 1997), p. 38.

17. Bolles, *What Color Is Your Parachute?* p. 173.

18. S. Murphy, "The Second Interview," *Santa Barbara News Press*, December 19, 1999, p. E1.

19. M. Richtel, "Online Revolution's Latest Twist: Job Interviews with a Computer" *New York Times*, February 6, 2000, p. E1. Accessed January 9, 2009, at **http://query .nytimes.com/gst/fullpage.html?res=9C04E2DC1F3FF 935A35751C0A9669C8B63&sec=&spon=&emc=eta1**.

20. "Ace Your Audition Interview," retrieved April 28, 2001, from **www.wetfeet.com/asp/article.asp?aid562**.

21. J. Trotsky, "Oh, Will You BEHAVE?" *Computerworld*, January 8, 2001, pp. 42–43.

22. P. Farmery, "Recruiters Offer a New View of the Job Interview," *Job Choices: Diversity Edition* (Bethlehem, PA: National Association of Colleges and Employers, 2000), pp. 61–64.

23. J. Ayres, T. Keereetaweep, P. Chen, and P. A. Edwards, "Communication Apprehension and Employment Interviews," *Communication Education* 47 (1998), pp. 1–17.

24. D. B. Goodall and H. L. Goodall Jr., "The Employment Interview: A Selective Review of the Literature with Implications for Communications Research," *Communication Quarterly* 30 (Spring 1982), pp. 116–22.

25. R. W. Eder and G. R. Ferris, eds., *The Employment Interview: Theory, Research, and Practice* (Newbury Park, CA: Sage, 1989).

26. H. A. Medley, *Sweaty Palms: The Neglected Art of Being Interviewed* (Belmont, CA: Wadsworth, 1978), p. 1.

27. Medley, *Sweaty Palms*, p. 19.

28. C. Caggiano, "'What Were You In For?' and Other Great Job-Interview Questions of Our Time," *Inc.*, October 1998, p. 14.

29. C. L. Cooper, "No More Stupid Questions," *Psychology Today* 26 (May–June 1993), pp. 14–15.

30. G. Martz, *How to Survive without Your Parents' Money* (New York: Villiard, 1996), p. 57.

31. Bolles, *What Color Is Your Parachute?* pp. 238–39.

32. S. M. Ralston and W. Kirkwood, "The Trouble with Applicant Impression Management," *Journal of Business and Technical Communication* 13 (1999), pp. 190–207. See also S. M. Ralston, "The 'Veil of Ignorance': Exploring Ethical Issues in the Employment Interview," *Business Communication Quarterly* 63 (2000), pp. 50–52.

33. P. Rosenfeld, "Impression Management, Fairness and the Employment Interview," *Journal of Business Ethics* 16 (June 1997), pp. 801–8.

34. R. H. Beatty, *The Interview Kit*, 3rd ed. (Hoboken, NJ: John Wiley & Sons, Inc., 2003), pp. 49–50.

35. S. Silverstein and N. R. Brooks, "And Be Sure to Mention Your Favorite Subject: You," *Los Angeles Times*, March 1, 1993, p. D3.

36. Quoted in C. Kleiman, "Passion Play," *The Salt Lake Tribune and the Deseret News*, February 16, 2003, p. F1.

37. H. Chen, "Can This Interview Be Saved? Maybe with a Proper Thank You Note and Follow Up." *Vault.* Accessed January 2, 2009, at **www.vault.com/nr/main_article _detail.jsp?article_id=8801822&cat_id=0&ht_type=10**.

38. Medley, *Sweaty Palms*, p. 164.

39. M. B. Dickson, *Supervising Employees with Disabilities: Beyond ADA Compliance* (Menlo Park, CA: Crisp, 1993), p. 107.

40. M. Z. Sincoff and R. S. Goyer, *Interviewing* (New York: Macmillan, 1984), p. 80. See also T. Washington, "Advice on Answering Illegal Interview Questions: Reply Candidly or Tactfully Decline," *The Wall Street Journal Career Journal*, retrieved April 24, 2001, from **www.careerjournal.com/emailfriend/sendmail1 .asp?txtTargetPage5http%3A//www.careerjournal.com/ jobhunting/interviewing/19971231-washington.html**.

41. J. K. Springston and J. Keyton, "So Tell Me, Are You Married? When the Interviewee Knows You're Asking an Illegal Question," *Proceedings of the 1988 Annual National Conference of the Council of Employee Responsibilities and Rights* 2 (1988), pp. 177–86.

42. J. Woo, "Job Interviews Pose Risk to Employers," *The Wall Street Journal*, March 11, 1992, pp. B1, B5.

43. E. McShulskis, "Be Aware of Illegal Interview Questions," *HR Magazine* 42 (June 1997), pp. 22–23.

44. R. Fry, *Your First Interview*, 4th ed. (Franklin Lakes, NJ: Career Press, 2002), pp. 157–58.

45. R. Townsend, *Further Up the Organization* (New York: Knopf, 1984), p. 153.

46. D. Fandray, "The New Thinking in Performance Appraisals," *Workforce* 80, no. 5 (May 2001), pp. 36–40.

47. K. Blanchard, "Rating Managers on Performance Reviews," *Today's Office* 22 (August 1987), pp. 6–11.

48. C. W. Downs, G. P. Smeyak, and E. Martin, *Professional Interviewing* (New York: Harper & Row, 1980), p. 167.

49. K. Blanchard, "Rating Managers on Performance Reviews," p. 7.

50. C. O. Longenecker, "Truth or Consequences: Politics and Performance Appraisals," *Business Horizons* 27 (November–December 1989), pp. 169–82.

51. D. Dauten, "Worker Appraisals Are Like Having the Cat Spayed," *Albuquerque Business Outlook Journal*, March 26, 2001, p. 13.

52. G. L. Wilson and H. L. Goodall, *Interviewing in Context* (New York: McGraw-Hill, 1991), p. 181.

53. L. Iacocca and W. Novak, *Iacocca: An Autobiography* (New York: Bantam, 1984).

54. J. L. Pearce and L. W. Porter, "Responses to Formal Performance Appraisal Feedback," *Journal of Applied Psychology* 71 (1986), pp. 211–18.

Chapter 8

1. R. Reich, *Tales of a New America* (New York: Time Books, 1987), p. 126.

2. D. J. Devine, L. D. Clayton, J. L. Phillips, B. B. Dunford, and S. B. Melner, "Teams in Organizations: Prevalence, Characteristics, and Effectiveness," *Small Group Research* 30 (1999), pp. 678–711.

3. M. V. Redmond, "A Plan for the Successful Use of Teams in Design Education," *Journal of Architectural Education* 17 (May 1986), pp. 27–49.

4. "Professional Occupations in Multimedia," *California Occupational Guide*, No. 2006 (Sacramento, CA: California State Employment Division, 1995), p. 4. See also *A Labor Market Analysis of the Interactive Digital Media Industry: Opportunities in Multimedia* (San Francisco: Reagan & Associates, 1997), pp. 15–29.

5. D. L. Welles Jr. and S. H. Hartley, "Teamwork and Cooperative Learning: An Educational Perspective for Business," *Quality Management Journal*, July 1994, p. 30; and A. Radding, "Skills They'd Kill For," *ComputerWorld* 31 (June 2, 1997), pp. 93–95.

6. "Basic Types of Virtual Teams," Free Management Library. Retrieved January 29, 2009, from www.managementhelp.org/grp_skll/virtual/defntion.pdf.

7. C. Lazzareschi, "Being Part of the Team at Work," *Los Angeles Times*, September 12, 1994, pt. 2, p. 13.

8. For a more detailed discussion of the advantages and drawbacks of working in groups, see J. D. Rothwell, *In Mixed Company: Small Group Communication*, 6th ed. (Belmont, CA: Wadsworth, 2007), pp. 70–74.

9. G. M. Blair, "Groups That Work," retrieved August 26, 2003, from www.rotman.utoronto.ca/~baum/mgt2003/gmbart0.htm.

10. D. J. Rachman and M. H. Mescon, *Profile Kit for Business Today*, 4th ed. (New York: Random House, 1990), profile 2.

11. See, for example, J. R. Katzenbach and D. K. Smith, "The Discipline of Teams," *Harvard Business Review* 86 (March–April 1993), pp. 111–20.

12. T. J. Peters and R. H. Waterman Jr., *In Search of Excellence: Lessons from America's Best Run Companies* (New York: Harper & Row, 1982), p. 32.

13. E. Bormann, *Small Group Communication: Theory and Practice* (New York: Harper & Row, 1990).

14. "Is Your Team Too Big? Too Small? What's the Right Number?" Published June 14, 2006, in Knowledge@Wharton. Retrieved January 26, 2009, from http://knowledge.wharton.upenn.edu/article.cfm?articleid=1501.

15. J. Gribas, "Organizational Sports Metaphors: Reconsidering Gender Bias in the Team Concept," *Communication Research Reports* 16 (1999), pp. 55–64.

16. See, for example, P. Michelman, "How Will You Make Your Team a *Team?*" (Cambridge, MA: Harvard Management Press, 2004).

17. R. E. Parker, "Distinguishing Characteristics of Virtual Groups," in *Small Group Communication: Theory & Practice*, eds. R. Y. Hirokawa et al. (Los Angeles: Roxbury, 2003).

18. K. Melymuka, "Tips for Teams," *ComputerWorld* 31 (April 28, 1997), p. 72.

19. B. J. Alge, C. Wiethoff, and H. J. Klein, "When Does the Medium Matter? Knowledge-Building Experiences and Opportunities in Decision-making Teams," *Organizational Behavior and Human Decision Processes* 91 (2003), pp. 26–37.

20. M. M. Montoya-Weiss, A. P. Massey, and M. Song, "Getting It Together: Temporal Coordination and Conflict Management in Global Virtual Teams," *Academy of Management Journal* 44 (2001), pp. 1251–62.

21. "Virtual Teams: Reaching across Space, Time and Organizations with Technology," *HR Magazine* 42 (July 1997), pp. 133–34.

22. S. L. Herndon, "Theory and Practice: Implications for the Implementation of Communication Technology in Organizations," *Journal of Business Communication* 34 (January 1997), pp. 121–29.

23. P. Mohta, "Virtual Networking via the Internet," *Computer Technology Review*, Winter 1996, pp. 12–13.

24. J. Blau, "Global Networking Poses Management Challenge/Risk," *Research-Technology Management* 40 (January/February 1997), pp. 4–5.

25. "The Knowledge," *Spirit Magazine*, November 2008, p. 50.

26. Rothwell, *In Mixed Company*, pp. 137–38.

27. K. Lewin, R. Lippitt, and R. K. White, "Patterns of Aggressive Behavior in Experimentally Created Social Climates," *Journal of Social Psychology* 10 (1939), pp. 271–99.

28. R. Foels, J. E. Driskell, B. Mullen, and E. Salas, "The Effects of Democratic Leadership on Group Member Satisfaction," *Small Group Research* 20 (2000), pp. 676–701.

29. L. L. Rosenbaum and W. B. Rosenbaum, "Morale and Productivity Consequences of Group Leadership Style, Stress, and Type of Task," *Journal of Applied Psychology* 55 (1971), pp. 343–58.

30. R. R. Blake and J. S. Mouton, *The New Managerial Grid* (Houston, TX: Gulf, 1985).

31. F. E. Fiedler, *A Theory of Leadership Effectiveness* (New York: McGraw-Hill, 1967).

32. P. Hersey and K. Blanchard, *Management of Organizational Behavior*, 4th ed. (Englewood Cliffs, NJ: Prentice-Hall, 1982); and K. Blanchard, "Selecting a Leadership Style That Works," *Today's Office* 23 (September 1988), p. 14.

33. Bormann, *Small Group Communication*. For a succinct description of Bormann's findings, see Rothwell, *In Mixed Company*, pp. 131–33.

34. R. Fisher and A. Sharp, *Getting It Done: How to Lead When You're Not in Charge* (New York: Harper Business, 1998).

35. R. S. Wellins, W. C. Byham, and J. M. Wilson, *Empowered Teams: Creating Self-Directed Work Groups That Improve Quality, Productivity, and Participation* (San Francisco: Jossey-Bass, 1991), p. 3.

36. P. A. Chansler, P. M. Swamidass, and C. Canmann, "Self-Managing Teams: An Empirical Study of Group Cohesiveness in 'Natural Work Groups' at a Harley-Davidson Motor Company Plant," *Small Group Research* 34 (2003), pp. 101–20.

37. The discussion of the first five types of power is adapted from the work of J. R. P. French and B. Raven, "The Bases of Social Power," in *Studies in Social Power*, ed. D. Cartwright (Ann Arbor: University of Michigan, Institute for Social Research, 1959). Information power was introduced by B. Raven and W. Kruglanski, "Conflict and Power," in *The Structure of Conflict*, ed. P. G. Swingle (New York: Academic Press, 1975), pp. 177–219. Connection power was introduced by Hersey and Blanchard, *Management of Organizational Behavior*, p. 179.

38. A. T. Pescosolido, "Informal Leaders and the Development of Group Efficacy," *Small Group Research* 32 (2001), pp. 74–93.

39. S. T. Loh, "You Say the Boss Is How Old?" *Los Angeles Times*, March 1, 1993, pt. 2, pp. 9–10.

40. M. Zey, ed., *Decision Making: Alternatives to Rational Choice Models* (Newbury Park, CA: Sage, 1992).

41. See R. Y. Hirokawa, "Group Communication and Problem-Solving Effectiveness: An Investigation of Group Phases," *Human Communication Research* 9 (1983), pp. 291–305; Edward R. Marby and Richard E. Barnes, *The Dynamics of Small Group Communication* (Englewood Cliffs, NJ: Prentice-Hall, 1980), p. 78; Norman R. F. Maier and Robert A. Maier, "An Experimental Test of the Effects of 'Developmental' vs. 'Free' Discussions on the Quality of Group Decisions," *Journal of Applied Psychology* 41 (1957), pp. 320–23; and Ovid L. Bayless, "An Alternative Model for Problem-Solving Discussion," *Journal of Communication* 17 (1967), pp. 188–97.

42. For a contemporary version of the reflective-thinking model, see D. Gouran, R. Hirokawa, K. Julian, and G. Leatham, "The Evolution and Current Status of the Functional Perspective on Communication Decision-Making and Problem-Solving Groups," in *Communication Yearbook* 16, ed. S. Deetz (Newbury Park, CA: Sage, 1993).

43. M. E. Mayer, "Behaviors Leading to More Effective Decisions in Small Groups Embedded in Organizations," *Communication Reports* 11 (1998) pp. 123–32.

44. See, for example, Zey, ed., *Decision Making*.

45. B. A. Fisher, "Decision Emergence: Phases in Group Decision Making," *Speech Monographs* 37 (1970), pp. 53–66. See also M. S. Poole and J. Roth, "Decision Development in Small Groups, IV: A Typology of Group Decision Paths," *Human Communication Research* 15 (1989), pp. 232–56.

46. B. W. Tuckman, "Developmental Sequence in Small Groups," *Psychological Bulletin* 63 (June 1965), pp. 384–99. The terms *forming*, *storming*, *norming*, and *performing* originate from this article.

47. T. Kuhn, "Do Conflict Management Styles Affect Group Decision Making?" *Human Communication Research* 26 (2000), pp. 558–90.

48. G. Buzaglo and S. A. Wheelan, "Facilitating Work Team Effectiveness," *Small Group Research* 30 (1999), pp. 108–29.

49. M. S. Poole and J. Roth, "Decision Development in Small Groups, V: Test of a Contingency Model," *Human Communication Research* 15 (1989), pp. 549–89. See also E. M. Eisenberg and H. L. Goodall Jr., *Organizational Communication: Balancing Creativity and Constraint*, 2nd ed. (New York: St. Martin's, 1996), pp. 267–68.

50. For a discussion of relational roles, see J. Keyton, "Relational Communication in Groups," in *Handbook of Group Communication Theory and Research*, ed. L. R. Frey (Thousand Oaks, CA: Sage, 1999).

51. E. Matson, "The Seven Sins of Deadly Meetings," *Fast Times* 2 (April 1996), pp. 122-25.

52. See, for example, M. E. Mayer, "Behaviors Leading to More Effective Decisions in Small Groups Embedded in Organizations," *Communication Reports* 11 (1998), pp. 123-32.

53. Joel A. C. Baum, "Running an Effective Team Meeting," *HomePage for Game Theory and Competitive Strategy* MGT 2056-Fall 2003, retrieved August 26, 2003, from **www.rotman.utoronto.ca/~baum/mgt2003/meetings.html**.

54. B. Day, "The Art of Conducting International Business," *Advertising Age*, October 6, 1990, p. 48.

55. "Using Consult Decisions," *Crucial Skills* 6 (May 14, 2008), p. 1.

56. "A Purpose and a Place," *News for a Change*, May 2001, p. 5 (publication of Association for Quality and Participation at **www.aqp.org**).

57. Ibid.

58. For a discussion of how norms develop, see C. M. Anderson, B. L. Riddle, and M. M. Martin, "Socialization Processes in Groups," in *Handbook of Group Communication Theory and Research*, ed. L. R. Frey (Thousand Oaks, CA: Sage, 1999).

59. Eisenberg and Goodall, *Organizational Communication*, p. 264.

60. L. Browning, "Reasons for Success at Motorola," paper presented at the conference of the International Communication Association, Miami, May 1992.

61. See, for example, P. W. Mulvey, L. Bowes-Sperry, and H. J. Klein, "The Effects of Perceived Loafing and Defensive Impression Management on Group Effectiveness," *Small Group Research* 29 (1998), pp. 394-415.

62. J. G. Oetzel, T. E. Burtis, M. I. Chew Sanchez, and F. G. Perez, "Investigating the Role of Communication in Culturally Diverse Work Groups: A Review and Synthesis," *Communication Yearbook* 25 (Mahwah, NJ: Lawrence Erlbaum, 2001).

63. Some sequences of escalating penalties for nonconformity have been described in the literature. See, for example, J. R. Wenberg and W. Wilmot, *The Personal Communication Process* (New York: Wiley, 1973); and T. D. Daniels and B. K. Spiker, *Perspectives on Organizational Communication*, 4th ed. (Dubuque, IA: Wm. C. Brown, 1997), p. 237.

64. Melymuka, "Tips for Teams," p. 72.

65. I. L. Janis, *Victims of Groupthink* (Boston: Houghton Mifflin, 1972), p. 9.

66. K. L. Gammage, A. V. Carron, and P. A. Estabrooks, "Team Cohesion and Individual Productivity," *Small Group Research* 32 (2001), pp. 3-18.

67. Adapted from E. G. Bormann, *Discussion and Group Methods*, 2nd ed. (New York: Harper & Row, 1975), pp. 176-95. See also P. Adler and P. Adler, "Intense Loyalty in Organizations: A Case Study of College Athletics," *Administrative Science Quarterly* 33 (1988), pp. 401-18.

68. Janis, *Victims of Groupthink*, p. 9. See also J. A. Ross, "Team Camaraderie: Can You Have Too Much?" in *Managing Teams for High Performance* (Cambridge, MA: Harvard Management Press, 2007).

69. V. Goby, "Business Communication Needs," *Journal of Business and Technical Communication* 21 (4), (2007), pp. 425-37. See also A. Sharon, "The Death of Groupthink," *Business Week* (February 5, 2008), retrieved January 26, 2009, from **www.businessweek.com/print/managing/content/feb2008/ca2008025_687188.htm**.

70. D. G. Myers and H. Lamm, "The Group Polarization Phenomenon," *Psychological Bulletin*, July 1976, pp. 602-27. For a more detailed discussion of how the risky shift operates, see A. BarNir, "Can Group- and Issue-Related Factors Predict Choice Shift?" *Small Group Research* 29 (1998), pp. 308-38.

71. S. P. Robbins, *Organizational Behavior: Concepts, Controversies, and Applications*, 4th ed. (Englewood Cliffs, NJ: Prentice-Hall, 1990), p. 289.

72. See, for example, E. Catmull, "How Pixar Fosters Collective Creativity," *Harvard Business Review*, September 2008, pp. 64-78.

73. J. Rae-Dupree, "For Innovators, There Is Brainpower in Numbers," *New York Times* (December 7, 2008), p. BU 3.

74. A. Osborn, *Applied Imagination* (New York: Scribner's, 1959). See also F. Hurt, "Better Brainstorming," *Training & Development*, November 1994, pp. 57-59.

75. New World Encyclopedia, retrieved January 21, 2009, from **www.newworldencyclopedia.org/entry/Linus_Pauling**.

76. K. Thompson, "Six Ways to Kill a Brainstorm," retrieved May 16, 2008, from **www.masternewmedia.org/news/2008/04/23/how_not_to_brainstorm_your.htm**.

77. W. H. Cooper, R. B. Gallupe, S. Pollard, and J. Cadsby, "Some Liberating Effects of Electronic Brainstorming," *Small Group Research* 29 (1999), pp. 147-78.

Chapter 9

1. "Meetings in America: A Study of Trends, Costs, and Attitudes Toward Business Travel and Teleconferencing, and Their Impact on Productivity" (Greenwich, CT: Infocom, 1998). Accessed March 20, 2006, from **http://e-meetings.mci.com/meetingsinamerica/uswhitepaper.php**.

2. L. Tuck, "Meeting Madness," *Presentations*, May 1995, p. 20.

3. M. Barr, "Virtual Meetings," *Indiana Business Magazine* 43 (May 1999), pp. 42-47.

4. S. G. Rogelberg, D. J. Leach, P. B. Warr, and J. L. Burnfield, "'Not Another Meeting!' Are Meeting Time Demands Related to Employee Well-Being?" *Journal of Applied Psychology* 91 (2006), pp. 83–96.

5. S. G. Rogelberg, C. Scott, and J. Kello, "The Science and Fiction of Meetings," *MIT Sloan Management Review* 48 (Winter 2007), pp. 18–21; and P. Sandwich, "Better Meetings for Better Communication," *Training & Development* 46 (January 1992), pp. 29–31.

6. S. M. Smith, "Managing Your Meeting from the 'Bottom Line Payoff,'" in *Innovative Meeting Management*, eds. R. A. Swanson and B. O. Knaps (Austin, TX: Minnesota Mining and Manufacturing, 1997), p. 53.

7. Rogelberg, Leach, and Burnfield, "Not Another Meeting!" pp. 83–96.

8. E. Matson, "The Seven Sins of Deadly Meetings," *Fast Company* 2 (April 1996), pp. 122–25.

9. F. Williams, *Executive Communication Power: Basic Skills for Management Success* (Englewood Cliffs, NJ: Prentice-Hall, 1983), p. 65.

10. J. Hill, "In-House Webconferencing Aids Company with Many Franchises," *Presentations*, November 2002, p. 15.

11. Adapted from S. D. Collins, *Communication in a Virtual Organization* (Cincinnati: Thomson, 2003), pp. 48–49; and *The Listening Leaders Newsletter*, December 8, 2004, accessed from the International Listening Leadership Institute at **www.ListeningLeaders.com**.

12. L. Tuck, "Brave New Meetings," *Presentations*, September 1996, pp. 28–36.

13. F. Stone, "We've Got to Stop Meeting Like This," *Getting Results . . . for the Hands-on Manager* 42 (February 1997), p. 5.

14. A. Luong and S. G. Rogelberg, "Meetings and More Meetings: The Relationship between Meeting Load and the Daily Well-Being of Employees," *Group Dynamics* 9 (2005), pp. 58–67.

15. From *Six Secrets to Improve Your Future Business Meetings* (Austin, TX: 3M Visual Systems); 3M Corporation, "Decide If a Meeting Is Needed," accessed at **www.3m .com/meetingnetwork/readingroom/aa_ae_me_meet ing_needed.html**; S. De Wine, *The Consultant's Craft: Improving Organizational Communication* (New York: St. Martin's, 1994), p. 162; and S. M. Lippincott, *Meetings: Do's, Don'ts, and Donuts*, 2nd ed. (Pittsburgh, PA: Lighthouse Point Press), 1999.

16. See, for example, J. M. Cook, "Tips for Planning an Effective Meeting," *Presentations*, August 1997, p. 26.

17. C. Allard, "Trust and Teamwork: More than Just Buzzwords," *En Route*, August 1992, p. 41.

18. 3M Meeting Network, "Building Great Agendas," retrieved August 28, 2003, from **www.3m.com/meeting network/readingroom/meetingguide_building.html**.

19. Ibid.

20. Cathy Olofson, "The Ritz Puts On Stand-Up Meetings," *Fast Company* 17 (September 1998), p. 62. Retrieved August 28, 2003, from **www.fastcompany.com/magazine/ 17/minm.html**.

21. C. O. Steele, "Make Your Meetings More Productive," *Black Enterprise* 24 (March 1994), p. 76.

22. De Wine, *The Consultant's Craft*, p. 165.

23. *Leading Meetings*, vol. 1 (Great Neck, NY: Xerox Learning Systems), pp. 15–17.

24. D. Tannen, *Talking from 9 to 5: How Women's and Men's Conversational Styles Affect Who Gets Heard, Who Gets Credit, and What Gets Done at Work* (New York: Morrow, 1994), p. 290. For an overview of the subject, see J. A. Bonito and A. B. Hollingshead, "Participation in Small Groups," *Communication Yearbook 20* (Newbury Park, CA: Sage, 1997).

25. For a detailed description of the nominal group technique, see S. A. Beebe and J. T. Masterson, *Communicating in Small Groups: Principles and Practices*, 5th ed. (New York: Longman, 1997), pp. 227–31.

26. *Leading Meetings*, vol. 1, p. 50.

27. 3M Management Institute, "Meeting Quality: A Chicken-Egg Question?" *Meeting Management News* 4 (June 1992), pp. 2–3.

28. Allard, "Trust and Teamwork," p. 41.

29. *Leading Meetings*, vol. 2, pp. 41–45.

Chapter 10

1. D. Z. Meilach, "Even the Odds with Visual Presentations," *Presentations*, November 1994, p. 51.

2. L. Tuck, "Profiling the Presentation Professional," *Presentation Products*, November 1992, pp. 35–42.

3. J. M. Lannon, *Technical Communication*, 9th ed. (New York: Longman, 2003), p. 639.

4. J. P. Wright, *On a Clear Day You Can See General Motors* (New York: Avon, 1979), p. 96.

5. H. M. Boettinger, *Moving Mountains, or The Art of Letting Others See Things Your Way* (New York: Collier, 1969), p. 6.

6. "The Conference Board," *Across the Board* 24 (September 1987), p. 7.

7. Toastmasters International Web site. **www.toastmasters .org/MainMenuCategories/WhatisToastmasters .aspx**, accessed February 13, 2009.

8. See, for example, R. S. Mathis and L. Carrell, "Communication Training for Clergy: Exploring Impact on the Transformative Quality of Sermon Communication," *Communication Education* 58 (2009), pp. 15–34; and D. R. Seibold, S. Kudsi, and M. Rude, "Does Communication Training Make a Difference? Evidence for the Effectiveness of a Presentation Skills Program," *Journal of Applied Communication Research* 21 (May 1993), pp. 111–29.

9. Ken Haemer, quoted in G. Zelazny, *Say It with Presentations* (New York: McGraw-Hill, 2006), p. 13.

10. L. Iacocca and W. Novak, *Iacocca: An Autobiography* (New York: Bantam, 1984), p. 117.

11. J. T. Molloy, *Molloy's Live for Success* (New York: Bantam, 1985), p. 16.

12. Personal correspondence from Steven Vasilion, September 24, 1997.

13. R. Naguib, "International Audiences," Toastmasters International. Retrieved March 6, 2009, from **www .toastmasters.org/MainMenuCategories/FreeResources/ NeedHelpGivingaSpeech/BusinessPresentations/ SpeakingGlobally_1/InternationalAudiences.aspx**.

14. C. J. Williams, "Jury Duty? You May Want to Edit Your Online Profile," *Los Angeles Times* (Sept. 29, 2008), p. A6.

15. Cited in *This Just In*, March 19, 1995 (**archie@netcom .com**).

16. B. E. Bradley, *Fundamentals of Speech Communication: The Credibility of Ideas*, 6th ed. (Dubuque, IA: Wm. C. Brown, 1991), pp. 58–61.

17. Meilach, "Even the Odds," p. 3.

18. "The Gray Flannel Sideshow," *Presentations*, November 1993, p. 50.

19. H. L. Marsh, "Summary Membership Remarks," speech delivered at a meeting of the New York Chapter of the Institute of Internal Auditors, New York, May 13, 1983.

20. S. Linver and J. Mengert, *Speak and Get Results: The Complete Guide to Speeches and Presentations That Work in Any Business Situation*, rev. ed. (New York: Fireside, 1994), p. 14.

21. J. Windsor, "Will You Pass the Two-Word Test for Ultimate Presentations?" *Presentations.com* (February 5, 2009). Retrieved March 5, 2009, at **www.presentations .com/msg/content_display/presentations/e3id425 eb6001d58ee77a43d3cb8ba6aa6c**.

22. For a discussion of research supporting the value of organization, see S. E. Lucas, *The Art of Public Speaking*, 10th ed. (New York: McGraw-Hill, 2009), pp. 192–93. Also, see N. R. Faylor, S. A. Beebe, M. L. Houser, and T. P. Mottet, "Perceived Differences in Instructional Communication Behaviors Between Effective and Ineffective Corporate Trainers," *Human Communication* 11 (2008), pp. 145–56.

23. Adapted from C. L. Bovée and J. T. Thill, *Business Communication Today*, 2nd ed. (New York: Random House, 1989), pp. 89–90. Student examples of moving from what audiences know to what they don't know are found in J. A. DeVito, *The Elements of Public Speaking*, 7th ed. (New York: Longman, 2000), pp. 364–65.

24. "President Discusses Strengthening Social Security in Florida," Tampa Convention Center, Tampa, Florida, February 4, 2005. Accessed March 31, 2006, from **www .whitehouse.gov/news/releases/2005/02/20050204-13 .html**.

25. For a discussion of nonlinear organizing patterns, see C. Jaffe, *Public Speaking: Concepts and Skills for a Diverse Society*, 3rd ed. (Belmont, CA: Wadsworth, 2001), pp. 174–77; and M. W. Lustig and J. Koester, *Intercultural Competence: Interpersonal Communication across Cultures*, 4th ed. (New York: Allyn & Bacon, 2003), pp. 243–52.

26. "Presentation Planning: Draw a Logic Tree," *Meeting Management News*, April 1993, pp. 1–2.

27. S. Hybels and R. L. Weaver II, *Communicating Effectively*, 6th ed. (Boston: McGraw-Hill, 2001), pp. 447–49; and M. Osborn and S. Osborn, *Public Speaking*, 5th ed. (Boston: Houghton Mifflin, 2000), pp. 378–80.

28. The uppermost limit of items people can usually recall from their short-term memory is seven. For oral presentations, however, limiting the number of main points to five increases the odds that listeners will retain them. See J. Katt, J. Murdock, J. Butler, and B. Pryor, "Establishing Best Practices for the Use of PowerPoint™ as a Presentation Aid," *Human Communication* 11 (2008), pp. 193–200.

29. D. Zielinski, "Perfect Practice," *Presentations*, May 2003. Retrieved March 6, 2006, from **www.presentations .com/presentations/delivery/article_display.jsp? vnu_content_id=1902958**.

30. R. Moran, "Tips on Making Speeches to International Audiences," *International Management* 44 (1989), p. 74.

31. James C. May, "Connecting and Protecting Our Planet: Transportation and the Environment," speech delivered October 30, 2008, to the European Aviation Club. From *Vital Speeches of the Day*, February 2009, vol. 75 (2), pp. 68–71.

32. "Errors Are Common in Credit Reports, Small Study Suggests," *The Wall Street Journal*, May 27, 1991, p. B7.

33. Quoted in J. W. Robinson, *Winning Them Over* (Rocklin, CA: Prima, 1987), p. 279.

34. Remarks as Prepared for Delivery by U.S. Attorney General Eric Holder at the Department of Justice African American History Month Program, February 18, 2009. Retrieved March 10, 2009, at **www.usdoj.gov/ag/ speeches/2009/ag-speech-090218.html**.

35. Ibid.

36. *Executive Speechwriter Newsletter* 8 (1993), p. 3.

37. "How to Close a Speech," retrieved June 9, 2003, from **www.public-speaking.org/public-speaking-closings-article.htm**.

Chapter 11

1. L. Poole, "A Tour of the Mac Desktop," *Mac World* 1 (February 1984), p. 16.

2. C. Spangenberg, "Basic Values and the Techniques of Persuasion," *Litigation*, Summer 1977, p. 64.

3. H. Anderson, "Day Care: Big Hit at the Office," *Los Angeles Times*, May 21, 1989, pp. 30–33.

4. J. Lawlor, "Offbeat Perks Can Perk Up Workers," *USA Today*, August 17, 1992, p. 2B.

5. J. Applegate, "Best, Worst Small-Business Names of 1994," *Los Angeles Times*, April 12, 1994, p. D3.

6. Ibid.

7. M. Poundsford, "Using Storytelling, Conversation and Coaching to Engage," *Strategic Communication Management* 11 (2007), pp. 32–35.

8. C. Gallo, "Use Storytelling to Strengthen Your Presentations," *Business Week Online* (September 12, 2008). Retrieved March 14, 2009, from **www.businessweek.com/smallbiz/content/sep2008/sb20080912_141650.htm**.

9. Ibid.

10. D. A. Small, G. Loewenstein, and P. Slovic, (2007). "Sympathy and Callousness: The Impact of Deliberative Thought on Donations to Identifiable and Statistical Victims," *Organizational Behavior and Human Decision Processes* 102 (2007), 143–53.

11. Adapted from J. A. Daly and I. N. Englebert, *Presentations in Everyday Life* (Boston: Houghton Mifflin, 2001), p. 311.

12. A. Rooney, "Sales vs. Service," *Executive Speechwriter Newsletter* 14 (May 1989), p. 5.

13. J. Slan, *Using Stories and Humor—Grab Your Audience!* (Boston: Allyn & Bacon, 1998), p. 12.

14. J. E. Lukaszewski, "You Can Become a Verbal Visionary," *Executive Speeches* 12 (August/September 1997), pp. 23–30.

15. L. L. Lindsey and K. A. Yun, "Examining the Persuasive Effect of Statistical Messages: A Test of Mediating Relationships," *Communication Studies* 54 (2003), pp. 306–21.

16. "Making Time and Money Real," *Executive Communication Report* 3 (March 1987), developed by *Small Business Report*, 203 Calle del Oaks Mount, Monterey, CA 93940.

17. S. J. Diamond, "Some Airlines' Ads Mislead without Lying," *Los Angeles Times*, June 13, 1991, p. E1.

18. C. Romans, "Numb and Number: Is Trillion the New Billion?" CNN.com, February 4, 2009. Retrieved online March 12, 2009, at **www.cnn.com/2009/LIVING/02/04/trillion.dollars/index.html?eref=rss_topstories**.

19. D. B. Yoffie and M. Kwak, "Judo Strategy: 10 Techniques for Beating a Stronger Opponent," *Business Strategy Review* 13 (Spring 2002), pp. 20–30.

20. J. Flaherty, "Recipe for a Business Best Seller: Analogies about Anything but Business," *The New York Times*, September 5, 2001, p. C14.

21. "Miners Deserve Better," *Los Angeles Times*, January 5, 2006, p. B12.

22. The quotes in this section were accessed March 22, 2006, from **www.woopidoo.com/business_quotes**.

23. "Paper Work Is Avoidable (If You Call the Shots)," *The Wall Street Journal*, June 17, 1977, p. 24.

24. D. R. Vogel, G. W. Dickson, and J. A. Lehman, "Driving the Audience Action Response," *Computer Graphics World* 5 (August 1986), pp. 25–28. See also D. R. Vogel, G. W. Dickson, and J. A. Lehman, *Persuasion and the Role of Visual Presentation Support: The UM/3M Study* (Austin, TX: 3M Corporation, 1986), pp. 1–20.

25. For more suggestions on how to use handouts, see R. W. Pike, "Handouts: A Little Charity to Your Audience Goes a Long Way," *Presentations*, May 1994, pp. 31–35.

26. T. Simons, "MultiMedia or Bust?" *Presentations*, February 2000, pp. 40–50.

27. I. Parker, "Absolute PowerPoint," *New Yorker*, May 28, 2001, pp. 76–87.

28. For a discussion of PowerPoint's limitations, see R. Ganzel, "Power Pointless," *Presentations*, February 2000, pp. 54–57.

29. E. R. Tufte, *The Cognitive Style of PowerPoint* (Cheshire, CT: Graphics Press, 2003), p. 22.

30. Parker, op. cit., p. 86. See also T. Simons, "Does PowerPoint Make You Stupid?" *Presentations*, March 2004, pp. 25–31.

31. G. Jaffe, "What's Your Point, Lieutenant? Just Cut to the Pie Charts," *The Wall Street Journal*, April 26, 2000, p. A1.

32. For more information on using visual aids effectively, see S. M. Kosslyn and C. Chabris, "The Mind Is Not a Camera, The Brain Is Not a VCR: Some Psychological Guidelines for Designing Charts and Graphs," *Aldus Magazine*, September/October 1993, pp. 33–36.

33. K. Medaris, "Purdue Expert Gives Do's and Don'ts of Visual Presentations," *Purdue University News*, October 6, 2008. Retrieved March 15, 2009, at **http://news.uns.purdue.edu/x/2008b/081006T-SmithPower.html**.

34. L. Tuck, "Improving Your Image with LCD Panels," *Presentations*, January 1994, p. 32.

35. L. Pearson, "The Medium Speaks," *Presentation Products*, June 1993, pp. 55–56.

36. See, for example, L. Tuck, "Using Type Intelligently," *Presentations*, April 1994, pp. 30–32; and S. Hinkin, "Not Just Another Pretty Face: 10 Tips for the Most Effective Use of Type," *Presentations*, January 1995, pp. 34–36.

37. J. Terberg, "Font Choices Play a Crucial Role in Presentation Design," *Presentations*, April 2005. Retrieved March 14, 2006, from **www.presentations.com/presentations/creation/article_display.jsp?vnu_content_id=1000875169**.

Chapter 12

1. R. Ailes, "You Are the Message," *Executive Communications*, January 1988, p. 1.

2. K. O. Locker, *Business and Administrative Communication*, 5th ed. (Boston: McGraw-Hill/Irwin, 2000), pp. 485–87.

3. M. Landis (Houser), "Taking the Butterflies Out of Speechmaking," *Creative Living* 9 (Spring 1980), p. 19.

4. D. Zielinski, "Perfect Practice," *Presentations*, May 2003. Accessed March 25, 2006, from **www.presentations.com/presentations/delivery/article_display.jsp?vnu_content_id=1902958**.

5. Adapted from L. Fletcher, *How to Design and Deliver a Speech*, 4th ed. (New York: Harper & Row, 1990), pp. 347–51.

6. J. Grossman, "Resurrecting Auto Graveyards," *Inc.*, March 1983, pp. 73–80.

7. W. L. Haynes, "Public Speaking Pedagogy in the Media Age," *Communication Education* 38 (1990), pp. 89–102.

8. Ailes, "You Are the Message," p. 5.

9. P. J. Stella, "Are There Any Questions?" *Presentations*, November 1994, p. 12.

10. K. E. Cleveland, *Agree for Maximum Impact* (Victoria, BC: Pertinent Information, Inc.). Retrieved July 2, 2003, from **www.pertinent.com/articles/persuasion/kenrickP2.asp**.

11. I. Wallace and D. Wallechinsky, *Book of Lists* (New York: Bantam, 1977), p. 469.

12. "The Speaker May Look Calm but Survey Confirms Jitters," *Los Angeles Times*, September 13, 1981, pt. 5, p. 13.

13. M. B. Stein, J. R. Walker Jr., and D. R. Forde, "Public-Speaking Fears in a Community Sample: Prevalence, Impact on Functioning, and Diagnostic Classification," *Archives of General Psychiatry* 53 (1996), pp. 169–74. See also "Addressing Fears," *Psychology Today* 29 (June 1996), p. 11.

14. A. K. Watson, "Taking the Sweat Out of Communication Anxiety," *Personnel Journal* 74 (1995), pp. 111–17.

15. See, for example, R. R. Behnke, C. R. Sawyer, and P. E. King, "The Communication of Public Speaking Anxiety," *Communication Education* 36 (April 1987), pp. 138–39; J. Burgoon, M. Pfau, T. Birk, and V. Manusov, "Nonverbal Communication Performance and Perceptions Associated with Reticence," *Communication Education* 36 (April 1987), pp. 119–30; and K. L. McEwan and G. Devins, "Increased Arousal in Emotional Anxiety Noticed by Others," *Journal of Abnormal Psychology* 92 (November 1983), pp. 417–21.

16. J. C. Humes, *Talk Your Way to the Top* (New York: McGraw-Hill, 1980), p. 135.

17. C. R. Sawyer and R. R. Hehnke, "State Anxiety Patterns for Public Speaking and the Behavior Inhibition System," *Communication Reports* 12 (1999), pp. 33–41.

18. A. N. Finn, C. R. Sawyer, and P. Schrodt, "Examining the Effect of Exposure Therapy on Public Speaking State Anxiety," *Communication Education* 58 (2009), pp. 92–109. Retrieved August 28, 2009 from **www.informaworld.com/smpp/title~content=t713684765~db=all~tab=issueslist~branches=58-v58**.

19. D. Pogue, "Panic on the Podium," *Mac World*, January 1995, pp. 97–98.

20. T. E. Smith and A. Bainbridge, "Get Real: Does Practicing Speeches Before an Audience Improve Performance?" *Communication Quarterly* 54 (2006), pp. 111–25.

21. Zielinski, "Perfect Practice."

22. J. A. Daly, A. L. Vangelisti, and D. J. Weber, "Speech Anxiety Affects How People Prepare Speeches: A Protocol Analysis of the Preparation Processes of Speakers," *Communication Monographs* 62 (1995).

23. See, for example, A. Ellis, *A New Guide to Rational Living* (North Hollywood, CA: Wilshire Books, 1977); and A. Beck, *Cognitive Therapy and the Emotional Disorders* (New York: International Universities Press, 1976).

24. D. Baskerville, "Public Speaking Rule #1: Have No Fear," *Black Enterprise* 24 (May 1994), pp. 76–81.

25. J. Ayres, T. Hopf, and E. Peterson, "A Test of Communication-Orientation Motivation (COM) Therapy," *Communication Reports* 13 (2000), pp. 35–44.

Chapter 13

1. J. C. Meister, *Corporate Universities*, revised ed. (New York: McGraw-Hill, 1998).

2. R. E. Wilkes, "Mortgage Megatrends," speech delivered at a meeting of the Austin Association of Professional Mortgage Women, Austin, TX, September 15, 1987, and reprinted in *Executive Speaker* 9 (1988), p. 9.

3. E. Graham, "High-Tech Training," *The Wall Street Journal*, February 9, 1990, p. R16.

4. M. Lowenstein and J. Spletzer, *Informal Training: A Review of Existing Data and Some New Evidence*, Report NLS 94-20 (Washington, DC: U.S. Bureau of Labor Statistics, 1994). Retrieved April 14, 2003, from **www.bls.gov/ore/pdf/nL940050.pdf**.

5. M. Molenda, J. A. Pershing, and C. M. Reigluth, "Designing Instructional Systems," in *The ASTD Training and Development Handbook*, ed. R. L. Craig (New York: McGraw-Hill), 1996, pp. 266–93.

6. K. Blanchard, "Managers Must Learn to Teach," *Today's Office* 22 (October 1987), pp. 8–9.

7. "How Lever's 'Hands-On' Demos Ignited Rep Enthusiasm," *Business Marketing Digest* 18 (Third Quarter 1993), pp. 29–32.

8. D. Bocher, "Chapter 11: Speak with Confidence," in *Powerful Presentations That Inform, Inspire and Persuade* (New York: McGraw-Hill, 2003).

9. Research summarized in T. H. Leahey and R. J. Harris, *Human Learning*, 2nd ed. (Englewood Cliffs, NJ: Prentice-Hall, 1989), p. 203.

10. J. E. Lukaszewski, "You Can Become a Verbal Visionary," *Executive Speeches* 12 (August/September 1997), pp. 23–30.

11. R. Kiyosaki in the forward to B. Singer, *$ales Dogs* (New York: Warner Books, 2001).

12. A. Fisher, "Willy Loman Couldn't Cut It," *Fortune* (November 11, 1996), p. 210.

13. Kevin Hogan quoted in V. Alonzo, "5 Steps to Bigger Sales," *Incentive* 174 (October 2000), pp. 117–19.

14. *Specialty Speeches* (Mission Viejo, CA: Toastmasters International, 1992), p. 10.

15. Quoted in N. Rackham, *Spin Selling* (New York: McGraw-Hill, 1988), p. 51.

16. Adapted from R. B. Adler and G. Rodman, *Understanding Human Communication*, 8th ed. (New York: Oxford University Press, 2003), pp. 404–7.

17. M. Burgoon and M. D. Miller, "Communication and Influence," *Human Communication: Theory and Research*, eds. G. L. Dahnke and G. W. Clatterbuck (Belmont, CA: Wadsworth, 1990), pp. 233–34.

18. R. E. Petty and J. T. Cacioppo, "Involvement and Persuasion: Tradition versus Integration," *Psychological Bulletin* 107 (1990), pp. 367–74.

19. For a detailed review of credibility, see R. H. Gass and J. S. Seiter, *Persuasion, Social Influence and Compliance-Gaining* (Boston: Allyn & Bacon, 1999); and S. E. Lucas, *The Art of Public Speaking*, 7th ed. (New York: McGraw-Hill, 2001), pp. 400–5.

20. This discussion of fallacies is adapted from R. B. Adler and G. Rodman, *Understanding Human Communication*, 10th ed. (New York: Oxford University Press, 2009), pp. 441–42.

21. J. Sprague and D. Stuart, *The Speaker's Handbook*, 3rd ed. (Ft. Worth: Harcourt Brace Jovanovich, 1992), p. 172.

22. "At Lanier a Better Mousetrap Isn't Quite Enough," *Fortune* (February 26, 1979), pp. 74, 76.

23. D. J. O'Keefe, "Social Judgment Theory," in *Persuasion: Theory and Research* (Newbury Park, CA: Sage, 1990). See also "Social Judgment Theory" in E. M. Griffin, *A First Look at Communication Theory*, 7th ed. (New York: McGraw-Hill, 2009).

24. Griffin, *A First Look*, p. 194.

25. M. Burgoon and J. K. Burgoon, "Message Strategies in Influence Attempts," in *Communication and Behavior*, ed. G. J. Hanneman and W. J. McEwen (Reading, MA: Addison-Wesley, 1975), p. 153.

26. M. Allen, "Determining the Persuasiveness of Message Sidedness: A Prudent Note about Utilizing Research Summaries," *Western Journal of Communication* 57 (1993), pp. 98–103. See also M. Allen et al., "Testing a Model of Message Sidedness: Three Replications," *Communication Monographs* 57 (1990), pp. 275–91.

27. For more information on cultural differences in styles of persuasion, see M. L. Lustig and J. Koester, *Intercultural Competence: Interpersonal Communication across Cultures*, 5th ed. (Boston: Pearson Education, 2006), pp. 239–48; and D. A. Lieberman, *Public Speaking in the Multicultural Environment* (Englewood Cliffs, NJ: Prentice-Hall, 1994), p. 16.

28. Adapted from J. A. Daly and I. N. Eisenberg, *Presentations in Everyday Life* (Boston: Houghton Mifflin, 2001), p. 344.

29. C. Osgood, *Osgood on Speaking: How to Think on Your Feet without Falling on Your Face* (New York: Morrow, 1988), p. 39.

30. Adapted from G. C. Gard, "Accepting an Award: How to Be Gracious and Effective in 30 Seconds," *Toastmaster*, November 1988, p. 20.

Appendix II

1. B. Lewis, "Make Sure You Actually Communicate Rather than Simply Offer Information," *InfoWorld*, November 22, 1999, p. 80.

2. J. Evers, *The Economy of Plain English* (Nanuet, NY: James L. Evers Associates), and "Five Phrases to Eliminate from Your Business Writing," *Manager's Intelligence Report*, September 2000, p. 1.

3. M. Bugeja, "Say What You Mean," *Successful Meetings*, October 2000, p. 135.

4. "Trim the Fat from Your Business Writing with These Ideas," *Manager's Intelligence Report*, January 2000, p. 4.

5. L. Baldrige and G. O'Brien, "Netiquette," *Kinko's Impress*, 2000, pp. 20–21.

6. P. Lucrezio, "Companies Must Develop, Enforce E-Mail Usage Policies," *Capital District Business Review*, February 2, 2000, p. 37.

7. A. Humphries, "E-mail for Careerists: Care Enough to Send the Very Best," September 29, 2000. Retrieved May 28, 2001, from **www.cnn.com/2000/CAREER/corporateclass/09/29/email.protocol/index.html**.

8. Hsu, Tiffany, "Crafting a Resume That Will Grab Recruiters," *Los Angeles Times*, March 29, 2009. Retrieved July 18, 2009, from www.latimes.com/business/la-fi-cover29-2009mar29,0,4601180.story?page=3.

9. C. D. Bass, "Unusual Résumé May Net That Job," *Albuquerque Journal*, June 18, 2000, p. I-1.

10. The Job Hunters Guide, prepared by the Bureau of Economic Research and Analysis, New Mexico Department of Labor, March 2000, pp. 10–13.

11. W. S. Enelow, "What Do Employers Really Want in a Résumé?" retrieved June 22, 2001, from **www.jobweb.com/catapult/enelow-r.html**.

12. R. Smith, "eRésumés 101: Choosing Your Best Electronic Résumé Format," retrieved June 5, 2001, from **www.eresumes.com/tut_eresume.html**.

13. S. J. Gerson and S. M. Gerson, *Technical Writing: Process and Product*, 3rd ed. (Upper Saddle River, NJ: Prentice-Hall, 2000), pp. 167–69.

14. Y. Parker, "Guide for a Scanner-Friendly Resume," retrieved on June 11, 2001, from **www.damngood.com/jobseekers/ScanGuide.html**.

15. Ibid.

16. K. Hansen, "Common Sense Steps Can Prevent Employer Backlash against Online Résumés," includes some citing of S. Armour, *USA Today*, July 15, 1999. Retrieved June 13, 2001, from **www.quintcareers.com/online_resume_guide.html**.

17. M. Tullier, "The Art and Science of Writing Cover Letters: The Best Way to Make a First Impression," retrieved June 22, 2001, from **http://resume.monster.com/coverletter/coverletters**.

credits

Text

Chapter 1:   **Page 5:** Reprinted from JOB OUTLOOK 2009–STUDENT VERSION, from Job-Web (www.jobweb.com), with permission of the National Association of Colleges and Employers, copyright holder; **p. 15:** DILBERT: © Scott Adams/Dist. By United Feature Syndicate, Inc.; **p. 17:** Adapted from Mark P. Orbe, and Carol J. Bruess, CONTEMPORARY ISSUES INTERPERSONAL COMMUNICATIO0N (Los Angeles: Roxbury, 2005), p. 309. Reprinted by permission of Oxford University Press; **p. 20:** Reprinted by permission of Harvard Business School Press. From *Inside Chinese Business: A Guide for Managers Worldwide* by Ming-Jer Chen. Boston, MA 2001, p. 64. Copyright © 2001 by the Harvard Business School Publishing Corporation; all rights reserved.

Chapter 2:   **Page 36:** Passel, J.S. and Cohn, D. U.S. Population Projections: 2005–2050. Washington, D.C.: Pew Research Center, 2008. Reprinted by permission; **p. 39:** E. Trompenaars, RIDING THE WAVES OF CULTURE (New York: McGraw-Hill/Irwin, 1994), p. 70. Reprinted by permission of The McGraw-Hill Companies; **p. 41:** Reprinted by permission of Harvard Business School Press. From *Inside Chinese Business: A Guide for Managers Worldwide* by Ming-Jer Chen. Boston, MA 2001, p. 136. Copyright © 2001 by the Harvard Business School Publishing Corporation; all rights reserved; **p. 45:** "Difference as Advantage: Maximize the Benefits of Your Cultural Identity on the Job" by Chandra Prasad from www.imdiversity.com. Chandra Prasad is the author *of On Borrowed Wings: A Novel* and the editor of *Mixed: An Anthology of Short Fiction on the Multiracial Experience.* You can read about her work at www.chandrapasad.com; **p. 51:** Reprinted by permission of *Harvard Business Review.* From "Cultural Intelligence" by P.C. Earley and E. Mosakowski, October 2004, pp. 139-146. Copyright © 2004 by the Harvard Business School Publishing Corporation; all rights reserved; **p. 54:** Philip R. Harris and Robert T. Moran, *Managing Cultural Differences,* 2/e, pp. 245-247. Copyright © 2007. Reprinted by permission of Elsevier; **p. 56:** Used by permission of Ted Goff; **p. 60:** Courtesy of Texas Instruments.

Chapter 3:   **Page 70:** © 2006 Ted Goff from cartoonbank.com. All Rights Reserved. Reprinted by permission; **p. 73:** Dilbert: © Scott Adams/Dist. By United Feature Syndicate, Inc.; **p. 74:** A.D. Wolvin and C.G. Coakley, PERSPECTIVES ON LISTENING (Norwood, NJ: Ablex, 1993), p. 115; **p. 76:** Domenici, K. and Littlejohn, S.W. *Facework: Bridging Theory and Practice.* Thousand Oaks, CA: Sage, 2006, pp. 130-131. Reprinted by permission; **p. 80:** Adapted from L. Barker and K. Watson, LISTEN UP (New York: St. Martin's Press, 2000); **p. 83:** © 2009 Ted Goff from cartoonbank.com. All Rights Reserved; **p. 86:** Used by permission of Marc Tyler Nobleman.

Chapter 4:   **Page 95:** © The New Yorker Collection 2000 Robert Mankoff from cartoonbank.com. All Rights Reserved; **p. 99:** © The New Yorker Collection 1987 Lee Lorenz from cartoonbank.com. All Rights Reserved; **p. 103:** Dilbert: © Scott Adams/Dist. By United Feature Syndicate, Inc.; **p. 109:** © The New Yorker Collection 2002 Frank Cotham from cartoonbank.com. All Rights Reserved.

Chapter 5:   **Page 126:** © Tribune Media Services, Inc. All Rights Reserved. Reprinted with permission; **p. 127:** "Boss's Angry E-Mail Sends Shares Plunging" from *The Daily Telegraph,*

Chapter 12:   **Page 378:** © Cowles Syndicate, Inc. King Features Syndicate. Reprinted by permission; **p. 394:** Dilbert: © Scott Adams/Dist. by United Feature Syndicate, Inc. Reprinted by permission.

Chapter 13:   **Page 408:** Reprinted by permission of NTL® Institute for Behavioral Sciences; **p. 411:** Dilbert: © Scott Adams/Dist. by United Feature Syndicate, Inc. Reprinted by permission.

Photos

Page 5: © Stephen Simpson/Taxi/Getty Images; **p. 9:** © Fat Chance Productions/Iconica/Getty Images; **p. 16:** © Digital Vision/Getty Images; **p. 27:** © Lars Niki/McGraw-Hill Companies; **p. 35:** © Brand X Pictures/Punchstock; **p. 38:** © BLOOMimage/Getty Images; **p. 42:** © Ingram Publishing/AGE Fotostock; **p. 49:** © ThinkStock/Punchstock; **p. 58:** © Digital Vision/Getty Images; **p. 69:** © Jason Hetherington/Stone/Getty Images; **p. 75:** © Cameron/Corbis; **p. 84:** © Blend Images / Getty Images ; **p. 91:** © Photodisc/Getty Images; **p. 98:** © age fotostock / SuperStock; **p. 103:** © Digital Vision/Getty Images; **p. 107:** © Jon Feingersh/zefa/Corbis; **p. 117:** © Digital Vision/Getty Images; **p. 125:** © Walter Hodges/Corbis; **p. 131:** © Stockbyte/Getty Images; **p. 137:** © age fotostock / SuperStock; **p. 142:** © Synaptik/Getty Images; **p. 145:** © Stockdisc/Stockbyte; **p. 159:** © Photodisc/Getty Images; **p. 173:** © Jiang Jin / SuperStock; **p. 177:** © Lifesize/Getty Images; **p. 187:** © Purestock/Getty Images; **p. 235:** Royalty-Free/Corbis; **p. 236:** © Andersen Ross/Blend Images/Getty Images; **p. 239:** ©Photodisc/Getty Images; **pp. 264, 273:** ©Digital Vision/Getty Images; **p. 289:** ©Peter Dazeley/Photographer's Choice/Getty Images; **p. 303:** © Photodisc/Getty Images; **p. 310:** © Image Source/Punchstock; **p. 318:** © Image Source/Getty Images; **p. 326:** ©Comstock/PictureQuest; **p. 347:** © Digital Vision/Getty Images; **p. 377:** © age fotostock/SuperStock; **p. 379:** © BananaStock/Punchstock; **p. 391:** © Photodisc/Getty Images; **p. 396:** ©Max Oppenheim/The Image Bank/Getty Images; **p. 401:** © Anthony Marsland/The Image Bank/Getty Images; **p. 402:** © Thinkstock Images/Jupiterimages; **p. 423:** © Ingram Publishing/Getty Images; **p. 425:** © Walter B. McKenzie/Stone/Getty Images; **p. 429:** © Noel Hendrickson/Riser/Getty Images; **p. 432:** © Comstock/PictureQuest; **p. 439:** © Stockbyte/Getty Images.

index

Note: Page numbers followed by "n" refer to footnotes.

A

Aberman, John, 14
Ability, credibility and, 424
Academy of Certified Administrative Managers, 70
Accents, 46, 76
Accepting an award, 440
Accommodation, 140, 141
Accuracy, teams and, 237
Acheson, Bill, 75
Acronyms, in instant messages, 26
Action-oriented listening style, 79
Action teams, 236
Active voice, 385
ADA (Americans with Disabilities Act of 1990), 49, 213
Adams, Scott, 14. *See also* Dilbert cartoons
Adaptive Path, 290
Ad hominem fallacy, 426
Advanced Public Speaking Institute, 439
Advertising careers, 6
African Americans
  condescending attitudes toward, 55
  disclosure and, 47
  eye contact and, 47
  nonverbal behavior and, 47, 106
  perception of whites by, 56
  verbal skills and, 47
  women, speaking with Euro-American women, 76
African cultures, supporting material and, 431
Agendas, meeting, 280–283, 286–287, 294
ahorita, 94
Ailes, Roger, 377, 388
Air Florida flight 90 crash, 140
Allen, Thomas J., 112
Ambiguity
  equivocal terms and, 93–94
  high-level abstractions and, 94–95
  nonverbal behavior and, 104
  strategic, 96–97
American Society of Civil Engineers, 36
Americans with Disabilities Act of 1990 (ADA), 49, 213
American Telephone and Telegraph, 78
Analogies, 355
Anchors, of listeners, 428
Andreotti, Lamberto, 385

Anheuser-Busch, 406
"Annuity University" workshop, 306
Anxiety, in presentations, 378, 393–396
Apologies, 136
Appearance. *See also* Personal attire
  in nonverbal communication, 106–108
  in presentations, 381–382
Apple Keynote, 366
Appraisal interviews. *See* Performance appraisal interviews
Arab cultures. *See* Middle Eastern cultures
Argumentum ad populum fallacy, 427
Asian Americans
  beckoning gestures and, 106
  holding hands and, 106
  silence and, 47
Asian countries. *See also* China; Japan
  collectivist culture in, 42
  gender roles in, 40
  long-term orientation in, 45
  low-context cultures in, 42
  silence in, 47, 77
Assurance, in impromptu presentations, 380
Asynchronous communication, 27, 242
Attention getters, 332
Attire. *See* Personal attire
Attitudes
  of audiences, 310
  condescending, toward African Americans, 55
  of interviewees, 163
  as listening barriers, 74–76
  nonverbal communication of, 104–105
  personal space and distance and, 110–111
Audiences
  analysis of, 306–310
  appeals to needs of, 427–432
  attitudes of, 310
  credibility and, 357, 423–425
  cultural style of, 431–432
  demographic characteristics of, 308–309
  eye contact with, 383
  hostile, 429–431
  imagining how appeals look to, 427
  for impromptu presentations, 380
  information needs of, 307
  international, 309

Audiences—*Cont.*
  key members of, 306–307
  knowledge of, 307
  opening statements and, 333–336
  personal preferences of, 307–308
  in presentation rehearsals, 395
  in question-and-answer sessions, 392
  reasons for listening, 332
  similarities to, 425
  size of, 309
  for technical reports, 405
  for training programs, 408–410
  well-informed, 431
Audition interviews, 197
Austria, task orientation in, 44
Authoritarian leadership style, 243
Authority
  leadership style, 243
  power distance and, 43, 44
  in presentations, 382
Authority rule, 257
Avoidance of conflict, 139, 141
Award presentations, 439–440

B

"Back channels," 241
Bandwagon appeal, 427
Bar charts, 362–363
Barge, J. Kevin, 62
Barnes & Noble, 56
Baryshnikov, Mikhail, 440
Baum, Joel, 255
Beckoning gestures, 106
Behavioral interviews, 197, 198
Belmont, Woody and Sandy, 300
Benefits, in sales presentations, 421–422
Bennis, Warren, 14–15
Berglos, Steven, 138
Berlin, Leonard, 112
BFOQ (bona fide occupational qualification), 213
Biased language, 98–99
Biden, Joe, 162
Birdwhistell, Ray, 47
Black & Decker, 40
Blacks. *See* African Americans
Blake, Robert, 243–244
Blanchard, Kenneth, 224, 244
Blogging, 28
Body language, 109–110, 383–384
Body relaxation, 110
Bolles, Richard, 190, 195, 205

Bona fide occupational qualification (BFOQ), 213
Book of Lists (Wallace and Wallechinsky), 393
Boomerang effect, 423
Boomers, 48–49
Borders, 56
Bormann, Ernest, 245–246
Brainstorming
  group creativity through, 267–268
  in negotiation, 148, 150
  for presentation ideas, 318, 319
  in problem solving, 250
Braithwaite, Dawn, 49
Brawn, Alan, 311
Briefings, 402–403
Broadcasting careers, 6
Brown, Scott, 129
Brownell, Judi, 71
Bryan, Wilhelmus B., III, 194
Bryant, Kobe, 239
Bureau of National Affairs, 194
Bush, George H. W., 162
Bush, George W., 162, 318–320
Business cards, 38
Business letters
  in post-interview follow-up, 212
  requesting employment interviews, 195–196
  requesting informational interviews, 192, 193–194
Business practices, cultural differences in, 37. *See also* Cultural diversity

C

Caldera, Louis, 369
Caldwell, Barry, 241
Capital letters, as shouting, 104
Career research interviews, 190–194
  choosing interviewees for, 190–192
  contacting prospective interviewees for, 192–193
  finding job leads through, 195
  following-up, 193–194
  gatekeepers and, 191
  personal contacts and, 190, 191
Career tips
  on adult learning styles, 407
  on art of the apology, 136
  on balancing logic and emotion, 426
  on careers in communication, 6
  on cell phone and voice mail use, 24
  on confidence-building strategies, 393
  on cubicle etiquette, 113
  on cultural differences, 45

Career tips—*Cont.*
  on emerging as a group leader, 245
  on finding photographs and videos, 366
  on getting recognized by your bosses, 14
  on getting through gatekeepers, 191
  on international audiences, 309
  on invitational rhetoric, 316
  on job fairs, 164
  on leadership from members, 282
  on minimizing audience interruptions, 390
  on negotiating a salary, 206
  on opting out of meetings, 292
  on organizational culture, 61–62
  on reframing complaints in meetings, 276
  on requesting a raise, 419
  on saying "no," 140
  on seating arrangements, 286
  on spirituality in the workplace, 131
  on standing in your audience's shoes, 427
  on standing or sitting during presentations, 382
  on technical reports, 405
  on telephone logs, 85
  on time for planning presentations, 305
Carlson, Ed, 13
Carr, Beau, 27
Carter, Susan, 119
Carubba, Frank, 242
Case studies
  angry e-mails, 127
  cheerleader sales reps, 385
  dramatizing presentations, 359
  Google goes low-tech, 8
  Griffin Hospital, 57
  interview blunders, 199
  language-misunderstanding lawsuit, 46
  The Redeem Team, 239
  selling to seniors, 306
  sexual harassment, 119
  (lap)topless meetings, 290
Casperson, Dana, 108
Cause–effect pattern, 323–324
Caux Round Table Principles for Business, 52
Cell phones, 24
Chalk boards, 364–365
Channels, in communication model, 7, 8
Charnow, Michael, 242
Children, at work, 113
Chile, social orientation in, 44
Chilton, Roger, 232

China
  collectivist culture in, 42, 44
  concerns and communication practices in, 41
  gestures in, 106
  intolerance for conflict in, 39
  long-term orientation in, 43
  negotiating styles in, 147
  networking in, 20
  social customs in, 38
Chronological context, 9, 147. *See also* Time
Chronological pattern, 322
Churchill, Winston, 423
Civil Rights Act of 1964, 117
CKE Restaurants, 276
Claims, 329–330, 348, 430
Clarity, from supporting material, 348
Clark, Tyrone M., 306
Clarke, Kenneth, 311
Clichés, 96
Clinton, Bill, 162
Closed questions, 167–168
Closing statements, in presentations, 337–338
Clothing. *See* Personal attire
Clubs for employees, 18
Co-cultures, 45–52
  disabilities, 49–52
  ethnicity and, 47
  generational differences, 48–49
  language mixes, 45–46
  regional differences, 46–47
Code of ethics, for business, 52
Coercion, 422–423
Coercive power, 247
Cohesiveness, 263–265, 267
Colangelo, Jerry, 239
Collaboration. *See also* Teams
  in conflict management, 141, 143
  geography and, 277
  in successful teams, 240
Collectivist cultures, 42–44
Column charts, 362–363
Commitment, teams and, 237, 240
Common-good approach, 10, 12
Common ground, 425
Communication
  careers in, 6
  climate for, 127–131
  contexts of, 8–9
  as culture, 36
  importance of, 5–7
  model of, 7–8
  principles of, 9–11
  as a process, 10–11
Communication apprehension, 378, 393–396

Communication channels
  blogging, 28
  e-mail (*See* E-mail)
  face-to-face, 23–24
  instant messaging, 25–26, 29, 242
  listening and, 73
  multiple, 30
  selection of, 28–30
  teleconferencing, 25, 29, 242,
    275–277
  telephone and voice mail, 24–25
  tone and, 29
  Twitter and text messaging, 26
  videoconferencing, 25, 29, 276–277
  voice mail, 15, 24, 29, 739
  written communication, 27–28, 29
Communication climate, 127–131
Communication networks, 12–23
  downward, 12–13
  horizontal, 16–17
  informal, 17–23
  inventory for, 22
  upward, 14–16
Communispond, 393
Community beauty, 145
Comparative advantages organization
  plan, 326–327, 414–415
Comparisons, as supporting material,
  350, 355–356
Competition, in conflict management,
  140–141, 143, 146
Complaints, in meetings, 276
Compliments, 131–133
Compromise, in conflict management,
  141, 143, 145
Computer displays, 365
Computer-mediated meetings, 288
Computer Solutions (strategic case),
  66–67
Concept mapping software, 329
Conclusions, to presentations, 336–
  337, 395, 433
Condit, Philip, 107
Confidence, in presentations, 382,
  393–396
Confidentiality, in interviews, 179
Confirming messages, 128–131
Conflict
  benefits of, 138
  categories of, 138–139
  cultural differences in tolerance for,
    39–40
  ego/identity issues in, 139
  norms for, 261–262
  as problem-solving phase, 251, 252
  seating arrangements and, 286
Conflict management, 139–151
  approaches to, 139–143, 146
  cultural differences and, 39–40, 147

Conflict management—*Cont.*
  in cyberspace, 144
  example of, 149–151
  negotiation as, 143–149
  reframing complaints in, 276
  saying "no" in, 140
  self-assessment of style of, 142
Conflict phase of problem solving,
  251, 252
Conformity, in groups, 265–267
Connection power, 248
Consensus, 256
Constructive criticism, 133–135
Content messages, 9
Content-oriented listening style, 79
Context, of communication, 8–9
Contingency approaches to leadership,
  243–245
Contractions, in presentations, 385
Control, distributions of, 10
Corning Glass, 18
Corporate social responsibility (CSR),
  11
Cose, Ellis, 56
Counterfeit questions, 82
Covey, Stephen, 69–70, 81
Creative thinking
  encouraging, 267–268
  in problem solving, 250
  recognition and, 14
Credentials, credibility and, 424
Credibility
  citing sources in presentations and,
    357
  in introducing another speaker, 436
  in persuasive presentations, 423–
    425
Crips, Desiree, 195
Criteria satisfaction organization plan,
  325–326, 414, 415–416
Critical incident questions, 170
Criticism, 133–137
  characteristics of constructive,
    133–135
  cooperative solutions to, 137
  in performance appraisal interviews,
    226–227
  responding to, 135–137
CSR (corporate social
  responsibility), 11
Cubicle etiquette, 113
Cultural context, 9
Cultural diversity, 35–56. *See also*
  Co-cultures
  advantages of, 45
  assumptions and behaviors in, 54
  in audiences, 308, 431–432
  communication styles and, 47,
    53–56

Cultural diversity—*Cont.*
  conflict management and,
    39–40, 147
  conflict tolerance and, 39–40
  cyberspace collaboration and, 277
  dialogue and, 55–56
  disabilities and, 49–52
  disclosure and, 47
  ethical issues in, 52–53
  ethnicity and, 47
  ethnocentrism and, 55
  eye contact and, 47, 106, 108–109
  formality and, 37–38
  gender-related language
    challenges as, 102
  gender roles and, 40, 44n
  generational differences and, 48–49
  group decision making and, 256
  group norms and, 263
  high- *vs.* low-context cultures as,
    40–42, 96–97
  individualism *vs.* collectivism as,
    42–44
  listening problems from, 76–77
  monochronic *vs.* polychronic
    cultures as, 39, 77, 113–115
  nature of culture and, 36–37
  networking and, 20
  nonverbal behavior and, 105, 106
  population by race and ethnicity, 36
  power distance and, 43, 44
  in problem-solving meetings, 292
  regional differences and, 46–47
  self-assessment of cultural
    intelligence, 51
  short- *vs.* long-term orientation and, 45
  social customs and, 38
  styles of dress and, 38–39
  task *vs.* social orientation and, 44
  trends toward, 35–36
  uncertainty avoidance and, 44
  values and, 43
  in virtual teams, 241
Cultural literacy, 53–55
Culture, nature of, 36–37
Culture, organizational. *See*
  Organizational culture
Customer support, instant
  messaging in, 25

D

Daniels, William R., 274
DBM, 190
Deardon, William, 237
Deaver, Dave, 172
Decision-making methods, 256–258
Decoding, 7, 8
Deferred thesis, 415, 429–430

Definitions, in presentations, 349–350
Dell Computer, 406
Delta Airlines, 28
Democratic leadership style, 243
Dempsey, David, 330
Descriptive statements, 128–129
Design, 368, 369–370
Designated leaders, 246
DeSilva, Gina, 156
Deukmejian, George, 335
Devil's advocate, 266
Dewey, John, 248
Diagnostic interviews, 160, 187
Diagrams, as visual aids, 360
Dietrich, Marlene, 440
Digital Natives, 48, 49
Digital portfolios, 209
Dilbert cartoons, 15, 73, 104, 224,
    249, 285, 334
Dilenschneider, Robert, 126
Direct questions, 168–169, 288
Disabilities, 49–52
    definition of, 213
    guidelines for interacting with
        people with, 50, 52
    height and, 110
    language and, 49
    reasonable accommodations for
        employees with, 213
Disciplinary interviews, 160
Disclosure, 47
Disconfirming messages, 128–131
Disfluencies, 388
Disney Productions, 61, 406
Distance
    cultural diversity in, 43, 44, 105
    in interviews, 172
    personal space and, 105, 110–111
    power and, 111
Distance zones, 105, 111
Dogmatism, 246
Dogster.com, 290
Dorsch, Elaine, 232–233
Downsizing, 61
Downward communication, 12–13
Dress. *See* Personal attire
Drucker, Peter, 75
Drummond, Mary-Ellen, 106
Dry-erase marker boards, 364–365
Dun and Bradstreet, 78

E

EEOC (Equal Employment Opportunity
    Commission), 213, 216
Effect–cause pattern, 324
Egocentrism, 74
Egypt, 38
Either–or fallacy, 426

Elaboration likelihood model of
    persuasion, 426
E-learning, 407
Electronic blackboards, 366
Electronic communication. *See also*
    E-mail
    cell phones, 24
    instant messaging, 25, 26, 29, 242
    videoconferencing, 25, 29, 276–277
Electronic résumés, 197
Elevator speech, 19, 164
E-mail
    advantages and disadvantages of,
        27–28, 29
    conflict management and, 144
    impact of negative, 127
    leveling of status differences in, 242
    popularity of, 27
    in requesting informational
        interviews, 192–193
Emergence phase of problem
    solving, 251, 252
Emergent leaders, 245–246
Emoticons, 104
Emotion, balancing logic with, 426
Emotional contagion, 117
Emotional intelligence (EQ), 126
Employee compensation, 145
Employee manuals, 2
Employment interviews, 194–223.
    See also Interviews
    answering questions briefly, 209
    anticipating questions for, 200–204
    asking questions in, 209–210
    background research for, 195, 200
    by computer, 197
    constructive thinking in, 198
    contacting potential employers
        for, 195–197
    contacting the person hiring for, 195
    digital portfolios for, 209
    emphasizing the positive in, 207–208
    enthusiasm in, 209
    following-up after, 212
    formats for, 197–198
    honesty in, 205, 207
    importance of, 194
    interviewer complaints about, 201
    legal issues in, 213–216
    negotiating a salary in, 206
    offering evidence in, 208
    personal attire in, 199
    recovering from blunders in, 199
    rehearsing for, 210
    responding to employer's needs
        in, 204–206
    sample, 216–223
    self-assessment of interview
        quotient, 211

Encoding, 7, 8
Enthusiasm, in presentations, 388
EQ (emotional intelligence), 126
Equal Employment Opportunity
    Commission (EEOC), 213, 216
Equality, 130
Equivocal terms, 93–94
Escalators, 18
Ethics
    in audience analysis, 306
    business code of, 52
    corporate culture and, 60
    diversity and, 52–53
    Golden and Platinum Rules in, 72
    in interviewing, 178–180
    in persuasion, 422–432
    in showing interest, 116
    standards for behavior and, 10, 11–12
    in strategic ambiguity, 96
Ethnicity. *See* Cultural diversity
Ethnocentrism, 55
Euro-Americans
    disclosure and, 47
    displays of emotions and, 431–432
    eye contact and, 47
    organizational patterns for
        presentations by, 320
    perceptions of African Americans
        by, 56
    verbal skills and, 47
    women, speaking with African
        American women, 76
Europe
    social customs in, 38
    task orientation in, 44
    time sense in, 39, 113–114
Evidence. *See* Supporting material
Examples, in presentations, 351
Exit interviews, 160, 187
Expectations check, 283
Expert opinions, 257
Expert power, 247
Extemporaneous presentations, 379
External noise, 7
Eye contact
    friendliness *vs.* hostility and, 110
    involvement and, 108
    misleading messages from, 109
    during presentations, 383
    respect and, 47, 106, 108

F

Facebook, 20, 217
"Face time," in virtual teams, 241, 242
Face-to-face communication, 23–24, 29
Facial expressions, 108–109, 110
Factual questions, 168
Factual stories, 353

Fairness or justice approach, 10, 12
Fallacies, 426–427
False cause fallacy, 426–427
Feasibility reports, 405–406
Features, in sales presentations, 421–422
Federal Express, 246
Feedback
    in communication model, 7
    constructive, 133–135
    desire for, 13
    in face-to-face communication, 23, 29
    in performance reviews, 223–226
Feminine style of speech, 100–101, 102
Ferry, Richard M., 44
Fictional stories, 352, 353
Fiedler, Fred, 243–244
Figurative comparisons, 355
Final reports, 404–405
The First Globals, 48, 49
Fisher, Aubrey, 251
Fisher, Roger, 129, 146, 246
Fitch, Stona, 36
Flip charts, 365
Focus groups, video, 171
Ford Motor Company, 118, 235, 241
Formal communication networks
    downward, 12–13
    horizontal, 16–17
    upward, 14–16
Formality, cultural differences in, 37–38
Forming phase of problem solving,
        251, 252
Franklin, Benjamin, 235
French, John, 246
Fresh Air Sports (strategic case),
        300–301
Friedman, Stew, 8
Friendster, 28
Froggatt, Kirk, 30
Functional role analysis, 252–254, 255
Functional roles, 253–255, 279

G

Gardner, Stephen, 335
Gatekeepers, getting through, 191
Gates, Bill, 359
Gathering spaces, 112
Gender differences
    in language, 99–101, 102
    in listening, 77–78
    in titles during introductions, 436
"Genderlects," 100
Gender roles, cultural diversity in,
        40, 44n
General Electric (GE), 13, 78, 406
General goals, 313–314
General Mills, 81, 246
Generation X, 48–49
Generation Y, 48, 49

Generative listening, 72–73
Georgakis, Paul, 232–233
Germany, 38
Gestures, 106, 109–110
*Getting It Done: How to Lead When
    You're Not in Charge* (Fisher and
    Sharp), 246
Getting to Yes (Fisher and Ury), 146
GF Business Equipment Company,
        109
Gibb, Jack, 128
Gifts, cultural differences in, 38
Goals
    general, 313–314
    group *vs.* personal, 258–261
    for interviews, 161, 162, 188–189,
        227
    for meetings, 282–283, 284
    for presentations, 310, 313–315,
        428–429
    specific, 314–315
    for training, 407–408
Golden Rule, 72
Goldwyn, Sam, 356
Gonzales, José Maria, 40
Goodwill speeches, 418
Google
    blogging consequences at, 28
    low-tech publicity at, 8
    multitasking at meetings, 290
    searching for yourself on, 217
Google Chat, 171
Google Translate, 92
Gore, Al, 162
GoToWebinar, 420
Governmental/political careers, 6
Granovetter, Mark, 191
Graphics. *See* Visual aids
Graphs, 363–364
Greece, low acceptance of uncertainty
    in, 44
Green, David, 395
Griffin, Em, 428
Griffin Hospital, 57
Group interviews, 197
Group presentations
    delivery of, 433–435
    introductions, conclusions, and
        transitions in, 433
    organization of, 432–433
    self-assessment of, 434
Groups. *See* Teams
Groupthink, 264, 265–267
Guided discussions, 377

H

Hall, Edward, 36, 40, 111
Hand holding, 106
Handouts, 309, 365–366

Handshakes, 199
Hanson, Jeffrey, 18
Harley-Davidson, 246, 406
Harmony
    accommodation and, 140
    ambiguous language and, 96–97
    cultural differences in, 39–40, 42
    group *vs.* personal goals and, 260
Hastert, Dennis, 70
Hearing problems, 50, 72
Heckman, Frank, 261
Height, power and, 110
Hersey, Paul, 244
Hewlett-Packard, 16, 18
Hidden agendas, 261
High-context cultures, 40–42, 96
High-level abstractions, 94–95
Highly structured interviews, 165–166
Hillel, Rabbi, 143
Hogan, Kevin, 71, 421
Holder, Eric, 335
Hollywood Video, 197
Honesty
    in communication, 129
    in employment interviews, 205, 207
    in persuasive presentations, 424–425
Hong Kong, 44
Honoring a person or institution,
        437–438
Horizontal communication, 16–17
Hostile work environment, 117–118
Hour-per-minute principle, 305
The Human Side of Enterprise
    (McGregor), 58–59
Humor, in opening statements, 336
Hypothetical questions, 169–170
Hypothetical stories, 352

I

Iacocca, Lee, 78, 125–126, 225, 306
IBM, 60, 107
"Iceberg tips," 84
"I" language, 128–129, 147
Illnesses, 113
IM. *See* Instant messaging
Immediacy, 116–117
Impartiality, 425
Impromptu presentations, 380–381
India, social customs in, 38
Indifference, 129–130
Indirect questions, 169
Individualistic cultures, 42–44
Indonesia, 39
Informal communication networks
    cultivating networks, 19–23
    functions of, 17–19
    value of, 17
Information-gathering interviews,
        187–189

Information overload, 17
Information power, 247–248
Information-sharing meetings, 274
Informative presentations, 401–413.
    See also Presentation delivery;
    Presentations
  briefings, 402–403
  goals of, 314
  organizational patterns in, 324
  reports, 403–406
  training, 406–413
In Search of Excellence (Peters), 70
Inspiration software, 329
Instant messaging (IM)
  acronyms in, 26
  advantages and disadvantages of,
    25, 29
  guidelines for, 26
  by virtual teams, 242
Intel Corp., 28, 280
Interactive presentations, 377–378
Intercultural sensitivity, stages of, 53
Interjections, 411
Interpersonal skills, 124–151
  building relationships, 138–139, 421
  communication climate and, 127–131
  giving apologies, 136
  giving constructive feedback, 133–135
  giving praise, 131–133
  importance of, 125–126
  managing conflict (*See* Conflict
    management)
  responding to criticism, 135–137
  unpleasant communication traits, 126
Interruptions, minimizing, 390
Interview quotient (IQ), 211
Interviews, 158–182. *See also*
    Employment interviews
  auditions, 197
  background information
    collection, 188
  behavioral, 197, 198
  career research, 190–194
  characteristics of, 160
  closings for, 177
  diagnostic, 160, 187
  disciplinary, 160
  ethics in, 178–180
  examples of, 156, 159
  following-up after, 193–194
  formats for, 197–198
  goals for, 161, 162, 188–189, 227
  identifying and analyzing other party
    to, 161–163
  information-gathering, 187–189
  interviewee's role in, 176–177, 180
  interviewer's responsibilities in,
    174–176, 179–180
  legal issues related to, 213–216
  length of, 171, 174

Interviews—*Cont.*
  motivation in, 174
  nonstructured, 165, 166
  nonverbal behaviors in, 169
  openings for, 172–174
  orientation in, 173–174
  panel, 197
  participation distribution in, 160
  performance appraisal, 160,
    223–228
  presidential debates as, 162
  questions for, 166–170, 175–176,
    189, 200–204, 209–210
  sample plan for, 180–182
  sample transcript of, 216–223
  self-assessment of skills for, 178
  settings for, 170–172
  structure for, 165–166
  topics list for, 164–165, 181–182
  types of, 160
  video, 171
Introduction of another speaker,
    436–437
Investigative interviews, 160, 187
Invitational rhetoric, 316
IQ (interview quotient), 211
Irreversible nature of
    communication, 10
Isenberg, Barry, 381
Italy, time sense in, 113–114

J

Janis, Irving, 265
Japan
  collectivist culture in, 44
  harmonious closings and, 432
  intolerance for conflict in, 39
  low acceptance of uncertainty in, 44
  personal space in, 105
  problem-solving meetings in, 292
  smiling in, 109
  social customs in, 38
  task orientation in, 44
Jargon, 95–96, 405
JCPenney, 61
Job fairs, 164
Job interviews. *See* Employment
    interviews
Jobs, Steve, 438
Journalism/publishing careers, 6
Judo Strategy (Yoffie and Kwak), 355

K

Kacmar, Michele, 208
Kahn, Robert, 13
Kaplan, Gary, 236
Katz, Daniel, 13
Katzman, Jerry, 94

Kelleher, Herb, 56
Kelly, Charles, 56
Kennedy, Del, 75
Kennedy, John F., 162
Keynote (presentation software), 366
Keynote listening, 76
Kiyosaki, Robert, 421
Kmart, 28
Knowledge, credibility and, 424
Krackhardt, David, 18
Krzyzewski, Mike, 239

L

LaFasto, Frank, 240
Laissez-faire leadership style, 243
Landis, Marilyn, 378
Language
  abstract, 94–95
  accents in, 46
  ambiguous, 96–97
  biased, 98–99
  body, 109–110, 383–384
  disabilities and, 49
  diversity of, 45–46
  gender-related challenges in, 99–103
  "I" *vs.* "you," 128–129, 147
  jargon, 95–96, 405
  lawsuit over misunderstanding of, 46
  masculine and feminine, 99–101, 102
  mixes, 45–46
  paralanguage, 105
  parallel wording, 331
  powerful, 97–98
  in presentations, 385–386
  relative words, 95
  slang, 95
  trigger words, 99
Laptops, banned at meetings, 290
Larson, Carl, 240
Lasorda, Tommy, 60
Lateral communication, 16–17
Lateral leadership, 246
Latin America
  displays of emotion in, 431
  personal space in, 105
  polychronic orientation in, 39
  social customs in, 38
  social orientation in, 44
Latino/a culture, 47, 106
Latitude of acceptance, 428
Latitude of noncommitment, 428
Latitude of rejection, 428
Layoffs, 61
Leadership
  centralized, 242–245
  contingency approaches to, 243–245
  designated, 246
  emergent leaders, 245–246
  lateral, 246

Leadership—*Cont.*
  life-cycle theory of, 244–245
  in meetings, 282
  in work groups, 242–248
Leadership Grid® (Blake and Mouton), 243–244
Leading questions, 170
Learning styles, adult, 407
Legal issues
  language-misunderstanding lawsuit, 46
  strategic ambiguity and, 97
  unlawful questions, 213–216
Letters. *See* Business letters
Life-cycle theory of leadership, 244–245
Lincoln, Abraham, 306–307
Listener Preference Profile, 80
Listening, 68–86
  20/80 rule in, 81
  assumptions in, 75–76
  egocentrism and, 74
  to emotional appeals, 86
  to evaluate, 85–86
  fear of appearing ignorant and, 74–75
  generative, 72–73
  importance of, 69–72
  in interviews, 175, 176
  keynote, 76
  length of time spent, 70
  listening noises, 77
  low accuracy of, 72
  mindless *vs.* mindful, 81
  nonverbal cues in, 84–85
  with an open mind, 130–131
  paraphrasing while, 82–84
  preoccupation and, 74
  sales presentations and, 421
  sincere questions and, 82
  talking and interrupting less while, 81–82
  talking *vs.*, 75–76
  to voice mail, 73
  withholding judgment while, 81
Listening barriers
  attitudinal, 74–76
  cultural, 76–77
  environmental, 73–74
  gender, 77–78
  lack of training and, 78
  physiological, 72–73
Listening noises, 77
Listening styles, 78–80
Lists, as visual aids, 360–361
Literal comparisons, 355
Locke, Don, 42
Logical fallacies, 426–427
Logic tree, 321
Long-term orientation, 45
Los Angeles Dodgers, 60

Lose–lose orientation, 144
Low-context cultures, 40–42, 96–97
Low-level abstractions, 94–95
Lukaszewski, James, 413

M

Macy's, 197
Madigan, John, 197
Majority vote, 256–257
Management teams, 236
Managerial styles, 243
Manipulation, 422–423
Manuscript presentations, 378–379
Marketing careers, 6
Marsh, Hugh, 312
Marshall, Bruce, 2
Martin, Judith, 55
Masculine style of speech, 101, 102
Mattel Corporation, 14
Matures, 48–49
May, James C., 334
MBWA (management by wandering around), 18, 160
McCormack, Mark H., 162
McCoy, Lee, 104
McDonald's Corp., 61, 73, 109, 406–407
McGregor, Douglas, 58–59
Media careers, 6
Medley, Anthony, 200
Meetings, 272–295
  agendas for, 280–283, 286–287, 294
  ban on mobile devices at, 290
  complaints in, 276
  computer-mediated, 288
  concluding, 292–294
  cost of, 273–274, 276
  decision-making, 275
  effectiveness checklist for, 294–295
  follow-up after, 294–295
  geography and, 277
  goals for, 282–283, 284
  improving participation at, 287–289
  information-sharing, 274
  keeping discussions on track, 289–291
  keeping positive tone during, 291
  opening, 284–285
  opting out of, 292
  parliamentary procedure in, 285–287
  pre-meeting work for, 283
  problem-solving, 275, 277–283
  ritual activities in, 275
  roles in, 278–279
  seating arrangements, power, and conflict, 286
  summarizing, 293
  time constraints for, 284–285, 289
  virtual, 275–277
  when to hold, 278–279

Mehrabian, Albert, 111
Mellinger, Michael, 188
Memorized presentations, 378–379
Men. *See also* Gender differences
  listening by, 77–78
  masculine speech, 101, 102
Mentors, 21–23
Message overload, 74
Messages. *See also* Verbal messages
  in communication model, 7, 8
  confirming *vs.* disconfirming, 128–131
  content, 9
  difficult, 97
  instant messaging, 25, 26, 29, 242
  message overload, 74
  problem-oriented, 129
  relational, 9–10
  silent, 112–115
Method of residues, 245–246
Mexican Americans, disclosure and, 47
Mexico
  high-context culture in, 42
  intolerance of conflict in, 40
  power distance in, 44
  time schedules in, 39, 94
  use of titles in, 38
Miami *Herald,* 46
Microphones, 387
Microsoft, 28, 30, 277
Microsoft PowerPoint, 366–367
Middle Eastern cultures
  gender roles in, 40
  as low-context cultures, 42
  supporting material in, 431
  time schedules in, 39
  women's clothing in, 38, 117
Mindful listening, 81
Mindless listening, 81
Minorities, mentors and, 21
Minority decisions, 257
Minutes, meeting, 286
"Mixed-gender strategy," 102–103
Models, as visual aids, 359
Moderately structured interviews, 166
Monochronic cultures, 39, 77, 115
Monologues, 377
Monster.com, 190
Moran, Robert, 332
Motions, in meetings, 287
Motivated sequence organization plan, 327–329, 414, 416
Motivation, communication and, 17
Motivational speeches, 418
Motorola, 235, 261
Mouton, Jane, 243
Multicommunicating, 73
Multimedia, teamwork in, 235
Multitasking, 175, 290
Murphy's Law, 365

Murrow, Edward R., 394
Museum of Springfield (strategic case), 232–233
Muslim cultures. *See* Middle Eastern cultures
MySpace, 217

N

Nakayama, Thomas, 55
Names, formality and, 38
Native Americans
  eye contact and, 47, 108–109
  silence and, 47, 77, 106
Negative self-talk, 198
Negotiation
  cultural differences in, 147
  definition of, 143–144
  example of, 149–151
  methods for conducting, 148–149
  preparation for, 146–148
  strategies and outcomes, 144–146, 149–151
Nemawashi, 292
Nervousness, in presentations, 378, 393–396
Net Generation, 48, 49
NETMA (Nobody Ever Tells Me Anything), 13
Networking, 19–23. *See also* Communication networks
  cultural factors in, 20
  definition of, 19–20
  mentors in, 21–23
  prospects for, 20
  referrals to secondary sources in, 21
  respect in, 20–21
Neuharth, Al, 130
NGT (nominal group technique), 287–288
Nichols, Ralph, 72
Nizer, Louis, 75
"No," how to say, 140
Noise
  in communication, 7–8
  in cubicles, 113
Nominal group technique (NGT), 287–288
Nonstructured interviews, 165, 166
Nonverbal communication, 103–117
  appearance and, 106–108
  characteristics of, 103–105
  emoticons as, 104
  face and eyes and, 108–109, 110
  immediacy of, 116–117
  improving, 116–117
  jury selection and, 169
  listening and, 84–85
  observing conventions in, 117
  personal space and, 105, 110–111

Nonverbal communication—*Cont.*
  physical environment and, 111–112
  posture and movement and, 109–110
  in presentations, 382–384
  self-assessment of, 114–115
  self-monitoring behavior of, 116
  time and, 112–115
  voice and, 105–106
Norming phase of problem solving, 251, 252
Norms, in groups, 261–263, 265
Notes, in presentations, 379, 382–383

O

Obama, Barrack, 162
Objects, as visual aids, 359
Odors, 113
Office space, 112
Ofsthun, Amy, 369
Ogden, C. K., 92
Ogilvy, David, 111
"1-week later" test, 321
One Minute Manager (Blanchard), 224
Online meetings, 275–277
Online networking groups, 21
Online translation services, 92
Opening statements, 333–336
Open mind, 130–131
Open questions, 167–168
Opinion questions, 168
Oracle, 171
Oral communication. *See* Verbal messages
Organizational careers, 6
Organizational charts, 12–13
Organizational culture, 56–62
  career planning and, 61–62
  communication channels and, 30
  communication rules in, 58
  creating and maintaining, 60–61
  definition of, 56
  downsizing and, 61
  employee's fit with, 57–58
  ethical behavior and, 60
  importance of, 58
  Theory X and Theory Y, 58–60
Organizational patterns, 321–329
  cause-effect, 323–324
  chronological, 322
  comparative advantages, 326–327
  criteria satisfaction, 325–326
  effect-cause, 324
  motivated sequence, 327–329
  problem-solution, 324–325, 418–419
  topical, 323
Orientation phase of problem solving, 251, 252

Osborn, Alex, 267
Overhead questions, 288
Overhead transparencies, 365

P

Pagliaro, Chris, 113–114
Panel interviews, 197
Paralanguage, 105
Parallel wording, 331
Paraphrasing, while listening, 82–84, 291
PAR approach, 208
Parliamentary procedure, 285–287
Participation, improving, 287–289
A Passion for Excellence (Peters), 70
Patagonia, Inc., 107
Patterson, Kerry, 130
Patterson, Neal, 127
Pauling, Linus, 267
Pauses, in presentations, 388
People-oriented listening style, 78–79
People skills. *See* Interpersonal skills
PepsiCo, 44
Performance appraisal interviews
  checklist for, 227–228
  explanation of, 223
  functions of, 160, 223–225
  steps in, 225–227
  written record of, 227
Performing phase of problem solving, 251, 252
Perkin Elmer Corporation, 274
Personal attack fallacy, 426
Personal attire. *See also* Appearance
  cultural differences in, 38–39
  dress codes, 2, 107–108, 117
  for employment interviews, 199
  for presentations, 381–382
  responses to, 107–108, 110
Personal contacts, 190, 206
Personalismo, 44
Personal pronouns, 385
Personal space and distance, 105, 110–111
Persuasion
  alternatives to, 422–423
  definition of, 422
  elaboration likelihood model of, 426
Persuasive presentations, 413–432. *See also* Presentation delivery; Presentations
  appeals to needs of audience in, 427–432
  credibility in, 423–425
  evidence in, 430
  goals of, 314, 428–429
  goodwill speeches as, 418
  hostile audiences in, 429–431
  logical fallacies in, 426–427

Persuasive presentations—*Cont.*
  logic and emotion in, 426
  motivational speeches as, 418
  opposing ideas in, 430
  organizational patterns in, 324,
    413–416
  proposals as, 418–420
  psychological appeals in, 427
  public service announcements
    as, 416
  requesting a raise as, 419
  sales presentations as, 420–422
  self-assessment of strategies in, 417
  social judgment theory and,
    423, 428–429
Peters, Tom, 70, 75
Peterson, Susan, 76
Philippines, 44, 53
Photographs, as visual aids, 359–360
Physical proximity, communication
  and, 17
Physiological noise, 7
Pickens, T. Boone, 243
Pictograms, 363
Pie charts, 361–362
Pillsbury Corporation, 15
Pitino, Rick, 82
Platinum Rule, 72
Platinum Sounds (strategic case),
  156–157
Podcasting, 409
Polychronic cultures, 39, 113–114
Portugal, 44
Position power, 247
Poster board, 365
Poster presentations, 412
Post hoc ergo propter hoc fallacy, 426–427
Post-it notes, as visual aids, 365
Posture, 109–110, 383–384
Power
  coercive, 247
  connection, 248
  expert, 247
  information, 247–248
  language and, 97–98
  position, 247
  power distance, 43, 44
  referent, 247
  reward, 247
  space allocation and, 111
Power distance, 43, 44
"Power pause," 382
PowerPoint, 366–367
Praising, 131–133
Presentation delivery, 376–396
  confidence in, 382, 393–396
  extemporaneous, 379
  focus of, 395
  in group presentations, 433–435
  impromptu, 380–381

Presentation delivery—*Cont.*
  manuscript, 378–379
  memorized, 378–379
  microphones in, 387
  minimizing audience interruptions
    in, 390
  mistaken beliefs about, 396
  mistakes in, 386
  patterns of, 377–378
  question-and-answer sessions in,
    389–393
  rehearsals of, 395
  self-assessment of, 389
  speaking style in, 385–386
  standing or sitting during, 382, 383
  verbal elements of, 384–388
  video analysis of, 386
  visual elements in, 381–384
  vocal elements in, 387–388
Presentations, 302–341. *See also*
    Presentation delivery; Supporting
    material
  accepting an award, 440
  allotted time for, 115, 311–312
  analyzing speaking abilities for,
    310–311
  audience analysis in, 306–310
  avoiding computer catastrophes
    in, 370
  of awards, 439–440
  basic organizational plan for, 318–320
  brainstorming ideas for, 318, 319
  citing sources in, 356–357
  conclusions to, 336–337, 395, 433
  context for, 312–313
  as dialogue, 316
  entertaining, 314
  facilities for, 311, 312
  goals for, 313–315
  group, 432–435
  informative, 314
  interactive, 377–378
  introducing another speaker, 436–437
  introductions to, 332–333, 395,
    410–411, 433
  main points in, 320–321, 329–331
  opening statements in, 333–336
  organizational patterns for,
    321–329, 340
  outlines for, 339, 419
  persuasive, 314
  planning time for, 305
  poster, 412
  thesis for, 316–317, 326, 330, 333
  toasts, 438–439
  topics for, 311
  transitions in, 338, 341
  tributes, 437–438
  types of, 304
  welcoming, 435

Presentation software
  advantages of, 366–369
  dangers of, 367–369
  examples of, 366, 367
Presidential debates, 162
Primary questions, 167
Privacy, in cubicles, 113
Problem-oriented messages, 129, 148
Problem-solution organization plan,
  324–325, 418–419
Problem solving. *See also* Conflict
    management
  meetings for, 275, 277–283
  stages of, in groups, 250–252
  systematic, 248–250
  win–win orientation in, 145–146,
    149–151
Procter & Gamble, 36
Productivity, teams and, 236
Professional ethic, 12
Progress reports, 403–404
Project teams, 236
Pronunciation, in presentations, 387
Proposals, 418–420
Proximity, 112
Psychological noise, 8
Public information careers, 6
Publicity, low-tech, 8
Publicity test, for ethical behavior, 12
Public service announcements
  (PSAs), 416
Puerto Ricans, 42, 47

Q

Question-and-answer sessions
  management of, 391–393
  respect in, 391–392
  timing for, 390–391
Questions
  anticipating, 200–204, 391
  direct and indirect, 168–169, 288
  to encourage participation, 288–289
  factual and opinion, 168
  hypothetical and critical incident,
    169–170
  for interviews, 166–170
  leading, 170
  during meetings, 291
  open and closed, 167–168
  overhead, 288
  primary and secondary, 167, 175–176
  relay, 289
  reverse, 288–289
  rhetorical, 333–334
  sincere *vs.* counterfeit, 82
  unlawful, 213–216
Quid pro quo sexual harassment,
  117–118
Quinn, Feargal, 71–72

Quotations
    as opening statements, 334–335
    as supporting material, 350, 356

R

Rapid thought, listening and, 72–73
Rapport talk, 100–101, 102
Raven, Bertram, 246
Reagan, Ronald, 162
Receiver, in communication model, 7
Recognition, by one's boss, 14
The Redeem Team, 239
Reductio ad absurdum fallacy, 426
Reference letter, ambiguous, 97
Referent power, 247
Reflective-thinking sequence, 248–250
Reframing, 276
Rehearsals, of presentations, 395
Reich, Robert, 235
Reinforcement phase of problem
        solving, 251, 252
Relational messages, 9–10
Relational roles, 253, 255
Relationship building, 138–139, 421
Relative words, 95
Relaxation, 110
Relaying praise, 132–133
Relay questions, 289
Relevancy challenges, 289–290
Reports
    feasibility, 405–406
    final, 404–405
    status, 403–404
    technical, 405
    types of, 403
Report talk, 101, 102
Research interviews, 160, 187
Respect, 130, 131, 180
Résumés, 195, 197
Reverse questions, 288–289
Reward power, 247
Rhetorical questions, 333–334
Richard, Brenda, 137–138
Richards, I. A., 92
Richman, Jim, 6
Rights approach, 10, 12
Risky shift, 266
Ritual activities, 275
Ritz-Carlton, 280
Rivalry, 16–17
Room arrangement options, 312
Rule of Seven, 370

S

Salaries
    appearance and, 107–108
    finding comparable, 206
    negotiating, 206, 419

Salaries—*Cont.*
    nonsalary compensation, 107–108
Sales presentations, 420–422
Santos, Jose, 46
Saving face, 41, 47, 135
Scandinavian countries, social
        orientation in, 44
Scannable résumés, 197
Scents, 113
Schaffer, William, 6
Schrader, R. C., 39
Schwartz, David J., 71
Seating arrangements, 286
Secondary questions, 167, 175–176
Secondary sources, in networking, 21
Selection interviews, 160
Self-assessment
    of conflict management style, 142
    of cultural intelligence, 51
    of employment interviews, 203
    of group presentations, 434
    of group's communication
            effectiveness, 259
    of interview quotient, 211
    of interview skills, 178
    Listener Preference Profile, 80
    of meeting effectiveness, 294
    of nonverbal immediacy, 114–115
    of persuasive strategies, 417
    of presentation delivery, 389
    of presentation organization, 340
    of supporting material, 371
Self-directed work teams, 246
Self-image, 163
Self-monitoring behavior, 116
Senders, 7
Senge, Peter, 72
Service teams, 236
Sexual harassment, 117–119
Shaking hands, 199
Sharp, Alan, 246
Short-term orientation, 45
Siemens Corp., 18
Signposts, 411
Silence
    cultural diversity and, 47, 77, 106
    listening and, 81–82
Sincere questions, 82
Singapore, 44
Six degrees of separation hypothesis, 21
Skills wanted by employers, 5
Skype, 171
Slang, 95
Slides, 365, 367
Slydial.com, 25
Small talk, 173
Smiling, 46–47, 109
Social context, 9
Social customs, 38. *See also* Cultural
        diversity

Social intelligence, 126
Social judgment theory, 423, 428–429
Social orientation, 44
Software, 329, 366–369
Solomon, Muriel, 14
South America. *See* Latin America
Space allocation, 111
Spatial pattern, 322–323
Specialization, communication and, 17
Specific goals, 314–315
Speeches. *See* Presentations
Speech of introduction, 436–437
Sperry Corporation, 78
Spirited Sales Leaders (SSL), 385
Spirituality, respecting, 131
Stage fright, 378, 393–396
Stamp, Dennis, 279, 292
Statistics, as supporting material, 350,
        354–355
Status reports, 403–404
Stefani, Jean, 139
Stengel, Casey, 235
Stennek, Hans, 422
Stone, Karen, 49
Stories, in presentations, 350, 351–353
Storming phase of problem solving,
        251, 252
Strategic cases
    Computer Solutions, 66–67
    Fresh Air Sports, 300–301
    Museum of Springfield, 232–233
    Platinum Sounds, 156–157
    Sundown Bakery, 2–3
"The Strength of Weak Ties"
        (Granovetter), 191
Stress interviews, 197
Style approach to leadership, 243
Success, nonverbal communication
        and, 105, 116
Summarizing, in presentations,
        392–393
Sundown Bakery (strategic case), 2–3
Supporting material, 346–372. *See also*
        Visual aids
    citing sources, 356–357
    claims and, 329–330, 348, 430
    clarity from, 348
    comparisons as, 350, 355–356
    computer catastrophes and, 370
    cultural differences in, 431
    definitions as, 349–350
    examples as, 350, 351
    guidelines for using visual aids as,
            369–372
    importance of, 347
    in impromptu presentations, 381
    interest from, 349
    presentation software and, 366–369
    proof from, 349, 354
    quotations as, 350, 356

Supporting material—*Cont.*
  self-assessment of, 371
  statistics as, 350, 354–355
  stories as, 350, 351–353
Survey interviews, 160, 187
Sutcliffe, Andrea, 71
Switzerland, task orientation in, 44
Synergy, 237

T

Tables, as visual aids, 360–361
Tales of a New America (Reich), 235
Talking from 9 to 5 (Tannen), 140
Tannen, Deborah, 78, 100, 140
Target, 197
Task orientation, 44, 243–244
Task roles, 253, 255
Team interviews, 197
Teams, 234–268
  becoming a leader in, 245–246
  centralized leadership in, 242–245
  characteristics of, 237–239
  cohesiveness in, 263–265, 267
  competition from outside, 265
  conformity in, 265–267
  creativity in, 267–268
  cyclical stages in, 254
  decision-making methods in,
      254–258
  functional role analysis in,
      252–254, 255
  functional roles in, 255, 279
  group vs. individual performance
      in, 236
  group vs. personal goals in, 258–261
  importance of, 235–237
  interviews by, 197
  norms in, 261–263, 265
  power of members in, 246–248
  problem-solving stages in, 250–252
  profile of successful, 239–240
  self-assessment of communication
      in, 259
  self-directed, 246
  size of, 237–238
  systematic problem solving in,
      248–250
  virtual, 240–242
Technical reports, 405
Technology tips
  on avoiding computer catastrophes
      in presentations, 370
  on blogging, 28
  on cleaning up digital dirt, 217
  on collaboration in cyberspace, 277
  on concept mapping software, 329
  on conducting video interviews, 171
  on conflict management in
      cyberspace, 144

Technology tips—*Cont.*
  on creating a digital portfolio, 209
  on generational preferences in
      communication technology, 48
  on instant messaging at work, 26
  on listening to voice mail, 73
  on online translation services, 92
  on podcasting, 409
  on using a microphone, 387
  on video analysis of presentation
      delivery, 386
  on webinars, 420
  on working in virtual teams, 241
Teinchek, Carol, 2
Teleconferencing
  advantages of, 25, 29
  guidelines for, 277
  procedure for, 275–276
  by virtual teams, 242
Telephone use
  advantages and disadvantages of,
      24–25, 29
  cell phone do's and don'ts, 24
  cultural differences in, 277
  telephone logs, 85
Texas Instruments, 60
Text messaging, 26, 29
Thailand, 38, 44
Thanking people
  by handwritten notes, 29
  at meeting conclusion, 293–294
  networking and, 20–21
  recognition and, 14
Theory X, 58–59
Theory Y, 58–59
Thesis, deferred, 415, 429–430
Thesis statement, 316–317,
      326, 330, 333
Third-party harassment, 118
3M Corp., 18, 78, 235, 261
Time
  conflict management and, 147
  interviews and, 171–172, 174
  listening and, 77, 79
  meetings and, 280, 284–285, 289
  monochronic vs. polychronic
      cultures and, 39, 77, 115
  norms for, 263
  silent messages and, 112–115
Time-oriented listening style, 79
Time zones, virtual teams and, 241
Titles, use of, 38
Toasts, 438–439
Topical pattern, 323
Total Leadership (Friedman), 8
Touch, cultural differences in, 106
Townsend, Robert, 224
Training, 406–413
  adult learning styles, 407
  audience in, 408–410

Training—*Cont.*
  delivery of, 410–412
  goals of, 407–408
  jargon in, 412–413
  podcasting in, 409
  program planning, 407–410
  retention rates in, 408
  value of, 406–407
Trait approach to leadership, 243
Transience, in oral communication, 25
Transitions, in presentations,
      338, 341, 433
Translation services, 92
Transparencies, 365
Triangle of meaning, 92–93
Tributes, 437–438
Trigger words, 99
Trustworthiness, 424–425
TTFM (ta ta for now), 26
Tufte, Edward, 368
Tupperware, 60–61
Twain, Mark, 305
20/80 rule in listening, 81
Twitter, 26, 29

U

Uncertainty avoidance, 44
Underwood, Anita, 282
United Parcel Service (UPS), 38–39
Uptalk, 106
Upward communication, 14–16
Ury, William, 146
USAA Insurance, 235
Utilitarian approach, 10, 12

V

Vars, John, 290
Venezuela, personal space in, 105
Verbal messages, 92–103. *See also*
      Messages
  biased language in, 98–99
  equivocal terms in, 93–94
  gender-related language challenges,
      101–103
  jargon in, 95–96
  low-level vs. high-level abstractions
      in, 94–95
  masculine and feminine language
      in, 99–101, 102
  misunderstandings in, 93
  powerful language in, 97–98
  relative words in, 95
  slang in, 95
  strategic ambiguity in, 96–97
  triangle of meaning in, 92–93
  trigger words in, 99
  in voice mail, 15, 24, 29, 739
Verizon, 277

Videoconferencing
  advantages of, 25, 29
  cost saving in, 276
  guidelines for, 277
Video interviews, 171
Videos, 364, 386
Virtual meetings, 275–277
Virtual teams, 240–242
Virtue approach, 10, 12
Visual aids, 357–372
  avoiding computer catastrophes
    with, 370
  bar and column charts, 362–363
  diagrams, 360
  functions of, 358–359
  graphs, 363–364
  guidelines for using, 369–372
  importance of, 357–358
  lists and tables, 360–361
  media for presenting, 364–366
  objects and models, 359
  photographs, 359–360
  pictograms, 363
  pie charts, 361–362
  presentation guidelines for,
    370–371
  presentation software, 366–369
  in technical reports, 405
  video, 364
Visual impairments, 50
Visualization, 416
Vocabulary
  in presentations, 386–387
  specialized, 95–96, 405

Vogel, Douglas, 369
Voice
  nonverbal communication in,
    105–106
  in presentations, 383–384,
    387–388
Voice mail
  advantages and disadvantages
    of, 29
  anonymous, 15
  do's and don'ts, 24
  information in messages, 24
  listening to, 739
Voice-to-text services, 73
Volunteering, 14

W

wa, 39
Wallace, Irving, 393
Wallechinsky, David, 393
Wal-Mart, 14, 38
Walton, Sam, 14, 188
Watson, Thomas, Jr., 60
Waugh, Barbara, 16
Web, used in presentations, 370
Web conferencing, 277
Webinars, 420
Weiss, Timothy, 53
Welcoming remarks, 435
Wells Fargo, 28
Weston, Mary, 232–233
Wheelchairs, 50
Why Generation, 48, 49

Williams, Otis, Jr., 396
Williams, Paulette, 53
Winger, Julia, 232
Win–lose orientation, 144
Win–win orientation, 145–146,
  149–151
Women. *See also* Gender differences
  cultural diversity in gender roles
    for, 40
  feminine speech, 100–101, 102
  height in, 110
  listening by, 77–78
  mentors and, 21
  in Muslim countries, 38, 117
  nonverbal cues and, 55
  uptalk by, 106
  upward communication and, 15
Work groups. *See* Teams
Working hours, 145
Written communication, e-mail *vs.*,
  27–28, 29

X

Xerox Corporation, 78

Y

"You" language, 128, 147

Z

Zhong he, 39
Zugsmith, Mike, 247